DICTIONARY
OF
LABOUR BIOGRAPHY

Volume IV

DICTIONARY
OF
LABOUR BIOGRAPHY

Volume IV

JOYCE M. BELLAMY

Senior Research Officer, University of Hull

and

JOHN SAVILLE

Professor of Economic and Social History, University of Hull

First published 1977 by
THE MACMILLAN PRESS LTD
London and Basingstoke
Associated companies in New York
Dublin Melbourne Johannesburg and Madras

ISBN 0 333 19704 6

Printed in Great Britain by
UNWIN BROTHERS LIMITED
The Gresham Press Old Woking Surrey
A member of the Staples Printing Group

Contents

ACKNOWLEDGEMENTS   vii

NOTES TO READERS   ix

LIST OF CONTRIBUTORS   x

LIST OF ABBREVIATIONS   xiii

LIST OF BIBLIOGRAPHIES   xix

BIOGRAPHIES   1

CONSOLIDATED LIST OF NAMES   209
IN VOLS I, II, III AND IV

GENERAL INDEX   217

Acknowledgements

The need for any explanation concerning the aims and purposes of the *Dictionary* becomes less as more volumes are published. Perhaps it is worth noting again that we are always conscious of the gaps in our coverage and that we constantly review the range and spread of entries. We wish to bring to the attention of our readers that we are proposing in volume VI to include an Addenda and Corrigenda section to cover the first five volumes and we shall be grateful to receive any additions and corrections.

The research for this volume has been made possible by a generous grant from the Social Science Research Council. Our debts to many individuals are considerable. We particularly wish to thank the members of our research group, Mrs Margaret 'Espinasse, Miss Ann Holt and Mrs Barbara Nield; and then several individuals whose advice and assistance we have frequently sought: Dame Margaret Cole; Mr T. A. K. Elliott, CMG; Edmund and Ruth Frow; and our former colleague, Dr David E. Martin. Among others to whom we record our especial thanks are: Dr R. Page Arnot, Miss Sue Barrowclough, Mrs Margaret H. Gibb, OBE, Mr G. I. Lewis, Dr R. W. Lyman, Mrs M. Miliband, Dr K. O. Morgan, David and Naomi Reid, Mr Martin Upham and Mrs I. Wagner. We also wish to thank our contributors and those whose names are listed in the Sources section of the biographies.

Among librarians and their staffs we owe a continuing debt to Dr Philip Larkin and his colleagues of the Brynmor Jones Library, Hull University. Other university staffs to whom we are indebted include Glasgow, Keele, King's College, London, Newcastle upon Tyne, Oxford, the University College of Swansea, and York. We are especially grateful to the Historical Records Project team at LSE; Mr R. A. Storey and Mrs J. Druker of the Modern Records Centre, Warwick University; the British Library, London and Boston Spa and the Newspaper Library, Colindale; the British Library of Political and Economic Science and the South Wales Miners' Library. Among the public libraries we wish to thank are those in Barnsley, Birmingham, Bridgwater, Bristol, Burnley, Calderdale, Cardiff, Carlisle, Chatham, Cleveland, East Sussex, Edinburgh, Huddersfield, Humberside; the London Boroughs of Bromley, Camden, Hackney, Hounslow, Islington, Kensington and Chelsea, Lambeth, Lewisham, Redbridge, and Richmond; Maidenhead, Manchester, Newcastle upon Tyne, Norwich, Reading, Ross and Cromarty, Salford, Sheffield, South Shields, Stoke-on-Trent, Sunderland and Wigan.

We are also indebted to the staffs of the following organisations: News Information Service and Written Archives Centre of the BBC; Co-operative Union; Durham County Record Office; General Register Offices in London and Edinburgh; Labour Party (Cardiff, Huddersfield and London); Royal College of Physicians, Edinburgh; Scottish Record Office; Miss I. H. Hoskins and the Theosophical Society in England, and Mr C. R. N. Swamy, Theosophical Society, International HQ, Adyar, India. The trade union offices consulted included: AUEW, London and Manchester; ITF; NUM in Durham, Northumberland, South Wales and Yorkshire; the TUC library; and USDAW. Editors of local newspapers have been most helpful in publishing our letters which have put us in touch with families.

We also wish to record our thanks to all those in the University of Hull and outside who have given typing assistance. We further acknowledge the help given in proof-reading by Ann Holt, Dr David E. Martin, Barbara Nield and Richard Saville and the work undertaken by Barbara Nield on the index, assisted by V. J. Morris and G. D. Weston. Finally we wish to thank our publishers and in particular Mr T. M. Farmiloe in the London office of Macmillan and Mr A. Bathe, Mr H. W. Bawden and Mrs A. Dyer at Basingstoke.

JMB
JS

University of Hull
August 1976

While this volume was in the press we learnt of the tragic death, by drowning, of Anthony Elliott, British Ambassador to Israel, at the end of August 1976. Mr Elliott had an unique collection of biographical information on twentieth-century Members of Parliament and his knowledge and help was given to us generously and without stint. In volume V we will try to make clear the assistance he gave us, and the great loss which we have suffered both in terms of academic scholarship and in our personal relations.

Notes to Readers

1. Place-names are usually quoted according to contemporary usage relating to the particular entry.
2. Where the amount of a will, estate value or effects is quoted, the particular form used is normally that given in *The Times*, or the records of Somerset House, London, or the Scottish Record Office, Edinburgh. For dates before 1860 the source will usually be the Public Record Office.
3. Under the heading **Sources,** personal information relates to details obtained from relatives, friends or colleagues of the individual in question; biographical information refers to other sources.
4. The place of publication in bibliographical references is London, unless otherwise stated.
5. P indicates a pamphlet whose pagination could not be verified. Where it is known, the number of pages is quoted if under sixty.
6. The *See also* column which follows biographical entries includes names marked with a dagger and these refer to biographies already published in Volumes I, II or III of the *Dictionary*; those with no marking are included in the present volume, and those with an asterisk refer to entries to be included in later volumes.
7. A consolidated name list of entries in Volumes I, II, III and IV will be found at the end of this volume before the general index.

List of Contributors

Dr John Baxter — Douglas Knoop Research Fellow, Department of Economic and Social History, Sheffield University

Professor Joseph O. Baylen — Department of History, Georgia State University, U.S.A.

Dr John Benson — Lecturer in History, Wolverhampton Polytechnic

Raymond Brown Esq. — Lecturer, Department of Economic and Social History, Hull University

Dame Margaret Cole — London

Mrs Margaret 'Espinasse — formerly Reader in English Language, Hull University

Kenneth Dallas Esq. — Pinner

Mrs Janet Druker — Project Officer, Modern Records Centre, Warwick University Library

Edmund Frow Esq. — Manchester

Mrs Ruth Frow — Manchester

Dr Brian H. Harrison — Fellow of Corpus Christi College, Oxford University

Dr Patricia Hollis — Lecturer, Department of English and American Studies, East Anglia University

Miss Ann Holt — Research Assistant, Department of Economic and Social History, Hull University

Dr David Howell — Lecturer, Department of Government, Manchester University

Professor Judith Fincher Laird — Department of History, Denison University, Ohio, U.S.A.

Dr Keith Laybourn — Lecturer, Department of History and Politics, Huddersfield Polytechnic

Dr John C. Lovell — Senior Lecturer, Department of Economic and Social History, Kent University

James McConville Esq. — Lecturer, School of Business Studies, London Polytechnic

Dr David E. Martin — Lecturer, Department of Economic and Social History, Sheffield University

Dr Anthony Mason — Lecturer, Centre for the Study of Social History, Warwick University

Maurice Milne Esq.	Lecturer, Department of Humanities, Newcastle upon Tyne Polytechnic
A. Leslie Morton Esq.	Clare, Suffolk
Mrs Vivien Morton	Clare, Suffolk
Dr Robert G. Neville	Department of Education, Leeds University
Mrs Barbara Nield	Research Assistant, Department of Economic and Social History, Hull University
Archie Potts Esq.	Principal Lecturer in Economics, Department of Economics, Newcastle upon Tyne Polytechnic
Gerald Rhodes Esq.	Capel St Mary, Ipswich
John J. Rowley Esq.	Research Assistant (History), Wolverhampton Polytechnic
Dr David Rubinstein	Lecturer, Department of Economic and Social History, Hull University
Professor James A. Schmiechen	Department of History, Illinois State University, Bloomington Normal, U.S.A.
John B. Smethurst Esq.	Eccles
Richard Storey Esq.	Senior Project Officer, Modern Records Centre, Warwick University Library
Dr Eric Taylor	Senior Lecturer in Modern History, Wolverhampton Polytechnic
Anthony J. Topham Esq.	Senior Lecturer, Department of Adult Education, Hull University

List of Abbreviations

AB	able-bodied seaman
ACIS	Associate of the Chartered Institute of Secretaries
Add.	Additional
ADM	Annual Delegate Meeting
AEU	Amalgamated Engineering Union
AGM	Annual General Meeting
Ald.	Alderman
Amer. Rev. of Revs	*American Review of Reviews*
AMWU	Amalgamated Marine Workers' Union
APCE	*Annals of Public and Co-operative Economy*
App.	Appendix
ASE	Amalgamated Society of Engineers
ASRS	Amalgamated Society of Railway Servants
ATS	Auxiliary Territorial Service
AUCE	Amalgamated Union of Co-operative Employees
AUEW	Amalgamated Union of Engineering Workers
BBC	British Broadcasting Corporation
BFCY	British Federation of Co-operative Youth
BLPES	British Library of Political and Economic Science, LSE
BM	British Museum (now British Library)
BMA	British Medical Association
BS	Bachelor of Surgery
BSP	British Socialist Party
BSU	British Seafarers' Union
C.	Command Paper (pre-1899)
CB	Companion of the Bath
CBE	Commander of the British Empire
CC	County Council
Cd	Command Paper (1900-18)
CH	Companion of Honour
Ch.	Chapter
CI	Communist International
CMG	Companion of the Order of St Michael and St George
CND	Campaign for Nuclear Disarmament
CO	Conscientious Objector

Co.	County
Col.	Colonel
Coll.	Collection
Communist Rev.	*Communist Review*
comps	compositors
Cont. Rev.	*Contemporary Review*
Co-op. Annual	*Co-operative Annual*
CP	Communist Party
CPGB	Communist Party of Great Britain
CPSU	Communist Party of the Soviet Union
CSU	Complete Suffrage Union
Cttee	Committee
d	old pence
DFM	Distinguished Flying Medal
DLB	*Dictionary of Labour Biography*
DMA	Durham Miners' Association
DNB	*Dictionary of National Biography*
Dod	*Dod's Parliamentary Companion*
Dublin Rev.	*Dublin Review*
Econ. J.	*Economic Journal*
Econ. Rev.	*Economic Review*
ed.	edited/edition
Engl. Hist. Rev.	*English Historical Review*
Engl.Ill. Mag.	*English Illustrated Magazine*
Engl. Rev.	*English Review*
et al.	*et alia/et alii* (Lat.): and others
ff.	pages following
Fortn. Rev.	*Fortnightly Review*
FRCS	Fellow of the Royal College of Surgeons of England
FRCSE	Fellow of the Royal College of Surgeons of Edinburgh
GFTU	General Federation of Trade Unions
GPO	General Post Office
Hist. J.	*Historical Journal*
ibid.	*ibidem* (Lat.): in the same place
idem	(Lat.): the same; author as mentioned in previous entry
ILO	International Labour Organisation
ILP	Independent Labour Party
Int. Co-op. Bull.	*International Co-operative Bulletin*
Int. Lab. Rev.	*International Labour Review*

Int. Lit.	*International Literature*
Int. Rev. Social Hist.	*International Review of Social History*
Int. Soc. Rev.	*International Socialist Review*
ITF	International Transport Workers' Federation
ITF J.	*International Transport Workers' Federation Journal*
J.	*Journal*
J. of Econ. Hist.	*Journal of Economic History*
JP	Justice of the Peace
Kelly	*Kelly's Handbook to the Titled, Landed and Official Classes*
Lab. Mon.	*Labour Monthly*
Labour Mag.	*Labour Magazine*
LCC	London County Council
LCMF	Lancashire and Cheshire Miners' Federation
LEA	Labour Electoral Association
Lib-Lab	Liberal-Labour
LP	Labour Party
LRC	Labour Representation Committee
LRCP	Licentiate of the Royal College of Physicians
LRCS	Licentiate of the Royal College of Surgeons
LRCSE	Licentiate of the Royal College of Surgeons, Edinburgh
LRD	Labour Research Department
LRFPS(G)	Licentiate of the Royal Faculty of Physicians and Surgeons (Glasgow)
LSE	London School of Economics and Political Science
Mag.	*Magazine*
MC	Military Cross
MD	Doctor of Medicine
MFGB	Miners' Federation of Great Britain
misc.	miscellaneous
MP	Member of Parliament
MRC	Modern Records Centre
MS(S)/ms.	Manuscript(s)
NAC	National Administrative Council
N. Amer. Rev.	*North American Review*
NASFU	National Amalgamated Sailors' and Firemen's Union
NATSOPA	National Society of Operative Printers and Assistants
NCB	National Coal Board
NCF	No-Conscription Fellowship
NCLC	National Council of Labour Colleges

n.d.	no date
NDL	National Democratic League
NEC	National Executive Committee
New Rev.	*New Review*
NLP	National Labour Press
NMA	Northumberland Miners' Association
NOGC	National Organisation of Girls' Clubs
n.s.	new series
NSFU	National Sailors' and Firemen's Union
NTWF	National Transport Workers' Federation
NUAW	National Union of Agricultural Workers
NUDAW	National Union of Distributive and Allied Workers
NUGMW	National Union of General and Municipal Workers
NUJ	National Union of Journalists
NUM	National Union of Mineworkers
NUS	National Union of Seamen
NUWSS	National Union of Women's Suffrage Societies
NUX	National Union of Ex-Servicemen
NY	New York
19th C.	*Nineteenth Century*
Obit.	Obituary
OTC	Officers' Training Corps
P	Pamphlet
PC	Privy Councillor
PL	Public Library
PLP	Parliamentary Labour Party
POEU	Post Office Engineering Union
Polish Rev.	*Polish Review*
Pop. Studies	*Population Studies*
PP	Parliamentary Paper
PRO	Public Record Office
Proc.	Proceedings
pt(s)	part(s)
PTS	President of the Theosophical Society
Q.	*Quarterly*
Q(s)	Question(s)
QC	Queen's Counsel
Railway Rev.	*Railway Review*
RAOC	Royal Army Ordnance Corps
R.C.	Royal Commission
RDC	Rural District Council
repr.	reprinted
Rev.	Reverend

rev.	revised
Rev.	*Review*
Rev. of Revs	*Review of Reviews*
s	shilling(s)
S.C.	Select Committee
Scottish Hist. Rev.	*Scottish Historical Review*
SDF	Social Democratic Federation
SDP	Social Democratic Party
ser.	series
SLP	Socialist Labour Party
Soc. Rev.	*Socialist Review*
Spec.	*Spectator*
SWMF	South Wales Miners' Federation
SYMA	South Yorkshire Miners' Association
TGWU	Transport and General Workers' Union
Trans	*Transactions*
Trans Roy. Hist. Soc.	*Transactions of the Royal Historical Society*
TUC	Trades Union Congress
UDC	Union of Democratic Control
UN	United Nations
Univ.	University
USDAW	Union of Shop, Distributive and Allied Workers
VE	Victory in Europe
vol(s).	volume(s)
WEA	Workers' Educational Association
WIC	Women's Industrial Council
WIL	Women's International League
WLL	Women's Labour League
WTUA	Women's Trade Union Association
WTUL	Women's Trade Union League
WWW	*Who Was Who*
YMA	Yorkshire Miners' Association (Yorkshire Mine Workers' Association from 1923)
YMWA	Yorkshire Mine Workers' Association
YWCA	Young Women's Christian Association

List of Bibliographies

The subject bibliographies attached to certain entries are the responsibility of the editors. The entries under which they will be found in Volumes I, II, III or IV are as follows:

British Labour Party

1900–13	LANSBURY, George	II
1914–31	HENDERSON, Arthur	I
Christian Socialism, 1848–54	LUDLOW, John Malcolm Forbes	II
Co-operation		
Co-operative Education	HALL, Fred	I
Co-operative Party	ALEXANDER, Albert Victor	I
Co-operative Production	JONES, Benjamin	I
Co-operative Union	HAYWARD, Fred	I
Co-operative Wholesaling	REDFERN, Percy	I
Co-partnership	GREENING, Edward Owen	I
International Co-operative		
Alliance	MAY, Henry John	I
Irish Co-operation	GALLAGHER, Patrick	I
Retail Co-operation		
Nineteenth Century	HOLYOAKE, George Jacob	I
1900–45	BROWN, William Henry	I
1945–70	BONNER, Arnold	I
Scottish Co-operation	MAXWELL, William	I
Guild Socialism	SPARKES, Malcolm	II
Mining Trade Unionism		
1850–79	MACDONALD, Alexander	I
1880–99	PICKARD, Benjamin	I
1900–14	ASHTON, Thomas	I
1915–26	COOK, Arthur James	III
1927–44	LEE, Peter	II
Scottish Mining Trade Unionism	SMILLIE, Robert	III
Welsh Mining Trade Unionism	ABRAHAM, William (Mabon)	I
New Model Unionism	ALLAN, William	I
New Unionism, 1889–93	TILLETT, Benjamin (Ben)	IV

ADAMS, David (1871-1943)

LABOUR MP AND ALDERMAN

David Adams was born on 27 June 1871 in Newcastle upon Tyne, the son of John Adams and his wife Agnes Brand (née MacGregor). He was educated at Dr Rutherford's School in Camden Street and then at the Science and Arts School. Subsequently he was apprenticed as an engineer with Harfield & Company, Blaydon, and later joined his father's firm of salvage contractors, metal merchants and shipowners.

Adams joined the ASE in 1902. He was an early member of the Newcastle branch of the Labour Representation Committee and served as chairman of the Committee (later the Newcastle LP) from 1903 to 1923. He was also a Fabian and a member of the ILP. He was a delegate to the International Socialist Congress in Copenhagen in 1910; a candidate for the NAC of the ILP in 1914 and a member of its committee on local taxation in that year. His long career in local government began in 1902 with his election to the Newcastle City Council as a nominee of Newcastle's LRC. He kept his seat for thirty-eight years, representing successively South Elswick, Armstrong and St Lawrence wards. During this time he served on many committees, but his particular interest was housing, and he was especially active on the committees of housing and health. He was one of the chief sponsors of the Corporation's Walkerville Garden City, and was a member of the National Housing and Town Planning Council.

During the 1920s and 1930s Adams was prominent in Newcastle civic life, becoming particularly identified with engineering and shipowning interests. In the early 1920s Adams became a partner in the firm of D. & T.G. Adams, shipowners, and in 1925 chairman of a new company, D. Adams & Co. of Newcastle. In the later part of his career he was also a director of other shipping companies. He was a member of the Tyne Improvement Commission, the Newcastle Commercial Exchange, the North of England Shipowners' Association and the North East Coast Institution of Shipbuilders. Throughout his long association with these public bodies and in his work on the City Council generally, he consistently tried to represent the Labour point of view on contentious issues. He fought hard to retain municipal ownership of the city's tram system, and on more than one occasion campaigned to keep the Town Moor as an open space for the free use of all. He played a prominent part in reviving the Temperance Festival on the Town Moor in the years after the First World War. He was made a JP in 1909 and was Sheriff of Newcastle from 1922 to 1923. In 1928 he became an alderman and Lord Mayor in 1930-1. In July 1940 he was awarded the freedom of the City.

In the general election of 1918 Adams contested the Newcastle West constituency but was decisively defeated by the Coalition Liberal candidate. In 1922, however, he was successful by a rather narrow margin, when the candidature of two Liberals resulted in a split in the Liberal vote. In the election of the following year, opposed this time by only one Liberal, C.B. Ramage, he lost the seat. Adams contested York City in 1924 and made a very respectable showing against the sitting Conservative member, Sir J.A.R. Marriott. He was unsuccessful again in 1931 at Barrow-in-Furness, but in 1935 he was returned for the constituency of Consett, County Durham, and continued to represent the town until his death in 1943.

In the House of Commons Adams remained a faithful supporter of the leadership of the PLP. Apart from routine constituency matters, which received particularly close attention in the war years, Adams continued his interest in housing, especially new housing programmes and their financing. In the debate on the Housing (No.2) Bill in 1923 he repeatedly pressed for increased government subsidies to be given to municipal authorities, so that the profits of speculative builders could be minimised. He gave his support to measures aimed at restricting rents and to proposals for regional development. On matters of foreign policy, he had long been committed to total international disarmament and the settlement of disputes by arbitration. In the 1920s he had favoured the withdrawal of Allied troops from the Rhineland and a large reduction in reparations, and had advocated the inclusion of all states, including Germany, in the League of

Nations. Adams was a member of the famous 1917 Club, founded to commemorate the first Russian Revolution.

David Adams died on 16 August 1943 in the General Hospital in Newcastle and was cremated at the West Road Crematorium. A memorial service was held in St Nicholas' Cathedral two days later. He was survived by his wife Elizabeth, the daughter of Captain John Patterson (a well-known shipmaster of Newcastle), whom he had married in September 1897, and by his family of two sons and a daughter. One of his sons, Ronald Shaw Adams, was a company owner and director, who died in Newcastle in 1974. The other son, David McGregor Adams, was in business with his brother and then emigrated to the Bahamas. Olga Adams became a doctor. In his will David Adams left effects to the value of £5864.

Writings: *The Planning and Development of the Walker and Willington Estates* [repr. from *Northern Echo*, 1914] 38 pp. [copy in Newcastle PL]; *The Relationships of the Medical Profession to Local Authorities in respect to Rate-provided Hospitals and Clinics* [paper read before AGM of British Medical Association, Newcastle 19-22 July 1921] 12 pp.

Sources: S.V. Bracher, *The Herald Book of Labour Members* (1923); *Dod* (1923) and (1943); *Hansard* (1923-43); *Labour Who's Who* (1924) and (1927); *Manchester Guardian*, 13 Oct 1924; *WWW* (1941-50); biographical information: T.A.K. Elliott, CMG; personal information: D.G. Adams, Monkseaton, nephew. OBIT. *Times*, 13 Aug 1943; *Newcastle J. and North Mail*, 17, 19 Aug 1943; *Stanley News* [Co. Durham], Aug 1943; *Daily Telegraph*, 6 Dec 1943.

BARBARA NIELD

ADAMSON, Janet (Jennie) Laurel (1882-1962)
CO-OPERATOR AND LABOUR MP

Jennie Adamson was born on 9 May 1882 in Kilmarnock, the daughter of Thomas Johnston of Kirkcudbright, who was a railway porter at the time of her birth but who probably had other occupations, including that of coachman. Jennie's mother, Elizabeth (née Denton) had married Thomas Johnston in 1871 and they had six children but she was widowed when quite young and turned to dressmaking to support the family. The daughters all helped their mother when they were old enough but the family were impoverished and the conditions of her early life influenced Jennie's subsequent private and political career. Jennie herself had a secondary school education but became a dressmaker although she also undertook some school-teaching. In 1902 she married William Murdoch Adamson, a journeyman pattern-maker who was subsequently a prominent member of the Workers' Union and later MP for Cannock (1922-31 and 1935-45).

In 1908 Mrs Adamson joined the Labour Party and three years later became a member of the Workers' Union. For some time the family lived in Manchester, where she worked with the Women's Suffrage movement and gave active support to her husband when he was involved as Workers' Union organiser in settling area disputes. In particular she helped during the Black Country strike of 1915. In that year her husband was transferred to Belfast, where Jennie Adamson continued to work actively for the Socialist and now also for the co-operative movement.

In 1921 William Adamson was appointed head of a new East Midland division of the Union, and they lived in Lincoln. There Jennie was closely involved with the women's side of the labour movement, and she served on the Board of Guardians for three years, concerning herself particularly with maternity and child welfare work. One of her more memorable campaigns was 'Boots for Bairns'. She was also a member of the Lincoln Co-operative Society's management committee.

In 1923, after her husband's election for Cannock Chase, the family moved to London. In the 1926 General Strike she was a member of the Women's National Strike Committee and in 1927 was on the executive of the London Labour Party. In 1928-9 she was chairman of the Standing Joint Committee of Industrial Women's Organisations of which she had been a member for some years and in 1929 also was chairman of both the London Labour Women's Advisory Committee and the Labour Women's National Conference. She was elected to the LCC and served for three years (1928-31); she was also a member of the TUC and LP Joint Committee on Workmen's Compensation for several years. From 1927 to 1947, except for a short period (1943-5), she was a member of the NEC of the Labour Party and served as chairman of the Party from 1935 to 1936. Her speech at the 1936 LP conference consisted chiefly of a detailed attack on the National Government's record both in domestic and foreign affairs. She spoke out strongly on the fear of Fascist aggression and the duty of Labour to defend peace and preserve democracy.

On several occasions in the 1930s she represented the Labour Party on the Labour and Socialist Women's International Committee and presided over international conferences in many European countries: in Vienna in 1931 and Paris in 1933; also in Belgium, Switzerland, Germany and Czechoslovakia. Though not a militant she was always an active supporter of women's rights, as was her husband also.

In 1935 Jennie Adamson contested the constituency of Dartford as Labour candidate, opposing the Conservative candidate, and eventual victor F.E. Clarke. On the death of the latter soon afterwards a by-election was held in November 1938, and this time Mrs Adamson won the seat and joined her husband in the House, defeating the only other candidate, the Conservative G.W. Mitchell, by 4238 votes in a very closely contested election. On most political matters she belonged to the right wing of the Labour Party. In October 1939 she protested against the Personal Injuries (Civilians) Scheme, which was part of the Emergency Provisions Act passed on the outbreak of war, as this excluded from compensation civilian women, not in employment. There were further debates on this issue, which was finally resolved after the publication of a Select Committee report in 1943 [Brookes (1967) 138-9]. During the years of the Second World War Jennie Adamson served in the Government as additional parliamentary private secretary to Sir Walter Womersley at the Ministry of Pensions. She abstained when Labour members pressed a division criticising the Government's handling of the Beveridge Report in 1943.

In the election of 1945 she contested Bexley as a Labour and Co-operative candidate (she was sponsored by the Royal Arsenal Co-operative Society). She faced a Conservative candidate, J.C. Lockwood, and a Liberal, W. Smith, and polled more than their combined total of votes. During the first year of the new Labour Government she remained with the Ministry of Pensions with responsibility for war orphans, and served as the Minister's parliamentary secretary; but in 1946 she decided to retire from the Commons to become deputy chairman of the National Assistance Board. She continued to hold this post until her retirement from active public life in 1953.

Throughout her life Jennie Adamson was a consistent champion of the cause of working mothers. She outlined her views on the importance of their role very clearly in her speech in the Commons on 8 March 1945 in support of the Family Allowances Bill. After applauding the House's acceptance of the fact 'that the children of the nation are its greatest asset' she went on to say:

> . . . the fact remains that the wife and mother has not the status to which she ought to be entitled. Her work is of the highest national importance, yet we have never valued her work, or given her that recognition which, in my judgment, was her due. We have always thought that her work was less important than that of her husband and less important than that of a woman in factory or workshop.

Mrs Adamson had continued her interest in the Standing Joint Committee of the Industrial Women's Organisations (from 1941 known as Working Women's Organisations) and on her retirement from it in December 1947 she spoke at a special House of Commons lunch which marked the occasion. After recalling some of the more memorable events in a long career, she concluded by stressing the responsibility which the present generation of women had of continuing the political and social work of the generation which was passing.

Jennie Adamson died on 25 April 1962 and was cremated at Honor Oak Crematorium, London. Her husband had died in October 1945, and the younger of her two sons, Flying Officer Thomas Johnston Adamson, DFM, had been killed on active service in 1944. Mrs Adamson was survived by two daughters and a son. William, a captain on cable ships, died in 1967; Elizabeth Denton and Annabella Findlay both became teachers and both are married and living (1976) in London. Mrs Adamson left effects to the value of £7023.

Sources: *Lincolnshire Forward*, 7 Dec 1929; *Stockport Express*, 21 Dec 1933 [photograph]; *Daily Herald*, 20 July 1936, 6 Dec 1947; *Labour Party Report* (1936); *Glasgow Evening News*, 26 Nov 1938; *Dod* (1939) and (1946); *Kelly* (1949); *WWW* (1961-70); P. Brookes, *Women at Westminster* (1967); R. Hyman, *The Workers' Union* (Oxford, 1971); biographical information: Dr M. Currell, Birmingham Univ.; T.A.K. Elliott, CMG; personal information: Mrs E. Kemp, Surbiton, and Mrs A. Redgrave, London, daughters. OBIT. *Labour Party Report* (1962).

BARBARA NIELD

See also: *William Murdoch ADAMSON.

ARNOLD, Alice (1881-1955)
TRADE UNIONIST AND LABOUR ALDERMAN

Alice Arnold was born in a Coventry workhouse on 19 January 1881, a daughter of Samuel Arnold and his wife Caroline (née Styles). Although her father was a skilled man, a grate-fitter by trade and a poacher by habit, the parents, with their six children, lived in extreme poverty, for he worked only intermittently. It seems likely that Alice's early experiences created in her the determination which she showed throughout her life to support the underdog.

She left school at the age of eleven and a series of factory jobs followed. Little is known of her early trade union experiences, and it was not until the years of the First World War that her abilities as an activist began to be known. Employed on war production at Rudge-Whitworth's Coventry factory, she was responsible as a shop steward for the recruitment of hundreds of women into the Workers' Union; she campaigned for better rates and conditions and in September 1917 led a successful resistance to the reduction of women's piecework rates in the plant. By the end of 1917 Miss Arnold had been appointed a full-time organiser for the Workers' Union in Coventry, second to George Morris, the Union's organiser there since 1913; and in that capacity she continued to take special responsibility for women's questions, gaining as she did so considerable experience of negotiation and a reputation as a fighter.

When the war ended Alice Arnold continued her work on behalf of the Workers' Union. In 1919 she stood as a trade union candidate for election to the Coventry City Council for Swanswell ward. After she was elected, she worked in alliance with other Labour representatives, although politically she was to the left of some of them, including S.G. Poole. Not until 1928, when it seemed that a Labour group could be formed on the City Council, did she stand as a Labour candidate.

During the 1920s Miss Arnold became a popular figure in Coventry, and her fellow-workers often discussed with her their personal as well as their work problems. But in 1931 she received perhaps the greatest blow of her career, for, with the amalgamation of the Workers' Union with the TGWU and the consequent restructuring of the organisation, her job in Coventry disappeared. She was offered a post in Birmingham. Unwilling to leave Coventry and her friends in the city she refused, only to be told that the alternative was dismissal. Anxious to see Miss Arnold's work in Coventry continued, a small delegation from the local Labour movement went to meet Ernest Bevin, but their efforts failed and she lost her post. A fund-raising campaign, chiefly organised by the co-operative movement and ward Labour Parties, was launched to help her set up in business, and as a result a small greengrocer's shop was purchased for her near the city centre. But she had little talent for this work and kept the shop for only a year or two. Again without any means of support, she was assisted this time by the Coventry and District Co-operative Society who employed her as a mutuality club collector and she continued with them, later becoming complaints officer, until her death.

Alice Arnold continued her civic activities throughout her personal difficulties. She showed a special interest in housing and public health, and campaigned to clear the slum areas of Coventry. She was made an alderman in 1931, and in 1936, in accordance with seniority, she was entitled to the mayoralty. But whether because of her objections to the monarchy – since it was Coronation year – or because the ruling coalition of Liberals and Tories rejected such a concession to the growing Labour influence, she was not given the position. In 1937 the mayoralty was again contested, since control of the council was in the balance and the Progressives (Liberals and Tories) claimed that she would use the mayoral position to further Labour's interests. Miss Arnold refused to compromise over her views or to accept special conditions regarding the mayoral position; but in spite of all this she became mayor of Coventry in 1937 – the first woman to hold the position. Always concerned with women's issues, and with widespread support among Coventry women, she recognised her particular responsibility to the women of the city, and she maintained this when the right of women to become freemen of the city, after apprenticeship, was contested. She was also a supporter of the republican side in the Spanish Civil War and attended meetings associated with it.

After her mayoral year, she continued her council activities until her death, although in her later years she became critical of the Labour movement and estranged from some of her friends. She was in failing health for some years before her death and this may have influenced her criticisms of the Labour Party. She did not let her Party membership lapse but was less active in the movement and, according to some of her contemporaries, was at times 'cantankerous and difficult'. But it is for her work in the Coventry labour movement during the inter-war years, especially on behalf of women, that she will be remembered. A fluent speaker, with a clear voice and cultured intonation, she was a principled character – often to her own disadvantage – who made her mark both as trade union organiser and in civic activities. Physically she was short and in later life inclined to be stout. She had dark hair and her facial expression suggested a determined, rather serious-minded person; but her niece recalls that it was her voice rather than her appearance which contributed to her impact at factory-gate meetings. Throughout her life she maintained an individual line and not infrequently refused to compromise with other people or organisations.

She had a long-standing interest in mysticism and helped to found the Parkside Spiritualist Church. After a period in High View Hospital, Exhall, Miss Arnold died on 22 November 1955. She left effects valued at £569. Her funeral service was conducted at Canley Crematorium on 25 November by Mr Joseph Capstack of the Parkside Spiritualist Church, and was attended by the Lord Mayor, Ald. T.H. Dewis, and six former mayors of the city. In his book on *Twentieth-Century Coventry* (1972), Kenneth Richardson wrote of Miss Arnold that: 'She probably never had much in the way of political ideas but her natural class instinct and honesty of purpose gave her a curious dignity and capacity to inspire an affectionate respect which is still not quite forgotten' [p.202].

Sources: (1) MSS: G. Hodgkinson, notes to K. Richardson (below): Modern Records Centre, Warwick Univ.; TGWU, Minutes (1931) [printed but not published]; Coventry LP Women's Section (All Saints), minute books (1936-7) in Coventry LP papers MSS 11; and B. Buxton, notes to R. Hyman (below), 17 Nov 1965, in Hyman papers MSS 51: all at MRC. (2) Other: *Workers' Union Record* (1917) and (1924) [includes photographs]; *Coventry Standard*, 1919-55 *passim*; *Midland Daily Telegraph* (later *Coventry Evening Telegraph*), 1919-55 *passim*; R. Hyman, *The Workers' Union* (Oxford, 1971); K. Richardson, *Twentieth-Century Coventry* (Coventry, 1972); personal information: Miss Edith Arnold, Coventry, second cousin; Mrs N.

Magson, Kenilworth, niece. OBIT. *Coventry Evening Telegraph*, 22 Nov 1955; *Coventry Standard*, 25 Nov 1955.

JANET DRUKER

See also: Stephen George POOLE.

BARBER, Jonathan (1800-59)
CHARTIST AND RADICAL

Jonathan Barber was born in 1800, and moved to Nottingham in about 1820 to work as a stockinger and silk glovemaker in the domestic hosiery industry. He married and had six living children in 1841, when he testified before the Children's Employment Commission. His children were put to work from the age of five at tambouring, lace running and seaming. As a worker in an obsolete and decaying trade, and a political leader of some notoriety, Barber experienced brief periods of steady work alternating with spells of unemployment, as in May 1847, when he was unemployed and dependent upon a small allowance from the Working Men's Association. In his later years his health failed and he obtained a bare subsistence as a street hawker of nuts and shrimps.

Barber was one of a small group of radical activists, including James Sweet and George Harrison of Calverton, who became prominent in the newly-formed Nottingham Working Men's Association in 1838, and gave continuity of leadership to local Chartism for more than a decade. His leadership was characterised by a profound distrust of co-operation with middle-class radicals, and a strong sense of frustration, injustice and class-consciousness, which imbued his speeches with violent rhetoric. At the flashpoints of conflict of August 1839, July 1842 and April 1848, however, he failed to provide the impetus for the sustained development of revolutionary organisation. During August 1839, Barber opposed the Sacred Month as impractical in organisational terms, but at a mass meeting on the outskirts of the town on 12 August he enjoined Chartists to procure arms. Police dispersed the crowd after several such speeches, and on the following day Barber and three others were arrested for riotous assembly. Tried in March 1840, at the Nottingham Assizes, he pleaded guilty and was discharged after entering into his own recognisances in the sum of £100 and providing two sureties of £20.

During 1840-1 Barber held local office in the Chartist movement and mounted attacks upon the Nottingham Auxiliary of the Anti-Corn Law League. He campaigned for the second petition of 1842 and, despite a violent speech in the Market Place, escaped prosecution after the so-called 'Battle of Mapperley Hills' on 23 August, when yeomanry broke up a Chartist rally and made mass arrests. During 1843-4 his energies were devoted to the organisation of the Framework Knitters' Petition, although he did not appear as a witness before the Royal Commission of 1845.

Barber was prominent once more in April 1848. On 1 April the *Northern Star* quoted *The Times* in reporting speeches 'containing sentiments of an inflammatory character' at a radical meeting, including a denunciation by Barber of royalty and the priesthood, a recurrent theme in his diatribes. At a mass rally in the Market Place on 10 April, he urged his hearers to 'have their just rights'. After 10 April a discernible split occurred within the Chartist ranks. Jonathan Barber and James Sowter, a cordwainer, became leaders of an ultra-radical cadre which held open-air meetings throughout the summer, with much physical-force language and denunciation of petitioning or any concession to middle-class sensitivies. During the autumn this faction started to meet at Smith's Temperance Coffee House on Low Pavement. There 'the Republicans of Nottingham' celebrated the anniversary of the French Revolution in February 1849, after which a dispute ensued between Barber and O'Connor on the merits of republicanism in the *Northern Star*.

Increasingly separated from the mainstream of radical activity in Nottingham, Barber turned to secularism. According to G.J. Holyoake, Smith's Coffee House was a place where 'a triple coterie of Chartists, Socialists and Theologians are nurtured on ginger beer, coffee and lemonade,' [*Reasoner*, *10* (1851) 352]. It provided a venue for the early meetings of the Nottingham Secular Society, which flourished 1851-3 with rooms in North Street and lecture visits from Holyoake, Robert Cooper and Charles Southwell. During these years Barber was the most articulate and controversial local secularist, replying to anti-infidel lectures by the Rev. W. Collison in March 1851 and the Rev. G.W. Condor in the spring of 1852, when other working-class members of the Society lacked the confidence to challenge clerical authority. From 1853, however, he was, by his own account, 'uneasy in his mind with regard to Christianity'. The onset of an ultimately fatal disease, probably consumption, in the summer of 1858, led to his dramatic conversion to Christianity by Canon J.W. Brooks of St Mary's Church. His conversion and the rumoured defection of other secularists was signalised by wide publicity, a paragraph in a Nottingham paper being reprinted in *The Times* of 5 August 1858 and in the provincial press. The Nottingham Secular Society repudiated the apostate via the columns of the *Reasoner*, hinting at bribery or derangement.

Jonathan Barber died professing his redemption on 17 January 1859.

Sources: *Northern Star*, 1838-52; *Nottingham Rev.*, 1838-59; Children's Employment Commission, *Trades and Manufactures* 2nd report Pt I App. 1843 XIV [Evidence of J. Barber collected by R.D. Grainger, no. 239 f87]; *Reasoner*, 1852-8; W.H. Wylie, *Old and New Nottingham* (1853); *People's Paper*, 15 Aug 1857; *Nottingham J.*, 18 Feb 1859; J.W. Brooks, *The Apology for renouncing Infidel Opinions of J. Barber . . . To which are added an Introduction, and Particulars of his State of Mind during his Last Illness* [1859] 18 pp.; C. Holmes, 'Chartism in Nottingham, 1837-1861' (Nottingham Univ. BA dissertation, 1960); R.A. Church, *Economic and Social Change in a Midland Town. Victorian Nottingham, 1815-1900* (1966); P. Wyncoll, *Nottingham Chartism* (Nottingham, 1966); J.J. Rowley, 'The Language of Physical-Force and Violence in Nottingham Chartism' (Sussex Univ. BA dissertation, 1971). OBIT. *Nottingham Rev.*, 21 Jan and 18 Feb 1859.

JOHN ROWLEY

See also: *Feargus O'CONNOR, for Chartism 1840-8; James SWEET.

BARNES, George Nicoll (1859-1940)
TRADE UNION LEADER AND LABOUR MP

George Barnes was born at Lochee, Forfarshire, on 2 January 1859, the second of five sons of James and Catherine Barnes. His father, a Yorkshireman by birth and a devout Episcopalian, was a journeyman machine-maker who travelled about doing various jobs; at the time of George's birth he was managing a jute mill in Dundee. Catherine Barnes's father was also a machine-maker (and screw-maker) from the Vale of Strathmore. When Barnes was seven years old the family moved to Tranmere on Mersey, and shortly afterwards to Middlesex, where James Barnes again managed a jute mill, at Ponders End. George received an intermittent education at the National School, and at the age of eleven began work in the jute mill. After about two years there he became apprenticed in 1872 to Powis, James and Company, a Lambeth engineering firm who manufactured woodworking machinery and by whom his father at that time was also employed. Having returned to Scotland, Barnes completed his apprenticeship with Parkers Foundry of Dundee. Throughout his apprenticeship he was a regular attender at evening classes, in the main to study technical drawing and machine construction.

After about five years at Parkers, Barnes returned to England and found employment in the Barrow shipyards. But in 'the black year of 1879', when there was widespread unemployment, he was driven to try his luck in London; and after tramping about all winter in search of work, was taken on in the shops of Messrs Lucas and Airds, a large building firm in Fulham. He worked there for eight years, and then became a draughtsman at Woolwich Arsenal. He later worked at the Millwall, the Victoria and the newly-constructed Albert Docks. While employed in the docks he joined the Amalgamated Society of Engineers, gradually became involved with its work, and associated with John Burns and Tom Mann. He was greatly influenced by the ideas of Henry George and started a class in Fulham to study *Progress and Poverty* and other writings of George's. He also read the first volume of Marx's *Capital*, and the works of other Socialists, including William Morris's *News from Nowhere*. Barnes remained an empirical and undogmatic Socialist, but he was 'much taken up' by the activities of the Socialist League, and in 1887 took part in the march on Trafalgar Square at which John Burns and Cunninghame Graham were arrested. He joined the ILP on its foundation in 1893, and continued his membership until the war. In the general election of July 1895 he stood as ILP candidate for Rochdale and polled 1251 votes in a three-cornered fight. The Conservative (who won) and the Liberal candidate each polled over 4000. Barnes was also a firm believer in co-operation; he helped to found the Chelsea and Fulham Co-operative Society of which, along with the Arsenal Society, he was a member for twenty years.

Barnes's main interest, however, continued to centre on the ASE. Like so many of his contemporaries he was greatly stirred by the success of the 1889 Dock Strike and the possibilities which were opening up for New Unionism. In that year he succeeded John Burns on the eight-man council of the ASE, and in 1891 he was secretary of the powerful London committee established on an *ad hoc* basis to promote the candidature of Tom Mann for the general secretaryship of the ASE. On a number of occasions he acknowledged his debt to Mann. 'But for my connection with Mr Mann', he once wrote, 'I dare say I should never have come into prominence in Labour circles, and very possibly I should have been content to go on working in the "shops" ' [*Pearson's Weekly*, 8 Mar 1906]. In 1892 Barnes was elected to the position of assistant secretary of the ASE, and three years later, in May 1895, he resigned in order to contest the position of general secretary. John Anderson, the incumbent, was a conservatively-minded trade unionist and the election was fought on issues of policy. Barnes was supported by a number of officials as well as by Tom Mann, and he conducted a vigorous campaign. 'Barnes stood on a policy of direct Parliamentary representation for the Society, increased militancy in trade policy, federation of all kindred societies, the transformation of the *Monthly Report* into a Journal for discussion of Society problems, and for fettering the powers of the executive council, which he claimed "enjoys a position of practical irresponsibility" ' [Jefferys [1945] 141]. In the election Barnes ran Anderson very close, polling 11,603 votes against the latter's 12,910. In the following year the executive council dismissed Anderson for 'wilful neglect of duty', and in the union election which followed, with eight candidates offering themselves, Barnes gained 8000 more votes than Anderson, who was the runner-up.

Barnes took office at a time of great uncertainty for the engineering industry. The central problem, for the unions as well as the employers, was the 'machine question'. The development of mass production techniques involved the replacement of the traditional centre lathes and planers by capstan turret lathes, millers and borers, and the crucial issue of policy was whether the new machines were to be operated by skilled workers. In the summer of 1896, about the time when Barnes became general secretary, there was established the Employers' Federation of Engineering Associations, and it was clear from its formation that the Federation was to be a fighting organisation. By the spring of 1897 the tensions between the unions and the employers were reaching a critical point, and the conflict came into the open over the demand by the London Joint Union Committee for an eight-hour day.

The London Union Committee threatened to withdraw their labour from those firms who still refused the eight-hour demand; and the Employers' Federation countered with a lockout in July 1897. Thus began one of the most bitter disputes in the engineering industry. At the outset the unions were confident of victory. Trade was brisk and morale high; but by September the Employers' Federation, which achieved a remarkable unity among engineering firms, was strongly on the offensive. The story has been told in detail in Jefferys [1945] 143 ff. and H.A.

Clegg et al. (1964) 161 ff. By the end of 1897, although the Federátion had failed in its attempt to deny the principle of collective bargaining, the unions were thoroughly beaten, and the terms of settlement were harsh. Barnes always argued, however, that since the crucial principle of collective bargaining remained, the major defeat which the ASE had undoubtedly suffered was not calamitous; and in this he was right.

In the winter of 1898, after the settlement of the strike, Barnes visited Germany, to study conditions generally and also to pass on personally the thanks of the ASE for the support they had received during the recent dispute. He was much impressed by the provisions made by German employers for the safety and general welfare of their workmen, and later wrote a series of articles in the Engineers' *Monthly Journal* describing his experiences in Germany. In the following year he went to Denmark and Sweden on a similar mission, and in 1902 spent three months in America with the Mosely Industrial Commission.

Barnes had long believed that the emancipation of labour could be achieved through working-class representation in Parliament. At the end of February 1900 he was the ASE delegate at the founding conference of the Labour Party; but the members of his executive council were for the most part lukewarm or hostile. A month after the establishment of the LRC, a ballot of all the Society's members produced only 2897 votes in favour of affiliation and 702 against. The smallness of the total vote enabled the executive council to postpone the issue, and at the same time a resolution was passed whereby officers of the Society could not be eligible to stand as parliamentary candidates with financial support from the union. It was not until the following year that the decision to affiliate was accepted by a delegate meeting – in June – and the ASE did not formally affiliate to the LRC until March 1902. By this time the Taff Vale judgement had been upheld by the House of Lords. Barnes himself reacted very sharply, and correctly, to the new legal situation created by the decision of the Lords, and showed himself much more realistic in appraising its consequences than many of his trade union contemporaries [ASE, *Monthly J.* (Aug 1901)]; and he fully supported the efforts of the TUC and the LRC to convince the labour movement of the need for fresh parliamentary legislation. Barnes was a member of the LRC executive committee in 1904, and of the Parliamentary Committee of the TUC in 1906, the year in which he first entered Parliament.

In the general election of January 1906 he stood in the Blackfriars and Hutchesontown (later Gorbals) constituency of Glasgow. He had been introduced to the constituency by Keir Hardie, and he fought the election on an ILP platform. Clydeside was not the most promising area for an official of the ASE at this time. In 1903 a strike on the Clyde had been opposed by the ASE executive council, who went to the length of stopping benefit; this action aroused considerable hostility, only partially abated in the following year when the Final Appeal Committee gave decisions against the executive and ordered payment of benefit to the Clyde men who had been on strike [Jefferys [1945] 167]. More important for Barnes, however, was the fact that the Blackfriars constituency had a large Irish Catholic vote – thirteen per cent. in 1910 – and this in the previous election of 1900 had gone to Bonar Law, the Unionist candidate, the Liberal being regarded as unsound on the Home Rule question. Barnes received the official support of the Irish Nationalist Party, and he achieved a majority of some 300 votes over Bonar Law. At all subsequent elections he steadily increased his majority until his retirement from politics in 1922.

From the outset of his career in the Commons Barnes gave his most active support to the cause of Old Age Pensions. In 1902 he had become chairman of the National Committee of Organised Labour for old age pensions set up a few years earlier by Charles Booth and sympathetic trade unionists. Frederick Rogers of the Bookbinders' Union was its secretary and only paid official, and Herbert Stead of the Browning Settlement in Walworth was another prominent member. Barnes made the pensions question the subject of his maiden speech in February 1906, and at the beginning of the 1907 session he moved an amendment to the King's Speech regretting the absence again of any reference to Old Age Pensions. In June 1908, at the second reading of the Pensions Bill, Barnes spoke in favour of the general principles upon which the measure was based, and of its basic provisions, but opposed the pauper disqualification clauses; he also urged that the pensions committees should be made more representative in character and should be largely based on town councils. In the debates on the National Insurance Bill of 1911 he opposed the exemption provisions and demanded that contributions be exacted from all employees, including those of the Government and local authorities.

From 1908 Barnes was able to devote more time to parliamentary affairs, as in that year he resigned the general secretaryship of the ASE. There were a number of fundamental issues on which disagreement and controversy within the union centred; and the history of the union in the first decade of the twentieth century was one of bitter debate and conflict. One unresolved question related to the machine operators of the new engineering technology. As George Barnes himself wrote in his last Annual Report of 1908: 'The average ASE member has indicated in the most unmistakable manner that the ASE shall remain an organisation of fully-skilled and trained men.' 'I believe he is wrong', Barnes added. Most of the controversial issues found expression in the relationship between the centralised authority of the executive council and the long-standing local autonomy of the districts; and it was the conflict between these two principles of organisation that provided the background to Barnes's resignation. In 1906 the Manchester District Committee and the Erith District Committee had been suspended for refusing to accept the instructions of the Central Conference and of the executive council; in 1908 the refusal of the North-East District Committee to accede to the executive decisions brought about Barnes's resignation from the ASE. As he explained at the time:

> there had been the development of an undemocratic feeling in the trade unions which worked out in the direction of mistrust of officials and officialdom . . . It seemed to him only reasonable on the part of the employers, on the part of the community, on the part of everyone outside trade unionism to say 'alright, we shall give you recognition, but we must have some agent through whom that principle can be given effect to' [ASE, *Monthly Report* (May 1908)].

Barnes's resignation deprived the ASE 'of one of the most efficient and able secretaries since William Allan' [Jefferys [1945] 168]. At the same time it must be appreciated that Barnes was escaping from 'an almost intolerable situation' [H.A. Clegg et al. (1964) 434]. Not only was he highly critical of the union's constitution, but also his general political ideas were shifting towards the right. His Socialism had always been somewhat restrained, and he was now becoming increasingly moderate in political and industrial affairs. He was one of a group of Labour and Lib-Lab MPs who supported the Labour Disputes Bill of 1911, designed to prevent strikes by making them illegal unless advance notice of thirty days had been given. Will Crooks, Arthur Henderson and Charles Fenwick were among those who also indicated their support. The Bill was not proceeded with, but Barnes and his colleagues were widely criticised within the trade union movement and at the September 1911 meeting of the TUC at Newcastle upon Tyne.

In the short Parliament that sat between the two general elections of 1910 Barnes was chairman of the PLP. It was not a very happy term of office for him. He was unwell for most of the year, and he probably handed over to Ramsay MacDonald with some relief. When war broke out in August 1914 Barnes had no hesitation in taking a patriotic line. He believed that Britain had no alternative but to defend her international obligations and uphold the supremacy of international law and the rights of neutral countries. In the early months he was active in recruiting campaigns all over the country. He took a particular interest in the pensions and allowances being paid to the families of recruits, and he demanded that soldiers should receive a minimum pay of £1 a week. When the Government set up a special committee to investigate the system of war pensions, Barnes was chosen, along with T.P. O'Connor, to represent the Labour point of view. Lloyd George, Austen Chamberlain, Bonar Law and R. McKenna were the other members. The committee sat throughout the winter of 1914, but before it made its report Barnes was sent to Canada with William Windham of the Ministry of Labour to persuade Canadian mechanics to migrate to England to replace the skilled engineers who had joined the Army. The mission remained in Canada from May until September, and received a substantial response:

about 1800 skilled men were enrolled for war work in English workshops. A similar number were recruited later in the year when, on this occasion accompanied by J. Gunning of the ASE, Barnes and Windham went to France to select skilled mechanics from among the British troops. Barnes's encounter, though it was brief, with front-line action, and the death of his youngest son, Henry, at the Battle of Loos in September 1915, reinforced his conviction that, if such sufferings and sacrifices were to be justified and deserved there had to be, above all, unity of purpose at home and the employment of the country's total resources.

In 1916 Barnes was made chairman of the Savings Committee, of which he was to remain a member after the end of the war. He was also a member of the Central Appeal Court, which heard pleas from conscientious objectors. It sat under the presidency of Lord Sydenham, and Barnes's parliamentary colleague on the tribunal was Sir George Younger. Barnes had been in favour of including in the Conscription Acts the clauses allowing conscientious objection.

On 7 December 1916 Lloyd George invited to the War Office a joint deputation of the Parliamentary Labour Party and the Party executive. Although the delegates were divided, the outcome was that Labour agreed by seventeen votes to twelve to join the second Coalition Government. The War Cabinet was increased to include Arthur Henderson (without portfolio); John Hodge became Minister of Labour and Barnes was appointed to the new Ministry of Pensions. Since the beginning of the war, the War Emergency Workers' National Committee had been working towards the centralised control of naval and military pensions under a Pensions Minister, and it was made a condition of Barnes's acceptance of the office that the Royal Warrant for the Army should be revised. Under Barnes's direction improvements were made in the payments to disabled servicemen, and a new system was introduced whereby some men could qualify for a pension that was related to their pre-war standard of earnings. In his reorganisation of the pensions administration Barnes drew heavily on the work already accomplished by the Statutory Committee, of which he had been a member. This body had set up a network of local pension committees, and these now formed the basis of the improved system.

When Arthur Henderson was sent to Russia in the summer of 1917 to attempt to persuade the Kerensky Government to continue the war, Barnes (without portfolio) replaced him in the War Cabinet. He undoubtedly found this period of 'real responsibility' a most difficult and trying one [*From Workshop to War Cabinet*, 146-50]; and he must have welcomed the opportunity afforded him of work that was more in his own field, when he was placed in charge of a Government Enquiry into Industrial Unrest. Eight regional Commissions were set up to take evidence, and Barnes had to summarise their findings and recommendations. This he did in a series of fourteen points [ibid., 153-4]; he also chose to list a series of 'psychological conditions' which were adding to the unrest, including 'the feeling that there has been inequality of sacrifice, that the government has broken solemn pledges, that the trade union officials are no longer to be relied upon, and that there is a woeful uncertainty as to the industrial future' [Pelling (1963) 156].

On Henderson's resignation from the Cabinet in the aftermath of the Stockholm Conference quarrel, Barnes again replaced him. John Hodge became Minister of Pensions. Since the Labour Party's Annual Conference at Manchester had endorsed the continuation of the Coalition, Barnes regarded himself as provided with a fixed mandate; he saw himself, G.H. Roberts, and other Labour members of the Government as 'custodians of Labour's good faith' for the duration of hostilities and until a peace treaty formally marked the end of the war.

When the war ended, the Labour Party's national executive had already taken the decision that their participation in the Coalition was to cease. This was confirmed at a special Party conference on 14 November 1918. Foreseeing this outcome, Barnes had already resigned his membership of the Party. He believed it was a grave mistake on Labour's part to deny itself the opportunity of exercising some influence at the peace conferences – indeed, it had been in the hope of achieving some such bargaining position that he had so strongly urged the continuance of the Coalition and the settlement of industrial disputes for the sake of a united national effort. Barnes was asked to attend the Paris Peace Conference as the Government's Labour representative, and he was subsequently one of the signatories of the Treaty of Versailles.

Since 1916 Barnes had been a prominent member of the League to Abolish War, established that year after a conference at the Browning Hall. Herbert Stead was a founder member and vigorous supporter, and Barnes found him an inspiring colleague. During the remaining years of the war Barnes became very much interested in the possibility of establishing some international machinery which, having the force of international law behind it, would lay down and guarantee the rights of working men, and thus offer some real opportunities for industrial reconstruction. Towards the end of 1918, with the advice of David Shackleton and other members of the Ministry of Labour (notably H.B. Butler and E.J. Phelan), he drafted a list of proposals which were to become the framework of the scheme which developed into the International Labour Organisation. In January 1919, on behalf of the British delegation, he presented this preliminary draft to the Commission for World Labour. It was the only detailed plan for a Labour Charter to be placed before the Commission. At this early point in the discussions Arthur Henderson, Charles Bowerman and J.H. Thomas travelled to Paris from the International Labour and Socialist Conference in Berne to confer with Barnes on some of the details of his proposals. At Berne the delegates had been discussing certain 'minimum requirements' which they wanted the League of Nations to incorporate in a 'code of international law'. These requirements concerned, among other matters, the education and employment of young persons, women's working conditions, hours of work and dangerous work, the right of combination, conditions of immigrant workers, the legal minimum wage, unemployment and social insurance and the administration of the labour laws; and many of them were included in Barnes's original proposals. Barnes piloted the whole plan through thirty-six sittings of the Commission, and saw it finally and unanimously approved. The Labour Charter and the provisions for the International Labour Organisation were later incorporated in Part 13 (often known as the Labour Chapter) of the Peace Treaty.

Barnes, not surprisingly, considered the acceptance of the Labour Chapter to be his most important achievement and was profoundly optimistic about its future. In 1919 he headed the British delegation to the first ILO Conference in Washington, at which forty-one countries were represented. Among other acts of the Conference was the establishment of a permanent Labour Office at Geneva. At that point Barnes felt that his mandate was exhausted and it was time for him to leave the Government. This he did in January 1920, and he was made a CH in the same year. After a short trip for the sake of his health to Egypt and Palestine, he returned to Parliament as a back-bench supporter of the Coalition.

His immediate concern was to persuade the Commons to ratify the six conventions of the Washington Conference. These included the employment of women, the eight-hour day, the night employment of young persons and the minimum legal age for industrial employment. They had to be put before the elected governments of the participating countries within twelve months of 26 January 1920. During the year Barnes made repeated requests for a Government statement on the conventions and for their early discussion in the Commons. They were eventually debated on 27 May 1921, with a marked lack of enthusiasm from the Labour benches (with the exception of Henderson), and were defeated. Barnes was bitterly disappointed at this result and at its implications for the future of the ILO.

The last few years in the Cabinet had been difficult ones for Barnes, not least because of the bitter criticism of his policies and of his personal position which had come from different sections of the labour movement. His continued participation in the Coalition Government after Henderson resigned, and later after Labour officially withdrew, had made him widely unpopular in the labour movement, and his own union had strongly opposed many of the Government's innovations and regulations in the munitions industry [Wigham (1973) 96-8]. Yet Barnes continued to justify the attitude he had taken on the conduct of the war as one of necessity and common sense. It is doubtful whether he appreciated at this time the degree to which his ideas and attitudes had moved away from those of his early years. Griffith-Boscawen, who served under Barnes at the Ministry of Pensions, and who was very complimentary to Barnes in his *Memories* (1925), had this also to say of him:

> Though called a Labour member, there was nothing of the modern Socialist-Labourite about him. I should describe him as being really an old-fashioned and very cautious Scottish Whig. He had read a great deal and travelled much, the duties of a Trade Union official apparently allowing him a good deal of spare time and leisure, which he had used to the best advantage. He knew his 'Robbie Burns' almost by heart, but curiously enough did not appreciate Scott. He was a great admirer of the works of Thomas Hardy, which was a bond of sympathy between us [p.195].

In the 'Coupon' election of December 1918 Barnes, standing as an unofficial Coalition Labour candidate (i.e. without the 'Coupon') defended his constituency of Gorbals against John Maclean, the official Labour candidate. His campaign was based mainly on his wartime services, his loyalty to the Labour Party and his unswerving anti-Bolshevism. At a private meeting he said that 'He was profoundly apprehensive of the evils and dangers of Bolshevism, and he was going to do all he could to combat it. Therefore in this contest if anyone were disposed to label him or call upon him to label himself, he wanted nothing better than to be called an Anti-Bolshevist. He believed that in Bolshevism madness lay. It was anti-social, based on mere feelings of revenge and class hatred. They wanted to pull down; he wanted to pull up.' Barnes won the election by 6811 votes, but in 1922, with the tide of opinion swinging strongly against him, he decided to withdraw from politics before the general election of that year. His chief regret was that the ILO would be left without a fully committed spokesman in the House of Commons.

In the years following his retirement Barnes gave much time to work in support of the ILO, and retained an active interest in the co-operative movement – he was for a number of years a director and, for a time, Chairman of the Co-operative Printing Society. He also continued to concern himself with the problems of industry, particularly demarcation questions and arbitration disputes. He believed that it should be possible to establish an organisation representing unions and employers which could draw up a series of industrial codes. These codes would fix wages in the various branches of an industry, would set up tribunals to decide demarcation disputes, and would draw up a basic scale of wages proportionate to output; they would also include provision for the administration of sick and unemployment pay by the industry itself, to prevent abuse, and for the publication of all profits. Barnes incorporated most of his ideas for the achievement of industrial harmony and co-operation in a book he published in 1924, *Industrial Conflict. The Way out*. He hoped to see a similar policy of moderation and co-operation developed within the Labour Party. It had always been his belief that Labour must be prepared to offer practical solutions and towards the end of his autobiography, published in 1923, he summarised his view of the Party's prospects now that its 'apprenticeship' had been served:

> The Labour Party has lived too much in the atmosphere of conferences and public meetings, and is too prone to forget that, however desirable it may be to make common cause with the workers of other countries, it should first of all faithfully serve those of its own kith and kin . . . The difficulty at present is in changing over from propaganda to practical politics . . . Class war, direct action, revolutionary propaganda, are all clearly out of date for a Party which has adopted Parliamentary and Constitutional means of improving the position of those for whom it speaks . . . The weakness of the Labour Party is not that it lacks the ability to govern, but that it has not adjusted itself to changed conditions . . . I believe that it will yet settle down to practical business on the basis of actual facts in the world in which we live, and use its political power to steer the cause of Labour into the main stream of the Nation's life.

To the end of his life he continued to be active in a number of liberal political causes and was a supporter of Harold Macmillan's Next Five Years Group in 1935. George Barnes died at his home at Herne Hill, London, on 2 April 1940. After a funeral at St Paul's Church, Herne Hill, he was buried at Fulham Cemetery. He was survived by his wife Jessie (daughter of T. Langlands, of Dundee) whom he had married in 1882, and by his son Robert and his daughter, Jessie. He left effects to the value of £3129. All his papers were lost when the house at Herne Hill was bombed in a German air raid on London.

Writings: *Trade Unionism: the case plainly stated* (1891) 8 pp.; *The History of the Amalgamated Society of Engineers* (1901); 'Uses and Abuses of Organisation among Employers and Employed. The Old Trade Unionism vs Wisely-organised Labour', *Engineering Mag. 20* (Jan 1901) 560-7; 'Report by Mr George N. Barnes of the Amalgamated Society of Engineers', in *Mosely Industrial Commission to the United States of America Oct-Dec 1902* (1903) 54-78; *America in its Social Aspects* (1903) 11 pp.; 'Wage Systems and their Bearing upon Output', *Engineering Mag. 27* (Apr-Sep 1904) 490-7; 'How I got on', *Pearson's Weekly*, 8 Mar 1906; *The Problem of the Unemployed* [1908] 16 pp.; (with A. Henderson), *Unemployment in Germany* [1908] 15 pp.; *Henry George* [1909] 20 pp.; *Karl Marx* [1909] 21 pp.; 'Labour Exchanges and what may come of them', *Labour Leader*, 18 June 1909; *Robert Burns* [1909] 12 pp.; *The Unemployed Problem* [1909] 12 pp.; Evidence before R.C. on the Poor Laws 1910 XLVIII Cd 5066 App. VIII Qs 82764-3133; 'Trade Unionism and Strikes', *Soc. Rev.*, 9 Aug 1912, 417-24; 'Co-operation in Relation to the Industrial System' in *Proc. of Royal Philosophical Society 44* (1913) 52-63; *The Development of Co-operative Effort* (1913) 28 pp.; 'Thirty Years of the Trade Union Movement', *Co-op. Annual* (1914) 189-210; *Summary of the Reports of the Commission of Enquiry into Industrial Unrest* 1917-18 XV Cd 8696; 'The Perils to the Workers from Materialism' in *The Religion in the Labour Movement* [Speeches of G.N. Barnes, Einer Li, A. Henderson and others at the International Conference on Labour and Religion held in London in 1919] [1919] 10-17; *The Industrial Section of the League of Nations* (Barnett House Papers no. 5: Oxford, 1920, repr. 1930) 16 pp.; 'The Scope and Purpose of International Labour Legislation' in *Labour as an International Problem* ed. E.J. Solano (1920) 1-37; *An Eastern Tour* (1921); *From Workshop to War Cabinet* [1923]; 'Wanted – An Industrial Magna Charta' *Pictorial Mag.*, 17 Nov 1923, 1-3; *Industrial Conflict. The Way out* (1924); 'Evolution or Revolution', *Weekly Westminster*, 3, 10 and 17 Oct 1925; 'Co-operation in the States of Today and Tomorrow', *Int. Co-op. Bull.*, 19 Oct 1926, 289-97; *The History of the International Labour Office* (1926); 'British Labour turns to Co-operation', *American Federationist 34* (Feb 1927) 165-70; *Co-operators and Peace: an appeal* [1934] 9 pp.

Sources: (1) MSS: Labour Party archives: LRC; Webb Coll.: BLPES [for letters from Barnes]. (2) Other: ASE, *Monthly Journals*: AUEW, London; *Labour Annual* (1896) 196; E. Aves, 'The Dispute in the Engineering Trades', *Econ. J. 8* (Mar 1898) 115-24; F.W. Hirst, 'The Policy of the Engineers', ibid., 124-7; *Rev. of Revs 6* (1906) 571-2; *Hansard*, 4th ser. vols *152-99*, 5th ser. vols *1-160* (1906-22); *Christian Commonwealth*, 16 Mar 1910; *Times House of Commons* (1910) 95, (1911) 87; H.M. Hyndman, *Further Reminiscences* (1912); *Labour Year Book* (1913); *Christian Commonwealth*, 22 Sep 1915; *British Citizen*, 1 Sep 1917; E.A. Parry and A.E. Codrington, *War Pensions: past and present* (1918); A. Griffith-Boscawen, *Memories* (1925); *The Book of the Labour Party*, 3 vols ed. H. Tracey [1925]; B. Turner, *About myself* (1930); *DNB* (1931-40); P. Snowden, *An Autobiography*, 2 vols (1934); M.A. Hamilton, *Arthur Henderson* (1938); G. Elton, *The Life of James Ramsay MacDonald (1866-1919)* (1939); J.C. Wedgwood, *Memoirs of a Fighting Life* (1940); J.B. Jefferys, *The Story of the Engineers* [1945]; *The British Labour Party 3* ed. H. Tracey (1948); G.D.H. Cole, *A History of the Labour Party from 1914* (1948); R.O. Clarke, 'The Dispute in the British Engineering Industry 1897-98: an evaluation', *Economica* (May 1957) 128-37; F. Bealey & H. Pelling, *Labour and Politics 1900-1906* (1958); P.P. Poirier, *The Advent of the Labour Party* (1958); H.

Pelling, *A Short History of the Labour Party* (1961); H. Pelling, *A History of British Trade Unionism* (1963); E. Shinwell, *The Labour Story* (1963); H.A. Clegg et al., *A History of British Trade Unions since 1889*: vol. *1: 1889-1910* (Oxford, 1964); W.G. Blaxland, *J.H. Thomas: a life for unity* (1964); R.K. Middlemas, *The Clydesiders* (1965); B.C.M. Weekes, 'The Amalgamated Society of Engineers 1880-1914' (Warwick PhD., 1970); L. Thompson, *The Enthusiasts* (1971); N. Milton, *John Maclean* (1973); E. Wigham, *The Power to Manage. A History of the Engineering Employers' Federation* (1973); C. Hazelhurst & C. Woodland, *A Guide to the Papers of British Cabinet Ministers 1900-1951* (1974); biographical information: T.A.K. Elliott, CMG. OBIT. *Manchester Guardian* and *Times*, 23 Apr 1940; *Brixton Free Press*, 26 Apr 1940; *Labour Party Report* (1940); *TUC Annual Report* (1940).

BARBARA NIELD

See also: *John BURNS; †Arthur HENDERSON, for British Labour Party, 1914-31; †George LANSBURY, for British Labour Party, 1900-13; *Tom MANN; Francis Herbert STEAD.

BARRETT, Rowland (1877-1950)
SOCIALIST AND PACIFIST

Rowland Barrett was born on 11 August 1877 at 1 Castle Street, Newcastle-under-Lyme, the son of James Barrett, a mechanic, and his wife Charlotte (née Turner). Details of his early years are not known but in 1894 he joined the SDF after hearing a debate on Socialism at St George's Young Men's Debating Society in that town. After an illness he left North Staffordshire in 1900 and thereafter moved around the country at frequent intervals in pursuit of his various occupations, until he settled in the North East for some eight years as a commercial representative and finally moved to South Devon, where the last three decades of his life were spent.

Barrett's career falls into a number of phases which are apparently unrelated but actually united by his crusading brand of reformist Socialism. This manifested itself most strongly in his work as a journalist in his thirties, as county secretary for the National Union of Agricultural Workers from 1927 to 1934 and as Labour Party propagandist in Devon, also in the inter-war years. His first occupation was upholstering: he held posts with a Bridgnorth firm, with Waring & Gillow Ltd, and with Anslow Ltd at Coventry. He was a member of the National Amalgamated Furnishing Trades Association from 1898 to 1912 and he was active in the cause of Socialism before going to Coventry, as is shown by testimonials from Crewe ILP, 1904, and Wolverhampton ILP, 1906; but it was in Coventry that his journalistic career began, as editor of the *Coventry Sentinel*, organ of the local ILP (of which he was chairman), 1908-10.

Employment in 1910 and 1911 as advertising salesman and general manager with the *Midland Counties Tribune* was followed by the editorship of the *Bedfordshire Mercury* from 1911 to 1912, one of the papers owned by the Liberal MP Sir Richard Winfrey, with whom Barrett was on friendly terms. In February 1913 Barrett received an invitation to edit the *Leicester Pioneer*, which he accepted. He remained with the *Pioneer* for two years, during which time he was sounded out for the editorship of the *Labour Leader*, invited to take charge of a revived *Coventry Sentinel*, and offered a permanent post by Winfrey. While he was at Leicester Barrett, who was a member of the NUJ from 1913 to 1915, was involved in a dispute with the proprietor, A.H. Reynolds, over the part played by the *Pioneer* in the 1913 by-election, in which Hartley stood as the British Socialist Party candidate against the Liberal, Gordon Hewart.

His journalism showed a continuing concern with such issues as the provision of public abattoirs (a major issue pursued by another Coventry Socialist, S.G. Poole), housing and local industrial disputes. An ending of the tied-cottage system was a particular preoccupation of Barrett's during his Devon period, and his RDC election address of 1931 coupled with it the issues of rural electricity supply and the protection of amenity.

Barrett's departure from journalism (with a good reference from Reynolds) seems to have come as a surprise to his friends. His experience of space-selling stood him in good stead for his new career as Newcastle upon Tyne area representative for Wm Brown & Co of Liverpool Ltd, fruit, rice and canned goods merchants. During this period he unsuccessfully applied for exemption from military service on medical grounds and subsequently suffered imprisonment at Wormwood Scrubs and Wakefield as a conscientious objector, having refused to wear uniform after his call-up. His objections were on religious grounds, that war was contrary to the teaching of Christ; and although he could be fiercely critical of the established Church he numbered several priests and ministers among his friends, notably the well-known Christian Socialist the Rev. P.E.T. Widdrington, chairman of the *Sentinel* board during Barrett's editorship, and the Rev. F. Seaward Beddows of Wycliffe Church, Leicester.

His imprisonment in May 1917 was followed by directed work on his release, and it was not until February 1919 that he was reinstated with Brown's. He married Marion Jackson on 19 July 1919. There were no children of the marriage. Surviving correspondence indicates that he was a successful and popular member of their staff, and he evidently saved sufficient capital while in their employ to purchase in 1923 what was intended to be a smallholding at Rockvale Cove, Stoke Fleming, near Dartmouth. However, experience led him finally to run this as a small, informal holiday camp for Socialists; and he combined with this activity campaigning on behalf of the Labour Party in Devon – where he was twice invited to offer himself for selection as parliamentary candidate – and on behalf of the NUAW, in Devon and Cornwall particularly, but also on occasions further afield.

Barrett seems to have been a natural fighter, constitutionally opposed to authority, but with a genial disposition, which won him numerous friends in the labour movement. Leaving school early, but working assiduously on Ruskin College correspondence courses, he had some of the faults of the autodidact, most noticeable in his concern for a very unwieldy system of reformed spelling which he developed in later years. However, his crusading journalism struck the right note of informed criticism to arouse the political consciousness of his readers, and the labour movement, particularly in Devon, had cause to be grateful for his work – carried on with great energy until somewhat affected by a serious motorcycle accident in 1934. He died on 26 September 1950 at his Stoke Fleming home and was cremated at Plymouth. In a ceremony conducted by A.W. Waddington, a lifelong friend, and Alderman F. Scardifield, chairman of Dartmouth Labour Party, his ashes were scattered among the pines he had planted at Rockvale Cove. He left an estate valued at £3866.

Sources: (1) MSS: Rowland Barrett papers: Modern Records Centre, Univ. of Warwick Library (MSS 83); these include volumes of annotated press-cuttings, MS 'Life and Letters' and some correspondence. Volume of annotated *Coventry Sentinel* and *Midland Counties Tribune* cuttings with a few letters in Coventry and Warwickshire Coll.: Coventry Reference Library (JN 335). (2) Other: J. Yates, *Pioneers to Power* [history of Coventry Labour Party] (1950); P.d'A. Jones, *The Christian Socialist Revival 1877-1914* (NJ, 1968). OBIT. *Dartmouth Western Guardian*, 5 Oct 1950.

RICHARD STOREY

See also: Stephen George POOLE.

BATTLEY, John Rose (1880-1952)
LABOUR MP

John Battley was born in Clapham on 26 November 1880, the son of George and Adah Elizabeth Battley (née Maderson). His father was then a general labourer, but later (from 1899) he ran a grocer's shop in Battersea; his mother was a seamstress. John Battley left Basnett Road School at the age of thirteen in 1894, and went as an apprentice to the printing works of the London, Chatham and Dover Railway at Victoria, and later to Marchbanks, printers in Battersea Rise, where he stayed until 1904. On the completion of his apprenticeship he joined the London Society of Compositors in 1902. At the end of 1904 he set up as a master printer in Queen's Road, Battersea, at first in partnership with his elder brother, George; the partnership was soon dissolved, but the firm continued to be known as Battley Brothers.

John Battley early became involved in philanthropic activities through his membership of the Victoria Baptist Church in Clapham, and while he was still an apprentice spent his Saturday afternoons teaching in a Shaftesbury Ragged School. He was an active member of the Church from about 1898 onwards; and for a number of years he ran bible classes for children. Religion was in fact one of the most powerful influences on his whole life, and at the time of the Boer War he became a convinced pacifist for religious reasons, and remained so during the First World War. He supported the No-Conscription Fellowship and the Fellowship of Reconciliation and himself became a conscientious objector in 1916. He was given conditional exemption and went to work in a market garden. As a young man he also strongly supported the temperance movement. Pacifism and temperance were both causes to which he remained attached throughout his life.

Battley joined the City of London ILP branch in 1913, but he was not active. He was, however, one of the leading figures in a move to re-start the Battersea ILP branch after the war; on its formation early in 1922, he became its first secretary (jointly with Oscar Raynor) and subsequently branch chairman. This, his first active political role, seems to have been inspired largely by his wartime experiences and, especially, the ILP's stand against conscription. Battersea ILP took a prominent part in the No More War campaign of the 1920s.

In 1923 he moved his printing works from Battersea to larger premises in Clapham, and although he continued as a member of the Battersea ILP until the end of the 1920s, it was as a prominent local businessman that he first became publicly known in Clapham. He was a founder-member of the Clapham Rotary Club in 1924 and its president in 1929, and was active in the Clapham and District Chamber of Commerce, among other local bodies.

In the early 1930s Battley had two breakdowns, probably largely the result of strain and overwork. The second of these, in 1932, was the more serious and necessitated a stay of several months in the Maudsley Hospital. After his recovery, he married, in March 1933, Dorothy Sybil Allchurch, the daughter of Stanley Allchurch with whom he had been associated particularly in the founding and running of the Lavender Hill Temperance Choir. Shortly after his marriage he began his close involvement with the Clapham LP which continued for the rest of his life. In November 1934 he was an unsuccessful Labour candidate for the north ward of Clapham in the Wandsworth Borough Council elections, and in the following year he was for the first time nominated to the general management committee of the Party. In 1937 he contested the LCC elections, and was also selected as prospective parliamentary candidate for Clapham. Although unsuccessful in the 1937 LCC elections he became in the following year the first Labour representative for Clapham on the LCC when he defeated the Municipal Reform candidate in a by-election by the narrow margin of fifty-seven votes. During these years he gave considerable financial help to the Party and was instrumental in securing for the first time the appointment of a full-time agent from the beginning of 1938.

From the time of his election to the LCC until 1946 when he ceased to be a member Battley was a conscientious and very regular attender both at committee and council meetings, but not a prominent speaker. He gave a great deal of time to helping individual constituents with their problems, holding a regular 'surgery' for this purpose throughout the war. In June 1939 he was appointed chairman of the casual wards sub-committee of the LCC's public assistance committee, and this led to a strong interest in the problems of vagrancy. At the same time he still had his business to maintain and was involved in many other public activities in Clapham, such as the Clapham Orchestral Society and the Clapham Exhibition of 1939, in addition to his temperance, pacifist and Rotarian interests. And in 1940 he was appointed a JP. The strain of all these activities began to tell on him and in November 1943 he sought to withdraw his parliamentary candidature, but was persuaded to continue.

In the general election of 1945 Battley won a majority of 5000 votes in a three-cornered fight and thus became Clapham's first Labour MP. He was, as in his LCC days, most assiduous in his attendance at the House, and he continued on an even larger scale the welfare role which he had adopted in his LCC days. He never spoke in a debate in the House, and asked few parliamentary questions but he carried on a large correspondence with Ministers and government departments, largely about constituents' problems. He did not stand for re-election in 1950, and died on 1 November 1952 after a long illness. He was cremated at the South London Crematorium, Streatham Vale.

John Battley was a man of strong moral and religious principles, but quiet and unassuming in manner. A self-made man of humble origins, a stern but paternalistic employer, he seemed destined until he was in his fifties to be known simply as an honest, respectable and respected member of Clapham society. Clapham meant much to him: he edited in the 1930s a Clapham guide which went into several editions, and built up an extensive collection of prints of Old Clapham. His Socialism, like his pacifism, was a sincerely held conviction springing largely from his religious outlook, but also coloured by his childhood experiences of deprivation and poverty. His pursuit of an active political career in his last twenty years marked a distinct new phase in his life. As a politician he generally followed an orthodox party line, especially in matters of social policy, his main interest. His rare disagreements with party policy were chiefly over questions which affected his innermost convictions, as when, along with a number of other Labour MPs, he voted against the National Service Bill of 1947. His political speeches, mostly in Clapham, were notable less for their expositions of policy than for the expression of his convictions, and he frequently adopted the style of a preacher. If he was known as 'Honest John' in Clapham he was also known as 'John the Baptist'. As a speaker he was at his best in small gatherings. But his main contribution was the individual case work to which he devoted so much of his time and energy as a member of both the LCC and Parliament.

Battley had two sons, David John, born in 1935, who became an actor; and Bernard, born in 1938, who took over the family printing business of Battley Brothers. He left an estate valued at £43,453.

Writings: *Impressions* (1917); (with E. Trent), *A Brief Survey of the Art of Printing* (1928) 23 pp., rev. ed. (1934) 36 pp.; *Sanctions: notes of an address to the Victoria Men's Christian Fellowship* [1935] 27 pp.; *Clapham Guide* (1935; later eds); *Clapham, Old yet ever New: an address* (1937); *45 Years of Print and the 45 Hour Week* (1938); *The Monasticism of the Casual Poor: a speech* (1940) 41 pp.; *A Visit to the Houses of Parliament with John Battley MP* [1947; rev. ed. 1949]. (All except the first edition of *A Brief Survey of the Art of Printing* were published by John Battley's own company.)

Sources: (1) MSS: John Battley papers: B. Battley, Clapham; Minutes of Clapham LP: Transport House, London. (2) Other: *Hansard* (1945-9); C. Bunker, *Who's Who in Parliament* (1946); *Dod* (1946); *WWW* (1951-60); biographical information: T.A.K. Elliott, CMG; personal information: B. Battley, Clapham, son. OBIT. *Times*, 4 Nov 1952; *Clapham Observer*, 14 Nov 1952.

GERALD RHODES

BENTHAM, Ethel (1861-1931)
DOCTOR, COUNCILLOR AND LABOUR MP

Ethel Bentham was born in London on 5 January 1861. Her father, an inspector, later secretary and finally general manager of the Standard Life Assurance Company in London, was William

Bentham, Justice of the Peace for the County of Dublin and a Quaker belonging to the same family as Jeremy Bentham; her mother was Mary Ann (née Hammond). Ethel Bentham spent her early years in Dublin, where she was educated at Alexandra School and College. As a young girl she accompanied her mother on charitable visits to the Dublin slums and an early excursion into social work, undertaken while she was still in Dublin, was a Sunday club organised for shop-girls.

Resolving to become a doctor as the best means of being able to affect the lives of the poor, she studied at the London School of Medicine for Women. Being forced to gain the statutory qualifications elsewhere, she took the Licentiate in Midwifery of the Rotunda Hospital, Dublin, in 1893; the triple Scottish qualification – LRCP, LRCSE and LRFPS(G) – in 1894, and the MD of Brussels University in 1895. She worked as assistant medical officer to the Blackfriars Provident Dispensary for Women and Children, and as clinical assistant at the New Hospital for Women for one year, then went into general practice in Newcastle upon Tyne with Ethel Williams. She remained there for some thirteen years, and during this time was an active suffragist. In 1909 she was a member of the executive committee of the National Union of Women's Suffrage Societies. She joined the Labour Party in 1902; and in 1907 was the first Labour candidate to contest a municipal election in Newcastle. In this contest, however, she was unsuccessful. She was on the list of ILP speakers in 1908.

She went to London in 1909 and continued as a general practitioner until a few years before her death. At this period she was closely involved with many of the women in the labour movement such as Marion Phillips, Mary Longman and Susan Lawrence, members of a group centred on Lansdowne Road, Holland Park, where she lived for a time at number 74. She also gave lectures in 1909-10 for the Women's Industrial Council on medical and related topics including nursery schools, and at her suggestion a baby clinic with a hospital in North Kensington (at 92 Tavistock Road and 1 Ladbroke Square respectively) was founded in 1911, in memory of her friends Margaret MacDonald and Mary Middleton. Dr Bentham became the senior medical officer, and at the time of her death she was still the consultant medical officer. The management of the hospital was taken over in 1937 by the Kensington Borough Council. The Baby Hospital had 20-26 beds for children under five years and it carried out specialised work in caring for sick children whose mothers were incapable of doing so, educating mothers in child care, and feeding problems. During the Second World War the buildings were used as a day nursery. At the present time [1976] the Tavistock Road building is a school treatment centre and the premises in Ladbroke Square are still in use as the 'Ladbroke Day Nursery'. Dr Bentham also worked for a time as senior clinical assistant in the Throat and Ear Department of the Royal Free Hospital. Her work for mothers and children was recognised in November 1930, when she was presented with an illuminated volume of the Clinic's Report, autographed by many of her associates.

She became a member of the executive committee of the Women's Labour League in 1910, and was its president in 1913. She was a candidate for the NAC of the ILP in 1913. She first stood for election to the LCC in North Kensington in 1910, and unsuccessfully contested a seat on the Borough Council in 1912. She was successful in 1913, and remained on the Council for thirteen years. One of her main interests was in improved housing and on the initiative of Dr Bentham and the other Labour members of the Council a block of working-class homes was built in North Kensington. Dr Bentham was one of the first women magistrates to be elected; she took a special interest in children's courts and lunacy cases. She served as government nominee on the Metropolitan Asylums Board, where she advocated the reform of casual wards. She also stood as a candidate for election to the LCC, being supported by the Fabian Women's Group.

Ethel Bentham served on many committees, and in addition to the WLL (later merged in the women's section of the LP) and the NUWSS, she was also on the executive of the Fabian Society and on the Standing Joint Committee of Industrial Women's Organisations. She was a member of the NEC of the Labour Party from 1918 to 1920, 1921 to 1926 and 1928 to 1931, and was a member of the Advisory Committees on Public Health and Foreign Policy. She was also for some time a director of the *Daily Herald*, and a member of the PEN Club and the 1917 Club: the latter, founded to commemorate the first Russian Revolution, was a meeting place for radicals and Socialists. On the medical side she was a member of the BMA and the Association of Registered Medical Women.

After three unsuccessful attempts in 1922, 1923 and 1924, she was elected to Parliament by the constituency of East Islington in 1929: she raised the Labour vote from nearly 6000 in 1922 to 15,000. Her election addresses showed her particular interests in health (especially maternity and child welfare), housing, education and peace. Her speeches in the House mirrored her chief concerns and are full of anecdotal material drawn from her experience as a medical practitioner of many years' standing. For instance, her long-term interest in the mentally ill is well illustrated in her speech on the Mental Treatment Bill, on 17 February 1930, in which is reflected her experience of private and Poor Law institutions and the difficulties of both patients and their families. As a doctor, she was also particularly concerned with questions of health and safety at work – in fact her maiden speech was during a debate on accidents in mines. Her concern, however, was also with workers other than those like the miners who were most obviously and dramatically at risk. She had a special interest in the plight of shop assistants [*Hansard*, 21 Mar 1930] and she gave evidence to the S.C. on Shop Assistants' hours. She was in favour of children's staying on longer at school, as this would prevent them from doing heavy work too soon [*Hansard*, 21 Mar 1930].

As a former suffragist, she must have been particularly delighted to move the second reading of the Nationality of Women Bill [*Hansard*, 28 Nov 1930]. If it had become law, this Bill would have meant that British women would no longer have lost their nationality when they married foreigners. It got no further than this second reading, but it did provide Ethel Bentham with an opportunity to protest against 'the principle which regards women as holding an entirely inferior status, classing them with lunatics and criminals'. She was a member of a Select Committee on Capital Punishment and an all-party Committee for the Protection of Coloured Women, set up in 1929, which was concerned with the condition of women in the colonies.

Dr Bentham joined the Westminster and Longford monthly Meeting of the Society of Friends in 1920. In her letter of application she stated that she was brought up in the Church of England, 'but have for many years been out of harmony with it'. She had, however, frequently attended Friends' Meetings in both Newcastle and London [minutes of Westminster and Longford Monthly Meeting, 18 Mar 1920]. She was a member of the Meeting at Friends' House, and took an active part in the Central Adult School held there on Thursday evenings.

Ethel Bentham died on 19 January 1931 at the age of seventy – the first woman MP to die in office – of pleurisy following influenza. She was cremated at Golders Green Crematorium, where a Meeting was conducted by the Society of Friends; and later a Memorial Meeting was held at Friends' House. She left an estate valued at £8552.

Writings: (with others), *Wage earning Mothers* (WLL, n.d.) 32 pp.; (with others), *The Needs of Little Children: report of a conference on the care of babies and young children* (WLL, 1912) 32 pp.; 'What should London think about?', *Nation* [London] *32*, no. 3, 21 Oct 1922, 111-13; 'Aspects of Birth Control', *Soc. Rev. 24* (Oct 1924) 101-8.

Sources: WIC, *Annual Reports* (1909-10); *Daily Herald*, 24 Oct 1924; *Labour Who's Who* (1924) and (1927); *Hansard* (1929-31); *WWW* (1929-40); *Medical Register* (1930); *Medical Directory* (1931); P. Brookes, *Women at Westminster* (1967); biographical information: T.A.K. Elliott, CMG; Kensington and Chelsea Borough Library; Library of the Religious Society of Friends, London; North West Thames Regional Health Authority; Royal College of Physicians, Edinburgh. Obit. *Islington Gazette* and *Times*, 20 Jan 1931; *Friend 71*, n.s., 23 Jan 1931; *Islington and Holloway Press* and *Lancet*, 24 Jan 1931; M.D. Shaw, 'Ethel Bentham MP: an appreciation', *Friend 71* n.s., 13 Feb 1931; *Labour Party Report* (1931).

ANN HOLT

BESANT, Annie (1847-1933)
SECULARIST, SOCIALIST, THEOSOPHIST, INDIAN NATIONALIST

Annie Besant was born in the City of London on 1 October 1847, the daughter of William Burton Persse Wood, a businessman with wide intellectual interests. He was a member of a minor branch of a family which included Sir Matthew Wood, MP, Lord Mayor of London; Field-Marshal Sir Evelyn Wood; Lord Hatherley, Lord Chancellor of England; and Katharine Wood, later O'Shea, still later Parnell. Her father was Irish on his mother's side; her mother was wholly Irish. Despite this impressive background, William Wood's family was left in straitened circumstances upon his early death in 1852. The young Annie Wood led a modest but genteel life, spent in considerable part in the home of Ellen Marryat, sister of the popular novelist Frederick Marryat. In 1866 she was introduced to radical politics through a family friend, the radical solicitor W.P. Roberts.

At the age of eighteen she met the Rev. Frank Besant, brother of the novelist Walter Besant. When she was twenty they were married. If Frank Besant was the stereotype of the masterful, insensitive mid-Victorian husband, his wife combined innocence with passion in a way which must have made trouble inevitable. As she noted in her *Autobiography* (1893), at the time of her marriage she was already 'a woman of strong dominant will' (p. 82), a trait which was to characterise her whole life. Her husband pocketed her first literary earnings and physically abused her. Personal illness and the illness of her two small children added to her problems, and during 1871-2 the young wife and mother found that her previously strong religious faith was leaving her. Through the unconventional clergyman Charles Voysey she met the freethinking publisher Thomas Scott, who published in 1873 her first major essay. Written under a pseudonym, it was entitled 'On the Deity of Jesus of Nazareth'. In the same year she was legally separated from her husband, taking her daughter Mabel but leaving her son Digby in his father's care. Frank Besant was left to lead the life of a rural clergyman in Sibsey, Lincolnshire, until his death in 1917. His sense of hurt and hostility towards his wife did not leave him, for when Digby was reconciled to his mother upon coming of age his father cut off all relations with his son [A.D. Besant (1930) 221-2].

Study of a variety of theological literature and the works of Mill, Darwin, Comte and Spinoza were steps towards persuading Mrs Besant that the theism which she professed in 1873-4 was an untenable faith. It was at this point that Charles Bradlaugh, the president of the National Secular Society, entered her life. Influenced by her friend Ellen Dana Conway, wife of the 'ethical' clergyman Moncure Daniel Conway, she began to read Bradlaugh's journal, the *National Reformer*. Early in August 1874 Mrs Besant heard Bradlaugh speak for the first time and made his acquaintance. She quickly became his most dependable and able lieutenant, writing a weekly column in the *National Reformer* under the pseudonym 'Ajax', later becoming co-editor and joint proprietor of the journal. She was also elected a vice-president of the National Secular Society.

Mrs Besant's relationship with Bradlaugh was one of the most productive in the history of modern British radicalism. They lived near each other in St John's Wood, London, and it is likely that they would have lived in the same house had it not been for the objections of Bradlaugh's two daughters. They not only worked but holidayed together, and may have hoped to marry, for Bradlaugh's estranged, alcoholic wife died in 1877 and Mrs Besant seems to have hoped to free herself from her husband. Certainly she considered that she and Bradlaugh were engaged, and she wrote to at least one correspondent in 1877 to say so [Tribe (1971) 179-83]. It is not known whether they were lovers, though Mrs Besant's principal biographer thinks not, nor, indeed, that she ever had a lover [Nethercot (1961) 110-15]. Certainly she was an extremely attractive woman with many friendships with men during the period before 1889, among them

Edward Aveling, John Mackinnon Robertson, George Bernard Shaw, Herbert Burrows and W.T. Stead. Nevertheless, her relationship with Bradlaugh was undoubtedly the longest and most fruitful of her pre-theosophical life. As to Bradlaugh, although he had already been superabundantly active in the secularist and radical movements for many years, Mrs Besant provided both political and personal assistance of great value to him. On the other hand, the always fractious secularist movement found in the Bradlaugh-Besant axis a new source of gossip and discord.

Mrs Besant's first public lecture was delivered in London on 25 August 1874, in the same month that she met Bradlaugh. Her lecture was evidently a very considerable success, as is shown in the lengthy, cautious, but awed account of it given by the Rev. Charles Maurice Davies in his book *Mystic London* (1875). Her subject was 'the political status of women', and Davies, hiding her identity under a pseudonym, commented that she knocked down the stock objections to women's suffrage 'like so many ninepins'. At the same time she attacked Christianity, saying that 'if Bible and religion stood in the way of Woman's Rights, then Bible and religion must go' [Davies (1875) 94-5]. Mrs Besant was soon widely acclaimed as a superb public speaker. Bernard Shaw, for example, remembered her as being in the 1880s 'the greatest orator in England, and possibly in Europe' [Shaw (1917) 12]. But the lecturing experiences were not always easy, especially at first. In her *Autobiography* (p. 200) she wrote of an engagement at Congleton in 1876 during the course of which she 'received a rather heavy blow on the back of the head from a stone thrown by some one in the room. We had a mile and a half to walk from the hall to the house, and were accompanied all the way by a stone-throwing crowd.' Nor was this occasion unique. Her speaking experiences at first faced constant interruption and her health broke under the strain. As she herself acknowledged, however, she suffered much less from riotous opposition than Bradlaugh and others had done in the earlier, heroic phase of the secularist struggle.

During her first three years as a secularist Mrs Besant was concerned above all with questions of Christianity and free thought. But she also wrote on a wide variety of other topics, including the land, the French Revolution, prostitution, and euthanasia. Her ceaseless activity and her ability made her a prominent figure before she was thirty.

It was in 1877 that she first became notorious, as a result of the famous birth control trial, *The Queen* v. *Charles Bradlaugh and Annie Besant*. Bradlaugh had advocated neo-Malthusian views since the early 1860s. Although support for such views among secularists was by no means universal, by the 1870s acceptance of family limitation was common to many advanced radicals, along with such other characteristic beliefs as land reform, republicanism and temperance. Self-help was still regarded even by many of the most progressive as the key to social progress. It was not until the liberating doctrines of Henry George in the early 1880s that they began to regard maldistribution of wealth, not over-population, as the principal cause of poverty.

Charles Knowlton's *Fruits of Philosophy* had first been published in the United States in 1832, and had sold moderately and without hindrance in Britain ever since. Upon the successful prosecution of a Bristol bookseller in 1876 for publishing an illustrated and allegedly obscene version, the edition published by the secularist Charles Watts was also prosecuted. Watts dismayed his friends by pleading guilty to the publication of an obscene book. Bradlaugh and Mrs Besant thereupon formed their own Freethought Publishing Company and brought out an edition of *Fruits of Philosophy* as a test case. Not only the right of poor people to limit their families but freedom of the press was at stake.

A prosecution was immediately brought, and though the identity of the prosecutors has never been disclosed, it is likely that either the Society for the Suppression of Vice or supporters of the Christian Evidence Society were the responsible party. Meanwhile the sales of *Fruits of Philosophy* had soared. Mrs Besant said at the trial that the annual sales of the pamphlet 'for years back' had been about 700 copies a year, but that in three months the Freethought edition had sold no less than 125,000 copies. In her speeches to the jury she laid stress upon the lives of the poor and the results of large, poor families, especially immorality and overcrowding. She pointed out that birth control literature was available to the wealthy, but not to the poor, who could not afford to purchase it; and she denied the charge of obscenity.

The defendants were found guilty but on appeal were freed on a technicality. There is no doubt that the trial made an enormous impact on public opinion at a crucial time, when it was ready to take birth control seriously. Mrs. Besant proceeded to write a more modern birth control manual, entitled *The Law of Population*. Published in 1877, this pamphlet was largely devoted to justification of birth control, discussion of methods of contraception occupying relatively little space. *The Law of Population* clearly met a great need, for 175,000 copies were published in England by 1891, and it was translated into a number of other languages. Mrs Besant was for a short time the secretary of the revived Malthusian League (1877), a body which agitated for the spread of birth control information and practice.

Although her courage, resourcefulness and ability had given the cause so great a fillip, the result was a personal disaster. Frank Besant applied to take her seven year-old daughter Mabel from her. The case was heard before the Master of the Rolls, Sir George Jessel, in May 1878. Jessel was openly antagonistic to Mrs Besant, partly because Mabel had not been given religious instruction, partly because of her mother's advocacy of birth control. The transfer to the father was now made: Mabel's intimacy with her mother was resumed when she came of age, and as in her brother's case this entailed breaking her ties with her father.

For the next dozen years the political life of Annie Besant was a microcosm of radical London; there was hardly a radical movement in which she did not take an important part. She joined demonstrations against the Disraeli Government's foreign and imperial policies in the years before its fall in 1880. She assisted Bradlaugh in his election victory in Northampton in 1880, and actively supported his prolonged and strenuous attempts to take his seat in the House of Commons, not without some risk to her own safety. She continued her lecturing, writing and editing for the *National Reformer*, and from this work came a steady stream of pamphlets and short books, expressed in vigorous, uncompromising language. Although she did not declare herself a Socialist until 1885, her publications after 1877 took on a markedly political and social bias, without weakening in her championship of secularism. She dealt with a wide variety of topics, putting forward always an advanced radical line. In foreign and colonial policy, both in Africa and Asia, she showed herself a vehement anti-imperialist. In Irish affairs she condemned the coercive policies of the Gladstone Government in the early 1880s, notably imprisonment without trial. She defended the rights of women and birth control, asking in a pamphlet on *The Social Aspects of Malthusianism* [1880?]: 'Has a woman no rights as an independent human being? We do not regard a man only as a husband and father: why should we regard a woman only as a wife and mother?' [p.4].

She wrote on numerous occasions on the land question, demanding the graduated taxation of large estates, the creation of peasant proprietors and the amendment of the existing land laws. Later, but still before her Socialist days, she supported land nationalisation. She advocated republicanism, claiming that 'The Republican spirit is the very core of English progressive thought' [*English Republicanism* [1878] 2]. Among her other topics at this time were free trade and its history, the reform of the divorce laws, vivisection and various scientific subjects. In common with many other secularists and advanced radicals of the period, Mrs Besant was attracted to the study of science. In general terms this attraction was due to the alternative which science seemed to pose to the dogmas of established religion. Science, it was widely thought, could replace belief in God with something as respectable but more rational, based as it was on natural laws and observed experiments. In Mrs Besant's case there were two other attractions. One, as she later said, was to find a distraction and a new type of useful activity after the loss of Mabel. The other was Edward Bibbins Aveling, science lecturer at London University and a new recruit to secularism in early 1879. With Aveling's assistance the National Secular Society arranged a number of classes in different scientific subjects. Mrs Besant's interest in science antedated her interest in Aveling, but it was with his encouragement that she attended science classes at London University, became qualified as a science teacher and attempted to gain a BSc degree on botany and then in chemistry. However, these attempts failed because of the opposition and prejudice of the university authorities. During the same period, between 1879 and 1883, her personal relationship with Aveling became very close.

In 1883, the year that her career as a student of London University came to an end, she began one of her most engaging and attractive publications. This was the literary monthly, *Our Corner*, which ran until the end of 1888. The journal contained an almost bewildering variety of 'Corners', most of them running simultaneously, among them an 'Art Corner', 'Chess Corner', 'Gardening Corner', 'Inquisitive Corner', 'Political Corner', 'Publishers' Corner', 'Science Corner' and 'Young Folks' Corner'. It also contained poetry, science, literature and various kinds of fiction, including the serialisation of two of Bernard Shaw's early novels. Mrs Besant's own *Autobiographical Sketches* was also published serially. *Our Corner* had a radical political outlook which became more prominent and more Socialist as the years passed. Not only Shaw, but Bradlaugh and many other radical and Socialist writers of the period were among the contributors.

Socialism in the early 1880s was a new and influential creed among advanced radicals in London, and it is not surprising that Mrs Besant should have taken an active interest in it. Her interest was stimulated by a personal factor. It was probably late in 1883 that Aveling began his liaison with Eleanor Marx which was to become a common-law marriage and to end in tragedy. Whether or not Aveling and Mrs Besant had been lovers, she certainly behaved like a conventional discarded mistress, making personal attacks on Eleanor Marx in the pages of the *National Reformer*. It was apparently at the beginning of 1884 that Aveling joined the Marxist body, the Social Democratic Federation. Soon afterwards Mrs Besant became friendly with George Bernard Shaw. This seems to have been the third of her three serious relationships with men in her radical and Socialist years; first Bradlaugh, deep and enduring; then Aveling, short but intense; then Shaw, brief and unsatisfactory. It seems that Mrs Besant wanted a much closer relationship than did Shaw and that this was the cause of their rupture. However, it is hard to believe that intimacy between the mocking, witty Shaw and the passionately earnest Annie Besant could in any case have been of long duration.

During 1884-5 Socialism made an increasingly strong appeal to her. Bradlaugh, to whom she remained devoted and whose own devotion to her survived her attachments to other men, was cast too strongly in the individualist radical mould to turn to a new philosophy in his fifties and Mrs Besant hesitated to give wholehearted support to a doctrine between whose adherents and Bradlaugh there was bitter antagonism. Nevertheless, she realised gradually that she had become a Socialist. A famous debate in April 1884 between Bradlaugh and the SDF leader, H.M. Hyndman, 'Will Socialism benefit the English People?' roused her, as she wrote in her *Autobiography*, 'to a serious study of the questions raised' [p. 301]. Without advocating Socialism as such, her writing and lectures became increasingly influenced by concern for social reform.

In 1885 she finally decided to embrace Socialism by joining the Fabian Society, partly, no doubt, under the influence of Bernard Shaw. However, this was not the only reason. The Fabian Society was the only Socialist body specifically catering for the middle classes and for intellectuals. In addition, it was less dogmatic and less antagonistic to radicals and secularists, in particular to Bradlaugh, than other Socialist bodies. But her decision to become a Socialist brought about the first rift in her relationship with Bradlaugh; a political and intellectual rift, for the personal link remained strong.

Not only the infant Fabian Society, which in 1886 had only forty members, but the Socialist movement as a whole was heartened and strengthened by the recruitment of the most prominent woman in political life and one of the most prominent of British radicals. Names like Shaw, Webb, Bland, Olivier, Quelch, Bax and Hyndman were little known to the general public in 1885, and among previous recruits to Socialism only William Morris could bring to the movement the prestige and publicity of Annie Besant.

At the same time she was a rather unusual Fabian, and it is unlikely that she was ever entirely at home among them. For Mrs Besant, although she wrote vigorously and spoke brilliantly, was no austere intellectual, and had little of the self-questioning, sometimes cynical wit which characterised the Fabians. She was never one of the ruling inner circle. Moreover, her stream of writing on secularist topics, a less than burning issue to most of the Fabians, continued throughout her Socialist phase. None the less, she took an active part in the work of the Society, speaking and writing for it, serving on its executive committee, and delivering a lecture in 1888 on 'Industry under Socialism' which was published the next year as one of the famous *Fabian Essays in Socialism.*

Her Socialism in the later 1880s did not follow a single clear line. Despite assertions by some writers to the contrary, she did not join the SDF until 1888 [Nethercot (1961) 253-4, 278]. Even when she did so, she remained a member of the Fabian Society. She also retained her neo-Malthusian convictions, which many contemporary Socialists did not share. Her Socialism, in short, was eclectic. It was based principally on her indignation and horror at the extremes of wealth and poverty which she saw about her, rather than on theory. However, she drew on various theories as she felt the need for them. She believed firmly that Socialism was a product of the working of laws of social evolution. She was also quite prepared to draw upon Marxist as well as gradualist sources. Thus in articles in *Our Corner* in 1886 (reprinted as *Modern Socialism*) she advised her readers to study a section of *Das Kapital*, and she went on to discuss favourably Marx's theories of value and surplus value. An article on 'The Socialist Movement' in the *Westminster Review* [*70* n.s. (1886) 212-30] shows clear Marxist influence:

> Slavery was, in truth, a necessary stage in social evolution . . . But in reality the 'free labourer' only obtains as wage such portion of the results of his labour as enables him to exist at the standard of living current for his class at the time, and the remainder of his produce goes to his employer . . . Here is this unpropertied class, this naked proletariat, face to face with landlord and capitalist, who hold in their grip the means of subsistence . . . Poverty will never cease so long as any class or any individuals have an interest in the exploitation of others.

Her views and her language were more direct and more radical than those of most Fabians but she was never a convinced Marxist. In the *Westminster Review* article she pointed in the fashion of Sidney Webb to 'an unconscious movement towards Socialism [which] has been steadily growing in strength'; and on 24 May 1887 she wrote to the *Pall Mall Gazette* in the wake of a controversy between Shaw and Hyndman, declaring roundly of Marx's theory of value: 'This quagmire of contradictions and bad metaphysics is no safe foundation for modern Socialism.'

Too militant and impetuous, too much of an activist for the Fabians, Mrs Besant was insufficiently Marxist for the SDF. The class war never had her wholehearted allegiance. The fact that in her Socialist phase she supported the underprivileged without equivocation but without a consistent ideological base, meant that she was able to support a variety of radical and Socialist causes without pinning herself down to any one party or faction, and that she favoured a greater measure of radical-Socialist unity than proved possible at the time. Her value to the movement lay in much more than her famous name. Later writers have sometimes implied that she was a woman of superficial intelligence, ruled by impulse rather than reason, notable for a pretty face and a fine voice rather than for intellectual ability. Such suggestions are wide of the mark. The range and abundance of her writing, her translations from several different languages, show that while she lacked originality, she had great ability and an immense capacity for hard work. However, her somewhat isolated position and her role as the only really prominent woman among early British Socialists must have imposed a considerable strain. She probably underwent periods of deep loneliness, and this position of isolation should be borne in mind when one is considering her later retreat from Socialist activism.

In October 1887 Mrs Besant ceased to be joint editor of the *National Reformer* with Bradlaugh, since their political views had by now diverged so widely, and also so as not to jeopardise his new Liberal political career. She continued to write for the paper, however, and remained its joint proprietor. It was during this period that unemployment led to many protests and processions in London. In the resistance to attempts to prevent these demonstrations, especially to prevent access to Trafalgar Square, Mrs Besant played a leading role. During the past decade probably none of her many radical and Socialist causes had burned so brightly as free speech, freedom of the press and the right of assembly. She was a leader in the famous 'Bloody Sunday' fracas in Trafalgar Square (13 November 1887) and its aftermath. Immediately after 'Bloody Sunday' she was instrumental in forming, along with the radical journalist W.T. Stead, the Law and Liberty League, whose aims were to defend free speech, the rights of the poor and other radical causes. The formation of such a League had been advocated by William Morris, and he and other radicals and Socialists gave it their firm backing. In support of its objectives Mrs Besant and Stead established a halfpenny journal called the *Link*. As the League's secretary she waged in the pages of this short-lived weekly her most famous campaign, leading to the strike of the East London match girls of 1888.

Following a meeting of the Fabian Society on women's work, and investigations of her own, Mrs Besant published an article in the *Link* on 23 June 1888 under the title 'White Slavery in London'. It was this article which led directly to the match girls' strike and which, in turn, played an important part in the upsurge of New Unionism. She attacked the employers, Bryant and May, who had paid a dividend of 23 per cent the previous year, but who were able to do this only at the expense of the workers. In summer they had a working day of eleven and a half hours, with an hour and a half for meals. Fines were imposed for such misdemeanours as talking, dirty feet or untidy floors. Wages of girls were as low as 4*s* 6*d* and 5*s* a week, and only four women earned as much as thirteen shillings. The company denied all charges and threatened to sue Mrs Besant. ('I await placidly the legal attention', was the published reply: no action ensued). After the dismissal of a girl for insubordination (allegedly for refusing to sign a paper saying that the girls were well treated and content), the strike broke out on 5 July. The total number of women and girls who joined the strike was variously estimated between 1100 and 1400. Mrs Besant, surprised by its suddenness, did not hesitate when asked to assume its leadership. She virtually turned the *Link*'s four pages into a strike sheet. She discovered that among the shareholders of Bryant and May were to be found three MPs and fifty-five clergymen, and bitterly contrasted the 'silky, clustering curls' of the country clergyman's daughter with the partial baldness of the fifteen-year-old match girls who carried boxes on their heads. She arranged a deputation to visit the House of Commons and opened a subscription fund which received wide support, from Socialists and others. Over £400 was collected, and two distributions of between four and six shillings were made to over 650 of the strikers. After nearly a fortnight in which other Socialists, among them Shaw and Herbert Burrows, also played important parts, the strike ended with the victory of the match girls. Annie Besant became the secretary of the Matchmakers' Union, which by early September had over 600 members. It was her finest hour, long remembered in the labour movement, and she followed it up by working in less publicised ways for many other groups of unskilled and unorganised workers in 1888-9.

Less well known than her leadership of the match girls' strike, Mrs Besant's election to and service on the London School Board, her last service to British Socialism and radicalism, was no less important. She had wanted to stand for the new London County Council, but legal difficulties over women's rights in this matter persuaded her to stand instead for the School Board. This was in November 1888. Her election meetings were later described by Shaw as 'unique and luminous in the squalid record of London electioneering' [Shaw (1917) 18]. Despite the many attacks on her, or perhaps because of them, the election result was a triumph for Mrs Besant. She finished top of the list of eleven candidates, five of whom were returned, and her 15,926 votes were nearly three thousand more than those of the next candidate. Her victory, and the victory in Hackney of Stewart Headlam, the Christian Socialist clergyman with whom she had been friendly for many years, were hailed by radicals and Socialists with great enthusiasm.

The aftermath was in a sense even more remarkable. Although the Board remained under the control of the Moderates (Conservatives), the initiative of Mrs Besant, Headlam and A.G. Cook of the London compositors was the decisive factor in a resolution passed early in 1889 to pay trade union wages in all Board contracts. The London School Board, the first elected body to take this decision, was soon followed by many others. In the same year Mrs Besant seconded a successful resolution in favour of setting up a committee to undertake a study of the problems of underfed children, the Board lacking legal powers to provide the required meals. In 1890 she moved an important resolution in favour of the abolition of school fees. This resolution, carried by twenty-four to sixteen against the advice of the Board's 'Moderate' chairman, played a part in the Government's introduction of free schools in 1891. Perhaps most remarkable was an historic resolution of the Board, passed in May 1889, in whose passage Mrs Besant was one of the moving spirits: 'All citizens have an equal right to send their children to schools built and supported by them, and . . . the Board are of opinion that there is considerable advantage in having children of all classes attending the same schools.' It is not surprising that Headlam should write in mid-1890 that Mrs Besant was 'the real leader of the advanced party' on the Board [Rubinstein (1970) 24].

Mrs Besant's acceptance of theosophy in 1889 was a momentous change which soon brought to an end her leadership in the secularist and Socialist movements. Theosophy is a mystical creed containing both pantheistic and supernatural elements, but without an exclusive or rigid set of theological doctrines. Many of its basic concepts are drawn from the East, notably from Hindu sources. Thus it could claim to be a bridge between the religions of East and West, and between believer and unbeliever. Mrs Besant had long been interested in India, and *Our Corner* had carried articles on India and Hinduism. She had also known of theosophy for a considerable time, having written about it in the *National Reformer* as early as 1882. Since about 1886 she had inquired with growing interest into psychological, supernatural and occult subjects, including Spiritualism, and early in 1889 she was given a copy of Helena Petrovna Blavatsky's *The Secret Doctrine* to review for W.T. Stead's *Pall Mall Gazette*. Her lengthy, thoughtful, half-convinced review appeared on 25 April 1889, and shortly afterwards Stead gave her an introduction to Madame Blavatsky, the co-founder and principal leader of the theosophical movement, little realising the significance of this step. Within a few weeks Mrs Besant had announced her conversion. Judging from her writings on the subject the conversion seems to have been due to disappointment with the motives of hatred, greed and selfishness which she found in the Socialist movement – and in some of the workers; interest in such psychological and supernatural phenomena as the nature of thought and clairvoyance; and attraction to a philosophy which seemed to provide complete knowledge, an outlet for emotion and a source of mental peace. Doubtless loneliness and other personal factors, of which she was probably not conscious, also played a significant part.

For a period Mrs Besant followed her usual activities, continuing her School Board work, attending the International Socialist Congress in Paris in 1889 and even speaking to secularist meetings. She claimed that there was no conflict between theosophy and her earlier activities. But her interest in them rapidly waned and at the same time her old comrades showed signs of unease or hostility. She withdrew from the Fabian Society, the SDF, and the National Secular Society in 1890-1 and did not stand again for the London School Board in 1891. For her old comrade Charles Bradlaugh, 'it was his last great disappointment' [Tribe (1971) 270].

Annie Besant's prolonged later career as a theosophist and Indian nationalist is, except in outline, beyond the scope of this *Dictionary*. Soon after the death of Madame Blavatsky in 1891 she became the effective leader of the main theosophical movement, and she was president of the Theosophical Society from 1907 until her death in 1933. She settled in India soon after her first visit in November 1893, declaring her belief in Indian culture and in the traditions of ancient Hinduism, from which she felt that theosophy drew its most important inspiration. Her lecturing and writing continued unabated, and her energy and magnetic speaking power lasted far into old age. She visited England frequently and retained some of her old friendships and links with the labour movement. She retained also her capacity to attract large crowds wherever she went. A meeting of the Fabian Society in London in 1910 or 1911 was later described by Lady Emily Lutyens, who had not then met Mrs Besant, but who was soon to become a theosophist and an intimate of hers. An overflow crowd of Fabian members was present. Lady Emily wrote: 'I was completely carried away, and felt myself face to face with something immeasurably greater than anything I had ever known' [Lutyens (1957) 18]. On numerous occasions during her visits to England before 1914 Mrs Besant spoke at large meetings in support of the campaign for women's suffrage, stressing in particular her sympathy with women who were poor, badly housed and exploited. In 1914 she set something of a precedent in labour relations during a London building lockout and strike by organising the construction of the Theosophical Society headquarters by trade union labour without reference to employers or contractors. In 1924 a London meeting held to commemorate her fifty years of public work attracted an audience of over two thousand people. Representatives of many different bodies with which she had been affiliated were present, and among the speakers were such leaders of the labour movement as Margaret Bondfield, George Lansbury, Marion Phillips, Emmeline Pethick Lawrence, Harry Snell, Ben Tillett and Ben Turner.

It was in 1914 that Mrs Besant turned her energies to the cause of Indian nationalism, establishing a daily paper, *New India*, to campaign for the cause. In 1916, after discussions with other nationalist leaders, she inaugurated the All-India Home Rule League. She was in fact the dominant figure in Indian nationalism during the First World War. In 1917 she was interned for three months for her political activities and was also elected president of the Indian National Congress for the following year. With the rise of Gandhi after the war her personal leadership and her brand of nationalism were superseded, but she maintained her belief in Home Rule and her stream of publications on the subject. In 1925 her Commonwealth of India Bill, seeking Dominion status for India within the British Empire, was introduced into the House of Commons by one of her old friends, George Lansbury, and supported by other Labour members, including Hugh Dalton. The Bill was introduced a second time, again under Labour auspices, in 1927. During this period she was a member of the Fabian Society, and apparently also of the Labour Party. If, as an ageing non-Indian out of sympathy with the militant phases of the nationalist struggle, she could no longer have a major influence on developments, her role had been significant in the earlier formative years. The importance of her Home Rule campaign was generously acknowledged by Gandhi, her successful rival, and also by Nehru, whom she initiated into a brief period of theosophy and fired with enthusiasm for Indian nationalism. Her work also influenced the thinking and policy on India of individuals and groups within the Labour Party. Her theosophical teachings helped to persuade Indians of the value of their cultural traditions and religion; as *The Times* pointed out in its rather snide obituary notice, she had a profound influence on young Hindus, whom she told that 'their gods, their philosophy, their morality were all on a higher plane of thought than the West had ever reached' [21 Sep 1933].

Dr Annie Besant (recipient in 1921 of an honorary Doctorate of Letters from the Benares Hindu University) died on 20 September 1933, shortly before her eighty-sixth birthday, in Adyar, India, home of the theosophical movement. Tributes were paid to her in many countries, above all in India and in Britain. Some observers, like the aged Gladstone [(1894) 318] judged her to have been superficial and complacent; like Besterman [(1934) 267], to have possessed overweening self-confidence, no matter what issue she was promoting; or, like *The Times* obituarist, as determined to control every movement she adopted. Here it may be sufficient to say that she laboured unceasingly in the radical, secularist and Socialist movements for about sixteen years. In the varied aspects of these movements she made an enormous impression on her time. Her writing and speaking ability, and her willingness to engage in public controversy made her one of the outstanding leaders of late nineteenth-century radicalism and Socialism. Hardly over forty when she turned to theosophy, she made as great an impact in early life as some leaders in a lifetime. The fascination which she exercised over so many people during her life and has continued to exercise since her death is some indication of her magnetism and her influence.

Writings: T. Besterman's *A Bibliography of Annie Besant* published by the Theosophical Society in 1924 (copies at BM; Theosophical Society, London and Adyar, India; and in *DLB* Coll.) provides a comprehensive guide to most of Mrs Besant's books and pamphlets up to and including the year 1924. Of the 412 items listed, 326 are entirely her own writings, twenty-five are in collaboration with others, and twenty-one are edited or introduced by her. Details of the periodicals which she edited are also included together with a list of publications containing extracts from her works. Another useful bibliography of her books and pamphlets is given in the *Theosophist* (Besant Centenary Issue 1847-1947) *69*, no. 1 (Oct 1947) 89-100. In the sections which follow only a selection of her writings are listed but they include many of her major works on Radicalism, Secularism, Birth Control, Socialism and India and also her autobiographical publications. Many of her periodical writings were subsequently published in pamphlet form and some rare items are included in *A Selection of the Social and Political Pamphlets of Annie Besant 1874-1890*, with a Preface and Bibliographical Notes by John Saville (NY, 1970).

Radicalism:
History of the Great French Revolution (1876; 2nd ed. 1883); *English Republicanism* (1878) 8 pp.; *Landlords, Tenant Farmers and Labourers* (1880) 8 pp.; *Free Trade versus "Fair" Trade* [lectures] (1881) 48 pp.; *Essays, Political and Social* [1881?]; *The English Land System* (1882) 8 pp.; *Coercion in Ireland and its Results* (1882) 8 pp.; *The Political Status of Women* [1885?] 14 pp.; *The Legalisation of Female Slavery in England* (1885) 8 pp.; *Liberty, Equality, Fraternity* [188-?] 8 pp.

Secularism (inc. Birth Control):
My Path to Atheism [Pamphlets] (1877); *The Law of Population: its consequences, and its bearing upon human conduct and morals* (1877) 48 pp.; *Marriage: as it was, as it is and as it should be* (NY, 1879) 52 pp.; *Social Aspects of Malthusianism* [1880?] 8 pp.; *Theological Essays and Debate* [1883?].

Socialism:
The Redistribution of Political Power (1885) 30 pp.; *The Evolution of Society* (1886) 52 pp.; *Modern Socialism* (1886) 52 pp.; *Radicalism and Socialism* (1887) 20 pp.; *The Socialist Movement* (1887) 24 pp.; 'Industry under Socialism' in *Fabian Essays*, ed. G.B. Shaw (1889; 6th ed. with an Introduction by A. Briggs, 1962).

India:
Wake up, India: a plea for social reform (1913); *India and the Empire* (1914); *How India wrought for Freedom: the story of the National Congress told from official records* (1915); *India: a Nation. A Plea for Indian Self-government* (1915); *The Future of Indian Politics* (1922); *India: bond or free? A World Problem* (1926).

Autobiographical:
Autobiographical Sketches (1885); *Why I am a Socialist* (1886) 8 pp.; *Why I do not believe in God* (1887) 23 pp.; *Why I became a Theosophist* (1889) 31 pp.; *1875 to 1891: a fragment of autobiography* [an address] (1891) 14 pp.; *Annie Besant: an autobiography* (1893).

Sources: (1) **MSS:** Correspondence in Bensusan Coll., Univ. of Essex; Add. MSS, BM and at Theosophical Society HQ., Adyar, India; see also the Besant letters in *The Bradlaugh Papers: letters, papers and printed items relating to the life of Charles Bradlaugh (1833-1891) arranged from the collection assembled by his daughter Hypatia Bradlaugh Bonner (1858-1935) and now in the possession of the National Secular Society 698 Holloway Road, London N19 3 NL; A Descriptive Index by Edward Royle, Lecturer in History, University of York* (EP Microform, Wakefield, 1975). Other material, cited by D. Tribe in his book on Bradlaugh (1971), included an MS. memoir of Mrs Besant by Hypatia Bonner but the present location of this is not known.

(2) **Biographical Works:** W.T. Stead, 'Mrs Annie Besant', *Rev. of Revs 4* (Oct 1891) 349-67 (repr. in W.T. Stead, *Character Sketches* [1892] and as a separate book by the Theosophical Publishing House, Adyar, India (1946)); *Labour Annual* (1898); C.J. Schuver, *Annie Besant* [in Dutch] (Haarlem, 1904) 58 pp.; Anon., *Mrs Annie Besant: a sketch of her life and her services to India* (Madras, 1908) 63 pp., 2nd ed. (Madras, 1917) 56 pp.; S.E. Gay, *The Life-Work of Mrs Besant: a review and comments* [1913] 36 pp.; G. Lansbury, 'Mrs Besant as a Politician' and articles by other hands in *Herald of the Star 6* (Oct 1917) [Mrs Besant's Birthday Number] 514-18; B.C. Pal [Vipinachandra Pala], *Mrs Annie Besant: a psychological study* (Madras, [1917]); G.B. Shaw, 'Mrs Besant as a Fabian Socialist', *Theosophist 39* (Adyar, Oct 1917) 9-19; A. Blech [L. Dalsace], *Annie Besant, Présidente de la Société Théosophique: un abrégé de sa vie* [in French] (Paris, 1918); Editor of *Justice*, Madras [T.M. Nair], *Evolution of Mrs Besant . . .* (Madras, 1918); *Dr Annie Besant: fifty years in public work* [articles by various hands] (1924) 32 pp.; *Annie Besant, D.L.: Queen's Hall Jubilee Demonstration, July 23rd 1924, Report of Speeches* (1924) 24 pp.; *Tributes to Dr. Annie Besant, DL, PTS, Servant of Humanity, from representative Indians and Europeans* (repr. from *New India*, Aug 1924); *Labour Who's Who* (1924); L. Heber, *Annie Besant: en moderne pioner* [in Norwegian], (Oslo, 1927)); G. West [G.H. Wells], *Mrs Annie Besant* (1927), idem, *The Life of Annie Besant* (1929); *WWW* (1929-40); *DNB* (1931-40) [by H.V. Lovett and P. Cadell]; C. Jinarajadasa, *A Short Biography of Dr. Annie Besant* (Adyar, 1932); G.M. Williams, *The Passionate Pilgrim: a life of Annie Besant* [1932]; T. Besterman, *Mrs Annie Besant: a modern prophet* (1934); E. Bright, *Old Memories and Letters of Annie Besant* (1936); *International Theosophical Year Book 1937* (Adyar, 1936) 181-3; S. Prakasa, *Annie Besant: as woman and leader* (Adyar, 1941); *A Woman World-honoured: Annie Besant, Warrior* [tributes] (Adyar, 1943); *The Annie Besant Centenary Book: 1847-1947*, ed. J.H. Cousins (Adyar, 1947); *Theosophist 69* (Besant Centenary Issue 1847-1947) (Adyar, Oct 1947); A.H. Nethercot, *The First Five Lives of Annie Besant* (1961); idem, *The Last Four Lives of Annie Besant* (1963); C.P. Ramaswami Aiyar, *Annie Besant* (Delhi, 1963); D. Rubinstein, 'Annie Besant', in *People for the People*, ed. D. Rubinstein (1973) 145-53.

(3) **Other Works:** C.M. Davies, *Mystic London: or, phases of occult life in the Metropolis* (1875); *In the High Court of Justice, Queen's Bench Division, June 18th 1877. The Queen v. Charles Bradlaugh and Annie Besant* [1877]; W.P. Ball, *Mrs Besant's Socialism* (1886) 36 pp.; S. Webb, *Socialism in England* (1890); G.B. Shaw, *The Fabian Society: what it has done and how it has done it* (Fabian Tract no. 41: 1892) 32 pp.; W.E. Gladstone, 'True and False Conceptions of the Atonement', *19th C. 36* (Sep 1894) 317-31 (see also Mrs Besant's reply, in the same journal and under the same title, *37* (June 1895) 1021-6; H.B. Bonner, *Charles Bradlaugh*, 2 vols (1894); M.D. Conway, *Autobiography* 2 vols (1904); H.S. Olcott, *Old Diary Leaves* 4th, 5th and 6th ser. (London, 1910; Adyar, 1932 and 1935); H.M. Hyndman, *Further Reminiscences* (1912); E.R. Pease, *The History of the Fabian Society* (1916, rev. ed. 1925, repr. 1963 with a new Introduction by M. Cole); T. Mann, *Tom Mann's Memoirs* (1923); M. Quin, *Memoirs of a Positivist* (1924); F. Whyte, *The Life of W.T. Stead* 2 vols (1925); F.G. Bettany, *Stewart Headlam* (1926); G. Lansbury, *My Life* (1928); A.D. Besant, *The Besant Pedigree* (1930); B. Tillett, *Memories and Reflections* (1931); N.E. Himes, *Medical History of Contraception* (1936); T. Gautrey, *'Lux Mihi Laus': School Board memories* [1937]; H. Pearson, *Bernard Shaw: his life and personality* (1942, rev. ed. 1961); J.A. and O. Banks, 'The Bradlaugh-Besant Trial and the English Newspapers', *Pop. Studies 7* (July 1954) 22-34; H. Pelling, *The Origins of the Labour Party 1880-1900* (1954, 2nd ed. 1965); E.P. Thompson, *William Morris: romantic to revolutionary* (1955); St.J. Ervine, *Bernard Shaw* (1956); E. Lutyens, *Candles in the Sun* (1957); B.R. Nanda, *Mahatma Gandhi* (1958); F.H.A. Micklewright, 'The Rise and Decline of English Neo-Malthusianism', *Pop. Studies 15* (July 1961) 32-51; M. Cole, *The Story of Fabian Socialism* (1961); A. Stafford, *A Match to Fire the Thames* (1961); A.M. McBriar, *Fabian Socialism and English Politics 1884-1918* (Cambridge,

1962); B.R. Nanda, *The Nehrus: Motilal and Jawaharlal* (1962); E.E. Barry, *Nationalisation in British Politics* (1965); E. Draper, *Birth Control in the Modern World* (Harmondsworth, 1965); P. Fryer, *The Birth Controllers* (1965); W.S. Smith, *The London Heretics, 1870-1914* (1967); P. Thompson, *Socialists, Liberals and Labour: the struggle for London, 1885-1914* (1967); D. Tribe, *100 Years of Freethought* (1967); C. Tsuzuki, *The Life of Eleanor Marx 1855-1898* (1967); *Shaw: an autobiography*, 2 vols, ed. S. Weintraub (1969-70); C. Rover, *Love, Morals and the Feminists* (1970); D. Rubinstein, 'Annie Besant and Stewart Headlam: the London School Board election of 1888', *East London Papers 13* (summer 1970) 3-24; E. Royle, *Radical Politics 1790-1900: Religion and Unbelief* (1971) [with bibliography]; D. Tribe, *President Charles Bradlaugh MP* (1971); biographical information: Theosophical Society, London and International HQ., Adyar, India. OBIT. *Times*, 21 Sep 1933; 'The Passing of Annie Besant' and 'Dr Annie Besant, Tributes', repr. from *Theosophy in India* (Oct 1933); *Labour Party Report* (1933).

DAVID RUBINSTEIN

See also: *Charles BRADLAUGH; †Stewart Duckworth HEADLAM.

BLATCHFORD, Montagu John (1848-1910)
SOCIALIST, JOURNALIST AND ARTIST

Montagu Blatchford was born in Aberdeen on 30 October 1848, the elder son of John Glanville and Georgiana Louisa Corri Blatchford, both provincial actors. John Glanville Blatchford was the illegitimate son of a Tavistock woman and a Cornish cadet of the family of Glanville. His wife was half Italian, the daughter of Montagu Corri, theatrical composer and a midshipman in Nelson's fleet at the Battle of the Nile.

When her husband died of tuberculosis in 1853, Louisa Blatchford continued for nine years to make a precarious living on provincial stages. In 1862 she settled her family in Halifax, where Montagu and his younger brother Robert worked at odd jobs to supplement her earnings. But she was determined to keep her boys off the stage and to put them to regular trades; so when in 1864 or 1865 she was able to secure steady work as a dressmaker, she apprenticed Robert in a brush manufactory and Montagu in a lithographic printing company, Messrs Stott Brothers in Mount Street. Both boys attended a nonconformist chapel.

According to Robert Blatchford in his reminiscences, and according to his biographers, Mont (as he was called) was the favourite son. His mother thought highly of his gifts both as a graphic artist and in music, while she regarded Bob as 'a dunderhead' (*My Eighty Years*, 6). In 1871, after a violent quarrel with Mrs Blatchford and just before completing his term of apprenticeship, Robert ran away from home, leaving Montagu to look after their mother; according to Laurence Thompson, 'Mont could not forgive Robert' for this [Thompson (1951) 117]. It seems likely that Mont too was almost out of his apprenticeship with Messrs Stott. He found work as a designer for a textile firm, John Crossley and Sons Ltd of Dean Clough Mills. There he met his future wife, Susan Emma, daughter of Samuel Greenwood of Halifax. Samuel's interests were remarkably in consonance with those of his son-in-law: by profession he was an 'engine tenter' – in charge of an engine at a mill – but in his spare time he did architectural drawings for builders, played in the theatre orchestra, and had been a bandsman in a cavalry regiment. His daughter Susan was a setter in the Dean Clough Mills; that is, she set out the designer's pattern in squares for the weaver to work from.

Montagu and Susan Blatchford had eight children but two died in infancy. The remaining six were Robert Frank, born 1872-74?, who died of typhoid fever at the age of 27 while serving as a Volunteer in the Boer War; Annie Louisa, born in 1875, who married Willie Thomas and had a son and daughter, both still living; Arnold, who later worked at the *Clarion* office; William and Clement, twins, who took over the block-making and engraving business in which their father had originally set up Robert and Arnold; but William subsequently became a teacher of higher mathematics and physics at Loughborough College. Neither of them married. The youngest child was Phyllis, born in 1890, who married James Fletcher, and has one daughter.

Montagu was a good designer; but like his mother he fired up easily. His daughter writes: 'All the Corris, having Italian blood in their veins, were very excitable. And as the head of Dean Clough Mills was also an Italian, Mr Marchetti, these two had only to meet and the fur would be flying.' During one of their disputes, in 1878, her father said, 'One of us will have to go, and I suppose it will be me', and he walked out.

He and his family then moved to London, in 1879, taking his mother, Louisa Blatchford, with them. Montagu hoped to make a living as a freelance artist for the illustrated papers. He had drawings accepted by a number of papers including *Punch, Fun,* and the *Sporting and Dramatic News.* His risky move out of steady employment in Halifax was perhaps made possible when, either now or rather earlier, Robert contributed something to their mother's support – a burden which Montagu had apparently carried alone up to then. When he married Montagu had rented a house near by for his mother, and he did the same in London.

In 1885, after six years in London, he returned to Halifax and to his old employment with Crossley and Sons. But he finally broke with the firm about 1888, and followed his brother on to the staff of the *Sunday Chronicle,* which was published in Manchester. He contributed drawings and verses and remained on the paper until the time of the famous quarrel with the proprietor, Edward Hulton, which led Robert Blatchford to resign in October 1891, followed in November by Alex. Thompson and the staff artist William Palmer, and by Montagu and Edward Fay in December.

Even before the dispute with Hulton the group had been considering the possibility of starting a Socialist weekly of their own. To the tiny capital of a few hundred pounds which they now managed to scrape together for the purpose Montagu contributed £50. The *Clarion* was launched in Manchester on 12 December 1891. Robert Blatchford wrote its leading articles, and he and Thompson edited it; Fay and Montagu were the other two staff journalists. They all wrote under the names they had already been using on other papers: Robert was 'Nunquam', Thompson 'Dangle', Fay 'The Bounder', and Montagu 'Mont Blong' (or 'Mong Blong').

The vast success and influence of the *Clarion* and of his articles in it, especially those which made up his book *Merrie England,* brought Robert Blatchford fame in the Socialist-Labour world, and he became so to speak the hero of the rapidly developing *Clarion* movement. Montagu was as ardent a Socialist as Robert, but a less flamboyant and dominating personality. The brothers seem to have been fairly intimate in the 1880s – Montagu was lending Robert money in 1885 – and in the 1890s when they were struggling together to establish the *Clarion,* yet Montagu is almost ignored in Robert's autobiographical writings and in the biographies of Robert composed by his admirers. Laurence Thompson does not mention him among the recipients of letters from Robert whom he enumerates in his 'Sources' – although William, Montagu's son, does appear there. And the Halifax newspapers do not list any member of Robert's family among those attending Montagu's funeral in 1910.

Montagu's work for Socialism would probably not be ignored if he had not performed so much of it in the shadow of his brother. In 1908 he sold his share of the *Clarion* to Robert for £2000; but up to 1908 he was still supplying the paper with political cartoons and comic drawings, 'miles of verse', and humorous pieces in prose. He was also a member of the Halifax Art Society and exhibited with them. He also contributed to and helped to edit other *Clarion* publications, among them almost certainly the Clarion Song Book used by the Clarion choirs; for it was Mont who created these choirs, the Clarion Vocal Unions, and for many years conducted the Halifax Union and, usually, the massed choir – the United Clarion Vocal Union. (His grand-daughter Christine Fletcher now possesses his baton of ebony and gold.) As Laurence Thompson observes (117-18), he 'spent time and temper and money and love bullying conducting and judging choirs, and brought much happiness into beauty-starved lives'. Thompson then quotes Montagu's own words:

Perhaps in thirty or forty years, when those who are young and ardent now, have grown old and worn, and a little sad perhaps, they may chance to hear or to remember a snatch of some of the music we have learnt and sung together. And then back in a flash from the shadows of the past will come for a moment the soaring voices that have grown worn and thin, the vast friendly audiences that have long since faded away, and perhaps a kindly recollection of the cantankerous little man who, whatever were his failings, was at least proud of the Clarion Vocal Union and fond of its members [Thompson (1951) 117-18].

In Halifax Montagu was a widely known and widely valued figure. He was an early member of the Halifax Fabian Society (established in May 1891) and vice-president in 1891-2. He was an able public speaker; he addressed meetings on behalf of Fabianism and also spoke at Labour Church gatherings. He was a founder member of Halifax ILP (1893) and president 1903-4; president likewise – the first president – of the reorganised Halifax Trades Council in 1907-8. In the municipal elections of 1895 he stood as a 'Socialist-Labour' candidate against a Liberal (the incumbent) and a Conservative. He lost in the three-way split of votes, but in 1902 he was elected councillor for Central ward and served for three years. He was a member of the School Board during the last two years of its existence, and he was one of the first members of the education committee. Although out of kindness he painted scenery for the entertainments got up by a Congregational Church attended by his daughter Louisa, he was himself a staunch agnostic.

In the midst of all his multifarious public activities he found time to write several books (among them a history of the co-operative movement in Halifax) and several light operas. He took pleasure in directing local amateurs in the production of operas he had written. He painted landscapes (as well as stage scenery), and still occasionally contributed drawings to *Punch* and the *Illustrated Sporting and Dramatic News*. He was a remarkably versatile man: a clever designer, a good black-and-white artist, a tolerable painter and an acute critic of art, an amusing comic writer in prose and verse; he was a conductor and a composer, a witty conversationalist, a formidable debater, a skilful chairman, a convinced Socialist, and a humanitarian.

After he returned from London in 1885 Montagu Blatchford lived in Halifax for the rest of his life. His home in the 1890s was 14 Gladstone Road; later it was 10 Park View. He died on 19 April 1910 from an attack of angina pectoris, after a long illness (he had Bright's disease), and was buried in the family grave he had bought in the cemetery of King Cross Wesleyan Church where his mother and later his wife were also buried. The service was conducted by the minister of the Harrison Road Congregational Church, and was attended by a large number of representatives of labour and Socialist organisations. Montagu was survived by his wife and five children, the youngest of whom is still (1975) living. He left an estate of £1831.

Writings: Librettos for comic operas: *Phyllis* (performed in Halifax in 1890), *Sylvia* (performed in Halifax in 1891) and *The Highwayman* (performed in Halifax in 1905); *The Art of Happiness* (repr. from the *Clarion*, 1896); *The History of the Halifax Industrial Society Ltd for fifty years* (1901); *The Prodigal Fathers. And other Sketches in Prose and Verse* (1902).

Sources: *Clarion*, 9 Nov 1895, 8 Sep 1900, 20 Dec 1901, 9 Oct 1903; R. Blatchford, *My Eighty Years* (1931); A.M. Thompson, *Here I lie* (1937); L. Thompson, *Robert Blatchford: portrait of an Englishman* (1951); J.A. Fincher, 'The Clarion Movement: a study of a Socialist attempt to implement the Co-operative Commonwealth in England, 1891-1914' (Manchester MA, 1972); biographical information: Calderdale Central Library, Halifax; Calderdale Museum Service, Greetland; personal information: Mrs P. Fletcher, Ascot, daughter. OBIT. *Clarion*, 22 Apr 1910; *Halifax Courier* and *Halifax Guardian*, 23 Apr 1910.

MARGARET 'ESPINASSE
JUDITH FINCHER LAIRD

See also: Robert BLATCHFORD.

BLATCHFORD, Robert Peel Glanville (1851-1943)
SOCIALIST JOURNALIST

Robert Blatchford was born on 17 March 1851 at Maidstone, Kent, the second son of a provincial strolling comedian and his actress wife. His father, John Glanville Blatchford, an illegitimate son of a Cornish cadet of the house of Glanville, was an admirer of Sir Robert Peel. His mother, Georgina Louisa Corri Blatchford (d. 1892), was the daughter of an Italian, Montagu Corri, and an Englishwoman.

Details of Robert's childhood are sketchy. Much of his early life was spent in the atmosphere of the stage. When his father died of consumption in 1853, his mother continued to make a peripatetic living on the stage for nine years. Her two sons, Montagu and Robert, often performed as comedians and dancers to supplement her income. Their combined earnings, however, were often insufficient to provide for their needs, and the family suffered constantly from cold and hunger. To the end of his life Blatchford always remembered cold as the bitterest experience of the poor.

In 1862 Mrs Blatchford settled in Halifax to give her sons the opportunity to learn a trade. Robert's first job was that of odd-job boy in a lithographic printing works at a salary of eighteen pence a week for a twelve-hour day. He had little formal schooling as a child, although he did attend school sporadically, first in Halifax, and later in Portsmouth for a few weeks. Even these brief experiences led him in his adult years to denounce the 'cram' method of education and the constant resort to corporal punishment which characterised the schools of his youth. In spite of his lack of systematic schooling, Blatchford had begun his self-education by the age of eight: he read the Bible, *Pilgrim's Progress*, Dickens, and any stories about battles he could get hold of. The time he had for reading was owed in part to his poor health; he was frail and sickly as a child, and doctors had repeatedly warned his mother that he would never reach adulthood. In 1864 or 1865, when his mother secured steady employment as a dressmaker, she apprenticed both her sons, Montagu to lithographic printing and Robert to brush-making. At the brush manufactory when he was sixteen he met the girl who was to be his wife. They also attended the same chapel. 'Within a few weeks . . . I told myself I would marry Sarah Crossley' (*My Eighty Years* (1931) 46); they were married in 1880.

But he came to dislike his work and his environment more and more, and, according to Laurence Thompson [(1951), 7] he left home in 1871 after a quarrel with his mother and just before he completed his term of apprenticeship. This explanation is queried by Blatchford's daughter Dorothea, who in a private communication (1974) stated that he decided on May Day 1871 to leave the town because 'he had had enough of his hard life in Halifax'. He wrote to his mother, walked to Hull where he worked for a few weeks, and then moved to London by way of Yarmouth. In London, after a short period of hardship, he enlisted in the Army for a period of seven years. Blatchford served with an Irish regiment, the 103rd Regiment, Dublin Fusiliers (known as the Ramchunders), and the 96th Regiment of Foot (later known as the Manchester Regiment). He owed his improved physique, his formal education and his love of sports to his Army experience. He enjoyed it wholeheartedly, and his enjoyment stimulated some of his best writing, in his reminiscences and stories of Army life. He enjoyed the physical exertion, the development and exercise of skills (he became a first-class marksman and a good cricketer), the discipline, the friendships, the jokes and foolery. In 1874 he achieved the rank of sergeant and the Army's second-class certificate of education.

In June 1877 Blatchford left the Army and transferred to the Reserves. He became a clerk (storekeeper) in the Weaver Navigation Company, an engineering firm in Northwich, Cheshire, at a salary of a guinea a week. In 1878 he served for a few months in the Reserves during the scare of war with Russia. Blatchford always used his spare time to continue his education. He learned grammar, syntax and shorthand by studying Cobbett's *Grammar, Webster's Dictionary* and a shorthand dictionary. After he left the Reserves he continued to read and was greatly influenced by Carlyle, Cobbett, Emerson and later, Omar Khayyám. Because he was largely self-educated, Blatchford in later years did not share the contempt of many of his Socialist comrades for Samuel Smiles's gospel but on the contrary greatly admired his famous *Self Help*.

Blatchford married his childhood sweetheart, Sarah Crossley, on 1 May 1880 in Zion Chapel, Halifax. His wife was the daughter of a domestic servant and a mechanic. Before her marriage she had worked both in the brush-shop where Robert was apprenticed and at a milliner's shop in Halifax. They settled down in Northwich, living on his salary, now thirty shillings a week. After his marriage Blatchford continued his interest in sports, particularly cricket and rifle shooting, and joined the Volunteers. Bored with his job, he wanted to become an artist, like his brother, but since there were no facilities for lessons in Northwich, he dabbled instead in writing.

His writing career began in 1882 when he published a sketch in a local paper, the *Yorkshireman*. His move into full-time journalism came through a new friendship with Alexander Mattock Thompson (1861-1948), then a writer for the Manchester *Sporting Chronicle*. The two men met in 1882 through a common friend, Joe Norris, a former army acquaintance of Blatchford's who had shared a house with him in Northwich. In 1884, through Thompson's influence, Blatchford began writing a weekly column for the Leeds *Toby*, a satirical journal. A year later Thompson persuaded Edward Hulton, owner of the *Sporting Chronicle*, to give Blatchford employment on his new London paper, *Bell's Life*. Blatchford became a general news reporter and columnist at a salary of £4 a week, and he and his family moved to Barnes in South London. It was at this stage in his career that he first met the exuberant and astonishing Edward Francis Fay, who was also on the staff of *Bell's Life*.

In August 1885 Blatchford began to write leaders, from London, for Hulton's new Manchester paper, the *Sunday Chronicle*. He took as his penname Nunquam Dormio ('I never sleep'). When *Bell's Life* failed, Hulton brought Blatchford back to Manchester to work full time on the *Sunday Chronicle*. The whole family moved north again in the autumn of 1887 after spending a brief holiday in the Isle of Wight, partly to recover from the shock of the deaths of two of their children earlier in the year.

At this time Blatchford was not yet a Socialist. The event which precipitated him into Socialism was probably the move back to the industrial North, for his particular kind of Socialism was very much a reaction against the cut-throat competitiveness of industrial society. One of the strongest influences upon Blatchford came from the South Salford SDF branch. One member of the branch, Joseph Waddington, claimed to have converted Blatchford to Socialism by taking him on a tour of Manchester's slums, and in 1889 Blatchford wrote a series of articles in the *Chronicle* which bitterly denounced the conditions of Manchester housing (the articles were reprinted as the *Nunquam Papers* in 1891); he also helped to organise two working men's Sanitary Associations. Another claim to have converted Blatchford to Socialism in 1889 was made by Henry M. Reade, later a member of the Manchester ILP branch. Blatchford himself attributed his conversion to his hatred of the social waste wrought by industrial capitalism, and he emphasised especially the influence of the famous pamphlet by Hyndman and Morris, *A Summary of the Principles of Socialism*, first published in 1884. But there were many influences playing upon Blatchford in these closing years of the 1880s. He had become interested in the ideas of Henry George during his London period, and their influence coloured his reporting of the land war in Ireland in 1888 when he toured that country with Fay, who was himself an Irishman. In Manchester Blatchford became actively involved in the labour movement. He helped to found the Manchester Fabian Society, in early December 1890, as a result of the urgent representations of Edward Pease; and he had close connections with the local SDF, with the Bradford Labour Union (formed in May 1891) and with leaders of the New Unionism such as Leonard Hall, James Bartley and John Burns.

The shift to a Socialist position was reflected in Blatchford's writings in the *Sunday Chronicle*, to the growing dismay of its proprietor. In 1891 Blatchford announced in his column that he had accepted the invitation of the Bradford Labour Union to become the Independent Labour candidate for East Bradford at the next election. One should add – though this is less important – that he had also been spending time and energy (and money) on the production of a comic opera with his own libretto and lyrics and with music by his cousin Clarence Corri. 'There is a reference in a letter from Blatchford to Thompson many years later to "*In Summer Days*, which as you know cost us our jobs" ' (Thompson (1951) 77). Whether this was really so is not quite certain. Early in October 1891 Blatchford left the *Sunday Chronicle* after Hulton had insisted that he should cease to use the paper for inculcating his Socialist views. Although he was able to find other journalistic outlets for the time being – in the *Workman's Times*, for example – his resignation from the *Chronicle* meant a severe cut-back in income, for Hulton had paid him £1000 a year.

Blatchford had been followed in his resignation from the *Chronicle* by four other members of its staff – in the order of their departing, Thompson, the staff artist, William Palmer (father of Robert, the present Lord Rusholme), Montagu Blatchford and Fay. This group determined to start a Socialist weekly of their own. Blatchford and Thompson mortgaged their insurance policies to raise £350, Montagu added another £50, and a young actor, Robert Courtneidge (later to be the father of Cicely, the famous actress) who was a friend of Thompson's, lent them £100 free of interest. One way and another, a few hundred pounds were raised and the first number of the new paper, the *Clarion*, was produced – under extraordinary difficulties: owing to a defect in the printing press, the first issue which appeared on 12 December 1891 was almost entirely illegible; and the posters advertising it had been destroyed by a furious storm. Forty thousand persons, however, bought or tried to buy it and it was soon to establish itself as the most popular radical journal of the day. The main *Clarion* journalists continued to write under the names they had been using on other papers: Palmer was 'Whiffly Puncto', Montagu was 'Mont Blong' (or 'Mong Blong'), Alex. Thompson 'Dangle', and E.F. Fay 'The Bounder'; Blatchford remained as 'Nunquam'. Besides them the staff consisted of a clerk (also from the *Chronicle*), Robert Suthers, and an advertising manager, Tom Wilkinson. After an initial sale of 40,000 the circulation of the *Clarion* remained for some years at about 34,000 until the popularity of *Merrie England* and then of *God and my Neighbour* shot it up; in 1910 it was 83,000. While the *Clarion* saw itself as a Socialist paper, it was far from devoting its columns entirely to Socialist or even to Labour questions. The content was as original as the style. There was poetry, comic and serious, there were stories and articles on a world of topics written in demotic English, colloquial, casual, droll, constantly interesting. As Margaret Cole wrote:

> There never was a paper like it; it was not in the least the preconceived idea of a Socialist journal. It was not solemn; it was not high-brow; it did not deal in theoretical discussion, or inculcate dreary isms. It was full of stories, jokes and verses – sometimes pretty bad verses and pretty bad jokes – as well as articles. It was written in language that anyone could understand, 'with no middle-class unction', to quote an unemployed carpenter friend of Thompson's; it believed that anyone whatever his condition or education, who could read plain English could be made into a Socialist, and that Socialism was not a difficult dogma, but a way of living and thinking which could make all men behave like brothers in the ordinary pursuits of life. In the confidence that its readers would back it up, it carried Morris's gospel of fellowship through the industrial areas in homely terms which Morris would never have been able to use; it made Socialism seem as simple and universal as a pint of bitter. It is pleasant to notice that Morris, two years before his death, expressed his appreciation of 'Mr. Blatchford's *Clarion*'. [*Makers of the Labour Movement* (1948) 195].

In January 1892 Blatchford formally withdrew from the candidature at East Bradford. No doubt the burden of paying his own election expenses proved a strain on his unsteady finances. He did not, however, abandon the political arena. He soon began siding publicly with the SDF against the Fabian permeation policy. The outcome of the *Clarion*-SDF agitation for an independent political course was the formation of the Manchester ILP on 14 May 1892 in the *Clarion* office. Blatchford drafted the constitution of the organisation, incorporating as its Fourth Clause the proposition that Socialists were to abstain from voting where no Labour or Socialist candidate was standing, thereby forcing a cleavage between the two existing political parties. The abstention policy became known as the 'Manchester Fourth Clause', and was generally associated with Blatchford, although it owed its origins to the SDF, and through them to a section of the Chartists.

When the ILP at its first conference in January 1893 refused to adopt the 'Fourth Clause', Blatchford moved closer to the SDF. In August he severed his ties with the ILP by resigning as president of the Manchester branch, and in December he publicly admitted himself to be a member of the SDF. He attacked what he considered the 'narrowness' of the ILP (Margaret Cole records that he asked Keir Hardie whether a Labour Party needed to be a Hard Labour Party), and turned his energies to promoting the formation of a Socialist party which would be social-democratic, rather than merely 'labourite'.

By 1893 Blatchford had become leader of a distinct clique within the ILP and Socialist-Labour movement, the Clarionettes. The group, composed of *Clarion* readers and sympathisers, was already distinguishable as a separate faction, for at least two Clarion Clubs had been formed. During the 1890s the Clarion organisations grew to encompass groups with political, social, recreational and educational interests – all sharing the prefix 'Clarion'. Blatchford carefully nurtured the organisations, for he considered it his duty as a Socialist journalist to educate the masses in the tenets of Socialism. His best-known work, *Merrie England*, had this aim. It was a 'series of letters on the labour problems addressed to John Smith, of Oldham, a hard-headed workman, fond of facts'. *Merrie England* was first serialised in the *Clarion*, and then issued in 1894 as a shilling book. Since it sold 20,000 copies very quickly, it was decided to take the much greater risk of publishing it at a penny; and eventually it sold over two million copies, and was translated into many languages. It was Blatchford's most successful piece of writing, and one of the most effective pieces of propaganda, perhaps the most effective, in the history of the British labour movement. In fact, 'many years later *The Manchester Guardian* wrote that for every British convert [to Socialism] made by *Das Kapital* there were a hundred made by *Merrie England* . . . For every hundred converts, moreover, there were a hundred more unconverted who . . . thought that there was "a great deal in it," and opened their minds and their hearts a little to Socialists' [Thompson (1951) 101]. Blatchford believed that the evolution of a Socialist state was inevitable, and that the function of Socialists was to ease its passage by removing obstacles such as the competitive system, ignorance and legal barriers. To that end he wrote additional books, pamphlets and articles to explain Socialism, published additional newspapers aimed at reaching different sectors of the public, and encouraged co-operative ventures – some of which bordered on the utopian – to educate the workers in the virtues of co-operation.

The *Clarion* writers and their comrades also formed organisations through which participants could be exposed to Socialist fellowship and become imbued with the values of Socialism. In the autumn of 1889 Blatchford himself established the Cinderella Clubs – social and educational clubs for slum children – and in 1894 the Clarion Scouts – youth groups often mounted on cycles to propagandise and canvass on behalf of the Socialist movement. To co-ordinate their activities Blatchford published the *Scout* (1895-6) and the *Clarion Scout* (1908-10). His brother Montagu established various organisations of which the most important were the Clarion Vocal Unions and the Clarion Glee Club, and the staff produced the *Clarion Song Book* (1906) for their use. Julia Dawson, the *Clarion* women's writer, organised the Clarion Handicraft Guilds, the Holiday Camps, and the Clarion Vans, which toured the country on propaganda journeys. A London Fabian, Harry Lowerison, founded the Clarion Field Clubs; and Tom Groom, a Birmingham Fabian, organised the formation of the National Clarion Cycling Club. Other Clarion organisations, such as the Clarion Fellowship, a group of *Clarion* sympathisers, appear to have had more spontaneous origins. Not only did the *Clarion* staff establish many organisations, but they also hoped to find among them a circulation base for the *Clarion* when sales were going down (as they did in 1894 after Keir Hardie turned the monthly *Labour Leader* into a weekly). In 1900, for example, Blatchford attempted to centralise the Fellowship with this aim. In their efforts to reach a larger public the staff also published a cycling journal, *King of the Road* (1897), and a women's paper (edited by Winifrid Blatchford), *Women Folk* (1909-10).

Although the Clarion movement spread quickly in the 1890s, assuming a distinctive character with a language, heroes and symbols of its own, it was not until the first decade of the twentieth century that its organisational structure reached its highest development. In larger perspective the movement represents Blatchford's success in moulding a part of the Socialist movement in his own image. He deliberately exacerbated differences within the ILP, encouraging rank-and-file opposition against the ILP leadership in the 1890s and first decade of the twentieth century. It was his often-repeated contention that the ILP membership resented 'labour leaders', as he disparagingly called Keir Hardie and the National Administrative Council.

The first revolt appeared within the county federations created by the ILP in 1894. By January 1894 Blatchford and other dissidents had begun urging the formation of a united Socialist Party to encompass all existing Socialist bodies, including the ILP. Blatchford temporarily threw his support behind Andrew Reid's movement which established the short-lived 'New Party and National Union of Socialists'. Blatchford's own campaign for a new party gained momentum when William Morris gave him support in October 1894 though endorsing Blatchford as a personality rather than as a political tactician. Between 1894 and 1896 Socialist unity forces gained control of a number of the county ILP federations, and agitated for the creation of a unified Socialist party at ILP conferences. Ironically, just as the rank-and-file appeared to reflect his views, Blatchford abandoned the field. The electoral reverses of 1895, coupled with personal ill-health – he had nearly died of influenza in 1894 – led to his refusing to appear at public meetings and to his resignation from the editorship of the *Clarion*, which left Thompson in charge. It was one of many periodic 'withdrawals' in Blatchford's journalistic career, occasioned in part by the ill fortunes of the Socialist movement and in part by his propensity to illness. His recurrent bouts of influenza led to periods of depression and melancholy and, apparently, considerable drinking – in his personal correspondence he periodically announced that he was 'teetotal' or that he had had to leave off whisky. The *Clarion*'s financial status also worried him. In October 1894 the staff formed a limited company, and in 1895 they moved the paper to London in the hope of securing a larger and more stable circulation – a hope which was realised; but Blatchford faced additional problems in London, for he refused to send his children to Board Schools and attempted instead to educate them himself. His ultimate solution for his son Corri was to enrol him in an independent, co-educational school founded by Harry Lowerison at Heacham on the north Norfolk coast in 1900.

At the ILP Conference of April 1896 the Socialist unity forces collided head-on with the NAC and were soundly defeated. The NAC successfully excluded from membership the sixteen existing county federations and abolished the federation structure. When several of the expelled federations reformed themselves as independent Socialist federations, Blatchford took heart and began editing the *Clarion* again. Between 1897 and 1900 he ignored the ILP – SDF strife and left the political direction of the paper largely in the hands of Thompson. Blatchford's principal interest at this time was in backing through the *Clarion* the efforts of P.J. King to set up a federation of trade unions. Together with King, Blatchford convened and financed a Federal Labour Parliament in Manchester in 1898; this Parliament set up a trades federation, the National and International General Federation of Trade and Labour Unions, which was governed by annually-elected Parliaments. King and Blatchford failed, however, to persuade the TUC to adopt the *Clarion* scheme, and the Federal Labour Parliament appears to have ceased to meet after 1902, when King resigned as general secretary.

The event that sharpened and clarified many of Blatchford's political and social attitudes was the Boer War, 1899-1902. He was unusual among contemporary British radicals in combining hostility to industrial capitalism with support for British imperialism. His army experience played a considerable part in this attitude. When the war began he attacked the pacifism and anti-imperialism of the Liberals, Radicals and Socialists. To give up parts of the Empire would be 'difficult and dangerous' for Britain, and of no use to the colonies themselves. His attitude to the war, and his vigorous denunciation of those who were opposed to a victory for British arms, antagonised and embittered many within his own following and even more in the wider movement. The ILP, for instance, instituted a boycott of all *Clarion* publications, and this further hardened Blatchford's hostility towards Keir Hardie and those around him.

Tariff Reform was another issue on which Blatchford inevitably took up a position against that of most of the labour movement. In *Merrie England* and *Britain for the British* he had attacked the doctrine of Free Trade as destructive of British agriculture and hence pernicious to the Empire. The agitation initiated by Joseph Chamberlain in 1903 was not formally backed by Blatchford and the *Clarion*, but the main aims of the Tariff Reformers – the revival of British agriculture and a self-sufficient Empire met with the *Clarion*'s full approval. Blatchford was always careful to distinguish between Tariff Reform as it would be applied by Tories and the Tariff as an instrument of Socialist policy; and R.B. Suthers used the same approach in his collection of *Clarion* articles, *My Right to Work*, published in 1906.

After the Boer War Blatchford continued to agitate for a united Socialist Party, and supported the London Progressive Party – who were the accepted Radicals in London – in the 1901 LCC elections, and the SDF candidate Harry Quelch at the Dewsbury election of 1902. The ILP, having contested Dewsbury in 1895, considered that it had a prior claim to the constituency, but when Harry Quelch persisted in his candidature, both the ILP and the local trades council decided to take no part in the election. In the event, although the Liberal and Conservative candidates polled 5660 and 4512 votes respectively, Quelch attracted unexpected support from the ILP rank and file and polled 1597 votes.

The most sensational new development of Blatchford's thinking came as a result of reading Haeckel's *Riddle of the Universe*. He reviewed the book enthusiastically in the *Clarion*, asserting that it demolished 'the entire structure upon which the religions of the world are based'. His articles attacking organised religion were reissued in two books: *God and my Neighbour* (1903) and *Not Guilty: a defence of the bottom dog* (1905). Blatchford's denunciation of religion as a barrier to social progress and a bastion of ignorance, coupled with his acceptance of determinism, lost the *Clarion* many readers, while attracting others of rationalist persuasion.

Blatchford's interest in political events revived in 1906 when the *Clarion*'s circulation soared as a result of the election to Parliament of twenty-nine Labour Representation Committee candidates. Soon after the election he began urging the revival of the Scouts and Fellowship as propaganda forces. A year later, at the Colne Valley by-election, the *Clarion* staff raised funds for the youthful Socialist orator and writer, Victor Grayson. The ILP had refused to endorse his candidature and had refused him financial support. Grayson won the seat in a sensational election on a straight Socialist ticket. His victory appeared as a vindication of the 'Fourth Clause' and served as further justification to Blatchford for his continuing attacks on the ILP and Labour Party. The gist of his criticism was that both bodies were too closely tied with the Liberals in the tradition of Lib-Lab politics. In the winter of 1907-8 Blatchford travelled throughout the North with Grayson, chairing his victory meetings and reorganising the Clarion Fellowship. Again in 1908, Blatchford appeared on the speaker's platform in unemployed demonstrations held throughout the North. The staff began to publish local editions of the *Clarion* in Manchester and Bradford, where Blatchford's success appeared most evident.

For all practical purposes Blatchford's political career ended in the summer of 1910, when he retreated to the cottage he had bought at Heacham, Norfolk, and his elder daughter, Winifrid, assumed the responsibility of editing the *Clarion*. Her father was discouraged by Grayson's defeat in the January general election and by the Labour Party's support for the Liberals. In addition, the *Clarion* paper, *Women Folk*, collapsed and the *Clarion*'s circulation was dropping steadily. Although Blatchford allowed Grayson to use the *Clarion* as a medium for organising the British Socialist Party (BSP) in 1909-10, he never threw the support of the *Clarion* wholeheartedly behind the movement. He feared the BSP would fail to unite the Socialist factions and so would merely augment factionalism. Many *Clarion* groups, however, took an active part in the formation of the BSP.

In the years before 1914 Blatchford was also embittered by Socialist reaction to his views on the threat of German militarism. He began advocating conscription in the autumn of 1909, after he had witnessed the German army manoeuvres as a correspondent for the *Daily Mail*. Later, in 1912, when troops were used for strike breaking, Blatchford turned against conscription; earlier, however, he had viewed it as a last resort to protect the Empire.

The fragmented *Clarion* movement virtually disintegrated when Blatchford swung his paper into support of the British Government at the outbreak of the First World War. Although the staff had consistently urged the Government to avert war, the journal began recruiting for the Army soon after war was declared. At the end of October 1914 Blatchford left the Socialist movement for ever. During the war he continued to oppose conscription – unless it was accompanied by a conscription of wealth – but continually ridiculed conscientious objectors.

During the war Blatchford wrote for the *Weekly Dispatch*, and the *Sunday Chronicle*. He occasionally reported from the battle front, and in November 1918 the *Chronicle* sent him to Rosyth to witness the surrender of the German fleet on H.M.S. *Malaya*. He left the *Chronicle* in early January 1924 to write for the *Sunday News*. After 1927 he was a freelance journalist. The *Clarion* continued to be published by the Fellowship until 1935 (the *New Clarion*, 1935, published by Odhams Press, was a different journal, effectively directed by Ernest Bevin).

At the beginning of the First World War Blatchford moved his family to Horsham, Sussex. In November 1916 they moved to a farm near Slinfold, and then back to Horsham. His wife died there on 19 December 1921, in the house Blatchford purchased after the war.   After his wife's death, Blatchford became a spiritualist, largely as a result of the earlier influence of W.T. Stead. In his early *Clarion* days he had also been a vegetarian and a believer in phrenology. In 1931 he published a romanticised autobiography, *My Eighty Years*. His views changed little over the years. He never swerved in his antagonism to the Labour Party, and in the general election of 1924 he voted for the Conservative Party. He was by this time quite without influence.

Blatchford was an unusual phenomenon among those who may be counted as of the British labour movement, although he was by no means unrepresentative of many working men of his own time. He was a passionate critic of the social evils of capitalism and of the ways in which human nature was warped and twisted by competitive individualism. Above all, he believed that 'the best way to realise Socialism – is to make Socialists', and that the most effective way of making Socialists was by the use of reason to dispel ignorance. So far Blatchford was well within one of the main streams of British radicalism. But he was also an anti-parliamentarian, an advocate of economic nationalism and a self-sufficient Empire, and in the years immediately before and during the First World War, a militarist and a jingoist. His great period was the early years of the *Clarion*, when he combined a savage indignation with a zest for life that offered exhilarating prospects to his enormous audience. As he wrote to A.M. Thompson in 1931:

. . . I was always a Tory Democrat and you a French Democrat. You remember that from the first the Clarion crowd and the Hardie crowd were out of harmony. It was a repetition of the old hostility between the Roundheads and the Cavaliers. The Labour Leader people were Puritans; narrow, bigotted, puffed up with sour cant. We both disliked them, because we were both Cavaliers. They were nonconformist, self-righteous ascetics, out for the class war and the dictation by the proletariat. We loved the humour and colour of the old English tradition. You know it was so. You know we could never mix . . . [Thompson (1951) 230].

Blatchford died on 17 December 1943 at Horsham, Sussex, survived by two daughters, Winifrid Norris Blatchford (1882-1968) and Dorothea Glanville Blatchford born on 19 August 1890, and a son, Robert Corri, born on 8 March 1888, who died in hospital in Chelmsford in 1966. He had joined the Army in 1915, but was discharged on account of illhealth in 1918. He became an actor, but his stage career was of short duration. Robert Blatchford was buried in his wife's grave in Horsham Cemetery. He left an estate valued at £4593.

Writings: *The Nunquam Papers* (Manchester, 1891); *Fantasias* (1892; 2nd ed. 1895); *Socialism: a reply to the encyclical of the Pope* (Manchester, 1892) 19 pp., later eds including *The Pope's Socialism* (1909) 23 pp.; *The Living Wage and the Law of Supply and Demand* (Manchester, 1893) 16 pp.; *How I became a Socialist* (SDF, 1894 and 1901); *Merrie England* (1894; later eds); *Three Open Letters to the Bishop of Manchester on Socialism* (1894) 16 pp.; *A Son of the Forge* (1894); *Some Tory Socialisms* (1895) 12 pp.; *Tommy Atkins of the Ramchunders* ([1895]; later eds); *The Bounder: his book* (2nd ed. [1895]); *The Clarion Ballads* (1896) 16 pp.; *The Mingled Yarn: a drama* (1897); (with P.J. King), *Trades Federation* (1897); *Impressionist Sketches* (1897); *The New Religion* ([1898?]; later ed.) 12 pp.; *A Bad Law . . .* (1898, 2nd ed. 1899) 20 pp.; *The Tramp and Bab's Fairy* (1898); *Altruism:Christ's glorious gospel of love against man's dismal science of greed* (1898) 16 pp.; *Competition: a plain lesson for the workers* (1898; another ed. 1906) 16 pp.; *Land Nationalisation* (1898, 3rd ed. 1906) 16 pp.; *Real Socialism: what Socialism is, and what Socialism is not* (1898) 20 pp.; *A Bohemian Girl and McGinnis* (1899); *Dismal England* (1899; 2nd ed. 1901); *My Favourite Books* (1899; rev. ed. 1900, repr. [1911]); *The Black MP's* (1899) 16 pp.; *Imprudent Marriages* (Chicago, [189-?]) 25 pp.; *Mr Pickard and the Independent Labour Party* [189-?] 4 pp.; *Love and Sympathy the Basis of Socialism* (New York, [189-?]) 4 pp.; *Julie. A Study of a Girl* [1900?]; *Tales for the Marines* (1901; later eds); *Britain for the British* (1902; another ed. [1908]); *A Book about Books* (1903); *God and my Neighbour* (1903; later eds); *Not Guilty: a defence of the bottom dog* (1906; later eds); *Christians and Infidels* [1907; repr. from the *Clarion*, 18 Oct 1907]; *The Sorcery Shop* (1907); *The Dolly Ballads* ([1907]; later eds); (with U. Sinclair), *Socialism and War* (Pass on Pamphlet, no. 27: [1908?]) 16 pp.; *Essays on Socialism* (Terre Haute, Indiana [19-]); *What is this Socialism?* [1908?] 11 pp.; 'After Eighteen Years', *Clarion*, 7 Jan 1910; 'A Socialist on National Defence', *Spec. 103*, 25 Dec 1909, 1090-1; *My Life in the Army* ([1910]; another ed. [1915]); *Chetham College "the Oldest Free Library in the World"* (Boston, 1910); *Germany and England* [1911] 48 pp. and repr. from the *Daily Mail* (13-23 Dec 1909) in rev. ed. as *The War that was foretold: Germany and England* [1915] 48 pp.; *General von Sneak. A Little Study of the War* (1918); *Spangles of Existence* (1921); *Stunts* [Essays] ([1922]; another ed. [194-?]); 'Is there Life after Death?', *Spec. 128*, 22 Apr 1922, 488-9; *English Prose and how to write it* (1925); *More Things in Heaven and Earth* (1925); *As I lay a-thinking. Some Memories and Reflections* [1926]; *Robert Blatchford* [Selected Essays] (1927); *Saki's Bowl* [Essays] (1928); *My Eighty Years* (1931); *Shadow Shapes: a sheaf of human documents* (1931); *What's all this?* [1940] and [1942?].

Sources: (1) MSS: Autograph letters to Alexander M. Thompson (1885-1943) 4 vols; Autograph letters to William Palmer (1912-36) 2 vols; Clarion Newspaper Co. Ltd [Accounts, balance sheets, printing estimates etc. 1891-95] and [Memorandum and Articles of Association, 1894]: Archives Department, Manchester PL; Dilke papers: BM; A.R. Wallace Coll.: BM; S.J. Berry, 'The Clarion Table: the record of a Manchester luncheon group; Written at the request of some of the members (1908-1943)' [typescript]: Archives Department, Manchester PL. (2) Theses: L. Bather, 'A History of the Manchester and Salford Trades Council' (Manchester PhD, 1956); D.F. Summers, 'The Labour Church and Allied Movements of the late 19th and early 20th Centuries' (Edinburgh PhD, 1958); R. Frow, 'Independent Working Class Education with Particular Reference to South Lancashire, 1909-1930' (Manchester MEd., 1968); R.N. Price, 'The Boer War and the British Working Class, 1899-1902: a study in working-class attitudes and reactions to Imperialism' (Sussex PhD, 1968); J.O. Springhall, 'Youth and Empire: a study of the propagation of Imperialism to the young in Edwardian Britain' (Sussex PhD, 1968); J.A. Fincher, 'The Clarion Movement: a study of a Socialist attempt to implement the Co-operative Commonwealth in England, 1891-1914' (Manchester MA, 1972).
(3) Newspapers: *Clarion*, 12 Dec 1891-June 1932; then *New Clarion*, 11 June 1932-19 Mar 1934; *King of the Road*, 1897; *Labour Leader*, 1894-1922; *Scout*, 1895-6; *Sunday Chronicle*; *Women Folk*, 1909-10. (4) Other: *Labour Annual* (1895) 162; Clarion Newspaper Co. Ltd, *A*

Catalogue of Books, Pamphlets etc. of Socialist and Advanced Literature for Social Reformer. (1895); A. Woollerton, *The Labour Movement in Manchester and Salford* (Manchester ILP Branch pamphlet no. 1: 1907); J.E. Rattenbury, *Robert Blatchford's New Religion* (1909); A.N. Lyons, *Robert Blatchford* (1910); H.M. Hyndman, *Further Reminiscences* (1912); M. Beer, *A History of British Socialism* (1920); H.W. Lee and E. Archbold, *Social-Democracy in Britain* (1935); A.M. Thompson, *Here I lie* (1937); *DNB* (1941-50) [by R.C.K. Ensor]; *WWW* (1941-50); G.D.H. Cole, *British Working Class Politics 1832-1914* (1941); M. Cole, *Makers o. the Labour Movement* (1948); J.R. Clynes, 'Robert Blatchford (Nunquam)' in *The British Labour Party*, ed. H. Tracey, *3* (1948) 325-8 and 'The *Clarion* and its Chiefs', ibid., 321-4; L. Thompson, *Robert Blatchford: portrait of an Englishman* (1951); H. Pelling, *The Origins of the Labour Party 1880-1900* (1954; 2nd ed. Oxford, 1965); F. Bealey and H. Pelling, *Labour and Politics 1900-1906* (1958); P.P. Poirier, *The Advent of the Labour Party* (1958); C. Tsuzuki, *H.M. Hyndman and British Socialism* (OUP, 1961); A.M. McBriar, *Fabian Socialism and English Politics 1884-1918* (Cambridge, 1962); B. Simon, *Education and the Labour Movement 1870-1920* (1965); L. Thompson, *The Enthusiasts* (1971); personal information: Miss D.G. Blatchford, Hove, daughter; Dame Margaret Cole, London. Obit. *Observer*, 19 Dec 1943; *Manchester Guardian*, 20 Dec 1943.

JUDITH FINCHER LAIRD
JOHN SAVILLE

See also: Montagu BLATCHFORD; †Henry Musgrave READE.

BLYTH, Alexander (1835-85)
SECRETARY OF MINERS' RELIEF SOCIETY

Alexander Blyth was born in 1835 at Spittal, near Berwick, but spent his early childhood at Coatbridge in Lanarkshire. His father died when he was twelve years old, and with his sister and two brothers he went to live with an uncle at Seghill, Northumberland. He never attended school, and it was not until be began work as a driver at the Dudley Colliery in 1847 that he learned to read and write, in the evenings.

At Seghill Blyth concerned himself with urging upon his fellow-miners the virtues of teetotalism and the advantages to be derived from attendance at mechanics' institutes. He was an enthusiastic supporter of the Liberal cause, but never joined the trade union movement. Indeed, even towards the end of his life he was still suspicious of many aspects of miners' unionism, writing for example to William Watson that the followers of Alexander Macdonald were 'a senseless lot' (23 Feb 1874).

A Miners' Provident Association was established in the Newcastle area in 1859, but mainly because of opposition from the employers, it soon collapsed. After the Hartley disaster of 1862, in which 204 miners were entombed, Blyth played a leading part in the establishment of the first miners' mutual insurance society. This was the Northumberland and Durham Miners' Permanent Relief Fund, which offered Northern coalminers the opportunity of insuring against financial loss caused by industrial accidents. Donations and honorary subscriptions were invited, while ordinary members of the society were required to pay an entrance fee of one shilling and a monthly contribution of sevenpence. In return, substantial benefits were allowed: when a member died without leaving dependent relatives, a grant of £23 was made; when dependants survived him, his widow received a five-pound funeral grant, five shillings a week for herself, and two shillings a week for each child. In cases of long-term disability the injured miner was allowed eight shillings a week until he was able to resume work.

In 1862 Blyth was elected the first general secretary of the Northumberland and Durham Miners' Permanent Relief Fund, and three years later he left Dudley Colliery in order to become a full-time official of the society. At first, most trade unionists were suspicious of the Fund, but by the early 1880s – and perhaps earlier – this suspicion had turned into general support. Tommy Burt, for example, recorded it as his opinion that the society had done the miners of Northumberland, Durham and Cumberland 'an incalculable amount of good' (*Provident*, 15 Apr 1884). During the twenty-three years of Blyth's secretaryship, the Relief Fund emerged as the major source of compensation for industrial accidents in the northern coalfield. The rivalry of the aristocratically-led, London-based National Association for the Relief of British Miners did not prevent 7500 Durham and Northumberland men from joining the local Permanent Relief Fund within three months of its foundation. By 1872 the society's 22,322 members represented a quarter of those employed in the coalfield; and thirteen years later, at the time of Blyth's death, more than three-quarters of the 108,752 miners working in the district were subscribers to the Fund.

Many coalowners had also been suspicious at first, regarding the society as the thin end of the Union wedge; but not all were hostile. In 1863, for example, the Hetton Coal Company provided the tent in which tea was served at the first anniversary meeting of the Durham district of the society (*Colliery Guardian*, 1 Aug 1863). The decline of hostility on the part of the colliery owners was reflected in their positive contribution to the Fund. Sympathetic managements agreed to deduct subscriptions at source, and by 1874 some 14,000 miners had their payments collected at the colliery office. Employers also paid a proportion of the men's subscriptions – about fourteen per cent. – and in 1880 a total of £5246 was received in this way.

But under the 1880 Employers' Liability Act, no contracting-out agreements were reached in the North-East, and many owners decided to end their financial support of the Fund. By 1883 three-quarters of Northumberland owners were refusing to subscribe, and many small Durham employers also stopped paying.

Blyth had supported the foundation in 1879 of the central body of the permanent relief fund movement, the Central Association for Dealing with Distress caused by Mining Accidents, and he served as a member of its council. He worked for the extension of the permanent relief fund movement into other coalfields, and was particularly involved in the formation of the West Riding of Yorkshire Miners' Permanent Relief Fund, becoming a close friend of its secretary, William Watson.

Blyth soon became an acknowledged authority on the compensation of North-Eastern coalminers and their families for industrial accidents, and in 1872 gave evidence to the Royal Commission on Friendly and Benefit Building Societies. He travelled in Italy, Spain, Egypt, Portugal, Gibraltar, Canada and the United States, and it was in Gibraltar that he died on 12 December 1885 and was buried. He was survived by his widow, Margaret, and by six children. He left the sum of £277.

Writings: Evidence before R.C. on Friendly and Benefit Building Societies, 1871-4 XXII Qs 27031-244.

Sources: *Annual Reports of the Northumberland and Durham Miners' Permanent Relief Fund* (1862-86); J. Benson, 'The Compensation of English Coal-miners and their Dependants for Industrial Accidents, 1860-1897' (Leeds PhD, 1974); J. Benson, 'English Coal-Miners' Trade Union Accident Funds, 1850-1900', *Econ. Hist. Rev.* 2nd ser. *28*, no.3 (Aug 1975) 401-12; personal information: Miss J.M. Watson, Barnsley. OBIT. *Newcastle Daily Leader*, 15 Dec 1885.

JOHN BENSON

See also: George Lamb CAMPBELL.

BROADHEAD, Samuel (1818-97)
MINERS' LEADER

Born the son of a miner at Outwood, near Wakefield, on 16 September 1818, Sammy Broadhead, as he was popularly called, entered the pit at an early age. He spent most of his working days at collieries owned by the Charlesworth Company. When Broadhead began work Yorkshire pits were relatively shallow, and in many cases the coal was still drawn to the surface by horse-operated gins. Samuel Broadhead remembered the introduction of steam engines at some of the West Riding collieries, and as a lad he assisted in operating an engine which could haul approximately four cwt of coal (to the surface) at a time. He worked as a coal-getter at the Chapel Pit and later at the Robin Hood Colliery, near Wakefield. In 1852, when wages were low in his part of Yorkshire he moved to Kilnhurst, near Rotherham, in the south part of the county, and obtained employment at Rawmarsh Colliery.

The first record of Broadhead's trade union activities belongs to 1844; this was two years after the Miners' Association of Great Britain and Ireland was formally established at the Griffin Inn, Wakefield, on 7 November 1842, with David Swallow elected as its first general secretary. 1844 was the year of the great strikes in the Durham and Northumberland coalfields and in other regions as well. The industry was going through a severe depression: orders were few, and work so scarce that if a man took home 9s a week he was regarded as doing well. In an effort to fight these conditions, a local miners' union was formed in South Yorkshire, of which Broadhead was secretary and treasurer, and which also had its headquarters at the Griffin Inn. The local union affiliated to the Miners' Association, but it is not clear whether Broadhead played any part in the national organisation. In later life he used to recount how he and other local leaders were allowed 4d per day for expenses during the strike, which in some Yorkshire pits lasted for more than three months. The story of the Miners' Association is told in Challinor and Ripley (1968); in Yorkshire the Association seems to have collapsed by about the middle of 1845.

Broadhead's more lasting involvement in trade union affairs began in 1858 when the South Yorkshire Miners' Association was founded. He was one of the first members of the union, and soon became treasurer of the Rawmarsh branch. He was associated with John Frith and other South Yorkshire miners' leaders at this time, and in 1875, after the death of John Normansell, Broadhead ceased to work underground and became the permanent treasurer of the South Yorkshire Miners' Association (SYMA). In the same year he became a board member and treasurer of the Shirland Colliery Co. Ltd. This enterprise, which is often wrongly described as a co-operative venture, was invested in heavily by the SYMA; and when it failed, the union suffered a considerable financial loss [Williams (1962) 146 ff.]. When the SYMA amalgamated with the West Yorkshire Miners' Association to form the Yorkshire Miners' Association in 1881, Broadhead became the treasurer of the new organisation. He continued to hold this office until his death at Kilnhurst on 20 December 1897.

Samuel Broadhead did not play a prominent part in the external affairs of the Yorkshire miners' unions of the nineteenth century, neither did he lead an important public life. But he was one of the pioneers of trade unionism in the Yorkshire coalfields and was associated with miners' unions for over fifty years. Although he was a quiet unassuming man, he was highly respected in the mining communities of Yorkshire, where he was a familiar figure, for it was he who for almost a generation travelled throughout the West Riding disbursing strike and victim pay from his famous leather bag. He was married in 1848, the ceremony taking place at Wakefield Parish Church. He left an estate valued at £1115.

Sources: B. Jones, *Co-operative Production* (Oxford, 1894); F. Machin, *The Yorkshire Miners* (1958); J.E. Williams, *The Derbyshire Miners* (1962); R. Challinor and B. Ripley, *The Miners' Association: a trade union in the age of the Chartists* (1968). OBIT. *Leeds Mercury, Sheffield Daily Telegraph* and *Sheffield and Rotherham Independent*, 21 Dec 1897.

ROBERT G. NEVILLE

See also: †John NORMANSELL.

BROOKE, Willie (1895/6?-1939)

TRADE UNIONIST AND LABOUR MP

It has not been possible to confirm the actual date of Willie Brooke's birth from official records. According to Debrett, *House of Commons* (1930), it was 18 June 1895 but in *WWW* (1929-40) it is given as 18 December 1896. His father was Fred Brooke, a wool-sorter, and his mother was Hannah, daughter of George Priestley of Bradford. His father died a few years after Willie's birth. After an education at the Carlton Secondary School, Bradford, Brooke's first job was as an office boy in the Amalgamated Society of Dyers, and he eventually became chief clerk at its Bradford headquarters. When the Society amalgamated with the National Union of Textile Workers and the Operative Bleachers', Dyers' and Finishers' Association (Bolton Amalgamation) under the title of the National Union of Dyers, Bleachers and Textile Workers, Brooke continued on the staff at the Manningham Lane headquarters.

During his earlier years as a trade union functionary Brooke was elected to the first scholarship offered by the Dyers and Bleachers at the Central Labour College. This was probably in October 1919 [Craik (1964) 114] and he remained at the college for three years. When he returned to Bradford he immediately began to take an active part in the political and trade union life of the city. He had joined the ILP in his teens, and for twelve years (1925-37) he was a member of the Bradford City Council, representing Tong and Bradford Moor wards, and was for a time junior whip for the Labour group. For a period he was president of the Bradford City Labour Party. In 1929 he was elected to Parliament, as a sponsored candidate of the Dyers and Bleachers, for the Scottish constituency of Dunbartonshire – a most unusual honour for an Englishman; and it is possible that his particular trade union connections were the reason.

Brooke lost his seat in the 1931 débâcle and returned to Bradford as a trade union official. In 1932 he was selected as prospective Labour candidate, in succession to Ben Turner who had retired, for the Batley, Morley and Ossett constituency. There was a good deal of local opposition in the divisional Labour Party about the invitation to Brooke, but it was probably the strong textile union support that was decisive. He did much to unite the Party before the general election of 1935, which he won with a majority of 2842 over the sitting Conservative. Part of his success was the switch of Liberal voters to his candidature, helped by the support of the local organisation of Lloyd George's Council of Action for Peace and Reconstruction, as well as by his own lifelong membership of the Methodist Church.

His main interests in the Commons were in working conditions and education. He was especially noted locally for his concern with educational provision for handicapped children. His health, however, rapidly deteriorated in the later 1930s, and the last two years of his life were spent mostly in sanatoriums. He attended Parliament during the last quarter of 1938, but became ill during the Christmas recess and died at the Bradford home of his widowed mother on 21 January 1939. The funeral took place at Bethel Chapel, Shelf. He left effects valued at £1233. Labour held the seat at a by-election in March 1939 with the election of Hubert Beaumont.

Sources: *Hansard*, 31 Oct 1929; *WWW* (1929-40); Debrett, *House of Commons* (1930); *Dod* (1931); *Yorkshire Observer*, 8 and 9 Nov 1935; *Hansard*, (1935-7); T. Jones, *Lloyd George* (Oxford, 1951); W.W. Craik, *The Central Labour College 1909-29* (1964); biographical information: Central Library, Bradford; T.A.K. Elliott, CMG. OBIT. *Bradford Telegraph and Argus*, 21 Jan 1939; *Times*, 23 Jan 1939; *Batley News*, 28 Jan 1939.

ANN HOLT

See also: *Ben TURNER.

BURNS, Isaac (1869-1946)
MINERS' LEADER

Isaac Burns was born on 9 November 1869 at Moor Row, Egremont, Cumberland, and was one of twelve children of Timothy Burns, an iron miner and his wife Mary Mossop. He received an elementary education at Newton-in-Furness, three miles from Barrow, and at the age of twelve started work in the iron ore mines of Yarlside, near Barrow-in-Furness. On his first day of employment his mother insisted that he should join the local iron ore miners' union. When his father was injured in an accident Burns was the breadwinner for the family.

In 1891 the Yarlside mines were flooded and Burns migrated to South Yorkshire, where he found work at South Kirkby Colliery, Hemsworth. In the same year, however, he decided to cross the Atlantic, and between 1891 and 1894 he worked in the copper, silver and gold mines of Arizona, Colorado, Utah, Oklahoma and Montana – 'often down but never out'. Returning to Hemsworth in 1895 he was again employed at the South Kirkby Colliery, and became an active member of the Yorkshire Miners' Association branch attached to the pit. He soon became auditor of the South Kirkby Lodge, and thereafter promotion came rapidly: he became secretary, collector, president, and from 1912 onwards branch delegate to the YMA Council. While he was president he was dismissed from his job for his trade union activities; but after he had been for ten months in receipt of YMA victimisation pay the union managed to secure his re-employment at the colliery – now as checkweighman. For fifteen years he was annually elected a member of the Yorkshire County Joint Wages Board, and in this capacity was one of those who signed the agreement which provided for a return to work after the 1926 dispute. He was also a member of the Yorkshire Safety First Committee. He frequently attended Miners' Federation of Great Britain conferences, and he was an elected branch official of the YMA for fifty years, his trade union membership spanning sixty-five years.

Burns was one of the early Socialists among the Yorkshire miners. Long before 1900 he had rejected the radical wing of the Liberal Party, and he was well known for flaunting rather than wearing his flaming red tie. During the famous Barnsley by-election of 1897 his cottage was the campaign headquarters of Pete Curran, the ILP candidate. In the First World War Burns was a pacifist. In August 1917 he ignored the advice of the Mayor and the Chief Constable of Barnsley and presided over a 'peace' meeting. The *Barnsley Chronicle*, reflecting popular opinion commented:

> The peace cranks had secured a large bacon box for a platform and around this. they assembled. Suddenly Mr Burns sprang upon the box, but no sooner had he done so than a soldier in khaki dashed forward and knocked him to the ground. The chairman, looking terrified, made a bolt across Cheapside followed by the infuriated crowd. At a gallop he reached Hayes Croft where he hid in a cottage and for a couple of hours afterwards the crowd waited about evidently anxious for Burns to come out into the open. But the Hemsworth man knew better than to do so and as the police guarded the cottage and the approaches he was able to rest within in safety. At a late hour he was smuggled away [*Barnsley Chronicle*, 18 Aug 1917].

The unpopularity Burns incurred from his pacifist views probably contributed to his defeat by Coalition Liberals in the Pontefract constituency in the general election of 1918 and the by-election of 1919. Although decidedly left wing, Ike Burns, as he was generally called, refused to join the Communist Party of Great Britain. Among those whom he admired was the one-time MFGB secretary, A.J. Cook; the two men were close friends.

For many years Burns was active in local government. He was the first, and for some years the only Labour member of the Hemsworth Rural District Council. During the period in which he sat on the Council (1897-1922) he had one term of office as chairman; and with the coming of urban powers to Hemsworth he continued to serve, now on the Urban District Council, and held the chairmanship on two occasions. Burns was also a member of the Hemsworth Board of Guardians from 1906 to 1922.

Throughout his life Burns was an ardent Roman Catholic whose faith was never in doubt. He had married Margaret Stevenson on 7 June 1897, and they had one son and two daughters. Burns was very much a family man; he refrained from drinking and smoking to ensure that his children should obtain a good education. Burns was a generous, courageous, forthright man who was always prepared to fight for his principles. He was one of the Yorkshire miners' leaders who had ability but who never managed to obtain a district official's position at Barnsley. Burns's home was in Hemsworth, but he died at St Helen's Hospital, Barnsley, on 7 February 1946. He left an estate valued at £960.

Sources: *Barnsley Chronicle*, 18 Aug 1917; *Yorkshire Telegraph and Star*, 19 June 1926; *Labour Who's Who* (1927); R. Page Arnot, *The Miners* vol. *1* (1949); biographical information: NUM, Barnsley; personal information: Miss M.G. Burns, Dodworth, daughter.

ROBERT G. NEVILLE

See also: †Thomas ASHTON, for Mining Trade Unionism, 1900-14; †Arthur James COOK, for Mining Trade Unionism, 1915-26; Peter (Pete) Francis CURRAN; †Benjamin PICKARD, for Mining Trade Unionism, 1880-99.

BUTLER, Herbert William (1897-1971)
TRADE UNIONIST AND LABOUR MP

Herbert Butler was born on 30 January 1897 in Hackney, one of the thirteen children of Frank Butler, a Vienna baker. He was educated at Sigdon Road School, Hackney, until he was fourteen, when he was apprenticed to the printing trade as a gold blocker. He continued as a printer after his apprenticeship was completed, and had joined the National Union of Bookbinders by the beginning of the First World War.

From 1916 to 1919 Butler served in the Navy as a stoker. On his return to civilian life he lost his job as a result of his union activities in the printing trade, and was unemployed for about two years. In 1919 he had joined the National Union of Ex-Servicemen (NUX). This was an organisation of and for the rank and file, consciously distinct from the other two associations of ex-servicemen: the Comrades of the Great War, which was limited to ex-officers, and the National Federation of Discharged Soldiers and Sailors, which had been formed by some high-ranking officers with the aims of deflecting leftist tendencies among the lower orders of ex-servicemen. (These two bodies later combined to form the British Legion – of which many years later Butler became a member.) The NUX was affiliated to the Labour Party. One of the members was a Hackney councillor called John Beckett, later Labour MP for Gateshead, and later still prominent in Oswald Mosley's British Union of Fascists; another member was Clement Attlee. The chief business of the NUX was to watch over and if necessary fight pension cases on behalf of its members. It provided a training ground for Butler's subsequent political career. In the words of a Labour Party and Borough Council colleague who was also a member, Albert Cullington, 'Herbert Butler was a very live member of the Hackney Branch and was one of the very few local members then capable of speaking at street corner meetings.' Butler also got experience in the South Hackney Labour Party, which he had joined in 1919.

In 1921 Butler got a job as shop assistant with a wholesale and retail firm selling carpets and linoleum in Whitechapel. He joined the Hackney branch of the National Union of Shop Assistants, Warehousemen and Clerks, and soon became branch secretary; when the Hackney branch had to be closed down, the membership was transferred to Dalston, of which Butler became vice-chairman and then chairman.

Butler became secretary of the Hackney Labour Party in 1920 and it developed into a flourishing organisation, 'contesting all elections, i.e. Boards of Guardians, Borough Council, LCC and parliamentary. Our share of the poll showed a progressive increase at all elections' [letter from A. Cullington]. In the general election of 1922, the Central Hackney Labour Party was determined to fight the seat, for the first time. The branch had no funds, no agent, and no premises. Five members, of whom Butler was one, borrowed a total of £350 (which was all repaid) and Butler was appointed agent and honorary secretary. With this rudimentary organisation the candidate, A.A. Lynch succeeded in winning 4507 votes (the Conservative had 9795, the Liberal 6825). Butler continued to act as secretary and/or chairman of the Central Hackney Party until his election to Parliament in 1945 for Hackney South – the seat held by Herbert Morrison in 1923-4, 1929-31 and 1935-45.

From 1928 to 1931 Butler was a Hackney Borough councillor, and in 1929 was made a JP. He was also chosen as a member of the London County Advisory Committee for the Appointment of Justices. He was a co-operator and a member of the Co-operative Political Council. In 1934 he was re-elected to the Borough Council, on which he continued to serve until 1959; he was deputy leader, then, from 1945 to 1947 leader. He served as mayor in 1936-7. The work for which he became widely known was in housing: under his chairmanship the housing committee effected great improvements in the housing situation in the borough. Butler was also for many years chairman of the Hackney Trades Council.

There was an important episode in the history of the Hackney Trades Council which illustrates on a small scale some of the struggles and conflicts of the period between the General Strike and the second Labour Government of 1929. In September 1926 the Labour Party disaffiliated the Hackney Trades and Labour Council for its Communist connections. The Council still remained affiliated to the TUC. A new Trades Council was established which was affiliated to the Labour Party but not to the TUC. In February 1928 the TUC formally disowned the Communist-dominated Council, and thereafter its membership declined sharply. By 1930 it had ceased to exist.

Albert Cullington was the first secretary of the new Labour Party Trades Council and he was followed by Butler who also acted as chairman until 1929, when he resigned the position of secretary but remained chairman. One incident during the existence of these two Trades Councils in Hackney involved A.J. Cook. A meeting was advertised to be held under the auspices of the disaffiliated Trades Council on 16 February 1928, at which the speakers were A.J. Cook and the three prospective Communist Party candidates for the Hackney constituencies (Wal Hannington, South Hackney; Mrs Helen Crawfurd, North Hackney; J.T. Murphy, Central Hackney). Butler sent a letter of protest to Herbert Smith, the president of the Miners' Federation saying that Cook, the secretary of an organisation affiliated to the Labour Party 'should not utilise his position as secretary to boost a section of people who are doing their utmost to retard the work of the Labour Movement'. Butler also wrote to Arthur Henderson and Herbert Morrison. Herbert Smith sent a copy of Butler's letter to Cook who then wrote to Butler in scathing terms, telling him to mind his own business: 'I am perfectly free to utilise my spare time in whatever way I choose, and being a member of my Trade Union and also a Socialist, Mr Smith has no control over my Socialist activities' [14 Feb 1928]. The affair was discussed by both the London Labour Party and the NEC of the Labour Party, and Cook met a deputation from the latter which included Arthur Henderson. The official account of the meeting, held on 17 February, suggests that Cook took a relatively moderate position, and one that was nothing like so intransigent as his earlier letters or public pronouncements, would have suggested. Cook explained that the invitation to speak had come from Wal Hannington, who asked him to address a meeting, the purpose of which was to raise funds for the unemployed. When he (Cook) learnt that the meeting was one in support of Communist candidates, he had not fulfilled the engagement.

There are some unexplained matters in the whole affair. Cook certainly did not speak at the meeting – which took place the night before his discussion with the NEC – and his absence was represented by the organisers as due to his being called away to a mining disaster in Whitehaven. Cook had submitted a long list of questions to the NEC deputation which from the official account of the proceedings were not pressed by Cook and did not receive serious attention. After this meeting Herbert Morrison of the London Labour Party, tried to take the affair further, but the NEC of the Labour Party refused, and the matter dropped. The whole incident, which is well documented in the LP archives, is important for the light it throws on Cook's political attitudes in the closing years of his life: the tensions and strains he was subjected to, and the political contradictions he was involved in.

In the later 1930s Butler took a part in rallying opposition to the Fascists, who frequently made trouble in East London, especially in Hackney. In 1937 Butler joined the Beaufort Lodge, no. 5244, of the Freemasons. He had already left the carpet and linoleum firm, of which he had become manager, in order to set up a similar business of his own. At some point he joined the Association of Supervisory Staffs, Executives and Technicians, of which he was still a member in 1969. [This union became the Association of Scientific, Technical and Managerial Staffs in 1968.]

In the Second World War Butler was Chief Warden in the Hackney Civil Defence organisation, and chairman of the Hackney Food Committee; he was also chairman of the Civil Defence Committee of the Standing Joint Committee of London Boroughs. In 1947 he received the freedom of the Borough of Hackney. Some time before 1950 he joined the British Legion and became vice-president of the Central and South Hackney branch.

In 1945 Butler contested South Hackney in the Labour interest, and won the seat. (Later, from 1955, after a redistribution of seats, his constituency was Central Hackney.) In his maiden speech (1 Apr 1947) he opposed the Labour Government's National Service Bill; but this cannot have been held against him, for in 1950 he was appointed parliamentary private secretary to Walter Edwards, Civil Lord of the Admiralty, and James Callaghan, its parliamentary and financial secretary. Over the years he spent in the House, however, his chief interests were housing (most of all), local government, unemployment, and health. In his own district he was involved in hospital organisation in the Health Service both at regional and at hospital group level: he served on a group Management Committee and on the North East Metropolitan Regional Hospital Board. In 1950-1 he played an active part in the campaign against the reimposition of prescription charges which was conducted by the Labour Party Health Group under its chairman L.A. Pavitt, MP, who contributed this information about Butler.

In 1964 Butler was again elected MP for Central Hackney by a large majority – 11,376. From about this time, however, he was less active in the House, spoke less often, and asked fewer questions. But from beginning to end of his parliamentary career of twenty-five years he was an admirable constituency member: intimate with conditions in Hackney, where he had lived all his civilian life; almost constantly accessible to his constituents, and tireless in attending to their problems and interests.

In 1969 he decided not to seek re-election to the Commons. He had served the labour movement for fifty years, and he wanted now to concentrate on his business. He hoped for a seat in the Lords; but perhaps because the Labour Government was defeated in 1970, perhaps for some other, unknown reason, he was not raised to the peerage. His successor as MP for Central Hackney, S. Clinton Davis, records that Butler 'left the warmest possible memories' in the House of Commons.

In 1969 Butler was vice-president of the Association of Municipal Corporations, and in 1971 he was made an alderman of the new London Borough of Hackney. His concern about housing persisted. After he had given up many other interests, he continued to support a housing association, the Abbeyfield Society, which provided sheltered accommodation for solitary people.

In his youth, Herbert Butler said in 1969, he had attended evening classes 'and studied Marxian economics, the Russian Revolution, the Third International, unemployed movements, Socialist philosophy and tactics' (*Hackney Gazette*, 28 Feb 1969). He continued to read widely, mainly in economics and politics. S. Clinton Davis mentions one rather unusual accomplishment of his: 'Although he was not Jewish, he could converse readily in Yiddish, which was something of an asset in this constituency.' He may have learned to speak Yiddish quite early – the proprietors of the firm he worked for in Whitechapel were Jewish, and it is likely that most or many of their customers were Yiddish speakers.

In 1925 Butler, with Albert Cullington and others, had formed an amateur dramatic group, 'The People's Players'; they presented, for instance, Shaw and Barrie plays in 1926. Eventually, according to Albert Cullington, 'the Communists infiltrated and took control'.

On 18 September 1926 Herbert Butler married Nellie Bingley, daughter of Henry William Bingley and Annie Elizabeth Bingley. Both her parents came from Sheffield, but Nellie, born and brought up in Hackney, was as much a native true as her husband was. Her father was a carpenter, a long-standing member of the ILP, and a Hackney Borough councillor. Herbert Butler died on 16 November 1971 in St Leonard's Hospital, Shoreditch. The funeral was on 22 November at Enfield, where he was cremated. On 28 November there was a memorial service in the church of St John-at-Hackney, conducted by the Rector of Hackney, the Rev. G.H. McKinley. Butler's wife had died in 1961, but three sons survived him: Michael, who had settled in America; Richard, an economist working for the Hong Kong Government, who married a daughter of Hackney Councillor Jack Dunning; and John, a commercial manager. Herbert Butler left an estate valued at £14,684.

On 6 July 1974 a plaque commemorating Butler's long and admirable work in housing was unveiled by the Mayor of Hackney. It was put up in a new housing estate, the Herbert Butler Estate at Swinnerton Street designed and in process of being built by the Hackney Borough Council, to be completed in 1977.

Sources: (1) MSS: personal papers, including election addresses of H.W. Butler: Greater London Record Office; Labour Party archives: LP/MIN/28/11-38. (2) Other: *Labour Party Report* (1927); *Hackney Gazette*, 20 Feb 1928; *Shop Assistant*, 31 Oct 1936; *Hackney Guardian*, 11 Nov 1936; *Dod* (1946); *Daily Telegraph*, 2 Apr 1947; *Hansard*, (1947-69); *Hackney Gazette*, 5 Aug 1960, and 28 Feb 1969; B. Donoughue and G.W. Jones, *Herbert Morrison: portrait of a politician* (1973); biographical information: BBC News Information; B. Burke, London [for details of the Hackney Trades Council]; T.A.K. Elliott, CMG; S.C. Tongue, London Borough of Hackney Archives Department; personal information: J. Butler, London, son; Counc. A. Cullington, London; S. Clinton Davis MP; Ald. M. Ottolangui, Hackney; L.A. Pavitt MP. OBIT. *Hackney Gazette*, 19 Nov 1971; *Times*, 20 Nov 1971; *Hackney Gazette*, 26 and 30 Nov 1971.

MARGARET 'ESPINASSE

See also: †Arthur James COOK.

CAMPBELL, George Lamb (1849-1906)
SECRETARY OF MINERS' RELIEF SOCIETY

Campbell was born at Scotter, Lincolnshire, on 12 May 1849, the son of the Rev. Hugh Campbell, a Free Church minister, and his wife Sarah (née Hall). Little is known of his early life except that his childhood was spent in Scarborough, where in his late teens he joined the staff of a local newspaper. In 1868 he moved to Lancashire and became a journalist for the *Wigan Observer*.

He became concerned with the problem of mining accidents during the years 1868 to 1871 when the Wigan coalfield experienced a series of disasters in which 317 miners were killed, leaving 150 widows, and 354 children fatherless. Local relief organisations were quite unable to cope with the large number of dependants, and, mainly through the vigorous advocacy of William Pickard, the agent for the Wigan district union, the Lancashire and Cheshire Miners' Permanent Relief Society was established in 1872.

Pickard's plan for the Relief Society was regarded with much suspicion by the working miners. At this time most coalowners organised their own schemes for sickness and accidents; and except in the cases of major disasters, there were advantages for them in this arrangement [Challinor (1972) 162]. This led the miners to regard the establishment of a pooled fund as likely to reduce the owners' incentive to concern themselves with safety measures and hence as a retrograde step, and it was for this reason that Pickard's scheme was viewed with so much hostility. What was needed, the miners argued, was a campaign for stricter mine regulations. Despite this opposition the new Relief Society was formed in 1872. Miners paid an entrance fee of one shilling and a weekly subscription of threepence, in return for which injured members received a weekly allowance of six shillings and free medical attendance; twenty pounds was paid upon the death of a miner leaving no dependent relatives, while the widow of a married man received a five-pound funeral grant, five shillings a week for herself and two shillings a week for each boy under twelve and each girl under thirteen.

When the scheme was first established there were certain administrative features to which great objection was taken. Working miners provided three-quarters of the total monies received; the coalowners one quarter. Control, however, was firmly in the owner's hands, both at county and at pit level. Administrative costs were reckoned to be too high, and there were allegations of inefficiency. In 1872 G.L. Campbell was appointed full-time secretary of the Relief Society, a position he was to retain for the rest of his life. At the end of its first year the Society had enrolled 10,424 miners (nearly 17 per cent. of those employed in Lancashire) and by 1879 more than half the miners eligible for membership had joined.

The passing of the Employers' Liability Act of 1880 brought a new element into the situation. The coalowners issued an ultimatum to the effect that their workers would remain members of the Lancashire and Cheshire Permanent Relief Society (thereby contracting out of the Act) or their employment would end on 1 January 1881. The notice came at a time when wage claims were being considered from the men's side, and in the long and bitter strike which followed, 'many issues intertwined in the dispute, causing chaotic confusion' [Challinor (1972) 164]. One thing, however, was clear: the hatred of the miners for the Relief Society. A result of the strike, which lasted through January and into February and was the biggest in the history of the Lancashire coalfield, was the enforced resignation of William Pickard as agent.

Despite initial hostility the Relief Society continued to increase its membership. In 1905, the last full year in which Campbell was secretary, the membership was 48,000, representing some 52 per cent. of the county's miners. There remained throughout a good deal of coercion on the part of the owners. When the first effective employers' liability act was passed in 1897, the coalowners were still able to compel many men to stay in the Relief Society, and although the Lancashire Federation campaigned against the owners, and indeed endeavoured to float their own accident and relief scheme, the Relief Society remained coalowner-controlled.

In addition to his position in the Lancashire Society, Campbell was consulting secretary of the North Wales Permanent Relief Society and the Monmouthshire and South Wales Miners' Permanent Provident Society; and he was also founder and general secretary of the Central Association for Dealing with Distress caused by Mining Accidents. At the time of his evidence before the R.C. on Labour, Campbell reported that there were nine regional associations affiliated to the Central Association, with a membership of 275,143 miners on 30 June 1891. The size of these associations varied markedly, and their administration and control were also different in different parts of the country.

Campbell became one of Britain's leading authorities on the compensation of coalminers and their dependants following accident or death. From his arrival in Wigan he was also associated with the administration of public funds which were raised after mine disasters; in 1878, for example, he was appointed secretary of the Haydock Colliery Explosion Fund. He was also consulted when the Lord Mayor of London appealed for subscriptions after serious colliery accidents. In several pamphlets, in numerous meetings and in an extensive correspondence, Campbell stressed the advantages to be derived from working-class self-help after mining accidents. He read a paper at the British Association meeting at Cardiff in 1891 on 'Miners' Thrift and Employers' Liability'.

He was a member of the governing body of the Wigan Mining and Mechanical School, and upon its absorption into the Wigan Mining and Technical College, became a member of the general committee. He was also one of the earliest promoters of the Free Library movement. A member of the Wigan Library authority from its establishment in 1876, he was also an honorary member of the Hindley Library Committee. For many years he was a member of the Council of the Library Association, whose annual meeting he helped to organise at Manchester in 1882. Seventeen years later he was appointed special local secretary to organise the Association's conference at Southport.

He was associated with the Wigan Infirmary from its foundation in 1873, and urged the adoption of the weekly contribution system. In 1888 he was elected to the Infirmary's board of management and in 1900 he was made a vice-president. He also maintained a lively interest in the Wigan musical scene. He served as organist of the Hope Church, sang in the parish choir and was one of the founders of the Trinity College choir. It was due to his efforts that the composer and conductor, Sir Julius Benedict, visited Wigan during the 1870s.

Campbell was an enthusiastic Freemason, becoming master of the Lindsay Lodge and Provincial Grand Organist of West Lancashire. During the late 1870s he was elected a Fellow of the Statistical Society, and in 1891 was made a JP for the borough of Wigan. He became particularly concerned about the practice of juveniles appearing in open court, and advocated the establishment of special courts to deal with young offenders.

G.L. Campbell married Ann Dunkerley Adamson of Scarborough and they had two daughters and three sons. He died in Southport on 7 June 1906 and was survived by his wife and children. The funeral service at Southport Cemetery on 9 June was conducted by the Rev. D.S. Rennard, chaplain of the Lindsay Lodge of Freemasons. Campbell left £2587.

Writings: *Permanent National Relief of Distress caused by Accidents in Mines* (Wigan, 1878) 18 pp.; *Miners' Insurance Funds: their origin and extent* (1880) 17 pp.; (with C.W. Sutton), 'Statistical Report on the Free Town Libraries of the United Kingdom', *Trans. Library Association* (1880); 'The Grouping of Populous Places for Library Purposes', *Trans. Library Association* (1880) 28-31; Introduction to *Wigan Public Library. Mr Folkard's Catalogue of its Reference Department* (Wigan, 1886) 25 pp.; Evidence before R.C. on Labour 1892 XXXIV Qs 8264-359; *Public Subscriptions and Permanent Funds* (Wigan, 1896) P; *The Permanent Fund and the Compensation Act* (Wrexham, 1898) P.

Sources: *Annual Reports of the Lancashire and Cheshire Miners' Permanent Relief Society*, 1873-1906; *Trans. Third AGM of Library Association* (1881) 3; *Southport Visiter*, 9-10 June 1906; R. Challinor, *The Lancashire and Cheshire Miners* (Newcastle upon Tyne, 1972); J. Benson, 'The Compensation of English Coal-miners and their Dependants for Industrial Accidents, 1860-1897', (Leeds PhD, 1974); idem, 'Colliery Disaster Funds, 1860-1897', *Int. Rev. Social Hist. 19*, pt 1, (1974), 73-85; personal information: A. Rhodes, general secretary (1974) of Lancashire and Cheshire Miners' Permanent Relief Society. OBIT. *Wigan Observer*, 8 June 1906.

JOHN BENSON

See also: Alexander BLYTH; †William WATSON.

CASASOLA, Rowland (Roland) William (1893-1971)
FOUNDRY WORKERS' LEADER

Rowland Casasola was born in Manchester on 14 May 1893, the son of Joseph Casasola, a journeyman baker, and his wife Letitia (née Roberts), and he claimed descent from a sixteenth-century Spanish cardinal, while other accounts suggested that Rowland's grandfather had reached Manchester from Mexico in the 1860s. Casasola was educated at an elementary school, and was apprenticed as an iron moulder. He joined the Friendly Society of Iron Founders on 6 July 1912, and later passed, as the result of amalgamation, into the National Union of Foundry Workers. He volunteered for the Army in 1914, and served in France with the Royal Engineers. He took part in the first Battle of Loos in September 1915, and ended with the rank of corporal. During his war service, he was wounded in the thigh, and lost a toe.

On his return from the war, he joined the Labour Party, in 1919, and over the next decade, he achieved some prominence as a propagandist in Lancashire. He was associated particularly with the ILP, and also took an economics course through the National Council of Labour Colleges. During the inter-war years he worked as a moulder at the Trafford Park works of Metropolitan-Vickers, but he was not involved prominently in trade union activities.

In October 1931, he supported the unsuccessful Labour candidacy of William Dobbie in the Stalybridge and Hyde constituency. This – and subsequent propaganda work – led to his selection as the prospective candidate for the division in May 1933. He faced a majority of 13,306, but he reduced this to 5073 in a straight fight in the 1935 election. When the sitting member retired in March 1937, Casasola was not selected to fight the by-election. The choice of the Rev. Gordon Lang led to considerable controversy, and eventually the local party officers published details of the selection conference. On a short list of four, Casasola had been eliminated on the second of the three ballots. He later claimed that his rejection had been due to his strong sympathy for Republican Spain. From 1937 to 1939 he was the prospective candidate for Bury, and was adopted later as a candidate in the two-member Stockport seat. He fought there in 1945, in tandem with Reginald Stamp, a London councillor. Casasola was still unsponsored, having failed in an attempt to become the official candidate of his union. As with some other north-western industrial seats, Labour did not capture Stockport in 1945: Casasola had forty-four less votes than Stamp, and 1162 less than the second Conservative.

Although his political ambitions seemed blocked, he made headway in the new Amalgamated Union of Foundry Workers. When the first elections for the national executive committee were held in 1946, Casasola was elected for the Area C seat. This covered Lancashire, Wales, the West Midlands and South West England. This was the way in which Casasola became prominent in Labour Party controversies. The characteristic anti-Communism of the period was not reflected in the Foundry Workers' pronouncements. On international affairs, wages policy and international trade union unity, the Foundry Workers remained critical of the Labour Government and the TUC. They promoted their views at Party conferences and the TUC, although Jim Gardner, the union's general secretary, was debarred as a Communist from attending Labour conferences, so that Casasola became the union's principal spokesman there; in contrast, he did not normally attend the TUC. In 1949 he advocated the nationalisation of the foundries, when the Party conferences debated future policy, while the following year he spoke on a similar theme and more controversially, seconded a critical resolution on foreign policy.

Casasola was now the union's official candidate and was adopted for the re-drawn Manchester Moss Side seat. In the 1950 election, the Conservative candidate died between nomination and polling, and the contest was postponed until 9 March. Casasola fought as an orthodox Labour candidate, being adjudged by one observer to be just 'a little left of centre' [*Manchester Guardian*, 8 Mar 1950]. A combination of orthodox views and fundamentalist oratory was not effective, and in a three-cornered fight he finished second, 8578 votes behind the Conservative. His last parliamentary contest came in October 1951, when he fought Blackburn West, a seat lost by Labour in 1950 by 1879 votes. Most of the publicity in Blackburn focused on Barbara Castle's fight to retain the neighbouring East constituency. Casasola still argued that trust between a Labour Government and the Soviet Union was feasible. This belated rendition of 'Left can talk to Left' struck no response, and he lost by 2701 votes.

He remained a leading exponent of left-wing views at the Party Conference, and continued to act as the chairman of his union's delegation. At the 1953 Conference, he moved an amendment to the policy document, *Challenge to Britain,* advocating the public ownership of engineering and related industries. It was based on the *Plan for Engineering* which had originated in wartime AEU discussions on the future of public ownership, and had become a focus of left-right antagonisms. The amendment was attacked vehemently by Arthur Deakin, and was defeated by 4,499,000 votes to 1,797,000.

Casasola's most important Conference contribution came in 1954 when he moved the critical resolution on German Rearmament, in a speech full of traditional Socialist slogans. For once it seemed that the critics might defeat the Executive, but the Foundry Workers' resolution was lost by 3,281,000 to 2,910,000. It was felt by some that the defeat was at least in part facilitated by the nature of the Foundry Workers' resolution. The *New Statesman* (2 Oct 1954) labelled it 'absurdly naïve'. It seems that at the pre-Conference meeting to consider the resolutions on German rearmament, a successful attempt was made to saddle the critics with a resolution that was not likely to gain support from marginal delegates. Casasola's involvement in the German controversy led to his going to Paris later in the year, along with Sydney Silverman and Ben Parkin. They held meetings with Communist and Gaullist opponents of German rearmament, and gave an interview to *L'Humanité*. These activities produced complaints from Guy Mollet to Morgan Phillips, secretary to the LP.

Casasola was elected as the Foundry Workers' chairman at the 1954 Annual Delegate Meeting in succession to Archie MacDougall. By then, the left-right divisions had become clearer within the union, and on several issues the position of the Foundry Workers as a whole remained well to the left of the Labour Party. This position was upheld by the new president. His addresses to the Annual Delegate Meetings of 1955-8 supported wider extensions of public ownership, condemned the Party's general moderation, advocated a major development of East-West trade, and were vague on the sensitive question of international trade union unity. At the 1957 Annual Delegate Meeting he spoke on the situation in Hungary following the Soviet intervention in the previous November: 'There was not a Socialist in the world', he said, 'who was not shocked by the happenings in Hungary. I never believed that such a situation could and would happen in a Socialist country. . . . There must have been many things that should have been adjusted to meet the wishes of the workers in a workers' state. Those who failed to make these adjustments did a great disservice to Socialism all over the world' [Foundry Workers' ADM *Report* (1957)]. He was, however, careful not to put himself in the position of Communist-baiter, and not all his statements went unchallenged by his union colleagues.

It was in this period that he became a member of the Labour Party's National Executive. He had stood for election to the trade union section seven times running, without success – a candidate from a relatively small and left-wing organisation stood little chance. In 1955 he finished in thirteenth place, but with 801,000 votes he was no less than 3,175,000 behind the last successful candidate. Early in 1956, however, a vacancy occurred in the trade union section. A.E. (Jock) Tiffin, general secretary of the Transport Workers had died in December 1955 and his successor, Frank Cousins, moved off the NEC to the General Council. He was duly replaced by the best loser, Casasola. It is rather surprising that he retained this seat at the 1956 and 1957 Conferences, although on both occasions he received by far the lowest vote of the successful trade union candidates. Casasola was a member of the home policy sub-committee, then developing revisionist policies on a wide range of issues, but he played no part in the study groups that produced the key policy documents. He left the NEC after the 1958 Conference.

Casasola resigned as the Foundry Workers' president on his sixty-fifth birthday in May 1958. He had also been a member of the executive of the Confederation of Shipbuilding and Engineering Unions, a position held by him until the following August. He emerged briefly from the obscurity of retirement in February 1961 when he announced his resignation from the Labour Party to become an 'unashamed and card carrying' member of the Communist Party, and to attack Labour's continued retreat from public ownership. He died at his home in Higher

Blackley, Manchester, on 29 March 1971. He was married but had no family. He left effects valued at £1592.

Casasola was an accomplished platform speaker. Although small in stature, he carried the full rhetorical armoury of an evangelical Socialist. His interest in industrial questions was unusually slight for a trade union leader; his principal concern was with political issues. It is clear that he was greatly influenced by the strong and attractive personality of his Communist general secretary, Jim Gardner; but on many issues, it would be difficult to claim that he held any very defined view. He always defended the domestic record of the Attlee Government, and usually appeared as a moderate in industrial matters. His principal importance was as a trade union advocate of a number of left-wing positions at a time when the Cold War made their spokesmen highly vulnerable to attack. It also made them scarce in number. It was this scarcity that helped to account for his prominence.

Writings: The principal source for Casasola's views is the Foundry Workers' *Journal* – available at the AUEW (Foundry Workers' Section), 164 Upper Chorlton Road, Manchester 16. This contains articles by him and reports of the ADM's including his presidential addresses. See also his 'Labour wants Socialism', *Lab. Mon.* (Nov 1954) 499-506; 'I stay where I belong', *Daily Worker*, 1 Mar 1961; and *Labour Party Conference Reports*, 1947-58.

Sources: For Casasola's election attempts see: *Hyde Reporter*, 13 May 1933; *Stalybridge Reporter*, 19 and 26 Oct, 2, 9 and 16 Nov 1935, 19 Mar, 2, 9, and 23 Apr 1937; *Stockport Express*, 7, 14, 21 and 28 June, 5 July 1945; *Stockport Advertiser*, 15 and 22 June 1945; *Manchester Guardian*, 5 and 8 March 1950; *Daily Worker*, 22 Feb 1950; *Blackburn Times*, 21 Sep, 12, 19 and 26 Oct 1951. Other: *Labour Party Reports*, 1949-50, 1952-5; 'Attlee, Attlee über Alles', *New Statesman and Nation*, 3 Oct 1954, 378; Foundry Workers' ADM *Report* (May 1957); H. Fyrth and H. Collins, *The Foundry Workers* (Manchester, 1959); M. Harrison, *Trade Unions and the Labour Party since 1945* (1960); M. Foot, *Aneurin Bevan: a biography*, vol. 2: *1945-1960* (1973); L. Minkin, 'The Labour Party Conference and Intra-party Democracy 1956-70' (York D.Phil., 1975); biographical information: R. Ward, Eccles. OBIT. *Foundry Workers' J.* (Apr 1971) 158.

DAVID HOWELL

CHARLTON, William Browell (1855/7?-1932)
MINERS' LEADER

The date and place of William Charlton's birth cannot be confirmed from the records of Somerset House. It is likely that his father was Ellison Charlton, a joiner of Birtley, Chester-le-Street, and it is probable that William was born in the same place. The exact date of birth was almost certainly between 1855 and 1857. When he was eight he started work coupling at the flats at Edmondsley Colliery; he later moved to Littleburn as a boiler-fireman. In 1874 he gained his certificate as winding engineman, and for the next twenty years he worked in various places in Co. Durham – Seaham, Hetton (where the township elected him to Durham CC), Usworth and Hamsteels; he returned to Littleburn in 1894. His connection with trade unionism began in 1888 when he was sent as Hamsteels Lodge delegate to the council of the Durham County Colliery Enginemen and Boilerminders' Association. In 1905 he became secretary to the Association, a post which he held with distinction for over twenty years, retiring in 1928 or 1929. He was for some time treasurer (succeeding Thomas Hindmarch) and for four years president. He published a history of his Association in 1925.

Charlton was also chairman, and later general secretary, of the National Federation of Colliery Enginemen and Boiler Firemen. For many years, including that most difficult year 1926, he was chairman of the Durham County Federation Board. Peter Lee paid public tribute to his work for the Board, referring to 'his wide experience and sagacious counsel'. Charlton was one of the founders of the Durham Aged Mineworkers' Homes Association – working with Joseph Hopper a prime mover in the venture – and was one of its most active supporters. When the Durham District Welfare Committee was established in April 1922 (being the regional organisation of the Miners' Welfare Fund, itself a by-product of the Sankey Commission of 1919) the chairman was the president of the Durham Coal Owners' Association, and Charlton was vice-chairman (in his capacity as chairman of the County Federation Board) [Garside (1971) 293].

William Charlton took a lively interest in local public affairs. He was the first chairman of Brandon Urban District Council, and one of the pioneers of the Brandon Co-operative Society. After he moved to Durham City, he was for many years a JP on the Durham bench, and was described by the Clerk of the Court as 'a regular attender, conscientious, and scrupulously fair'.

He was a devout Wesleyan Methodist, a local preacher and a long-standing member of the Old Elvet Church in Durham. Charlton died at his home, 26 Western Hill, Durham, on 30 January 1932, after an illness of some weeks. The funeral service was held at the Old Elvet Church, and he was buried at St Cuthbert's Church.

At the age of nineteen, Charlton married Mary Green, daughter of the overman at Littleburn where he was then working. His wife died in 1924 or 1925, but three children of the marriage survived their father: his son, the Rev. R. Charlton, a Methodist minister in Quebec, and his two daughters, Miss Isabel Charlton, organiser for the Liberal Party in Yorkshire, and Mrs Matthew Waller. He left effects valued at £198.

Writings: *A Fifty Years' History of the Durham County Enginemen's Boilerminders' and Firemen's Association* (Durham, 1925).

Sources: J. Oxberry, *The Birth of the Movement: a tribute to the memory of Joseph Hopper* [Durham Aged Mineworkers' Homes Association] [1924]; R. Page Arnot, *The Miners* (1949); R.F. Wearmouth, *The Social and Political Influence of Methodism in the Twentieth Century* (1957); W.R. Garside, *The Durham Miners 1919-1960* (1971). OBIT. *Durham County Advertiser*, 5 Feb 1932.

MARGARET 'ESPINASSE
ANTHONY MASON

See also: †John ADAIR; James CLARK.

CHATER, Daniel (Dan) (1870-1959)
CO-OPERATOR AND LABOUR MP

Daniel Chater was born in Walnut Tree Walk, Lambeth, on 17 November 1870, the eldest child of Henry Chater, who before his marriage was a sergeant in the regular Army, in which he served for ten years, seven of which were spent in India. Daniel's mother was Maria Snell, who with her sister, had been brought up in an orphanage until of an age to be placed in domestic service. At the time of her marriage to Henry Chater she was employed as a nursemaid in the household of a London civil engineer and it was her reluctance to live in army barracks that persuaded her husband to leave the service. He obtained work in the Great Eastern Railway works at Stratford as a boilermaker's labourer. Frequently he was put on short time and when Daniel was born Henry Chater gave his occupation as 'letter carrier'. His wife did sweated work at home, making buttonholes for a local shirt factory for a wage of $2\frac{1}{4}d$ per dozen holes. The family (there were five children) suffered severe hardship.

After a little education at a dame's school, Daniel Chater attended the local Board school from the age of eight but only irregularly, since he was often required to help at home. At the age of twelve he started work as a solicitor's clerk. Subsequently he became an office-boy in a small firm owned by the son-in-law of the family by whom his mother had been employed as nursemaid; but this particular office proved uncongenial, and two years after the death of his mother he left both the job and his home at the age of seventeen. There then followed a variety of short-lived clerking jobs (he had taught himself shorthand and typing) until he was offered employment, in 1895, with a firm of stockbrokers. He had married in the previous year and soon afterwards he and his wife, Kate (née Wood), settled in Ilford, where they continued to live for the rest of their lives.

About 1905 Daniel Chater became a keen Socialist and, in his own words, 'voraciously devoured its literature'. For a time he was a *Clarion* vanner and also a member of the Ilford Socialist Party, which later merged with the local branch of the ILP. Chater remained an active member until a branch of the Labour Party was formed in the area which then joined with the ILP. He was also a member of the National Union of General and Municipal Workers and of the Plebs League, and an enthusiastic supporter of the London Co-operative Society.

From 1919 to 1922 Chater represented the Hainault ward of Ilford on the Essex County Council and he served on the Metropolitan District Smallholdings and Allotments Committees. The allotments movement was a long-standing interest of his since the years before the First World War, when he was chairman, then secretary, of the Seven Kings and Goodmayes Horticultural Society, which had a very successful allotment section. During the war years the movement greatly expanded. Chater became active in the Vacant Lands Cultivation Society, which was in large part responsible for the establishment in Birmingham of the National Union of Allotment Holders. By the end of the war this had become the recognised organisation of practically all allotment societies in England. Chater became its first general secretary and held the post until changes in his employment necessitated his resignation. He did, however, also remain active in the movement locally. In 1920 he was invited by the Agricultural Wholesale Society (a farmers' co-operative venture which served as a central buying agency for the purchase of machinery, tools, feed-stuffs, etc.) to manage an allotments department. Many difficulties arose, caused in the main by general slump conditions, and the scheme was not a success. Chater found himself unemployed for some months. He then had a series of posts – from one of which he was dismissed for being a Socialist.

In the general elections of 1923 and 1924 Chater contested the Ilford constituency in the Labour interest, but on both occasions lost to the Conservative candidate. From 1924 until 1926 he was chairman of the Ilford Labour Party and Labour leader in the Ilford local parliament, which he had helped to found. In 1927 he was nominated by the political committee of the London Co-operative Society, of which he was chairman in 1926, as prospective candidate for South Hammersmith. He was subsequently approved by the constituency Labour Party. The seat had been a safe Tory one for forty-five years and the Labour Party fought a very hard contest. Chater was elected in 1929 with a majority of only 412 votes, one of the nine Co-operative candidates to be returned. In a short congratulatory article, the *Daily Herald* noted that Chater had given more than twenty-five years of service to the co-operative movement and had acted as its spokesman at many conferences and congresses. He lost his seat, however, in the Labour débâcle of 1931, and for the next four years he was organiser for the political committee of the London Co-operative Society, lecturing and writing on its behalf.

In 1933 Chater was invited to become the Labour and Co-operative candidate for the constituency of Bethnal Green, North-East. At the general election of 1935 he was returned with a sizeable majority over the Liberal candidate, and he continued to represent the division for fifteen years, retiring in 1950 when the constituency disappeared as a result of local government reorganisation.

Chater seldom voted against the official Party line in his earlier years in Parliament. His attitude during the first phase of the Second World War was a common one – anti-Chamberlain and pro-Churchill. During his later years as an MP he moved somewhat to the Left. During the war he voted on several important occasions against the Government – on Purchase Tax and the Means Test in 1941 and in 1942 on the omission of civilian women from the war-time Personal

Injuries Act. In 1943 he spoke out vigorously against the release of Oswald Mosley. After the Labour victory of 1945, he was highly critical of the way nationalisation was carried through, especially in the matters of the overgenerous compensation to the former owners, and the insufficient number of workers promoted to managerial posts. He was unhappy about the Cold War developments in foreign policy, and continued to believe in the possibility of peaceful co-existence with the Soviet Union, and insisted upon the importance of good trading relationships between the two countries.

Dan Chater died on 25 May 1959 in Whipps Cross Hospital at the age of eighty-eight. About five years before he had been injured in a collision with a motorcycle and had since been crippled. He was buried in Ilford Cemetery. At his own request there was no church service, and only members of the family and representatives of the Bethnal Green Labour Party were at the graveside. In his youth he had attended a Wesleyan chapel but in later life he became an agnostic. He left effects valued at £4631. His wife had died twenty years before, but he was survived by his family of four sons and two daughters. After elementary schooling all Chater's children went to Ilford County High School, where there was one or another of them on the roll from 1908 to 1926. The eldest son, Sidney Walter, became a bank clerk in 1912, joined the Territorial regiment of the London Rifle Brigade in 1913 and went to France in 1914. He was commissioned in 1916 and awarded the Military Cross and promoted to acting captain in 1917. In 1924 he emigrated to South Africa. After farming for a while he worked for a Labour paper, and in 1932 accepted the editorship of *Co-operation,* the official organ of the agricultural co-operative movement. He succeeded in having this paper – renamed the *Primary Producer* and later *Organised Agriculture* – made the official organ of the South African Agricultural Union, and continued as editor until 1961. Sidney Chater became prominent in the South African co-operative movement, and at a co-operative congress held in Cape Town in 1974 was thanked for his important services to the movement by the president of the South African Agricultural Union – of which Chater was chairman until 1971 and a director until 1974.

The second son, Eric (who also served in the Forces, from 1914 to 1919), was one of the LCC's eight assessment officers until this post was abolished by the passing of the National Health Service Act. He was then employed in the NHS at Lewisham Hospital. He retired in 1957 but still (1976) works, for a firm of chartered accountants. The third son, Alfred, worked for the London Co-operative Society until his early death in 1934; and the fourth, Cyril Norman, retired after thirty years of foreign service for one of the Shell companies and now (1976) works for a solicitor at Sidmouth. The youngest son, Percy, was a district auditor with the civil service. Kate and Eva Chater, who both married, worked as a secretary and in banking respectively.

Writings: 'The problem of Labour Unity', *Lab.Mon. 24* (Apr 1924) 108-9; autobiography (untitled) [typescript] [1951?]: E. Chater, Ashtead, and copies in Ilford Central Library and the Brynmor Jones Library, Univ. of Hull.

Sources: (1) MSS: Labour Party archives. (2) Other: *Times,* 16 Nov 1923; *Labour Who's Who* (1927); *West London Observer,* 3 May 1929; *Financial Times,* 5 June 1929; *Daily Herald,* 15 June 1929; *Hansard* (1929-31) and (1935-50), *Dod* (1931), (1936), (1949); C. Bunker, *Who's Who in Parliament* (1946); *Daily Worker,* 14 Apr 1948; *WWW* (1950-61); biographical information: T.A.K. Elliott, CMG; personal information: E. Chater, Ashtead, son. Obit. *Recorder* [Ilford], 28 May 1959; *Times,* 30 May 1959.

BARBARA NIELD

See also: †Albert Victor ALEXANDER, for Co-operative Party; †William Henry BROWN, for Retail Co-operation, 1900-45.

CLARK, Gavin Brown (1846-1930)

RADICAL MP, LAND REFORMER AND SCOTTISH NATIONALIST

Gavin Clark was born in 1846 at Kilmarnock, Ayrshire, the third son of William Clark, an insurance agent, and his wife Jessie, daughter of John Brown of Fenwick, Ayrshire. Soon after Gavin's birth the family moved to Glasgow, where he spent his early years. When he was about thirteen he ran away to sea and served as an ordinary seaman for some four years. He then spent two years in India and other colonial countries; how he supported himself is not known.

After he returned to Scotland he studied medicine for three years (1869-72) at Glasgow University. He then moved on to Edinburgh University, where he matriculated as a fourth-year medical student in 1872. He qualified as LRCS, FRCS and MD, all of Edinburgh; and he held various appointments in Edinburgh hospitals. During his student years Clark became interested in the temperance movement. He joined the Independent Order of Good Templars, at the same time edited their journal, and in 1874 was elected chief officer for the South London and Surrey area of the Order. It was this organisation which first brought him into contact with Keir Hardie, who joined it in 1873.

When, presently, Clark moved to London he was apparently still studying medicine at some, presumably advanced, level; and he had a medical practice in London for some years. But he was becoming more interested in Radical politics than in medicine. In 1872 he had been a member of the British section of the First International, and collaborated with John Hales and S. Tyler in drafting the programme for a congress held in Nottingham. In 1876 Clark supported Gladstone's campaign denouncing the Turkish massacres of Bulgarians, and was a leading organiser of the demonstration on 9 October in Hyde Park. In the same year he was one of three representatives from London at a conference held in Birmingham with the object of uniting the various Liberal Associations in the country. From this conference there emerged the National Federation of Liberal Associations. Two Bulgarians brought by Clark gave details to the conference of the atrocities and the tyranny of Turkish rule. Agitation on behalf of the subject peoples of the East carried on by the Liberal Associations helped to prevent the Disraeli administration from fighting on behalf of Turkey and, in the phrase of the former Chartist Henry Vincent, 'put the hook through the Tory nose on the Eastern question' [DLB, 1 (1972) 332]. Also in 1876, Dr Clark gave up his medical practice. He spent the next two years in travelling about the world, and after his second marriage in 1879, he and his wife had a prolonged honeymoon abroad. He returned to London shortly before the general election of 1880, at a time when there was widespread ferment and agitation over the land question, with strong pressure for reform of the land laws. Henry George (whose *Progress and Poverty* was published in America in 1880, in England in January 1881 and his *Irish Land Question* in March and April 1881) visited the British Isles several times in the 1880s, publicising the conditions of the peasants in Ireland and the crofters in Scotland, and urging reform.

In 1881 Clark attended the preliminary meetings of the Democratic Federation, but he resigned membership when the Federation adopted firmly Socialist principles in its manifesto of 1883. In the later 1880s he joined the Fabian Society. But his chief interest from 1880 onwards was the land question. In the autumn of 1880 he addressed Liberal clubs on the necessity for fundamental reform of the landholding system, and in 1881, at the invitation of the Irish Land League, he visited Ireland and was able to compare peasant conditions there with those of the crofting communities in the Highlands of Scotland. In 1882, he took the chair at a meeting in London called to support the crofters in Skye who were claiming the restitution of their ancient rights to the land. The West Highlands were at this time in a state of unrest, with a campaign going on for withholding rents, and some cases of seizing grazing land.

By 1882 many Liberals, particularly in the Highlands, were urgent for some reforming action to relieve the difficulties of the crofters – difficulties which had been exacerbated by a failure of the corn and the potato crop in that year; in September the TUC passed a resolution in favour of land nationalisation; and with pressure from one source and another, by February 1883 the

Government was induced to set up, though with reluctance, a Royal Commission of Inquiry (an action it had refused to take in 1882). The recommendations of the Commission were rejected by both Government and Opposition; but enough alarm remained to produce the Crofters' (Holding) Act of 1886.

But before this time Clark was in Parliament. His arrival there was partly due to the foundation in 1882 of the London Highland Law Reform Association, whose establishment was in turn due to a suggestion of Clark's; and Clark was elected chairman of its executive committee. (In 1885 the London Association amalgamated with its Edinburgh counterpart to form the Highland Land League.) These associations planned to return 'crofters' candidates' to Parliament. In 1883, as chairman of the Highland Law Reform Association, Clark made a tour of the Highlands; and he was adopted as (the first) 'crofters' candidate' for Caithness by the Caithness Working Farmers' and Crofters' Committee. He won the seat from the Liberal, Major Clarence Sinclair, in 1885 and held it until 1900.

He played an active parliamentary part in the passing of the Crofters' Act of 1886. This gave the Crofters' Commission power to fix rents and to cancel arrears of rent. Clark was said at this time to be 'the most aggresive champion in Parliament of Scottish land reform'. In the election of 1892, like the other crofters' candidates, Clark stood as a Home Rule Liberal and won by a large majority. He was at the time vice-president of the Scottish Home Rule Association and had already in 1889 introduced in Parliament a motion for Scottish Home Rule. He introduced it again in 1892. Clark was also vice-president of the Scottish Labour Party, although he was always more Lib. than Lab. Along with Keir Hardie, he was one of its founders in 1888. Cunninghame Graham was elected president, the other vice-president was John Ferguson and Hardie was secretary [Lowe (1919) 4]. Later Clark was to provide financial support for Tom Johnston's *Forward*, first established in 1906.

Apart from the question of land reform in Britain, Clark's interests were chiefly colonial. He was a constant supporter of the Boers from their rebellion of 1880-1 onwards, and was elected secretary of the Transvaal Independence Committee. When he was returned to Parliament in 1885 he was acting as Agent General of the South African Republic (as the Transvaal was renamed in 1884), and he held this post for ten years. (In 1887 an attempt was made to deprive him of his parliamentary seat on the grounds that he was holding that office; but it was an unpaid post, so the attempt failed.) In 1884 a deputation from the South African Republic's Volksraad was received by the Prime Minister, Gladstone, and the Minister for the Colonies, Lord Derby. In the Address approved by the Volksraad on 11 August, thanking the English for the reception of their delegates, Dr Clark figured much more prominently than the Ministers. The printed Address devotes nine of its twenty lines to a eulogy of 'that unwearied champion of truth and justice – that second knight "without fear or blemish" – Dr Clark', assuring him that 'his name is ingraved in shining letters on the grateful and tremulous hearts of the people of the South African Republic'. He continued unwearying support for the Boer cause during the closing years of the century, including the publication in Belgium of certain documents relating to the Jameson Raid. It is not surprising that with all this activity on behalf of the Boers, he lost his seat in the general election of 1900. He stood as an Independent Liberal.

His Radical activities after his enforced retirement from the House of Commons seem to have declined, or at least they have not been documented. In 1909 there was a revival of the Highland Land League. At the inaugural meeting Clark argued that only the nationalisation of the land would produce the necessary fundamental changes in the landholding – particularly the crofting – system. He was elected president of the resuscitated League, but it lasted for no more than a year or two.

During the First World War Clark was an active member of the Wounded Allies Relief Committee, which set up hospitals in France and in Serbia. For his services during the war he was made Knight Commander of the Serbian Order of St Sava, and Knight (Cross) of the Belgian Order of the Crown.

Clark was a competent and prolific writer both on land reform questions and in support of

Boer independence. His main period of activity within the British labour movement was in the 1880s when he became widely known; but it is likely that in the long run his Scottish nationalism was the more influential of his activities. He died at Hampstead on 5 July 1930, leaving an estate of £13,814. Clark was married twice: first, in London in 1872, to Cecilia Lillias, daughter of James Scotland; secondly, in Glasgow in 1879, to Ann, daughter of John Brown, a minister in that city. He had two sons, the younger of whom, Captain W.B. Clark, was killed in the First World War, and one daughter, Mrs W.A. Brand.

Writings: *British Policy towards the Boers: an historical sketch* (1881) 56 pp.; *Our Future Policy in the Transvaal: a defence of the Boers* (1881) 32 pp.; *A Plea for Nationalisation of the Land* [a lecture] [1882] 40 pp.; *The Transvaal and Bechuanaland* [1883]; 'Our Boer Policy', *Fortn. Rev. 40* (n.s. *34*) (Aug 1883) 278-89; *The Highland Land Question: an abstract of the report of the Royal Commission to enquire into the condition of the crofters and cottars in the Highlands and Islands of Scotland* [1885] 40 pp.; *The Transvaal Crisis* [speech] [1899] 7 pp.; Correspondence between Clark, President Kruger, General Joubert and Joseph Chamberlain: PP. 1900 LVI Cd 369; edited *The Official Correspondence between the Governments of Great Britain, the South African Republic and the Orange Free State which preceded the War in South Africa* (1900); *Our Boer Policy: an historical sketch* (1900) 32 pp.; 'The Land Problem in the Highlands', *19th C. 75* (July 1914) 131-7; 'The International: recollections', *Soc. Rev.*, no. 70 (July-Sep 1914) 249-55.

Sources: *International Herald*, 27 July 1872 [account of Nottingham Congress of British Federation of the First International]; *Medical Directory* (1877) and (1883); A.R. Wallace, 'How to nationalize the Land', *Cont. Rev. 38* (Nov 1880) 716-36; 'The Land Reform Union', Supplement to the *Christian Socialist* (July 1883) 4pp.; R.C. on the Condition of Crofters and Cottars in the Highlands of Scotland 1884 XXXII-XXXVI; 'Acknowledgment of Thanks to England', in Transvaal Correspondence: P.P. 1884-5 LVII [c.4252]; 'G.B. Clark, M.D. F.R.C.S.E. Crofter Candidate for Caithness', *Crofter*, 1 Sep 1885, 83-4; *Caithness Courier*, 23, 30 Oct, 6 Nov and 4 Dec 1885; *Times*, 26 Nov 1885 and 30 June 1886; *Dod* (1886) and (1899); *Hansard*, 3rd ser. *302-56* (1886-91); 4th ser. *1-88* (1892-1900); N.M. Marris, *The Right Honourable Joseph Chamberlain* (1900); 'Will History repeat itself?', *Labour Leader*, 7 May 1909; H.M. Hyndman, *Record of an Adventurous Life* (1911); D. Lowe, *Souvenirs of Scottish Labour* (Glasgow, 1919); M. Beer, *A History of British Socialism* (1919); *WWW* (1929-40); H.W. Lee and E. Archbold, *Social-Democracy in Britain* (1935); J. van der Poel, *The Jameson Raid* (OUP, 1951); J.S. Galbraith, 'The Pamphlet Campaign on the Boer War', *J. of Modern History 24*, no.2 (June 1952) 111-26; T. Johnston, *Memories* (1952); D.W. Crowley, 'The ''Crofters' Party''', 1885-1892', *Scottish Hist. Rev. 35* (1956) 110-26; E.P. Lawrence, *Henry George in the British Isles* (Michigan State Univ. Press, 1957); M.S. Wilkins, 'The Non-Socialist Origins of England's Most Important Socialist Organisation', *Int. Rev. Social Hist. 4* (1959) 199-207; A.J. Peacock, 'Land Reform 1880-1919: a study of the activities of the English Land Restoration League and the Land Nationalisation Society' (Southampton MA, 1961); C. Tsuzuki, *H.M. Hyndman and British Socialism* (1961); H.A. Clegg et al., *A History of British Trade Unions since 1889 1:1889-1910* (Oxford, 1964); J.G. Kellas, 'The Liberal Party in Scotland', *Scottish Hist. Rev. 44* (1965) 1-16; H.J. Hanham, *Scottish Nationalism* (1969); idem, 'The Problem of Highland Discontent, 1880-1885', *Trans Roy. Hist. Soc.* 5th ser. *19* (1969) 21-65; R. Price, *An Imperial War and the British Working Class: working-class attitudes and reactions to the Boer War 1899-1902* (1972); S. Koss, *The Pro-Boers* (1973); K.O. Morgan, *Keir Hardie: radical and socialist* (1975); biographical information: Professor H.J. Hanham, Massachusetts Institute of Technology; Professor T.C. Smout, Edinburgh Univ.; Royal College of Surgeons and Royal College of Physicians, Edinburgh; Univ. of Glasgow Library. OBIT. *Lancet*, 19 July 1930.

MARGARET 'ESPINASSE

See also: Roderick MACDONALD

CLARK, James (1853-1924)
MINERS' LEADER

James Clark was born in Castle Eden, Co. Durham, in 1853. His parents moved to Felton Fell when he was a child, and James began work in the local colliery. The family moved again, to Burnhope, where James Clark became a hewer and then a deputy. Later he was a deputy at Westwood. He joined the Durham County Deputies' Mutual Aid Association, and when in 1906 the Association decided to appoint a secretary, Clark was chosen. The post was at first part-time, later full-time. The Association's headquarters were at Ebchester until 1910, when they were transferred to Durham.

The deputy was directly responsible for the safety of men in the pit. The Durham Deputies' Association had been established in 1875, at a time when a number of separate organisations were founded representing special interests including colliery enginemen, cokemen and colliery mechanics. Most of these sectional groupings, including the Deputies' Association, came together with the major union, the Durham Miners' Association, to form the Durham County Federation in 1878 [Arnot (1949) 65-6]. But there was always friction, sometimes open, between the DMA and the Deputies' Association. The latter had the support of the coalowners in 1875 at its foundation, and there was always the fear among working miners that the deputies' membership of a separate organisation might perhaps encourage a leaning towards the employers' side. In 1890, after a bitter strike at Silksworth Colliery, the principle was agreed that deputies who wished to transfer membership from the DMA to the Durham Deputies' Association should be allowed to do so after the issue of a 'clearance card'. It was not a popular agreement with the DMA, and the problems involved between the two organisations remained throughout Clark's career as an official, and long after his death. By no means all Durham deputies belonged to his Association; in 1919 some 2188 deputies were members of the DMA, and 1731 of the Deputies' Association (with only six belonging to neither body). In 1919, the DMA decided to cancel the 'clearance card' agreement, and the conflict between the two organisations remained sharp throughout the inter-war period [Garside (1971) 90-2].

James Clark was a moderate, practical man with an immense knowledge of the Durham coalfield. For several years before his death he had suffered ill-health, but he continued in office until a fortnight before his death. About twelve months before he died he was honoured with a presentation in Durham Town Hall. He died on 12 December 1924 following an operation at the County Hospital, Durham. The funeral service was held in the Bethel Church – Clark was a devout Wesleyan Methodist – and he was buried in St Margaret's Cemetery. He had married in 1874, and was survived by his wife and five children, two of whom were in America. He left effects valued at £350.

Sources: R. Page Arnot, *The Miners* (1949); R.F. Wearmouth, *The Social and Political Influence of Methodism in the Twentieth Century* (1957); W.R. Garside, *The Durham Miners 1919-1960* (1971); biographical information: Dr A. Mason, Warwick Univ. OBIT. *Durham County Advertiser*, 19 Dec 1924; NMA, *Minutes* (1925).

JOHN SAVILLE

See also: †Samuel COULTHARD.

COOMBES, Bert Lewis (Louis) (1893-1974)
MINER AND AUTHOR

Born in Wolverhampton on 9 January 1893, Bertie Louis Coombs Griffiths was the son of James Coombs Griffiths, then a grocer, and his wife Harriett (née Thompson). When and why he adopted the name of Coombes is not known (spelt Cumbes at the time of his marriage). At some point in his youth the family moved to Herefordshire where his father rented a smallholding. When Coombes was eighteen years old, with a view to earning a better living, he left his father's employ to find work in the South Wales coalfield and obtained employment at the Resolven pit as a miner's helper. This was the beginning of a full working life of forty-two years spent underground. Although he moved from one pit to another within the area, he never left South Wales. On 29 September 1913 he married Mary Rogers, whose father was checkweigher at Resolven and secretary of the local lodge.

Coombes himself in later life served on several pit committees. Yet, in general, he was without strong political inclinations or trade union ambition, and if he had any religious affiliations, they remain unknown. He does record that he volunteered for military service in 1914, but was turned down because of bad eyesight. He tried to enlist again later in the war under the Derby Scheme but this time was refused because of his occupation.

Bert Coombes is known chiefly for four books which he wrote in the late 1930s and early 1940s. One is autobiographical, and the others draw in large part on his own experiences. They describe in a concise and unemotional way the living and working conditions – in particular the inseparability of the two – of the Welsh miners he knew. There is a basic Socialist commitment in the books, but the tone is matter-of-fact, modest and avoids political polemic. The tendency towards understatement when he is retailing, for example, accounts of accident, death or extreme courage, makes the content even more telling.

With little formal education on which to draw, Coombes spent several years in studying 'to learn the tricks' of authorship. He had much encouragement with his early writing from John Lehmann, the poet and writer, who at the time was editor of *New Writing* and who described Coombes in the first volume of his autobiography *The Whispering Gallery* as 'This small, hard-bitten miner, with his small, square head, his pale, rough-hewn, serious face', and then went on to give his opinion of Coombes's writings:

> What struck me at once about *The Flame,* the first sketch he sent me late in 1936, was the simplicity and unforced, quiet movement of the writing with its occasional small touches that revealed the natural way of talking of the West of England. . . . Coombes felt very deeply about the wrongs of the miners during the years of unemployment, their neglect by the country as a whole, and the need to modernize the mines. . . . He was active in the political struggle to improve the miners' lot: but what was admirable in his writing was the absence of propaganda and deliberate over-painting of suffering and injustice. I was one of many who had their imagination awoken and their heart stirred by the vivid human appeal of these stories, their sensitive, unhysterical truth with a just perceptible undercurrent of stolid bitterness; . . . so I believe that B.L. Coombes' writing about the lives of the miners may have had much to do with the great stirring of national conscience which eventually made the nationalization of the mines a priority no party could withstand [Lehmann (1955) 259-61]

In 1938 Coombes was awarded a silver medal for an original story at a Borough of Leyton Eisteddfod; and in 1939 his first book, *These Poor Hands,* dedicated to John Lehmann and published by the Left Book Club, sold 60,000 copies in three months. It received very favourable reviews by J.B. Priestley and Cyril Connolly among others. It and the books which followed were translated into many European languages, including Russian. From his initial successes with short stories he went on to submit pieces to *Argosy, British Ally, Fortnightly,* the *Geographical Magazine, New Writing, Reader's Digest,* and *Picture Post.* For at least fifteen years he wrote a regular weekly article in the *Neath Guardian.* His subjects included industrial problems and current local and national affairs in addition to mining matters. He wrote the scripts of several documentary films and assisted Jack Lindsay with his play *Face of Coal* which was produced at the Scala Theatre in 1946. By May of that year, when Coombes was elected to membership of the Society of Authors, he had already written over four hundred articles.

He also made twenty-two broadcasts in features and talks. One of the earliest, entitled 'In Britain now; coal miner at home' was transmitted on 25 May 1942. He wrote the Country Magazine programme, on the Vale of Neath, broadcast in September 1950 and one of his last broadcasts was a recorded interview in 'A Tribute to a Miner Novelist' in October 1963.

He was three times winner of the Sir Arthur Markham Memorial Prize at Sheffield University and shared it on two other occasions. In 1955 he was joint winner, with Marjorie Proops, of a literary competition organised by the *Daily Mirror,* in which many thousands of entrants had submitted essays on international friendship. At a conference in Hamburg which followed in May of that year, winners of similar competitions in the other eight participating European countries met together. A Hamburg newspaper offered a £10 prize for the best account of the week's activities and Coombes was the winner.

With the proceeds of his books, which he later said 'never made me a rich man but . . . smoothed out some of the rough times we lived through', Coombes and his wife bought Nantyfedwen, a farm of 160 acres, in Onllwyn in the Vale of Neath, which had formerly been a public house and a chapel. They ran the farm together, Mary Coombes having a milk delivery round and Bert continuing to work as a collier. In 1914 he had been one of the first men in the South Wales field to use the new mechanical coal-cutters and in his later working life he was a specialist in this means of getting coal. In addition to his writing, farming and local union activities, Coombes also served on the management committee of the Miners' Rest Home in Porthcawl. He was a founder member of the St John's Ambulance Brigade in Resolven, and played an important part in its rescue work underground. Later he became its secretary and in 1972 was awarded the Vellum Vote of Thanks of the Priory of Wales for a remarkably long period of service. In the mid 1920s he had been attached to the Military Hospital Reserve and had undertaken a period of training at Aldershot. His recreations were cricket (he had helped to start a cricket club in Resolven during the General Strike) and music; he was secretary and playing member of the Resolven orchestra. He retired from work early after a roof fall had almost broken his back. He had suffered two previous accidents of a similar kind in 1930 and 1934.

Bert Coombes died on 4 June 1974 at the Adelina Patti Hospital, Craig-y-Nos, where he had been a patient since January. Before that, since the death of his wife in July 1970, he had lived alone in the farmhouse. Most of the farm land had been sold. In 1972 he was awarded a pension by the Royal Literary Fund, in recognition of his work. He was buried at St Mary's Church, Resolven, where he had been married and where his wife was also buried. His coffin was draped with the St John's flag and four officers from the Neath County District formed a guard of honour. He left an estate valued at £7348. There were two children of the marriage, Rosemary and Peter. Rosemary moved away from South Wales but one of her four children, Vivien Davies, who lived with his grandfather for many years, inherited the farm.

Writings: 'Better off', *Left Rev. 3,* no. 14 (Mar 1938) 869-72; *I am a Miner* (Fact no. 23: 1939); *These Poor Hands: the autobiography of a miner working in South Wales* (1939); 'This is the Problem', *Picture Post 10,* 4 Jan 1941; (with Lord Meston), *The Life we want* (1944) 24 pp.; *Those Clouded Hills* (1944); 'Dusty Retort', *New Statesman and Nation,* 10 June and 8 July 1944; *Miners Day* (NY, 1945); 'The Mines Today', *Fortn. 180* n.s. *174* (Oct 1953) 243-7. In addition to these books and articles, Coombes had stories published in *Argosy, British Ally, New Writing* and *Penguin New Writing* and articles in Australian, British, New Zealand, Russian and South American national papers; articles (weekly) in the *Neath Guardian,* in *Coal* for the Ministry of Information and also articles for the Ministry of Fuel and Power. He also wrote scripts for the BBC and gave a number of radio talks.

Sources: (1) MSS: Coombes papers: V.I. Davies, Onllwyn, Glamorgan. (2) Other: B.L. Coombes, *These Poor Hands* (1939); J. Lehmann, *The Whispering Gallery: autobiography*, vol. *1* (1955); The Editor, 'B.L. Coombes – this is the Story of your Success', *Neath Guardian*, 9 Mar 1956; C. John, 'He sent the Message of the Miner around the World', ibid., 27 Sep 1963; 'B.L. Coombes: coal miner' in *Useful Toil: autobiographies of working people from the 1820's to the 1920's*, ed. J. Burnett (1974) 107-15; B. Lipman, 'Bert Coombes', *Planet 23* (summer 1974) 17-20; *Western Mail*, 3 July 1974; D. Smith, 'Underground Man: the work of B.L. Coombes, "Miner Writer"', *Anglo-Welsh Rev.* (winter 1974) 10-25; biographical information: Miss J. Kavanagh, BBC Written Archives Centre, Reading; G.I. Lewis, Univ. College of Swansea; Midland Bank Trust Co. Ltd, Swansea; Mrs D. Shine, Society of Authors, London; N. Thomas, *Planet*, Tregaron; W. Thomas, *Neath Guardian* Newspapers, Neath; Miss H. Tuschling, Victor Gollancz Ltd, London; personal information: V. Bonham-Carter, Royal Literary Fund, London; V.I. Davies, Onllwyn, Glamorgan, grandson; C. John, *Steel News*, Port Talbot; Councillor F.R. (Bob) Langdon, O.B.St.J., JP, Resolven; Jack Lindsay, Castle Hedingham. Obit. *Times*, 12 June 1974; *Neath Guardian*, 14 June 1974; B. Langdon, 'B.L. Coombes: a fitting final chapter' [letter], *Neath Guardian*, 28 June 1974.

BARBARA NIELD

CURRAN, Peter (Pete) Francis (1860-1910)
TRADE UNIONIST AND LABOUR MP

'Pete' Curran was born in Glasgow in March 1860, of Irish Roman Catholic parents. At the age of ten he began work as a junior hammer-driver in the blacksmith's shop of an iron and steel works. He subsequently worked as both driver and striker in many large engine works in and around the city. A keen student of contemporary economic and social problems, he soon developed a special interest in the cause of Irish land reform, and by the early 1880s he was a conspicuous figure at meetings of the Irish Land League, later the Irish National League and then the United Irish League.

The branch of the Land League to which he belonged was sharply divided between Charles Parnell and Michael Davitt on the issue of land nationalisation, a policy denounced by the Parnell group as visionary and impracticable. Curran read widely on this question, being particularly interested in parallel problems of land monopoly in Scotland. After Henry George's lecture tour of Scotland in 1884, which Curran found most inspiring, he joined the Scottish Land League. In spite of the disapproval of some older members of the Irish League, he maintained his association with it until the end of that year, when he joined the SDF.

An extremely able, if somewhat unpredictable and fiery propagandist, Curran addressed many street corner and open-air meetings, particularly on Glasgow Green. H. M. Hyndman recalled that 'his street-corner speeches were perfect in their way' [*Further Reminiscences* (1912) 123]. Curran was not, however, without misgivings about the Social Democratic Federation. He later argued that if it 'had been conducted from the outset more on British and less on Continental lines, there would have been no other Socialist Party in this country' [*Labour Leader*, 1 Oct 1909].

In 1888 Curran decided to leave Glasgow, since his growing reputation as a Socialist agitator was causing problems for him in his workshop. He went to London, where he obtained work at the Royal Arsenal, Woolwich, again as a blacksmith's striker. There he helped to found the Gasworkers' and General Labourers' Union, and in September 1889, a newly appointed organiser, he moved to live in the west of England as district secretary.

In October 1890, in the course of a strike at the Plymouth coal harbour, Curran, George Shepheard of the Dockers' Union, and John Matthews, secretary of the Bristol, West of England and South Wales Trade Operatives, attempted to persuade the coal merchant G.F. Treleaven to employ only union labour, on the threat of a possible extension of the strike. Such action was judged to be intimidation (under the 1875 Conspiracy and Protection of Property Act) by the local magistrates, and their sentence of a £20 fine or six months' hard labour was upheld at Quarter Sessions. After a nation-wide campaign, conducted mainly by the Plymouth Trades Council, an appeal was allowed and was heard in July 1891 before Lord Chief Justice Coleridge. When Sir Henry James, defending Curran, succeeded in getting the lower court's decision reversed and the Employers' Association liable for costs, the result was hailed as a great trade union victory. *Curran* v. *Treleaven* [1891 2QB 545] became established as a leading case in Labour Law, since the Court of Appeal held to previous judgements whereby 'intimidation' must involve violence to the person or damage to property. Shortly afterwards Curran was elected national and general organiser of the Gasworkers' Union.

Throughout the 1890s Curran was an active delegate to Trade Union congresses, where he was firmly behind the cause of 'New Unionism'. In the later years of the decade, when the younger Socialist delegates of the TUC parliamentary committee established something of a left wing 'opposition', the most consistent spokesman of any stature was Curran. In January 1899 he was elected president of the General Federation of Trade Unions, established after a special TUC conference. A constitution for such a Federation had been drawn up several years before by the parliamentary committee, but it had remained a paper project. In 1897 a special committee had been set up to devise a full scheme, the principal aim of which was the provision of a permanent system of strike insurance; and Curran co-operated closely with this committee. He remained president of the GFTU until 1910.

He became a member of the Fabian Society in the early 1890s, and in 1893 attended the Inaugural Conference of the Independent Labour Party at Bradford and became one of four Fabians to be elected to its first National Administrative Council, of which he remained a member until 1898. When in February 1900 the Fabian Society held a postal referendum on whether it should denounce imperialism in general and the Boer War in particular, the result was in favour of making no pronouncement. Curran was among the fifteen members who left the society over this issue; the others included J.R. MacDonald, J.F. Green and G.N. Barnes. During these years, and later as an MP, Curran was a firm believer in the necessity of international arbitration; at the International Socialist Congress in Paris in 1900 he was very outspoken and impassioned against the war. Hyndman recalls that his speech was one of the features of the Congress and he delivered it with such terrific energy and fire that he roused the enthusiasm of every delegate present, though not one out of ten understood the meaning of a single word he was saying, and sat down amid a thunderous burst of applause' [*Further Reminiscences* (1912) 123].

With MacDonald and Keir Hardie, Curran was prominent in the setting up of the Labour Representation Committee. At the LRC Conference of 1903 he successfully moved the resolution to establish a distinct and separate Parliamentary Labour Party. As one of the Trade Unionist members of the LRC Executive Curran attended Labour conferences in France, Germany, Belgium, Holland and the U.S.A.

He first stood for Parliament in 1895, as ILP candidate for Barrow-in-Furness, but polled a mere 414 votes in a three-cornered fight against a Unionist and a Liberal. Two years later, in October 1897, as the nominee of the Trades and Labour Council, he contested the by-election at Barnsley. This was a working-class constituency with a high proportion of miners in its electorate, and it had been a safe Liberal seat for many years. Barnsley was also the headquarters of the Yorkshire Miners' Association, dominated at this time by powerful Lib-Lab leaders such as Ben Pickard, Ned Cowey and William Parrott. This by-election was the first time that the ILP had contested a mining constituency, and it aroused considerable interest in political circles. The Liberal candidate was Joseph Walton, a Cleveland coalowner, who supported the eight-hour day and who was vigorously backed by the Yorkshire miners' leaders. Curran's election address read as follows:

TO THE MEN OF THE BARNSLEY DIVISION

Electors!

On the joint invitation of the Barnsley and District Trades and Labour Council and the Independent Labour Party, I have agreed to become the Candidate for the vacancy caused by the raising of your former member to the Peerage.

As a Workman, I am a Democrat in politics, and desire to see all political power in the hands of the people. Adult Suffrage, Payment of all Members of Public Bodies, including Juries, so as to give the workers a free opportunity of being represented thereon, and the Abolition of the House of Lords as being unnecessary and dangerous, are urgent questions for immediate settlement. In this connection I may add that, being the son of Irish Parents, I have all my life taken an active part in the Irish Home Rule movements. Growing years only confirm my faith in the necessity for this measure of reform. I also desire earnestly the release of the Irish political prisoners.

Generally, I am opposed to any kind of class privilege in the Government of the Nation, and in favour of every proposal for democratising the system of Government.

As a Trade-unionist of many years' standing, I have at the Trade-union Congress and elsewhere advocated and voted for the advanced proposals of that body, including a Miners' Eight Hours Bill with no exemptions, a Legal Eight Hours Day for all Trades – save where by reason of technical difficulties, a hard-and-fast rule could not be enforced, as in some departments of the glass trade – the Nationalisation of Land, Mines, Minerals, Railways and the like, and the Municipalisation of Gas, Water, Trams, and other Public Services as stages leading to the development of Socialism.

The evils inseparable from the Private Ownership of Land and Minerals cannot be overcome by small and ineffective Reforms. They are too deep for that.

I would give the People full and direct control over the Liquor Traffic and empower School Boards to supply meals to hungry children. I would seek to place all Taxation on unearned incomes, so as to relieve Labour and Trade of this onerous burden.

I feel strongly that the right to work should be secured to every able-bodied citizen.

If returned as your Representative, I will carry my Trade-Unionist principles into the politics of the House of Commons, and consider all Questions that come before me there from the Workman's point of view. The great struggle in the Engineering Trade, the gloomy outlook in the Textile Industry, the well-grounded discontent in the Mining Trade, with its Low Wages and Tyrannical Rules and Bye-Laws, all tell of the growing power of Landlordism and Capitalism, and of the great need there is for the Workers of the country having men in Parliament who will attend to their interests without regard to convenience of any political Party.

The extension of our Foreign Markets, with its consequent War and Slaughter of Savage Tribes, is the only proposal which politicians have to offer for the improvement of your position. As a Socialist, I am in favour of the development of our Home Markets, by securing to the worker the whole of the Product of his Labour.

Inviting your hearty co-operation in winning a victory for Labour,

I am, yours with respect,

PETE CURRAN

Barnsley, 24th Sept, 1897.

[*Labour Leader*, 2 Oct 1897]

It was an extremely bitter contest. One afternoon in that October the miners of Wombwell stoned the Socialist candidate. Curran had few well-known local miners to speak out in his support, and there was great pressure from the YMA officials against those who took an independent line. William Lunn, president of the Rothwell branch of the YMA, Isaac Burns, and James Walsh, checkweighman to the South Kirkby Collieries, were among the most prominent of Curran's local supporters. From outside the constituency there came Robert Smillie, Tom

Mann and the best woman speaker of the ILP, Enid Stacy. On the other side were Havelock Wilson MP and Edward Harford, the general secretary of the railwaymen's union (ASRS).

Walton came at the top of the poll of 11,000, with Curran receiving just over 1000 votes. It was a serious defeat for the ILP. 'Barnsley altogether', wrote Keir Hardie to a member of the *Labour Leader* staff, 'is the worst thing we have done.' For Curran it was 'the most emphatic indication we have yet had of the parting of the ways between Liberal-Labourism and Socialism.'

He did not stand again for Parliament until 1906, when he unsuccessfully contested Jarrow. The bulk of his support probably came from the mining element in the constituency [Poirier (1958) 259]. He had spent the previous four years, as prospective candidate, working in the constituency, helped considerably by the strong Chester-le-Street branch of the ILP. During this time he had also been involved in the setting up of a co-ordinating committee, composed of representatives from the GFTU and the Labour Party, which aimed at a new trade union Act to invalidate the Taff Vale decision. In 1905 he was active on the committee of the – entirely Socialist – National Right to Work Council, of which G.N. Barnes was chairman.

In the Jarrow by-election of July 1907 that followed the death of the sitting member, Sir C.M. Palmer, Curran secured the seat by a decisive margin in a four-cornered fight. This was the first time that the Irish Nationalists had contested the seat; previously their vote had gone to the Liberals.

His parliamentary career was to be short-lived. After his maiden speech, which was made on 15 July 1907 during a debate on colonial preference, and in which he pressed for public ownership of industries and railways, he was congratulated by Col. Seely, a Conservative, 'upon having so successfully "caught the tone of the House"' [Hyndman (1912) 123]. He subsequently helped to prepare Labour's draft recommendations for an Unemployed Bill, and he was also among the small group of Labour activists pressing for urgent government action on unemployment and the eight hour day. He continued to be closely associated with the Peace movement, a policy which was rather unpopular in Jarrow because of the implied threat to local naval orders. In addition to his other activities he was a JP for Essex, the first Labour member on the county's magisterial bench.

In the election of January 1910 Curran was narrowly defeated by Godfrey Palmer, the son of the late Baronet. He had been recurrently ill for the previous few months, and soon after the election underwent a serious operation at the London Hospital. After a sudden relapse he died at his home in Pretoria Avenue, Walthamstow, on 14 February. The funeral, arranged by Will Thorne, took place at Leytonstone Roman Catholic Cemetery, and was attended by many hundreds of representatives from the major labour and trade union organisations. One unusual tribute was from the Variety Artistes Federation, in appreciation of Curran's work on behalf of the music hall profession. The obituary notices all mentioned Curran's 'uniform kindness', his many services to trade unionism, his political honesty, and the vigour with which he conducted his advocacy of his Socialist principles. 'For him also', wrote one commentator, 'The question of the right treatment of the black races was one of considerable interest; and it was one of his sources of gratification that he wore on his finger a ring which was presented to him by the negroes of one of the States of America, for services which he had rendered their cause.' The same obituary number of the *Jarrow Guardian* (18 Feb 1910) summed up editorially:

Whether people agreed or disagreed with the political policy of the deceased, everybody admired his manly, straightforward way of conducting a contest. He would not stoop to take the least advantage of an opponent; he hit hard, but, in the language of the ring, always above the belt. Fearless in his advocacy of the principles in which he believed, he never shirked awkward questioning, but boldly met each and every adversary, and when 'Pete' had his back to the wall, his opponents were always made aware of it. Mr Curran was courteous to everybody, of lively disposition, and in social circles a very companionable [*sic*] man. Few men have worked harder for the Labour movement than did Mr Curran, and to the last he showed that sincerity of purpose which was the distinguishing characteristic of a short but very busy life.

Pete Curran was survived by his wife, two daughters and two sons. He left an estate of £119.

Writings: (with others), *The Law of Intimidation: what does it mean?* (Plymouth, 1890) 36 pp.; 'Socialism in English Trade Unions', in *Int. Soc. Rev. 2* (Sep 1901) 185-7; *Human Documents: character sketches* [1908/9?] [repr. from *Reynolds' Newspaper*] 20 pp.; 'From the Steam Hammer to Parliament', *Labour Leader*, 1 Oct 1909; (with D. Irving), *H.M. Hyndman and 'Real Reform'* [n.d.] 16 pp.

Sources: *Workman's Times*, 3 Feb 1894; *Labour Leader*, 15 June 1895, 2 Oct 1897, 12 July 1907, 1 Oct 1909; *Labour Annual* (1896); *Reformers' Year Book* (1905); *Hansard*, 15 July 1907, 426-30; *Socialist Annual* (1911); H.M. Hyndman, *Further Reminiscences* (1912); W. Thorne, *My Life's Battles* (1925); J. Sexton, *Sir James Sexton, Agitator: the life of the dockers' MP. An Autobiography* (1936); J.J. Lawson, *The Man in the Cap* (1941); *The British Labour Party: its history, growth, policy and leaders*, ed. H. Tracey, vol. *1* (1946); P.P. Poirier, *The Advent of the Labour Party* (1958); B.C. Roberts, *The Trades Union Congress 1868-1921* (1958); J. Saville, 'Trade Unions and Free Labour: the background to the Taff Vale decision', *Essays in Labour History* ed. A. Briggs and J. Saville (1960) 317-50; A.M. McBriar, *Fabian Socialism and English Politics 1884-1918* (Cambridge, 1962); H.A. Clegg et al., *A History of British Trade Unions since 1889 1: 1889-1910* (Oxford, 1964); H. Pelling, *The Origins of the Labour Party 1880-1900* (1954, 2nd ed. Oxford, 1965); B. Simon, *Education and the Labour Movement, 1870-1920* (1965); H. Pelling, *Social Geography of British Elections, 1885-1910* (1967); P. Thompson, *Socialists, Liberals and Labour: the struggle for London 1885-1914* (1967); K.D. Brown, *Labour and Unemployment, 1900-14* (1971); L. Thompson, *The Enthusiasts: a biography of John and Katharine Glasier* (1971); S. Pierson, *Marxism and the Origins of British Socialism* (Cornell, 1973). OBIT. *Times*, 16 Feb 1910; *Cotton Factory Times, Jarrow Guardian* and *Labour Leader*, 18 Feb 1910; *Reynolds' News*, 20 Feb 1910; *Labour Leader*, 4 Mar 1910.

BARBARA NIELD

See also: George Nicoll BARNES; †George LANSBURY, for British Labour Party, 1900-13.

DALLAS, George (1878-1961)
TRADE UNION OFFICIAL AND LABOUR MP

George Dallas was born in Glasgow on 6 August 1878, the son of a shoemaker of the same name and of Mary Hay. At an early age he moved with his family to Kilmaurs, Ayrshire, where he grew up and went to school. He left school at twelve, his first job being at a coalmine; later, he studied at the Royal Technical College, Glasgow; and, as an adult, at the London School of Economics.

Dallas's earliest political activity was when he joined the Christian Socialist League at the age of sixteen. Other early influences on his political views were Keir Hardie, Robert Blatchford and the *Clarion*, Robert Owen and William Morris. He went to London at the time of the Boer War, worked as a clerk in a coal merchant's business and soon became involved in anti-war activity. He helped to organise public meetings, which sometimes became violent, for the 'pro-Boer' cause; and he himself spoke to hostile audiences in Hyde Park.

About the turn of the century Dallas returned to Glasgow, where he first worked as an assistant in a haberdasher's shop and began his trade union activity, soon becoming secretary of the Shop Assistants' Union for the Glasgow and West of Scotland district (not a paid post). In the latter capacity he helped to start many new branches of the union. Dallas later had his own men's wear shop in Motherwell, but he became too absorbed in politics to be successful as a shopkeeper. He was active in the ILP in Motherwell, where he stood, unsuccessfully, as a Socialist candidate in the municipal elections of 1907. Under the pseudonym 'Dalziel', he wrote about Motherwell local politics in the first issue of the Glasgow weekly *Forward*, founded by Tom Johnston in 1906, and he was later a frequent contributor to this paper in his own name.

In 1908 Dallas was appointed organising secretary of the ILP in Scotland, working from Glasgow, and he remained in that post until 1912. It was a period of intensive propaganda activity during which many new ILP branches were formed in Scotland. In the course of his Socialist propaganda and organising work Dallas gave assistance on a number of occasions to groups of workers who became involved in industrial disputes at a time when the trade unions were still very weak in Scotland outside the skilled trades. He was associated in particular with strikes of girl thread workers at Neilston, Renfrewshire, in 1910, in which the National Federation of Women Workers was concerned, and of dye workers in the Vale of Leven, Dunbartonshire, in 1911, in which both the Amalgamated Society of Dyers and the National Federation of Women Workers were involved. During the latter dispute public exposure by Dallas of the low wages, long working hours and unhealthy working conditions, especially of the girl workers, in the turkey-red dyeing industry in the area led to an action for slander being started by the employers against him and against *Forward*. Subsequently, however, after the dispute had been settled, the company decided not to proceed with the action. In addition to the formation of new branches and these sporadic industrial victories, one of Dallas's achievements in the ILP post lay in encouraging others, of whom James Maxton became the best known, to take up propaganda work.

Early in 1912 Dallas moved to London to become chief organiser for the National Federation of Women Workers, of which Mary Macarthur was general secretary; but he did not stay long in that post, apparently because of disagreement with Miss Macarthur (whom he had known since his shop assistant days ten years earlier) over 'methods of working'. Early in 1913 he was appointed as the first London divisional organiser of the Workers' Union. This was at the beginning of a period of expansion for the union, and the London organising staff was soon increased. Dallas's responsibilities at that time covered not only London but also a wide area of the Home Counties on all sides of London. A number of strikes which occurred in small towns within this area gave him the opportunity to organise and expand branches of the union. He had a notable success in securing a settlement of a strike at the Crittall metal window factory at Braintree in 1913 and in converting the owner into supporting trade unionism in his works. This led to Crittall becoming a highly progressive employer for his time in the conditions which he provided for his employees.

Dallas was a trade union official during the First World War. He was an opponent of militarism, and took a critical attitude to the introduction of conscription, on which he differed from the leadership of his union. From 1916 to 1918 he edited a monthly journal, the *Trade Union Worker*, published by his division of the union. The union grew rapidly at this time, particularly among workers in government factories, where it catered for the unskilled and the semi-skilled, but also in the rural areas, organisation spreading from the small towns in which it was already established to the surrounding countryside. Nationally, the Workers' Union shared the organising of agricultural workers with the National Agricultural Labourers' Union (later the National Union of Agricultural Workers). When the first Agricultural Wages Board was set up in 1917 under the Corn Production Act Dallas was appointed to it as one of the Workers' Union members, and became secretary of the workers' side. He threw himself energetically into the task of organising farm workers, which he saw at the time as aiming 'to show the farmers and landlords that the workers of England mean to end the tyranny of the countryside'. It was as a representative of agricultural workers that Dallas became widely known from then onwards, and his association with the Wages Board brought him into contact with a wide range of agricultural interests and opinion. In 1919 he was appointed to the R.C. on Agriculture, under the chairmanship of Sir William Barclay Peat, and he was one of the minority signatories of the Commission's interim report in the same year – there was no final report.

Dallas had other interests at this time. He was active nationally in the Workers' Educational Association as a member of its central council during the First World War, when William Temple was its president; and he was associated with the WEA's work on educational reconstruction. Dallas had married in 1913 Agnes Brown, who had been one of the thread workers on strike at Neilston in 1910 and who had subsequently been first an official in Scotland of the National Federation of Women Workers and then a national organiser for the Women's Labour League. She died in 1916 at the age of twenty-eight. In 1920 he married Agnes's younger sister Mary, and they went to live at Welwyn Garden City – of which they were among the first inhabitants – early in 1922. Dallas soon became very active in the public and political life of the new town, and he was appointed a JP for Hertfordshire in the early 1920s. He stood unsuccessfully as Labour parliamentary candidate for Maldon (Essex) in 1918 and 1922, and in 1923 and 1924 he stood, again unsuccessfully, for Roxburgh and Selkirk.

He became prominent in the Labour Party nationally in the 1920s through his role in the formulation of the Party's agricultural policy. As chairman of the Party's advisory committee on agriculture and rural problems he played a leading part in preparing the report on Labour's agricultural policy, which was approved by both the TUC and the Labour Party in 1926. Ramsay MacDonald moved the adoption of the report at the Party Conference of that year, and Dallas, though not at the time a member of the NEC, replied to the debate. As MacDonald said, the report 'laid down quite definitely as a fundamental principle the Nationalisation of the Land'; but the reference in this case was specifically to agricultural land. Nationalisation was justified on the grounds that private landlords were ceasing to supply the necessary capital for agriculture and that to give state assistance for this would merely put money in the landlord's pocket. Following the adoption of the policy, Dallas was active in the late 1920s and in the 1930s in developing the Party's campaign to make it known and accepted in the country.

The Workers' Union encountered increasing difficulties, especially financial difficulties, throughout the 1920s. There was growing criticism of the leadership from within, and in 1927 Dallas, who was chief agricultural organiser of the Union, stood (though unsuccessfully) for the office of president against John Beard, who had held it since 1913. In 1929 the Union was absorbed by Bevin's now larger Transport and General Workers' Union. Dallas did not fit easily into the larger union though he remained an official of it until he retired. He was elected MP for Wellingborough, however, at the 1929 general election in a three-cornered contest, and he was also elected in October 1929 as a constituency party representative on the Labour Party NEC. Dallas was a backbench MP in the 1929-31 Parliament. Most of his parliamentary speeches were on agricultural matters, and he was particularly concerned about the worsening condition of British agriculture and the unrestricted import of wheat to which it was subject. Outside Parliament, he was a leading speaker in 1930 at large outdoor agricultural demonstrations representing landowners, farmers and farm workers, held in different parts of England to draw attention to the plight of the industry. He had already got to know something of agricultural conditions in North America from a visit there in 1923, when he had toured through rural areas; and he made a second visit in the summer of 1930 to attend an international conference of agricultural economists. Dallas's other parliamentary activities included membership of the all-party Committee on Electoral Reform set up by MacDonald in December 1929, which failed to reach agreement on the subject. In the following year he was elected to the Consultative Committee which maintained liaison between the PLP and the Cabinet. Dallas remained loyal to the Labour Party in the 1931 crisis, and in common with most of his parliamentary colleagues he was defeated at Wellingborough in a straight fight with a Conservative in the general election of that year.

Although a disastrous year in other respects, 1931 marked the beginning of a new interest for Dallas which was to absorb much of his time and energy over the next twenty years. When the River Nene Catchment Board was set up under the Labour Government's Land Drainage Act of

1930, Dallas, whose Wellingborough constituency in which he had lived since 1929 lay in the Nene valley, was appointed as the statutory 'Minister's member'. His fellow-members were representatives of local authorities and internal drainage boards, and they elected him first chairman of the Board. Dallas remained chairman throughout the life of the Catchment Board, until 1951, and was also chairman for a short time of its successor body, the Nene River Board. He became closely identified in the public mind with the river, and when he died the Northampton *Chronicle and Echo* headed his obituary notice 'Man who tamed the Nene'.

During the 1930s Dallas served on a number of government committees connected with agriculture, and was active in national agricultural affairs. The Labour Government had appointed him to a committee on tied cottages in agriculture which reported in 1932, but which was divided equally on the subject of their retention or abolition, Dallas and two of his colleagues arguing for abolition. In 1934 he was appointed to the Cattle Committee set up by the National Government to advise Ministers on arrangements for paying subsidies to cattle producers; and in 1937 to its successor body, the Livestock Commission. In 1936 he was the only member from England on a committee investigating the system of employment and remuneration of farm workers in Scotland; it recommended a system of statutory machinery for wage regulation in Scotland such as existed for England and Wales. Dallas was also prominent, as a representative of agricultural workers, in the successful campaign in the early 1930s to save the British sugar beet industry, which provided much employment in rural areas, and which was threatened with withdrawal of the Government subsidy. In 1933 he was elected chairman for the year of the National Council of Agriculture for England, of which he had been a member for many years.

At the 1935 general election Dallas failed narrowly, by 372 votes in a straight fight, to regain his parliamentary seat at Wellingborough, and soon after he gave up his candidature there. He was later adopted as candidate for Belper in Derbyshire but gave that up also before the 1945 election. According to George Brown, it was Dallas who organised his adoption as Labour candidate for Belper in 1945 (*In my Way*, 41-2). Dallas continued to be re-elected each year, until he retired in 1944, to the NEC, of which he was vice-chairman in 1936-7 and chairman in 1937-9, presiding over the 1939 Party Conference at Southport. In 1936-7 he was a member, along with Hugh Dalton and Mrs Barbara Gould (with the addition of Labour MPs in the areas concerned), of the Labour Party Commission of Enquiry into the Distressed Areas. At the 1937 Party Conference Dallas, on behalf of the NEC, moved the proposed changes in the Party constitution, which were adopted in spite of some trade union opposition, to enable an increased number of constituency party representatives on the NEC to be elected by direct and separate election instead of by vote of the whole conference. Dallas's period as chairman of the NEC (October 1937 to June 1939) was marked not only by the anxiety of the Labour movement about the worsening international situation but also by the internal controversy in the Party over the advocacy of a Popular Front by Sir Stafford Cripps and others. Dallas himself shared the view of the majority of the NEC in opposing Labour participation in a Popular Front.

Dallas became increasingly involved during the 1930s in international policy questions. He was a delegate to the Congress of the Labour and Socialist International in Vienna in the summer of 1931; and as a member of the International Sub-Committee of the NEC from 1931 onwards he represented the Labour Party on numerous occasions at conferences of continental Socialist parties and at meetings of the LSI (the International). At a critical period in the summer of 1938 he was one of a Labour Party delegation conveying greetings to the Czech Social-Democratic Party which was celebrating its sixtieth anniversary. He belonged to the pro-rearmament group of the NEC in foreign policy matters, being particularly close in his standpoint to Dalton, whom he succeeded as chairman of the International Sub-Committee in 1940 when Dalton joined the Government.

When war came in 1939 Dallas stood for a vigorous prosecution of it and like a number of other Labour leaders he held strong anti-German views of the type labelled 'Vansittartite'. His most important work during the Second World War was in connection with home timber supplies. In June 1940 he was appointed by the new Coalition Government as chairman of the Timber Control Board which was set up to co-ordinate efforts to secure a large and rapid increase in the use of home-grown timber; and although the Board was disbanded in 1942, Dallas remained involved in timber production questions throughout the war. As the end of the war approached, however, Dallas became increasingly concerned about the direction of Soviet policy and came to regard the treatment of Poland as a test case of this. After the war, he was a strong supporter of the 'Free Polish' cause, and he shared platforms with the Duchess of Atholl and Bertrand Russell to protest against Soviet encroachment. From about 1948, however, his concern shifted to the advance of Chinese Communism: his view was that there would be great dangers for international peace if the huge numbers of the Chinese people were harnessed to international Communism.

By 1945 Dallas had retired from all his trade union and political posts. He was awarded the CBE in the 1946 New Year's Honours. In the same year he was appointed to the inter-departmental committee, under the chairmanship of Lord Lindsay of Birker, on the expenses of members of local authorities; this led to the provisions for loss of earnings by local councillors which were enacted in the Local Government Act of 1948. After the war Dallas was active in Northamptonshire, where he lived and where he had been a JP since 1938. He was impatient to see social progress in the rural areas and played a leading part in founding the Northamptonshire Rural Community Council; and he was chairman for several years of the parish council of his own village, Great Doddington, near Wellingborough.

Long after his retirement Dallas retained a lively interest in national and international politics. He intervened suddenly and prominently in a national political debate in the summer of 1953 when the Labour Party was again discussing its agricultural policy, and Aneurin Bevan and his supporters had decided to press for the nationalisation of 'rented land'. Dallas, as a long-time supporter of land nationalisation (but not only of rented land), engaged in controversy in several newspapers with Richard Stokes MP, and others, who argued for taxation of land values as an alternative to nationalisation. Dallas continued to support public ownership of land as a way of promoting a more efficient agriculture. In 1956 Dallas took a step which he had been planning for several years when he joined with others in founding the Friends of Free China Association, of which he became chairman, with the Duchess of Atholl as president. In announcing their intention to form the Association he said:

> We believe that the existence of a Free China is indispensable to the existence of a Free Asia. So long as mainland China remains under Communist domination, there can be no real peace in the Far East and no country in Asia can be safe from Communist aggression. . . . By helping the Free Nationalist Chinese we shall be assisting in the world struggle against Communism.

This became Dallas's main activity in the last years of his life. In 1957, at the age of seventy-eight, he led a delegation from the Association to Formosa (Taiwan). It was the first such delegation from Britain to visit the island under Nationalist rule. It was a cause, however, which was undermined by events and the passage of time, and which received little support from official opinion in Britain.

All his adult life Dallas was a convinced Socialist and a firm democrat. In spite of the strong anti-Communist views of his later years he remained a radical in politics, and never considered being anti-Communist as an excuse for being reactionary. For most of his life he was an atheist, and he remained so until his death. He was proud of being a Scot, but had lived too long away from his native land to be a narrow nationalist. Dallas was an avid reader, mainly on political subjects, and he built up a large collection of books and pamphlets on a succession of subjects in which he was interested. His collection of agricultural pamphlets is housed in Nottingham University library. A genial disposition helped to ensure Dallas a wide range of friends, political and otherwise, and he was highly respected in the different circles in which he moved. He was a forceful platform speaker and had a very characteristic appearance by which he became well known, certainly from his middle years onwards. He had a large bushy moustache; the crown of his head was bald but he had bushy hair at the sides. He was of medium height and increasingly stout as he got older. The characteristic features of his dress were his stiff wing-collars and large hats. His jacket pockets usually bulged with papers.

Dallas died on 4 January 1961 at Bishop's Stortford, where he had lived for the last six years. He was cremated at Cambridge on 7 January: those present were members of his family and representatives of some of the bodies with which he had been closely associated. His oldest friend, James Welsh, former Labour MP for Paisley and ex-Lord Provost of Glasgow, gave a non-religious address. His estate came to £863. He was survived by his wife Mary, who died in 1973, and their two sons Kenneth and Ronald. Kenneth [the author of this biography] had graduated in economics at Glasgow University and was employed successively in the economic department of the TUC, the International Confederation of Free Trade Unions and the National Economic Development Office; Ronald also graduated at Glasgow University, worked for a short period as a journalist on *Forward*, then in the Labour Party press department and later as a lecturer in a technical college.

Writings: (with E. Selley), *Farm Workers fight for a Living Wage* (1920) 12 pp.; *Farm Workers' Greatest Betrayal; an exposure of the Coalition Government* (1921) 12 pp.; *What Labour has done for Agriculture* (1934) 12 pp.; (with others), *A Programme of Immediate Action: interim report of the Labour Party Commission of Enquiry into the Distressed Areas* (1937) 16 pp. – this was followed by five regional reports in the same year; 'A New Charter for Agricultural Workers?', *New Statesman and Nation*, 9 Mar 1940, 302; 'Ourselves and Russia' [letter], *Spec.*, 22 Feb 1946, 193; *River Nene Catchment Board: a brief record of some of the work* (Oundle, 1951) 52 pp.

Sources: *Workers' Union Record* (Feb 1915); *Trade Union Worker*, Jan 1916-Apr 1918; E. Selley, *Village Trade Unions in Two Centuries* (1919); F.E. Green, *A History of the English Agricultural Labourer 1870-1920* (1920; 2nd ed. 1927); *Labour Party Annual Reports*, 1926-44; J.W. Robertson Scott, *The Dying Peasant* (1926); *Challenge* [Wellingborough] (May 1929); F.H. Crittall, *Fifty Years of Work and Play* (1934); G. McAllister, *James Maxton: the portrait of a rebel* (1935); T. Ireson, *Northamptonshire* (1954); *Socialist Commentary* (July 1956); H. Dalton, *The Fateful Years* (1957); G. Brown, *In my Way* (1971); R. Hyman, *The Workers' Union* (Oxford, 1971); *WWW* (1961-70); biographical information: T.A.K. Elliott, CMG; personal knowledge. OBIT. *Chronicle and Echo* [Northampton], 4 Jan 1961; *Scotsman* and *Times*, 5 Jan 1961; *TGWU Record* (Feb 1961); *Labour Party Report* (1961).

KENNETH DALLAS

See also: †Mary MACARTHUR

DIXON, John (1850-1914)
MINERS' LEADER

John Dixon was born on 28 September 1850 at the village of Grendon, near the market town of Atherstone in North Warwickshire; he was the eldest of seven children of James Dixon, a labourer, and his wife, Elizabeth (née Blood). After an elementary education at the Bentley Schools, he began work at the age of ten, at the Baddesley Collieries; but for several years attended evening classes to further his education. Dixon lived with his parents until he was twenty-one, when he moved to Mexborough and obtained employment at the Denaby Main Colliery. He became increasingly involved in the affairs of the South Yorkshire Miners' Association, and his work for the Denaby miners resulted in his election as branch secretary in 1874. So creditably did he perform his duties that after twenty-five years' service the branch presented him with a clock and other presents in recognition of their appreciation. Dixon ceased to work underground in January 1879 when he was chosen as the men's checkweighman and in the following year he became one of the YMA auditors. (In 1881 the South and West Yorkshire Miners' Associations had amalgamated to form the YMA.) Here he gained valuable experience, and acted as assistant to John Frith, the YMA financial secretary. It was this experience which helped him to win the election for the post of YMA financial secretary when Frith died in 1904. John Dixon now left Mexborough and went to live in a house next door to the miners' offices in Barnsley. During the decade which followed he worked strenuously to increase the numerical strength and general position of the Association.

During the preceding thirty-odd years in the Mexborough district, besides doing a great deal of hard work on behalf of the YMA, Dixon had devoted much energy to the service of the local community. He was a member of Mexborough Education Authority for twenty-one years; a member of Mexborough Urban District Council for eleven years (1893-1904) and chairman for one year; a member of Mexborough School Board for twenty-one years (1883-1904) and a member of the Burial Board. In addition, as a firm believer in the advantages to the worker to be derived from friendly societies, he was an ardent supporter of Court 5348 of the Wath-upon-Dearne and Mexborough district of the Ancient Order of Foresters. He rendered such valuable assistance to his Court that about the turn of the century he was presented with an illuminated emblem of the Order. He also engaged in hospital work in the Mexborough district.

In 1875 Dixon had married Miss F. Beaman of Bewdley, Shropshire; they had two sons and two daughters. His wife predeceased him by six years. John Dixon was a quiet, unobtrusive, affable man, who was well liked by his colleagues. His death on 11 December 1914 was not unexpected, for he had been in ill-health for some time, and for the last few weeks of his life had been unable to leave his house. The funeral took place on 15 December 1914. After a service at the Regent Street Congregational Church, Barnsley, where Dixon had been a highly respected member, a large cortège journeyed to Mexborough, where over 200 miners representing nearly every YMA branch in South Yorkshire joined the mourners, marched in procession to the cemetery, and lined the pathway to the graveside. He left an estate valued at £2603.

Sources: *Barnsley Chronicle,* 4 June 1904; biographical information: J. Macfarlane, Sheffield Univ. Obit. *Barnsley Chronicle* and *Mexborough and Swinton Times,* 19 Dec 1914; YMA, *Annual Report* (1915).

ROBERT G. NEVILLE

See also: †Thomas ASHTON, for Mining Trade Unionism, 1900-14; †John FRITH; †Benjamin PICKARD, for Mining Trade Unionism, 1880-99.

DREW, William Henry (Harry) (1854-1933)
TRADE UNION LEADER

William Henry Drew was born in Exeter in 1854. Little is known of his early life except that he began work in agriculture and became interested in politics in the mid-1860s when John Duke Coleridge QC (who was later Lord Chief Justice of England), was contesting Exeter for the Liberal Party. When he was eighteen Drew migrated to Jarrow and, after a short stay, moved to Shipley, where he commenced work as a woolcomber at Pricking Mill. Later he became a warehouseman at Airedale Mills, Shipley, and was eventually employed as a worsted weaver. He joined the West Riding Power Loom Weavers' Association in 1887, and from that date until 1907 acted as an organiser for the Association, serving on its executive committee for most of the time.

Drew was one of a number of personalities in the West Riding of Yorkshire who were the pioneers of both textile trade unionism and of independent Labour politics. When the *Yorkshire*

Factory Times was established in 1889 Drew, together with Allen Gee and Ben Turner, were recruited as correspondents. When the Manningham Mills strike began in December 1890 it was these three who provided the leadership in what was to prove a major event in West Riding labour history [Pearce (1975)]. The strike lasted almost nineteen weeks and at its peak involved between four and five thousand workers; and although it ended in failure it gave a new impetus to trade unionism in the region and led immediately to a strong movement for independent political action. Within a month from the end of the strike the Bradford Labour Union was established, and this in turn led to the formation of the Independent Labour Party in 1893. In all these developments Drew took a leading part.

Physically he was a most unlikely person to emerge as a labour leader. He was a thin, narrow-chested man, with bent shoulders, a high-pitched voice and he suffered for many years from bronchitis. But despite these physical handicaps Drew was a man of great determination and stamina. He became president of the Bradford Labour Union, and in November 1891 he stood successfully on the Labour Union ticket for the Bradford School Board. In 1892 he gave evidence, along with Ben Turner, to the R.C. on Labour. Certain of his statements in this evidence were publicly refuted in a vigorous attack upon him by H.H. Illingworth, a local Bradford manufacturer, and in August Drew unsuccesfully sued Illingworth for slander. His inability to pay costs compelled him to file a petition for bankruptcy in January 1895, when he was found to have a deficit of £116.

Throughout the middle years of the 1890s he continued his political activities unabated. He helped found the Bradford Central Labour Club, of which he became president, to resign in 1895 when the Club changed its rules to permit non-unionists to hold office. In December 1893 the Bradford Unemployed Emergency Committee was established, uniting the ILP, the Bradford Trades Council and the Social Reform Union, a non-conformist group, in an attempt to tackle the problem of unemployment. Drew became one of its leading figures. The Committee conducted its own survey of unemployment, ward by ward, and wholly refuted the complacent statements of the Bradford Board of Guardians.

Drew had been a member of the Bradford Trades Council since 1887, and became secretary in 1898, following the resignation of James Bartley. Ben Turner wrote of his work:

> . . . he put the Trades Council on to its wider basis. He paved the way for the full time work of Trades Council Secretary. He began the noted Trades Council Year Book. He began the compensation work; . . . [Turner (1920) 125].

Drew further promoted an inquiry into the working conditions of the woolcombers in 1899, and he played a leading role in the opposition of the local trade union movement to the 1902 Education Act. He also attempted, with no great success, to involve the Trades Council in support for bimetallism through the Trade Union Monetary Association, of which he himself was secretary.

Towards the end of 1906 Drew gave notice that he intended to emigrate and would be resigning from the secretaryship of the Trades Council. His decision was taken probably for health reasons, and he left for Canada in early March 1907. Little is known about the remainder of his life except that he later returned to Bradford and worked as a clerk in the Labour Exchange. He died on 29 January 1933. No will has been located.

Writings: Articles to *Yorkshire Factory Times*, 1889-1906; Evidence before R.C. on Labour 1892 XXXV Group C vol.1 Qs 5374-842; 'The National ILP; Its Origin', in Bradford Trades and Labour Council, *Year Book 1907*(for 1906), 97, 99-100.

Sources: (1) MSS: Bradford Trades and Labour Council, Minutes: Textile Hall, Bradford. (2) Other: *Bradford Observer*, 28 Apr 1891, 11 Aug 1893, 5 Jan 1894, 25 Jan 1895; Bradford Unemployed Emergency Committee, *Manifesto* (Bradford, 1894); *Bradford Labour Echo*, 1 June 1895; Bradford Trades and Labour Council, *Year Book* (1899) 86 and *Year Book 1907*(for

1906) 17 and 19; B. Turner, *Short History of the General Union of Textile Workers* (Heckmondwike, 1920); *Independent Labour Party 1893-1943 Jubilee Souvenir* (1943); F. Brockway, *Socialism over Sixty Years: the life of Jowett of Bradford (1864-1944)* (1946); C. Pearce, *The Manningham Mills Strike, Bradford, December 1890-April 1891* (Univ. of Hull, 1975). OBIT. *Yorkshire Observer*, 30 Jan 1933; *Bradford Pioneer*, 14 Feb 1933.

KEITH LAYBOURN
JOHN SAVILLE

See also: †James BARTLEY; †Allen GEE; *Frederick William JOWETT, for Independent Labour Party, 1893-1914.

EDWARDS, Alfred (1888-1958)
LABOUR (later INDEPENDENT) MP

Alfred Edwards was born on 22 March 1888 at Middlesbrough, one of nine children of Thomas Edwards, a journeyman joiner with the North Eastern Railway Company, and his wife Sarah (née Bamford). He attended the Victoria Schools, Middlesbrough, was interested in sport and his first job was with a Middlesbrough cycle dealer. He became an expert racing cyclist and organised events in the Cleveland and Hull districts where for a time he ran a billiards saloon and also competed in the Amateur Billiards championship. He then returned home and after a period of unemployment found work in 1912 as an unskilled labourer at the Diamond Grit Atlas Foundry of Harrison Brothers (England) Ltd at Middlesbrough.

In his early youth he had studied the Bible and the works of Mary Baker Eddy, the founder of Christian Science, and was a devout follower of this faith throughout his life. His interest in Socialism began when he was seventeen. George Lansbury became a candidate for Middlesbrough in the general election of 1906, standing against Havelock Wilson and a Conservative. Lansbury's candidature was a complicated one in that he was supported by the ILP but not by the LRC, and he was easily beaten into third place. But the Socialist campaign he ran made a considerable impact, and Edwards was among those who were influenced [Purdue (1973)]. On his return to Middlesbrough Edwards had continued the self-education which enabled him, after two years at the Foundry, to become manager of the works. Then two years later, with assistance from friends, he became controller and eventually owner of the business. He first went to America in 1916 and made annual visits between the wars, initially on business but later also on lecture tours, speaking on economic subjects and Anglo-American relations. He was an active Rotarian all his working life.

Edwards entered politics late in life. He did not join the Labour Party until 1931 and at one stage his *Who's Who* entry said that he had joined the Labour Party 'on the desertion of its leaders'. From 1932 to 1935 he served as a Labour councillor on the Middlesbrough Town Council. At the general election of 1935 he won Middlesbrough East with a majority of only 67; this was a seat which had been held by Ellen Wilkinson from 1924 until 1931.

In political matters Edwards was middle-of-the-road, but during the war he was a fairly persistent critic of the Coalition Government. He called for the resignation of the Labour Party from the Government in 1942; he voted against the Government in support of Mavis Tate's amendment to the King's Speech on equal compensation for women with war injuries; he was against the release of Oswald Mosley in 1943 and he also voted against the Government on a vote of confidence in 1944. It was not however, until after the Labour victory of 1945 (at which he was returned with a large majority) that he began to have major doubts about the Party's policies, especially nationalisation. When the Bill to nationalise iron and steel was introduced, Edwards expressed his total opposition, both in the House and outside. He went on a country-wide tour, speaking at sixty-seven meetings in seventy-seven days. Inevitably disciplinary measures were taken, and late in 1948 he was expelled from the Labour Party. He found his position as an Independent ineffectual, and in 1949 he applied for, and was granted, the Conservative whip. He insisted on facing his old electorate at the general election of 1950, but was decisively beaten by H.A. Marquand, the Labour candidate. At the general election of 1951 he stood as a Conservative for Newcastle East, but was again unsuccessful; and thereafter his business commitments, which continued to expand, took priority. He had sold the Middlesbrough foundry during the war but he also had a building and a mason's tool business and in 1953 he bought Wilson's Foundry and Engineering Co. Ltd, Bishop Auckland, which he developed successfully.

Edwards died on 17 June 1958 at his home at Hemble Hill, Guisborough, survived by his wife Anne Raines (née Hoskison), whom he married in 1917, and by two daughters. One daughter lived in the U.S.A. and the other, Sybil, still farms (1976) from the family home, and is a magistrate and chairman of the family foundry. His funeral was held privately at the Darlington Crematorium and was followed later by a memorial service. He left an estate valued at £43,019 (£425 net) [*Times*, 27 Feb 1959].

Writings: 'Excess Profits Tax' [letter], *New Statesman and Nation*, 26 Apr 1941; *Why Socialism does not work* (1949) P; 'We took off our Coats', *Rotarian* (Oct 1952); articles in *Christian Science Monitor, Reader's Digest* and trade papers.

Sources: *Northern Echo*, 18 Nov 1934, 17 Dec 1935; *The Times House of Commons* (1935); *Hansard*, 11 Dec 1935, 15 Dec 1948; *North Eastern Daily Gazette*, 12 Dec 1935, 22 Sep 1936, 19 and 30 Jan, 10 Aug, 29 Oct 1945, 29 Mar 1946; C. Bunker, *Who's Who in Parliament* (1946); *Dod* (1948); *Yorkshire Post*, 17 May 1948; 'Mr Alfred Edwards', *Voice of Industry* (July 1950); *Kelly* (1952); A.W. Purdue, 'George Lansbury and the Middlesbrough Election of 1906', *Int. Rev. Social Hist. 18*, pt. 3 (1973) 333-52; biographical information: County Libraries Service, Cleveland; T.A.K. Elliott, CMG; personal information: Miss S.K. Edwards, JP, Guisborough, daughter. OBIT. *North Eastern Daily Gazette*, 17 June 1958; *Northern Echo* and *Times*, 18 June 1958.

JOYCE BELLAMY

EWART, Richard (1904-53)
TRADE UNIONIST AND LABOUR MP

Richard Ewart was born on 15 September 1904 at South Shields, Co. Durham, the only son in a family of six daughters. When Ewart was born his father's occupation was registered as 'general labourer' and it is known that he worked for several years as a municipal lamplighter. Ewart's mother's name was Sarah McFadden and she made her 'mark' on his birth certificate. Ewart was educated at St Bede's Roman Catholic School, South Shields, which he left at the age of fourteen, and worked at Whitburn Colliery. At the age of twenty-one, while working as a hewer, he suffered a back injury and had to leave the pits. Unemployment was very high in South Shields in the 1920s, and the only work he could find was that of marker in a local billiards hall. He eventually became manager of this hall.

Throughout his working life Ewart was an active trade unionist. During his period of employment in the mines he was a member of the Durham Miners' Association, and when he left the pits he immediately joined the National Union of General and Municipal Workers. In December 1936 he became a full-time branch secretary of the union, and in August 1938 was appointed a union organiser. In 1943 he was transferred to the Cleveland district to help union officials to cope with the wartime expansion of trade union work on Teesside and he was responsible for the local iron-stone mining membership of the NUGMW.

Ewart joined the Labour Party in 1925, and in 1932 was elected to the South Shields Town Council for the Holborn ward, to become its youngest member at that time. He served on the

South Shields Council until 1943 and was chairman of its housing committee from 1936 to 1939 and vice-chairman of its public assistance committee in 1937. After his transfer to Cleveland he was elected a member of the North Riding County Council in March 1943. He sat on the public health, housing and sanitary committee, the Cleveland Guardians committee and the Morris Grange visiting committee, and was a representative of the Council on the North Riding insurance committee and the Langbaurgh assessment committee. In December 1943 Ewart appears in the council minutes as a member of the North Riding mental hospital committee, and hence sitting on the committee for the care of the mentally hanidcapped. He was appointed a JP in 1944, and served as chairman of the Cleveland and District Labour Party from January to July 1945.

In July 1945 he successfully stood as parliamentary Labour candidate for the double-member constituency of Sunderland as a sponsored candidate of the NUGMW. His selection was made at short notice after the last-minute withdrawal of the previous Labour candidate, T.F. Peart, who preferred to fight the Workington constituency. Ewart's Labour partner, F.T. Willey, topped the poll with 38,769 votes. Ewart was second with 36,711 votes, thus defeating the two sitting members, a National Liberal and a Conservative. The Communist candidate, T.A. Richardson, received 4501 votes. When double-member constituencies were abolished, Ewart stood as Labour candidate for the Sunderland South constituency in 1950 and held the seat against a Conservative and a Liberal. In a straight fight against a Conservative candidate in 1951 Ewart again held the seat, but only by a narrow majority. After Ewart's death in 1953 the Conservative Party won the seat in the subsequent by-election.

Ewart's first parliamentary duty after his election to the House of Commons was to join the British parliamentary delegation to Germany in 1946. He also visited Spain in the spring of 1948, and in the *Catholic Herald* of 16 April Ewart advocated Marshall Aid for Spain. 'In these days', he wrote, 'when dangers are threatening the great Christian heritage, Spain should share in the Western Union' [*Daily Worker*, 30 Apr 1948]. These were sentiments which brought him much criticism from trade unionists in his constituency. But for most of his parliamentary career he confined himself almost entirely to regional and industrial affairs. He was anxious about the effects of the steel shortage on the shipyards of the Tyne and Wear, and was concerned that the North East was not getting its fair share of defence contracts. From 1950 until his death in 1953 he was secretary of the North East Group of Labour MPs and led fact-finding visits of MPs to trading estates, shipyards and airports in the North Eastern region. He also pressed in Parliament for the North East to be given its own regional radio service, and urged that the extension of television services to the North East should be speeded up. His links with the NUGMW remained strong after his election to Parliament, and he continued to play an active part in the internal affairs of the NUGMW, although his intervention was viewed with mixed feelings by some of the union's full-time officials. On 8 June 1951 Ewart was appointed parliamentary private secretary to Sir Hartley Shawcross, President of the Board of Trade, and he retained this post until the defeat of the Labour Government in October 1951.

Ewart died on 7 March 1953 at St Andrews Hospital, Willesden of a gastric complaint after an illness lasting several months. He had never married. Throughout his life he was a devout Roman Catholic, and from 1949 to his death he served as chairman of the management committee of St Raphael's, Potters Bar, Herts, a residential school for mentally handicapped boys run by the Brothers of St John of God. In recognition of his services to the school Ewart was buried in the little cemetary attached to St Raphael's as an honorary member of the Order of St John. He left £9207 gross.

Sources: *Minutes* of South Shields Borough Council and the North Riding County Council; *Hansard* (1945-53); files of the *Shields Gazette* and *Sunderland Echo*; *Daily Worker*, 30 Apr 1948; *Dod* (1951); *WWW* (1951-60); biographical information: T.A.K. Elliott, CMG. Obit. *Manchester Guardian*, *Shields Gazette*, *Sunderland Echo* and *Times*, 9 Mar 1953; *J. of the*

NUGMW 16, no. 5 (May 1953); G. Foster, *Adventure into the Past* (Sunderland Labour Party, 1954) P.

ARCHIE POTTS

FINLEY, Lawrence (Larry) (1909-74)
TRADE UNIONIST AND COMMUNIST

Larry Finley was born in Liverpool on 12 July 1909, the son of Edward James Finley and Annie Finley (née Batch). His parents had lived in Salford, but his father emigrated to Canada to prepare a home and Larry was born while his mother waited in Liverpool to take passage and join him. However, she died in childbirth and the child was brought up in Salford by his father's brother, a Socialist docker and his wife, a deeply religious Methodist. He went to Seedley Council School and also to the Socialist Sunday School at Hyndman Hall in Liverpool Street. There he came under the influence of Sam Farrow, who was described as 'the theoretician of Hyndman Hall'. Thanks to his tuition, Finley acquired an extensive knowledge of Marx's *Capital*.

In 1923, he began working at W.H. Bailey's in Oldfield Road. He could not afford indentures and he worked in a quick succession of factories learning the trade of toolmaker the hard way. He joined the Salford 2nd branch of the AEU and became active in the Labour Party League of Youth. He was elected a delegate from the League of Youth to Salford City Labour Party.

In 1926, the year of the General Strike, the North Salford League of Youth, under the leadership of Ron Hicks, and South Salford, led by Finley, provided a contingent to the May Day demonstration. Their banner, made by Jack Williams in the cellar at Hyndman Hall, displayed a portrait of Lenin with the caption, 'Our Guiding Star'. James Openshaw, the chief marshal, ordered the banner-bearers to take it down. They refused and when the main contingent moved off the League of Youth contingent marched away in the opposite direction.

In the early thirties Finley was out of work and became active in the National Unemployed Workers' Movement. After the mass demonstrations of October 1931, when the leaders of the Manchester and Salford movement were arrested, Finley took over the leadership and continued the agitation. Among those active in the political scene in Salford was a young girl, Ellen O'Neill, a member of the Young Communist League. Within a short time, on 1 April 1935, he married Ellen and cemented a comradeship which continued until her death in 1970. He also joined the Communist Party of which he was a loyal member for over forty years.

Finley always took a broad view of political work. He was the inspirer and leader of the Workers' Art Club, which operated from Hyndman Hall and embraced a wide range of cultural and sporting activities; these included a boxing club where two young dockers, Joe and George Norman, trained themselves and other youngsters. Finley was also involved in the organisation of the Workers' Film Society, which eventually took over the running of Hyndman Hall.

In 1933 Finley, together with Sam Knight, Jim Claxton and a French comrade who used the name of C.H. White, founded Marx House, Manchester. The two years' syllabus included classes in astronomy and physics, geology, biology and sociology, as well as a systematic study of the works of Marx and Engels. The final months of the second year had a course entitled 'The Everyday Struggle of the Revolutionary Movement'. Both Finley and his wife were tutors at the school. Marx House, Manchester was closed down in 1946.

In 1937, Finley obtained work at L. Gardner and Sons Ltd, in Peel Green, Eccles, where he was rapidly elected a shop steward and representative to the AEU district committee. During the Spanish Civil War, he volunteered for the International Brigade, but was rejected because of his leg, which he had broken at the age of twenty-two and which had never been properly set. He persuaded the Gardner shop stewards' committee to support the 'Voluntary Aid for Spain' programme organised under the auspices of the executive council of the AEU. A group of volunteers set to work in a brick shed with a borrowed lathe and bench. An appeal was circulated to union members to donate old motor cycles. So many decrepit machines were towed in that the works overflowed into the back premises of Eccles Trades Council. After some weeks of hard work, often continuing into the night, six reconditioned machines were sent to Spain.

At the beginning of the Second World War, in 1940, Finley was released from his job at Gardner's and directed to work at Fords. When the Ford Company reopened its factory in Trafford Park, the hundred men in the toolroom included twenty-five displaced shop stewards. Finley and Arthur Wilde took the initiative in building the union organisation and in 1941 were elected as shop stewards. The management decided to get rid of him: Finley was stopped at the works gate and given his cards, and when a deputation from the toolroom met the management, the spokesman, Arthur Wilde, was immediately discharged. The men ceased work, and eventually Wilde was reinstated, but Finley remained outside.

He then moved to London, in May 1941. He obtained work at Napiers, was soon elected a shop steward and also played an active part in the large Communist Party organisation in the factory. He became a member of the North London district committee of the AEU. In London Finley continued all those activities which he had begun in the North West. In line with his belief that political activity was broader than the Communist Party, he played a part in a long-established debating society, the Cogers, which met every Saturday night in a pub in Fleet Street. There, he sharpened his political understanding against the wit of journalists and print workers. He was honoured by being elected as 'Grand', or chairman, for a term of office.

When his health began to fail, he decided to return north with the intention of preparing a home to which he and his wife could retire. While they were apart, they corresponded at length on many aspects of Marxist theory. But the home he had prepared was abandoned when he learned that Nellie had cancer and would not live long. He returned to London to be with her until she died. He then left London to spend the rest of his life in a cottage at Hollins, near Bury. True to his principles, he did not exert political pressure on his three children; Sylvia qualified as a doctor, and Lawrence and Helen were teachers. But he noted with considerable pride and pleasure that each of them acquired understanding and made a contribution to the working-class movement.

While Finley lived in Hollins, he continued his work on Marxist theory. He completed one section of work on the subject of 'Labour from Primitive Communism to Capitalism'. In May 1974 he contributed to the discussion in *Marxism Today* on 'Inflation and Marxist Theory'. He finished a further contribution the day he died. His death took place on 27 October 1974, and he left an estate valued at £3261. He was given a secular funeral at Rochdale Crematorium; the coffin was draped with a red flag, and the Red Flag and the Internationale were sung.

Writings: 'Inflation and Marxist Theory', *Marxism Today 18*, no. 5 (May 1974) 152-4; 'Labour from Primitive Communism to Capitalism' (1974) [typescript] 27 pp.

Sources: Private papers; personal knowledge.

EDMUND AND RUTH FROW

FLANAGAN, James Desmond (1912-69)
CO-OPERATIVE JOURNALIST

James Desmond Flanagan was the only child of the Co-operative journalist James Aloysius Flanagan, and his wife Elizabeth (née McCormick). He was born in Glasgow on 14 June 1912, and was educated first at a primary school there and then, after his father moved to Manchester, at the Xaverian College, Manchester. When he was seventeen he followed his father into the co-operative movement and worked in the Labour Department of the Co-operative Union; later on, he moved to the Union's Publication Department, and in 1948 he became librarian, a post which he held with distinction until his death. Under his direction the library gained an international reputation as a centre of information about the movement and its history – of which he himself had an unusual knowledge.

He was a member of the committee of the Working Party of Librarians and Documentation Officers of the International Co-operative Alliance. His research and his duties brought him into close association with the UN, with British and overseas government departments, and with other institutions which looked after co-operative organisations in the developing countries.

He was for many years tutor in International Co-operation at the Co-operative College, Stanford Hall, Leicester, and at other times acted as external examiner for the College. He belonged to the NUJ and was the father of the Co-operative Union Chapel.

Besides a number of pamphlets and numerous newspaper articles on various aspects of co-operation, Desmond Flanagan wrote centenary histories for several Co-operative Societies. His centenary history of the Co-operative Union, a scholarly and well-written account, was published shortly before his death.

On 14 September 1943 he married Mary Toner. They had four children: the daughter is a teacher of languages; one of the sons is a Common Law assistant with a local government authority, another is with the Canadian Treasury Department, and the third has a managerial post in industry.

Desmond Flanagan died in hospital after a short illness, on 22 December 1969. Requiem Mass was celebrated in St Cuthbert's Church, Withington, and he was buried in Southern Cemetery, Manchester. He was fifty-seven years old and had served the co-operative movement for forty years. He left an estate valued at £9390.

Writings: *Captain Grim. A pirate play for young co-operators* (Co-op. Union, 1932) 15 pp.; *Functions of the Co-operative Press – National and International* (1934) 11 pp.; *Co-operators salute Peace. A review of major international events since the Great War* (Co-op. Party, [1938] 23 pp.; 3rd ed. 1939-40) P.; *The Co-operative Movement's First 100 Years, 1844-1944* (1944) 48 pp.; *The Path of Progress: centenary of the Halifax Co-operative Society, 1851-1951* (Halifax, 1951) 24 pp.; *Something to remember: our centenary of co-operation 1856-1956* (Brighouse, 1956) 15 pp.; *Triumph at Leek: the centenary story of Leek and Moorlands Co-operative Society – 100 years of progress 1859-1959* (Manchester, 1959) 18 pp.; *The Gleaming Record of Fifty Years: golden jubilee, 1912-1962* [United Co-operative Laundries Association] (Manchester, 1962) 24 pp.; Translated (with J. Letargez) from the French, P. Lambert, *Studies in the Social Philosophy of Co-operation* (Co-op. Union, 1963); 'The British Co-operative Movement since the Independent Commission', *APCE 35*, no. 4 (1964) 251-63; *1869-1969: a centenary story of the Co-operative Union of Great Britain and Ireland* (Co-op. Union, 1969); *Men and Women who have made our History* (Co-op. Union, n.d.) 44 pp.

Sources: Personal information: Mrs M. Flanagan, Manchester, widow; R. Garratt, Co-op. Union, Manchester. OBIT. *Co-op. News,* 27 Dec 1969; *Co-op. Rev. 44,* no. 1 (Jan. 1970).

MARGARET 'ESPINASSE

See also: †Albert Victor ALEXANDER, for Co-operative Party; †Arnold BONNER, for Retail Co-operation, 1945-70; †William Henry BROWN, for Retail Co-operation, 1900-45; †James Aloysius FLANAGAN; †Fred HALL, for Co-operative Education; †Fred HAYWARD, for Co-operative Union; and †Henry John MAY, for International Co-operative Alliance.

GILLILAND, James (1866-1952)
MINERS' LEADER AND LABOUR COUNCILLOR

James Gilliland was born at East Rainton, Co. Durham, on 11 May 1866, the son of David Gilliland, a miner, and his wife Elizabeth (née McCullough). His early days were spent in the

Crook district. He too became a miner, and in 1897 was elected as checkweighman at Lintz Green Colliery, a post he held for ten years. Later, he was checkweighman at the Ouston 'E' pit at Birtley, and he retained this position until his appointment as agent in 1925.

He first attempted office in the union in 1915 when Samuel Galbraith became an MP. Gilliland was among the last five names to be voted on for agent by individual ballot of members, but he was unsuccessful. Then in October 1919 he was defeated by Peter Lee for the position of financial secretary. He came second again in an election for agent in May 1923, being defeated on this occasion by J.E. Swan, who had lost the constituency of Barnard Castle in the general election of 1922. Finally, Gilliland was elected agent in 1925, the defeated candidate being John Herriotts, ex-Labour MP for Sedgefield. When W.P. Richardson died in 1930, a rearrangement of the duties of the remaining officials made Gilliland compensation secretary of the DMA; and there was a further rearrangement of positions in the middle thirties, following the deaths of the president, James Robson, in September 1934 and of the general secretary, Peter Lee, in June 1935. J.E. Swan took Lee's position and Gilliland became president. Both retired in 1945, under Rule 19 of the newly-established National Union of Mineworkers.

Following his election as agent in 1925, Gilliland began to play a part in the national movement. He represented Durham on the executive committee of the MFGB in 1925, 1927, 1929, from 1931 to 1934 and again in 1936 and 1939. In 1932 he was a member of a delegation which went to meet the Mining Association of Great Britain to discuss action that might follow the expiry of the Coal Mines Act of 1931 [Arnot (1961) 86 ff.]. In 1937 he was a member of the committee established by the special conference of the MFGB (20 Apr 1937) to take forward negotiations in the long-drawn-out case of the Spencer Union in Nottinghamshire (the other members were J.A. Hall (Yorkshire), Arthur Horner (South Wales) and James Bonar (Northumberland)).

Gilliland was a staunch Labour man. He was a member of the Tanfield Urban District Council for nine years, and in 1925 he was elected to the Durham CC as representative of Birtley. He was vice-chairman and then till 1949 chairman of the education committee, and it was especially for his work in the field of education that he was best known by the general public in Durham. He became an alderman and did not retire from Council work until 1951. In 1932 he was appointed a JP; and was awarded the OBE.

Gilliland was a devout Methodist, a local preacher for sixty-five years. He was a voracious reader and possessed a fine private library, of which he was proud. He died on 27 December 1952 at his home in Lower Barn, Durham City. The funeral service was held at the Jubilee Methodist Church, and the interment was in South Road Cemetery. Gilliland was survived by his wife, three sons and two daughters, and left effects valued at £3017.

Sources: R.F. Wearmouth, *The Social and Political Influence of Methodism in the Twentieth Century* (1957); R. Page Arnot, *The Miners in Crisis and War* (1961). OBIT. *Northern Echo*, 29 Dec 1952; *Durham Chronicle and Seaham Weekly News*, and *Durham County Advertiser*, 2 Jan 1953.

ANTHONY MASON

See also: †John HERRIOTTS; †Peter LEE, for Mining Trade Unionism, 1927-44; †John Edmund SWAN.

GOSLING, Harry (1861-1930)
TRANSPORT WORKERS' LEADER AND LABOUR MP

Harry Gosling was born at 57 York Street, Lambeth, on 9 June 1861. The home into which he was born was a relatively prosperous one. His father, William Gosling, was a journeyman lighterman at the time of his birth. His mother, Sarah Gosling (née Rowe), was a school teacher, and continued to follow her profession after marriage. The family owed its prosperity to Harry's great-grandfather, who built up a substantial business on the river, becoming the owner of several sailing barges. Harry's grandfather and father continued in the trade, but were content to operate in a small way of business. Harry Gosling himself was a delicate child, and hardly seemed suited to work on the river. Family tradition, however, counted for a great deal in this trade, and so in 1875, at the age of fourteen, he was bound apprentice to his father at the traditional ceremony held in the Hall of the Watermen's Company.

Gosling's formal education ended when he was thirteen – he filled the gap between leaving school and being apprenticed by working as an office-boy. Many years later Herbert Morrison described him as a man 'of quite limited education but well-spoken' [An Autobiography (1960) 76]. He had had eight years of formal schooling, at the British and Foreign School in Marlborough Street (later Grey Street), near Waterloo Road, Blackfriars, where for a long period there was only one master to look after 250 boys. Had things worked out differently, Gosling's schoolteacher mother might have been an influence prolonging and enriching his education, but she died when he was only seven. His father was rather an unusual character. A man of varied interests, he was later described as a 'dreamer' by his son. He loved music and the theatre and, possessing a fairly large house, delighted to let part of it to actors. He must have given his son a broader view of life than that acquired by most children in Lambeth.

The Goslings' sphere of employment on the river was untypical. In the second half of the nineteenth century the lighterage trade of the Thames was passing into the hands of large concerns, and journeymen who had once expected to set up in business for themselves found that they were condemned to become permanent employees. This was particularly true in the downstream areas, and here the men formed a trade union in 1872 – the Amalgamated Society of Watermen and Lightermen. In the upstream areas, however, the old world lingered on. The Gosling family owned boats and worked for themselves. They were one of a group of families that specialised in towing rafts of timber from the docks to builders' wharves in Lambeth and other upstream areas. The union had no influence in this sector. Instead the men belonged to the old Turnway societies [Up and Down Stream (1927) 51 ff.]. Harry Gosling's connection with this old-fashioned, almost pre-industrial, world continued unbroken for some years. He finished his apprenticeship in 1882, and married in 1884; his wife was Helen Martin, daughter of the engineer Joseph Law Duff. In 1887, however, he had a sudden collapse. The breakdown in his health was so bad that for three years he was unable to work on the river, and when not in St Thomas's Hospital, was forced to eke out a living as a salesman. Although he tried to resume as a lighterman in 1890, he broke down again the following year, and that was the end of his work on the river. His health had been a source of anxiety from his earliest days, and it was to remain so for the rest of his life. Remembering him later, Morrison wrote: 'he had a weak heart which compelled him to avoid excitement and to impose a strict discipline on himself' [p.76]. He was a lifelong abstainer from alcohol.

Between 1887 and 1890, while he was exiled from river work, Harry Gosling was able to commit himself to his beloved trade of lighterman in a new way. The 1889 dock strike created an enthusiasm for trade unionism amongst all waterside workers in London, and in that year Gosling joined the Amalgamated Society of Watermen and Lightermen (known for short as the Lightermen's Union). In 1890 he became president of the Lambeth branch and a member of the union's executive council. Early in 1893 he was elected to the full-time post of general secretary, a position he held until 1921. It was enthusiasm for the New Unionism which had brought Gosling into the industrial movement, and he always remained a progressive, if moderate, union leader. His membership, however, consisted of conservative craft unionists. As men who had served their apprenticeship they were freemen of the Watermen's Company, proud of the ancient traditions of their craft, and disdainful of most other waterside workers. Yet despite their view of themselves as an élite, their working conditions were poor. The large lighterage concerns emerging at this time had little regard for craft sentiment, and they introduced new methods – tug haulage and larger barges – which undermined the position of the journeymen and permitted increased employment of boys and non-apprenticed workers. In order to improve the situation Gosling sought to modernise the union, but the task proved difficult. His executive had to be convinced that a typewriter and a telephone would be useful in the union office. Gosling nearly despaired of his members, and at one point asked Tom Mann whether he should give up his job with the Lightermen and work for the Dockers' Union instead. Mann told him to stay where he was. The most fundamental weakness of the Lightermen's Union was its insularity. It was not interested in the numerous river workers who had not served an apprenticeship – the so-called non-freemen – and although these men were increasingly used by employers it would not admit them to membership. Gosling worked hard to convince his members of the need to enrol the non-freemen, arguing that without them the union would never be able to regulate the trade. At last in 1900 he finally succeeded, and the organisation opened its ranks.

The object of reform within the society was obviously to give it the capacity to confront the employers to some purpose. Gosling was a mild man and would have preferred negotiation to industrial action, but the employers had little patience with collective bargaining. By a mixture of force and negotiation he was able to make some progress. In 1900 he called a strike to compel the employers to adhere to an agreement made in 1889; the men stayed out for seventeen weeks. In 1909 the apprentices were called out in a similar defensive action, the stoppage lasting fourteen weeks. In both cases the union carried its point. In the interval between these two strikes Gosling was able to negotiate with the employers' association a set of working rules. These came into force in 1908, and represented the first serious attempt to regulate the trade by means of collective agreement.

While Gosling was dragging a reluctant Lightermen's Union into the twentieth century, he was also developing an interest in the wider Labour movement. In 1895 he contested Rotherhithe in the London County Council election as a Labour Progressive candidate. Rotherhithe was a waterside district, and a number of dockers rallied to his cause; but his own members remained firmly Tory. He lost that election, but fought, again as a Progressive, in 1898, at Clapham. He was defeated again, but received an alderman's seat, and so became a colleague of John Burns and Will Crooks in the small Labour group that operated within the Progressive Party. After serving his six years as an alderman Gosling stood for the waterside constituency of St George's and Wapping in the election of 1904, and was duly returned. He continued to represent this constituency on the Council until it disappeared under the redistribution of 1918; he developed a great affection for the people of the neighbourhood, and showed a particular interest in the welfare of the children. In 1908 Gosling became a member of the newly-created Port of London Authority, and continued to serve on this body until his death. He tried to use his influence to promote enlightened employment practices, but the trade union members really had little control of policy. Gosling came to know the Authority's chairman, Lord Devonport, quite well, and even managed to interest him in the welfare of the Wapping children. Devonport, however, was far from well disposed towards the waterside unions, and Gosling was to find him an implacable adversary in the 1912 strike.

During these early years of the twentieth century Harry Gosling was beginning to make his presence felt in the Trades Union Congress. He first attended Congress in 1893, and in 1908 was elected to the parliamentary committee, holding his seat on that body right up to the reorganisation of 1921. Before Gosling's influence within the TUC had reached its peak, however, events in the port industry had already made him into a national figure. In July 1910 Ben Tillett, acting on behalf of the Dockers' Union, invited both London and provincial waterside unions to a conference on federation. The conference met in September, with sixteen unions represented. Gosling took the chair at that meeting, and when the National Transport Workers' Federation was formally inaugurated on 1 March 1911 he was elected president; James Anderson of the Stevedores' Union was elected general secretary. The task of Gosling and

Anderson was an onerous one. Both retained their posts in their own unions, and were only able to devote part of their time to the Federation. They had virtually no staff to help them in this work. Before the two officers had any opportunity to improve the machinery of the Federation they became involved in the wave of transport strikes that spread throughout the country in the summer of 1911. The position of Gosling was especially difficult. His own union was deeply involved in the disputes of 1911, yet at the same time, as the NTWF president, he found himself called upon to represent the general body of port workers – particularly in London where the Federation was firmly based.

In the first round of negotiations which began in London on 10 July, Gosling tried to extract two major concessions from the employers: recognition for all the unions involved in negotiations, and a uniform scale of payment throughout the port. Opposition from the employers led to compromise in these objectives, and in the end he and the other Federation leaders were faced with the choice of either accepting an unsatisfactory agreement as better than nothing or standing out for something better. Believing that the NTWF was still too weak to face a major strike, they chose the former course. This proved to be a mistake. The men rejected the compromise settlement and started to come out on strike. The employers then accused Gosling and his fellow NTWF leaders of bad faith. Forced into a major stoppage, Gosling determined to use the occasion to promote unity of action amongst the London port workers and so make a reality of the federal idea. Addressing a huge mass meeting in Trafalgar Square on 6 August, he exhorted the men to stand together, and to permit no resumption of work until *all* the various sections of port and road transport workers had achieved a satisfactory settlement. To a considerable degree this policy worked, and the Government was obliged to intervene in order to bring the stoppage to an end. Gosling was then involved in a seemingly endless series of negotiations, first at the Board of Trade and later at the Home Office. By the end of August, when a full resumption of work was finally achieved, he had appended his signature to no less than ten separate agreements. Being now something of an expert on industrial disputes, Gosling was appointed by the Government to the newly-formed Industrial Council, in October 1911.

Although the NTWF achieved a considerable triumph in London in 1911, it aroused great hostility amongst the employers, and relations remained extremely strained. In the provinces, meanwhile, the Federation had hardly made its presence felt at all. The machinery of the organisation stood in urgent need of development, and at a special meeting held in February 1912 Gosling proposed that a full-time general secretary should be elected. The proposal was accepted. Anderson decided not to stand, and Robert Williams was elected to the post in the following June. Before the new régime had been established, however, the storm that had been threatening in London finally broke. Gosling was involved with the disastrous 1912 London dock strike in all its stages. It was a series of disputes involving his own Lightermen's Union that caused the stoppage, although in fact almost all sections of port workers had pressing grievances, and the issue of the closed shop which was the main cause of trouble in the lighterage trade concerned most other port workers as well. The port-wide stoppage, called by the NTWF in support of the lightermen, began on 23 May, and immediately the Government set up an inquiry into the origins of the dispute. Gosling gave evidence, and his tone was one of bitterness and intransigence. He was convinced that the employers intended to break the Federation, and he was determined not to let that happen. On the opening day of the inquiry he declared his position: 'We say we are not going to work with non-unionists, and we are not going to do that until we are starved into doing it, and I believe even if the men are starved into submission, as soon as they get fat and well they will be out again for the same principle.' Neither the inquiry nor subsequent initiatives by the Government were able to break the deadlock, for the port employers under the leadership of Lord Devonport were even more intransigent than the Federation. Gosling and Tillett undoubtedly hoped that they could win by calling a national strike of the NTWF, and this action was taken on 10 June; but the response from the provinces was negligible. London was therefore left to fight on alone, and without hope.

The 1912 strike was called off on 27 July. In the later stages the strain on Gosling was great, for funds were running out and the families of the strikers were being subjected to great hardship. His sense of responsibility for the welfare of his members and their families was intense, and this was a profoundly unhappy time for him. But the disaster strengthened his determination to do all in his power to improve the workers' organisation, so that a defeat of this kind would be unthinkable in the future. In the autumn of 1912, together with the NTWF executive, he visited nearly every port in the country and launched a campaign for the complete amalgamation of all port and road transport unions. While the amalgamation project was unfolding Gosling had to steel himself to face the electors of St George's and Wapping in the March 1913 LCC election. Transport workers who had been involved in the 1912 strike constituted a very large proportion of the electorate, and Gosling had little hope that they would return him. To his surprise, however, he came top of the poll. No doubt many of the waterside workers in the neighbourhood followed the advice of the docker who got up at Gosling's eve-of-poll meeting and shouted: 'Never mind, boys, whether it was his fault or not. If Gosling doesn't get in, then Lord Devonport licks him.'

When the NTWF conference assembled at Newport in June 1913 Gosling made the need for amalgamation the main theme of his presidential address. 'It is a heavy task that I am proposing', he said, 'and one that will require great judgement and tact to carry through.' In fact it was very nearly carried through before the First World War, and on a much more ambitious scale than had been originally envisaged. The General Labourers' National Council had been preparing an amalgamation scheme, and in the second half of 1913 it joined forces with the NTWF to produce a single set of proposals for a general labour amalgamation. Gosling was a member of the joint sub-committee of six which drafted the plan. A combined conference of the two organisations was held in London in July 1914, and this approved the project and left the sub-committee to make arrangements for the ballot. But the war intervened, and the matter had to be shelved.

Gosling's attitude to the war was one of total support, and the years of war increased his responsibilities. In 1915 the Government set up the Port and Transport Executive Committee to deal with congestion in the ports. No union representative was appointed to the Committee; but when the Federation protested, Gosling was invited to become a member, and later on he was joined by several other NTWF leaders. In 1916 Ernest Bevin was elected to the NTWF executive, and he quickly became the driving force behind the organisation. Gosling remained, however, very much at the centre of affairs, and the trio of Gosling, Williams and Bevin dealt with most of the major policy decisions. It was during these years that the Federation first became effective as a *national* body; in 1917 a national wage campaign was mounted which achieved considerable results.

In some respects the war years represented the peak of Gosling's career. In 1915 he was elected chairman of the parliamentary committee of the TUC, and he presided at the Annual Congress the following year. He made good use of the opportunity to address Congress as its president. His speech was described by B.C. Roberts, the TUC's historian, as 'the most memorable feature of the 1916 Congress', and 'outstanding in its quality'. It mentioned the need for a number of improvements: 'for a more sympathetic understanding between capital and labour, for a new era in business, for the workman's right to a voice in all the vital conditions of his work' [*Up and Down Stream* (1927) 131]; one necessary improvement he dwelt on with great emphasis. Gosling's whole career in the trade union movement had been devoted to breaking down sectionalism and developing the scale and efficiency of labour organisation. Up to this time his efforts had been concerned almost solely with the transport industry, but he now turned his attention to the TUC. Looking to the future, he told the delegates: 'the work of the parliamentary committee will be greater than ever. Its offices and its staff must be added to . . . We must not be satisfied until organised Labour is as important in its greater and more national aspects as any Department of State, with its own block of offices and civil service, commodious and well appointed.' Gosling's words were not without effect. At that Congress a sub-committee was appointed to consider ways in which the machinery of the TUC could be developed, and its recommendations were accepted by Congress the following year. The improvements were modest, but they were a beginning.

In 1917, because of his services to the Allied cause, Gosling was created a Companion of Honour. He was also appointed to the Imperial War Graves Commission in that year. With the disappearance of his old constituency under the redistribution of 1918 Gosling had planned to give up his work on the LCC, but the London Labour Party was formed just after the war, and he was prevailed upon to stand as a Labour candidate at Kennington in the 1919 election. He was victorious, together with fourteen other Labour men, and the new party elected him as leader. Herbert Morrison, as party secretary, used to attend the group's meetings. He has left us this picture of the party leader. 'It was always a pleasure to watch Harry Gosling in the Chair. Sometimes he would open the discussion, but more often he let the others talk. There was often some doubt as to whether he had fully read the Council agenda, but he had an extraordinary capacity for picking up the threads, and for reconciling conflicting points of view. Often, at the end of a discussion he would say, "Well, it looks to me as if you want to do this . . .". And nearly always they did' [p. 76]. Gosling continued on the LCC until 1925, with a short break in 1922, when he was defeated at Kennington but re-elected by the same constituency shortly afterwards.

In the industrial movement Gosling was at the centre of affairs during the turbulent post-war period. In 1920 he was a member of the Shaw Court of Enquiry into dock labour. In 1921 he was vice-chairman of the Triple Alliance and was intimately involved in the sequence of events that led up to 'Black Friday'. He had also been closely involved in the NTWF initiative which brought the 1919 railway strike to an end. In all these activities he worked closely with Bevin, and it was in association with Bevin that he played his part in achieving the transport workers' amalgamation of 1921, and also the setting up of the TUC General Council in the same year. Gosling became the full-time president of the new transport workers' union, an office he held until the last year of his life. He was the Transport and General Workers' Union's first and only president, as the office was abolished after his death. His part in bringing about the amalgamation had been substantial, for he had chaired all the amalgamation conferences and had been a member of the sub-committee of three which drafted the scheme in detail. Gosling's role in the creation of the TUC General Council was also a major one. He had been campaigning for increased powers and resources for the TUC since 1916, and in 1919 was involved in setting up the Co-ordination Committee. This Committee went on to devise the scheme for a General Council, and it was Gosling who presented its reports to successive Congresses. He became a member of the first General Council, and continued on that body until 1924.

In February 1923 Gosling was elected to Parliament for the first time. He had been unsuccessful in three previous contests [Lambeth-North (Dec 1910), Uxbridge (1918) and Lambeth-Kennington (1922)], but was now returned at a by-election in the Whitechapel and St George's division of Stepney. Gosling continued to hold the Whitechapel constituency for Labour until his death, and he served as Minister of Transport and Paymaster General in the first Labour Government. He was responsible for the passage of the London Traffic Act in 1924, and his handling of the Bill, arising out of the strike of tramway and omnibus workers, led to some criticism from Labour back-benchers. After the fall of the Government he took relatively little part in the work of Parliament, for his health began to deteriorate. Gosling did not regard his entry into Parliament, or his gaining of ministerial position, as a climax to his career. He had been in touch with Westminster, lobbying on behalf of his members, for many years before he became an MP, and the place held little magic for him. When Gosling had become Minister of Transport, he resigned the presidency of the TGWU, assuming that he would return to the position when Labour went out of office. When the Labour Government fell in October 1924, Gosling appeared at the next meeting of the union's council and requested the restoration of his former office. Bevin and the council decided against him – it was really Bevin's decision – but the storm of protest was such that the decision was rescinded and Gosling was restored to office.

The incident was widely interpreted as an indication of Bevin's dislike of any but subordinates in the organisation.

Gosling died at his home in Twickenham on 24 October 1930, after a long illness. He was aged sixty-nine. He left a widow but no children, and an estate valued at £2651. His body lay in state at Transport House, and hundreds came to pay their respects – including Lloyd George and Lord Devonport. The funeral was held at Golders Green Crematorium, and afterwards the mourners returned to Transport House, where a tablet was unveiled behind the presidential chair that he used to occupy. It was an appropriately situated memorial, for Harry Gosling was, above all, the perfect chairman.

Writings: *Peace: how to get and keep it* [1917] 15 pp.; *Up and Down Stream* (1927).

Sources: National Transport Workers' Federation, *Reports of General Council Meetings,* 1911-14; *Report upon the Present Disputes affecting Transport Workers in the Port of London and on the Medway* (1912) Cd 6229; *DNB* (1922-30); 'Mr Harry Gosling, CH., JP., MP., LCC. Labour's First Minister of Transport' in *The Book of the Labour Party,* ed. H. Tracey [1925] 264-7; H. Gosling, *Up and Down Stream* (1927); *Daily Herald,* 31 Oct 1930; R.W. Lyman, *The First Labour Government 1924* [1957]; B.C. Roberts, *The Trades Union Congress* (1958); A. Bullock, *The Life and Times of Ernest Bevin,* vol. 1:.1881-1940 (1960); H. Morrison, *An Autobiography* (1960); J. Lovell, *Stevedores and Dockers* (1969); biographical information: T.A.K. Elliott, CMG, Helsinki. OBIT. *Richmond and Twickenham Times* and *Times,* 25 Oct 1930.

JOHN LOVELL

See also: †William CROOKS; †Allen Clement EDWARDS; *Tom MANN; Benjamin (Ben) TILLETT, and for New Unionism, 1889-93.

HICKS, Amelia (Amie) Jane (1839/40?-1917)
SOCIALIST AND TRADE UNIONIST

Amie Hicks was born about 1839 or 1840 but the only details known of her early life are that she was the child of a Chartist and learnt 'her ideas of social right and wrong from her father's mother' [interview, *Woman's Signal,* 29 Mar 1894]. In 1865 she and her husband, William James Hicks, emigrated to Auckland, New Zealand, where she was employed in ropemaking. Illness compelled them to sell their home and return to England in the early 1880s with their family of six children [Lee and Archbold (1935) 89]. By the spring of 1883 William and Amie Hicks and one of the daughters, Margaretta, had joined Hyndman's Democratic Federation – from August 1884 the Social Democratic Federation, at which time Mrs Hicks was elected to its executive committee. Amie and her husband and their three eldest children were active workers for the SDF. When members of the Federation broke away late in 1884 to form the Socialist League with William Morris, Mrs Hicks, with John Burns, Herbert Burrows, H.H. Champion and others, stayed with Hyndman and the SDF [Tsuzuki (1961) 57-67]. In 1885 and again in 1888 Amie Hicks contested the London School Board elections as an SDF candidate. Her programme embraced free, compulsory, secular and technical education, and a daily free school meal; but on neither occasion was she successful.

Her active involvement with SDF affairs, however, continued: as open-air speaker and lecturer – on topics such as 'Shall the State feed Starving School Children?' and 'Women and Socialism' and as distributor of the SDF newspaper, *Justice.* In the free speech campaign of 1885 she was charged with obstruction while addressing a crowd in Dod Street, London and fined £20 to keep the peace for six months [*Times,* 1 Sep 1885]. She also took part with her son, Alfred, a compositor, in the unemployment agitations of 1885-6. Alfred and his father were among signatories of letters in *Justice* in 1885 appealing for funds to assist its publication when the paper faced competition from *Commonweal*, the journal of the Socialist League [Tsuzuki (1961) 68]. At this time the family lived in West Hampstead. The notoriety of their political activities resulted in the closure of a small private school being run there by Mrs Hicks's eldest daughter [Lee and Archbold, 89].

By 1888 Mrs Hicks had moved to Kentish Town and during the next two decades she lived at various addresses in the adjacent district of Camden Town. When she contested the school board elections her occupation was given as 'accoucheuse' [midwife]; she was a member of the Ladies' Medical College and had taken part in the agitation against the Contagious Diseases Acts which were repealed in 1886. Amie then became involved in trade union activities. Immediately after the London Dock Strike of 1889 she joined with John Burns, Clara James and others to form the Women's Trade Union Association. The object of the WTUA was to help women and girl workers to form unions, the funds of which were to strengthen their position in various trades rather than to provide financial benefits since the women could not afford adequate subscriptions for this purpose [Bulley and Whitley (1894) 79]. Mrs Hicks's own work in London's East End brought her in touch with Clementina Black of the WTUA, who had previously been a member of the Women's Trade Union League, founded by Emma Paterson. The WTUL refused to allow its members to belong to the WTUA so Miss Black left the League [interview, *Woman's Signal*, 29 Aug 1895]. The sweated working conditions of women ropemakers in the East End of London had prompted the WTUA to form the East London Ropemakers' Union in 1889 and Amie Hicks was elected their secretary. Her previous ropemaking experience was an asset for this work and she held the post for ten years.

As the ropemakers' secretary she gave evidence before the R.C. on Labour on the same day in 1891 as Clara James, who represented the confectionery workers. Repeated applications to give evidence had been made before they were allowed to do so [Drake [1920] 28]. At that time Mrs Hicks's union had a membership of 250-60 but it represented some 1000 women ropemakers and about 1500 jute workers, many of whom did not join, as Mrs Hicks told the Commissioners '. . . from fear of the employer – from fear of dismissal' [Q. 818). She and Clara James, who was a close family friend, had both testified to the unhealthy, immoral, unregulated and underpaid conditions in their trades. Amie Hicks appealed for the appointment of women factory inspectors, medical inspection of women's work, government regulation of profit and wages and amendments to the Employers' Liability Act. The first woman factory inspector was appointed in 1893.

For a six-month period Mrs Hicks represented the women ropemakers on the London Trades Council. She was the first woman to sit on a trades council but was asked to leave as she 'had not worked in the trade in England' [*Woman's Signal*, 29 Mar 1894]. Her expertise as a trade unionist was recognised however when, in the autumn of 1894, she was appointed a delegate with John Burns and David Holmes (of the Weavers) to the American Convention of Labor. Severe illness on her arrival in America prevented her attendance at the Convention but while recuperating in Boston she addressed a strike meeting, lectured on 'Women and the Labour Movement' to members of the Twentieth Century Club, and visited a number of workshops [*Woman's Signal*, 28 Feb 1895].

The founders of the WTUA realised, after a few years that trade unions did not always help the poorest working women, many of whom could not afford to join such organisations. But it was apparent that other activities, such as recreative clubs, training in certain skills and possible alterations in the law, could be of assistance. There was also a need for the systematic collection and publication of facts about the conditions of women's work. At a conference held in Holborn Town Hall on 26 November 1894 the Women's Industrial Council was formed to continue the work of the WTUA but on a broader base, by means of inquiries and specialised committees – the latter being suggested by another of Mrs Hicks's daughters, Frances Amelia, the secretary of the London Tailoresses' Union. Frances (sometimes called Amy) had been elected to the London Trades Council executive in 1893, joined the Technical Education Board of the LCC in February

1894 and in the same year spoke at a demonstration in Hyde Park in favour of the Employers' Liability Bill organised by the London Trades Council. She was appointed the first secretary of the WIC at a salary of £100 per annum but she only held office from April to October 1895. She resigned on her marriage to Henry J. James, a mariner, in September 1895 but continued to serve the Council as secretary of its organisations committee, of which her mother was chairman, and she also gave lectures on technical education and the Factory Acts. Miss Catherine Webb of the Women's Co-operative Guild succeeded Mrs James as secretary of the WIC [see *DLB 2* (1974) 397]; and Clara James, who was also a gymnast, was the drill instructor for the organisations committee.

Amie Hicks served on the executive of the WIC from its foundation until 1908. Her especial interest was the Clubs' Industrial Association, founded in 1898 by the organisations committee of the Council, and of which she was president for a number of years. The Association had forty-five working girls' clubs affiliated to it and arranged business and social meetings and lectures on industrial, social or educational questions. The Association's aim was to promote understanding of industrial law among working girls and women and encourage them to assist the factory inspectors. It disseminated copies of the Factory and Workshop Act abstracts and other industrial literature and protected workers who reported violations to the inspectors.

By this time Mrs Hicks was a well-known speaker on many subjects relating to working women. She attended the Socialist and Trades' Union International Congress held in London in August 1896, where conditions of women's labour in various countries were discussed; and she presented a resolution to the Congress for the Prohibition of women from working in factories for six weeks before and after confinement and for the grant of maintenance from a State Maternity Department. The motion was seconded by Herbert Burrows and carried unanimously [*Women's Industrial News* (Oct 1896)]. Amie Hicks attended the Conference on Home Work in November 1897 and the International Conference of Women held in London in June 1899 where she read a paper on 'Child-bearing Women' and where Beatrice Webb was also a speaker [*Labour Leader*, 1 July 1899].

In addition to her work for the WIC she was a member of the London Reform Union, a non-political organisation whose object was 'to reform London in every possible way, irrespective of parties' [interview, *Woman's Signal*, 28 Feb 1895]. It was concerned with social and moral reforms and with better housing and improvements in the municipal government of London, but Mrs Hicks favoured the Progressive Party's approach and disapproved of the action of the ILP which, in 1895, was withholding its support for the Progressives in the County Council elections.

Mrs Hicks continued her association with the WIC at least until 1910 and in her last years was vice-president of the National Organisation of Girls' Clubs [*Englishwoman's Year Book* (1914)]. The NOGC was formed in 1911 by amalgamation of the Girls' Clubs and Rest Rooms Committees of the National Union of Women Workers and the Clubs' Industrial Association (of the WIC). Amie Hicks's daughter, Margaretta, was secretary of the Women's Council, formed in 1912 as an auxiliary of the British Socialist Party, to organise and educate women in Socialist principles. In October 1914 the Council severed its connection with the BSP and then concentrated on propaganda work concerned with the wartime national food supply. It seems likely, although it cannot be confirmed, that Margaretta was living with her mother as her address in 1916 was 21 Rochester Square – the last address we have for Mrs Hicks. The WIC itself appears to have been disbanded about 1918 with its last-known publication (in 1916) relating to conditions of employment in domestic service.

Amie Hicks died in the Middlesex Hospital on 2 February 1917 after a long illness. No will has been located and nothing more is known about her husband, who at the time of Frances's marriage was a pianoforte maker. Although the *Women's Industrial News*, the WIC journal, carried an 'In Memoriam' tribute and recalled 'her personal note of sympathy for the particular case . . . her passionate sense of justice and . . . her eager, youthful spirit' no obituaries have been found in *The Times* or the contemporary press. Yet Amie Hicks was among the prominent women of the early Socialist and trade union movements. She had small, strong features with deep-set eyes and a determined mouth which bore the marks of a stressful life and in Ramsay MacDonald's biography of his wife Margaret he described Mrs Hicks as 'a quiet, simple, honest working woman of direct ways and the centre of a worshipping family'; and also as 'of some note as a Socialist worker, with a strong motherly face, a firm independent character, a great store of good simple common sense . . .' [(1912) 112 and 137]. MacDonald recalled how Mrs Hicks had inspired his wife and he quotes Margaret MacDonald's own words:

> I had a long talk with Mrs Hicks at her house [in early 1896] . . . she is very real and earnest; so unaffected and downright, and yet you feel a deep emotion impelling her and consecrating what she does [ibid. 112-13]

Margaret Bondfield in her own memoirs, *A Life's Work*, gives glimpses of the Hicks's family life and her close friendship with them and also quotes from an account written by Mrs Gilchrist Thompson, a member of the WIC, who helped to finance its surveys into working conditions. Mrs Thompson is recounting the early life of Clara James and tells how Miss James '. . . came under the influence of a heroic Labour leader, Mrs Amie Hicks, who, when I came to know her, typified to me what must have been the aspect of one of the minor prophets – denouncing the greed and cruelty of the society of his day' [pp. 32-3].

Writings: Letter to *Justice*, 14 June 1884 [on Malthus and Poverty]; 'Women and Socialism', ibid., 25 Apr 1885; 'Lust and Legislation' [on Contagious Diseases Act], ibid., 1 Aug 1885; Letter from Mrs Hicks defending prostitutes, ibid., 29 Aug 1885; Evidence before R.C. on Labour 1892 XXXV Group C vol. I Qs 8176-286; P.L. Parker, 'The Women in Hyde Park; an interview with Mrs Amie Hicks', *Woman's Signal*, 29 Mar 1894 [photograph]; S.A. Tooley, 'Labour Problems and the L.C.C.: an interview with Mrs Amie Hicks', ibid., 28 Feb 1895; 'Fines and Deductions in Factories and Workshops', in *Women Workers: the official report of the Conference held at Manchester on 27th-30th October 1896* (1896) 41-5.

Sources: *Justice*, 19 Jan, 14 June, 9 Aug, 6, 13 and 20 Sep 1884; *Times* 1 Sep 1885 and 26 Nov 1888; *Justice*, 17 Nov 1888 [Election Address]; *Workman's Times*, 5 June 1891; Evidence of Clara James before R.C. on Labour Group C vol. I 1892 XXXV Qs 8398-694; Women's Industrial Council, *Annual Reports*, 1894-1915; A.A. Bulley and M. Whitley, *Women's Work* (1894); *Woman's Signal*, 15 and 22 Feb, 18 Oct 1894; 18 July and 29 Aug 1895; *Women's Industrial News*, Oct 1895, Jan, Oct and Nov 1897, Dec 1901, June 1903; *Labour Annual* (1899) 83; J.R. MacDonald, *Margaret Ethel MacDonald: a memoir* (1912; later eds); *Englishwoman's Year Book and Directory*, ed. G.E. Mitton (1914); B.L. Hutchins, *Women in Modern Industry* (1915); *Labour Year Book* (1916) 363; B. Drake, *Women in Trade Unions* [1920]; H.W. Lee and E. Archbold, *Social-Democracy in Britain* (1935); M. Bondfield, *A Life's Work* [1949]; G. Tate, *London Trades Council 1860-1950* (1950); C. Tsuzuki, *H.M. Hyndman and British Socialism* (Oxford, 1961); M. Ramelson, *A Century of Struggle for Women's Rights* (1967); P. Thompson, *Socialists, Liberals and Labour: the struggle for London 1885-1914* (1967); biographical information Anna Davin, London; Mrs M. Miliband, Leeds; R.A. Storey, MRC, Warwick Univ. OBIT. *Women's Industrial News* (Apr 1917).

JOYCE BELLAMY
JAMES A. SCHMIECHEN

See also: †Margaret Grace BONDFIELD; *John BURNS; *Margaret Ethel Gladstone MACDONALD; *Emma Anne PATERSON; †Catherine WEBB.

HOLBERRY, Samuel (1814-42)
CHARTIST

Samuel Holberry was born on 18 November 1814 at Gamston, Nottinghamshire, the youngest of the nine children of John and Martha Holberry. The family occupied a cottage on the estate of the Duke of Newcastle, for whom the father worked as a farm labourer. In his childhood Samuel acquired a rudimentary education at Sunday school and for a short time at a day school. This was cut short when he began work in a cotton mill at Gamston. In his later teens he was employed as a farm servant, but he soon grew discontented with the drudgery of the life. One of his brothers had joined the Army, and Samuel, an impressionable youth, was eager to follow his example: he made a false statement of his age and was enlisted in March 1832 in the Thirty-third Regiment of Foot at Doncaster. He spent three years in the Army, serving at Gosport, Woolwich, Northampton, and for a short time in Ireland. Part of his duty was the suppression of radical activities – whether working-class, trade unionist, or, if it was in Ireland, those of the Whiteboys and similar organisations, we do not know, but it was probably this duty which caused or assisted the development in Holberry of radical sympathies. He had been a member of the Orange Order during some part of his Army service, but left it early in 1835. Shortly afterwards, in April of the same year, he purchased his discharge from the Army with £20 borrowed from his parents and friends. While he was stationed at Northampton he had attended an evening school where perhaps something in the teaching had exposed to him the falseness of his youthful impressions of military life. At all events, after his discharge he returned home for a short stay, during which he destroyed all the letters he had written to his family while he was a soldier. His repudiation of the past was total.

In the summer of 1835 Holberry went to Sheffield. There he obtained work with a cooper, with whom he stayed for twelve months. He then worked with Messrs Baines & Company as a rectifying distiller for eighteen months, until he was laid off in the autumn of 1837. He spent the following ten months in London, employed by a distillery in Upper Thames Street. It was at this time that he became a Chartist; but nothing is known of his early political activity. At the request of his former employers, Messrs Baines, he returned to Sheffield in the summer of 1838 to resume work with them. In October he married Mary Cooper, an Attercliffe girl, whom he had known since he first came to Sheffield. According to her, it was in the winter of 1838 that he joined the Sheffield Chartists, then meeting as the Sheffield Working Men's Association.

Little is known of his activities during the following year. He did not appear as a platform speaker either at any of the public meetings leading up to the presentation of the National Petition in June 1839, or at those held later from June to August – when they were banned. But he was a prominent figure in the 'church-going' activities carried on from August to the end of October by the Sheffield Chartists after the ban: by assembling on Sundays at their Parish Church and crowding into it they asserted their continuing right to meet. And during these months mass 'silent' meetings and 'camp' meetings of a politico-religious nature increasingly characterised Chartist activity in South Yorkshire. At this time Holberry was a member of the Baptist Church, but it is difficult to estimate how far his religious beliefs influenced his actions. While some Yorkshire Chartists were engaged in these religious manifestations of 'moral force' Chartism, new leaders were emerging, men prepared to use armed force, traditionally the ultimate defence against political despotism. Among the foremost of these new men in Sheffield was Holberry. He was well equipped for leadership, a devoted adherent to the cause, an intelligent and literate young man and a capable debater. When he was laid off from work in November 1839 (because of a dispute between the partners of the firm), he became increasingly involved in revolutionary activism, stimulated by the events of the winter.

The Newport rising of 3-4 November and consequent concern for the fate of its leader, John Frost, provided a critical stimulus to action for the physical force party among Chartists throughout the country. Already its leaders were being driven to contemplate action by the intensified harassment of Chartists during these winter months. The Sheffield leaders were no exception. A raid on their Fig Tree Lane meeting room by the police in late November further impressed on them the class nature of this political repression. Together with like-minded groups in the West Riding and further afield, they became more and more involved in secret preparations for simultaneous risings, with the aims of obtaining the Charter and freeing the Welsh prisoners. Action was first planned for late December, but was postponed. Holberry travelled to meetings as delegate of the Sheffield Chartists, in December, and again in the first week of January 1840. This time he attended the secret meeting of delegates assembled at Dewsbury to make the final plans for simultaneous risings in the West Riding on the night of 11 January. In Sheffield, the military 'classes' of the Chartists were to fire the barracks and to take and hold as Chartist 'forts' the Town Hall and the Tontine Inn. After attending the meeting Holberry visited the North Midland towns as far south as Nottingham, informing Chartist groups of the arrangements; he travelled south with the delegate who was taking news of the plans to London, and he then returned to Sheffield to take part in the final preparations there.

On the evening of 11 January the Sheffield Chartists' plans were betrayed by James Allen, a Rotherham publican, who had become involved in them. The authorities were alerted, and only a partial turnout of the 'classes' took place that night. Holberry and his wife were arrested at midnight in their home at 19 Eyre Lane, where in the garret the police found both arms and incendiary devices. The latter were to have been used in the Chartists' ultimate contingency plan of firing the whole town ('Moscowing' was the term they used). Holberry, who was the author of this plan, was to have been responsible for implementing it if necessary. It was only at the moment of his arrest that his political creed was recorded for the historian. It was a very blunt statement. Asked by the arresting officer, who had just found a dagger on Holberry's person, 'Surely you would not take life?' Holberry replied, 'But I would, in defence of liberty and the Charter. Mind, I am no thief or robber, but I will fight for the Charter and will not rest until we have got it, and to that I have made up my mind.' He and his wife were taken to the Town Hall for questioning. Mary Holberry (who was expecting a child) refused to betray her husband, and was held for forty-eight hours, until for want of evidence against her she was released on the morning of Tuesday 14 January. That day Holberry with eight others was committed for trial and removed to York Castle under escort.

At the Yorkshire Spring Assizes which began on 5 March 1840, Holberry and four of his comrades, James Duffy, Thomas Booker, William Booker and William Wells, were charged with 'having unlawfully conspired and confederated with other persons at Sheffield, on the 12th January, 1840, to create a breach of the public peace, and with obtaining arms and other instruments for the purpose of more effectually accomplishing their object'. The case against them began to be heard on 16 March. The Attorney-General, Sir John Campbell, led for the prosecution and Sir Gregory Lewin for the defence. The defendants were found guilty and Holberry received the severest sentence of four years' imprisonment.

In Northallerton House of Correction where he was first confined, he experienced the brutality of class justice. He spent every day for the first four weeks on the treadmill. This was illegal, because he had been sentenced only to imprisonment; the penalty of hard labour was reserved for those who had been caught rioting. The authorities were well aware of this, but they turned a blind eye, as letters among the Treasury Solicitor's papers show. Moreover, the prison food was poor, and the prisoners suffered under the 'silent' system, which cut communication among them to a minimum. Communication from the outside world was also restricted; for three months Holberry heard from no one. His health deteriorated rapidly. On 30 January 1841 John Clayton, another Sheffield Chartist, who had been tried on the same day as Holberry, died in Northallerton gaol. This led to greater exertion by the Sheffield Chartists on behalf of Holberry and his remaining companions in the prison. In June petitions were sent to the Queen for their release or at least their removal to the county gaol. The Bookers and Duffy were freed, but it appears that the authorities were determined to make an example of Holberry, who was not released. His health was so bad, however – he was by this time suffering from advanced tuberculosis – that in September he was transferred to York Castle, where the conditions were less severe.

During the winter months he became steadily worse, and by the spring of 1842 he was close to death.

He was now allowed to write and receive letters. Some of those that he wrote were published in the *Northern Star* under the heading 'Voice from the Hell Hole' (*Northern Star*, 3 July, 14 Aug, 4 and 18 Sep 1841), and others appeared in the *Sheffield Mercury* (June 1842). From these letters his sufferings can be traced in intimate detail. In the last of them, dated 28 May 1842, he complains bitterly, 'York Castle is a queer place for a sick man. I wish I was back in Northallerton Hospital (hospital, mind) till I get better.' His friends were renewing their efforts: in May 1842 memorials from Sheffield, Barnsley, York, and from as far away as Brighton were forwarded to the Home Office. A month passed, however, before the authorities gave way. On 17 June Holberry was offered a conditional release; on 21 June, early in the morning, he died.

The Sheffield Chartists determined to make his funeral, arranged for 27 June, a public ceremony. In the main streets shops were shut as a mark of respect. Chartists appointed as stewards took over the maintenance of public order for the day. Tens of thousands witnessed the procession as it moved from the Coopers' cottage in Attercliffe where the body lay, and then back through the main streets of the town to the General Cemetery. The 'O'Connorite' contingent, men of the National Charter Association and women of the Female Charter Association, walked at the head, next to the hearse. They carried a black banner inscribed, 'Thou shalt do no murder', 'Clayton and Holberry martyrs to the People's Charter', 'Vengeance is mine, I will repay, saith the Lord'. They were followed by the moral force advocates, members of the Political Institute, a smaller group, better dressed, each wearing a black scarf. Their white banner carried texts like the others: 'Birks, Clayton and Holberry, Martyrs to the People's Charter', 'The Lord hateth the hands that shed innocent blood'. A huge crowd gathered in the cemetery to hear George Julian Harney's funeral oration. In an impassioned outburst he called upon the multitude to continue the struggle:

> Here, by the grave-side of the patriot; . . . swear, to unite in one countless moral phalanx, to put forth the giant strength which union will call into being . . . If ye do this and act upon your vow, . . . our children will rejoice that he died not in vain! but that from his ashes rose, phoenix-like, his dauntless spirit . . . [*Northern Star*, 2 July 1842, 5]

Reports from Sheffield printed in the *Northern Star* showed that Holberry's death (and Harney's oratory) had not been in vain: a revival of Chartism in Sheffield followed (*Northern Star*, 23 July, 6 and 13 Aug 1842).

The political actions carried out by Holberry during his short life were neither numerous nor important; but the interpretation of his death as a martyrdom and its incorporation into Chartist folklore gave his life and struggle significance in Chartist history. The legend was transmitted in lines such as these from J. M'Owen's poem, 'Father, who are the Chartists?':

> And they've sworn at a Holberry's grave, my child,
> That martyr so noble and brave, my child,
>> That come weal or come woe,
>> Still ONWARD they'll go
> Till Freedom be won for the slave, my child!

(Northern Star, 2 July 1844)

Mary Holberry remained widowed and childless for a few years – her son, Samuel John, had died while her husband was in prison and was buried with his father in Sheffield's General Cemetery. Later, she married a man named Pearson, by whom she had a son whom she christened Holberry. Holberry Pearson became a publican in Sheffield, and his son, Herbert (in his eighties in 1974) had worked in a number of different jobs, including the trade of silversmith.

Sources: (1) MSS: Home Office papers, HO 20/10 (Prisons correspondence), HO 40/51, 40/57 (Disturbances correspondence), HO 48/33 (Law Officers Reports and correspondence); Treasury Solicitor's papers, TS 11/813 (misc.), TS 11/814/2679 (misc.), TS 17816/2688 (Sheffield Treason, *Queen* v. *Holberry*): PRO; Letters sent to Holberry in York Castle: A.J. Peacock, York Educational Settlement. (2) Newspapers: *Northern Star, English Chartist Circular and Temperance Record*, nos 118-21 (these contain a series of biographical sketches based on interviews with his wife); *Sheffield Independent, Sheffield Iris* and *Sheffield Mercury*. (3) R.G. Gammage, *History of the Chartist Movement* (1854; 2nd ed. 1894, repr. with an Introduction by John Saville, New York, 1969); M. Hovell, *The Chartist Movement* (1918); A.R. Schoyen, *The Chartist Challenge* (1958); *Chartist Studies*, ed. A. Briggs (1959); A.J. Peacock, *Bradford Chartism* (York, 1969); *The Early Chartists*, ed. D. Thompson (1971); personal information: Herbert Pearson, Sheffield, son of Holberry Pearson.

JOHN BAXTER

See also: *George Julian HARNEY.

HOPKIN, Daniel (1886-1951)
LABOUR MP

Daniel Hopkin was born at Llantwit Major, near Cardiff, on 11 July 1886, the son of a farm labourer, David Hopkin, and his wife Ann (née Price). His father died in 1893 and his mother, the daughter of a Merthyr miner, supported the family of two boys and a girl by her earnings as cleaner of the Llantwit village school and by taking in washing. Later in life Hopkin said he had had the supreme advantage of a great mother. His first part-time job was in the fields when he was about seven. He also delivered newspapers and would read selections to those who could not read themselves. He was much encouraged by his headmaster, Mr D.J. Williams at the Llantwit village school where in 1900 he became a pupil teacher. He then won a two-year scholarship at Carmarthen Training College and, after qualifying, taught for a while at Blaengarw Council School. In October 1910 he won an exhibition to St Catherine's College, Cambridge, where he read history. While an undergraduate, in order to support his mother and sister who were living with him, he took on some private teaching.

In 1912, he became part-time tutor to the four sons of Dr Redcliffe Salaman, scientist and author of the classic *The History and Social Influence of the Potato* (1949). The Salaman family lived at Barley, fourteen miles from Cambridge and Hopkin travelled there daily by motor cycle. He took his BA in 1913 and an LLB the following year. He then moved to Barley as full-time tutor to the Salaman children, and formed a lasting friendship with the family. As Dr Myer Salaman, the eldest son recalls, 'he organised many new activities in the village – a debating society, football and hockey teams, tennis, boxing – in which he got all to join. It was from him I learned that people could and would co-operate, regardless of class or education, in response to the stimulus of an enthusiastic and truly kindly person' [personal letter, Apr 1976].

Hopkin remained with the Salaman family until he joined the Army shortly after the outbreak of the First World War. He served with the East Yorkshire Regiment in Gallipoli and in France, where in October 1916 he won the MC. He subsequently transferred as a major to the 39th Battalion, Royal Fusiliers (part of the 'Judeans' or Jewish Regiment), where he served with his friend Dr Redcliffe Salaman, who was the regimental MO, through Allenby's Palestine campaign of 1918. Salaman records in his letters home, published in 1920, that 'Hopkin is worth his weight in gold. He inspires the men with spirit and staying power, is cheerful at all times and a jolly fine commander' [*Palestine Reclaimed* pp. 61-2]. Hopkin had a continuing interest in Palestine for the rest of his life.

During his war service, he met in Cairo Edmée Viterbo, daughter of an Italian family settled there. She was a wealthy woman whose qualities of intellect and character were to be of great value to him in his future career. They were married in 1919 in London and returned to Cairo, where Hopkin worked for two years in an engineering firm owned by his brother-in-law. They then moved to San Remo where they bought a house with the intention of starting a school; but Hopkin had joined Gray's Inn in July 1919 and decided to make law his career. He returned to England and was called to the Bar in July 1924. He practised in London and on the South Wales circuit.

Hopkin then began to take an active interest in politics. In the years before the First World War he had already taken part in the labour movement: he joined a Christian Socialist organisation in 1912 – although which one is not known, and he later considered himself an agnostic – and he became a member of the Fabian Society in 1913. In 1928 he was narrowly defeated when he stood as a Labour candidate at a by-election for Carmarthen – then a Liberal stronghold – and at the general election in the following year he won the seat. His maiden speech argued for a national development board for Wales and for the greater involvement of the Welsh people in the processes of governmental decision-making. His political opinions were radical but middle-of-the-road, and during his career in the Commons he concentrated especially upon the problems of hill-farmers and of the mining community. Most of his own relatives were working miners, and his concern was often vividly expressed, as in the following passage:

> In 1928, there were 1,009 fatal accidents, and 161,790 non-fatal accidents. Let us try to visualise what this means. It means a procession 35 miles long, four abreast and one and a half yards apart; at every 14 yards you have an ambulance, and at every 60 yards you have a hearse [*Hansard*, 6 Nov 1929].

Hopkin lost his seat in 1931, but regained it in 1935, and continued as member for Carmarthen until he resigned in 1941. He was very much a constituency man and held regular monthly 'surgeries' for the discussion of constituents' problems, before such activities were generally undertaken by MPs. He pioneered the cause of leasehold enfranchisement by introducing a private member's bill, but it was many years before such a measure reached the statute book. He often spoke on Egypt – whose nationalist aspiration he supported – and Palestine. His support for a Jewish homeland was unequivocal.

At the outbreak of the Second World War Hopkin rejoined the Army as a major in the Pioneer Corps; then in 1941 he left the Army and Parliament to become a Metropolitan magistrate, first at Old Street, later at North London and finally at Marlborough Street. At one period he was chairman of the Magistrates' Association of Great Britain. He collapsed while sitting in court on 30 August 1951 and died the same day in hospital. He was cremated at Putney Vale and his ashes were buried in his mother's grave in the Baptist churchyard at Llantwit Major. He was survived by his wife, who died in 1965, and a son and a daughter, both of whom became barristers. The son served initially in the office of the Director of Public Prosecutions and later became a magistrate at his father's old Court in North London. The daughter joined the legal staff of the Inland Revenue. Hopkin left an estate valued at £6727.

Daniel Hopkin was of medium height and stocky build, with handsome, strong features and fair complexion, twinkling grey eyes and thick wavy hair. He had great physical energy and an infectious vitality, and could inspire a deep and lasting affection in people which transcended the usual political divisions. Professor Glyn Daniel, archaeologist and Fellow of St John's College, Cambridge, whose father was headmaster of the Llantwit village school in the 1920s, wrote to the editors of the *DLB* about Hopkin:

> My father's family came from just north of Carmarthen, and were his constituents, and it was intensely interesting to see the members of my family, who were typical Welsh Liberals, voting Labour when he became a Labour candidate, because of their devotion to him as a person. He had a great personality and, as you know, an enormous following in Wales [2 Mar 1976].

Some thirty-five years after he ceased to represent Carmarthen, and twenty-five years after his death, the memory of Daniel Hopkin in 1976 was still green in his old constituency.

Sources: R.N. Salaman, *Palestine Reclaimed: letters from a Jewish officer in Palestine* [1920]; *Western Mail*, 3 July 1924; *Liverpool Echo*, 7 July 1924; *Labour Who's Who* (1927); *Hansard*, 23 July and 6 Nov 1929, 5 Dec 1935, 24 Mar 1936, and 29 June 1937; *Kelly* (1932); *Western Mail*, 24 Jan 1941; *Evening Standard*, 30 Aug 1951; *WWW* (1951-60); biographical information: T.A.K. Elliott, CMG; Gray's Inn Library, London; St Catherine's College, Cambridge; personal information: Mrs Ann Boyd, London, daughter; Professor Glyn E. Daniel, Cambridge; David Owen, MBE, JP, Carmarthen; Dr M.H. Salaman, London. Obit. *Times* and *Western Mail*, 31 Aug 1951.

JOYCE BELLAMY
ANN HOLT

HOSKIN, John (1862-1935)
MINERS' LEADER

John Hoskin was born on 17 February 1862 at Upper Moor, Brampton near Chesterfield, the son of John Hoskin, a coalminer, and his wife Ann (née Gill). When he was very young the family moved to Barrow Hill, Staveley, where they lived in a house owned by a colliery company. Hoskin's father worked at the 'Do Well' Colliery and was an ardent trade unionist. In 1867 the family was evicted from their home after Hoskin's father was victimised because of his trade union activities. As a result, John Hoskin together with his brothers and sisters and his parents, walked to Yorkshire, pushing a dray which carried their belongings. Hoskin's father found work at Aldwarke Colliery, but was fatally injured in an accident at the pit in 1874. He was survived by his widow and nine children, the eldest of whom was fifteen and a half years old and the youngest only six weeks old. Hoskin's mother received no compensation: the West Riding Miners' Permanent Relief Fund Society was not established until 1876 and there was no State compensation; neither did the law in practice make colliery owners legally responsible for their own negligence, even if this could be proved; so for several years afterwards the family endured extreme poverty.

Immediately after the death of his father Hoskin started work at Roundwood Colliery and soon joined the South Yorkshire Miners' Association. From 1889 to 1904 he was secretary of the Roundwood Branch of the Yorkshire Miners' Association and had the distinction of never being opposed in elections for the position. In 1904 he was elected general treasurer of the Association. Coincidentally his predecessor, John Frith, had also been a miner at Roundwood Colliery and secretary of the local branch. During the 1890s Hoskin was frequently elected as branch delegate to the YMA Council, and in 1895 he was Roundwood Branch representative at local panel meetings (a panel being a group of branches). Later on he became a member of Rawmarsh Urban District Council, a position he held for several years. In 1897 he was appointed checkweighman at Roundwood Pit.

By the late 1890s he was well known and respected and as a result, in 1900, he was elected to serve on the Joint Boards (South and West Yorkshire) of owners' and miners' representatives. He held the position without interruption for twenty-four years. During the famous Denaby and Cadeby Conspiracy Case, which came in the wake of the Taff Vale decision, Hoskin acted as treasurer to the Relief Fund, for which there was collected in Yorkshire and in other counties a sum of £23,840. The YMA had been sued for conspiracy for £125,000, and 720 families had been evicted from their homes. After a long legal battle the YMA, at this time the third largest trade union in Britain, won its case against the Denaby and Cadeby Colliery Company, with costs, in 1905. About the year 1910 Hoskin was elected a member of the English Federation Conciliation Board, and in 1914 was chosen as treasurer of the workmen's side of the Board. In

1915, after the death of John Dixon, Hoskin was appointed general financial secretary of the YMA, without a ballot vote, because he received a majority of branch votes over the other candidates. Two years later he was chosen to represent the Association on the executive committee of the Miners' Federation of Great Britain; he continued to hold that position until July 1920, when on account of increasing pressure of work from the YMA financial department, he withdrew from nomination. In the 1921 lockout Hoskin was faced with enormous financial problems, but he efficiently carried out the complex administration involved in dealing with hundreds of private tradesmen and several co-operative societies. Hundreds of thousands of vouchers had to be scrutinised and the amounts they stood for discharged. Eventually he was forced to mortgage the Miners' Hall and Offices, but a debt of over £400,000 was still outstanding. One commentator observed: 'that debt harassed him, he could not have been more concerned if it had been his personal liability. He was determined that it should be repaid at the earliest possible moment.' He successfully urged that contributions should be increased by 1 s 6 d per week, and the debt was quickly cleared.

John Hoskin did not take an active part in the political life of the YMA, nor did he play a prominent role in the general affairs of the Association. He was respected as an industrious YMA official and a gifted accountant, admired for the clarity of his financial statements.

He had married the daughter of a Rawmarsh miner in 1890. His wife died at Easter 1923, and he had retired from his trade union activities by the beginning of the following year. He died on 20 January 1935 and his funeral took place at Rawmarsh. He left £5271 in his will.

Sources: *Yorkshire Mine Workers' Quarterly J.*, 30 June 1923; YMA, *Minutes* (1924) and (1935); H. Bunting, 'The Romance of the YMA', *Sheffield Mail*, 22 June 1926; R. Page Arnot, *The Miners: years of struggle* (1953); *Sheffield Telegraph*, 6 May 1955. OBIT. *Barnsley Chronicle*, 26 Jan 1935.

ROBERT G. NEVILLE

See also: John DIXON (1850-1914); †John FRITH.

JACKSON, Thomas Alfred (1879-1955)
WRITER, LECTURER AND COMMUNIST

Thomas Alfred Jackson was born in Tysoe Street, Clerkenwell, on 21 August 1879. His father, Thomas Blackwell Jackson, was a compositor with radical views. It was a family of craftsmen. TAJ (as he liked to be called) was the great-great-grandson of a blacksmith and armourer, his great-grandfather was a locksmith, his paternal grandfather a watchmaker, and his maternal grandfather a highly-skilled gun and tool-maker and die-sinker. This family tradition reinforced the trade unionism which his father preached to him as 'the very basis and foundation of all virtue'. As the only boy in a family of four children, Tommy was often entertained by his father with stories even more beguiling than those conjured up by the pictures in the family Bible, and the Cassell's *Illustrated History of England*, which were the all-engrossing study of the shy little boy until, at the age of nearly five, he learned to read. His father described, for instance, the great Reform demonstration in 1867 when a huge crowd wrenched out the railings of Hyde Park; a bomb-explosion outside Clerkenwell Gaol which had been attributed to Fenians, but which had not shaken his father's support for the struggle for Irish Home Rule; and the memorable day when Thomas Blackwell and his fellow 'comps' took time from work to file past the open grave in Westminster Abbey in which Charles Dickens had been buried that June morning in 1870. Sunday afternoon walks directed their steps to Dickens's London; and while mending the children's boots on a Saturday afternoon, Tommy's father often talked radical politics, and names such as Gladstone, Parnell and Bradlaugh were soon familiar ones. The seeds of TAJ's involvement with history, literature and Ireland's cause were all sown in these very early days.

Born with severe astigmatism and not provided with spectacles until he went to school, the little boy found lively games hazardous. This, together with his very early devotion to books and to serious reading, rendered him quite unable to comply with his houseproud and most unscholarly mother's constant pleading to him to 'be like other people'.

From the age of seven to thirteen TAJ attended the Duncombe Road Board School in Upper Holloway. The staff here were keen trade unionists, and though conditions were hopelessly inadequate, he had the benefit of an intelligent class teacher whose interest in general science enabled him to extend his scope beyond history and literature. Despite the size of the class and the lack of equipment, Tommy received a grounding not only in mechanics, physics and chemistry but even in what were still the revolutionary theories of Darwin. The curriculum also included Greek mythology, and opened up an avenue which was to lead TAJ to Frazer and 'the immensities and infinitudes of *The Golden Bough*'.

Leaving school at thirteen and a half, TAJ was six months too young to start an indentured apprenticeship; his first job was as a reading-boy at a large printing works. Some 120 compositors and thirty to forty apprentices were employed here, and TAJ's father was a foreman. Young Tommy had to read aloud from hand-written manuscripts, sitting in a little cubby-hole called a 'reading closet'. It took him some time to get acclimatised to the stench accumulating through the ill-ventilated floors. But the drabness was alleviated by the brightly-coloured posters put up by young Socialist apprentices, and the tradition of craft-solidarity at which compositors excel was a new form of education. Yet at first the lad was not ready to read the Socialist literature, such as *Merrie England*, which was proffered by his older work-mates. Devilry and pranks were indeed almost a duty, to avoid the stigma of being the goody-goody son of a foreman; and he had a natural bent for fun and against 'piety'.

Still, reading for pleasure was so far the main purpose of his life, and there was now at last the opportunity to start building up a library of his own. On his errands of delivery of proofs all over London, Tommy was able to stop at the second-hand book stalls, where the classics might be bought for ha'pence and pence.

> Books became for me what in a measure they still remain: an absolute necessity of life, often more necessary than food or clothes. To get books I have gone hungry. Often my dinner money went for books, found in Old Booksellers' Row. My breakfast and tea bread and butter (or better still, dripping) has, judiciously rationed, kept me going . . . As I reached the age of responsibility, I counted it a sinful waste of book-money to buy clothes other than second-hand. To get the time to read books I have neglected all sorts of duties, suffering in consequence deserved reproof. My book-hunger amounted to a mania. If I have regained a measure of sanity and a more balanced attitude, it is due more than anything to Socialism, and the need to *do* things, to translate Socialist convictions into Socialist effort [MS. Memoirs].

The transition from 'an orgy of book-worming to an organised dedication to a cause' was begun when TAJ found a copy of George Henry Lewes's,. *A Biographical History of Philosophy*. 'I devoured it like a novel . . . thereafter I wallowed in philosophy as I had previously in poetry, in translations from the classics, in English literature . . . I was acquiring a grasp of the universe . . . as a unity in multiplicity in perpetual process of self-transformation. I was, though I would not have known what you meant if you had told me so, preparing myself for Marx.'

By the time he reached his twenty-first birthday, TAJ had finished his apprenticeship and was learning to be a Socialist. 'For me, as for most of my generation, the adoption of Socialism meant a cruel wrench, a breaking of all personal ties, an alienation of friends and relations, the setting up of a barrier of division between oneself and one's parents, and all that they had hoped we would become.' The early anguish soon gave way to an ever stronger conviction as he joined the Social Democratic Federation in 1900 and read what books they had available. It was not easy to get them, but as he enriched his library one by one with the works of Marx and Engels, the spark burst into flame. Of his first introduction to the *Communist Manifesto*, TAJ wrote: 'when I came to read it I all but wept with delight. It gave me just what I had been groping towards for years . . . here, in essence, was a sound working concept of that becoming-process of human society which would in its further development make possible and ensure the coming of Socialism and Communism.'

In his early twenties this shy, withdrawn boy was able to master the art of public speaking. Later to become a highly successful orator, he was 'literally ill – a nervous wreck – for a fortnight' after speaking for less than five minutes as chairman of an open-air meeting. 'My second attempt, some time later, was made from a light waggonette . . . So much did my knees knock together, you couldn't hear what I said for the creaking of the springs . . . At my third attempt I drove away eight hundred people as fast as if a hose-pipe had been turned on them.' This seemed to the poor lad to be final, but he continued to attend the regular open-air meetings addressed by his Socialist friends. One of these, a discerning Irishman, coerced TAJ into agreeing to take the chair for him. The Irishman then slipped away, leaving the young man to struggle on until his return. This time the initial shyness was absorbed in his subject and a youthful eagerness to share his enthusiasm for the Cause. He forgot himself and remembered his audience, and from then on it was merely a question of conscious polishing of technique; but an audience always remained for him a gathering of real live individuals. It was not long before he was revelling in opposition at meetings, and he never failed to rout hecklers.

In his mid-twenties Jackson met and later married Katharine Sarah Hawkins, Socialist and suffragette. They suffered many deprivations, including the death, probably from malnutrition, of their first child Eleanor Michel (named after a daughter of Marx and a heroine of the Paris Commune, Louise Michel).

When, on the dramatic date of January the first 1900, TAJ emerged from his apprenticeship, he was not offered the customary opportunity to stay on as a journeyman at the same printing-works. He had already been blacklisted as a hobnobber with Socialists and the leader of any organised demonstration among the apprentices. As his reputation grew as a street-corner orator and a seller of Socialist pamphlets, it became more and more difficult for him to obtain work in the printing trade. Of these lean years in his late twenties TAJ wrote, 'We tasted bitter poverty and extremes of destitution, and all this concurrently with the feverish excitements and exaltations of incessant propaganda . . . I have more than once spoken at six meetings on a Sunday . . . We used to stage all-day meetings in one or other of the London parks . . . They were run on the relay system, and if, as happened, one's "relief" failed to turn up, there was nothing for it but to keep straight on . . . One day I was speaking for four hours before relief came.'

In the summer of 1909 TAJ accepted a month's engagement as a lecturer for the Bristol ILP. This was extended, and followed by lectures in Newport, Mon., and the South Wales valleys, so that he was able to keep his wife and his year-old second daughter in Newport until the summer of 1911. Dissension then arose out of his too militant Marxism and too outspoken atheism. He left Newport and returned to London for long enough to settle his wife (who was expecting another baby) at his parents' house, and went to try his luck in the north. His first job on arrival in Leeds was as lecturer for the National Secular Society. 'But here, as usual, I ran into trouble. In the ILP in South Wales there had been acrimonious complaints that I habitually paraded my atheism on the Socialist platform. Now I found some of the old Bradlaughites complaining that I habitually waved the Red Flag over the Free-thought platform . . . I accepted the inevitable, and took over the conduct of the agitation in Leeds as a free-lancer responsible to nobody but myself and my audience.'

For the next couple of years before the outbreak of war in 1914, TAJ spoke from the plinth of the Queen Victoria statue in Leeds Town Hall Square, every night in the week and twice on Sundays: the weather had to be very bad indeed for him to stop for lack of support. And to the fullest extent of his powers he reciprocated the fidelity and devotion of his audiences. With the aid of a small library of Marxist works, including the three volumes of *Capital*, he prepared new matter conscientiously, and won a reputation for hardly ever repeating himself. The pennies which his faithful followers threw into a hat at the end of each meeting were sufficient, if only barely so, to keep him, his wife and two daughters above starvation level and with a roof over their heads, until the outbreak of war compelled him to take a job, and limited his open-air speaking to Sundays. TAJ in Leeds is still vividly remembered:

> On certain weekday nights as well as every Sunday, and on the occasion of any special demonstration, Socialist speakers would address considerable crowds which always gathered and which, after the speeches, would break-up into small arguing groups. The speaker whom I most admired was Tommy (TA) Jackson. He was an engineer [sic] by trade; a self taught Marxist, who would learnedly expound the Marxian theories night after night. Thin, with a sallow complexion and a black lock of hair falling over his forehead like Jimmy Maxton, he was a master of his subject, with a line of satire and invective to match. Later, when I read Marx, I felt I really knew it all from his lectures [Lipman MS].

Two long-remembered pre-war public meetings were, in 1912, on Anti-Semitism, and in 1913 on Irish Nationalism. Later in 1913 James Connolly visited Leeds. He told TAJ: 'When we get through this trouble, I must try to get you to Dublin to give the boys a few lectures on Marxism.' In 1916, shortly before the Easter Rising, his old comrade Con Lehane wrote to TAJ: 'Our friend James in Dublin has some work we might do together.' TAJ wrote later: 'It may be fanciful in me, but I can never shake off the feeling that, but for a mere chance, I might have finished in the G.P.O. Dublin in Easter Week 1916.' When Connolly was executed, TAJ denounced the murder in a blazing fury from an emergency platform in Leeds. In his autobiography TAJ criticises himself; 'I was as good as insane with grief and rage . . . all the same, a really good political leader will never let himself get worked up into a state like that.'

Shocked and bewildered by the readiness of leading Socialists all over Europe to support the war, and in the absence of any collectively thrashed-out line, TAJ could only in his propaganda speak out against jingoism and in favour of the international solidarity of the working class. He was soon arrested and charged with sedition under the Defence of the Realm Act, under which John Maclean had already received a sentence of three years. TAJ was extremely lucky to have his case dismissed by an enlightened magistrate.

For the rest of the war TAJ had a job as a storekeeper in a small engineering works owned by a highly idiosyncratic pacifist. When the time came for the call-up of his age group, TAJ put in an appeal on the grounds of physical condition (his eyes and feet), domestic, mental and moral hardship. The chairman of the Tribunal, having listened to TAJ's arguments, agreed that this was a clear case of conscientious objection and granted him a certificate of exemption on condition that he continued to do work of national importance.

Although he was never conscripted into the Army, he was virtually conscripted into the Socialist Labour Party, on any occasion when they needed a first-class partisan for an important debate. The Revolution of March 1917 aroused intense excitement in Leeds, many of whose Jewish citizens were of Russian extraction. TAJ and his fellow SLP members defended the right of the Russian people to make a revolution, but in the absence of information their propaganda had to be confined to the general basic anti-war issue. Then came the thunderclap of the Bolshevik Revolution. The reaction of the capitalist press to this gave TAJ a clue, and when one newspaper quoted from a revolutionary manifesto in the very words of the *Communist Manifesto* of 1848, his hopes were confirmed: as the months went by the tone of his anti-war propaganda underwent an exhilarating change as it became clearer that the Bolsheviks were not to be defeated.

In the autumn of 1919 the National Council of Labour Colleges offered TAJ the post of full-time lecturer for their north-eastern district. This was certainly a job more suited to his talents, but for the family it meant a removal from a relatively warm back-to-back brick terrace-house to an isolated wooden bungalow in a remote field overlooking the rocky coast and a North Sea frequently lashed by bitter north-east gales. At times the cold was so intense that

Katharine would faint from inadequate circulation in an undernourished body. Of frail build and always delicate health, Katharine suffered privations from which she was never to recover: five years later she fell seriously ill, undermined both in nerves and physique by the excessive efforts she had made since her early 'teens, first for the cause of Socialism alone, and then to meet the ever-daunting incompatibility of providing adequately for the welfare of the family while at the same time battling by her husband's side for the cause which was equally hers.

For TAJ also there was much physical exposure involved in travelling without a car in all weathers. He made long journeys by rail and bus to mining villages all over the Northumbrian and Durham coalfield. These often meant long waits in driving rain or snow, or miles of walking against the gale-force winds. But for him there was rich compensation at the end of the road, in the meetings with the miners. He wrote later, 'to say that I came to love them is to be guilty of a gross understatement.' The war had given a great impetus to the idea of study-classes, and in them it became far easier to propagate the concept of class struggle and revolution than it had been by soap-box agitation.

In July 1920 the Communist Party of Great Britain was founded. TAJ was to have been present at the inaugural meeting, but was detained in the north. He soon started a branch in Newcastle which at once did a great deal of useful work. As delegate from this branch TAJ attended in January 1921 a Communist Unity Conference, at which he was invited to help in editing the first British Communist Party journal, a weekly called the *Communist*. This invitation was soon backed by an urgent call from Party headquarters.

For the next eight years TAJ was employed by the Communist Party, first as editor or sub-editor of the official party journals, then as an agitator-propagandist and finally on the left-wing *Sunday Worker*. From early 1924 to the end of 1929 he was a member of the Party's central committee, with special duties in the field of education and propaganda.

Of his early years as a foundation member of the Party, TAJ wrote: 'We had to do the best we could . . . given our all-too-insufficient preparation for so stupendous a task . . . I pulled my own Marxism to pieces, examined every piece closely and critically in the light of objective practice . . . helped by the works of Lenin as they appeared in English . . .' Of the contribution of Lenin to his personal studies he writes:

> I have a vivid memory of walking out of the optician's shop wearing my very first pair of spectacles, a little before my eighth birthday . . . It had all the effect of a miraculous revelation: I could see things for the first time . . . All that had been before a blurred, rather muddled vagueness, now took on specific shape and perspective, and became therefore gloriously available for confident practice. It was a world made new. And thus likewise it was with me when I was first made able to see Marx and Engels through the spectacles provided by Lenin and Leninism.

During his years as a journalist TAJ paid visits abroad, to Ireland and to Russia; first to Dublin in the autumn of 1921, to make contacts for an article in the *Communist*. Dublin was then rife with armoured cars and soldiery. He saw the hollow, smoke-blackened shell of the G.P.O., pitted with bullets. He was taken on a Sunday morning to inspect a parade of the Irish Citizen Army. The Colonel Commandant was the Countess Constance Markievicz; she was the first woman to be elected to the British Parliament but did not take her seat. He was also introduced to Charlotte Despard and Maud Gonne-MacBride. A few months later he was present as a reporter at the meeting of the Dail which led to the final ratification of the Partition. As editor of the *Communist*, he returned to London with a heavy heart, and published the news of the launching of the Irish Free State with the headline 'The Royal Irish Republic'. In 1923 TAJ attended an enlarged Plenum of the CPSU, travelling to Moscow with Harry Pollitt. The sight of the Red Flag flying over the Kremlin was a high peak in his life; the only sadness of this visit being that Lenin was forbidden by his doctors to see the British delegation, despite his expressed wish to meet them.

During the General Strike of 1926 TAJ's work was exclusively editorial. The weekly paper was to be turned for the duration into a daily, the *Workers' Daily*. TAJ prepared the first issue, to appear on the first day of the strike, and after weathering the panic of the printers it duly appeared; but the entire printing, except for a few copies which escaped in London, was captured by police stationed for the purpose all over the country. The TUC leaders then put a ban on all newspaper-printing, even of bulletins supporting the strike. So TAJ and his colleagues decided to issue a typewritten bulletin run off duplicators set up in as many secret places as possible. These had more success and supplies were distributed outside London, in spite of many police raids; but eventually TAJ was arrested and joined the other executive committee members in Wandsworth Prison. He was able to profit in a literary way from this enforced leisure, rereading Gibbon's *Decline and Fall of the Roman Empire* and discovering, belatedly, the charms of Jane Austen, whose novels he strained his eyes to finish in the fading light of the cell, and whose works were his first purchase on being released.

His next Party job was in the Agitation and Propaganda Department. He spent much time in the coalfields, endeavouring to put new heart into the miners, who were suffering from their recent betrayal. With the crushing of the miners' resistance in 1926 came a cruel setback to the whole working-class movement in Britain, and some eighty per cent. of CP members were themselves unemployed and battling against disillusionment. TAJ was racked with personal as well as political anguish. The Party being unable to pay its workers a living wage, the Jacksons accumulated arrears of rent for their flat, which had since 1923 been a hideout for political refugees from all over the world. One morning in the autumn of 1925 the bailiffs moved in, and the Jackson girls came home from school to find their home gone. Their father's precious books, their own childish treasures, and the furniture of the first comfortable home their mother had known since her childhood, were all confiscated and never seen by them again. For many months the family survived under appalling conditions which led to the death, early in 1927, of Katharine Jackson.

Returning to journalism, TAJ joined Walter Holmes on the *Sunday Worker*, a well-produced and highly successful newspaper which ceased publication at the end of 1929. He lost his place on the executive after finding it impossible to vote for the costly project of running a daily newspaper if it meant, as it must, abandoning at a stroke all the goodwill built up around the Sunday paper with its wide cultural scope. In later years TAJ admitted that he had made a mistake in voting against the launching of the *Daily Worker* at the end of 1929. He had been wrong, not in his estimate of the financial cost of the venture, but in his estimate of the power of the working class to meet this. A few months before his death he wrote 'this lack of faith on my part does sadden me, and that all the more because it is the type of error to which I am not prone: my political faith is rooted in a belief in the infinite creative potentiality of the "great, faithful, splendid, common people". And for once I allowed my faith to falter. I have tried to make up for it since.' (This last sentence is a reference to his articles and regular features in the *Daily Worker*). So far as we know, he never differed from the Party again.

His own account, however, from which the quotation above is taken, tells only a small part of the story of 1929. TAJ was always a man of independent ideas. In the debates which followed the reorganisation of the CPGB in 1923-4 he had taken a very critical attitude towards the political leadership (*Communist Rev.*, Apr 1924); and in the late 1920s the bitter controversies over the Comintern's new line found TAJ on the side of the majority of the executive committee and against the minority who supported the Comintern's policies. In an article in the *Communist Review* for February 1929 headed 'Self-Criticism' TAJ vigorously accused the 'ultra-lefts' of heresy hunting within the Party. In turn he was singled out for attack by the famous *Closed Letter* dated 27 February 1929 which the Presidium of the Communist International sent to the British Communist Party (repr. as App. G in L.J. Macfarlane (1966), 308-19). 'We must put a stop to the philistine twaddle about self-criticism,' wrote the C.I., 'a good example of which is the already mentioned article by Comrade Jackson in the *Communist Review*.' TAJ's opposition to the closing down of the *Sunday Worker* was not simply based upon scepticism regarding the viability of a daily paper; it was much more his principled objection to the sectarianism which the Comintern's new line represented, and which now became official policy of the CPGB.

In 1927 TAJ had married Lydia Packman, who was then working in the Labour Research Department. On the closing down of the *Sunday Worker* at the end of 1929 his wife urged him to take this opportunity of turning his attention to less ephemeral writing. To facilitate this they went to live in Sussex, but it was not until 1936 that his first book was published. The full title was *Dialectics. The Logic of Marxism and its Critics: an essay in exploration*. This essay, a volume of 648 pages, started life as a review article on Fred Casey's *Method in Thinking*. Experts in Moscow recommended that this essay should be expanded to a full-scale exposition, a task in which TAJ relied throughout on the advice and support of Dona Torr. The book proved far more popular than he had expected. It was timely, and something new for England, where Marxists had hitherto considered themselves as lagging behind the continent in political theory. However, TAJ himself said, 'My *Dialectics* is as full of faults as a dog is of fleas . . . but with all its faults it did embody the results of the reading of a lifetime.'

His next book was published the following year, 1937. *Charles Dickens: the progress of a radical* was occasioned by a special request from the Editor of *International Literature*, who wanted 'a nice long article' on the much-debated question whether Dickens strengthened or weakened his Radical views as he developed his art. The article soon, of course, grew into a book in which TAJ maintained that Dickens's Radicalism grew steadily until finally he became sceptical about Radicalism itself, and so ripe for further progress. This view was distorted by George Orwell, who attacked the book, into a suggestion that TAJ had actually presented Dickens as a Marxist. This TAJ categorically disclaimed, but the damage was done, and many bourgeois critics took their cue from Orwell, with the result that *Dickens* did not have the success in England that it might otherwise have had. TAJ's own criticism was: 'For a new edition I would wish to expand the analysis of Dickens' first-period novels . . . also the contemporary historical background could be elaborated.'

Later in 1937 Lawrence and Wishart published his *Trials of British Freedom*. These reports were based on articles originally drafted for a series in the *Sunday Worker*. The subjects range chronologically from Wilkes to the Trial of the Twelve Communists in 1925. TAJ commented later: 'For a new edition I would wish to expand considerably the historical-political background to the trials of John Wilkes, and I would draw attention to the notable respect in which my treatment of Chartism – especially in its Third Period – conflicts sharply with the conventional histories of Chartism which have most of them been written by Fabians with a strong anti-revolutionary and anti-proletarian bias.'

Next came a pamphlet issued by the Communist Party in July 1945. *Socialism: what? why? how?* was based on a series of lectures he had given in various parts of the country during the war, and was written up at the request of many from his audiences who desired a more permanent record. The work reveals TAJ's devotion to Engels and his admiration for Engels's expository technique. Before this booklet appeared, TAJ had completed the Marxist history of Ireland that he had projected and in part attempted as far back as 1904. Although finally achieved early in 1944, it was published, by the Cobbett Press, only in 1946. The title of what TAJ always referred to as his magnum opus was *Ireland Her Own: an outline history of the Irish struggle for national freedom and independence*.

Of *Ireland Her Own* TAJ wrote: 'Dear though my *Dialectics* must be to me as my "firstborn", it could not be quite the same to me as the book which should have been my first, but with which I had to toil and struggle, repeatedly baffled but always returning for a new endeavour – for the major part of forty years.' From the original draft compiled in 1904, TAJ worked when opportunity allowed it. 'I worked at the job of building a living body around the skeleton . . . I found that my grasp of Marxist theory was insufficient for the task . . . later . . . the opposite difficulty arose . . . my knowledge of the history of Ireland was far too superficial and far too little based on original sources. . . . This process of bound and rebound went on and on. When in 1943-4 I completed the book, it was my twelfth attempt.' But this moment of triumph was marred. 'When at last I took to the publishers the MS. complete in 240,000 words – as had been agreed upon – they broke to me the cruel news that, it being wartime, they could only find the paper for a book of half that length. It was all the more of a blow because I had already excluded from my MS everything that did not seem essential. . . . There was no easy way out. . . . Line by line, sentence by sentence, I re-wrote it . . . down to the space prescribed.' The history received high praise in Ireland. Of individual tributes perhaps the most moving to its author was a letter from an old Fenian of ninety-three, a former close associate of O'Donovan Rossa, who wrote that he 'had never expected to see the reading of his lifetime packed into a single volume. . . . You have done it, with nothing forgotten and nothing mis-stated.'

In 1943, before his *Ireland* was ready for the press, TAJ suffered personal loss in the unexpected death, after a minor operation, of his second wife. His daughter Vivien – who had had difficulty in visiting her father during his second marriage because of the hostility of her step-mother – was now able to be with him at this time, and helped him to recover from the shock not only of his wife's death but also of finding, when her will was read, that she had left the house to her sister, so that TAJ was rendered homeless at the age of sixty-four. But he was immediately offered a refuge by a neighbour, the painter Anne Day (formerly Anne Verner-Jeffreys), who put at his disposal her best room, which was large enough to contain all his books, and treated him as if she were a daughter, with all possible gentle care and attention; he lived there for ten years. When he had completed the final preparations for the publication of his magnum opus, *Ireland*, TAJ decided to embark on a fresh course of propaganda work. During the years 1930 to 1943, while living the 'retired' life prescribed for him by Lydia, he had done his best to confine his activities to writing. But it was not in his very warm and outgoing nature to be a recluse, nor would the militant working class allow him to remain one. Wherever he was, they claimed him for their own, and so it was, even in quiet Sussex. Within forty-eight hours of their arrival in Three Bridges, T.A. Jackson's name and repute were circulating among the trade unionists of this small railway-based community; and he had not paid many visits to the local co-operative stores before he had been nominated and elected to the management and education committees and had been asked to deliver a series of lectures. During the whole period of his intensive literary work he averaged one lecture a month locally. At one point he was offered a post as official lecturer for the NCLC, but this he refused, since it was made clear that if he accepted the job he would be expected to give up his journalistic connection with the *Daily Worker*, to which he was regularly contributing reviews and articles. Throughout the thirteen-year period, TAJ was able to carry on useful propaganda work and constantly tried to find fresh ways of stating the Communist case. He was in fact representing his Co-op. at an NCLC Conference when Hitler launched his attack on the Soviet Union. Soon after a highly-successful local 'Help Russia' week, whose organisation had been prompted by TAJ, he was able to widen his scope and be once again employed by Party headquarters. It was arranged that he would cover the country by districts, staying several weeks in each. This would enable the smaller branches to have the benefit of an experienced speaker without being involved in the heavy expense of railway fares. From the beginning of 1944 until the end of 1949 (from the ages of sixty-three to seventy) he visited every district as lecturer in Communist Theory for the education department of the Communist Party. It meant being away from home for eight or nine months each year. He visited Belfast and Dublin as well as the Scottish Highlands and the mining villages of South Wales. It was a great joy to him to return to places and people he had known in earlier days. Often he was greeted by young people who told him that their parents had urged them to come and listen to TAJ. Veteran Socialists in extreme old age turned out to remind him of old struggles.

The last five years of his life (1950-5) were spent largely in reading and writing. He published two more books. The first, *Old Friends to keep* (1950), was a collection of essays, revised versions of *Daily Worker* articles on the classic English novelists. He added an introductory essay on the Marxist approach to literature. In 1953 appeared what was intended to be the first part of a two-volume autobiography, entitled *Solo Trumpet*. This short book was the much-compressed narrative of his life story until 1921. Part II, which owing to publisher's difficulties never appeared, would no doubt have proved interesting to a wider public. TAJ had arranged it in quite a different way from Part I. His recollections were drawn together under a dozen subject-headings, so that the author's views on the major interests of his life are given full scope without the danger of an exhaustingly lengthy narrative. It also had the advantage of being readable like a series of essays, from which the reader might take his pick. The first essay was 'designed to emphasise the great historical significance of the founding of the Communist Party. . . . The concluding essay is recommended to all those non-members of the Party who will . . . see how duty and inclination have combined to make me take for myself the motto which Karl Marx took from Lucretius [*sic*, for Terence] "I am a man, and nothing human is alien to me."' The title of this final section was 'All The Fun Going'. After dealing with athletics and sport, he ends with a description of his delight in travelling round the British Isles:

> In the Isle of Man you can see a sight you might travel the world over and not beat – the sight of the sun setting behind Ireland, so that for several seconds the Mountains of Mourne stand out sharp-edged in solid silhouette. . . . It is with a full and deeply-rooted sense of the infinite beauty and magnificence of these Islands and their cities – along with much else of an opposite kind that we must and will some day amend – that I react to the politics and propaganda of those who will, if we let them, reduce this lovely land to a blighted and blasted wilderness totally uninhabitable to man . . . so long as I have strength and the ability to direct a pen, or the power to use my voice, I pledge myself to use those capacities to the uttermost to defeat and destroy the potential enemies and would-be destroyers of the entire human race. . . . According to my lights I have served the cause I believed in, regardless of consequences, and have used every faculty I possessed, to the full, in the service of that cause.

His fighting spirit and will to live enabled him to survive for over six months a major operation for cancer. During this time he lay in bed, rereading his dearest favourites among the classics of English literature. He died at the home of his daughter Vivien and her husband A.L. Morton, in Clare, Suffolk, where he had lived these last months of his life, surrounded by his beloved books, on 18 August 1955, three days before his seventy-sixth birthday. The general secretary of the Communist Party, Harry Pollitt, together with the editor of the *Daily Worker*, Johnny Campbell, and many other comrades escorted the coffin, draped in the banner of the central committee, through the ancient village of Clare. At the graveside, Harry Pollitt spoke a deeply felt tribute; a week-old baby and a veteran of over eighty were present. It was a manifestation TAJ would have found profoundly moving and inspiriting. His daughters (to whom he had always been a most affectionate and enlightened father) had had carved upon the gravestone: 'I believe in the eventual triumph of the Good Old Cause.' A flood of small contributions in his honour to the Fighting Fund of the *Daily Worker* soon totalled over £200. The majority of the tributes stressed his rare combination of wit and gaiety with profound study and dedication, and a supreme ability to speak simply.

Writings: 'Three Centuries: Jacobin '93; Communard '71; Bolshevik '17, *Socialist*, 18 Mar 1920 [repr. *Plebs 13* (Feb 1921) 39-43]; (with R.W. Postgate), 'Four Years: the story of the Russian Revolution', *Communist 2*, no. 66 (Nov 1921) 5-14; *What is the British Empire to you?* [1922?] P; *The British Empire* (1922) 35 pp.; 'The Party Conference', *Communist Rev.* (Apr 1924) 537-41; 'The British Empire', *Plebs 16* (May 1924) 171-6; 'Revolutionary Significance of the General Election', *Communist Rev.* (Dec 1924) 387-94; 'The Ides of March', *Plebs 16* (Mar 1924) 95-9; 'The Greatest Utopian', ibid. *17* (July 1925) 273-5; 'The American Civil War and British Labour', ibid. *18* (May 1926) 171-7; 'Self-Criticism', *Communist Rev.* (Feb 1929) 132-6; 'Essays in Censorship', *Lab. Mon. 11* (Apr 1929) 233-9; 'The Evolution of War', *Plebs 22* (Aug 1930) 171-4; 'Japan and World Revolution', ibid. *24* (June 1932) 133-8; 'The

Historical Roots of Irish Nationalism', ibid. *24* (Aug 1932) 175-81; 'Marx and Engels on Ireland', *Lab. Mon. 14* (Oct-Dec 1932) 643-8, 710-15, 769-75; *The History and Working-Class Associations and Traditions of Clerkenwell Green* (Marx House [1933?]); 'Marx himself', *Plebs 25* (Mar 1933) 51-6; (with J.M. Hay), 'A Discussion of Dialectical Materialism', *Lab. Mon. 15* (Aug 1933) 505-11; 'The "Underground" route to Socialism', *Plebs 25* (Sep 1933) 199-201; 'Underground and Overground. A Rejoinder', ibid. *25* (Dec 1933) 274-6; 'Walter Scott – who made the Novel a Necessity', ibid. *26* (Jan 1934) 4-7; 'William Morris – Artist-Craftsman, Socialist and Man', ibid. *26* (Apr 1934) 76-82; *A Great Socialist, Frederick Engels* (NCLC, 1935) 24 pp.; *The Jubilee – and How* [1935?] 30 pp.; *Dialectics. The Logic of Marxism, and its Critics: an essay in exploration* (1936); 'Marx and Shakespeare', *Int. Lit.* no. 2 (1936) 75-97; 'For a British Popular Front', *Plebs 29* (Jan 1937) 28-30; 'In Defence of a British Popular Front', ibid. *29* (Apr 1937) 86-7; 'The Monarchy Fetish', *Lab. Mon. 19* (May 1937) 283-7; 'Towards a Marxist Philosophy of Art', ibid. *19* (Aug 1937) 512-15; (edited with others), *Ralph Fox, a Writer in Arms* (1937); *Charles Dickens: the progress of a radical* (1937, NY, 1938); 'Communism, Religion and Morals' in *The Mind in Chains: Socialism and the cultural revolution,* ed. C. Day Lewis (1937) 205-33; (with W.J. Denman), *Fifty Years* [Story of Crawley and Ifield Co-operative Society Ltd.] (1938) 28 pp.; edited D. Guest, *A Textbook of Dialectical Materialism* (NY, 1939); 'History: Marxian and otherwise', *Plebs 31* (Sep 1939) 230-4; 'Literature and the struggle for Socialism', ibid. *31* (Nov 1939) 276-8; *Trials of British Freedom* (1940, rev. ed. 1945) [originally published in *Sunday Worker* (1928-9)]; 'The Study of Literature', *Plebs 32* (Apr 1940) 90-3; 'Marx, Hegel and Progress', ibid. *33* (Feb 1941) 30-1; 'The Study of Literature: The Art of Propaganda I', ibid. *33* (June 1941) 106-8; 'The Study of Literature: The Art of Propaganda II', ibid. *33* (July 1941) 131-2; (with J. Braunthal and W.J. Colyer), 'Socialism and Morality again' ibid. *34* (Aug 1941) 152-5; 'Some Flowers for Marx's grave', ibid. *35* (May 1943) 52-4; 'Marx and Determinism', ibid. *36* (Oct 1944) 124-6; *Socialism: what? why? how?* (1945; translated into Dutch, Amsterdam, 1946); Edited with an Introduction, M. Thorez et al., *Essays on the French Revolution* (1945); 'Marxism a Guide to Action' [Review], *Lab. Mon. 27* (May 1945) 160; *Ireland Her Own: an outline history of the Irish struggle for national freedom and independence* (1946, NY, 1947); 'Humanity vindicated', *Lab. Mon. 31* (Nov 1949) 348-51; *Old Friends to keep: studies of English novels and novelists* (1950); *Solo Trumpet. Some Memories of Socialist Agitation and Propaganda* (1953); 'Francois Rabelais', *Lab. Mon. 35* (May 1953) 215-20.

Sources: (1) MSS: T.A. Jackson's unpublished memoirs and other papers in the possession of his daughter, Mrs V. Morton, Clare, Suffolk; Lipman MS.: DLB Coll. (2) Other: *Communist,* 25 Mar 1922; H. Pollitt, *Serving my Time: an apprenticeship to politics* (1940); W. Rust, *The Inside Story of the Daily Worker: 10 years of working-class journalism* [1940] 23 pp.; idem, *Daily Worker reborn* (1943) 16 pp.; idem, *Voice of the People* [The Story of the Daily Worker] [1944] 16 pp.; J. Redman, *The Communist Party and the Labour Left 1925-1929* with Introduction by John Saville (Reasoner Pamphlets, Hull, 1957); H.M. Pelling, *The British Communist Party: a historical profile* (1958); L.J. Macfarlane, *The British Communist Party: its origin and development until 1929* (1966); A. Marreco, *The Rebel Countess: the life and times of Constance Markievicz* (1967); H.R. Vernon, 'The Socialist Labour Party and the Working-Class Movement on the Clyde, 1903-21' (Leeds MPhil., 1968); J. Klugmann, *History of the Communist Party of Great Britain 1: 1919-24* (1968), *2: 1925-7* (1969); W. Kendall, *The Revolutionary Movement in Britain 1900-21: the origins of British Communism* (1969); personal knowledge. OBIT. *Lab. Mon. 37* (Sep 1955).

VIVIEN MORTON
JOHN SAVILLE

See also: *J.R. (Johnny) CAMPBELL; *Harry POLLITT.

JENKINS, John Hogan (1852-1936)
TRADE UNIONIST, ALDERMAN AND LABOUR MP

John Jenkins was born on 27 May 1852, in Prospect Place, Pembroke Dock, the son of Thomas Night Jenkins, a shipwright in the Government Dockyards and a local Wesleyan preacher, and his wife Lettice (née Hogan). After an elementary school education John Jenkins tried to get employment in the Government Dockyards but was judged to be below the necessary weight. He was determined, however, to follow the trade of his father and grandfather, and became apprenticed in the locality as a shipwright. At the age of sixteen, owing to the bankruptcy of his employers, he moved to Cardiff, where he completed his indentures with the shipbuilding firm of John Batchelor, to whom, the family recalls, he had offered a Bible when asked for a testimonial. Like his father, Jenkins was a Wesleyan Methodist. He was a founder of the Lord's Day Observance Society in Cardiff, and in the evenings throughout his apprenticeship, and for long afterwards, he taught in the town's Ragged School. For fifteen years he was its superintendent. His political philosophy owed much to Christian Socialism, with its roots in the traditions of radicalism and non-conformity.

When he became a journeyman shipwright, Jenkins formed a society for the trade in Cardiff, and within a year became president, a post he held for ten years. When this group, the Cardiff Shipwrights' Society, became part of the Bristol Channel District of the Associated Shipwrights' Society in 1893, he was elected local representative and subsequently technical adviser. He represented the District at various conferences, and in 1895 he presided over the TUC, which met that year in Cardiff.

Jenkins was a member of the local Marine Board from its establishment, and for four years was president of the Cardiff Trades Council. In addition to his work for his own union, he assisted in the formation of branches of six other trade unions: the Labourers' Union, the Seamen's and Firemen's Union, the Dockers' Union, the Bakers' Society, the Waggon and Carriage Workers' Union, and the Shop Assistants' Union. He was often called upon to arbitrate between them. He was also actively interested in local government; he was first elected to Cardiff Town Council in 1890 as a member for the Grangetown ward. He was made a JP in 1893, subsequently became an alderman, and from 1903 to 1904 served as mayor of the town. His was the last mayoralty before Cardiff became a city.

In the 1906 general election Jenkins was elected Labour MP for the borough of Chatham and Gillingham, in which constituency he had spent two-and-a-half years working as Labour's prospective candidate. His election platform covered a wide range of subjects, and included firm commitments to support the further devolution of powers to countries within the British Isles, and to Free Trade, which he believed would be beneficial to the shipbuilding industry. Jenkins spoke frequently on the latter policy in particular, and this may have been instrumental in gaining for him the declared support of the Liberal Party, who were not themselves putting up a candidate. He also stressed his total opposition to the 1902 Education Act, and wanted to see an educational system which was unsectarian, completely free, and administered by popularly elected bodies. The main issue in the election contest, however, was undoubtedly the future prospects of the Royal Dockyards. An increasing number of men were being discharged by the Admiralty, and there was growing concern in the area about unemployment. As a shipwright, Jenkins had particular knowledge of the issues involved and pledged himself to press in Parliament for the revitalisation and expansion of the construction yards.

During his years in the House of Commons Jenkins, who was a tall austere-looking man, made the grievances of the dockyard workers on the subject of reorganisation his chief responsibility. He supported in particular the demands of the lowest-paid workers in the State shipyards, insisting that full trade union rates should be paid and adequate compensation schemes implemented. He also urged that a fairer system of distributing work should be brought about, and expressed concern at the lack of dry and floating dock accommodation, especially for vessels of the *Dreadnought* type. In addition he wanted to see a tightening-up in the qualifications of tradesmen, for instance carpenters working on board ship, and a clearer separation of their jobs and their duties as seamen.

In January 1910 Jenkins lost the seat of Chatham to a Conservative lawyer, G.F. Hohler, after a closely fought contest, during which Margaret Bondfield, among others, visited Chatham to address meetings. The issues before the electorate were substantially those of the previous election, and the result was something of a surprise to the local Labour movement. After his defeat Jenkins lived in Cardiff, where he remained an alderman and a JP and served on the Board of Guardians; he was also a hospital governor. From 1910 to 1920 he was technical adviser for the West and South West Coasts/Bristol Channel Shipwrights and he continued to be an active member of the Shipwrights' Society until 1925.

Jenkins married Sarah Dalin Williams, probably in 1875, in the chapel in Loudon Square, then the centre of Cardiff's dockland. She was the daughter of a Cardiff shipwright who worked in the yards along the river Taff and in her younger days was a professional singer. She is remembered as being a small, quiet and dignified woman. Of her eleven children, nine survived. She predeceased her husband in 1918. For the last years of his life, from 1920, Jenkins lived with his daughter Winnie and her family in Romilly Road, Cardiff. Another daughter, Beatrice, was the wife of David John Boon, who served on the Barry Town Council for forty-eight years, as councillor, alderman and mayor. He was a JP and also received the freedom of the town.

John Jenkins died at his home on 9 December 1936. The funeral service was held there and he was buried near his wife in Heath Cemetery. He left no estate, having distributed it among his family in the last years of his life. He was survived by three sons and six daughters, all of whom were musical. Of the sons, Thomas became manager of a large insurance company in Cardiff; Morley was chief clerk for the Diamond Shipyard and the third son, Wesley, became, at the age of twenty-three, the youngest chargeman-shipwright in the Bristol Channel area. Brian Jenkins, Wesley's son recalls that 'J.H. Jenkins became, indeed, a prophet without honour. How I wish I had known him more!' [personal letter, 11 July 1976].

Writings: 'How I got on', *Pearson's Weekly*, 12 Apr 1906.

Sources: *Reformers' Year Book* (1905) [photograph]; *Chatham, Rochester and Gillingham Observer*, 9 and 16 Dec 1905, 6, 13, 20 Jan and 17 Feb 1906; *Chatham, Rochester and Gillingham News*, 6 and 13 Jan 1906, 6, 8, 15, 22 Jan 1910; *Hansard* (1906-10); *Dod* (1909); *Pall Mall Gazette 'extra'* (Jan 1911); *WWW* (1929-40); F. Bealey and H. Pelling, *Labour and Politics 1900-1906* (1958); K.O. Morgan, *Wales in British Politics 1868-1922* (Cardiff, 1963; 2nd ed. 1970); personal information: R.W. Boon, Barry, grandson; J.B. Jenkins, Blundell's School, Tiverton, grandson; C.W. Jenkins, Cardiff, son; Dr C.C. Lewis, Cardiff, grandson. OBIT. *Western Mail*, 10 Dec 1936; *Cardiff Times*, 12 Dec 1936.

BARBARA NIELD

See also: †Alexander WILKIE.

JUPP, Arthur Edward (1906-73)
CO-OPERATOR

Arthur Edward Jupp was born on 29 December 1906 at Stratford, in East London, the son of William George Jupp, a railway engineer, and Elizabeth Ann Jupp (née Green). Both parents were active in the labour and co-operative movements: his father was a branch official in the National Union of Railwaymen and a member of the local Labour Party; his mother was a member of the Women's Co-operative Guild. Growing up in this environment, Arthur Jupp became a convinced Socialist and co-operator. After early education at local council schools, he won a scholarship to go to a secondary school. He left in 1922 at the age of fifteen, but later won a scholarship to the Co-operative College, Manchester, which he attended from 1929 to 1930 and where he gained the Co-operative Secretaries' Diploma.

At the age of sixteen he joined the British Federation of Co-operative Youth and became joint national secretary in 1927 serving for five years. The Federation was formed from local co-operative youth associations called Comrades' Circles; it is described by Bonner as 'a lively, vigorous but perhaps somewhat aggressively independent body' which 'undoubtedly assisted in producing co-operative leaders' (p.186-7). He was the delegate of the London Co-operative Comrades' Circles at the World Youth Peace Congress, held at Eerde, Overijssel, Holland, in August 1928.

His working career began when he was employed, after leaving school, as a clerk in the office of a wholesale furrier in the City of London. After his period at the Co-operative College he went into the central office of the London Society as a clerk, and in 1938 became its assistant education officer, education having been an interest of his since his days with the BFCY. This interest continued throughout the Second World War, when he served for four years in the Army Education Corps.

On his return from the war, Arthur Jupp became education secretary to the London Society. In 1952 he was appointed secretary of the Co-operative Productive Federation in Leicester and in 1960 joined the Co-operative Union in Manchester to become dry goods trades officer and secretary to the Co-operative Dry Goods Trade Association, a position he held until his early retirement in 1970.

Jupp served on many committees, including the central executive of the Co-operative Union and the Distributive Industry Training Board. In 1960 he was president of the Co-operative Congress held at Blackpool. In his public speeches to Congress he stressed the danger of losing sight of co-operative ideals in the necessary tasks of buying, producing and selling; equally dangerous was the reliance on capital from outside the movement and on trading with outside customers to the prejudice of the traditional democratic participation by members. He regarded the sustaining of co-operative ideals as the best hope for the future strength of the movement.

In 1936 Arthur Jupp had married Katherine Keeble and there were two children of the marriage, a son Alan Jupp, MA, ACIS, a computer consultant, and a daughter, Kathryn Jupp, MB, BS, a doctor. Arthur Jupp was a prolific writer in co-operative movement publications and was willing to work for local Labour Party candidates in both local and general elections. After a period of ill health he died at his Thorpe Bay home on 9 March 1973 at the age of sixty-six. His funeral was at the local crematorium and he was survived by his wife and family. He left effects valued at £13,357.

Writings: Co-operative pamphlets and articles in co-operative journals, in particular, the *Co-operators' Year Book,* 1954-60.

Sources: *Co-op. Congress Report* (1929); G.D.H. Cole *A Century of Co-operation* (Manchester [1945]); *Reynolds News,* 2 Mar 1952; *Co-op. Productive Rev.* (Mar 1952) 61; *Co-op. Rev.* (June 1954) 132-3; *Co-op. Congress Report* (1960); *Co-op. Rev.* (Jan and July 1960); A. Bonner, *British Co-operation* (Manchester, 1961; rev. ed., 1970); personal information: the late H.F. Bing, Loughborough; R. Garratt, and A.R. Perkins, Co-op. Union, Manchester; Mrs K. Jupp, Thorpe Bay, widow.

ANN HOLT

See also: †Arnold BONNER, for Retail Co-operation 1945-70; †William Henry BROWN, for Retail Co-operation 1900-45; †Fred HALL, for Co-operative Education.

LOWERY, Robert (1809-63)

CHARTIST AND LECTURER

Lowery was born on 14 October 1809 at North Shields, the son of a sailor and eldest of four boys. His mother had been born in North Shields and his father had moved there from Newcastle. Lowery's education started in a dame school in North Shields, and he was then sent to a master who taught him writing, arithmetic and grammar. When he was about five years of age his father moved to Banff and sailed from there as mate on a whaling ship. For several years Lowery went to school in Banff, and then his parents moved to Peterhead where his father continued to sail in the Greenland whale fishery ships. Lowery attended school in Peterhead but his father became ill and the family moved back to the north of England, to Sheriff Hill, near Gateshead. Lowery was nine years old at the time. As his father could work no longer, Lowery's formal education then ended, and he began working at a pit-head job were he earned 5 s a week, while his mother opened a school for girls. On his father's death, when Lowery was thirteen, his mother returned to North Shields and, according to his own wish, had her son apprenticed as a sailor. But this career lasted for only two years, because an illness, which began at sea, lamed Lowery for life. While convalescing he read widely, especially in theology and romantic literature; his favourite poet was Burns. His next apprenticeship, to a Newcastle tailor, gave him further opportunities for self-improvement. He married at eighteen years of age and happily, and had two daughters before he was twenty-one. His wife encouraged him in self-improvement, and the couple sometimes bought books in place of food.

Lowery entered political life in his early twenties through a political discussion-group. He trained himself in public speaking, and became secretary to the North Shields Political Union. By 1834 he was on Newcastle Town Moor addressing a meeting of 100,000 working men. He was active in breaking down privilege within Newcastle tailoring unions, whereby the older members monopolised available work, but as a leading trade unionist – he was secretary to the Tailors' Branch of the Consolidated Trades' Union – he was dismissed by his employers. For a time he was reduced to carrying out slop work, but although sometimes near starvation, he persisted with his reading, and began distributing unstamped radical newspapers. From 1835-8 he lived at South Shields. First he worked for James Mather, a radical wine and spirit merchant who encouraged him to publish his first, and fiercely anti-Anglican, pamphlet. *State Churches* (1837) is unoriginal, somewhat stagey in its language, and stuffed with literary, theological and historical references. For a few months Lowery kept his own public-house; but he regretted it, and in 1838 moved to a Newcastle post which involved promoting the sales of the radical *Northern Liberator*. By 1838 he was prominent enough to gain election as Newcastle delegate to the Chartists' Palace Yard meeting of 17 September, at which he stressed that Newcastle Chartists were ready to defend themselves against the Government by force if necessary. His (often repeated) attacks on writers who betrayed the working people were rebutted in *The Times* the following morning. Lowery attended the Kersal Moor meeting with O'Connor and Stephens, lectured in Carlisle and elsewhere in England, and then moved on to lecture in Scotland with Abram Duncan.

At this time, Lowery had an emotional and high-flown oratorical style. His early speeches displayed a radical optimism; but at the same time they voiced his deep distress at the suffering he saw around him. He took pains with his public speaking, and his deep interest in the art of communication still pervades the autobiography he wrote many years later. 'In person', said the *Charter* on 28 April 1839, Lowery '. . . is short, and is slightly built; his face, albeit it is somewhat stern, is expressive of intelligence and benevolence.' Lowery was courageous, sane and independent-minded, less earnest than some of the London Chartists, and at times almost mischievous in his taunting and mimicking of authority, though he was less colourful than the northern Chartist leaders.

He received his political education from middle-class radicals – from the star orators of the Northern Political Union like Doubleday and Charles Attwood, from his Primitive Methodist master-tailor at Newcastle, and from his radical employer James Mather. His radicalism owed much to his strong sense of history, to his belief in lost rights, and in a golden age of proletarian prosperity which had existed at some unspecified point in the past. He thought that the Reformation had weakened social welfare provision but had liberated the spirit of inquiry from Popish authoritarianism. He felt that the Anglican Church should never have been set up, and his sympathies lay entirely with puritans and covenanters. 'The spirit which brought the first Charles to the block was not yet extinct', he told a Tolpuddle protest-meeting in 1834. The American revolution is more prominent in his speeches than the French, and his autobiography gives G.J. Harney very short shrift. Recent memories of Tory repression at Peterloo, and of Whig betrayal after 1832 convinced him that the working classes must set up for themselves in politics. He was intensely proud of his class, which he thought was becoming more self-reliant and harder to deceive. 'We are now born again', he declared at Carlisle in 1838; working men were as moral as any other class, and were beginning to lose their internal differences. They were also becoming conscious of their power, which had only to be displayed for the oppressive political system to collapse of its own accord. 'It is said that England is great and glorious', he declared, 'but who made her so? The working classes.'

Lowery attributed the 'unnatural state' of society in the 1830s to a corrupt, pension-bound, central government: to a 'profligate money system, to London-based financial manipulators and to effete political parties.' 'What was the use of industry', he asked, 'if a man could not maintain himself and his family in comfort?' Yet his speeches hardly mentioned the factory owners, and he had little knowledge of the Chartist heartland in the manufacturing areas of the Midlands, Lancashire and Yorkshire. His route to the better life lay through franchise extension, which by bringing working men into the political system would purge government of its extravagance and excessive power. An expanded electorate would win free trade, reduce taxes, eliminate the national debt and abolish the corn laws. But Lowery's moralistic and anti-aristocratic diagnosis made no allowance for the unprecedented nature of the problems faced by early-Victorian governments, nor for the primitive administrative machinery at their disposal; and his libertarian policies hardly accelerated governments' emancipation from dependence on social and economic theories which were ill-suited for curing the evils of an urban and industrial society.

Such was the man who was elected, at Christmas in 1838, as a Newcastle delegate (with Harney and Dr John Taylor) to the Chartist Convention. He arrived in London with a reputation for violent language and physical-force views, but his actions were in fact more moderate, and the *Charter* of 28 April 1839 described him as 'hitting the happy medium between senseless violence and hesitating timidity.' Enthusiastic northern audiences pushed him occasionally into extravagant language, but much of his oratory was cautiously phrased and designed to warn the Government against encroaching further on popular rights. The people should use physical force only in self-defence, he said, when moral force had failed in protecting their rights. On the two occasions when Lowery decisively influenced Chartist policy, he can be found among the moderates. During the Frost rising, he strongly opposed physical force, which he felt could only harm the working classes.

The Chartist Convention sent Lowery and Duncan as missionaries to rouse Cornwall, a politically backward area. They were obstructed by employers, religious revivalists, clergymen, teetotalers, magistrates and Methodists, and after holding meetings in several places, they returned to London. Lowery's next mission was to Dublin, where he was strongly opposed by O'Connellites; it was an unsuccessful visit, but educated him still further in the size of the task the radicals had set themselves. In the Convention during the summer of 1839, he tried to damp down exaggerated estimates of popular readiness for a national holiday, and by August believed that any attempt at a general strike would fail. He refused to co-operate in plans for a Welsh rising, and published a pamphlet recommending a system of exclusive dealing which would strengthen working-class unity, help redress economic grievances, and make other classes aware of working-class power. He took up bookselling in Newcastle for a short time before lecturing again with Duncan on Chartism in Scotland; this helps to explain how he escaped arrest in these months. He always preferred Scottish audiences, because of the Scots' strong historical sense and their deeply-felt religious sensibilities. He attended the secret second session of the Chartist Convention in London as representative for Dundee and Forfar, hoping to restrain the extremists. His autobiography provides our only inside account of it, but during its debates from 19 December 1839 to 8 January 1840, Lowery contented himself with keeping a wary eye on the firebrand Beniowski and 'with standing mostly by the fireside flinging in a word or two of objection and advice when I had an opportunity.' When the Convention broke up, he returned to Newcastle.

At this point, three influences combined to draw Lowery into more gradual courses – an illness, Urquhartism and teetotalism. His illness in winter 1839-40 induced a religious experience which encouraged political quietism, and Urquhartite aid during this personal crisis inclined him towards their doctrines. In the autumn of 1840 he was sent by the Urquhart group to Paris to assure Frenchmen that British working men did not support Palmerston's Russian *entente*. Lowery was strongly attracted by Urquhart, whose 'power of attaching men of different classes and opinions to his views . . . was amazing.' At the same time, then, as government prosecutions exposed Chartist weaknesses, middle-class offers of political and personal help encouraged Lowery into new strategies. He had always wanted the middle and working classes to join together in assaulting aristocratic values, but he was now readier to encourage working men into attracting allies by making concessions.

On returning from Paris, he showed at the Leeds Parliamentary Reform Association's meeting in January 1841 that when attacked by middle-class radicals or, as he put it, by 'men pluming themselves upon their station in society', he could still forcibly assert his dignity and independence as a working man. Yet he was drifting further apart from O'Connor, to whom he had never in any case been closely attached. In January and February 1841, he gave lectures in Scotland based on Lovett and Collins's *Chartism: a new organisation of the people* (1840), and when O'Connor failed to pay the promised fee for reports of them Lowery protested strongly in the correspondence columns of the *Northern Star*. A signed supporter of Lovett's 'New Move', Lowery refused to retract when pressed by the O'Connorites. Though he did not attack O'Connor, he doubted O'Connor's capacity for leading a political agitation. His move, about this time, from extremist Newcastle to the more moderate Edinburgh probably accelerated his withdrawal from O'Connorite Chartism. He delighted in embarrassing the Edinburgh Whigs with his radical activities, and stood as radical candidate at the 1841 general election at both Edinburgh and Aberdeen. He scorned both political parties, and though victorious at the Edinburgh show of hands, was defeated at the poll.

So far, Lowery had been unaffected by the temperance movement, whose doctrines he misunderstood and even disliked. But at this stage, some Aberdeen teetotalers induced him to take the pledge. He had always opposed drunkenness, but had previously regarded teetotalers as attacking symptoms rather than causes. His life was henceforward linked with Scottish teetotalism. He signed Sturge's Complete Suffrage declaration, and refused to recant. At the April 1842 Complete Suffrage Union conference, he deplored Chartist obstruction of other radical movements, and spoke of the CSU as 'so just and necessary in itself, and so promising in its commencement.' He was an active committee-man at the Chartist convention of 1842 – seeking new ways of promoting the cause, restraining internal squabbles, and heading off any recurrence of the mistakes which had been made in 1839. At first he admitted that the name Chartist should be retained, but by the winter of 1842 his revisionism had made him unpopular with some Edinburgh Chartists, who disputed his election as their delegate to the December CSU conference. His recognition that O'Connorite Chartism was in danger of entering a political blind alley aroused a clannish and sectarian Chartist conservatism against him. He kept silent at the second Complete Suffrage conference, and attended no further Chartist conventions. He did not immediately abandon his Edinburgh Chartist connexions, but henceforward he became increasingly attached, as a paid lecturer or missionary, to socio-religious organisations.

He was never as prominent in the teetotal as in the Chartist movement. For this reason, and because his autobiography stops at 1841, his later career is relatively obscure. In 1845 he was keeping a temperance hotel in Aberdeen, and in 1846 he lectured for the Scottish Temperance League. In 1846-7 he publicly deplored the fact that during the Irish famine, grain was still being frittered away in distilleries and breweries. In 1848 he lectured for the Central Temperance Association, and was appointed first secretary to Lovett's Peoples' League. In 1849 he praised the freehold land movement, and recommended 'a fair day's wages for a fair day's work', but also stressed the even greater importance of wise personal expenditure. In 1851-2 he lectured for temperance organisations in Yorkshire and Norfolk, and then in 1852 went as domestic missionary to West Bromwich. In 1854 he went on a Scottish temperance tour, and at a London Temperance League conference in 1855 strongly upheld Sunday closing of public houses as a working man's cause. Between 15 April 1856 and 30 May 1857, he anonymously published his well-balanced, reflective, self-critical, surprisingly detached, eminently readable and at times brilliantly descriptive 80,000-word autobiography in the *Weekly Record of the Temperance Movement*, unofficial organ of the moderate and Quaker-dominated National Temperance League. The autobiography's occasional vagueness and reticence, its periodic irrelevances and its abrupt conclusion by no means outweigh its great merits, though it has been little used by historians of Chartism. The same good-humoured and unpretentious Lowery of the 1830s is still there in the autobiography, and as romantic as ever; he could seldom resist an opportunity for enthusing over historic localities and dramatic scenery which, be believed, deeply influenced the personality of those who lived in them.

But Lowery the autobiographer differs interestingly from Lowery the Chartist. His language is less aggressive and stagey, his mood is somewhat nostalgic for the lost enthusiasms of youth, and on some issues his ideas have changed. Whereas in the 1830s he had flirted with Owenism, by the 1850s he decisively rejected it, though less peremptorily than did Lovett in 1876. His earlier suspicions of the sabbatarian and temperance movements vanished. And his emphasis lay heavily on removing social evils through individual moral reform rather than through political action. These changes can be attributed partly to his greater age, partly to his experiences between 1839 and 1841, and partly to the fact that after 1841 he was no longer being pushed into extremism by eager Chartist audiences. Urquhart and his own illness had driven home the lessons he was already learning in 1840-1 from the Chartist defeats of 1839. 'Hitherto I had simply applied my mind to forms of government and popular rights, thinking that if these were attained improvement would be at once achieved', Lowery writes: but Urquhart 'turned my mind to the fact that all law was dead unless its spirit was in the people...'. Furthermore by 1856 Lowery was far more closely acquainted with the personalities and attitudes of religious organisations. One senses no strain, in the autobiography, between Lowery and his teetotal readership, for he had come to share the teetotalers' aspirations and methods. Lowery himself emphasises one further factor which altered his political strategy: the fact that social class relationships had been transformed between the 1830s and the 1850s. There was a new spirit of social responsibility abroad among aristocracy, middle classes and Anglican clergy. Lowery's aim was now to push this beneficial change in social class relationships still further, by explaining and justifying the working classes to their superiors, and by encouraging working men to develop their respectability and political maturity by learning from his own mistakes.

The scale of Lowery's political shift should not be exaggerated nor did social ambition ever lead him to forsake his class. In 1856-7, as in the 1830s, Lowery was proud to be a working man. His autobiographical tone, despite its self-criticism, is not apologetic: he stoutly defends the integrity and intelligence of working-class leaders, shows how extremism grew out of appalling social conditions, and strongly condemns the 1834 Poor Law Amendment Act. Lowery's ideas had not changed very much. In the 1830s, despite his dalliance with Owenism, he had never been a disciple of O'Brien, and had never attacked the political economy which he read so avidly. In the 1830s his links with the Grand National Consolidated Trades' Union were not founded upon the belief that trade unions should be weapons of class solidarity against their employers. He had used the concept of the general union only to subvert the exclusiveness of the

Newcastle tailors, and was quite prepared to take on slop work when it suited him. In the 1850s he still shared an Owenite belief in the influence of environment on human character. In the 1830s he had never repudiated Christianity, and had warmly supported the dissenters. His dissenting allegiance persisted into the 1850s, but his autobiography shows no liking for insistence upon total depravity, for exclusive concentration on the next world, for the concept of an avenging Old Testament deity, for religious obscurantism or hysterical revivalism. His enthusiasm for respectability, self-improvement, sobriety and providence runs throughout his career. Even as a Chartist he had attacked pot-house politicians and (at the 1842 Convention) recommended abstinence from intoxicating drinks.

By the 1850s his motive for urging abstinence was less directly political, and the prominence he gave to it in his social analysis suggests that his ideas had narrowed. During the ten months ending July 1858 that he worked as a temperance missionary on the Hull dockside, he preached that drink was the chief source of its demoralisation. 'Religion, obedience to the law of God, becoming godly or godlike, living righteously', he said 'is the only way in which men can be happy in this world.' In their minute books temperance organisations praised his temperance work, and when rheumatism and a failing voice ended his lecturing career in 1862, they raised a public subscription for his support. In September 1862 he emigrated to Canada to join his married daughter there. But his bad health persisted, and he died at Woodstock on 4 August 1863.

Writings: *State Churches destructive of Christianity and subversive of the Liberties of Man* (1837) 38 pp.; 'The Collier Boy' [poem], *Charter*, 23 June 1839; *Address to the Fathers and Mothers, Sons and Daughters of the Working Classes on the System of Exclusive Dealing and the Formation of Joint Stock Provision Companies* (Newcastle, 1839); thirty-three autobiographical articles in *Weekly Record of the Temperance Movement* (1856-7).

Sources: (1) MSS: Add. MSS, 34245A ff. 17, 18, 148, 169, 178 and 34245B ff. 121-2, 129-31, 153-4, 165, 167, 169, 175: BM; Urquhart MSS: Balliol Coll., Oxford; National Temperance League Minutes, 4 Mar 1859: National Temperance League Archives, Sheffield. (2) Newspapers and reports: *Newcastle Press*, 7 Dec 1833, 4 Jan, 27 Mar, 24 May 1834; *Newcastle Chronicle*, 1834; *Northern Liberator*, 1837-40; *Sun*, 18 Sep 1838; *Times*, 18 Sep 1838; *Carlisle Journal*, 1838-9; *Falmouth Express and Colonial Journal*, 23 Mar 1839; *True Scotsman*, Mar-Apr 1839; *Charter*, 1839 (especially the memoir in number for 28 Apr 1839); *Northern Star*, 1839-44; *Leeds Times*, 23 Jan 1841; *Leeds Mercury*, 23 Jan 1841; *Scotsman*, July 1841; *Nonconformist*, 13 Apr, 14 Dec 1842; *Scottish Temperance Rev.*, 1845-7; *British League*, May 1847; *National Temperance Advocate*, Nov 1849; *British Temperance Advocate*, 1 Aug 1851, p.87, 1 Mar 1852; *Abstainers Journal*, Oct-Dec 1854; *Proceedings at the Annual Conference of the . . . London Temperance League . . . Sept 11th, 1855* (1855) p.17; *Weekly Record of the Temperance Movement*, 1856-63. (3) Secondary: R.G. Gammage, *History of the Chartist Movement* (1894; repr. with an Introduction by J. Saville, New York, 1969); G. Robinson, *David Urquhart* [a biography] (Oxford, 1920); A. Wilson, 'John Taylor, Esq. M.D. of Blackhouse, Ayrshire (1805-42)', *Ayrshire Archaeological and Natural History Society Collections*, 2nd ser. *1* (1947-9); J.H. Gleason, *The Genesis of Russophobia in Great Britain* (Harvard Univ. Press, Cambridge, 1950); L.C. Wright, *Scottish Chartism* (Edinburgh, 1953); Yu. V. Kovalev, *An Anthology of Chartist Literature* (Moscow, 1956); F.C. Mather, *Public Order in the Age of the Chartists* (Manchester, 1959); R. O'Higgins, 'The Irish Influence in the Chartist Movement', *Past and Present 20* (Nov 1961) 83-96; W.H. Maehl, 'Chartist Disturbances in North-Eastern England, 1839', *Int. Rev. Social Hist. 8* (1963) 389-414; H.G. Weisser, 'Polonophilism and the British Working Class, 1830-1845', *Polish Rev.* (Spring 1967) 78-96; B. Harrison and P. Hollis, 'Chartism, Liberalism and the Life of Robert Lowery', *Engl. Hist. Rev. 82* (July 1967) 503-35; A. Wilson, *The Chartist Movement in Scotland* (Manchester, 1970); D.J. Rowe, 'Some Aspects of Chartism on Tyneside', *Int. Rev. Social Hist. 16*, pt 1

(1971) 17-39; *The Early Chartists*, ed. D. Thompson (1971); B. Harrison, 'Teetotal Chartism', *History*, *58*, no. 193 (June 1973) 193-217.

BRIAN HARRISON
PATRICIA HOLLIS

See also: *George Julian HARNEY; *Ernest JONES.

MACDONALD, Roderick (1840-94)
RADICAL MP AND LAND REFORMER

Roderick Macdonald was born in 1840 at Fairy Bridge near Lonmore, Skye, the son of Angus Macdonald, a crofter, and his wife Elizabeth, daughter of R. Macneil, merchant, of Stein, Skye. He attended the Lonmore Free Church School, where he became a pupil teacher. He then went on to the Free Church Normal School (for the training of teachers) in Glasgow. After teaching for two years at Lonmore School he returned to Glasgow, to study for the Free Church ministry. At some point (it is not known when – or why) he turned to medicine instead and qualified in Edinburgh as LRCP and LRCS in 1867. Much later, in 1883, he became FRCS of Edinburgh and MD of Durham University.

For ten years after 1867 Dr Macdonald practised medicine in a number of places in Scotland and England, and was a ship's surgeon, before settling in 1877 in London, where he lived for some time in Poplar and had a practice in the East End; he also studied law in the Middle Temple.

As a crofter's son brought up in Skye, and as a practising doctor in Ardnamurchan, Argyll, for three of the years before he came to London, Roderick Macdonald was well acquainted with the condition of the Scottish crofter, his difficulties and his aspirations. After 1877 he kept strong links with the Highlands and was president of the Gaelic Society of London. More important, he was treasurer of the Crofters' Aid and Defence Fund. It was natural for a man with this background and these connections to be drawn into Radical politics, in particular into the movement for land reform, at that time very active. Along with Dr G.B. Clark he was a member of the Highland Land Law Reform Association, and became its vice-president in 1883. About the same time he was adopted as 'crofters' candidate' for the constituency of Ross and Cromarty. Although he lost the by-election of 1884, he won the seat in 1885 with a majority of 2017. Described as an 'advanced Liberal', he advocated a sweeping measure of reform of the House of Lords.

His constituency was inconveniently distant from his daily work in London, and this work must have demanded, one would think, almost all his time and attention. For in addition to his private practice Dr Macdonald held a number of public and medico-legal posts: he was certifying factory surgeon for Poplar and district medical officer to the Poplar Union, divisional police surgeon for the Isle of Dogs and, later, coroner of North East Middlesex. It might be thought difficult for so busy a man to spend much time among his constituents in Ross and Cromarty. But for a few years at least they were apparently satisfied with the degree of his attention to their problems. He was, in fact, a diligent and conscientious MP, asking numerous questions regarding Scottish affairs particularly relating to the Crofters (Scotland) (No. 2) Bill of 1886. He was re-elected in 1886, but in 1892 he did not stand.

Roderick Macdonald died at his home in Camden Road, Middlesex on 9 March 1894 and his funeral took place on 14 March at Charlton Cemetery. His wife, who was a great-granddaughter of Spencer Perceval, had died in 1892; there were no children. He left an estate valued at £19,868 (later resworn at £24,181); and after several bequests, the residue of the estate was left in trust for the benefit of six London hospitals.

Sources: *Medical Directory* (1883); *Crofter,* 1 Sep 1885; *Times,* 26 Nov 1885 and 30 June 1886; *Dod* (1886); *Pall Mall Gazette* (1886); *Hansard* (1886-92); biographical information: Durham Univ. Library; Edinburgh Univ. Medical School; Middle Temple Library, London; Newcastle upon Tyne Univ. For further source references *see* Dr G.B. CLARK. OBIT. *Times,* 10 Mar 1894; *Ross-shire J.,* 16 Mar 1894; *British Medical J.* and *Durham Univ. J.,* 24 Mar 1894.

MARGARET 'ESPINASSE

See also: Gavin Brown CLARK.

McSHANE, Annie (1888-1962)
CO-OPERATOR AND LABOUR ALDERMAN

Annie McShane was born Annie Bromwich on 13 December 1888 at Sun Rise Villas, Bloxwich Road, Walsall, the daughter of Frederick William Bromwich, a commercial traveller, and his wife Mary Matilda (née Brownhill). She was the second of three children, having an elder sister and a younger brother. Her maternal grandfather, T.P. Brownhill, was mayor of Walsall in 1893.

After attending school in Walsall she qualified as a teacher and taught intermittently in the Walsall area until retirement. In December 1917 she married John James McShane, a Scotsman of Irish descent who had recently moved to Walsall to take up a teaching post. John McShane was a Roman Catholic and a member of the ILP. Mrs McShane never adopted Catholicism, but she shared her husband's political persuasions and played a prominent part in the two parliamentary election campaigns he fought in Walsall. In 1929 he defeated the sitting Conservative and a Liberal to become the town's first Labour MP, but lost the seat to a National Liberal two years later.

Her involvement in her husband's work led naturally to Mrs McShane entering political life herself, and in July 1930 she was elected to Walsall Town Council at a by-election in Birchills ward. She quickly established herself as a leading figure in the minority Labour group on the Council, becoming chairman of the Maternity and Child Welfare Committee and later of the wartime Communal Feeding Committee. During this period she also served as chairman of both Birchills Co-operative Women's Guild, of which she was a founder member, and the women's section of Walsall Labour Party. Her main interest outside politics was voluntary hospital work and she was a member of the 134th (Staffordshire) detachment of the British Red Cross Society.

In 1942 Mrs McShane became the second woman mayor of Walsall, with her elder daughter, Moira, acting as mayoress. Her year of office was particularly noteworthy for a series of fund-raising campaigns. These brought an enthusiastic response from the people of Walsall, and £40,000 was raised for causes ranging from the provision of comforts for merchant seamen to the endowment of beds in a Stalingrad hospital.

In 1945, when the Labour Party won control of Walsall Council for the first time, Mrs McShane was elected an alderman. She continued her council work over the next decade, but frequently came into conflict with her colleagues in the Walsall Labour group until eventually she ceased to attend group meetings and stopped paying her party contributions. Her nominal connection with the Party finally came to an end following a clash over the question of council house rents. This arose from the advice of the NEC to Labour groups on local councils that where rent increases became necessary they should 'relieve lower-paid tenants from the worst effects of such increases by bringing into operation some scheme of rent rebates' [*Newsletter for Labour Groups* (Mar 1956)]. When the Walsall group chose to reject this advice Mrs McShane attacked the decision on the grounds that 'they did not consider the predicament of the small wage earners . . . the Socialist principle that had to be applied to the rents question was: "to each according to his need; from each according to his ability" ' [*Walsall Observer,* 5 July

1957]. She duly voted against the Labour group on the issue and in July 1957 the party whip was withdrawn.

At the aldermanic elections in the following year Mrs McShane was removed from office by the Labour group, but when control of Walsall Council changed hands in May 1959 she was elected alderman for the newly-created Bloxwich East ward by the Independent group and held this position until her death. She was never reconciled with her former colleagues, but when she died the leader of the Walsall Labour group, Alderman John Whiston, paid this tribute to her: 'The life she led and the contribution she made to this town was such that she had few equals. We are all the poorer on her passing. Many of us could look to her as an example' [*Walsall Observer*, 23 Feb 1962].

Mrs McShane died on 17 February 1962 at her home, 259 Birmingham Road, Walsall, after a short illness. She was buried in Ryecroft Cemetery, Walsall, four days later, following a service at St Mary's, The Mount, the principal Roman Catholic Church in Walsall. No will has been located. She was survived by her husband, two daughters and a son. Both daughters were educated at Queen Mary's High School, Walsall, and Birmingham University. Moira is now married to George Luckyj, Professor of Slavonic Languages at the University of Toronto. The younger daughter, Eileen, is a consultant anaesthetist at the Manor and General Hospitals, Walsall. She is married to Geoffrey Hoggins, an oral surgeon. Mrs McShane's son, John, trained as a teacher and is now (1976) secretary of the Walsall branch of the NUT. None of Mrs McShane's children have any political or religious affiliation.

Sources: Reports of Co-operative Society and Labour Party activities in *Walsall Observer*, 1930-62; *Walsall Times*, 1930-54; F. Hall, *From Acorn to Oak, being the History of the Walsall and District Co-operative Society Limited 1886-1936* (Birmingham, 1936); K.J. Dean, 'Parliamentary Elections and Party Organisations in Walsall 1906-45' (Birmingham MA, 1969); idem, *Town and Westminster: a political history of Walsall from 1906-45* (Walsall, 1972); personal and biographical information: J.D. McShane, Walsall, son, Feb 1976; Bryan Stanley, POEU, London. OBIT. *Walsall Observer*, 23 Feb 1962.

ERIC TAYLOR

See also: †William ABBOTTS; *Gertrude CRESSWELL; †Charles DEAKIN; †Jane DEAKIN; †Joseph Thomas DEAKIN; †Henry HUCKER; *John James MCSHANE; Dora Miriam MIDDLETON; †William MILLERCHIP; †Joseph THICKETT; *John WHISTON.

MADDISON, Fred (1856-1937)
TRADE UNIONIST AND LIB-LAB MP

Fred Maddison was born on 17 August 1856 at Boston, Lincolnshire, the son of Richard Maddinson, a hotel worker, and his wife Mary (née Yates). (It is not known when or why Fred Maddison dropped the 'n' from his surname.) He was educated at the Adelaide Street Wesleyan School, Hull, and on leaving school was apprenticed to the trade of compositor. Later he served as chairman of the Hull branch of the Typographical Association for three years.

As a very young man Maddison developed radical views. In the early 1880s he was a prominent member of the Hull Radical Club, and like so many of his local contemporaries he became an enthusiastic advocate of labour representation in both local and national politics. In 1886 he was elected president of the Hull Trades Council, and when the TUC held their annual congress in Hull in that year Maddison gave the presidential address. (It was, it should be noted, normal practice for the host town to provide a local trade unionist for the position of president.) In his address Maddison offered an advanced Radical platform, advocating the eight-hour day, land nationalisation, and payment of MPs; he ended by deploring the division between skilled and unskilled workers. Maddison was always a staunch supporter of the Liberal Party, and in

1887 he became president of the Hull branch of the Labour Electoral Association, whose aims were the election of working men within the orbit of the Liberal Party. The Liberal Party at the centre took almost no notice of the LEAs, and their activities were often much resented by local Liberal associations. A case in point was the refusal of the East Hull Liberals to adopt Edward Harford, general secretary of the Amalgamated Society of Railway Servants, as their parliamentary candidate in 1887. Maddison was outraged, and gave the warning that if working-class candidates were rejected, 'then of a certainty the friends of labour representation would have to form a separate labour party and run a candidate of their own, which would mean in nine cases out of ten, the success of the Tory Party.' These were opinions that were coming to be increasingly accepted, and the Liberal Party suffered a long attrition of working-class support through its failure to comprehend the spirit of the times. For Maddison, however, the ties with Liberalism never seriously weakened; and on this particular occasion he was attacked for not encouraging Harford to run as an independent Labour candidate.

In June 1887 Maddison had led the Hull trade unionists in their refusal to take part in the celebrations attending the Jubilee of Queen Victoria; because, Maddison said, 'he had not the slightest amount of respect for the object of the Jubilee.' In November of the same year he became the first working man to win a seat on the Hull Town Council, and in the next year his republican sentiments found further expression when he refused to join with the rest of the Council on a vote of condolence to the bereaved family of the German Emperor. The latter was, said Maddison, 'a typical continental tyrant', and 'if he had died sooner, the world would have been a better place.'

In this decade of the 1880s Maddison was articulating the ideas of advanced radicalism. On the Town Council, for example, he campaigned for the principle of Fair Contracts, whereby all contractors to the Hull Corporation had to pay trade union rates to their employees; and in 1889 he was successful in getting the Council to adopt the principle. He left Hull for London in 1889 to become editor of the *Railway Review*, the journal of the Amalgamated Society of Railway Servants. He was offered the post by the Society's general secretary, Edward Harford, in place of W. Foreman, the acting editor, who was circulating anti-Harford gossip. Maddison was inevitably regarded as a Harford man and was received by many in the union with hostility and suspicion; but he was notably successful as an editor. Harford was dismissed in October 1897 for unsatisfactory conduct – alcoholism – and Richard Bell, the organising secretary, took his place. There was almost immediately a clash between the new acting general secretary and Maddison. Bell had been instructed by the October conference to launch an all-grades campaign for improved terms of service. Maddison expressed doubts in the *Railway Review* about the wisdom of a head-on confrontation, with the companies when many of the railwaymen were not yet organised. Bell was outraged, and the executive committee unanimously regretted the appearance of the article; but Maddison refused to be disciplined, and in December 1897 he resigned from the *Review*. He was given a month's wages in lieu of notice [Bagwell (1963) 187-8].

In that same year Maddison had become MP for the Brightside division of Sheffield. During the nineties he had emerged as a vigorous anti-Socialist. He had twice stood unsuccessfully for Central Hull; first in 1892, when he was adopted as Lib-Lab candidate for the constituency and was supported by both the Central Hull Liberal Council and the Trades and Labour Council. His platform included an eight-hour day for the miners, the nationalisation of mining royalties, Home Rule for Ireland, allotments for agricultural labourers, the disestablishment and disendowment of all State Churches, and a graduated income tax. On the drink question, his election address contained a constantly-iterated passage:

> I am a social reformer, and therefore an opponent of the drink traffic. As a workman, I know the ravages which this traffic makes among my class, and, as I earnestly desire to curtail its power for harm, I would leave it entirely in the hands of the people. I am for the direct popular veto. Sunday closing, the prevention of the sale of drink to children, and all

measures calculated to lessen the evils which arise from the present system of licensing would receive my support. Nothing will counteract the demoralising influences of the huge brewers' syndicates, whose members often escape detection, but the placing of the traffic under the direct control of the people. As the law recognises no obligation to renew a license, I am rigorously opposed to compensation . . .

Maddison encountered a degree of Socialist opposition which, however, was much more vociferous at the subsequent general election of 1895, when he again contested Central Hull. He had been narrowly defeated by Seymour King in 1892 (the Conservative majority was only 476), but in 1895 he lost many votes: the Conservative, Sir H.S. King had 5476, Maddison 3515. The labour movement in Hull had become highly critical of the Liberal Government for its conduct during the seven-week dock strike of 1893, and the ILP had made considerable progress in the town. Maddison's electoral programme was similar to that which he had issued three years earlier, but with a rather greater emphasis upon social reform and a specific pledge to curb the power of the House of Lords. It became clear during the 1895 election that Maddison's radicalism was becoming somewhat old-fashioned for the advanced working men of Hull. He was able, however, to transfer his candidature to the Brightside division of Sheffield, which fell vacant on the death of the sitting member A.J. Mundella; two years later Maddison won the seat, though by a majority of only 183 votes. His candidature was again vigorously opposed by the ILP, but Brightside had a very strong Liberal tradition.

During his early years in London Maddison was elected to the Tottenham School Board, and served from 1891 to 1897. He had also been offered, in 1893, the position of labour correspondent to the Board of Trade, at a salary of £300 p.a. Maddison later told a meeting of the electors of Central Hull that although he did not believe he would ever again receive such a lucrative offer 'he felt his place was in the fight . . . he could serve his days best in the open in advocating those principles which he believed [to be] for their interest.'

Maddison lost his seat at Brightside in the general election of 1900 – the 'khaki' election. He was a bitter critic of the Boer War, and he never lacked the courage to state unpopular views. His 1900 election address concentrated on domestic, particularly industrial reforms; but Maddison did not hesitate to devote an outspoken paragraph to the War and the future of South Africa. But he was faced with two difficult problems. The first was that Sheffield, as a steel-manufacturing centre, was heavily dependent upon armament orders; and the second, more important perhaps, was that the local Liberal Party, like the national Party, was seriously divided over the war issue. H.J. Wilson, the dominant figure in Sheffield Liberalism in this period, was passionately anti-war; but the pro-war faction was also powerful. It included John Derry, the editor and part-proprietor of the *Sheffield and Rotherham Independent*, J. Skinner, the agent for Hallam, and two local MPs: Sir F.T. Mappin (Hallam) and J.B. Langley (Attercliffe); throughout Maddison's election campaign, the *Independent* supported him on domestic issues, but treated his anti-war views in a half-apologetic way that did considerable disservice to the Liberal campaign [Price (1972) 41]. Maddison lost his seat by 964 votes.

After leaving the *Railway Review* in 1897 Maddison became an organiser for the Labour Association for the Promotion of Co-operative Production (which in 1902 was renamed the Labour Co-partnership Association and in 1927 the Industrial Co-partnership Association). He served on the executive of the Association for over forty years and was at one time its president. He returned to Parliament in the general election of 1906, when he stood for Burnley. His main opponent was H.M. Hyndman of the SDF. In Burnley, largely as a result of the organising work of Dan Irving the local SDF organiser, there was 'an exceptionally strong and independent Socialist movement' [Pelling (1967) 262], and altogether Hyndman stood four times in the constituency. In 1906 he achieved his best result and in a total poll of 15,184 was only about 350 votes behind Maddison. The political confrontation between an old-style working-class radical and a leading Socialist makes this contest a particularly interesting one for the historian. Along with H.H. Vivian, Maddison was censured by the TUC for opposing Pete Curran's candidature at Jarrow in 1907 [Clegg et al. (1964) 406]. Maddison lost Burnley to the Unionist by only 95 votes in the general election of January 1910 and he lost again, though only by 406 votes, when he contested Darlington in the December 1910 general election. He never stood for Parliament on any later occasion; his political career, on a national level, was now at an end, although on some occasions, for example in the debates on conscription which he had with the medieval historian, G.G. Coulton, he reached the national headlines.

Like many of his radical contemporaries, Maddison was always concerned with international problems and the prevention of war; and on the death of Sir W. Randal Cremer in 1908 he became secretary of the International Arbitration League, and for the next twenty-nine years was active in its cause. He travelled widely, both at home and abroad, on behalf of the League.

He lived for many years at Ealing and then, for the last seven years of his life, at Hounslow. He was a magistrate for the County of London, and he retained his membership of the London Society of Compositors up to the time of his death. He was a Unitarian in religion. In reply to W.T. Stead's well-known inquiry in 1906 concerning books which had been influential in his life Maddison said that of all writers Joseph Mazzini had been quite the most important, particularly the essays on *The Duties of Man*. 'He has shaped my political, economic, and religious thinking, and no one has gained so entirely my agreement.' [*Rev. of Revs* (1906) 577]. In 1877 Maddison had married Jane Ann Weatherill of Bewholme, Yorkshire, the daughter of a farmer. He died on 12 March 1937 in an Isleworth nursing home in his eighty-first year. His funeral service was held at Golders Green Crematorium and he was survived by his wife and three daughters. He left effects worth £1578.

Writings: *The Store, the Workshop and the Trade Union* [1898] 7 pp.; 'The Labour Representation Conference', *The Speaker*, 3 Mar 1900, 592-3; 'Why British Workmen condemn the War', *N. Amer. Rev. 170*, no. 4 (Apr 1900) 518-27; 'Some Impressions of the Co-operative Congress', *Econ. Rev. 10* (July 1900) 363-67; 'The Co-operative Congress', ibid., *12* (July 1902) 333-8; 'The Trade Union Congress', ibid., (Oct 1902) 468-72; Introduction to A. Watson, *A Great Labour Leader: being the life of the Right Hon. Thomas Burt M.P.* (1908); 'The Labour Co-partnership Association', *Econ. Rev. 20* (July 1910) 314-17; *Debate on Compulsory Service at Northampton Town Hall, Dec 17 1912 between Mr F. Maddison and Mr G.G. Coulton* (Cambridge, [1912]) 30 pp.; *Debate between Mr G.G. Coulton . . . and Mr Fred Maddison . . . Woodford . . . January 31, 1913 (That Universal Military Service as proposed by Lord Roberts is necessary for National Defence and desirable on Social Grounds)* (Cambridge, [1913]) 32 pp.

Sources: (1) MSS: H.J. Wilson papers: Sheffield City Library. (2) Other: *Election Addresses for Central Hull*, June 1892 and 9 July 1895; *Eastern Morning News*, 2, 5 and 8 July 1892, 6 and 9 July 1895; *Dod* (1898) and (1909); *Sheffield Weekly News*, 23 Sep 1899; *Election Address for Brightside Division of Sheffield*, 18 Sep 1900; *Sheffield Independent*, 15, 19, 26 and 28 Sep 1900; *Sheffield Telegraph*, 25 Oct 1900; *Burnley Gazette*, 6 Jan. 1906 [for Election Address]; *Rev. of Revs 6* (1906); H. Evans, *Sir Randal Cremer: his life and work* (1909); W.J. Davis, *The British Trades Union Congress: history and recollections* vol. *1* (1910); *WWW* (1929-40); *Kelly* (1932); G.G. Coulton, *Four Score Years* (Cambridge, 1943); F. Bealey and H. Pelling, *Labour and Politics 1900-1906* (1958); B.C. Roberts, *The Trades Union Congress 1868-1921* (1958); H.A. Clegg et al., *A History of British Trade Unions since 1889*, vol. *1: 1889-1910* (Oxford, 1964); H. Pelling, *Social Geography of British Elections 1885-1910* (1967); R. Price, *An Imperial War and the British Working Class: working-class attitudes and reactions to the Boer War 1899-1902* (1972); biographical information: Burnley Central Library; Sheffield City Library. OBIT. *Times*, 15 Mar 1937; *Middlesex Chronicle*, 20 Mar 1937; *Railway Rev.*, 26 Mar 1937.

RAYMOND BROWN

See also: †Richard BELL; *William Randal CREMER; †Henry Harvey VIVIAN.

MELLOR, William (1888-1942)

SOCIALIST JOURNALIST AND PROPAGANDIST

William Mellor died in his early fifties, in the middle of a war during which journals had little space for lengthy obituaries. He had written no reminiscences, and aside from his journalism only one unimportant book and two or three pamphlets. It is not surprising, therefore, that in company with others who were stronger in the spoken than in the written word his forceful personality, commanding if not invariably wise, was almost forgotten soon after his death.

His deep and fine-sounding voice had an accent which led those who met him to take him for a Yorkshireman; in fact he was born at Crewe on 7 September 1888, the son of a Unitarian minister also named William. The family, though not poor, was not by any means well-off. Young William went to elementary school; but he had good brains and succeeded in getting himself to Willaston Grammar School, and thence to Exeter College, Oxford. The intention was that he should enter the Unitarian ministry like his brother Stanley, who was long a successful preacher in Liverpool. But he reached the university at the time of the great Liberal landslide, and became a Socialist and an agnostic; he was soon a vocal member of the Oxford University Fabian Society which included so many brilliant young men, including G.D.H. Cole, Kingsley Griffith, who became a county court judge, Ivor Brown, later editor of the *Observer*, Sir George Clark the historian, afterwards professor and provost of Oriel College, Maurice Reckitt; and others who were to die in the coming war. The OUFS, which before long became part of the University Socialist Federation headed by Clifford Allen from Cambridge (later Lord Allen of Hurtwood and the hero of the extreme war resisters), played a vigorous part in the Webb's 1909 campaign for social security and the break-up of the Poor Law. But some of the members developed a resistance to the methods of the Webbs and quarrelled on principle with the strictly collectivist brand of Socialist thought which the Webbs and their supporters within the Fabian Society were then promulgating. They were more inclined to embrace the propaganda for Syndicalism and workers' control – then being preached by Tom Mann, by the South Wales miners, by the teachers and students of Ruskin College who had seceded to set up the Central Labour College in London, and by the newly-founded and explosive *Daily Herald* – and were particularly interested in the Guild Socialist theories proffered by S.G. Hobson and A.R. Orage in the *New Age* weekly. There were resounding arguments within the Fabian Society, many of whose younger members, in the universities and outside, joined the rebels. The Webbs resisted strongly (though Bernard Shaw was not altogether unsympathetic); but the movement against them rode higher than the earlier revolt headed by H.G. Wells. For a brief while in 1913 Mellor was made secretary to the Fabian Research Committee which the Webbs had set up in an attempt to canalise the energies of the new rebels – they miscalculated the abilities of the latter, who before long completely captured the Committee (which later became the independent Labour Research Department); and in the final battle for the control of the Fabian Society itself, fought a few months after the outbreak of war, the rebels lost by one vote only. Cole then resigned from the Fabian Society; only a few followed his example, but so many of his younger supporters became involved in war – or, later, in anti-war agitation – that the battle was never resumed in that form. Cole's first major book, *The World of Labour* (1913), had meantime become 'prescribed reading' for militant Socialist youth; and he and Mellor were together writing for the *Herald* (under the pen-name of JUDEX) a regular column of industrial and trade union notes.

Mellor himself was against the war, for industrial rather than strictly pacifist reasons; and his contributions to the *Herald* were strongly in support of 'direct action' – strikes and the like. Because he had been an elementary schoolboy, he tended always to regard himself as a member of the working class who understood their mentality much better than his middle-class friends at

Oxford and the acolytes of the *New Age*. This was not quite true; but he was certainly a very effective speaker to working-class audiences, and in journalism and pamphleteering his down-to-earth style was a check upon a slight tendency of Cole's to talk above the heads of his readers. They made a strong and influential team on the left; their 'Notes', continued when after the outbreak of war the *Herald* became a weekly, were read eagerly not only by the middle classes but also by shop stewards and other manual workers just beginning to feel the power given them by war conditions. Later they were referred to as 'the Mellor-and-Cole Board' on the analogy of Lloyd George's Liquor Control Board.

Mellor was an important leader in the Guild Socialist movement. He attended the discussion which produced the 'Storrington Document' – the first thoroughgoing statement of Guild policy; and when the National Guilds League was formed in 1915 he was its first secretary. In the technical sense, he was not a very good one; he was arbitrary in his choice of new entrants, and casual in his accounting – he tended to leave unidentified piles of small change lying about in his lodgings at the unfashionable end of Grosvenor Road. He became, of course, involved in the shop stewards' movement, and for some time, like Cole, he 'advised' the Amalgamated Society of Engineers. But these activities were checked when the Military Service Acts caught up with him, and he was for a while 'on the run'. His place as secretary of the NGL was filled by Monica Ewer (wife of the future foreign editor of the *Daily Herald* who was then doing national service as pig-keeper to the Astors at Cliveden); for her he nourished a protective *tendresse* which slightly amused his associates. The ASE had made an effort to keep him out of the Army (as they had Cole) on the grounds of 'work of national importance'; but this was unsuccessful, largely because, unlike Cole, he insisted on haranguing the Tribunal himself. His appeal was dismissed, and he was jailed. But his ordeal did not last very long; for having consented to take 'alternative service', he was drafted to be assistant to a market gardener, in whose service he almost at once suffered an exceptionally violent attack of nose-bleeding. Having covered the vegetables with gore, he was immediately dismissed by his outraged employer; and then reappeared in the movement. In the disputes within the National Guilds League which followed the October revolution in Russia he took a strongly left-wing line, and joined the British Communist Party at its formation; he did not, however, stay very long in it.

When the war ended the need for keeping even partly under cover ended also. In March 1919 the *Herald* became once more a daily, with George Lansbury as editor; and Mellor, now fairly well known, joined the staff as industrial correspondent and industrial editor. He served Lansbury and his successor Hamilton Fyfe, and in 1926 became editor himself. He was not particularly successful; it was not an easy assignment in the troubled years which followed the General Strike, and the circulation never reached a satisfactory level. In August 1929 the TUC signed a partnership agreement with Odhams Press to produce a new *Daily Herald*. The driving force on the TUC side was Ernest Bevin, with J.S. Elias as managing director of Odhams Press. The first issue of the new *Herald* appeared in March 1930. Mellor was retained as editor, but he was soon out. There was no quarrel; he became assistant managing director of the Press itself, and retained this post until 1936. In 1933, it should be mentioned, he also took on the editorship of a not very distinguished journal called the *Town and County Councillor,* an assignment which lasted until 1940; its importance to Mellor lay in the fact that it brought him into contact with the able Socialist journalist Frank Betts, long editor of that well-known paper the *Bradford Pioneer,* and with his daughter Barbara (afterwards Barbara Castle).

But now there appeared to be another chance for a left-wing movement. The second Labour Government, elected in 1929, soon began to disappoint its Socialist supporters; and by the autumn of 1930 Mellor was joining in the discussions at Easton Lodge, initiated by G.D.H. Cole, which resulted in the formation of the Society for Socialist Inquiry and Propaganda (SSIP) with Ernest Bevin as chairman and Cole as vice-chairman. Mellor was not a member of its original executive committee, but joined it early in the following year, and played a large part in its propaganda until the summer of 1932, when it came to an end because of events within the Independent Labour Party.

The ILP had begun to quarrel with MacDonald in the mid-twenties, and at the very start of his new Government had received from him a stern warning against 'sniping'. Nevertheless, the ILP continued to formulate policies of its own, to which it expected MPs sponsored by it to adhere, whatever the rest of the Labour Party did or thought. The Labour Party countered by stiffening its own standing orders; and by the spring of 1932 it was apparent that the ILP was likely to disaffiliate. But there was a considerable minority, led by E.F. Wise, the former civil servant, Patrick Dollan of Glasgow, and David (afterwards Lord) Kirkwood, which had no stomach for going out into the wilderness. When disaffiliation was carried by the majority led by James Maxton, and the ILP split, SSIP at first hoped to enrol the dissidents. These, however, had other ideas, and approached SSIP for an amalgamation, which Cole opposed, but was outvoted on his own executive. Wise and his friends then joined with SSIP (less a dissenting minority) to form a new body called, in reminiscence of William Morris, the Socialist League, which sought affiliation to the Labour Party in time for the latter's Annual Conference in the autumn of 1932. Part of the terms of agreement was that Wise, and not Bevin, should be chairman of the new body; Bevin did not openly protest, but regarded himself as having been betrayed once again by unstable intellectuals. The chief financial support came from Stafford Cripps, George Strauss, MP, G.R. (later Lord) Mitchison, and D.N. Pritt, KC; Cole, after standing by his executive's decision for a time (during which SSIP was wound up) found himself in growing disagreement with its tactics and resigned; and as Wise died unexpectedly in 1933, the League was in practice led by Cripps, with Mellor as second string.

Mellor was responsible for a League success at the 1932 Party Conference, when his personal contacts with trade unions induced the delegates of the NUR to cast their union block vote in favour of an amendment adding to a resolution for nationalising the Bank of England the words 'and the joint stock banks' – though it may be observed that no Labour Government, then or thereafter, has suggested putting this resolution into effect. It was carried in the angry mood which was the outcome of the 1931 electoral disaster; and as an achievement it stood alone. No other policy resolution of any importance promoted by the Socialist League was carried; many were defeated by large majorities, and the big battalions of the Party gradually became convinced that the League was following the example of the ILP and trying to force separate policies of its own upon the Party as a whole. The merits or demerits of any particular resolution – sixty-seven of them were sent in to a single Conference – had little to do with the case; but disciplinary action was almost certain to come. And in January of 1937 the League precipitated matters by joining with the (disaffiliated) ILP and the Communist Party in issuing the once-famous Unity Manifesto calling for a 'united front of the whole of the working class . . . in the struggle for immediate demands, and the return of a Labour Government'. It was a militant-sounding document, listing a whole series of 'simple things the workers need', to be obtained by 'active demonstrations' without waiting for general elections. The collaboration with the Communist Party produced an immediate effect: the Labour Party's NEC issued a circular letter on 'Party Loyalty' condemning any association with other parties, whether for a United Front or a Popular Front, and at the end of the month expelled the Socialist League. The League, in an attempt to save its membership from being driven out of all local Party organisations, decided in May to dissolve itself, Mellor dissenting. This was the end of the Socialist League, though not of the purging of its most prominent members such as Cripps, Strauss and Aneurin Bevan.

During these years, Mellor had not been without a public voice. He could not write for the *Daily Herald;* but in January 1937 Cripps and others established the *Tribune* as a weekly supporting the Socialist League, in addition to the League's own house-organ; and Mellor was asked to edit it. Cripps, George Strauss, Ellen Wilkinson, Harold Laski, H.N. Brailsford and Nye Bevan were members of the Board of Control. Michael Foot and Barbara Betts, who had become great friends and admirers of Mellor's, wrote a regular column of trade union notes after the manner of the Mellor-and-Cole Board. 'Working with Mellor', Michael Foot wrote in the biography of Aneurin Bevan (vol. *1*, 245), was like living on the foothills of Vesuvius. On slight provocation the molten lava would pour forth in protest against the imbecilities of the world in general and anyone who dared to cross him in particular. All who might be suspected of betraying the Cause were in peril of being consumed by his private supply of hell-fire. A wonderful gentleness and generosity mixed with these ferocities but both the lowly and the great went in dread of his wrath – all except Bevan.

Tribune, despite its editorial talents, continued to run at a loss, and after about eighteen months its backers made an agreement with Victor Gollancz's Left Book Club whereby it became more or less an organ of the Club. The Club leaders, however, were at that time getting too close to the Communist Party line to be acceptable to Mellor, who in any case was not a man to submit easily to dictation; so part of the bargain was to get rid of him – much to the indignation of some of his contributors. After a while he went back to work on the *Daily Herald;* but his public career was over, and he died, of an operation following an attack of pneumonia, on 8 June 1942. His wife, Helen Edna Thomson, daughter of a master brassfounder in Liverpool, whom he had married in September 1919, survived him, with one son. He left an estate valued at £679.

Mellor was a big well-built dark-haired man. His sallow face was too heavy to be handsome, but he had an attractive smile and a most incongruous dimple. He was something of an outdoor man, with a great interest in cricket; also something of a *bon viveur* when he was in funds and had the company at hand. He was an excellent speaker and propagandist, partly because his emotions were easily aroused; and formidably effective in argument. His style of controversy was dominating, sometimes coming near to bullying, and lesser lights hesitated to challenge him unless they were very sure of their ground. As a tactician he was too temperamental to be always a safe guide, and too quick to quarrel. He stood for Parliament twice, at Enfield in Middlesex in 1931 and 1935, and at the time of his death was prospective candidate for Stockport. In the circumstances of his time his enthusiasms were fated for disappointment; but he was a vigorous and powerful leader who attracted affection as well as attention.

MARGARET COLE

Writings: (with G.D.H. Cole), *The Greater Unionism* (1913) 20 pp.; 'The National Guilds League' [letter], *Plebs* 7, no. 7 (Aug 1915) 159-60; (with G.D.H. Cole), *The Price of Dilution of Labour* (1915) 8 pp.; (with G.D.H. Cole), *Trade Unionism in War-time* [1915] 14 pp.; (with G.D.H. Cole), *Safeguards for Dilution: what circulars L2 and L3 mean* (1916) 12 pp.; (with G.D.H. Cole), *The Meaning of Industrial Freedom* (1918) 44 pp.; *Direct Action* (1920); (with G.D.H. Cole), *Gildensozialismus* (Cologne, 1921) 53 pp.; 'A Critique of Guild Socialism', *Lab. Mon. 1* (Nov 1921) 397-404; *The Claim of the Unemployed* [1932?] 16 pp.; (with G.D.H. Cole), *Workers' Control and Self-Government in Industry* [1933] 19 pp.; *The Co-operative Movement and the Fight for Socialism* (n.d.) P.

Sources: *Labour Who's Who* (1927); *Labour Party Report* (1935) 170-2, 232-3; A. Hutt, *The Post-War History of the British Working Class* (1937); J.T. Murphy, *New Horizons* (1941; repr. 1942); M.B. Reckitt, *As it happened: an autobiography* (1941); A.F. Brockway, *Inside the Left* (1941); G.D.H. Cole, *A History of the Labour Party from 1914* (1948); M.I. Cole, *Growing up into Revolution* (1949); E. Estorick, *Stafford Cripps: a biography* (1949); *Beatrice Webb's Diaries 1912-1924*, ed. M.I. Cole (1952); F. Williams, *Ernest Bevin* (1952); R.J. Minney, *Viscount Southwood* (1954); *Beatrice Webb's Diaries 1924-1932*, ed. and with an Introduction by M. Cole (1956); C.A. Cooke, *The Life of Richard Stafford Cripps* [1957]; A. Bullock, *The Life and Times of Ernest Bevin*, vol. *1: 1881-1940* (1960); M. Cole, *The Story of Fabian Socialism* (1961; repr. 1963); M. Foot, *Aneurin Bevan: a biography*, vol. *1: 1897-1945* (1962); L.J. Macfarlane, *The British Communist Party: its origin and development until 1929* (1966); P. Thompson, *Socialists, Liberals and Labour: the struggle for London 1885-1914* (1967); W.

De'ath, *Barbara Castle: a portrait from life* (1970); M. Cowling, *The Impact of Labour 1920-1924: the beginning of modern British politics* (1971); B. Pimlott, 'The Socialist League: intellectuals and the Labour Left in the 1930s', *J. Cont. Hist. 6*, no.3 (1971) 12-38. Obit. *Manchester Guardian*, 9 June 1942; *Daily Herald* and *Times*, 10 June 1942; *Stockport Express*, 11 June 1942.

See also: *Aneurin BEVAN; *Samuel George HOBSON; *Alfred Richard ORAGE; †Edward Reynolds PEASE; †Malcolm SPARKES for Guild Socialism; †Beatrice and Sidney WEBB.

MIDDLETON, Dora Miriam (1897-1972)
CO-OPERATOR AND LABOUR ALDERMAN

Dora Middleton was born Dora Went on 16 June 1897 in Cannock, Staffordshire, the daughter of George Went, a stonemason, and his wife, Elizabeth (née Turner). She was one of three sisters and there were also six sons of her parents' marriage. While Dora was still very young the family moved to Walsall and she was educated at Hillary Street School. She left school at an early age, becoming first a fancy leather worker and then a tailoress. In 1919 she married Frederick George Middleton, a caster in a foundry. He later worked in the building trade and finally became an agent for the Co-operative Insurance Society.

Mrs Middleton became interested in politics while she was still at school and at the time of her marriage she was already an active member of Walsall Labour Party. During the 1920s and 1930s she served on all the main party committees and also became a leading member of Walsall Co-operative Society, in turn holding all the principal offices in the Women's Guild; at the Walsall municipal elections in November 1935 she stood unsuccessfully as the Labour and Co-operative candidate for Hatherton ward. In July 1944, under the terms of the wartime political truce, she was co-opted to Walsall Town Council to fill the vacancy in Palfrey ward arising from the death of Mrs Gertrude Cresswell, and in the following year won the seat in her own right.

Mrs Middleton's main interests in the field of local government were health, housing and old people's welfare. She was chairman of the health committee of Walsall Council for many years, and vice-chairman of the housing committee for a shorter time. She also founded the Palfrey Sisters of Rest Club (now Palfrey Senior Citizens' Club) and served as chairman of the Joint Walsall Sisters of Rest Clubs. In terms of political attitudes she belonged to the right wing of the Labour Party, certainly in her later years. Thus, in 1957, she found no difficulty in accepting the Walsall Labour group's decision to reject the advice of the NEC that rent rebates should be introduced to relieve lower-paid council house tenants from the effects of rent increases [for which see Annie McShane].

In 1959 Mrs Middleton's services to Walsall were recognised by her election as mayor. In addition to carrying out the usual civic duties, and particularly the speaking engagements, with distinction she established twin town links between Walsall and Mulhouse, France, and organised a series of fund-raising efforts on behalf of World Refugee Year. These brought an enthusiastic response from the people of Walsall and almost £7000 was raised.

Mrs Middleton was made an alderman in 1964 and held this position until 1969, when she gave up council work, after representing Palfrey ward continuously for twenty-five years. She died on 17 June 1972, at the home of her second daughter, Brenda, 23 Boscobel Road, Walsall, and was buried in Ryecroft Cemetery on 23 June, following a service at St Mary and All Saints Church, Palfrey. She was survived by three daughters and a son, her husband having predeceased her in March 1955. She left effects valued at £937. Her eldest daughter, Grace, works as a chemist's dispenser for Walsall Co-operative Society. She is married to Clifford Leslie Tomkinson, an engineer. Mr and Mrs Tomkinson are leading figures in the labour movement in Walsall and in 1966 Mrs Tomkinson was awarded the TUC gold medal for her trade union work. Mrs Middleton's son Frederick George Middleton is a business executive. Her two other daughters are both married.

Sources: Reports of Co-operative Society and Labour Party activities in *Walsall Observer*, 1920-69, *Walsall Times*, 1925-54; F. Hall, *From Acorn to Oak, being the History of the Walsall and District Co-operative Society Limited 1886-1936* (Birmingham, 1936); K.J. Dean, 'Parliamentary Elections and Party Organisations in Walsall 1906-45' (Birmingham MA, 1969); idem, *Town and Westminster: a political history of Walsall from 1906-1945* (Walsall, 1972); personal information: Mr and Mrs C.L. Tomkinson, Bloxwich, son-in-law and daughter. OBIT. *Birmingham Sunday Mercury*, 18 June 1972; *Walsall Observer*, 23 June 1972.

ERIC TAYLOR

See also: †William ABBOTTS; *Gertrude CRESSWELL; †Charles DEAKIN; †Jane DEAKIN; †Joseph Thomas DEAKIN; †Henry HUCKER; Annie McSHANE; *John James McSHANE; †William MILLERCHIP; †Joseph THICKETT; *John WHISTON.

MORLEY, Iris Vivienne (1910-53)
NOVELIST, HISTORIAN AND COMMUNIST

Iris Morley was born in Carshalton, Surrey, on 10 May 1910, the elder daughter of Lyddon Charteris Morley, at the time a captain in the Hampshire Regiment. He later became Colonel of the Regiment. Her mother was Margaret Gladys Vivienne Braddell, daughter of Sir Thomas de Multon Lee Braddell, Chief Judicial Commissioner of the Federated Malay States, and his wife, Ida Violet Nassau, who was descended from the Earls of Rochford, and through them, from William the Silent via several 'natural children' who 'had all been recognised'. This was to have a powerful influence, in a rather unexpected way, upon Iris's later development. Her ancestry on her father's side was not unimportant either. After George Morley, Bishop of Winchester in the time of Charles II, there was a string of army officers and a long association with the county of Hampshire, which she always regarded as her home ground in a special sense. And her father, a quiet, unassuming and capable soldier who had served at Gallipoli and as liaison officer with the 'Whites' in Siberia (an experience which left him, on the whole, rather favourable to the 'Reds' than not) was interested in books, in history and in ideas, and a great admirer of Oliver Cromwell. It should be added that for all their historic connections no part of the family was at all rich; they depended upon their earnings, and these never seemed to afford any margin for accumulation.

Iris was a lively passionate child who liked to be admired and to dominate. Her uncle Maurice Braddell (who was only ten years her senior and more like an elder brother than an uncle) who has provided much material about her early years, says that she 'came roaring into the world'. Her admiring audience included various cousins. He writes:

> We were both very romantic and she and I were fed on Grimm's *Fairy Tales* and Andrew Lang's. Both of us had an unnatural craze for dressing up and acting plays, for which we conscripted all our small cousins and ruled them with the rod of a film director. In my teens we worshipped the Duke of Monmouth and Charles II and *all* the Orange family from whom we were proud to be descended. William of Orange was a sacred name and Iris was a Dutch republican and an English royalist – and why not?

She early developed a passion for dancing and said later that she would have been a ballet dancer if she had not grown too tall. This passion remained: after the war she published two books on ballet and she was ballet critic of the *Daily Worker* until she became ill in autumn 1951.

The Morley family lived the semi-nomadic life of the pre-war regular Army, a life described with irony and humour in the early chapters of her novel, *Rack*. The consequence was a succession of short-time homes and changes of schools. These included Ocklynge at Eastbourne, the Royal School at Bath, and, finally Mannamead, Plymouth. She disliked school, but did well at the things that interested her – English, history and dramatics.

After Mannamead she was for a short time at the Royal Academy of Dramatic Art in London, but found that her voice was not strong enough for stage work. In any case it seems clear that in spite of her love of the theatre her real bent was for writing. She devoured historical novels – Dumas was a particular favourite – and early began to try to write them. None of these early efforts survive but already she had the eye for significant detail and the vivid descriptive power that was to mark all her work.

In 1929 she married Captain Gordon Coates of the Devonshire Regiment and went with him to India. The marriage was not a success and ended with a divorce in 1934. She then married the journalist Alaric Jacob and went with him to America when he became Reuters' Washington correspondent. Up to this time her life had been that of any lively and beautiful girl with an Army background and 'good' social contacts, and her political ideas, so far as they existed, those of her class. In the mid 1930s all this began to change. The social conditions of the 'hungry thirties' could not be ignored – later she spoke of the deep impression made by the arrival of the 1934 hunger marchers in London. She began to read Marx and Lenin and some of the Marxist-inspired books being written at this time, like John Strachey's *The Coming Struggle for Power*.

This reading transformed her understanding of history. The romantic admirer of William of Orange became the cool analyst, trying to understand the real motive forces of historical change. All the same, she remained a romantic, and it is this romantic involvement, combined with a Marxist insight and realism, which makes her historical novels so outstanding. Certainly it is the romanticism which is still most apparent in her first book *The Proud Paladin* (1936) a medieval story of a girl who should have been a boy and who became a successful soldier. No one was more conscious of the shortcomings of this prentice work than Iris Morley herself – she used to say it was based on nothing more than a reading of Froissart. Yet it has a clarity and brightness of colour which sometimes remind one of the illuminations of a fourteenth-century manuscript.

And, as in all her novels, there is a definite autobiographical element. It is interesting to note, for example, that the one sport in which she really excelled was fencing, at which she was accustomed to meet men on equal terms. Her great height, muscular strength and cool nerves must have made her a formidable opponent. Always, of course, transmuted, this autobiographical element is present not only in her novels of contemporary life, but, if less directly, in the historical ones. In *Cry Treason* and *The Mighty Years*, for example, a good deal of her can be recognised both in Henrietta Wentworth and Elizabeth Villiers, who may, indeed, be said to reflect opposing aspects in her nature.

Much of *The Proud Paladin* was probably written before she left England. In America she lived first on 12th Street, New York, but from 1936 in Washington. Here she began, in the Library of Congress, the serious study of the later seventeenth century which was to produce *Cry Treason*. She worked, too, in a left-wing bookshop and art gallery which was patronised by Eleanor Roosevelt and was one of the offshoots of the progressive ferment around the New Deal. At some point she joined the Communist Party of the U.S.A., of which she remained a member till she and Alaric Jacob returned to England soon after the outbreak of the war.

With *Cry Treason* she emerged as a clearly major writer. She once said that she expressed in this book all her deepest feelings about the Spanish Civil War, and this remark is perhaps a key both to its quality and to her attitude towards history. The war in Spain taught her to understand why and how Englishmen had fought at Sedgemoor, and the years she spent learning to understand this made it easy later to see how and why the Russian people fought against Hitler.

However, she was too scholarly to fall into the error of dressing present day problems and attitudes in the costume of the past, and her three novels of the seventeenth century make a real contribution to historical understanding. *Cry Treason* (published in 1940) is a long and detailed account of the struggle of the New Country Party under Monmouth and Shaftesbury against the Stuart attempts to put the clock back. She saw them, not as the traditional Absalom and

Achitophel, feather-brained dupe and unprincipled schemer leading ignorant peasants to destruction, but as the heirs of the old Commonwealth Party and even of the Levellers, whose defeat marked the extinction of the plebeian left in the English Revolution and opened the way both for the end of the Stuart counter-revolution and the compromise of 1688 which determined the course of England's development for the next century.

Cry Treason was a wide panorama, in which a whole society and period were surveyed. *We stood for Freedom* deals with the same events from a more limited and individual standpoint, describing the preparations for revolt in the West and its effect upon a small group of people. If less massive it is perhaps more movingly personal and its note of triumph arising from apparently irrecoverable defeat is even more marked. It is perhaps relevant that it was being written at the time of Dunkirk. Its title was taken from the lines by Gerrard Winstanley, a writer whom she greatly admired and liked to quote:

> When these clay-bodies are in grave, and children stand in place,
> This shews we stood for truth and peace, and freedom in our daies [Winstanley (1649)].

After the return to England Alaric Jacob served as war correspondent in France, in Africa and in the Far East. Iris lived sometimes at Fleet in Hampshire but mainly in London, working again in a left-wing bookshop and with the Society for Cultural Relations with the U.S.S.R. From 1941 to 1943 she lived at 5 Willow Road, Hampstead. The atmosphere of these years is admirably caught in her first novel dealing with contemporary life, *Nothing but Propaganda*, published in 1946.

During 1941 and 1942 the third and last of her seventeenth century novels, *The Mighty Years* (1943) was being written. Like *Cry Treason* this is a long book into which a great deal of thought and reading has gone, a remarkable achievement in a life packed with other activities. It deals with William of Orange and the 'Glorious Revolution' of 1688. And, as a prefatory letter says, 'the William of this story bears no resemblance to the stainless hero of my childish scribbles.' Quoting Marx's dictum that the Revolution 'brought into power, along with William of Orange, the landlord and capitalist appropriators of surplus-value', she comments:

> Yet he [Marx] did not mean to infer that the Stuart-Roman Catholic alternative was preferable. On the contrary, if the particularly odious form of government that Charles II and James II tried to force upon the country had been successful in maintaining itself, the English people would doubtless have experienced the terrible degradation that was the lot of the French from the times of Louis XIV till the Revolution.

If the movement led by Monmouth and Shaftesbury had won, she says, we can imagine that:

> England would have been a sweeter place during the eighteenth century and our forefathers spared much loathsome drudgery. But it did not. The struggle was lost and William of Orange, the peers and the Bank of England inherited. Which brings us back to poor William. I say 'poor' because I do not think he was either the cold-hearted schemer of the Jacobites or the rather repulsive super-statesman of the Whigs . . . Essentially William was a man who struggled against the evils he knew and not for a good he imagined . . . his Common Cause had no relation to the great progressive philosophy that was called the Old Cause.

Paradoxically, perhaps, while *Cry Treason* and *We stood for Freedom* describe defeats and *The Mighty Years* a success, it is a sadder book than its predecessors. They record the heroic end of an heroic age, it records the triumph of reason and compromise which inaugurated the eighteenth century. Yet as a novel it is in no way inferior to its predecessors.

At the end of 1943 Iris Morley was appointed the *Observer* correspondent in Russia (from which Alaric Jacob had just returned), and in January 1944 they sailed together on one of the Arctic convoys to Molotovsk on the White Sea. She was one of the very few women to make this voyage, whose perils are vividly described in a letter to her sister:

The convoy ran into a terrible storm. A 12 force gale – the maximum: a hurricane. I have never seen anything like it – great walls and valleys of water, all the surface whipped into a foamy yeast and the sky clouded with spray. You don't nowadays imagine storms wreck ships, do you? But they do. In the middle of the afternoon the engines stopped and they thought she was going. But they got them going again and she was alright – only minor damage. But others weren't so lucky.

After the storm they took refuge, while the convoy regathered, at Reykjavik which to their surprise they found 'all lighted up. No blackout. We went ashore and it seemed like fairyland: sugar cakes in the shops, silk stockings, tweeds, Lux, jam etc: all unrationed.' A few days of 'this Cinderella existence' was only a respite before the further ordeal of a heavy attack by German submarines and planes in which many ships were lost [see Roskill, vol. *3* (1960) 242, 268-9].

Eventually they reached Moscow and remained in the Soviet Union till the summer of 1945. In addition to her work for the *Observer*, Iris Morley also wrote for the *Yorkshire Post* and in Moscow they found themselves members of the group of British correspondents, among whom their main friends included James Aldridge the novelist, Ralph Parker, first of *The Times* and later of the *Daily Worker*, and Alexander Werth of the *Sunday Times*. Alaric Jacob represented the *Daily Express*. It was a strange and often frustrating life, in which occasional visits to the front were interludes in long periods of forced inaction in Moscow, where they gathered such crumbs of news as could be found. Iris Morley was fortunate in being able to make full use of her passion for and knowledge of the ballet. She was soon welcomed at the Bolshoi, became friendly with Ulanova and other leading dancers and even took lessons herself. The outcome of her visits was her book *Soviet Ballet* (1945) illustrated with photographs taken by herself. This book was an immediate success; it was the first, and perhaps is still the best book in English on the Soviet ballet. In 1949 she published a comparison of ballet in England and in Russia, *The Rose and the Star*, written in collaboration with Phyllis Manchester.

They visited Leningrad soon after the siege was raised, and were struck by the contrast between the historic beauty of the city and the destruction caused by the siege and the sufferings its people had endured. They were also among the first party of journalists to visit the Nazi extermination camp at Maidanek in Poland and to write a full account for the outside world. One of her letters says:

I can't express really what it was like. The horror of this great slaughter house, this *industry* far exceeding the horrors of massacres or battlefields – it frightens you in the most terrible way . . . The warehouses were the worst. The greatest department stores in the world couldn't have been more completely fitted up. Have you any idea what eight hundred and twenty thousand pairs of shoes look like, all off the feet of people sent to the foulest deaths?

She went to Moscow a firm friend of the Soviet Union and her experiences there only strengthened her admiration. Unlike some of her colleagues, who were ardent Russophiles while this was expedient and quick to show their true feelings when the wind changed, she retained her convictions till the end of her life. Some of her comments on the time-servers were unprintable, but may be guessed at from a reading of her novel *Not Without Fantasy* (1947) which gives a striking picture of the war as seen by the foreign correspondents in Moscow. The tedium and the frustrations come through, but so does the sense of a great people fighting a just and necessary war.

Shortly afterwards the Jacobs returned to England by way of the Balkans, where they saw something of the beginnings of the new Socialist countries emerging from the war. They reached London in August. Iris Morley returned to the U.S.S.R. for a further three months in 1947, after which the development of the Cold War made British papers increasingly disinclined to keep correspondents in Moscow, especially if they were known to be sympathetic to the Soviet regime. In 1950 she was able to make a short visit as one of a delegation of women, and returned very impressed by the speed with which the devastation of the war was being repaired.

Early in 1946 she and her husband bought a bomb-damaged Georgian house, Chetwynd House at Hampton Court, which was to be her home for the rest of her life. And in May 1946, her daugher was born. Her name, Aurora, was characteristic, originating partly from the well-known ballet and partly from the cruiser *Aurora* which played a symbolic role in the October Revolution. Hampton Court, which she already loved and knew well (she wrote about it in *The Mighty Years*), made a fine setting for her style and her love of history, and in 1951 she wrote, and published herself, a booklet *Hampton Court* which is a guide with a difference. It not only describes the Palace and how it came to be built, but also goes into some detail about what it cost and how the builders were paid. She loved the elegance of the Wren buildings and sometimes expressed regrets, not perhaps entirely serious, that he never completed his plan for tearing down the Tudor parts and rebuilding the whole in a uniform classical style.

Once settled at Hampton Court she began to resume political activities. Her articles as ballet critic for the *Daily Worker* were of outstanding quality. She became a most popular lecturer on behalf of the British-Soviet Friendship Society and the Society for Cultural Relations. She began to take part in the work of the History Group of the Communist Party, especially in a series of discussions aimed at clarifying problems of the sixteenth and seventeenth centuries. About the end of 1949 or the beginning of 1950 she joined the British Communist Party, from which, indeed, she had never been divided by any substantial differences. She became active, too, in the peace movement, especially among her fellow writers.

In 1946 she began to write *A Thousand Lives*, 'an account of the English revolutionary movement of 1660-1685'. In this she developed the thesis, implicit in *Cry Treason* and *We stood for Freedom*, of the Monmouth rebellion as the last act of the English Revolution and as resuming the political struggle of the Levellers and other left elements of the Commonwealth. It is a remarkable book which has never had the recognition it deserves, perhaps partly because the quality of its writing has aroused academic disquiet. Professor V.G. Kiernan calls it 'the first serious British study inspired by Marxist thinking of this neglected period'. After remarking that it 'is based throughout on a systematic study of the evidence', he adds:

> Still more striking is the historical imagination at work in it. It is the work of an author most of whose books were novels, and it has humanistic qualities lamentably rare in the academic history-writing of today. To the study of society and its solid economic foundations she added an absorbing interest in individuals, in motive and psychology and the often unpredictable interaction of character and circumstance . . . It will stand as an inspiring lesson in how scholarship and imagination can again be brought together [*Lab. Mon.* (Feb 1955) 92-3].

Christopher Hill praised it in similar terms. It is 'a brilliant study of a neglected period in the revolutionary history of the English people . . . Miss Morley tells the moving story with great skill and vivacity. It is a tragedy that so talented a writer was cut off in her prime; but this is a noble legacy' [*Daily Worker*, 25 Nov 1954].

A Thousand Lives, with the three novels based on seventeenth-century history, will probably prove to be the most durable part of her literary work. Yet it met with considerable difficulties at the start. Finished in 1950, it was rejected by several publishers with more or less polite excuses, and was only published, by André Deutsch, more than a year after her death. After completing *A Thousand Lives* she wrote her last novel, *Rack* (1952). In this she returns to the memories and experiences of her early life, though a reader who assumed that every character or episode must have an actual counterpart would be seriously mistaken. This, indeed, is true of all her novels of contemporary life: her own experience is used but is also transformed. What is real is the accurate reflection of the atmosphere and society in which they move.

About the time *Rack* was completed she had to undergo an operation in St Mary's Hospital, Paddington for what appeared to be an ovarian cyst, but proved to be a malignant tumour in such an advanced state as to give no hope of recovery. The surgeon estimated her probable expectation of life at no more than six months, though in fact she lived almost two years, soon in a state of increasing pain and weakness. During these years her courage and resolution never failed.

She was not told of the actual facts of her condition and continued to work in hope of ultimate recovery. Almost at once she began what was intended to be a major novel on the life of Nelson, with the whole panorama of revolutionary and Napoleonic Europe as a background. At the time of her death perhaps a quarter was written – not enough for publication, but enough to show that it might have been a book of no less power and distinction than the best of her other work.

In July 1953 she went for a holiday in Cornwall, hoping that this would assist her recovery. At this point she had certainly no thought of death, but was making eager plans for the future. But after a few days she became critically ill and was brought back to Trimmer's Hospital, Farnham, where she died on 27 July. Her funeral was at Fleet, Hampshire, and she was buried in the local cemetery. A striking tribute from a correspondent appeared in *The Times* [7 Aug 1953]. Iris Morley was survived by her husband and their daughter, Aurora, then seven years old. Aurora subsequently considered following her mother into RADA or her step-mother, Kathleen Byron, the actress, into the Old Vic but decided not to. She married Laurence Way and later trained as a teacher.

Writings: *The Proud Paladin* (New York and London, 1936; repr. 1971); 'Miss Britannia', *Good Housekeeping* (June 1940); *Cry Treason* (1940); *We stood for Freedom* (1941; New York, 1942; repr. Bath, 1973); *The Mighty Years* (1943); *Soviet Ballet* (1945); *Nothing but Propaganda* (1946); *Not without Fantasy* (1947); (with P.W. Manchester), *The Rose and the Star. Ballet in England and Russia compared* (1949); *Hampton Court. How the palace was built* . . . (1951) 30 pp., repr. as *Here's Hampton Court* (1952) 30 pp.; *Rack* (1952); *A Thousand Lives. An Account of the English Revolutionary Movement, 1660-1685* (1954).

Sources: G. Winstanley, *A Watch-word to the City of London, and the Armie* (1649); *Daily Worker*, 25 Nov 1954; S.W. Roskill, *The War at Sea 1939-1945*, vol. *3* (1960); *Winstanley: the Law of Freedom and other writings*, ed. with an Introduction by C. Hill (Penguin, 1973); personal information: M. Braddell, New York, uncle; Mrs D. Manser, Crookham Village, Hampshire, sister; A. Jacob, London, husband; personal knowledge. OBIT. *Times*, 28 July and 7 Aug 1953.

A. LESLIE MORTON

OAKEY, Thomas (1887-1953)
MINERS' LEADER

Thomas, or Tom Oakey, as he was usually called, was born the son of John Oakey, a miner, at Fryston, near Castleford, on 1 August 1887. Throughout his life he was connected with the mining industry of Yorkshire and never lived more than two miles away from the mining community into which he had been born. When he was only three years old his father was killed in an accident at Fryston Colliery. Another three members of his family also died in pit accidents. In 1897, during a strike in which his elder brothers were involved, the family were evicted from a company-owned house and forced to move to Castleford. Three years later Oakey left school and started work as a pony driver at Glass Houghton Colliery, Castleford. In his early years he was strongly influenced by Herbert Smith, who was then the Glass Houghton branch delegate of the Yorkshire Miners' Association and a checkweighman in the Haigh Moor seam where Oakey worked, and who sustained and enlarged Oakey's interest in miners' trade unionism. Herbert Smith – who was to become not only the most prominent Yorkshire miners' official but also president of the MFGB – and Oakey were to enjoy a close friendship.

Oakey remained at Glass Houghton from 1900 to 1912 and then moved to Fryston Colliery, where he became a deputy. His career as a miner, however, was interrupted by the First World War, when he joined the Army, and for a short period was a machine gun instructor at Pirbright, Surrey, attached to the Guards' Machine Gun Regiment. Two years after the end of the war Oakey returned to Glass Houghton Colliery, where he quickly became involved again in the affairs of the Yorkshire Miners' Association. After being employed for seven years as a face-worker he was elected by the Glass Houghton lodge as their delegate to council meetings of the YMA.

During the years that followed Thomas Oakey played an increasingly important part in the organisation and administration of the Association. By this time he had gained a reputation as a competent pit man and trade union official. In 1931 he was one of sixty candidates nominated for the position of auditor of the YMA and was elected by a comfortable margin. Oakey succeeded Levi Dyson of the Barrow lodge, near Barnsley, who had worked together with James Ballance of the Wheldale branch, Castleford. When Ballance retired a few years later Oakey continued to carry out his functions as an auditor single-handed. In 1939 when Joseph Hall was elected president of the union, and a new financial secretary had to be appointed, Oakey was chosen as his successor. Oakey was also a member of the South and West Yorkshire Joint Boards, which were concerned with disputes and grievances occurring at individual collieries; and in addition he served on the Yorkshire Regional Coal Board. In 1948 he represented Yorkshire on the executive committee of the National Union of Mineworkers.

In 1952 Oakey retired from all trade union activity at the same time that Joseph Hall retired from the presidency of the YMA. A ceremony attended by many NUM and YMA officials, together with a number of MPs, was held in Barnsley in October of that year, in honour of both men. Many tributes were paid to Oakey's work for the miners, and W.E. Jones (then vice-president of the NUM and general secretary of the YMA) presented him with a cheque and a case of pipes. Over the years Oakey had given valuable advice on research relating to safety in mines; and it was this aspect of his service which was particularly stressed by Arthur Horner, the general secretary of the NUM, in his address.

Oakey was a physically large man, with a quiet personality. 'Communication' wrote one of his colleagues, 'was never a strong point with Tom on any subject.' In politics, as in industrial matters, he was firm but moderate in all his opinions and actions; and there is no doubt about his popularity with his own generation of miners. Outside his trade union work and family responsibilities Oakey had little time for other activities; he was, however, a keen supporter of Castleford Rugby League Club and was considered a good judge of the game.

On 18 May 1953, less than a year after his retirement, and after an illness lasting over eighteen months, Thomas Oakey died at his home in Townville, Castleford. He was survived by his wife Catherine and by his two daughters. A Requiem Mass was celebrated on 21 May at St Joseph's Church, Castleford, of which Oakey was a member; he was buried in Castleford Cemetery. He left £3391 in his will.

Sources: *Pontefract and Castleford Express,* 17 Mar 1939 and 24 Oct 1952; biographical information: NUM (Yorkshire). OBIT. *Yorkshire Evening News,* 18 and 19 May 1953; *Yorkshire Post,* 19 May 1953; *Pontefract and Castleford Express,* 22 May 1953.

ROBERT G. NEVILLE

See also: †Joseph Arthur (Joe) HALL; †Herbert SMITH.

PALIN, John Henry (1870-1934)
TRANSPORT WORKERS' LEADER AND LABOUR MP

John Henry Palin was born at 7 Renfrew Road, Lambeth, in London, on 19 July 1870, the son of John Palin, a joiner who came from Nottingham, and his wife Elizabeth (née Shipman). He was educated at St Nicholas's Boys' School, Nottingham, and began work at the age of twelve as an apprentice joiner. Eventually, having changed jobs on a number of occasions, he went into service in 1891 with the Great Northern Railway as a porter at Kings Cross Station, London, then in Nottingham, Retford and several other stations before moving to Laisterdyke Station, Bradford, in 1895. He left railway service in 1899 in order to devote more time to politics.

It was trade unionism which first brought Palin into public life, although his trade union associations in the early years of the century are somewhat confusing. He was secretary of the Laisterdyke branch of the ASRS in 1896 and represented it on the Bradford Trades Council. Although he was apparently no longer a railwayman he was on the EC of the ASRS in 1901-2, an ASRS delegate to the 1903 Conference of the LRC and chairman of the ASRS conference in 1906. In 1903 he became the secretary of the Bradford branch of the Amalgamated Association of Tramway and Vehicle Workers – this was presumably a paid job – and during the first ten years of office he increased the local membership from 150 to 1500.

Palin's major contribution however, came in the field of Labour politics. He had been a member of the ILP since 1896, and rose quickly to local prominence. In 1904 he was elected as the councillor for Bradford Moor ward and was returned for this ward at every election until the 1920s. Although he was a member of the ILP (in 1913 a member of the NAC) he nevertheless stood with the support of the Workers' Municipal Federation, an organisation which had been formed in 1901 and 1902 in order to unite the various factions of the Labour movement at municipal elections. In 1901, along with four ILP colleagues – Edwin Halford, Frederick Jowett, Dr Hector Munro and Julia Varley – Palin was elected to the Bradford Board of Guardians. He spent three years on the Board, where he campaigned especially for the construction of old people's cottage homes. In his early years his town council work was mainly directed towards improving the condition of tramway workers and dealing with educational questions. In the latter field he was particularly concerned with school meals for the children of the working classes. In these and other matters he was a staunch supporter of Jowett, and when Jowett was returned to Parliament for Bradford West, in 1906, Palin assumed the leadership of the Bradford Labour Movement on all educational matters. He neatly presented the main arguments on the school meals question in a short pamphlet, *Bradford and its Children: how they are fed* [1908?]. In 1909 and again in 1912 Palin was a candidate for the NEC of the Labour Party.

In 1913, one newspaper described Palin as a 'young man in a hurry.' In Labour circles he is not only notable locally, but he is considered to be the coming man in the larger sphere of Parliamentary representation [*Bradford Weekly Telegraph,* 3 Oct 1913]. Palin disagreed politically with most of his colleagues in the leadership of the ILP in supporting the First World War, and he served as a sergeant in the ordnance department of the Royal Engineers. After the war he continued to serve as secretary of the Bradford Tramway and Vehicle Workers until 1921 when, on the formation of the TGWU, he became secretary of the Passenger Trade Group for the No. 9 area, holding this position until 1925. In 1918 and again in 1922 he unsuccessfully contested Bradford North in the general elections of these years, but was unexpectedly returned for Newcastle West in the 1924 'Zinoviev scare' election and again in 1929, being defeated there in 1931. He was adopted as candidate for Shipley in 1932. His career in the Commons was undistinguished, and none of his main concerns – the raising of the school-leaving age to sixteen and the other demands of the Bradford Charter – were carried on to the Statute Book.

Palin was an excellent debater and exerted much influence over his Bradford contemporaries. He was Lord Mayor of Bradford in 1924-5. Palin was a member of the Church of England, and was a speaker for the St Mary's Mission in Nottingham during the early 1890s. He was a co-operator all his life and an anti-vaccinationist. He married Annie, daughter of John Bettison, on 8 October 1895, and they had two sons and five daughters. Palin died on 22 May 1934. W. Leach, ex-MP for Bradford Central, wrote of him that 'Bradford has produced two really great trade union secretaries and both are now dead. One was Joseph Hayhurst and the other was John

Henry Palin, and which was the greater I do not know' [*Bradford Pioneer*, 25 May 1934]. No will has been located.

Writings: *Bradford and its Children: how they are fed* [1908?] 12 pp. [repr. from *Socialist Rev. 1* (1908) 207-19].

Sources: (1) MSS: Bradford Trades and Labour Council, Minutes: Textile Hall, Bradford. (2) Other: Bradford Trades and Labour Council, *Year Books*, 1904-23; *Yorkshire Factory Times*, 15 July 1904; *Bradford Weekly Telegraph*, 3 Oct 1913; *Newcastle J.*, 16 Oct 1924; *TGWU Record*, (Jan 1924) and (June 1934); *Labour Who's Who* (1927); *Times Guide to the House of Commons* (1929); *Times*, 24 May 1934; F. Brockway, *Socialism over Sixty Years: the life of Jowett of Bradford* (1946); biographical information: Bradford Central Library; T.A.K. Elliott, CMG. Obit. *Bradford Pioneer*, 25 May 1934.

KEITH LAYBOURN

See also: *Frederick William JOWETT, for Independent Labour Party, 1893-1914; †Samuel SHAFTOE.

PETCH, Arthur William (1886-1935)
SOCIALIST, CO-OPERATOR AND TRADE UNION LEADER

Arthur William Petch was born on 3 March 1886 in the village of Hornby near Lancaster in the hundred of Lonsdale. He was the son of Nathaniel Petch, a police sergeant in the Lancashire Constabulary, and his wife Emma (née Fletcher). His early life was spent moving from place to place as the Lancashire Constabulary demanded of his father. The family finally settled down at Swinton, Lancashire, where Arthur attended the St Peter Church of England School for 1 d per week. He left school in 1900 at the age of fourteen and began work as a junior clerk with the Eccles Provident Industrial Co-operative Society (later Eccles and District Co-operative Society). As a young man he was very keen on physical culture; he practised wrestling and boxing, and won a bronze medal for weight-lifting. He became an instructor and ran a physical culture group at the Blue Ribbon Hall, Pendlebury; but he suffered a severe heart strain which forced him to give up his athletic pursuits and kept him out of the First World War.

He joined the Eccles branch of the Amalgamated Union of Co-operative Employees in 1908 – the only member of the office staff in the union – and for four years acted as secretary to the Eccles Co-operative Employees' Social Committee. He left the service of the Society in February 1914 upon being appointed as shorthand-typist to Alfred Hewitt, the general secretary of the AUCE. In August 1914 he was chosen to be the secretary of the Eccles branch of the AUCE and was responsible for the building of the Eccles branch from 170 members in 1914 to 726 members in 1916, with a 100 per cent membership of all local employees. He was responsible for the formation of the Manchester Federation of the branches of the AUCE. He remained in branch office, first as organising secretary and later as financial secretary, until 1920, and he was elected to the North Western District Council of the AUCE in 1916.

In addition to his union work within the co-operative movement he also became involved in the activities of the local labour movement. He was a delegate to the Eccles Trades and Labour Council from the Eccles branch of the AUCE in 1910, and when the demands of the First World War robbed the Council of its officials in 1914 he became the secretary, and was elected president of the Council in 1916. It was he who brought about the establishment of the Irlam and Cadishead Trades Council in 1914 and the Swinton and Pendlebury Trades Council in 1917. He was secretary to the Eccles Parliamentary Divisional Labour Party from 1916 to 1920, and an unsuccessful Labour candidate in the 1919 Eccles municipal election.

A major break in his union career came in 1920 when he was appointed manager of the general section of the AUCE under Joseph Hallsworth. When the AUCE joined with the Warehouse Workers' Union to form the National Union of Distributive and Allied Workers (NUDAW) in 1921, Petch was appointed financial secretary and office manager. He was an extremely efficient administrator, and continued in the head office of the union until his death.

Although he had resigned all his positions in the local labour movement in 1920, Petch continued to be active in the Eccles co-operative movement. In 1918 he had been elected a director of the Eccles Provident Industrial Co-operative Society and served until 1921; he was re-elected in 1922 and served continuously until 1931, when he became president. He retired from this position in January 1934 on the ground of ill health.

Petch was an excellent debater, and in the 1920s he became a NCLC lecturer. He devised the NCLC course for secretaries – being a Fellow of the Institute of Secretaries' Association – and he was an assiduous examiner of the correspondence courses in the subject. He was a lecturer at NCLC summer schools, and contributed to *Plebs*, to the earlier AUCE *Journal* and to the later *New Dawn*, in which he wrote the 'Central Office Notes'. He also wrote under the pseudonym of 'Autolycus' as well as under his personal signature.

His wife died on 6 August 1935 after a short and painful illness. The shock of her death placed Arthur Petch under a tremendous strain. He died peacefully during the night of 16 August 1935, only ten days after his wife, at the early age of forty-nine. His funeral took place at Manchester Crematorium and he left effects valued at £1231. Their only son, Arthur Logan Petch, after gaining an LLB degree at Manchester University became a barrister.

Writings: *Trade Unionism; What every Worker should know* (NCLC, 1934) 28 pp.; articles in *Eccles Co-operative Record* and *New Dawn*; *A Manual of Trade Union Branch Administration* [n.d.] [n.p.].

Sources: (1) MSS: Arthur Petch papers: Eccles PL. (2) *Eccles Co-operative Record* (1910-1935); *New Dawn,* 7 Jan 1922; *Labour Who's Who* (1927); *Eccles Co-operative Record* (Aug 1934) 185; J.B. Smethurst, 'History of Eccles Trades Council and Labour Party' [unpublished MS]; biographical information: P.H. Jones, USDAW; personal information: Miss K. Anders and H. Pridmore, USDAW; A.L. Petch, Manchester, son. OBIT. *Eccles and Patricroft J.*, 23 Aug 1935; *New Dawn*, 24 Aug 1935; *Eccles Co-operative Record* (Aug 1935).

JOHN B. SMETHURST

PICTON-TURBERVILL, Edith (1872-1960)
SOCIAL REFORMER AND LABOUR MP

Edith Picton-Turbervill was born at Lower House, Fownhope, Herefordshire, on 13 June 1872, the twin daughter of John Picton Warlow, then a captain in the Madras Staff Corps, and his wife Eleanor (née Temple) daughter of Sir Grenville Temple, Bt, of Stowe. She changed her name to Picton-Turbervill at the same time as her father, when in 1891 he inherited the Turbervill estate of Ewenny Priory in Glamorgan. The estate was of over 3000 acres and her father was a mine royalty owner and a Conservative; he was a JP and a member of the Penybont RDC. Edith was educated at the Royal School, Bath. Both her family environment and her school encouraged her in the belief that life was essentially something active, preferably on behalf of others; she was also deeply religious. It was social and philanthropic work which drew her to the labour movement, leading her to conclude 'that fundamental changes in law were necessary to obtain better conditions of life for the people' [*Life is good,* 154]. She grew up in a family which was aristocratically connected, although not particularly affluent until she was grown-up.

Her first experience of social work was among navvies working on the building of the Vale of Glamorgan Railway, near her home. They were living in squalid conditions, isolated from the local community, and Edith attempted their moral improvement through religion and the provision of a reading room. At this time her interests were mainly in evangelical work, and she attended a training school for missionaries in London as a preparation for missionary work in the East. Part of the course consisted of slum visiting, which brought her into contact with the slums of Shoreditch and the evils of sweated labour.

As a young woman she had met in America the Hon. Emily Kinnaird, of the Young Women's Christian Association, and it was through her that Edith Picton-Turbervill first developed an interest in that organisation. In 1900 she went to India to work for the YWCA, mainly among Anglo-Indians and Indian women students, until ill health compelled her to return home in 1906. She went back to India after her illness and became travelling secretary of the YWCA Students' Department in South India, finally leaving in 1908. She never lost her interest in India, and later was active in Indian debates during her two years in the Commons. On returning home she became head of the YWCA Foreign Department from 1909. At this time she was also involved in the agitation for women's suffrage, but definitely on the constitutionalist side, regarding Mrs Millicent Fawcett as her leader rather than Mrs Emmeline Pankhurst, for whom, however, she had a very high regard.

One of her lifelong wishes was that women should be allowed to take orders in the Church of England. Soon after the end of the First World War she became the first woman to preach a sermon at a statutory service of the Church of England, at North Somercotes, in Lincolnshire. She was also one of a number of women who preached at St Botolph's Church, Bishopsgate, at the invitation of the rector, G.W. Hudson Shaw. She held the Bishop of London's Inter-diocesan Diploma for evangelical work; and all her life the place of women in the Church remained a central concern.

She was national vice-president of the YWCA from 1914 to 1920 and from 1922 to 1928, and was, for a time, director of appeals for the Association. During the First World War she was actively involved in YWCA work to provide hostels and canteens for women munitions workers and for members of the Women's Army in France. She received the OBE for this in January 1918. It was during the war years that she seems to have made her first contact with Labour personalities, among them George Lansbury and Margaret Bondfield. Margaret Bondfield seems to have especially influenced her, although Edith noted in *Life is good* (1939), p. 155, that she was greatly impressed by Arthur Henderson's *The Aims of Labour* (1918). Exactly when she became a Socialist is not clear from her autobiography, but she joined the Labour Party early in 1919, and became a parliamentary candidate for North Islington at the general election of 1922. Maude Royden and Isabella Ford were among those who gave her active support in her campaign, and although she had little hope of winning the seat she increased the Labour vote. In the 1923 general election she did not stand herself, but worked in Port Talbot for Ramsay MacDonald, with whom she remained on friendly terms until his death, although her comments on him in her autobiography are by no means uncritical. She was the unsuccessful candidate for Stroud in Gloucestershire in 1924 and had some sharp comments on MacDonald's silence on the Zinoviev letter scare, noting that 'it had a devastating effect upon Labour candidates at the election'. In December 1925 she was adopted as candidate for the Wrekin division of Shropshire – like Stroud, a largely rural constituency with, however, a mining community of about four thousand; and she became a close friend of the local miners' agent, William (Bill) Latham – 'A splendid looking old man, he was a strong chapel man and his speeches full of Old Testament phraseology and references' [*Life is good,* 166]. Although an Anglican, she was frequently asked to preach in the local chapels in the Wrekin, and at the general election of 1929 she won the seat by nearly 3000 votes. When the result was announced 'some in the vast crowd, sang the Doxology "Praise God from whom all blessings flow" – this was caught up by a large number and swelled into a loud chorus' [*Life is good,* 170].

In 1929 there were fourteen women in the new House of Commons with just over 600 men; and the account of the 1929-31 Parliament in Miss Picton-Turbervill's autobiography is worth reading. She was never a militant feminist but always deeply concerned with the inferior status of women, and always vigorously supported reforming measures. Because of her wide knowledge of canon law, she was nominated by the Government – the first woman to be nominated – to the Ecclesiastical Committee of Parliament (July 1929). In her politics she was consistently a moderate and an admirer of MacDonald, but in the crisis of 1931, after a period of hesitation – she abstained from voting on the first vote of confidence asked for by the National Government – she decided to stay with the Labour Party. Henderson and William Graham, especially the latter, were mainly responsible for her decision. At the general election of 1931 she lost her seat – which she fully expected – and in her own account of these days emphasised the enormous influence of the radio broadcasts of MacDonald and Snowden in winning support for the National Government. As she wrote later: 'The panic, however, that had been created with regard to money was so great that I verily believe if a chimpanzee had stood in that election for the National Government he would in some constituencies have been returned to Parliament' [Life is good, 268].

During her time in the Commons, she achieved the rare success of having a Bill she introduced under the Ten Minutes rule become law. This was the Sentence of Death (Expectant Mothers) Bill. In her handling of this issue Edith Picton-Turbervill showed her essential humanity and sensitivity. The law did not permit the execution of a pregnant woman, and in fact women had not been executed even *after* the birth of their child for sixty years when the Bill was proposed; but the ugly charade of pronouncing the death sentence still went on, and it was this Edith Picton-Turbervill wished to prevent. She succeeded in getting government support for the Bill, which became law.

She had travelled widely all her life, and after losing her seat in Parliament she went to Russia in 1932 (which did not impress her) and to Kenya in the following year. In 1935 she visited Turkey as head of the British delegation to the International Congress of Women Citizens, and as such met Ataturk. She visited Copenhagen in the same capacity in 1939. In 1935 she was a member of the Next Five Years Group and in 1936 was asked to join a Government Commission to Hong Kong and Malaya to inquire into the *mui-tsai* question. This was a subject on which she had spoken many times while in Parliament. Under this system, young girls were transferred from their natural parents to another household, in return for money, to become domestic servants. It was obviously open to abuse, and was, in fact, illegal but still widespread. An attempt had been made to register and inspect existing *mui-tsais* in 1929, but there was still a good deal of disquiet on the subject. Her investigations led Edith Picton-Turbervill to write a Minority Report. The two other commissioners, Sir Wilfrid Woods and Mr C. A. Willis, retired members of the Ceylon and Sudan Civil Services respectively, thought that the existing legislation simply needed to be more actively enforced. They thought it politically unwise to do as Miss Picton-Turbervill suggested in her report – to extend the system of registration and inspection to all transferred children, whether they were called *mui-tsais* or whatever. Both reports were published by the Colonial Office in 1937, and in 1939 the Governments of Hong Kong and Malaya both accepted the principle of the Minority Report.

During the Second World War Edith Picton-Turbervill worked for the Ministry of Information from 1941 to 1943. In 1944 she was president of the National Council of Women Citizens. From 1940 she lived in the Cheltenham area, continued to write, lecture, and support the many causes in which she had worked, and also appeared on radio and television. She died on 31 August 1960 at Cheltenham, aged eighty-eight, and left an estate valued at £25,555.

Edith Picton-Turbervill was an impressive figure physically, tall and strong-featured. Her speeches in Parliament were forthright, based upon strongly-held and well-argued opinions. She had a wide circle of friends, including left-wing Labourites, and her political moderation was by no means the mark of a weak personality. On the contrary, she always acted according to her conscience, and her moral courage was undoubted. Coming as she did from an old and famous family, the labour opinions she developed were sharply in contrast with her family and general social background; but her relations with her family remained warm and affectionate. Almost all her close friends were women, most of them from the middle or upper class, and with a marked social or religious conscience; they included the Hon. Emily Kinnaird, who visited India for the last time at the age of eighty-one for the purpose of spreading the Gospel among the untouchables of the South; Maude Royden; and Elizabeth Cadbury.

Writings: 'The Coming Order in the Church of Christ', *19th C. and after 80*, nos. 475 and 477 (1916) 521-30, 1000-7; (with B.H. Streeter), *Woman and the Church* (1917); 'The Liturgy of the Church of England', *Cont.Rev.113* (Jan 1918) 76-9; *Christ and Woman's Power*, with an Introduction by Lady Frances Balfour (1919); *Musings of a Lay-woman on the Life of the Churches* (1919); *Christ and International Life* [1921]; *The Coming Order in the Church of Christ, Women in the Church* (1923) 11 pp.; 'New Turkey's Dictator', *Sat.Rev.159*, 29 June 1935, 811; Commission on Mui Tsai in Hong Kong and Malaya: *Report* (Jan 1937) Colonial No.125 non-parl., Minority Report on pp. 214-49; 'Childhood in Brighton and Bruges', in *Myself when young*, ed. Countess of Oxford and Asquith (1938) 313-60; *Life is good: an autobiography* (1939); *In the Land of my Fathers* (Cardiff, 1946); *Should Women be Priests and Ministers?* [repr. from B.H. Streeter and E. Picton-Turbervill, *Woman and the Church* (1917)] [1953] 52 pp.; Preface to A.B. Temple, *The Story of Algar Temple and the Indian Mutiny* [Cardiff, 1957?].

Sources: *Labour Who's Who* (1924); *Hansard* (1929-31); *Dod* (1931); *Kelly* (1932); L. Abercrombie et al., *The Next Five Years: an essay in political agreement* (1935); G.A. Greenwood, 'A Woman on the Track of Slavery', *Great Thoughts* (Oct 1936) 26-8; *Myself when young* and *Life is good* [see **Writings** above]; *International Who's Who* (1945-6); *WWW* (1951-60); biographical information: Dr M.E. Currell, Birmingham Univ.; T.A.K. Elliott, CMG; Mrs B. Wilson, YWCA, Hull. OBIT. *Gloucestershire Echo*, 2 Sep 1960; *Manchester Guardian* and *Times*, 3 Sep 1960; *Labour Party Report* (1960).

ANN HOLT

See also: †Arthur HENDERSON, for British Labour Party, 1914-31.

POOLE, Stephen George (1862-1924)
LABOUR COUNCILLOR

Stephen George Poole was born in Earlsdon, Coventry, on 23 January 1862. His father, George Poole, was a watch finisher, a skilled workman and a regular attender at chapel. His mother Ellen (née Dolbey) came from a more comfortable background. In spite of his careful and thrifty behaviour, George's father experienced financial difficulties during the trade depression of the late 1860s, and in 1868 the family left Coventry, living successively in Manchester, Warrington and Preston; they later returned to Coventry. Moreover, ill health in the father left the family in great need, and they lived in the poorer quarters of the city.

Stephen George's education was interrupted when his father fell ill, and at the age of nine, the young George took a job as an errand boy. He then became a half-timer in a cotton mill, and as soon as he had passed the required educational level, worked full-time at the mill, supplementing his education by attending a night school. On the family's return to Coventry, he worked for a short time in a cotton factory. He then found a situation at Owen Bros, where he was apprenticed for seven years as a ribbon designer and jacquard stamper. During his apprenticeship the family home was broken up, his mother, brothers and sisters left Coventry for London, and George was left to live on his apprentice's pay. In 1883 he became a journeyman and a freeman of the city. A year later he married. He left Owen Bros in 1886 to become a designer with Corey Franklin, a ribbon manufacturer, where he remained until 1900. In that year he started in business for himself as a textile designer at 19 Much Park Street and was also known for his work on illuminated addresses, some of which were produced for trade union branches.

As a young man, Poole took an active interest in social matters. His activities were first channelled through the Holy Trinity Young Men's Association, which campaigned on social questions; but later he became a leading member of the SDF in the city. He was one of the founder members of the Coventry ILP and LRC. He first stood in a municipal election in 1896, as a candidate for Gosford Street ward, but polled only 172 votes. In 1905 he again stood as a Labour candidate, this time in Harnall ward, where he was second on the poll for a single seat. A by-election for the same ward followed only three weeks later; Poole was this time successful and so became Coventry's first Labour councillor. He concentrated his attention on the reform of sanitary conditions and on housing. His name is associated in particular with the campaign to abolish private slaughter-houses in Coventry and to establish a public abattoir. In 1908, impressed by Upton Sinclair's *The Jungle,* he produced a pamphlet entitled *Coventry's Jungle* to publicise the need for a public abattoir. But in spite of his persistence in the matter, the abattoir was not established until eight years after his death.

Poole tackled many other issues in his years as the only representative of Labour. He suggested measures to deal with the refuse which had contributed to the high infant mortality rate in the north-eastern quarter of Coventry in the summer of 1906. He campaigned for the establishment of secondary schools in the city where places would be free: for supplying workmen's cottages with electricity and gas at reasonable prices, and against the unwholesome conditions prevailing in and around many of the poorer quarters of the city.

Poole's main success was undoubtedly in the field of housing. In March 1906 he tabled a motion in Council calling for a committee of inquiry into housing in Coventry and indicating that municipal housing should be provided. This led to an agreement on the Council, one year later, to provide workmen's flats in Short Street and houses in Narrow Lane which were completed in 1908. Other schemes followed, so that by the outbreak of the First World War there were nearly two hundred municipal houses. George Poole was a member of the housing committee between 1906 and 1920 (except for 1907-8 when he was not on the Council) and was chairman in 1913-16. Under his chairmanship other building schemes were encouraged. His interest in housing was not confined to his work on the City Council. In 1911 he was also involved in a scheme to establish a garden suburb at Radford, although it was not until 1914 that the necessary capital was promised by Coventry Co-operative Society.

In conjunction with Rowland Barrett, Tom Hutt, and other Coventry Socialists, Poole was involved with the publication of an ILP paper, the *Coventry Sentinel* (1908-12). In 1909-10 he was the prospective ILP parliamentary candidate for Coventry, but did not pursue his candidature. With the outbreak of war in 1914, however, Poole became much more conservative in his views; and he was active in the British Workers' National League, a 'patriotic' body which was virulently hostile to the pacifist cause. In 1918 he was appointed a JP but thereafter he became increasingly at odds with the local labour movement and he retired from the Council, and from active political life, in 1921. After a period of failing health he died at his son's home at Bingley on 21 July 1924. He was buried at Coventry Cemetery and the address at the funeral was given by the Rev. P.E.T. Widdrington. He left a widow, eleven children and effects valued at £996.

Sources: (1) MSS: Notes in Coventry and Warwickshire Coll. (John Yates's book): Coventry Reference Library. (2) Other: *Coventry Herald* and *Coventry Standard*, 1900-24 *passim;* S.G. Poole, *Coventry's 'Jungle': the case for a public abattoir* (Coventry ILP, 1908) 8 pp.; J. Yates, *Pioneers to Power (Coventry LP, 1950);* K. Richardson, *Twentieth-Century Coventry* (Coventry, 1972). OBIT. *Coventry Standard*, 25-6 July 1924.

JANET DRUKER

See also: Rowland BARRETT.

REED, Richard Bagnall (1831-1908)

RADICAL REFORMER

Richard Bagnall Reed was born in Winlaton, County Durham in 1831. After receiving an elementary education he was apprenticed to the trade of a blacksmith, specialising in chainmaking. He subsequently edited, for a short time, the news-sheet of the Chainmakers' Union. He continued to educate himself in his leisure time and took a particular interest in political questions. This was natural since the Bagnalls and Reeds among his forbears shared the radical sympathies of the Winlaton ironworkers, who had been radicals since the time of 'Crowley's Crew' (in the works originally established there by Ambrose Crowley); it is to be noted that the committee of the Winlaton and Blaydon Health Association, founded on 26 January 1848, included R.S. Bagnall, James and John Reed, all of Winlaton. The inauguration of the Winlaton Mechanics' Institution on 1 February 1847 gave R.B. Reed the opportunity for self-improvement, particularly when a Reading Room was opened in Winlaton on 27 September of the same year. Reed, aged sixteen, is recorded as speaking at the latter occasion, when he remarked on 'the advantages of this step, as illustrated in his own person.' He became an active member of the Mechanics' Institution and, at its fourth anniversary meeting, delivered an address on the theme 'Civilization – may it reign victorious in every clime.' Reed is mentioned in Ward's local Directory for 1851 as the librarian of the Mechanics' Institution. The secretary of this body was Joseph Cowen, junior, who was to be Reed's lifelong colleague. Although only two years older than Reed, Cowen was the dominant figure in the partnership, partly through force of character and partly through Cowen's wealthier family background. Throughout, Cowen provided the leadership and the resources, and Reed the painstaking zeal. Their views were similar: interest in Mechanics' Institutes, support for the co-operative movement, hostility to the game laws, and, above all, commitment to radical reform of the franchise. It would be tempting to dismiss Reed as a mere carbon copy of his dynamic companion, but this would do less than justice to Reed's own qualities and achievements.

Newcastle in the 1850s had considerable potential as a radical centre. Cowen, the leading radical personality, was an active supporter of revolutionary movements abroad and of radical reform at home. It was he who brought George Julian Harney to Newcastle to edit the *Northern Tribune* in 1854. Together they founded the short-lived 'Republican Brotherhood' in 1855, and worked to gain control of the Newcastle Foreign Affairs Committee. When franchise reform was promised in the Queen's Speech at the opening of the 1857-8 session, Cowen immediately took the initiative. He convened a meeting of 'the friends of political reform', in the Chartist Hall, Nun Street, Newcastle, on 27 December 1857. R.B. Reed moved a resolution that local reformers should meet in one week's time, 'to consider the desirability of forming an organisation for agitating the northern counties in favour of a radical measure of parliamentary reform'. Reed's proposal was carried unanimously and the meeting duly took place on 2 January 1858, when the decision was taken to establish the Northern Reform Union. Its purpose was declared to be the mobilising of public opinion on behalf of a measure of parliamentary reform, based on manhood suffrage, the secret ballot, and the abolition of the property qualification for members of parliament. Cowen was elected treasurer and Reed secretary, which laid down the lines of their subsequent relationship: the paymaster and the organiser. Reed had given up his trade of chainmaking at the end of 1857 and received a salary in his new position.

The veteran radical, Thomas Doubleday, was invited to compose an address, which was published in March 1858. Its style and tone probably did the Union more harm than good. Reed's quiet efficiency was already beginning to attract sympathetic attention in the local press, even if editors could not fully espouse the Union's programme. The Address was a different matter. Couched in Chartist language, with resentment at 'class-favouring legislation' and the self-seeking of the 'landed and monied oligarchy', and sustained by an idiosyncratic view of history, the Address was unlikely to attract support from middle-class radicals. Yet Cowen and

Reed, from the outset, wished to avoid suffering the fate of the Chartists through alienating the middle classes. Although taking their stand upon the working-class claim for manhood suffrage, neither Cowen nor Reed demanded the vote for all men without exception or restriction. They agreed that paupers, criminals and lunatics should be excluded, and Reed considered that the elector should be a person who 'by a fixed residence gave proof of his being an honest citizen'.

In September 1858 Cowen issued an appeal to middle-class reformers. His printed letter eschewed 'the antagonistic and personal policy of past days'. Middle-class reformers were invited to adhere to the Northern Reform Union, or, if personal objections prevented this, to work for reform through their own organisation. Reed tried to recruit tradesmen to local committees of the Union and relied on moderation of manner to allay middle-class suspicions. Surveying the first ten months' work of the Union, Reed observed:

> No undue excitement had been indulged in, no bombastical declamation had been used, but a fair effort was made to show to the commercial classes that the faults and errors of the past had given the more advanced reformers an amount of experience by which they were determined to profit [Newcastle Daily Chronicle, 25 Nov 1858].

Thus, although the programme of the Northern Reform Union contained three of the six points of the People's Charter, the emphasis was placed upon the moral justification for manhood suffrage, and the spectre of 'knife and fork' Chartism was avoided. George Jacob Holyoake, writing as 'Disque' in an article first published in the Daily News and subsequently reprinted in the Newcastle Daily Chronicle, commented shrewdly on the Union:

> Its demand for reform is not the cry of empty stomachs shouting politics owing to a deficiency of soup, but the demand of sensible men who ask for what they ought to have, and will continue to ask until they get it [29 Nov 1859].

The work of building up the Northern Reform Union fell largely upon Reed's shoulders. He handled most of the correspondence, assisted in the creation of local branches, addressed public meetings and conducted relations with the press. Together with Cowen, he was the most active member of the seven-man executive of the Union. The president, William Cook, was old and infirm. The general management of the Union was entrusted to a council consisting of thirty members, according to the constitution, although in reality this figure was exceeded through the adhesion of prominent radicals, who did not normally attend at meetings. In this category were to be found G.J. Holyoake, W.J. Linton and G.J. Harney.

The subscription of at least one shilling annually was low enough to attract the working-class recruits who formed the rank-and-file of the membership. Early meeting-places, before the Union obtained its own office in Grainger Street, Newcastle, in 1859, serve to indicate sources of support: Primitive Methodist and Unitarian chapels, Temperance and Oddfellows Halls, and various taverns. Eventually a network of forty branches was established in north-east England. The main strength, outside the large towns, lay in the colliery villages. This was territory which Reed knew well, and he appears to have had more success here in his recruiting campaigns than among the shipbuilding and engineering workers of Tyneside. Reed's missionary work also took him amongst the lead-miners of Alston and the farmers of rural Northumberland. Significantly, the Northern Reform Union did not venture to hold a large open-air demonstration with trade union support, on the lines later adopted by the Northern Reform League in 1867. Indoor meetings were the rule, usually addressed by Cowen, Reed and one or two other speakers. At the end of 1859, the Union's busiest year, Reed claimed that 220 meetings had been held.

The other main campaigning tactic was the collection of petitions, with care taken to avoid impostures, in the light of Chartist experience. The climax of this work was the presentation to Parliament by the veteran General Perronet Thompson of forty-one petitions collected by the Union, simultaneously with the introduction of the Conservative Government's Reform Bill in February 1859. The petitions contained 34,676 signatures, evidence of Reed's diligent work. Although most of the signatories were working men, Reed claimed that, as regards Newcastle, the response was proportionately better from 'the professional class, such as clerks, accountants, etc.' Reed was particularly anxious to ensure that the Union received full and favourable coverage in the press. To this end, he sent reports to local editors and also contacted newspapers in London and elsewhere. From July 1858 until July 1859, the Union published its own monthly newspaper, the *Northern Reform Record*, which was then replaced by a series of cheap political tracts. The *Newcastle Daily Chronicle*, under the editorship of J. Baxter Langley from December 1858, could usually be relied upon to report meetings of the Union and to comment sympathetically upon them. This favourable treatment could not be guaranteed, however, until Cowen, already a part-owner, took over the paper in December 1859. By then, the Northern Reform Union was about to enter upon a decline which even the acquisition of the *Chronicle* could not arrest. The causes were the Newcastle election fiasco and the 'Berwick affair'.

In May 1858 the Reform Union adopted P.A. Taylor as manhood suffrage candidate for Newcastle at the next election. The initiative came from Cowen, who thereby opened up a feud with another body of local reformers, the Ratepayers' Association, better known as the Carstairs party, after the name of their candidate at the previous general election in 1857. In addition to strict temperance, municipal economy and pious moralising, Carstairs had offered the electors his support for an extension of the suffrage, with the ultimate goal of the vote for all men. This platform attracted the advocacy of the *Northern Daily Express*, the first daily paper to be established in the region, and Carstairs obtained 1672 votes. The victorious Whig/Liberal candidates, G. Ridley and T.E. Headlam, obtained 2445 votes and 2133 votes, respectively. Carstairs had done well enough to deserve another opportunity to re-contest the borough. However, the introduction of Taylor now threatened to split the reformers' vote. Carstairs' supporters, after a vain attempt to prevent the adoption of Taylor, therefore withdrew in dudgeon. The *Northern Daily Express* fulminated against the 'Blaydon atheism' which had introduced the Unitarian Taylor into the local arena. Other local newspapers were less hostile, but even the *Chronicle* disagreed with the timing of Taylor's candidature. Taylor, moreover, did not appear well-versed in the subtleties of electioneering. Reed later wrote of him:

> I feel sorry for Taylor. There are so many good points about him, but his entire absence of all tact will I am afraid prevent him from ever getting into the House.

Reed's pessimism proved to be exaggerated, for Taylor did enter Parliament, but not by courtesy of the electors of Newcastle. A deputation from the Northern Reform Union urged Taylor to quit the contest and avoid mutual embarrassment. What had been intended as a display of the Union's strength was clearly going to have the reverse effect. Yet Taylor resolved to fight on and the Union felt bound to play its part. In the general election of 1859 the sitting members were returned, Headlam with 2687 votes and Ridley with 2680 votes. Taylor received a derisory 463 votes. Disappointment at the Newcastle result, and a determination to convince middle-class voters of the corruption of the existing electoral system, led Cowen and Reed to publicise the malpractices that had taken place in Berwick-upon-Tweed at the general election and at an ensuing by-election. Their main target was a Whig, D.C. Marjoribanks, who had narrowly defeated Richard Hodgson, a Conservative, at the by-election. At Cowen's instigation, Reed now brought a private prosecution under the Corrupt Practices Act of 1854.

Reed had once expressed an interest in becoming a lawyer and embarked on his suit with enthusiasm. The Union obtained solicitors to assist him, but the politicians of Berwick were seasoned in the arts of electoral manipulation. There had already been petitions for misconduct after eight elections in the previous half-century, four of which were subsequently withdrawn. Reed's campaign, together with a petition from Hodgson, did at least cause Parliament to set up a Commission to investigate the Constituency. It sat throughout the summer of 1860 and eventually found that bribery had occurred at both the general election and the by-election. Marjoribanks, however, was exonerated and Berwick retained both its seats until the Redistribution Act of 1885.

The failure to unseat Marjoribanks, and the withdrawal in the same year of the Whig

Government's Reform Bill, had a disheartening effect upon the Union. The public mind was now more concerned with the alleged French menace and the exploits of Garibaldi than with electoral reform. The branch organisation of the Union began to crumble, although the Union still retained links with other reforming societies in the country. Reed was much involved in liaison work, being on the Council of the Ballot Society and a member of the Liverpool Financial Reform Association. He maintained a deferential correspondence with Lord Teynham, who was sympathetic to the Union's programme. It was apparently in response to a letter from Reed that Teynham lent his support to the idea of a national organisation. A national conference of reformers met at Leeds in November 1861, although neither Cowen nor Reed was present [Gillespie (1927) 238-9]. By this time the Northern Reform Union was approaching its end, and in any case, Reed was no longer the secretary.

In February 1861, J. Baxter Langley ceased to be editor of the *Newcastle Daily Chronicle*. The paper had become Cowen's dominant preoccupation and he decided that Reed's energies, like his own, could be more productively employed in journalism than in persevering with the Union. Reed at first functioned in an editorial capacity, writing an occasional leading article. Thereafter he found his true *métier*, as manager of the *Chronicle*. He became so preoccupied with the work that he did not play a leading part in the Northern Reform League, which organised local agitation at the time of the Second Reform Bill.

Reed earned the praise of distinguished contemporary journalists. G.J. Holyoake referred to Reed's 'journalist's instinct for incidents', and W.E. Adams wrote of him:

> Newspaper success depends even more upon skilful management than upon skilful writing. One of the most skilful managers of the time of which I am writing, and long afterwards, was Richard Bagnall Reed. No shrewder intellect than his, I think, was ever connected with the press. If he did not write much himself, he knew how to instruct and inspire others to write. And his energy was amazing. Nothing in any department of the paper escaped his watchful eye. Added to untiring zeal was a marvellous capacity for gauging the tastes and requirements of the reading public. Mr Reed was a newspaper genius who, had his lines been cast in other walks of life, would have attained distinction wherever he sought it. To him must be ascribed the credit of raising the press of the North of England from the parochialism of an earlier day to the rank and dignity it has ever since enjoyed [*Memoirs of a Social Atom* (1903) 493].

Reed's practical background helped him to appreciate new developments in printing technology and enabled the *Chronicle* offices to be among the best equipped in the country. He himself contributed to technical progress by inventing an improved device for casting stereotype plates, patented in 1880. In 1889 the *Chronicle* became the first British newspaper to install a 'Linotype'. Examples of Reed's managerial enterprise could be multiplied, but his work in this context belongs to the history of journalism rather than radicalism. It should, however, be stressed that the *Newcastle Daily Chronicle* owed its position as one of the most successful and influential of provincial radical newspapers in considerable part to Reed's management.

Joseph Cowen's breach with the Liberal Party over the Eastern Question, 1876-8, when Cowen's Russophobia proved stronger than his allegiance to Gladstone, caused a conflict of loyalties at the *Chronicle* office. The editor, James Annand, departed, but Reed remained. In the 1880s, Cowen's vendetta with the Party – over Ireland and Egypt in particular – led him and his newspaper to adopt a standpoint of bitter hostility towards Gladstonian Liberalism. It is impossible to establish Reed's opinion of these developments, but, whatever his sentiments, they did not prevent his remaining at Cowen's side. He is recorded as appearing, but not speaking, in support of Cowen at local meetings which Cowen addressed on 31 January 1880 and 8 January 1883. Reed's duties at the newspaper office were the probable reason for his absence from Cowen's numerous election meetings in November 1885. He was present, however, at the eve of poll meeting. Cowen's decision not to contest the Newcastle constituency in 1886 put an end to his platform appearances and to Reed's opportunity (or obligation) to display his allegiance.

Reed was an enthusiastic Freemason, rising to the high office of Deputy Provincial Grand Mark Master Mason, which he held between 1889 and 1898. He retired from the *Chronicle* in 1900, following the death of his wife and of Joseph Cowen in the same year. He spent his last years, in failing health, in a substantial house on the outskirts of Newcastle. R.B. Reed died on 27 February 1908 at Dinsdale Park, near Darlington. His funeral service took place at Longbenton on 1 March and he was buried in the family vault in the churchyard. He left an estate valued at £30,447, and was survived by twelve of his fourteen children, one of whom, Joseph, had already succeeded him as manager of the *Chronicle*. Joseph Reed later became an honorary colonel of the Tyneside Scottish volunteer regiment and received a knighthood in 1922. He relinquished his managing directorship in 1925 and retired to Horton Grange in Northumberland. Thus, only one generation separated Colonel Sir Joseph Reed, country gentleman, from R.B. Reed, the onetime chainmaker from Winlaton.

Sources: (1) MSS: Cowen papers: Newcastle PL [especially section C, no.6 for the Minute Book of the Northern Reform Union; section D, no.17; C 729 (for draft of letter to Lord Teynham, 6 Sep 1859) and C 1441 (for letter Lord Teynham to Reed, 7 July 1860)]; Holyoake papers: Co-op. Union, Manchester [especially 1102 and 1232] and Bishopsgate Institute, London. (2) Other: W.E. Adams, *Memoirs of a Social Atom*, 2 vols (1903; repr. in one vol. with an Introduction by J. Saville, New York, 1968); F.E. Gillespie, *Labor and Politics in England, 1850-1867* (Duke Univ. Press, 1927; repr. 1966); C. Muris, 'The Northern Reform Union 1858-1862' (Durham [King's College, Newcastle] MA, 1953); A.R. Schoyen, *The Chartist Challenge* (1958); M. Milne, *Newspapers of Northumberland and Durham* (Newcastle, 1971). OBIT. *Newcastle Daily Chronicle* and *Newcastle Daily J.*, 29 Feb 1908; *Newcastle Weekly J. and Courant*, 7 Mar 1908.

MAURICE MILNE

See also: †George Jacob HOLYOAKE; †Joseph COWEN.

RICHARDSON, Thomas (Tom) (1868-1928)
TRADE UNIONIST AND LABOUR MP

Tom Richardson was born at Usworth, Co. Durham, on 6 June 1868, the son of Robert Richardson, a miner. He was educated at the Usworth Board School, and started work in the pits at the age of eleven. In early adult life he was made a checkweighman at Washington Colliery, a post he held until he entered Parliament in 1910.

Richardson soon began to interest himself in politics, trade unionism and local government. He was elected to Washington School Board at the age of twenty-two, and was on the parish council for six years; he was a member of Chester-le-Street RDC for seventeen years, vice-chairman of the Council and of the Board of Guardians for three years, and chairman of the Highways Committee for six years; and he served for seven years on Durham County Council, where he was vice-chairman of an education sub-committee. He also served on the Durham Miners' executive and the Durham Coal Conciliation Board, and was vice-chairman of the Northumberland and Durham Miners' Permanent Relief Fund.

Tom Richardson was one of the pioneers of the Labour movement in the North East. He was an early member of the ILP and an active propagandist for Socialism, trade unionism and co-operation. He stood as Labour candidate for Whitehaven in the general election of December 1910. Sponsored by the ILP, he had the endorsement of the national executive of the Labour Party, and the support of the Lib-Labs. The large programme he put before the electors ranged from nationalisation of the mines through Home Rule for Ireland and a Women's Franchise Bill to Poor Law reform on the lines of the famous Minority Report. In a straight fight against the sitting MP, a Tory, Richardson won, nearly doubling the Labour vote and becoming the first Labour MP for Whitehaven.

In the House he does not seem to have spoken very often, but in 1913 he strongly supported the bill to nationalise the mines. He was a pacifist or at least was opposed to the War, and he was a member of the ILP minority led by Keir Hardie. In 1915 he asked questions in the House about the treatment of COs, and in 1916 he asked about the seizure by the police of ILP pamphlets and other literature held by branches of the ILP [*Hansard, 82,* 18 May 1916].

In 1918 he stood again for Whitehaven, but his anti-war activities had now made him so unpopular at this 'Coupon' election that he was mobbed at an open-air meeting in Whitehaven and had to be escorted by police to the house of the Whitehaven miners' agent, which the crowd then stormed and ransacked, without, however, finding him.

In 1919 Richardson decided to try to start a new career in Canada. He took his family to Vancouver, where he engaged himself in local Labour politics, and in 1920 stood as a Labour candidate for Vancouver City in the provincial elections. Politically, however, British Columbia could hardly be called radical or progressive at that time, and the Government won most of the seats. One way or another, Richardson did not succeed in making his way in British Columbia. Two daughters returned home within a year or two. The elder son chose to remain in British Columbia, where he was engaged in a course of study; but Richardson himself, his wife and his younger son returned to England in 1924.

Richardson was by then fifty-six, his financial resources appear to have been minimal, and he found it difficult to organise a way of life anything like his former one. He did propaganda work for labour causes, and was, for instance, useful in many of the by-elections which took place in the next few years. Latterly he became a regular propagandist for the London co-operative movement. But this rather exhausting work proved to be too much for his health. He developed heart trouble, and after a period of illness had finally to enter St Thomas's Hospital, where he died on 22 October 1929.

Richardson was a devout Primitive Methodist and lay preacher (as was his friend J.W. Taylor, MP, for whom he was election agent). He was a brother of W.P. Richardson, treasurer of the MFGB from 1921 to 1930. Tom Richardson had married Mary, daughter of John Purvis on 6 June 1888, and there were three sons and three daughters of the marriage. His wife survived him, along with five of the children. The two eldest daughters were secretaries at the House of Commons, of whom Nance was secretary to the Rev. Herbert Dunnico, MP, first in London and then at the United Nations in Geneva. The third daughter, Mrs Williams, lives (1976) in Los Angeles. Two of the sons had careers in Canada, one of whom was a lawyer, and the third son was a civil servant. Tom Richardson was buried at Streatham Vale Cemetery and left effects valued at £30.

Writings: *Profits and Wages in the Durham Coal Trade* (Darlington, [1909?]) 19 pp.; 'How I won Whitehaven', *Labour Leader,* 9 Dec 1910; (with J.A. Walbank), *Profits and Wages in the British Coal Trade, 1898-1910* (Newcastle, 1911); (with others), *Baths at the Pithead and the Works* (Women's Labour League, 1914) 16 pp.; *Labour's Struggle in Canada* (NLP, [1919?]) 4 pp.

Sources: (1) MSS: Labour Party archives: LRC. (2) Other: *Labour Leader,* 2 Dec 1910; *Whitehaven News,* 8 Dec 1910; *Hansard* (1913-17); *WWW* (1916-28); *Dod* (1918); *Daily Province* [Vancouver], 29 Nov and 2 Dec 1920; R. Page Arnot, *The Miners: years of struggle* (1953); R. Gregory, *The Miners and British Politics 1906-14* (Oxford, 1968); biographical information: Vancouver PL; personal information: Miss A. Gaunt, Roehampton, niece and Mrs May Robson, Whitley Bay, niece. OBIT. *Manchester Guardian and Times,* 23 Oct 1928; *Durham County Advertiser* and *Whitehaven News,* 25 Oct 1928; *Labour Party Report* (1929).

JOYCE BELLAMY
MARGARET 'ESPINASSE

See also: †William Pallister RICHARDSON; †John Wilkinson TAYLOR.

ROBERTS, George Henry (1868-1928)

TRADE UNIONIST AND LABOUR MP

Of the nine children born to George Henry Roberts and his wife Ann (née Larkman) only George Henry Roberts junior survived beyond infancy. He was born on 27 July 1868 (not 1869, the date usually given) at Chedgrave, near Loddon, Norfolk, where his father was the village shoemaker. From the age of five when his family moved to Norwich he attended St Stephen's National School, where he became a paid monitor at eleven. Delicate health during childhood precluded outdoor games but encouraged the companionship of books, especially the novels of Dickens, and Bunyan's *Pilgrim's Progress*, which he read several times. Roberts's poor health frustrated an ambition to become a schoolmaster when he was advised that the teaching profession would be too great a strain, and instead he was apprenticed at the age of thirteen to a firm of general printers, J.C. Pentney & Co. He continued to improve his education by attendance at evening classes in biology and physiology. Darwin's theory of evolution made a considerable impression on him, while through reading the works of William Morris and Russell Lowell's *Biglow Papers* he became interested in democratic ideas. Other books which influenced him were Henry Drummond's *Ascent of Man*, Benjamin Kidd's *Social Evolution* and the works on social questions published by Swan Sonnenschein. The 'democratic poets' – Roberts's phrase – Burns, Walt Whitman, Gerald Massey and Shelley, interested him most [*Rev. of Revs* (1906) 578].

When still an apprentice he agitated for improved conditions in the printing trade, but being unsuccessful, he moved to London in 1889. There he joined the London Society of Compositors and learned about the practical side of trade unionism. After a time he returned to Norwich and quickly became active in organising the local trade union movement. He was successively president and secretary of the Norwich branch of the Typographical Association. From 1892 to 1904 he was employed by Coleman and Co.

Having overcome his bad health, Roberts began a busy period of travelling and speaking. He was a leading spirit during the early years of the Norwich Trades Council, of which he was for many years president. In the early 1890s his political stance was that of a radical Liberal and he belonged to the local Gladstone Club. In 1896, however, he threw himself into the work of the Independent Labour Party and quickly became a leading figure in the Norwich branch of the movement, which he served as both secretary and president. He was also well known locally as an active member of the Friendly Society and Co-operative movements. He joined the Norwich Co-operative Society and was instrumental in getting branch funds invested in the Leicester Co-operative Printing Society. In 1899 his successful candidature at the School Board election was supported by the ILP, and in the following year there was a move to nominate him as the Socialist candidate in the general election; but he declined to let his name go forward, and two Conservatives were returned unopposed.

In January 1904 Roberts was at the centre of a controversial by-election that divided the LRC. Herbert Gladstone and MacDonald had agreed in 1903 that at the next general election the double-member constituency of Norwich should be contested by one Liberal and one Labour candidate; but after the death of one of the Conservative MPs, Roberts, who had been adopted as LRC candidate in February 1903, decided to seek election. The Liberals had selected as their candidate Louis Tillett, who was sympathetic to labour representation, but on this occasion urged that the progressive, free trade vote should not be split. Within the LRC Richard Bell firmly supported Tillett, publicly expressing his regret at the splitting of the progressive vote and Will Crooks gave tacit approval, while the TUC parliamentary committee endorsed both candidates. Though Arthur Henderson and a majority of the LRC did back Roberts, Tillett won the seat comfortably above the Conservative and Roberts was a poor third with 2440 votes. Bell telegraphed his congratulations to Tillett. This Norwich by-election was an interesting staging post in the evolution of the LRC. Roberts's defeat was not, however, the result only of national dissensions. Fred Henderson, a prominent Norwich member of the ILP, deserted him for Louis Tillett on the grounds that Roberts had no chance of victory; and there was a general weakness of trade unionism in the city which hindered the cause of independent labour [Bealey and Pelling (1958) 240ff].

In June 1904 Roberts became a full-time trade union official when he was appointed as the southern organiser of the Typographical Association. His last job as a working printer was as overseer in the printing department of Coleman & Co.'s Wincarnis Works. By the time of the general election of 1906 the local parties at Norwich had come to terms: Tillett stood for re-election and appealed to his followers to cast their second vote for Roberts. The result of the by-election was reversed, with Roberts at the top of the poll securing 11,059 votes. His election campaign was greatly assisted by the Typographical Association, which bore the cost of an agent and a large part of the expenses. He was sometimes known as the 'Printers' MP', and he retained his post as organiser at an annual salary of £350. Although he did little work for the Association outside Westminster, after the payment of MPs in 1911 he continued to draw some financial support from it [Musson (1954) 314].

He was returned to the Commons at the two general elections of 1910, on both occasions coming second to the Liberal. Locally he had a reputation as an approachable MP who was painstaking in helping with constituents' problems. His standing with Labour colleagues in the Commons was high; he was elected to the executive committee of the Party and was a Whip from 1907 to 1914 (Chief Whip 1912-14), positions that tended to make him increasingly favourable to co-operation with the Liberal Party. As chairman of the Labour Party Conference that met in London in January 1913, Roberts argued against direct action and violence in the industrial world. On several occasions he travelled abroad as a representative of the trade union movement, and in 1911 was a TUC delegate to the American Federation of Labor. He was one of the directors of the *Daily Citizen* in 1913.

On the declaration of war in August 1914 Roberts immediately gave support to the Government. He broke with the ILP and became one of the most active of Labour MPs in the war effort. As well as appearing regularly on recruiting and national savings platforms, he urged upon the trade union movement the need to make the defeat of Germany their highest priority. He was associated with the National Alliance of Employers and Employed, an organisation that was supported by several 'ultra-patriotic' trade union leaders, including Ben Tillett, James O'Grady, Havelock Wilson, W.J. Davis, J.T. Brownlie and W.A. Appleton, with the object of promoting co-operation between employers and employed [*Industrial Peace* (Oct 1917) 24-6].

With the establishment of the Coalition Government in May 1915 Roberts accepted the post of Junior Lord of the Treasury (in effect, a Whip), an appointment he held until Lloyd George became Prime Minister in December 1916, when he moved to the Board of Trade as parliamentary secretary. He served on the Departmental Committee appointed by the President of the Board of Agriculture and Fisheries in 1915 to consider the settlement and employment on the land of discharged sailors and soldiers, and, with two other members, E.G. Strutt and L. Scott, he submitted a minority report in the following year which was subsequently published in book form in 1917. In the latter year he was created a Privy Councillor, and held a joint secretaryship to the Parliamentary Munitions Committee, an office that involved a number of visits to the front. He firmly opposed Labour Party acceptance of an invitation to the Stockholm Conference, and when in May 1917 MacDonald sought, unsuccessfully, to travel to Petrograd, Roberts was nominated to make the journey as a representative of the pro-war standpoint. In August 1917 he succeeded John Hodge as Minister of Labour, an important post in view of the need for flexible industrial relations, and one that carried a seat in the Cabinet. By this time sections of the labour movement had come to regard Roberts as merely a creature of the

Government, intent on subordinating trade union claims to the furtherance of the war effort. His appointment as a minister required him to seek re-election for Norwich, and although in the outcome he was returned unopposed, the Norwich Trades Council and Labour Representation Committee decided by forty-one votes to fourteen not to nominate him as their candidate.

For his own part, Roberts did little to mend the breach. At national level he severed another contract early in 1918 by resigning from the Labour Party executive on the ground of the pressure of parliamentary duties. During his tenure of the Ministry of Labour, Roberts was involved in the establishment of the Joint Industrial Councils recommended by the Whitley Committee and the extension of the Trade Boards Act to cover industries in which there was no effective machinery for wage regulation. He expressed his views on industrial relations in an article published in 1917:

> Particularly desirable is co-operation between the employing and employed classes. Aloofness and misunderstanding between these important sections are a potent contributory to industrial inefficiency. Unless a closer degree of partnership can be effected, the future of industry will be extremely turbulent. Some employers are too prone to regard an approach from their workpeople as an impudent interference with their business. 'We intend to run our business in our own way' represents the attitude of this type. But these employers must learn that the way they run their business is a matter also of social concern, and that they cannot regard labour as they do inanimate things. Every one they employ is a human being, instinct with feeling and need, aspiration and possibility, like themselves. Gladly does one observe the growing disposition to have recourse to conciliation and arbitration in the settlement of disputed questions. Yet that is not sufficient: the highest interests of industry are of as much concern to employed as employer and they should be invited to consultation as to the means of furthering those interests.

He was chairman of the S.C. on Emergency Legislation in 1918 and in the 'Coupon' election of that year he stood as a Coalition Labour candidate. He headed the poll with a large majority over a Labour opponent. He then finally broke with the Labour Party by accepting the post of Food Controller in succession to J.R. Clynes who had, in accordance with party policy, resigned from the Coalition. At this point the executive committee of the Typographical Association, which had been in accord with Roberts's wartime activities, cancelled his appointment as parliamentary representative and organiser.

He remained Food Controller until February 1920, when he resigned. In May of that year he was appointed chairman of the S.C. on the Indemnity Bill. Having identified the Labour Party with class-war doctrines and the trade union movement with industrial unrest, he moved further towards the political right. At the 1922 general election he stood as an Independent. Following his re-election to the Commons he joined the Conservative Party in 1923, and as one of its official candidates contested Norwich for the last time in the general election of December 1923, when he lost his seat; both Norwich seats were won by Labour candidates, W.R. Smith and Miss D. Jewson. During his last years in Parliament he served as chairman of the Ministry of Health's Departmental Committee on Causes and Prevention of Blindness.

One interesting movement he supported in the years after 1918 was that for birth control. He took the chair at a large public meeting in the Queen's Hall, London, at the end of May 1921, and his opening words are worth quoting:

> I want to say, as one who has been identified with the working-class movement throughout the whole of my adult life, I am aware of the fact that women of the well-to-do classes have the benefit of knowledge on this subject, and I desire that the women of my own class shall be as adequately informed and intelligently equipped as the women of any other class in society. It is a deplorable fact today that while the better-to-do possess this knowledge, and are, in my opinion, ordering their lives so as to give their children greater and fairer opportunities, the class to which I belong, grovelling in their ignorance, are still producing in

excessive numbers, and producing a race which is not fitted for the Empire which we have to govern.

He further demonstrated his convictions by appearing as a witness for Dr Marie Stopes in the famous libel case of 1923: *M. Stopes* v. *Dr Halliday Sutherland*. Patrick Hastings, soon to become Attorney-General in the first Labour Government, was counsel for Dr Stopes. Roberts's cross-examination showed that he had read most of Marie Stopes's books, and that he thoroughly approved of the 'tact and delicacy' with which she approached her subject. He made it plain, while in the witness box, that he was wholly in favour of the widest possible dissemination of birth control information among young men and women before they were married.

In 1918 Roberts had been given the freedom of Norwich in recognition of his work in the war. He continued to live in the city, which he also served as a JP. In later life he had several business interests: he was a director of Home Grown Sugar Ltd in 1923; chairman of the Hecate Burner Co. and Western Advertising Services; and a director of Coleman & Co. and the Scholey Construction Co.

He died of heart failure on 25 April 1928 at an hotel in Sevenoaks, Kent, during a business trip. Roberts had married in November 1895 Anna (Annie) Marshall, the daughter of a shoe manufacturer; his wife, three sons and a daughter survived him. One of his sons, George Herbert, was a farm manager. His funeral was held at St Thomas's Church near his home, and he was buried in the local cemetery. He died intestate, leaving property to the value of £7110 (£1514 net). T.P. O'Connor MP wrote in a tribute:

> Georgie – as he was invariably called – always looked, and to a certain extent always remained, a boy. The short stature, the chubby cheeks, the very bright and striking eyes, the soft manner, they all suggested one of the Peter Pans of political life. He had keen differences of opinion, especially with former associates; he spoke clearly and vigorously; he worked incessantly and adroitly . . . George soon developed, in addition, that instinctive talent for leading men which is one of the first necessities of a politician's career. In time he came to have a commanding position in his own trade as secretary of the Typographical Association, and he also became president of the Trades Council in Norwich.
>
> With his diminutive person, his pleasant, musical, but not stentorian voice, these great positions could not be attained by anything but sheer merit and the power of getting that recognised [*Daily Telegraph*, 26 Apr 1928].

Writings: 'How I got on', *Pearson's Weekly*, 17 May 1906; *The International Correspondence Schools* [Report of a speech, with portrait 1912] 14 pp.; *Report of the Departmental Committee on Settlement or Employment on the Land of Discharged Sailors and Soldiers* 1916 XII Cd 8182, Cd 8277 and *M. of E.* Cd 8347; (with E.G. Strutt and L. Scott), *British Agriculture the Nation's Opportunity: being the minority report of the Departmental Committee on the Employment of Sailors and Soldiers* (1917); 'The Relations between Capital and Labour', in *After-War Problems*, ed. W.H. Dawson (1917) 149-69.

Sources: (1) MSS: Labour Party archives: LRC. (2) Other: *Reformers' Year Book* (1905); *Rev. of Revs 33* (June 1906) 578; *Daily Citizen*, 29 Feb 1913; *Dod* (1907-22); *WWW* (1916-28); *Industrial Peace* (Oct 1917) 24-6; *DNB* (1922-30) [by H.T. Tracey]; M.A. Hamilton, *Arthur Henderson* (1938); A.E. Musson, *The Typographical Association: origins and history up to 1949* (1954); J.H. Stewart Reid, *The Origins of the British Labour Party* (Minneapolis, 1955); F. Bealey and H. Pelling, *Labour and Politics 1900-1906* (1958); P.P. Poirier, *The Advent of the Labour Party* (1958); K. Briant, *Marie Stopes: a biography* (1962); M. Box, *The Trial of Marie Stopes* (1967); H.M. Hyde, *Their Good Names: twelve cases of libel and slander* (1970); biographical information: T.A.K. Elliott, CMG, Helsinki. OBIT. *Daily News, Daily Telegraph, Morning Post* and *Times*, 26 Apr 1928; *East Anglian Daily Times*, 26 and 27 Apr 1928; *Eastern*

Daily Press, 26 and 27 Apr, 1 and 2 May and 19 July 1928; *Norfolk Chronicle*, 27 Apr and 4 May 1928.

DAVID E. MARTIN

See also: †Richard BELL; †John HODGE; †James Ramsay MACDONALD.

ROEBUCK, Samuel (1871-1924)
MINERS' LEADER

Samuel Roebuck was born at Attercliffe, Sheffield on 17 April 1871, the son of Joseph Roebuck, a coalminer and his wife Catherine (née Barton). In 1876 his parents moved to Wombwell, near Barnsley, and it was here that he spent his boyhood. He went to the Low Valley Wesleyan Day School, and seems to have spent most of his pocket money on theological books. At the age of twelve, without his father's consent, he started work at Mitchell's Main Colliery, where his first job was carrying picks and assisting the pick sharpener. He passed on to the screens, worked at several different grades and finished his career at this pit as a surface worker employed on the coke ovens. When he was about fourteen Roebuck began work underground as a pony driver at the neighbouring Darfield Main Colliery. At the age of sixteen he was tramming for his father (pushing full tubs away from the coal face and supplying the hewer with a constant supply of empty tubs), and by the time he was twenty he was a fully qualified hewer, a job at which he continued until he was forty-one years old.

From an early age Roebuck was deeply religious. He became a Sunday School teacher when he was seventeen, and at twenty he was the president of a Young Man's Improvement Class which became famous for many miles round Wombwell. In 1890 he became a local preacher in the Barnsley Circuit of Primitive Methodism, and he continued with this service for the next ten years, until the pressure of his trade union work forced him to give it up.

As a young man he began to take an active interest in the trade union and friendly society movements. When he was only nineteen the Darfield Main branch of the YMA elected him as their delegate to Council meetings at Barnsley, and in 1902 he was chosen as branch secretary, a position he held until 1912. In 1911 he was nominated, along with more than thirty others, for the position of junior general secretary of the Yorkshire Miners. After seven ballots he was finally elected. He took up his post on 1 March 1912 – the day the national Minimum Wage strike began; and shortly afterwards he moved house from Wombwell to Barnsley. When John Wadsworth, the general secretary of the YMA, was taken seriously ill, Roebuck had to undertake most of the Association's secretarial work. On 22 January 1923, after Wadsworth's death, Roebuck was unanimously appointed general secretary without a ballot vote being necessary.

Roebuck became well known at national level as well as within the Yorkshire coalfield. He was one of the YMA representatives on the executive committee of the MFGB between the years 1912 and 1923. In 1919 he was a candidate for the position of general secretary to the MFGB, at the time when Frank Hodges was elected. In the Yorkshire miners' movement Roebuck was extremely active: he was a member of many committees; on the board of management of the West Riding Miners' Permanent Relief Fund Society (and on one occasion candidate for the position of secretary); a member of the South and West Yorkshire Joint Board; the Oaks and the Wharncliffe relief funds; the Miners' Lamp Committee and its Research sub-committee; and the Board of Mining Examinations. He represented the YMA and the MFGB at numerous national and international conferences, and as a member of the executive of the MFGB was fully involved in negotiations with succeeding British Governments. Like most miners' leaders, Roebuck played a full part in pit rescue work; on one occasion, he and Herbert Smith were presented with a testimonial by the Yorkshire Colliery owners as a tribute to their bravery at a fire at Darton Main Colliery.

Before he moved to Barnsley, Roebuck was active in the public life of Wombwell. He served on the Urban District Council for three years from 1904, and in his second year of office became chairman of the Gas and Water Committee, a position in which he showed his usual energy and common sense: he was the first chairman whose management produced a net profit while at the same time wages were increased and the price of gas reduced. Roebuck also persuaded every worker at the gas plant to join the appropriate union.

In 1914 Roebuck was chosen as prospective parliamentary candidate for the Doncaster constituency [Gregory (1968) 118]; but he later withdrew. When the war began he took a patriotic stance, and just after it ended he was awarded the OBE.

His health became seriously undermined in the post-war years, and after a long illness he died in Barnsley on 23 April 1924. He was survived by his wife, one son and three daughters. He left an estate valued at £1639.

Sam Roebuck continued his trade union work and his multifarious public duties until almost the end of his life. He was a JP for Barnsley, and an enthusiastic supporter of the local Beckett Hospital, and often spoke at the Sunday Festivals held on its behalf. Roebuck was an excellent speaker and a kindly, courteous man. Although self-educated after the age of twelve, he was well read; on his own evidence Carlyle, Ruskin, Charles Kingsley, Milton and Macaulay were among his favourite authors.

Writings: *The Gainsford Scheme or the 'Great Illusion'* (YMA, 1920) P.

Sources: *Doncaster Gazette*, 10 Apr 1914; *Barnsley Chronicle*, 26 Apr 1924; *Yorkshire Mine Workers' Q.J.*, 31 Dec 1923; *Sheffield Telegraph*, 6 May 1955; R.G. Neville, 'The Yorkshire Miners 1881-1926: a study in labour and social history' (Leeds PhD, 1974). OBIT. *Barnsley Chronicle*, 26 Apr 1924.

ROBERT G. NEVILLE

See also: †Thomas ASHTON, for Mining Trade Unionism, 1900-14; †Arthu. Iames COOK, for Mining Trade Unionism, 1915-26; †Herbert SMITH; †John WADSWORTH.

SCURR, John (1876-1932)
SOCIALIST AND LABOUR MP

John Scurr was born on 6 April 1876 in Brisbane, Queensland, Australia, the son of Louis James Rennie of Poplar, London, a captain in the Merchant Navy. His mother died when he was an infant and at the age of six months he was adopted by her brother, Captain John Scurr, also of the Merchant Navy, who was resident in Poplar when not away at sea. Consequently, it was in the East End of London that John Scurr grew up and he was to spend almost all his working life in the borough of Poplar. He was educated at George Green's School there and later at King's College School. He first started work in an office in Poplar in 1892 and subsequently had a number of clerical and minor managerial positions. Then for some years he carried on his own business, a retail hardware store.

From the late 1890s he became increasingly active in Labour politics in the area. He joined the SDF, where he worked with Will Crooks, George Lansbury and others, and for a period served on its executive committee. One of his earliest political activities was to work as lecture secretary for the Metropolitan Radical Federation. He was a member of the Poplar Labour League from 1897, and in time became its secretary; he later took an active part in the Poplar Trades and Labour Representation Council, and was its president in 1911. In 1906 he appeared on the official list of ILP speakers, but he seems also to have remained a member of the SDF for he was on its executive committee in 1910. In the period of industrial unrest, 1910-11, Scurr played a conspicuous part in the dock strike as district chairman of the Dockers' Union. Shortly afterwards George Lansbury, with whom Scurr had developed close personal and political ties, offered him employment with the *Daily Herald*. His wife was also an active member of the Labour movement – she was a member of the Poplar Board of Guardians in 1907 – and she was especially prominent in the suffrage movement: in June 1914 she led a deputation on sweating, organised by the East London Federation of Suffragettes, to the Prime Minister. Scurr supported women's suffrage, and on one occasion was arrested in Norwich for delivering an inflammatory speech on the suffrage issue; but he was subsequently discharged. He was a staunch supporter of Sylvia Pankhurst in her social welfare work, and after the war moved to live in Bow near to the Kingsley Hall, one of her centres.

During the First World War Scurr was a pacifist, and was active in support of conscientious objectors. He was a member of the London District Committee of the LP; and at the Party's 1917 Conference, a member of its Standing Orders Committee. He was elected to the Poplar Borough Council and in 1919 was made an alderman. Towards the end of the war Scurr became associated with the British Auxiliary of the Indian Home Rule League, of which Annie Besant was president. With two other ILP members, George Lansbury and David Graham Pole, Scurr served for a period on the executive committee of the London branch [Gupta (1975) 41] and succeeded Pole as secretary. After the First World War, almost certainly in 1919, Scurr visited India and wrote of the conditions of Indian workers on his return. When the British Auxiliary was disbanded in 1920, Scurr continued his association with Indian Home Rule through the Parliamentary Committee on India formed in 1919, whose membership included Theosophists, trade unionists and labour politicians and of which Scurr was secretary [Cook et al. (1975) 113].

As chairman of the Stepney Board of Guardians, he favoured the policies of outdoor relief and the rates equalisation fund that came to be called 'Poplarism'. In 1921, with twenty-nine other council members, one of whom was his wife, he was imprisoned for six weeks for contempt of court, in refusing to collect the rates. Following his release from Brixton in October 1921 Scurr was appointed chairman of the Metropolitan Boroughs Standing Joint Committee (he had been vice-chairman from 1919 to 1921), and he served as mayor of Poplar from 1922 to 1923. For a time he was chairman of the Poplar Pensions Committee and the London 'Right to Work' Council, and from 1925 to 1929 he was an LCC alderman.

Over a long period of time Scurr had been attempting to enter the House of Commons but since he was unwilling, until 1918, to stand as anything other than a Socialist, his main intention was probably to evangelise. He contested South-West Bethnal Green in July 1911 and polled 134 votes against the Liberal C.F.G. Masterman. Just over two years later the death of the member for Chesterfield, J. Haslam, led to a by-election, and Scurr was put forward by the recently-formed *Daily Herald* League, to oppose Barnet Kenyon. On this occasion he polled 583 votes. In February of the following year, 1914, he returned to Bethnal Green after Masterman had to stand for re-election following his appointment as Chancellor of the Duchy of Lancaster. Although Scurr more than doubled his previous result there, the outcome was a very narrow victory for the Conservative. A few months later, at Ipswich, where Masterman also contested the seat, the election results were very similar, Scurr being third on both occasions.

In the general election of 1918 Scurr contested the constituency of Buckingham, this time standing as a Labour candidate. The seat went to the Coalition Conservative candidate, but Scurr achieved a very respectable 7481 votes, more than double those of the Liberal. In 1922, the year after his prison sentence, he stood for Stepney Mile End but was again unsuccessful, coming a close second to the Conservative candidate. In the following year, however, this result was reversed by a much more decisive margin and at the two subsequent elections, 1924 and 1929, Scurr greatly increased his majority.

At the time of his election to Parliament Scurr was a long-standing member of the Fabian Society and the ILP. He was a candidate for the post of ILP treasurer in 1924, and chairman of the Party's parliamentary group to 1925. In the early 1920s he was a member of the ILP committee (chaired by Ramsay MacDonald) which sought to define relations between the ILP and the Labour Party and to work out generally acceptable policies. Scurr was a supporter of

Guild Socialism and of Clifford Allen, and was a collaborator with the group that published a draft programme in the *Labour Leader* on 8 December 1921, stressing the need for workers' control. When MacDonald became Prime Minister in January 1924, Scurr took over the editorship of the *Socialist Review* and contributed regularly to it in 1924 and 1925.

In the House of Commons Scurr tried to give full expression to his political opinions. In July 1924 he introduced a Bill 'to amend the Constitution of the Port of London Authority' so that Labour representation on it, at that time very slight, could be increased. He wanted trade unionists in the docks industry to elect nine members and he wanted more local authority representation. In the later years of the 1920s he took an active part in the debates on the Rating and Valuation Bills and on the Bill to amend the powers of the LCC; he repeatedly pressed for increased funds to be placed at the disposal of the Poor Law Guardians. He was also deeply concerned with the problems affecting labour in the colonies, particularly in South Africa, Kenya and India. In an article in the *Socialist Review* in August 1924 he had examined some of the more pressing colonial problems and had demanded the end of economic exploitation. He supported self-government for India, and believed that to alienate India would bring about a great Asiatic combination against Britain. In 1925 he was one of the eleven Commons members of the Standing Joint Committee on Indian Affairs (R.C. Wallhead was a fellow-ILP member) and in the same year he was on the B Committee which reviewed the Government of India (Civil Services) Bill and presented its report in December 1925.

Scurr's assessment of his responsibilities as a Socialist in the House of Commons was clear-cut; he had expressed his feelings unequivocally and at length in a *Socialist Review* article entitled 'Thoughts on Revolution' in September 1925:

. . . I do not care a brass farthing whether we have a Labour Government or not, if the game is to be played under the present rules. A Labour Government will only be useful if it is going to use its power on behalf of the working class and against the interests of the possessing class . . . I conceive that the duty of a working class political party is to challenge the fundamental basis on which our social system is founded. To expose, in season and out of season the evil thing which it is. We have not got to make the task of Government easy. We have got to make it difficult.

Scurr was, however, soon to change his mind, and to become increasingly hostile to the critics of the leadership of the PLP. In 1928 he resigned from the ILP in protest against the intransigent policy of the NAC, and during the 1929 Labour Government he was chairman of the consultative body between the Party and the Government which for months, according to Foot 'had been busy devising new methods to discipline the ILP' [(1962) 133]. Foot described Scurr as 'one of the most loyal of the "loyalist" MPs' [ibid.]. Scurr's shift to the Right had come within a few years, since in the earlier part of the 1920s he had been a member of the Anglo-Russian Parliamentary Committee and on the executive committee of the Labour Research Department, both useful indices of his political position, and there is, in addition, the evidence of his writings in the *Socialist Review* in 1924-5.

While serving as chairman of the consultative body, however, Scurr brought about a serious government defeat in the Commons, over the controversial issue of the Education Bill. He was a Roman Catholic by upbringing and was a prominent defender of the Catholic point of view in matters affecting voluntary schools, such as the appointment of teachers. In earlier years in Poplar, where the Irish had formed a distinct community, he had been a member of the executive council of the United Irish League between 1900 and 1906; but like many Irish Radicals he had chosen to work with the general radical movement rather than with one that was specifically Irish [Thompson (1967) 27]. When in January 1931 the Education (School Attendance) Bill came up for its third reading, Scurr moved a pro-Catholic amendment which sought to postpone the operation of the Bill 'until an Act has been passed authorising expenditure out of public funds . . . to meet the cost to be incurred by the managers of non-provided schools in meeting the requirements of the provisions of this Act.' [*Hansard*, 21 Jan 1931]. He pressed his opposition to a vote and thirty-five Labour members voted against the Government. Although MacDonald tried to minimise the extent of his defeat, the Lords were encouraged to reject the Bill and Sir Charles Trevelyan resigned as Minister of Education in protest against the Party leadership [Skidelsky (1970) 357-8]. In the general election of 1931 Scurr was defeated by Dr W.J. O'Donovan, the Conservative candidate, by 2661 votes. There was a 10 per cent fall in the turnout at the polls.

Towards the end of his life, owing to many months of illness (he had been in indifferent health for several years) Scurr suffered financial difficulties; and only a month before his death Father Bernard Whelan of Westminster Cathedral had made an appeal through *The Times* for subscriptions to a testimonial. He died on 10 July 1932 in the Manor House Hospital, Golders Green, at the age of fifty-six. After a service at St Joseph's Church, Highgate Hill, he was buried in St Patrick's Cemetery, Leytonstone. He had married Julia O'Sullivan, daughter of John O'Sullivan from Co. Cork, in 1910. His wife had predeceased him in 1927 but he was survived by his family of two sons and a daughter. One of his sons, John, made his career in local government and the other, Maurice, in insurance. His daughter, Monica, became a nurse and married a doctor. John Scurr left effects to the value of £1026.

Writings: *Casting the Silver Bullets* [1915]; *To destroy Militarism* [n.d.]; *Labour in India* [1920] 18 pp.; 'The Sovereign State', *Soc. Rev. 17* (1920) 116-24; *The Rate Protest of Poplar* [1922] 15 pp.; *Labour and the Rates* [n.d.]; 'The Need for the ILP', *Soc. Rev. 20* (1922) 202-8; *Local Government: an outline* [1923?, 2nd ed. [1925]] 32 pp.; 'Labour and the Empire', *Soc.Rev. 24* (1924) 6-16; 'The Future of Socialism', ibid. 83-7; 'A Statistical Journey through Great Britain', ibid. 117-24; 'A Reminiscence or Two', ibid. 165-7; 'Whither are we drifting?', ibid. *25* (1925) 25-30; 'A Basic Living Wage', ibid. 145-53; 'Watchman! What of the Night?', ibid. 211-23; 'The Fundamental Motive of British Foreign Policy', ibid. *26* (1925) 5-24; 'Thoughts on Revolution', ibid. 104-22; *The Reform(!) of the Poor Law* (1927) 16 pp.; *Unemployment, Engineering and the Russian Market* (1930) 29 pp.

Sources: *Justice*, 22 July 1911; S.V. Bracher, *The Herald Book of Labour Members: 1924 Supplement* (1924); *Hansard* (1924-31); H. Gosling, *Up and Down Stream* (1927); *Labour Who's Who* (1927); *WWW* (1929-40); H.W. Lee and E. Archbold, *Social-Democracy in Britain* (1935); L.M. Weir, *The Tragedy of Ramsay MacDonald* [1938]; F. Brockway, *Socialism over Sixty Years* (1946); C.R. Attlee, *As it happened* (1954); J. McNair, *James Maxton: the beloved rebel* (1955); M. Foot, *Aneurin Bevan 1: 1897-1945* (1962); A. Marwick, *Clifford Allen: the open conspirator* (1964); R.J.A. Skidelsky, *Politicians and the Slump: the Labour Government of 1929-31* (1967; Pelican ed., 1970); P. Thompson, *Socialists, Liberals and Labour: the struggle for London* (1967); P.S. Gupta, 'British Labour and the Indian Left, 1919-1939' in *Socialism in India*, ed. B.R. Nanda (1972) 69-121; C. Cook et al., *Sources in British Political History 1900-1951* vol.1 (1975); P.S. Gupta, *Imperialism and the British Labour Movement 1914-1964* (1975); G. Richman, *Fly a Flag for Poplar* (1975); biographical information: T.A.K. Elliott, CMG; P. Woods, London; personal information: M.J. Scurr, Wood Green, son. OBIT. *Times*, 11 July 1932.

BARBARA NIELD
JOHN SAVILLE

See also: †Clifford Reginald ALLEN; Annie BESANT; †Arthur HENDERSON, for British Labour Party, 1914-31; †George LANSBURY, for British Labour Party, 1900-13.

SHAW, Fred (1881-1951)
TRADE UNIONIST AND SOCIALIST

Fred Shaw was born on 25 May 1881 at Lindley, near Huddersfield. He was the son of John Albert Shaw and his wife Ellen (née Markham). He attended the local elementary school and the

Lindley Zion Sunday School and took his first job in the iocal Wellington Mills. The factory made woollen and worsted cloths, but Fred Shaw worked in the blacksmith's shop under his father, who was the foreman (and in politics a lifelong Liberal). Exactly when and why Fred Shaw became a Socialist is not known, but it was not later than early adult life, for by 1903 he was propaganda secretary of the Lindley Labour Representation Committee. In 1905 he was a founder-member of the local Clarion Cycling Club, and remained an enthusiastic cyclist, and later motor-cyclist, to the end of his life. In the same year, 1905, he helped form the Huddersfield branch of the Socialist Labour Party. It must have been about this same time that he became the first agent in Britain for the Chicago firm of Kerr and Co., a company publishing Socialist literature, whose books became well known in Britain before the First World War. Shaw was always an active trade unionist, and in 1912 he was elected secretary of the Huddersfield No. 2 branch of the ASE. By this date Shaw had joined the British Socialist Party and was already one of their national propagandists, speaking all over the country on ILP and BSP platforms. He was also a vigorous advocate of industrial unionism and in his own area carried on a sharp debate with more orthodox trade unionists such as Ben Turner. Shaw was an indefatigable agitator, and a prolific and fluent writer of letters and articles in the Socialist press, especially the *Huddersfield Worker* and the *Yorkshire Factory Times*. Like many of his young Socialist contemporaries, he was intensely interested in scientific matters and their relationship to social change, and he lectured on an extraordinarily wide variety of subjects: evolution, astronomy, eugenics and sociology in addition to the more usual political themes. In 1908 he wrote a long letter to the *Huddersfield Worker* explaining that he had become secretary of a new society at Lindley whose purpose was to establish a working-class educational institute. The letter is interesting mainly for its statement of what a typically self-educated working-class militant considered necessary for a Socialist curriculum. To raise money for the proposed institute, Shaw explained, they had started 'a non-profit sharing boot and clogging business, with an experienced man in charge as manager'. The letter continued:

. . . The present shareholders are all members of the Clarion Scouts and of the ILP, and they are determined to do all they can to push the scheme forward.

Starting with an economic basis on the writings of Smith, Ricardo, Marx, Rogers, etc., through the histories of Gibbon, Buckle, Green, Draper, Macaulay, etc., and philosophy and science from the writings and epitomes of Democritus, Plato, Epicurus, up through Bacon, Hobbes, Descartes, Locke, Newton, Hume, Kant, Dalton, Lyall, Darwin, Buckner, Spencer, Comte; through the various standard Sociological works, we should develop a set of personalities capable of holding their specific philosophical ideals against all comers, besides providing the movement with embryonic speakers and writers. All this can be realised by your support. Drop us a card for repairs or inquiry; we do the collecting at our own expense. Don't forget to look us up any time for further information. In conclusion let me appeal to you all, to remember that scientific socialism is but a small factor in our political and social life at present, but its growth will aid to bring that future arrangement of society we all are fighting for, and remember that this ideal is the only one worth living and striving to gain, and if you don't feel deeply the spirit that underlies the Socialistic ideals, at least aid us who intend making it our life's work.

During the First World War Shaw took the anti-war side within the BSP. He himself was exempted from military service because of his occupation, but he openly supported the anti-war movement, and did all he could for his friends who were conscientious objectors. In 1916 he accepted election to the national executive of the BSP, and in 1918 was its national chairman. Like many other Socialists his wish to attend the international Socialist meeting at Stockholm in the summer of 1917 was frustrated by the refusal of a visa. At the end of the war he stood unsuccessfully in the general election of 1918 as a Socialist candidate for Greenock, polling two and a half thousand votes out of a total of over twenty thousand. On the ground that he was taking too much time off for his candidature, his firm David Brown's dismissed him; but his workmates at once came out on strike, and he was reinstated. With the ending of the post-war boom he was dismissed again in 1921, this time finally.

As a leading figure in the BSP Shaw took an active part in the complicated negotiations to establish a unified Communist Party in Britain. He was present at the Unity Convention of 31 July–1 August 1920, and was elected to the first national executive of the newly established Communist Party of Great Britain [Klugmann (1968) 49; Kendall (1969) ch. 11]. His own BSP branch in Huddersfield joined the CPGB, and the next year Shaw made a vigorous though unsuccessful effort to achieve the affiliation of the Huddersfield CP to the local Labour Party.

During these years immediately following the end of the war, Fred Shaw was involved in a multitude of political and industrial activities, and these were probably the busiest years in a very active life. On a national level, in addition to his part in the formation of the CPGB he was on the national committee of the 'Hands off Russia' movement, whose successful campaign against British intervention in the Russian civil war culminated in the movement of August 1920. At the local level, Shaw was continuously involved in political and industrial work. In 1919 he was elected president of the Huddersfield Trades Council, and was again president from 1922 to 1929. He was also president of the regional Allied Engineering Trades Federation. From 1919 to 1922 he was a Socialist councillor for Longwood Ward, Huddersfield. He served with energy and commitment on four committees of the Town Council, including the finance committee; but lost his seat in 1923. On the industrial side he was at the centre of many trade union struggles in the Huddersfield area. He was several times a delegate to the national committee of the AEU, and he was inevitably involved, by virtue of his official positions, in the bitter conflicts with the engineering employers in 1921-2 [Jefferys [1945] 218 ff.]. The peak of his industrial career came in 1922, when he led the Huddersfield AEU committee at the time of the national lockout. The committee co-ordinated the picketing and welfare of all locked-out engineering workers. The lockout lasted thirteen weeks, and it ended in June 1922 in defeat. Henceforth Shaw was blacklisted by engineering firms in his area, and he never worked again at his trade. Until he was selected by the NCLC in 1924 to become their Yorkshire organiser he worked at a number of different jobs. It was a hard time, for him and his family.

Shaw left the Communist Party in 1923, and over the years became a loyal supporter of the Labour Party. In 1924 he applied for the position of assistant secretary to the TUC, was on the short list of six, given an interview but was not successful. Walter Citrine was appointed. From 1924 Shaw concentrated his main attention upon working-class education, and his more uncompromising attitudes of his younger days began to change. He was a militant Socialist all his life, typical of those who belonged to the left wing of the ILP and of most of the BSP in the years before 1914; as good an exemplar as one could find of the sort of men and women who made up rank-and-file activists of the British labour movement in the twentieth century. But like the overwhelming majority of these activists Shaw was not a revolutionary in the usual sense of that term. His election letter when he was a municipal candidate in 1919, at a time when he was at his most militant, offers useful insight into his political attitudes. At the end of the letter he summarised his programme:

1. That Huddersfield shall become a Communal City.
2. That the ownership of all the land within the Borough shall be vested with the Town Council for the time being.
3. That all Labour be employed direct for all Municipal Service, and for future developments. In all public departments, Labour shall have representation upon the Committee of Management, such representation to be elected from and by the Workers' Committees, established in those departments.
4. That all banking and credit organisations shall be vested with the Commune.

5. That the modes of Production and Distribution that can be communally owned shall be vested in the Commune.
6. That we scrap the existing Educational System and institute it upon a Communal basis.
   IMMEDIATE.   UNEMPLOYED.
   That we advocate and organise a continual reduction in working hours until the unemployed are absorbed.
   If you want to know what type of a man the Candidate is, come and have a shot at him.

Yours for Socialism,
FRED SHAW

Shaw's work for the NCLC was thoroughly congenial, and he carried it out devotedly: he lectured up and down Yorkshire and became well known and liked all over the county. He had always been a warm supporter of the Central Labour College and the Plebs League, and indeed was mainly responsible for the affiliation of the AEU to the National Council of Labour Colleges in 1923. Throughout his many years as an educational organiser he continued to play a part in the general politics and life of the West Riding labour movement. He was inevitably very active during the General Strike of 1926, and his account of what happened in Yorkshire during the strike [*Plebs 18* (1926) 249-51] is a helpful record for the historian. For many years he was on the executive of the Yorkshire Federation of Trades Councils, and was chairman in 1928. He served on the Court of Referees at the Huddersfield Employment Exchange between 1922 and 1927. He retired from full-time work at the end of 1946, but still acted as tutor for some classes; and he remained secretary of his AEU branch up to the time of his death.

Fred Shaw died of bronchial pneumonia on 22 January 1951, at the age of sixty-nine, and was buried on 25 January at the Lindley Zion Methodist Church graveyard. During the service, W.E. Lawn, secretary of the Huddersfield Co-operative Society Education Committee, read part of an essay written, he said, over a hundred years ago by 'that grand philosopher, Dr. William King'. Shaw left effects valued at £433. He had married Jane Hughes in 1907, whom he had met at the annual gathering of the Yorkshire and Lancashire Clarion Cycling Clubs. His wife was born at Oswaldtwistle, Lancashire, on 1 January 1882, and went into domestic service as a mother's help at the age of ten. Fred and Jane had six children, three sons and three daughters. When young, the children attended the Huddersfield Socialist Sunday School. Jane herself actively supported her husband's work, and often went to NCLC meetings with him on the pillion of his motor-bike. But the family life of an active working-class Socialist is never easy. The survivors of Fred Shaw's family write in warm terms of their father, and some of the flavour of their lives, and of the man himself, comes through in the extract given below:

> When we (the children) were small we saw very little of father, as he was in great demand going to meetings, speaking etc. We saw him while he was having his tea. We had to keep quiet. He did not talk much to us, as his mind and thoughts were far away. After tea he would dash away to his meetings, and when he returned home, he was busy studying and reading until the early hours of the morning. Books were revered in our house, no misuse of them, borrowing or lending. Weekends he carried on his work; sometimes we only saw him Saturday dinner-time, when we gathered around him for our Saturday 1 *d*.
>
> It was left to mother to bring us up, while father carried on with the working-class struggle. Times were hard, especially during the war years, when the threat of being called up, and knowing father would go to prison instead of fighting. Even young children could feel the tensions . . . My father was a very gifted, talented and well-read man. He had a few thousand books. There was hardly a subject he could not talk about. He was very fond of outdoor life, and held many of his meetings and day schools outdoors, at beauty spots in the country.
>
> It was a great pleasure when we were young for father to take my sister and myself occasionally for a walk. He would tell us about the flowers, trees, birds, animals, sky, cloud formations, anything interesting we came across. At night he sometimes would bring his

telescope out, and we would look at the moon and stars. If only he could have seen a man on the moon.

Father made his own wireless sets, and we had one as far back as 1926, he would sit up late at nights listening in to foreign stations.

After he retired he took up photography, and set off to visit castles in England and Scotland, and then wrote up all the historical data, and made drawings. The Huddersfield Library got father a book from Oxford on Crusader Castles, but he could not bring it home, so he went to the library and copied all the book and drawings. Father was also interested in studying drama and dramatists throughout the ages. He was making a TV set in 1950, and was waiting for a small part which arrived the day after he died, but he managed for a few seconds on Christmas Eve to get a picture of Trafalgar Square, he was delighted. [Letter, 7 Feb 1973].

Fred Shaw was survived by his wife (she died in 1968) and his six children. It is worth noting that he and his wife managed to send all six – daughters as well as sons – to grammar school. They seem to have inherited a good deal of their father's ability. The four – two sons and two daughters who were called up during the Second World War all became NCOs, while the eldest son, who made his career in the Regular Army, rose from private to major, was in charge of the post-war Jewish camps in Cyprus, and in 1958 was awarded the MBE for service in Malaya.

After Fred Shaw's death a memorial fund was raised by the Divisional Council of the NCLC: part of the money was used for an annual scholarship to send a Yorkshire student to the NCLC summer schools and the rest went to purchase what remained of Shaw's library, which has been placed in Wortley Hall near Sheffield as the 'Fred Shaw Memorial Library'.

Writings: 'BSP and Industrial Action', *Call*, no. 162, 15 May 1919, 4; 'Thoughts on Tactics', ibid., no. 192, 11 Dec 1919, 6; 'A Page from Trade Union History', *Plebs 14*, no. 6 (June 1922) 164-6; 'Another Page from Trade Union History', ibid., no. 7 (July 1922) 210-13; 'An Old Minute-Book', ibid., no. 9 (Sep 1922) 302-7; 'Strike History. Stories of the Nine Days from North and South: Yorkshire', ibid., *18*, no. 7 (July 1926) 249-51; 'William Godwin' [Review], ibid., *21*, no. 4 (Apr 1929) 80-3. Shaw also wrote many short articles and letters in newspapers and journals, especially in the *Huddersfield Worker*, and *Yorkshire Factory Times*.

Sources: (1) MSS: personal papers including diaries in the possession of Miss Marion Shaw, Huddersfield and on microfilm at Brynmor Jones Library, Hull Univ. and York Univ. Library. (2) Other: J.B. Jefferys, *The Story of the Engineers* [1945]; *Huddersfield Citizen* (Jan 1947); J. Klugmann, *History of the Communist Party of Great Britain* vol. 1: *1919-24* (1968); W. Kendall, *The Revolutionary Movement in Britain 1900-21* (1969) [Ch. 11]; B. Barker, 'Anatomy of Reformism: the social and political ideas of the Labour leadership in Yorkshire', *Int. Rev. Social Hist. 18* (1973) 1-27; idem, 'The Politics of Propaganda: a study in the history of educational Socialism and its role in the development of a national Labour Party in London and the West Riding of Yorkshire' (York MPhil., 1973); biographical information: Mrs A.L. Gardiner, Huddersfield; A.J.E. Waite, Huddersfield LP; personal information: Miss M. Shaw and Mrs L. Woodhead, Huddersfield, daughters. OBIT. *Daily Herald* and *Huddersfield Examiner*, 24 Jan 1951; W.M. Lawn, *Fred Shaw – In Memoriam* (1951); *Plebs 43*, no. 2 (Feb 1951).

NOTE: The editors are indebted to Bernard Barker, Barnet, and Margaret 'Espinasse for earlier drafts of this entry.

JOHN SAVILLE

See also: Robert BLATCHFORD; *Ben TURNER.

STEAD, Francis Herbert (1857-1928)

CHRISTIAN SOCIALIST

Stead was born in Howdon-on-Tyne on 20 October 1857, the third son in a family of eight. His father, the Rev. William Stead, was an Independent minister. His brothers were the crusading editor and world peace advocate, William Thomas Stead (1849-1912), and the renowned metallurgist, Professor John Edward Stead (1851-1923). Like his brothers and sisters, Herbert Stead was educated by his father at home, and until the age of seventeen assisted him with his pastoral duties in Howdon. A friend later recalled that 'as a boy, Herbert was more familiar with Latin for some time than with his native tongue, thanks to the daily grinding in his father's study'. He was preparing to follow his father in the ministry, but he felt before undertaking theological studies he should see something of life away from home. In 1874, therefore, he joined his brother William, then editor of the *Northern Echo* in Darlington, and served as a reporter for the *Echo* and the *Northern Daily Express* from 1874 to 1876. The contrast between these two early experiences, life at home and life as a reporter, profoundly influenced Stead's subsequent career and work.

In 1876 Stead left journalism to study for the Congregational ministry at Owens College, Manchester, and Airedale College, Bradford. From Airedale College he entered Glasgow University, where he was a Buchanan medallist and a Williams divinity scholar and graduated with honours in Classics and Philosophy. He then went on to advanced study on the Continent at the Universities of Halle, Göttingen, Giessen, and Berlin. In 1884 he was called to the pastorate of the Gallowtreegate Church in Leicester. It was during his service here that he married (in 1887) Bessie Macgregor, the daughter of the Rev. G.D. Macgregor of Paddington Chapel; they had a family of four children, one son and three daughters. In Leicester, Stead distinguished himself as a member of the Leicester School Board (1888-90) and by his interest in the lot of the unemployed and the destitute aged.

While he was working in Leicester, Stead was greatly influenced by the Rev. Wilfrid Richmond's book, *Christian Economics* (published in 1888), with its emphasis on the concept of economic conduct as a matter of Christian duty and on the need for the establishment of 'a Political Economy which shall be a branch of morals'. At a meeting of the Congregational Union in October 1888, Stead presented a paper on 'Christian Economics' in which he called for 'a Christian science of economics to replace the unethical orthodox political economy' and presented a Christian Socialist outlook based on the thought of Richmond [*Christian Socialist 6* (Nov 1888) 166 ff.]. Stead was also very much influenced by Tolstoyan ideas: as he later wrote, it was his reading of Tolstoy's works which in 1890 inspired him and his wife to give up 'comfortable Christianity' by resigning his pastorate in Leicester. He moved to Oxford, where he took a small workman's cottage off the Iffley Road, and for the next two years devoted himself to reading and study at home and in the Bodleian.

In 1892 Stead accepted the position of editor of the *Independent and Nonconformist* which he held until the journal was sold in 1894. 'The Purpose which had detached me from the ordinary pastorate, and from the claims of academic study', Stead later recalled, 'had now broken me loose from religious journalism.' His great 'Purpose' was to help the poor, and in spite of the attempts of many friends and some of his family, who urged him to make good use of his years of education at British and German universities by entering the teaching profession, Stead decided to live among the London poor and to serve them. He had heard, he declared, 'the approaching trample of the Labour Movement in Religion'; he was convinced that 'the future belonged to the working-classes, and [he] felt the need of serving their spiritual aspirations'. The opportunity for such social service came early in 1894, when Stead and his wife were invited by a committee of the Browning Hall Mission on Walworth Road to accept the vacant post of superintendent of the Mission. On obtaining the committee's agreement to transform the Mission into a Settlement with himself as Warden, Stead accepted the position, but did not begin his work at Browning Hall until October. Two months later, on 13 December 1894, the Mission officially became a Settlement house.

While preparing to move to Browning Hall, Stead began his long service as assistant editor of his brother's very successful monthly periodical, the *Review of Reviews*, which W.T. Stead had established in 1890. Until his death (on the *Titanic* in 1912), he often relied on Herbert to serve not only as assistant editor, but also as acting editor during his many absences in the United States and Europe, and as a regular reviewer of books and articles on religious subjects and labour problems. In 1893 Herbert Stead was dispatched to the Chicago World's Fair as 'Special Commissioner' for the *Review of Reviews* and wrote an article on 'The Civic Life of Chicago' which presaged W.T. Stead's memorable exposé of political corruption and vice in Chicago, *If Christ came to Chicago* (Chicago and New York, 1894). Herbert Stead was profoundly impressed by the work of Jane Addams at the Hull House Settlement in Chicago and by the 'Social Gospel' movement in the United States. He was especially interested in the attempts of the Chicago Congregational College to 'socialise the ministry of the future by founding a Chair of Christian Sociology' and 'by drilling its two hundred students in actual social work'. 'The sociologising of theology' seemed to Stead one of the best means of focusing the attention of the Church on social problems. What he had seen and learned in Chicago and especially at Jane Addams' Hull House, Stead sought to apply at the Browning Settlement. Above all, his objective was to 'reconcile' the Churches to the growth of organised labour.

From 1894 until his retirement in 1921, Stead made Browning Hall a settlement which worked 'corporately and explicity for Labour' and a trade union centre. At Browning Hall, he launched and actively participated in campaigns for slum clearance and public housing, succour for the unemployed, cheap transport, industrial peace, disarmament and the abolition of war, national homes for the aged, and old age pensions. His contribution to the long-drawn-out campaign for old age pensions was especially notable. The issue of pensions had been discussed and debated for about twenty years before the National Committee of Organised Labour for the achievement of old age pensions was established in 1899, with Frederick Rogers as its organising secretary. Stead was indefatigable in the campaign, support for which however remained patchy and uneven. Stead himself, for instance, wrote personally to every member of the House of Commons in 1902, urging support for pensions, but received only forty-seven replies. It was not until two years after the Liberal victory of 1906 that the first pensions bill reached the Statute book. Alongside his commitment to old age pensions Stead continued to work for other social causes. He was active in encouraging unemployed demonstrations during 1905, and worked closely on this issue with George Lansbury. But his overriding concern during the last thirty years of his life was with matters of war and peace. He was a lifelong pacifist, an advocate of international arbitration and a vigorous proponent of the limitation of armaments. On these issues he worked together with his brother, W.T. Stead, until the latter's death in 1912. William Stead was an important figure at the first Hague Conference of 1899, and during the next decade they both campaigned vigorously to promote Anglo-German friendship. In 1909, for example, Herbert Stead organised (with the help of trade union friends) a 'Peace Tour' of twenty British Labour MPs in Germany at Whitsuntide. When war finally broke out in August 1914 Stead supported the Allies but he became ever more dedicated to the cause of international agreement and the outlawing of war. In 1916 he organised a conference at Browning Hall which led to the establishment of a League to Abolish War, and the main aims being an association of nations with an international army to conduct its peacekeeping functions.

On his retirement as warden of Browning Hall in 1921, Stead continued to labour on behalf of international and industrial peace. In 1927 he travelled through Finland speaking in churches and on public platforms in support of the League of Nations and international amity. On the eve of his death he was arranging for a series of meetings urging the international banning of war as an instrument of national policy. He died on 14 January 1928 at his Blackheath home and his funeral was at Brookwood. He left effects worth £2116 gross (£776 net).

Writings: Autobiographical information by F.H. Stead in W.T. Stead, *Father and Son* (1884) pt. 2, 1-8; 'Christian Economics', *Christian Socialist 6* (Nov 1888) 166-71; *A Hand-book on Young People's Guilds* (1889); *The English Church of the Future: its polity. A Congregational Forecast . . . together with Letters from Leaders in the Principal Denominations of British Christians* (1892) 40 pp.; Editor of *Independent and Nonconformist* (1892-4); 'The Opening of the World's Fair. Glimpses by a Passing Guest', *Rev. of Revs 7* (1893) 656-9; *The Kingdom of God. A Plan of Study*, 3 pts (Edinburgh [1893]); *The Kingdom and the Church* (1893); 'The Civic Life of Chicago. An Impression left on a Guest after a Visit of a Dozen Days', *Rev. of Revs 8* (1893) 93-6; Edited with W.F. Aldeney, *The Story of Christ and his People* (1897); 'Browning as a Poet of the Plain People', *Amer. Rev. of Revs 15* (1897) 191-2; 'Model Industrial Village', ibid., *29* (1904) 433-5; 'Progress with Unemployed in England', *Charities and the Commons 15* (1906) 579-82; *How Old Age Pensions began to be* [1909]; 'Herbert Stead on American Peace Plans', *Survey 34* (1915) 1-2; 'How to unify the Peace Movement', *Amer. Rev. of Revs 51* (1915) 736-7; 'International Labour Week', *Survey 34* (1915) 249-50; 'A Dynamic View of the Deed of Christ', *Constructive Q. 3* (1915) 428-43; *Browning Hall and Settlement: eighteen years in the Central City Swarm* (Letchworth, 1916) 47 pp.; *To abolish War. At the Third Hague Conference. An Appeal to the Peoples* (Letchworth, 1916) 47 pp.; *No more War!: truth embodied in a tale* (1917); *Mary Isabella Stead, 1847-1918* (Letchworth, 1918) 16 pp.; *The Unseen Leadership: a word of personal witness* (1922: 2nd ed. Inverness, 1925); *To my Friends: a word of personal witness to a divine drama* (1922) 11 pp.; *The Proletarian Gospel of Galilee in some of its Phases* (1922); *The Story of Social Christianity* 2 vols (1924); *The Deed and Doom of Jesus* (Edinburgh, 1927).

Sources: (1) MSS: Lansbury correspondence: vol. 2, BLPES; T.R. Marr papers: National Library of Scotland; W.T. Stead papers: W.K. Stead, Flushing, Cornwall, great-nephew; J. Heatley, Jr. 'Recollections of the Stead Family', 29 May 1891 [typescript]: F. Whyte Coll., Newcastle Univ. Library. (2) Other: *WWW* (1916-28); G.N. Barnes, *From Workshop to War Cabinet* (1924); *Congregational Yearbook* (1929) 231-3; R.T. Jones, *Congregationalism in England, 1662-1962* (1962); B.B. Gilbert, *The Evolution of National Insurance in Great Britain: the origins of the Welfare State* (1966); J.O. Baylen, 'A Victorian Editor's Instructions to a "Cub" [Reporter]', *Journalism Q.* 44 (1967) 558-60; P. Thompson, *Socialists, Liberals and Labour: the struggle for London 1885-1914* (1967); P. d'A. Jones, *The Christian Socialist Revival 1877-1914* (Princeton, 1968); J. Harris, *Unemployment and Politics: a study in English social policy* (Oxford, 1972); H.Y. Emy, *Liberals, Radicals and Social Politics 1892-1914* (Cambridge, 1973). OBIT. *Times*, 16 Jan 1928.

JOSEPH O. BAYLEN

See also: George Nicoll BARNES; †Frederick ROGERS.

STOTT, Benjamin (1813-50)
TRADE UNIONIST AND RADICAL POET

A sketch of Stott's life is contained in the short 'Memoir' which precedes his *Songs for the Millions and Other Poems*. There is little further information, though something may be gathered from his dedications: the whole volume was dedicated to a well-known radical MP, Thomas Slingsby Duncombe; one of the poems, 'The Poet of Nature', is 'inscribed to John Bolton Rogerson, Esq.' who was a fellow member of the literary club to which Stott belonged (see below) and the next poem is 'A Dirge to the Memory of William Grant, Esq., the Philanthropist. Inscribed to J.F. Blandwood Halstead, Esq.', probably also a member of the literary club. The Grant brothers were well-known philanthropists who are believed to have provided a model for the Cheeryble brothers in Dickens's *Nicholas Nickleby*. It seems, therefore, that Stott had acquaintances among the local radical and humanitarian gentry and wealthy merchants.

He was born in Manchester on 24 November 1813. His father, a hairdresser and later an auctioneer, came of a family settled near Rochdale; his mother, who had been a Miss Hall, belonged to an old family, possibly miners and sheep farmers, who had for centuries lived near Hope and Bradwell in the High Peak of Derbyshire. Benjamin was the youngest of thirteen children. Both his parents died before he was six years old, and he was brought up by an unmarried sister of his mother's, who worked as a fustian cutter. He attended the National Free School in Granby Row, Manchester, where he learned to read and write. He seems to have shown promise, for when he was nine some friends of his father's got him a place in Cheetham's Hospital, where he remained for five years. In 1827 he left school and was apprenticed to a bookbinder for seven years, and when he was out of his indentures he worked as a bookbinder and stationer in Manchester for the remaining years of his life.

In the 'Memoir' he is said to have left Manchester only once, we are not told in what year, 'when the business of a society to which he belonged' led him to the Isle of Man. This society may have been the Odd Fellows in praise of whom he wrote a long poem, and of whose National Independent Order he was, according to his epitaph, 'an influential member and by them much esteemed.' But the society in question might conceivably have been the Bookbinders: during the 1830s this union was passing through formative struggles, and the Manchester lodge took the lead in trying to co-ordinate the activities of the various lodges. At all events, Stott was a keen trade unionist: his poems include 'Lines sacred to the memory of John Roach, a Chartist and pioneer activist in the boilermakers' society', verses which were printed and sold to members of Roach's union. In August 1842 Stott was a delegate from the Bookbinders to the Trades Conference called in connection with the Chartist general strike. In spite of a rather pessimistic estimate by Stott of the chances of success, fifty-eight of the eighty-five delegates voted in favour of the strike (*Northern Star*, 20 Aug 1842). Stott himself was a strong supporter of the Charter, as he shows in his Chartist song, 'Old England', addressed to 'ye men of Great Britain', adjuring them to claim 'the only hope left ye – your glorious Charter'.

He was well known locally as a poet, and he belonged to a Manchester and district literary circle which met at the Sun Inn, and which published a collection of contributions read at a meeting on 24 November 1842 and called *The Festive Wreath*. It was edited by John Bolton Rogerson, and Stott's contribution was the elegy on Roach, which was reprinted in his *Songs for the Millions and Other Poems* published together in one volume in 1843 (Middleton: printed and published by W. Horsman). The nineteen songs are Shelleyesque (but Christian) political poems in a high rhetorical strain, on such subjects as famine, liberty, the dungeoned patriot. Although full of apostrophe and abstractions, they are lucid, direct and not ineffective. The complex and elaborate metres and rhyme schemes which he often chooses are as a rule deftly handled.

Stott died on 26 July 1850 at 32 Chorlton Street, Manchester, at the early age of thirty-six. He was buried in Northenden churchyard. One of the literary circle to which he belonged thought so highly of him as to go to Northenden and copy Stott's epitaph; this gives his age and date of death, mentions his connections with the Odd Fellows and ends, appropriately, with five rhyming couplets in praise of his qualities [Proctor (1860) 102].

Writings: 'A Dirge' in *The Festive Wreath* (1842); *Songs for the Millions and Other Poems* (1843).

Sources: *Northern Star,* 20 Aug 1842; *The Festive Wreath,* ed. J.B. Rogerson (Manchester, 1842); 'Memoir' in *Songs for the Millions* (1843); *North of England Mag. 2* (July 1843) 143-4; D.W. Proctor, *Literary Reminiscences and Gleanings* (1860); D.C. Cummings, *History of the United Society of Boilermakers and Iron and Steel Ship Builders* (Newcastle upon Tyne, 1905); E. Howe and J. Child, *The London Bookbinders 1780-1951* (1959).

MARGARET 'ESPINASSE
EDMUND AND RUTH FROW

See also: John TEER.

SUMMERBELL, Thomas (1861-1910)

TRADE UNIONIST AND LABOUR MP

Thomas Summerbell was born on 10 August 1861 at Seaham Harbour, Co. Durham. He was the son of Thomas Summerbell, a coal trimmer, and his wife (née Matthews). He left school at the age of twelve, and after working for a hairdresser and as errand boy to a grocer, he was apprenticed to a printer.

At the end of his seven years' apprenticeship he was dismissed from his work on the *Seaham Weekly News* and found a job as journeyman printer in Felling, then in Jarrow; but his employer there did not keep to trade union hours, and Summerbell was a member of the Typographical Association, so he left. His next post was in South Shields, as a reporter on the *Argus*; he then moved to Hartlepool, from there to Newcastle, where he came under the influence of the Radical reformer Joseph Cowen, and finally to Sunderland, where he settled. At first he worked for the *Daily Post,* then in 1894 he started his own printing business. In his early years he was for some time a Gladstonian Liberal, but he came to see that labour had nothing to hope for from Conservatives or Liberals, but must be independent of them. He became a Socialist, a member of the ILP, and active in municipal and trade union affairs. His union sent him to the Trades Council, of which he became secretary in 1888. His work on the Council roused his interest in the organisation of unskilled labour, and he helped to found the Tyneside and National Labour Union (which became the National Amalgamated Union of Labour). In 1892 he was elected to the Sunderland Borough Council as member for Hendon ward, and he remained on the Council until his death. An advocate of municipalisation he was instrumental in persuading the Council to buy out the old tramways company and install a system of electric trams. He was vice-chairman then chairman of the tramways committee.

Summerbell was also an active member of the Housing Reform Council, the Land Nationalisation Society and the Labour Information Bureau, and he was secretary to the League of the Blind. He was also a trustee of the Robin Hood Court of the Foresters' Friendly Society. In 1906 he was elected for Parliament as a Labour Representation candidate but lost his seat at the January 1910 election about a month before his death. He was a member of the R.C. on Coast Erosion appointed in 1906 and in Parliament was a most active and conscientious MP. His Liberal colleague, James Stuart, the other member for Sunderland, left local affairs entirely to him, and he attended to them faithfully. But he also asked questions or spoke on a wide range of subjects. He developed a special interest in the West Indies – he was sometimes facetiously called 'the member for Trinidad' – because of his deep concern over the consequences of the indentured labour system, both to immigrants and to the native population of the West Indian islands. He thought that the Government was ignoring them, and that sweeping reforms – in the provision of education and housing, for example – were urgently needed. The workers of Trinidad sent a contribution to his expenses in the first 1910 election.

Both Stuart and Summerbell lost their seats on this occasion. There was severe unemployment in the town but their defeat was also due to the work of Samuel Storey, one of the successful Conservative candidates, who had made Sunderland 'the best organised constituency in the North of England' [Pelling (1967) 325 n.2].

As a boy Summerbell's favourite reading was Dickens; later on Samuel Smiles's *Self Help,* Robert Blatchford's *Merrie England* and *Britain for the British,* William Booth's *In Darkest England,* the works of Henry George and the literature issued by the ILP and the Land Nationalisation Society.

Summerbell died suddenly, of a seizure which attacked him during a Sunderland Council meeting on 10 February 1910. He left an estate of £1574 gross, £975 net. He was survived by his wife and his three children, Thomas (21), Walter (13) and Ethel (11). Thomas, born in 1889, carried on the family printing business and was, like his father, active in local Labour politics. He was a pacifist, although he served with the RAOC in the First World War. He was a member of the Sunderland Borough Council from 1930 to 1944, when ill health forced him to retire; the first Socialist mayor of Sunderland, from 1935 to 1937, and a JP. On 22 February 1954 he became the first man in the country to be made a life member of the Labour Party. He died unmarried on 14 October 1955, aged sixty-six, and left an estate valued at £51,428. Walter, born in 1896, started his working life in the Borough surveyor's office. During the First World War he was a CO and a member of the NCF and, after serving a term of imprisonment for his beliefs, worked as a gardener at the Wakefield Work Centre until the war ended. His former employers would not reinstate him so he joined his brother in the family firm. He remained a pacifist all his life and a supporter of the Fellowship of Reconciliation, Peace Pledge Union and the War Resisters' International. He married and had one daughter Joyce, born in 1924. He died on 28 August 1963. Ethel, born in 1898, attended Armstrong College, Newcastle, where she obtained a BSc. degree of the University of Durham. She taught in various secondary schools and Sunderland Training College, from which she retired in 1965. She was mayoress of Sunderland during her brother's mayoralty but was not active politically.

Writings: 'How I got on', *Pearson's Weekly,* 22 Mar 1906; *Afforestation: the unemployed and the land* (1908) 16 pp.; *Election Address* [1910?] [giving details of his parliamentary record] 16 pp.

Sources: (1) MSS: Labour Party archives: LRC. (2) Other: *Hansard* 4th ser. *152* (1906) to 5th ser. *13* (1909); *Dod* (1906); *Rev. of Revs 6* (1906) 580; *Reformers' Year Book* (1907); *Sunderland Year Book* (1907) 16-17 and (1910) 10-12; A.E. Musson, *The Typographical Association: origins and history up to 1949* (Oxford, 1954); *Sunderland Echo,* 14 and 17 Oct 1955; H.A. Clegg et al., *A History of British Trade Unions since 1889* vol. *1: 1889-1910* (Oxford, 1964); H. Pelling, *Social Geography of British Elections 1885-1910* (1967); personal information: Miss E. Summerbell, Sunderland, daughter. OBIT. *Sunderland Daily Echo,* 10, 11 and 14 Feb 1910; *Sunderland Echo,* 14 and 17 Oct 1955 [for T. Summerbell Jr.].

MARGARET 'ESPINASSE

See also: †George LANSBURY, for British Labour Party, 1900-13.

SUTHERS, Robert Bentley (1870-1950)
SOCIALIST WRITER

R.B. Suthers was born on 21 October 1870 in Chorlton upon Medlock, Manchester. He was the son of Bentley Suthers, a draper, and his wife Annie (née Maguire). Robert was an intelligent boy. Before he was twelve years old he won a foundation scholarship from Chorlton elementary school to Manchester Grammar School, which he entered in 1882.

When he left school in 1889 he was employed as a clerk in the office of the *Sunday Chronicle,* the Manchester paper started by Edward Hulton. Robert Blatchford had been writing for the *Chronicle* (under the pen-name of 'Nunquam') since 1885, and by 1887 was working full-time on the paper, until Hulton objected to his Socialist articles in 1891 and he walked out. Blatchford was undoubtedly the chief formative influence on Suthers at this time. In 'Reminiscences', his contribution to the *Clarion Coming-of-Age Supplement* (6 Dec 1912), Suthers wrote that even before he met Blatchford (as opposed to seeing him at meetings) he was 'imbibing Nunquamese sermons on the higher wisdom and the beauties of literature'; and he went on to recount in terms of mock horror his first encounters with Blatchford, and with Alexander Thompson and Edward Fay. When these three, together with Blatchford's brother Montagu and the staff artist William Palmer, left the *Chronicle* and started their Socialist weekly, the *Clarion*, at the end of 1891, Suthers went with them. His official job was looking after the accounts, but he did a number of other things as well.

In 1895 the *Clarion* moved its office to London, and Suthers moved with it, still keeping the accounts and doing various office jobs. He seems to have been slow to realise his talent for writing: it was not until 1901 that he began contributing regularly to the *Clarion*. He had entirely grasped the salient features of the *Clarion* manner – lucidity, pungency and humour. Although his first book, *A Man, a Woman, and a Dog,* published in 1901, was merely a comic novel, in the next few years Suthers became known as a Socialist pamphleteer and in particular as an authority on and propagandist for municipal Socialism. An advertisement for the *Clarion* in 1909 urged the public to read the paper for, among other features, 'Facts and Arguments on Progressive Municipalism', by R.B. Suthers. Between 1903 and 1905 he wrote several *Clarion* pamphlets on the subject, and in 1905 published what is perhaps his best book, an argument for supporting municipal trading, addressed to the ordinary citizen, with the title *Mind your own Business.* This book was brought up to date for the Fabian Society in 1929, and again in 1938. Bernard Shaw called his own work, *The Commonsense of Municipal Trading,* and Suthers's *Mind your own Business* 'the only two books on the subject worth reading'.

The other books and pamphlets on political and economic subjects which Suthers produced between 1906 and 1910 were concerned with national aspects of contemporary capitalism as contrasted with Socialism; for instance, he wrote in a series called 'Pass on Pamphlets', *John Bull and Doctor Socialism, John Bull and Doctor Free Trade, John Bull and Doctor Protection* (all in 1908). He likewise produced several compendiums of useful arguments for Socialism, and rebuttals of arguments against it. He seems to have agreed with Blatchford on many wide political issues: he supported Blatchford's scheme for national (Socialist) self-sufficiency, in which tariff reform was to be used as an instrument of Socialist policy (see *My Right to Work,* 1906, and the last two of the pamphlets listed above); and he endorsed Blatchford's warnings against German militarism (see *Behind German Dreadnoughts,* 1909).

In 1910 Hulton invited Suthers to become editor of his journal *Ideas,* and he moved back to Manchester. His reasons for leaving the *Clarion* are not known. In 1910 Blatchford had retreated to the cottage he had bought in Norfolk and left the *Clarion* to be edited by his elder daughter Winifrid. In 1913, however, there is evidence that he was editing the paper again and Suthers responded to a plea for his return to London as assistant editor. It was not the best moment to rejoin the paper since its support for the First World War helped to diminish the *Clarion's* influence in the labour movement, and Blatchford was to take final leave of Socialism in 1914. But Suthers stuck to the paper until 1925, when he resigned and became a freelance labour writer. He contributed to the *Daily Herald* and to a number of trade union journals. He was asked by NATSOPA to write the history of their union, and from August to November 1930 was acting editor of the *Miner.* During the 1930s he wrote a number of articles in the *Labour Magazine* and elsewhere, mainly on trade union history. In 1947 he produced a pamphlet, *How Russia gets Output,* which was one of the Labour Party's Discussion Series. He was still writing three articles a month in the year of his death.

He died in Paddington General Hospital on 20 September 1950, and was cremated at Golders Green. He left an estate valued at £775. On 30 September 1897 he had married Alice Elizabeth Watts, and they had two sons and one daughter, Dorothy. All his family survived him except the elder son, who was killed in the First World War. The second son, Harold, born on 12 June 1901, had a career in insurance, and was finally head of the pensions and insurance branch of the National Coal Board, and a member of the joint social security committee set up by the NCB and the European Coal and Steel Community. When he retired in 1966 he accepted the part-time job of correspondent for the European Economic Community on the British social security system.

His sister, Dorothy Violet Suthers, was born on 26 February 1905, and held various secretarial posts until her retirement in 1965.

Suthers took no active part in politics or in the trade union movement; he worked for Socialism with his pen, and a very effective instrument it was. He had considerable talent, and a mind of his own.

Writings: *A Man, a Woman, and a Dog* (1901); *Does Municipal Management pay?* (1903) 56 pp.; (with H. Beswick), *The Clarion Birthday Book* [1904?]; Clarion Pamphlets: *The Truth about the Trams* (no. 39: 1903) 16 pp., *The Citizen and the Council* (no. 42: 1905) 15 pp., *'Killed by High Rates' – or Rent?* (no. 43: 1905) 12 pp., *Seventeen Shots at Socialism* (no. 47: 1908) 22 pp.; *Mind your own Business: the case for municipal management* (1905; rewritten, 1929, rev. ed. 1938); *My Right to Work* (1906); *Jack's Wife* [tales] (1907); Pass on Pamphlets: *John Bull and Doctor Socialism* (no. 1: [1908] 15 pp., *John Bull and Doctor Free Trade* (no. 2: [1908] 15 pp., *John Bull and Doctor Protection* (no. 3: [1908]) 15 pp., *John Bull's Rent and Interest* (no. 7: [1908]) 15 pp., *100 Points for Socialism* (no. 19: [1909] 31 pp., *Behind German Dreadnoughts* (no. 21 [1909]) 15 pp., *Socialism and the Dead Level* (no. 23 [1909]) 15 pp.; *Common Objections to Socialism answered* (1908); *Political Economy for Plain People* (1909); *Free Trade Delusion* (1910); 'Reminiscences', *Clarion Coming-of-Age Supplement*, 6 Dec 1912, 6; *Is there Money?* [1919] 15 pp.; *Cheap Food: the nation's first duty* (1925) 16 pp.; *The Story of 'Natsopa' 1889-1929* [1930]; *Simple Simon – the Socialist Scoundrel* (1932) 15 pp.; *Socialism or Smash!* (1932) 16 pp.; *How Russia gets Output* (LP Discussion ser. no 14: 1947) 15 pp. Suthers also wrote a number of articles in the *Labour Mag.* between Feb 1929 and July 1933 and in *Labour* (July-Sep 1939).

Sources: *Labour Who's Who* (1927); *Author's and Writer's Who's Who* (1934); A.M. Thompson, *Here I lie* (1937); M. Cole, *Makers of the Labour Movement* (1948); L. Thompson, *Robert Blatchford* (1951); M. Cole, *The Story of Fabian Socialism* (1961); personal information: Miss D.V. Suthers, Caterham, daughter.

MARGARET 'ESPINASSE

See also: Montagu John BLATCHFORD; Robert BLATCHFORD; *Alexander Mattock THOMPSON.

SWANWICK, Helena Maria Lucy (1864-1939)
AUTHOR, PACIFIST AND SUFFRAGIST

Helena Sickert was born in Munich in 1864, the only daughter among the eight children of Eleanor and Oswald Adalbert Sickert. Her father, an artist and cartoonist, was born a Dane and became necessarily a German when the Prussians conquered his part of Slesvig. Her mother was the illegitimate daughter of a Fellow of Trinity College, Cambridge.

In 1859, when he married, Oswald Sickert was employed as a black-and-white artist on the staff of the *Fliegende Blätter* in Munich, and for some time the family continued to live in Munich for the winter months and in the country round about for the rest of the year. In 1868 they moved to England, where Oswald Sickert became naturalised. They lived first in Bedford, and then in Notting Hill.

In 1870 Helena fell ill with scarlet fever followed by rheumatic fever. She emerged so feeble and frail that by 1872 the family doctor insisted that she ought to live near the sea. She was sent to Neuville, to a private school where her mother had spent a happy girlhood as a boarder *en famille*. But the school had deteriorated; only a few pupils and one teacher remained, and Helena learned almost nothing during her four years there, except to talk French like a native and to do fine sewing. The school finally collapsed in 1876, and Helena spent the next two years at home. In 1878 she was sent to Notting Hill School where she was exceedingly happy, being, as she put it, 'ravenous for discipline, teaching, books, friends and leaders' [*I have been young*, 73]. She came to know the Burne-Joneses and the Morrises, William De Morgan, the sisters of Walter Raleigh, Bernard Shaw, and other well-known people. Oscar Wilde was already a family friend. The Sickert family were all gifted in art or music or both. Helena's eldest brother Walter was already showing his talent for painting and drawing.

From Notting Hill School Helena went up to Girton College, where she took the Moral Sciences Tripos and was awarded a second class. In the same year, 1885, she was appointed lecturer in psychology at Westfield College. Before leaving Cambridge she had met Frederick Swanwick, who had given up a tutorship at Cavendish College in order to return to Manchester, where his parents lived, and to become a lecturer in mathematics at Owens College. Helena and he became engaged in 1886 and were married in 1888.

The move to Manchester meant that Helena had to give up full-time work; but she lectured occasionally for the University Extension courses and contributed to journals, including the *Manchester Guardian*. Among the many friends she made were C.P. Scott, the *Guardian*'s editor, and Mary Agnes Adamson, later Mary Hamilton. She undertook work which brought her into touch with the Labour movement: she organised social clubs for workers, lectured to branches of the Women's Co-operative Guild, and became a member of the Women's Trade Union Council. In 1900, after the death of her husband's surviving parent, his mother, the Swanwicks moved out from Manchester (whose climate was bad for Helena) to Knutsford, where she at first devoted herself to gardening and recovering her health.

But the suffrage movement claimed her especial interest. She joined the North of England Society, whose chairman was Margaret Ashton, later to be Manchester's first woman councillor. This society was affiliated to the National Union of Women's Suffrage Societies (NUWSS), the non-militant body presided over by Mrs Fawcett. Mrs Swanwick held that the franchise could be obtained only by constitutional means, by organisation, education, and peaceful political action. She was strongly critical of the militant suffragettes, found a self-imposed martyrdom repugnant, and objected to the dictatorial methods of the Pankhursts. She worked very hard for the NUWSS, addressing meetings all over the country and undertaking organising and committee work. In 1908 she was elected to the executive, and in the following year became editor of the newly started journal, the *Common Cause*. In 1910 she gave evidence to the R.C. on Divorce.

It was soon clear that the *Common Cause* ought to be published in London; and since Frederick Swanwick was soon to retire from the chair of mathematics at Manchester University, Helena moved to London, preceding her husband by a few months, in 1911. But she felt her editorial freedom restricted by the decision not to attack the policies of the militants. So, although she had made a success of the paper, she resigned the editorship in 1912, and returned to freelance writing, chiefly for the *Manchester Guardian*, but also for others such as the *Observer*, the *Nation*, the *Daily News*. In June 1913 she attended in Budapest what was to be the last meeting for some years of the international Suffrage Alliance Congress. In the same year she published her book, *The Future of the Women's Movement*.

Mrs Swanwick was passionately opposed to the First World War. She was convinced that force was no alternative to negotiation but merely sowed the seeds of future wars; and she believed that their foreign policy made the Allies as 'guilty' as Germany. So when the Union of Democratic Control came into being (in August 1914) its views were altogether congenial to her, and she joined it in September – the same month as her old friend Mary Agnes Hamilton. The UDC was founded, with the aim of promoting a lasting post-war settlement, by E.D. Morel and others and by September Ramsay MacDonald was a member. MacDonald became chairman and Morel secretary. For fourteen years Mrs Swanwick took a leading part in UDC activities, and she wrote its history in 1924, in *Builders of Peace*. Her work in the UDC (added to Labour's support for women's suffrage) induced her to join the ILP before the war ended.

Government obstruction and other difficulties, including a recent serious operation, prevented Mrs Swanwick from attending the Dutch congress of women suffragists at The Hague in April 1915. The opposition in the NUWSS to this congress and, indeed, to the idea of peace by negotiation, led her to resign from that organisation and to take the lead in forming the British section of the Women's International League (WIL). Its aims were the settlement of international disputes by other means than war; women's suffrage; and Labourism. Mrs Swanwick was elected chairman and held office for seven years. In 1916 she became chairman of the Peace Negotiations Committee founded by the Rev. Herbert Dunnico, Charles Roden Buxton and herself. This body held that Britain should speedily take the lead in peace negotiations, since the prolongation of the conflict would produce a punitive settlement containing the seeds of a future war. Mrs Swanwick also helped to establish the 1917 Club, founded to commemorate the first Russian Revolution of 1917 and to provide a meeting place for Radicals and Socialists.

After the war Mrs Swanwick continued to work actively for both the UDC and the WIL. She opposed the Versailles Peace Treaty, particularly the clauses on indemnities; she also opposed intervention in Russia, continuation of the blockade of Germany in 1919, government policy in Ireland, and the French occupation of the Ruhr. As a member of the Advisory Committee on International Questions she helped to formulate Labour Party foreign policy in the twenties. In her WIL work she followed the same lines, but gave more attention to arousing political interest among women. She attended the Women's Peace Conference at Zurich in 1919 and at The Hague in 1922, and organised 'International House' in London and also in Manchester.

Mrs Swanwick was an early advocate of the plan for a League of Nations, and she was a member of the League of Nations Union; but she resigned when enemy nations were excluded from the actual League. Later, however, she came to believe that the League could be reformed. The Labour Government appointed her substitute delegate to the Fifth Assembly (1924), where she acted as *rapporteur* for refugees. After it, she rejoined the League of Nations Union, as vice-president.

After the death of E.D. Morel in November 1924, Mrs Swanwick undertook the editorship of the UDC organ, *Foreign Affairs*. She felt that new conditions demanded a new approach, and she successfully converted the paper into a larger and more expensive journal (the price was raised from 3*d* to 6*d*). But some new members of the UDC executive joined some older members who demanded a return to the old propaganda sheet and the old price. Mrs Swanwick therefore resigned the editorship in November 1927. The paper ceased publication soon after.

In 1928 she was elected to the executive of the Royal Institute for International Affairs, and in 1929 was appointed chief woman delegate to the Tenth Assembly of the League of Nations. Ill health restricted her activities in both capacities. In 1931 she received the Order of Companion of Honour for her work for peace and for the enfranchisement of women.

During the thirties she became increasingly aware of the dangers of aerial warfare, foreseeing the Pearl Harbour type of attack without a declaration of war, and 'first strike' defensive action. She advocated aerial disarmament as a prelude to total disarmament, and fought against the proposal to create a 'pooled' air force for use against aggressors. Her views on a pacifist policy for security were set out in *New Wars for Old* (1934), *Collective Insecurity* (1937) and *The Roots of Peace* (1938).

Frederick Swanwick died on 27 July 1931. In December Mrs Swanwick, with her faithful housekeeper Martha Agnes Rushton, moved to a cottage, 'Satis', in Maidenhead where she appears to have died from heart disease accelerated by an overdose of sleeping tablets, deliberately taken, on 16 November 1939, at the age of seventy-five. She left to her nephew, Lionel Temple Swanwick, an estate of £1184.

Writings: Mrs Swanwick edited the *Common Cause*, 1909-12, and *Foreign Affairs*, 1924-8, and she also contributed to journals and newspapers, including *Nation*, *Socialist Rev.*, *Daily News*, *Manchester Guardian* and *Observer*. Her principal books and pamphlets are: *The Small Town Garden* (1907); *The Future of the Women's Movement* (1913): *Women and War* (UDC pamphlet no. 11: [1915]) 13 pp.; *Women in the Socialist State* (NLP, 1921); *Builders of Peace: being ten years' history of the Union of Democratic Control* (1924); *The Geneva Protocol* [1925]; *The Extraordinary Assembly* [of the League of Nations] (UDC, 1926) 19 pp.; *Labour's*

Foreign Policy: what has been and what might be (Fabian Tract no.227: 1929) 44 pp.; *New Wars for Old: a reply to the Rt Hon. Lord Davies [The Crisis of Confidence in the League] and others* (WIL, 1934) 45 pp.; *Frankenstein and his Monster: aviation for world service* [a sequel to *New Wars for Old*] (WIL, 1934) 22 pp.; *Pooled Security: what does it mean?* [A reply to some critics of *New Wars for Old*] (WIL, 1934) 30 pp.; *I have been young* [autobiography] (1935); *Collective Insecurity* [on the League of Nations] (1937); *The Roots of Peace* [A sequel to *Collective Insecurity*, being an essay on some of the uses, conditions and limitations of compulsive force in the prevention of war] (1938).

Sources: (1) MSS: UDC records: Brynmor Jones Library, Hull Univ. (2) Other: Mrs Swanwick's *Builders of Peace* (1924) and *I have been young* (1935) are the main sources but other works include: R. Strachey, *'The Cause': a short history of the women's movement in Great Britain* (1928); *WWW* (1929-40); E.S. Pankhurst, *The Suffragette Movement* (1931); E. Windrich, *British Labour's Foreign Policy* (Stanford Univ. Press [1952]); H. Dalton, *Call back Yesterday: memoirs 1887-1931* (1953); A.J.P. Taylor, *The Trouble Makers* (1957); M. Cole, *The Story of Fabian Socialism* (1961); R.E.Dowse, 'The Entry of the Liberals into the Labour Party 1910-1920', *Yorkshire Bulletin of Economic and Social Research 13*, no. 2 (1961) 78-87; C.A.Cline, *Recruits to Labour* (Syracuse Univ. Press, 1963); M. Swartz, *The Union of Democratic Control in British Politics during the First World War* (Oxford, 1971); biographical information: B.H. Sadler, Warwick Univ., to whom the editors are indebted for an earlier draft of this biography. OBIT. *Reading Mercury* and *Times*, 18 Nov 1939; *Maidenhead Advertiser*, 22 Nov 1939; *Labour Party Report* (1940).

MARGARET 'ESPINASSE

See also: *Charles Roden BUXON; *Mary Agnes HAMILTON; Edmund Dene MOREL.

SWEET, James (1804/5?-79)
CHARTIST AND RADICAL

James Sweet was born in Northampton in 1804 or 1805. His origins are obscure, but he was probably a grandson of William Sweet, hatter, who died in 1814. At an early age James moved to London, where he worked as a tailor. Obliged to leave the metropolis by circumstances unknown, he joined his elder brother Thomas in Nottingham in about 1826, and commenced business as a hairdresser. Trade rivals sought to oust him by reducing prices, and by 1832 he was also dealing in books, periodicals and stationery. These remained his occupations for the rest of his life, and his premises in Goosegate, which were close to the Market Place and the 'Democratic Chapel', Barkergate (rented as a Chartist Hall, 1839-45), became the centre of radical Nottingham. Like the Dudley Chartist draper, Sam Cook, Sweet used his shop for the dissemination of news and propaganda, and derived a certain freedom of action from his shopkeeper status.

From 1838 to 1854 Sweet was the main co-ordinator of radical activity in the Nottingham area, acting as treasurer and banker to working-class movements. In 1853 he claimed to have handled some £5000, including a variety of Chartist funds and subscriptions to the Nottinghamshire Miners' Association during 1844-6. Sweet emerged as a leader of the Nottingham Working Men's Association in 1838. After the failure of the National Holiday he consistently opposed any resort to a strategy of violence, and emphasised the need for efficient organisation for a long-term struggle, with the onus upon working-class self-improvement. His *Address to the Working Classes on the System of Exclusive Dealing . . . by a Member of the Nottingham Co-operative Store* (1840) advocated co-operation and exclusive dealing to develop class self-dependence and remind shopkeepers of their reliance upon working-class support. He himself ran one of several short-lived stores.

As Nottingham correspondent of Cooper's *Midland Counties Illuminator* in 1841, Sweet reported a weekly cycle of Chartist activity, embracing religious services, lectures, singing class, mutual instruction group, schools, tract society and total abstinence society. He was deeply committed to the provision of facilities for 'alternative education,' supporting a Chartist Sunday School and a scheme in 1845 to create an independent operatives' hall as a base for working-class clubs and societies. The project foundered, but Sweet later became a vice-president and trustee of the People's Hall, a democratised mechanics' institute established in 1854 with financial support from George Gill, a Unitarian lace factor, and with a constitution drawn up by William Lovett. Sweet was also a temperance advocate, associating drunkenness with election corruption and political exploitation. His enthusiasm was tempered, however, by an awareness of the importance of the pub as a centre of radical organisation, and of the danger of exciting internal divisions within Chartism. He criticised the official temperance movement for intolerance.

In the late 1840s the Land Company provided a further focus for Sweet's radical commitment. He became sub-treasurer of the Nottingham locality and promoted a mutual assistance society to assist allottees with the problem of initial expenses. Working-class audiences were urged to 'keep out of alehouses, and buy land with the money'. He also presided over the Land Conferences at Birmingham (December 1846), Lowbands (August 1847) and Snig's End (August 1849). For Sweet, as for many other radicals, land ownership continued to present a viable alternative to industrial poverty.

Sweet remained in the forefront of the Chartist movement during the upsurge of activity in spring 1848, and the subsequent decline. On 10 April, he spoke at a mass rally in the Market Place, rebuking the violent rhetoric of local militants in a characteristic speech of studied moderation – 'we tell the authorities that a sabre cannot cut down an argument, and that a bullet cannot pierce an opinion.' Sweet was a close friend and admirer of Feargus O'Connor, managing his Nottingham election campaign of 1847, in which a Tory-Chartist alliance first forged in 1841 was successfully revived. During 1853 he organised the national relief fund for O'Connor, visiting him at Chiswick in March and April and attending the Lunacy Commission Enquiry into his state of mind. The fund realised only £31 and became a source of dissension: Sweet's financial probity was questioned, and he withdrew indignantly from further Chartist activity in April 1854.

His political commitment unshaken by this dispute, Sweet turned to municipal affairs. He had gathered experience of local administration as a member (from 1842) of the Board of Highways of St Mary's parish and later its chairman, combating the threat of cholera in 1849, and pressing for improvements in the drainage and paving of the parish. He became secretary of the Friar-Lane Provident Society and, in November 1854, won election to the Town Council for Byron ward as an ultra-Liberal. Sweet sat on the Council from 1854 to 1860 and from 1867 to 1870, and served on the Baths and Wash-houses Committee. During these years he was a leading left-wing critic of the ruling Whig clique, 'Number 30' (so called from a committee room in which the group habitually foregathered). Opposition to Number 30 crystallised in the 1861 by-election, when Sweet and a group of former Chartists supported the candidature of the Tory-Radical baronet Sir Robert Clifton. Their support, however, was conditional upon Clifton's reforming zeal, as Sweet indicated: 'If Sir Robert gets in he will have to go on, or else I shall be very close behind him and give him a shove.' The warning went unheeded, and in 1865 the radicals, irritated by Clifton's conservatism, supported the Liberals Samuel Morley and Charles Paget. In an election remarkable even in Nottingham for its violence, Sweet narrowly escaped injury; his shop was damaged and looted by a Tory mob. He obtained compensation from the town, and raised a subscription for other sufferers.

James Sweet remained politically active, appearing regularly on Reform League platforms where he declared himself 'a Chartist still', until his retirement from public life in 1872. He died on 15 April 1879, survived by his widow Martha – the marriage was childless – and was buried in the church cemetery. His effects were valued at under £800. Sweet commanded the support of

Nottingham radicals by reason of his integrity, his remarkable energy and, above all, his determination to ally himself with the cause of the working classes; 'he is the only middle-class man amongst them', as one local militant declared in April 1848. His speeches contained few religious references and there is no clear evidence of his religious beliefs.

Writings: *Address to the Working Classes on the System of Exclusive Dealing . . . by a Member of the Nottingham Co-operative Store* (Nottingham, 1840). He published the *Nottingham Illustrated Magazine and Monthly Advertiser* (Nottingham, 1861).

Sources: Pigot's *Directory of Nottingham* (1828); White's *Directory of Nottinghamshire* (1832); *Nottingham Rev.*, 1832-65; *Northern Star*, 1838-52; *Nottingham Mercury*, 1839-40; *Midland Counties Illuminator*, 1841; *Notes to the People*, 1851-2; *People's Paper*, 1852-8; Portrait of James Sweet [Nottingham Reference Library, source unknown, c.1870]; R.G. Gammage, *History of the Chartist Movement 1837-1854* (1894; repr. with an Introduction by John Saville, NY, 1969); 'Recollections of the Past', *Nottingham Weekly Guardian*, 27 Apr 1907; A.C. Wood, 'Sir Robert Clifton, 1826-69' *Trans of the Thoroton Society, 57* (1953) 48-65; A.R. Griffin, *The Miners of Nottinghamshire 1: 1881-1914* (Nottingham, 1955); C. Holmes, 'Chartism in Nottingham, 1837-1861' (Nottingham Univ. BA dissertation, 1960); R.A. Church, *Economic and Social Change in a Midland Town. Victorian Nottingham, 1815-1900* (1966); P. Wyncoll, *Nottingham Chartism* (Nottingham, 1966); J.J. Rowley, 'Drink and Temperance in Nottingham, 1830-1860' (Leicester MA dissertation, 1974) [copies at Victorian Studies Centre, Nottingham Univ. and Nottingham PL]. OBIT. *Nottingham Daily Express* and *Nottingham J.*, 16 Apr 1879; *Nottingham Daily Guardian*, 17 Apr 1879.

JOHN ROWLEY

See also: *Samuel COOK; *Thomas COOPER; *Feargus O'CONNOR for Chartism, 1840-8.

TAYLOR, Robert Arthur (1886-1934)
TRADE UNIONIST, ALDERMAN AND LABOUR MP

Arthur Taylor was born on 17 October 1886 in Byrom Street, Hulme, Manchester, the son of John Taylor, a joiner and organ-builder from Metheringham in Lincolnshire, and his wife Annie (née Holmes), a farmer's daughter from Hogsthorpe, also in Lincolnshire. The Taylor family moved back to Lincoln when Arthur was seven years old and for four years he attended St Peter-at-Gowt and St Botolph's schools.

In 1898 he returned with his family to Manchester, where he continued his education for a short time. When he was thirteen he first started work as an office boy and he also attended night school classes. But shortly afterwards he entered the tailoring trade, and when he returned to Lincoln in 1904 he continued to follow this trade. In 1909 he became a member of the Shop Assistants' Union and in 1912 started a tailoring business in the city with his brother.

Soon after his return to Lincoln Taylor became actively involved in Labour politics in the area. He was one of the founders, about 1906, of the Lincoln branch of the ILP, and he worked strenuously during its early years to strengthen the influence of the Labour movement in Lincoln and the surrounding rural areas. He was successively president and secretary of the Lincoln Trades Council and Labour Party. In a by-election for the City Council in July 1913 Taylor was returned for Park ward as the city's first Labour councillor. He continued to represent this ward until in May 1918 he enlisted as a private in the Inns of Court OTC. On his return to civilian life in 1919 he was re-elected and continued to represent the ward until he was made an alderman in 1930. In 1924 – the same year he was elected MP for Lincoln – he became Lincoln's first Labour mayor and was a member of the finance committee and chairman of the watch committee. At that time the Labour Party had nine representatives on the Council compared with two before the war. Taylor's particular interests were housing and education, and he served on the housing committee for many years. His appointment to the aldermanic bench was the outcome of a six months' strike campaign by the Labour group to secure for Labour councillors full representation on important committees and in the Council's affairs.

In 1920 Taylor had won a Working Men's Club and Institute Union scholarship to Ruskin College, but in 1921, for business and domestic reasons, he was compelled to give up a second year extension of the scholarship. He was anxious to enter Parliament and contested the Lincoln constituency on three occasions before he was elected, by a narrow majority, in 1924. At the 1918 election he had expressed at some length his support for the League of Nations and for the recognition of international minimum standards of labour conditions; and always maintained his support for the League's attempts at arbitration, and for disarmament. In his 1922 election campaign he had stressed the need for an overall national plan to be implemented for labour and a full state system of maintenance introduced which would supersede the 'dole'. He advocated a policy of co-operation by all sections of industry for reconstruction, although he fully supported the 1926 General Strike. His majority was substantially increased at the 1929 general election but he lost his seat in 1931 to the National Unionist, W.S. Liddall, although his result was less disastrous than in most parts of the country.

During his seven years in Parliament, Taylor devoted much time to the question of Anglo-Russian commercial relations, and, in particular, to the effects which their breakdown was having on heavy engineering industries in his constituency. In his maiden speech in December 1924 he emphasised that before the war Russian markets had absorbed much of the Lincoln area's production of agricultural implements, and that the rupture of these links created heavy losses for many firms and rising unemployment. In the mid-1920s he visited Russia in an effort to secure orders; and he spoke frequently, both in the House and locally, against the political discrimination which was being exercised against Russia through the Trade Facilities Act and the Export Credits Scheme. He also supported for the same reasons improved trade links with the Colonies and Dominions.

As the parliamentary representative of the National Amalgamated Union of Shop Assistants, Warehousemen and Clerks, Taylor consistently defended shop assistants' rights when hours and conditions of work were under debate. In 1927 he served on the Departmental Committee which reviewed the Shops (Early Closing) Acts of 1920 and 1921. In the following year he gave his general support to the private Shops (Hours of Closing) Bill presented by Sir Park Goff, which aimed, among other matters, at shortening the working week of the shop assistants; but he was critical of its restricted objectives and its failure to cover other parts of the distributive trades. In 1930 Taylor was appointed a member of the S.C. on Shop Assistants, which reported in 1931. Its conclusions were not acted upon until a few months after his death.

In 1931 Taylor strongly opposed MacDonald's break with the Labour Party, although up to that time he had been a loyal supporter of the leadership. In his 1931 election campaign Taylor declared unequivocally his support for public ownership policies. He believed that only nationalisation could overcome the financial crisis, remove Britain from control by foreign bankers and restore the workers' standard of living. After leaving Parliament, Taylor became, in March 1932, a special organiser for the Shop Assistants' Union. He resigned his aldermanic seat on the Lincoln Council and left the city. His home for the last years of his life was Sidcup in Kent, although he remained Lincoln's prospective Labour candidate.

Taylor had married in 1909 Laura Webber, the daughter of Benjamin Webber of Sleaford. She came from a politically active family (both her father and maternal grandfather were prominent in the local Conservative Club). At the age of eighteen she joined the women's suffrage movement. Throughout the years that the family lived in Lincoln she was a committed Labour Party worker and a popular platform speaker. She was one of the first members of the women's section of the Party, inaugurated in 1917, and in 1923 was appointed president of the women's group in the constituency Party. She was a stalwart supporter of her husband in his council and constituency work, especially in the 1929 election campaign.

Arthur Taylor died on 5 April 1934 in the Miller Hospital, Greenwich, from coronary thrombosis. He had suffered recurring periods of illness. In 1928, on health grounds, he visited the West Indies and Canada, but was taken seriously ill during his stay. His visit was extended to six months and during this time he recorded in diary form his impressions of the social and labour conditions in these countries. In his younger days, however, before illness overtook him, he was a football enthusiast and amateur sportsman: at one time he had been given a trial by Everton Football Club.

Taylor was survived by his wife and two daughters, his only son Robert having died in August 1924 at the age of twelve. After a funeral service on 9 April 1934 in St Martin's Church, Lincoln, attended by hundreds of representatives from all sections of the city's trade union and Labour movements, as well as other civic groups, Taylor was buried in St Helen's churchyard, Boultham Park. Many hundreds of people lined the streets, and among the large number of messages was a telegram from Ivan Maisky (the Soviet Ambassador in London) in recognition of Taylor's efforts on behalf of Anglo-Soviet co-operation. Arthur Taylor left an estate valued at £1151. In September 1936 the *Daily Herald* reported that the new offices being planned for the Lincoln Labour and trade union movements would be a memorial to Taylor and in December 1973, nearly forty years after his death, three trees were presented to Lincoln by the Labour women's group to be planted in Arthur-Taylor Street in memory of Arthur and Laura Taylor and of their daughter Maisie and her husband Leslie Mills, who was Labour mayor of the city in 1944.

After her husband's death Laura Taylor was secretary of the Mary Macarthur Holiday Home for Working Women at Ongar from 1934 to 1939. She moved to Stansted in 1939 to be hostess of a new Macarthur home there until 1948 and then for two years worked in the same capacity at the home in Poulton-le-Fylde. In 1962 she was involved in a serious car accident in which her elder daughter, Rosalie May (Maisie) was killed and subsequently (until her death in 1966) she lived with her second daughter, Anne, in Cottingham, East Yorkshire. Maisie was employed initially by the LCC in work with the blind; after war service in the ATS she married and became a Labour member of the Nottinghamshire County Council. After the death of her husband in 1954 she lived with her mother and worked in LCC Day Centres for the physically and mentally handicapped. Anne, who had married in 1945 Frances John Walker, a technical brewer, is (1976) a JP on the City of Hull bench, a magistrate member of the Humberside Police Authority and a member of the Mental Health (Yorkshire area) and Social Security Review Tribunals.

Sources: (1) MSS: Personal diary, 16 Mar-21 Sep 1928: Mrs A. Walker, Beverley and copy in Brynmor Jones Library, Hull Univ. (2) Other: *Hansard* (1924-31); *Lincolnshire Chronicle,* 1 Nov 1924; *Shop Assistant,* 15 Nov 1924, 20 June 1925; *Tailor and Cutter,* 9 Apr 1925; *Dod* (1925); *Labour Who's Who* (1927); *Lincolnshire Forward,* 29 Sep 1928; *Thames Valley Times,* 8 Apr 1931; *Daily Herald,* 25 Sep 1936; *Lincolnshire Echo,* 13 Dec 1973; F. Hill, *Victorian Lincoln* (Cambridge, 1974); biographical information: T.A.K. Elliott, CMG; personal information: Mrs A. Walker JP, Beverley, daughter. OBIT. *Lincolnshire Echo,* 5 and 9 Apr 1934; *Times,* 6 Apr 1934; *Lincolnshire Chronicle and Leader,* 7 Apr 1934; *Shop Assistant,* 21 Apr 1934; *Lincolnshire Echo,* 25 and 26 Apr 1966 [Mrs Laura Taylor].

BARBARA NIELD

TEER, John (1809?-83?)
TEXTILE WORKER, TRADE UNIONIST AND POET

In the brief autobiography which he prefixed to his book of poems, *Silent Musings,* Teer gives a sketch of his life up to 1869, the year of its publication. He was born in Manchester during the Napoleonic Wars of poor parents, and was sent at the age of seven to the Lancasterian School. He had two years' schooling, and then began work as a piecer in a cotton mill. He worked in various mills as piecer, then spinner, until he was twenty-eight. 'During the whole of this time, and for many years afterwards' he attended a Catholic Sunday School, urged on by that passion for learning which marked so many intelligent working men; and he studied grammar, read a great quantity of poetry (mostly eighteenth-century) and wrote some poems which were published in local newspapers. His first attempt at public oratory, he tells us, was on the need for a Ten Hours Bill, and was presumably therefore in the 1830s or 1840s; he spoke at the Mechanics' Institute, and his 'remarks were noted for their eloquence and force. I do not say this from egotism, but from a sense of gratitude that I felt for the pains I had taken in self-culture, under disadvantages which those only can comprehend who toiled in a cotton mill during the long hour system.'

It is presumed that Teer spent all his life in Manchester but at some unknown date he left the mills and was for many years employed in a warehouse. In 1842 the Operative Dyers prevailed upon him to become their secretary. Unfortunately for Teer, this was the year of the Chartist general strike or Plug Plot. The Dyers joined in the march, 'but not as rioters or disturbers of the public peace. In the sad disorder which ensued I took no part whatever, except what I deemed to be my duty as secretary to the men whose servant I was.' Nevertheless Teer was arrested, and was sentenced to '*two years' imprisonment*, with hard labour, and to find bail in £200, for my good behaviour for two years more.' He was convinced that his arrest was due to mistaken identity. His solicitor drew up a memorial, signed by four county magistrates and the chief superintendent of police, in an effort to get commutation of the sentences on Teer and those arrested with him; but the appeal was rejected.

Teer now turned his attention to the task of continuing his self-education in prison, and even of teaching fellow-prisoners. The governor and the visiting magistrates granted him 'a large amount of time for my own improvement and also that of many others'.

When he was released he again took up the position of secretary to the Dyers, and held it for twelve years. In 1854 he was a delegate to Ernest Jones's Labour Parliament. The circumstances in which his employment came to an end he leaves obscure, but it followed a strike which he had advised against, but had supported loyally while it lasted; it failed after nearly twenty weeks. He ends his account with some bitterness: 'as I acted with perfect sincerity, honesty, and uprightness throughout, I became eventually, like many others, a sufferer.'

Teer's autobiographical preface concludes with a statement of his position: the author

has devoted the last twenty-five years of his life in doing his utmost to ameliorate the condition of that most noble order of men, the working classes. . . . There are some who may consider that I have been a promoter of strikes and a sower of discord between employers and their workmen; but such is not the fact. I have been invariably opposed to them [sc. strikes], and through my instrumentality and mediation, I have had the satisfaction of preventing many; and those who have heard my address in the Town Hall, Corn Exchange, Carpenters' Hall, and other large meeting-rooms, will bear testimony to the fact.

But in what capacity he was making these public speeches we are not told.

Teer published two volumes of poetry, *The Progress of Catholicism and Other Poems* (Liverpool, 1841), a work sympathetic to Catholics, and *Silent Musings*, published in Manchester in 1869. The second contains three sets of verses, 'Prison Poems', 'Miscellaneous Poems', and 'Elegies' (these mostly on ministers who were good shepherds of their flocks). The last two sets are strongly moral and religious, and are not outstanding in quality. The most interesting set is the 'Prison Poems', where the author repeatedly but variously expresses his grief at being cut off from the sights of the countryside, as in 'When you behold the Splendid Sky', and from liberty, symbolised by the birds whose songs he can hear in his cell. Throughout the book the author shows his piety, and his resignation is motivated by hopes of heaven.

The metres used are in general simple. Teer is fond of the four-line ballad stanza, with its variations, and also of rhyming couplets. His diction shows some eighteenth-century poetic usages, which is not surprising in view of the list of writers studied by him which he gives in the preface: Blair, Addison, Johnson and Pope. He might have added Beattie, from whom he quotes at the head of his first 'Elegy'. Altogether, his poetry is simple and sometimes touching; he has not so much skill or so much spirit as his fellow-poet and fellow-citizen Benjamin Stott. After the publication of the 1869 volume we have no further information about him and it is not known when he died. A search through the General Register Office records after 1869 has revealed only one John Teer who died in Manchester on 6 January 1883. His occupation was given as beerhouse keeper. No records after 1890 have been consulted.

Writings: *The Progress of Catholicism and Other Poems* (Liverpool, 1841) 56 pp.; *Silent Musings* (Manchester, 1869).

Sources: Introduction to Teer's 1841 volume of poems; *Manchester Times*, 20 Aug 1842; *British Statesman*, 6 Oct 1842; *Times*, 31 Aug, 6 and 21 Sep 1853; *People's Paper*, 27 Aug 1853–9 Nov 1853 *passim*; Preface to Teer's 1869 volume of poems; J. Saville, *Ernest Jones, Chartist* (1952).

MARGARET 'ESPINASSE
EDMUND AND RUTH FROW

See also: Benjamin STOTT.

TILLETT, Benjamin (Ben) (1860-1943)
TRADE UNION LEADER AND LABOUR MP

Ben Tillett was born on 11 September 1860 at Lower Easton, Bristol, the eighth and youngest child of Benjamin Tillett, labourer, and his first wife, Elizabeth (née Lane). His mother, who was of Irish stock, died when Tillett was one year old, and his early childhood was spent in extreme poverty. His father worked in a comb factory, his elder brothers in the South Wales coalfield. He received spasmodic maternal attention from a series of step-mothers and other relatives, an experience which produced 'acute unhappiness'. When he was six years old, and had made two unsuccessful attempts to run away, he was sent to work in a brickyard for 1s6d a week. At the age of eight, being threatened with the loss of a dog which he had taken into the house because of its injured leg, he made a third attempt to run away; on this occasion he succeeded in joining a circus. A year or so later he was brought home again by an elder sister and sent to a National School in Stafford. Up to this point, his only education had been in 'hell-fire theology' at Sunday School. He was dismissed from the school after a few days for assaulting a bullying teacher who struck him. At the age of thirteen he joined the Royal Navy for 6d a week. Following a shipboard accident three years later, he underwent an operation for hernia, left the service, and joined the merchant marine, sailing from Bristol and later from London in full-rigged sailing ships on the Atlantic trade to the United States and the West Indies. During the following years and before his rise to prominence in the union movement, he worked as a casual labourer on the docks, acquired some knowledge of the trade of a shoemaker and continued from time to time to sign on with merchant ships, coasters and Baltic and Russian traders.

At this period Tillett lived at the house of his sister's mother-in-law in Bethnal Green. According to a statement much later in his life (*Hansard*, 20 Nov 1930) he could hardly read or write until he was seventeen; but as a young man he became a voracious reader, and later claimed acquaintance with the work of Charles Lamb, Hazlitt, Wordsworth, Samuel Johnson, Huxley, Spencer, Darwin, Newman, Carlyle and Ruskin. He tried to learn Latin and Greek, attended lectures at the Bow and Bromley Institute, then an educational centre for East London, and cherished a secret ambition to become a barrister. Although he was aware of the secularist trend of the period represented by Charles Bradlaugh, and admired its lucidity of thought, he retained a basically Christian outlook, attended the Congregational Church and later had considerable experience as a lay preacher. He identified with the temperance movement, through which he came to know Cardinal Manning and joined a Good Templar's Lodge. In 1882 he married Jane Tompkins, and they lived for a time in a small rented room in Bethnal Green, into which a family of children came to be crowded. Two daughters survived to grow up, other children died in infancy. Tillett also felt deeply the death, from tuberculosis, of a favoured adopted son. From time to time he obtained periods of more regular employment on the docks, and had a variety of jobs with the Nanking Tea Company. For six years or so he worked as a cooper at the Monument Tea Warehouse, near London Bridge.

In July 1887 workers in a tea warehouse in Cutler Street called a meeting to oppose a reduction in wages. Tillett proposed the organisation of a Tea Operatives' and General Labourers' Association (also known as the Tea Coopers' Association), and this being agreed, he was appointed secretary at a salary of £2 a week. He had some experience of trade unionism since he was already a member of the Boot and Shoe Operatives' Union. The new union led a struggling and largely ineffective existence, its numbers fluctuating between 300 and 800. Casual labour was notoriously difficult to keep together and union organisation on the waterfront in the 1880s had also fallen into disrepute as a result of the activities of Thomas Kelly and Samuel Peters, key figures in the proliferation of bogus unions in the East End of London. Only the specialist grades of stevedores, corn-porters, crane-drivers and watermen had managed to build stable organisations.

Tillett, however, had large ambitions. He was physically a small man in rather poor health, but he had considerable natural ability and a vigorous personality, and he was soon to reveal himself as one of the great orators of the labour movement – in spite of having as a young man a serious impediment in his speech. There were a number of factors working in his favour. Harry Orbell, a man of integrity and an excellent organiser, became president of the Tea Operatives. Even more important, Tom McCarthy, the secretary of the Amalgamated Stevedores' Union, was Tillett's closest associate in the early days of the new union; and like Tillett, McCarthy had far-ranging ideas about unionisation of the London waterfront. Moreover, the closing years of the 1880s were generally favourable to union growth. Trade was on the upswing; public opinion was becoming somewhat less ignorant about the working and living conditions of casual labourers; and the young Socialist movement – especially the SDF – was to prove very helpful in general propagandist work. It was, indeed, propaganda that Tillett was chiefly engaged in; and he used every opportunity to present his case before the public; for instance in his evidence before the House of Lords Committee on the Sweating System in 1889.

In the months before the great London dock strike, Tillett's union was organised around three branches. Its headquarters was Wroot's Coffee House in Poplar; the other two branches met at a coffee house in Barking Road and at the Assembly Hall in Mile End Road. Tillett's own account of the London Dock Strike in his autobiography, *Memories and Reflections* (1931), is defective. There is an excellent contemporary account in H.L. Smith and V. Nash, *The Story of the Dockers' Strike* (1889), and a good summary in the Webbs's *History of Trade Unionism* (1894); the most useful modern accounts are in H.A. Clegg *et al.* (1964) and (especially) John Lovell, *Stevedores and Dockers* (1969). The strike began effectively on Wednesday 14 August 1889, and within a few days the stevedores had joined – an action which was crucial for the outcome of the struggle, since they brought much-needed experience and discipline into the strike committee. Many of London's well-known Socialists also provided organisational and propagandist help, among them Eleanor Marx and H.H. Champion. It was, however, the working-class Socialists – John Burns and Tom Mann – who supplied the day-to-day leadership of the strike along with Tillett. At the beginning of the struggle Tillett's union had a few hundred members and a few shillings in its funds. At the peak of the strike, 100,000 workers were involved, including every class of waterfront labour. Tillett's roles in the strike were diverse: he took his place with Burns and Mann at the head of the daily marches, and spoke regularly from Tower Hill; he shared with Mann the responsibility for the picket lines; and he took a continuous part in the negotiations, both with the dock directors and with the Mansion House Committee which was attempting outside mediation. Tillett greatly admired and respected Cardinal Manning, whom he regarded as 'the dockers' friend from the first'. At the end of August, when the endurance of the strikers was nearly at breaking point, the strike committee issued a call for a general strike of all London trades. The 'No-Work Manifesto' was issued on 30 August, but withdrawn almost immediately, Tillett being among those who argued vigorously against its publication. He was concerned to retain the sympathy of the established craft unionists, and he was assisted in his moderating attempts by the news of the arrival of the first monies from Australia: the beginning of the stream of funds that was to make such a significant contribution to final victory. The withdrawal of the general strike call also strengthened the position of the outside negotiators. At one stage during the tortuous negotiations involving the Mansion House Committee and the dock companies, Burns and Tillett were inclined to accept the Companies' offer of 6d an hour payable from January 1890; but this was rejected by the full strike committee which by then (early September) numbered between fifty and sixty delegates. The settlement which was finally agreed on awarded the 6d rate from 4 November 1889.

The dock strike raised Tillett to a position of national importance in the labour movement. His Tea Operatives' union was reorganised to become the Dock, Wharf, Riverside and General Labourers' Union of Great Britain and Ireland, with a weekly contribution of 2d, and with a single cash benefit of 10s a week strike pay. He himself became its general secretary at a salary of £160 a year, and he held this position until the amalgamations of 1922 which resulted in the formation of the Transport and General Workers' Union. By the end of November 1889 there were 30,000 members in the new union, and branches were being established in most ports. Major problems, however, showed themselves immediately. They were rooted in the economic structure of the industry, and particularly in the casual system of labour hiring, the central institutional weakness of waterside organisation. Hence the attempts by the union in the aftermath of the strike to establish the closed shop; and on the other side the strenuous efforts by the employers of dock labour to break the waterside unions and establish a system of 'free labour', a term that entered increasingly into public discussion. For a year or so these and other problems were largely obscured from the union side by the continuation of boom conditions and the corresponding high level of employment; but with the downturn of trade in the winter of 1890-91 the insecurity of the dockers' work situation was starkly revealed. The employers' offensive against all the newly organised waterfront unions – beginning with Havelock Wilson's Sailors' and Firemens' Union – went right round the ports of Britain in the three years after 1890, and by the summer of 1893 the new unions were effectively broken – in many ports almost wiped out of existence. Tillett's autobiography is again far from reliable for this complicated story. At the time some serious mistakes were made by the union leaders. It must, however, be appreciated that they were working in conditions of extreme difficulty, with the whole apparatus of the state mobilised against the unions in times of crisis. Tillett himself made a speech at Bristol in 1893 defending the right of workers to militant self-defence against official violence; for this speech he was indicted on a charge of incitement to riot and tried at the Central Criminal Court. He was, however, acquitted.

During this and the following year, Tillett was the object of a sustained press campaign designed to show that he had become wealthy at the union's expense, and that he had lost the sympathy of the dockers. In 1894 the newspaper *Morning* published a report of a meeting of dockers in Bethnal Green which had been addressed by him. It alleged that he was heckled and driven from the platform by his angry members. Tillett had at this time become an enthusiastic cyclist and had received, as a present, a road-racing model from the newly-formed Whitworth Cycle Company. Fleet Street made much of this incident to demonstrate Tillett's affluence. He issued a writ for libel against the *Morning*, which was represented in court by Edward Carson. The defence produced evidence of Tillett's own verbal extravagances against well-known politicians, (he once referred to 'Mr Gladstone's mind' as being 'like an open sewer') and he lost the case. This involved him in payment of costs, which forced him to sell his house. He was saved from total ruin by 'a friend and his unexpected help'. By 1895 he had moved from Bethnal Green to Leytonstone.

The decade following the London dock strike saw the decline of Tillett's union from a peak membership of 40,000 to about 10,000. In London, by 1900, the Dockers' Union was moribund 'and only subsidies from the provinces enabled it to maintain a presence in the metropolis' [Lovell (1969) 216]. Some stability for the union was the result of the recruitment of tin-plate workers in South Wales, where Tillett followed a policy of support for voluntary conciliation machinery. In 1910, on the eve of the next upsurge in dockers' militancy, the union had 119 branches, sixty-seven of which were in South Wales, including twenty-nine tin-plate branches. These latter contributed one-fifth of the union's income, compared with one-twentieth from the ten London dock branches.

One of the many problems confronting the union was undoubtedly the failings of Tillett as an administrator. 'He was an unstable man; highly emotional, over-sensitive to criticsim, and lacking in application' [Lovell (1969) 95]. He was also much involved in activities other than those connected directly with his own trade union. In 1892 he was made an alderman of the London County Council and remained on it until 1898, serving on the Housing Committee. He represented the Dockers' union at the TUC in 1890, and was a member of the parliamentary committee from 1892 to 1894. He took a New Unionist, Socialist position in these years, and successfully moved a resolution at the 1893 Congress calling for the establishment of a separate political fund to assist independent Labour candidates in local and parliamentary elections. He lost his seat on the parliamentary committee in 1895, following the revision of the TUC's constitution [Roberts (1958) 150ff.]. At this period he was a member of the Social Democratic Federation, and much later wrote warmly if not entirely uncritically of Hyndman in his *Memories and Reflections* [p. 189]. But Tillett was temperamentally ill-attuned to the Marxism of the SDF, and in 1893 he was at the founding Conference of the ILP in Bradford, becoming a member of its first NAC. In the previous year he had unsuccessfully contested West Bradford at the general election, and he stood again in 1895. As Philip Snowden noted in the preface he wrote to Tillett's *Memories and Reflections*, 'Tillett's parliamentary campaigns were an important factor in the growth of the ILP in the West Riding.' The 1892 election was particularly important in the history of Labour politics in Bradford. The growing conflict between the Bradford Labour Electoral Association and the supporters of an independent Labour position was greatly sharpened by Tillett's intervention. The Bradford Trades Council, hitherto controlled by the LEA, now voted to support Tillett, and from this time the LEA began to lose its political position in the town.

Tillett would have made more impact upon the TUC in the 1890s had he been less erratic and inconsistent in some of the lines of his policy. The principal issue on which he lost support, from both the left and the right of Congress, was his advocacy of compulsory arbitration. It was his visit to Australia in 1897 which had impressed him with the usefulness of the compulsory element in arbitration, and he first moved a resolution in its favour at the TUC in 1899, when it was defeated by a majority of two to one. He was, clearly, much influenced also by the situation in his own union, where the port employers had so weakened the bargaining position of dockers that only legal compulsion could achieve any improvement. The defeat of Tillett's motion became an annual event for several years at the TUC. His conversion to the virtues of legal enforcement was so thorough that at the 1900 TUC he cautioned delegates not to fall into panic and alarm about the Taff Vale judgement; and he found himself in the position of having to express confidence in the objectivity of the judges. Tillett was not alone among trade union leaders in advising prudence in future policy decisions. At the 1901 TUC, C.W. Bowerman, in his presidential address, recommended Congress 'to make haste slowly', and it was only gradually that opinion hardened in favour of a far-reaching reform of the law [Clegg et al. (1964) Ch. 8].

Tillett contested Eccles in 1906 and Swansea in January 1910; but by the latter year he had shifted to a thorough-going anti-parliamentary position. In 1908 he published a bitterly worded pamphlet entitled *Is the Parliamentary Labour Party a Failure?* In this he denounced the Labour Party leaders in Parliament as 'toadies' and as 'press flunkies to Asquith'. When Tom Mann returned from Australia in 1910 (Tillett had met him again on his own second visit in 1908) he immediately suggested to Tillett that the time was opportune for the development of the unity of port labour; and in July 1910 Tillett wrote to the executive committees of other unions inviting them to a conference with this purpose. This initiative led directly to the formation in September 1910 of the National Transport Workers' Federation, composed of the sixteen leading unions in transport other than railways. Mann had come back to Britain an advocate of industrial unionism with a strong admixture of syndicalist ideas. He published a series of monthly pamphlets in 1911, under the title of *The Industrial Syndicalist*, and was the foremost propagandist for a new fighting trade union movement on a class basis. His influence on trade unionists, including his old comrade and colleague Tillett, was considerable; and while Tillett himself was never clear-cut in his ideological position, his actions and words set him squarely in the main-stream of the phase of militant direct action that dominated parts of the trade union movement in the years immediately preceding the outbreak of war in August 1914.

The great unrest burst out into a flood of strikes in the early summer of 1911; and while in 1911 the dockers won most of their demands by essentially local action in a number of ports, the Transport Workers' Federation was severely defeated in the summer of 1912 in its attempt to provide nationwide support for the London port-workers and to achieve recognition of the Federation itself. It was during this struggle that Tillett was supposed to have uttered his notorious prayer 'God strike Lord Devonport dead'. The defeat of the strike was especially serious for the Dockers' Union, in which the decline of membership was particularly marked [Lovell (1969) Ch. 7]. Tillett's general attitudes, however, remained unchanged. In his annual report to the union in 1912, he expressed a continued faith in syndicalist action by the Workers' Union; and he described Parliament as 'a farce and a sham, the rich man's Duma, the employers' Tammany, the Thieves' Kitchen, and the working man's despot'. In his Annual Report of 1914 he remained an ardent advocate of mass militancy. In politics, Tillett had long had connections with the SDF, and he was especially active in the years before the outbreak of war. He was a member of the executive committee of the SDP in 1910-11, and of the executive of the BSP in 1912-13.

The *Herald* newspaper, which first appeared as a compositors' strike-sheet in 1911, had given important support to the London dock strike of 1912, and Tillett became an active member of the Committee set up in the latter year to establish the paper on a permanent footing. He worked hard to raise funds for the new paper, on one occasion issuing a frantic appeal for money under the head-line 'AT ONCE! AT ONCE!! AT ONCE!!!' When bailiffs called on the *Herald*'s office in 1912, he stood in the doorway with George Lansbury and Robert Williams to prevent them from taking furniture. He used to claim that he drank with a friendly banker until he had reduced him to a benevolent state in which he gave Tillett bearer bonds of considerable value 'for the sake of the workers'.

Tillett was now, however, about to make another major change of direction. The outbreak of war in the summer of 1914 found him prepared to justify it as having been caused by Germany's 'ruling and sordid class'. He inveighed against the British capitalist class who sat at home 'in comfort and security' while the landed gentry and the working class fought at the front; and he quickly moved to a position of total patriotic support for the war. He became a member of the Socialist National Defence Committee, playing a very active part in the recruitment campaign and asserting his 'right as a Briton to love his King and Country'. He now claimed that 'German trade unionists [had] openly boasted in their cafés of what they were going to do when the great War came'; and at the 1915 TUC Congress he affirmed that 'if we should lose in the struggle we should lose more than any other country. And, on the other hand, we shall gain more if we win. We shall gain trade and prestige, and we cannot allow the Germans to take from us the liberties we have so hardly won.' He visited the Western Front in order to raise the morale of the troops, and mixed freely with the leading Generals and political leaders of the war period. The

Commander-in-Chief, Sir John French, said of him that 'by his knowledge of men and methods, he reached a class who would not generally attend meetings or lectures'. He campaigned for a co-ordinated war transport policy, and supported the formation of a Transport Committee on which shipowners and dockers were represented. He intervened to obtain rum rations for the troops in the trenches, and for the maintenance of the quality of beer supplied to the dockers at home. He represented the General Federation of Trade Unions on the War Emergency Workers' National Committee convened by Arthur Henderson and consisting of representatives from the GFTU, the TUC and the Labour Party. In June 1917 he attended the Leeds Convention called by the ILP and the British Socialist Party, and supported by many trade union and Socialist organisations, which – following the example of the Russian February Revolution – called for the setting up of a British Council of Workers' and Soldiers' Delegates, and which took a strongly anti-war position. Tillett said little at this conference, however, and was clearly out of place, since he was associated so strongly with the patriotic wing of the labour movement.

Tillett first entered Parliament in 1917, winning a by-election at North Salford. He retained the seat at the 'Coupon' election of December 1918; like Sexton, Jimmy Thomas, J.R. Clynes, Will Thorne, and Havelock Wilson, he enjoyed electoral support as a representative of the patriotic wing of the Labour Party, while the Labour Party as a whole won only 57 seats out of its 363 endorsed candidates. He remained an MP until 1924, when he lost the North Salford seat; but he was returned for the same constituency in 1929. In 1931 he lost the seat and did not stand again. During the immmediate post-war period, when the Labour Party and the trade union movement turned towards the left, Tillett formed part of an 'old guard' which urged constitutional action, rather than a general strike or militant confrontation, to bring pressure to bear on the Government to withdraw from its involvement in the anti-Bolshevik campaigns in Russia.

Tillett had now reached a point in his career where he preferred the status and social life of a public figure and a Member of Parliament to that of a trade union organiser. He was often criticised for his habit of dining in the West End of London – an indulgence which he defended by saying that 'nothing but the best was good enough for the working man'. He had no taste for the routine of day-to-day administration of a large trade union and by 1918 the membership of the Dock, Wharf, Riverside and General Workers' had reached 85,000. Moreover, the union remained a constituent part of the National Transport Workers' Federation, which constituted, with the miners and the railwaymen, the Triple Alliance. Leadership of the Dockers' Union, of which Tillett, as general secretary, remained the titular head, was therefore a key post in the formative years of the early twenties. While Tillett neglected this role, Ernest Bevin increasingly occupied the position of power thus vacant. (Even earlier, during the war, Tillett had relinquished his seat on the executive of the NTWF (1916) and allowed Bevin to replace him.)

Bevin had first been appointed as a full-time officer of the Dockers' Union in 1911, as a local organiser in Bristol, which had always been a stronghold of Tillett's organisation. In 1914, out of 235 branches, 109 were in the Bristol Channel and South Wales areas. Because of this, and possibly also because of his childhood connections, Tillett was a frequent visitor to Bristol before the war. He and his wife were members of the Bristol Socialist Society. (Bevin used to call Mrs Tillett 'Madame Defarge', because of her habit of knitting at Socialist meetings.) As the man who first appointed him to union office, Tillett was later to claim that he had 'found and made' Bevin. There is no evidence, however, that after his initial appointment, Bevin relied at all upon Tillett's patronage; there is evidence, on the other hand, that from an early stage in their association Bevin harboured considerable reservations about Tillett's showmanship and emotionalism. In 1920 Bevin was appointed assistant general secretary to Tillett, with the unanimous nomination of all the branches, and it was Bevin who represented the dockers at the famous Shaw Enquiry of that year, although Tillett was appointed a member of the Board which assisted Shaw.

The scheme for the amalgamation of eighteen unions to form the Transport and General Workers' Union was largely of Bevin's design, and Tillett – although remaining in principle an advocate of amalgamation – played little part in the negotiations leading to the merger. It was clear that Bevin was the favoured and indispensable candidate for the post of general secretary in the new organisation. Another official of the Dockers' Union was proposed as treasurer, and so, unless the other unions participating in the amalgamation were to suspect that the whole scheme was designed to aggrandise the Dockers' Union, it was necessary that the post of president should be filled by someone other than a Dockers' official. Bevin's support for the post went to Harry Gosling, the president of the Transport Workers' Federation and leader of the Watermen and Lightermen's union. But Tillett also had ambitions to become the president of the TGWU: and the collision of wills between Bevin and himself over this issue resulted in permanent estrangement between the two men. Bevin compelled Tillett to withdraw his nomination, in order to avoid a divisive election for the presidency; indeed, Gosling had declared that if Tillett ran, he would not oppose him; and this in Bevin's judgement threatened to undermine the amalgamation before it could be formed. Tillett later complained publicly that he had been 'jockeyed' and 'elbowed out'. But he was compensated for the loss of office of president by the post of international and political secretary in the new union, at his former salary, and he was allowed to retain his membership of the House of Commons. He had also obtained a seat on the General Council of the TUC in 1921, and he kept this position until his retirement in 1931. He was allowed to continue in his union office until the age of seventy; then, after several personal appeals to the National Executive Council, his retirement was further postponed for another year. At that point, he appealed again, to the full Biennial Delegate Conference, claiming the right of a pioneer to die in harness. The conference rejected his appeal by a majority of 225 to 21.

Tillett had helped to found the International Transport Federation in 1896, and in the 1920s he represented his own union at the conferences of the Federation. He was a member of the TUC delegation to the U.S.S.R. in 1924. He was also a member of the Special Industrial Committee of the TUC established in 1925 to deal with the mining dispute, but he was not at all active, and played no significant part in the conduct of the General Strike. In 1927, in response to a letter from Sir Alfred Mond addressed to the General Council of the TUC proposing top level discussions with a group of leading industrialists, Tillett supported J.H. Thomas's motion to accept the invitation. In the autumn of 1928, having succeeded Ben Turner as chairman of the General Council, he shared the chairmanship of these joint discussions. In 1929 he was president of the TUC Congress in Belfast. In the same year he was appointed as one of four TUC directors to the board of the reorganised *Daily Herald*, now based upon a joint partnership between the TUC and Odhams Press.

After his retirement in 1931 he lived on until 1943, 'small, wizened, loquacious, with bright bird-like eyes, sitting in a corner of the Trade Union Club telling of triumphs long ago and of the way in which Bevin, the man he had "found and made" had pushed him to one side' [Williams (1952) 109]. There is some evidence that Tillett ran into financial difficulties during the twenties, but the details are obscure [James (1969) 188]. In the thirties he had a pension from the TGWU. His autobiography, published in 1931, is an interesting document, unreliable and sentimental, but giving something of the flavour of his personality. He belonged to the New Welcome Lodge (of Freemasons) during the 1930s, but when he joined Freemasonry is not known. In his last years he was much influenced by the Moral Re-Armament movement, and evidently became a close friend of Frank Buchman's. A commemorative pamphlet published soon after Tillett's death (*Ben Tillett: Fighter and Pioneer*) included a personal sketch written by George Light, who had introduced Tillett to Buchman:

A few days before he died, I visited him in hospital. He was very cheerful. "How is Dr. Buchman," he asked, knowing that he had been ill, and had been the subject of an unscrupulous attack. "He's improving and beginning to talk again", I said. "Thank God for that. Tell him to go on fighting. Give him my love and tell him I wish him the best of luck. Tell him, you have a great international movement. Use it. It is the hope of tomorrow. Your movement will bring sanity back to the world".

Tillett died in Manor House Hospital, London, on 27 January 1943, only a few days after the death of John Burns, and a year after the death of Tom Mann, at whose funeral in Leeds he had been a pall-bearer. Ernest Bevin delivered the funeral address at Golders Green Crematorium. Later a memorial service was held in St Martin-in-the-Fields, attended by fifteen hundred people. Tributes were paid by C.R. Attlee and Arthur Deakin, and by Miss Anne Loughlin, the chairman of the TUC. No will has been discovered, but his wife, who died in 1936, left £168.

Writings: *A Dock Labourer's Bitter Cry*: by a docker [an address by B. Tillett] with a preface by George Blaiklock (1887) 12 pp.; *The Legislature and Labour: an address* (Cardiff, [n.d.]) 12 pp.; Evidence before S.C. of the House of Lords on the Sweating System 2nd report 1888 XXI Qs 12513-976; 'The Dockers' Story', *Engl. Ill. Mag.* 7 (1888-9) 97-101; (with T. Mann), *The New Trades Unionism* [1890] 16 pp.; 'The Labour Platform: new style', *New Rev.* 6 (Jan-June 1892) 173-80; Evidence before the R.C. on Labour 1892 XXXIV Group B vol. I Qs 3555-4081; *Prosecution of Ben Tillett: speech delivered in Horsefair, Bristol 18 Dec 1892* (Bristol, 1893) 8 pp.; 'Our Naval Weakness', *Nat. Rev.* 27 (Mar-Aug 1896) 872-80; *Trades Unionism and Socialism* (Clarion pamphlet, no. 16: 1897) 16 pp.; 'The Alleged Industrial Invasion of England by America', *Independent* (NY) 53 (1901) 3073-6; *Is the Parliamentary Labour Party a Failure?* [1908] 16 pp.; Evidence to Joint S.C. on the Port of London Bill, 1908 X (H of C paper 288) Qs 9336-85 and paper presented to Cttee bound as App. 8 'Statement of Labour Conditions', 677-82; *Dock, Wharf, Riverside and General Workers' Union: a brief history of the Dockers' Union commemorating the 1889 Dockers' Strike* (1910) 47 pp.; *History of the London Transport Workers' Strike, 1911*, with an Introduction by H. Quelch [1912] 71 pp.; *Industrial Germany* [1912] 16 pp.; *Who was responsible for the War – and why?* (1917) 11 pp.; (with A. Creech Jones and S. Warren), *The Ruhr: the report of a deputation from the Transport and General Workers' Union* (1923) 64 pp.; *Some Russian Impressions*, with a foreword by G. Hicks (LRD, [1925]) 24 pp.; Preface to W.P. Coates, *Why Anglo-Russian Diplomatic Relations should be restored* (1928); 'New Tasks for Trade Unionists', *Labour Mag.* 7 (Sep 1928) 204-6 and (Oct 1928) 268-71; Foreword to A.A. Purcell, *The Trades Councils and Local Working-class Movement* (Manchester and Salford Trades Council, [1931]); *Memories and Reflections* (1931); *An Address on Character and Environment* (Manchester, [n.d.]) 16 pp.; 'The Renascence of Spain', *Labour Mag.* 12 (June 1933) 89-90; 'Mighty Democracy', *Lab. Mon.* 20 (Jan 1938) 29-30; 'Tom Mann, a Revolutionary Working-Class Fighter', ibid. 23 (Apr 1941) 171.

Sources: (1) MSS: papers of Ben Tillett: Modern Records Centre, Warwick Univ.; Labour Party archives. (2) Other: E.M. Clerke, 'The Labour Market of East London' and C.S. Devas, 'The Great Strike and the Social Question', *Dublin Rev.* 22 3rd ser. (Oct 1889) 386-406 and 406-16; H.L. Smith and V. Nash, *The Story of the Dockers' Strike* with an Introduction by S. Buxton [1889]; *Monthly Record of the Dock, Wharf, Riverside and General Labourers' Union*, no. 2 (May 1890) 1-2; S. & B. Webb, *The History of Trade Unionism* (1894, rev. ed. (1920) repr. 1926 and 1950); *Labour Annual* (1895) 188; *Times*, 16 Sep 1897; H.M. Hyndman, *Further Reminiscences* (1912); S.V. Bracher, *The Herald Book of Labour Members* (1923); H. Gosling, *Up and Down Stream* (1927); *Labour Who's Who* (1927); *DNB* (1941-50); G.D.H. Cole, *A Short History of the Working Class Movement* (1948); idem, *A History of the Labour Party from 1914* (1948); F. Williams, *Ernest Bevin* (1952); H. Pelling, *The Origins of the Labour Party, 1880-1900* (1954); R.V. Sires, 'Labor Unrest in England, 1910-1914', *J. of Econ. Hist. 15*, no. 3 (Sep 1955) 246-663; B.C. Roberts, *The Trades Union Congress, 1868-1921* (1958); A. Bullock, *The Life and Times of Ernest Bevin*, vol. *1: 1881-1940* (1960); H.A. Clegg et al., *A History of British Trade Unions* vol. *1: 1889-1910* (Oxford, 1964); R.R. James, *Memoirs of a Conservative: J.C.C. Davidson's memoirs and papers, 1910-37* (1969); J. Lovell, *Stevedores and Dockers* (1969); G.A. Phillips, 'The National Transport Workers' Federation 1910-27' (Oxford DPhil., 1969); *Grimsby Evening Telegraph*, 22 Jan 1972; biographical information:

T.A.K. Elliott, CMG, Helsinki. OBIT. *Ben Tillett: Fighter and Pioneer* with a foreword by Lord Sankey (1943) 15 pp.; *Bristol Evening Post, Evening Dispatch* and *Star*, 27 Jan 1943; *Birmingham Post, Daily Express, Daily Telegraph, Glasgow Herald, Irish Press, Liverpool Daily Post, Morning Advertiser, News Chronicle, Nottingham Guardian, Times* and *Yorkshire Post*, 28 Jan 1943; *Hendon and Finchley Times*, 29 Jan 1943, *Highland News*, 30 Jan 1943, *Reynolds News*, 31 Jan 1943; *Islington Gazette*, 2 Feb 1943; Neil A. Johnston, 'Ben Tillett is dead', *Perthshire Advertiser*, 3 Feb 1943; *Church of England Newspaper*, 5 Feb 1943; *Int. Lab. Rev. 47* (Mar 1943) 344.

JOHN SAVILLE
A.J. TOPHAM

See also: *John BURNS; †Allen Clement EDWARDS; Harry GOSLING; *Tom MANN; *James SEXTON; †William James THORNE; Joseph Havelock WILSON; and below: New Unionism, 1889-93.

New Unionism, 1889-93:

(1) **MSS:** Booth Coll., BLPES; John Burns papers, BM; Clement Edwards Colls, Mitchell Library, Glasgow and J.C.G.C. Edwards, Bexhill; Howell Coll., Bishopsgate Institute, London; Stevedores' Union records, National Amalgamated Stevedores' and Dockers' Union, London; Tillett Coll., Modern Records Centre, Warwick; Webb Trade Union Coll., BLPES.

(2) **Theses:** C.L. Wheble, 'The London Lighterage Trade: its history, organisation and economics' (London MSc. (Econ.), 1939); G. Evans, 'Trade Unionism and the Wage Level in Aberdeen from 1870-1920' (Aberdeen PhD, 1951); D.W. Crowley, 'The Origins of the Revolt of the British Labour Movement from Liberalism, 1875-1906' (London PhD, 1952); J. Walton, 'History of Trade Unionism in Leicester to the end of the Nineteenth Century' (Sheffield MA, 1952); A.E.P. Duffy, 'The Growth of Trade Unionism in England from 1867 to 1906 in its Political Aspects' (London PhD, 1956); P.J. Head, 'The Status, Functions and Policy of the Trade Union Official, 1870-1930' (Cambridge MLitt., 1956); S. Maddock, 'The Liverpool Trades Council and Politics 1878-1918' (Liverpool MA, 1959); J.C. Lovell, Trade Unionism in the Port of London, 1870-1914' (London PhD, 1966); R. Brown, 'The Labour Movement in Hull 1870-1900 with Special Reference to New Unionism' (Hull MSc. (Econ.), 1966); E.L. Taplin, 'The Origins and Development of New Unionism 1870-1910' (Liverpool MA, 1967); P.W. Donavan, 'Unskilled Labour Unions in South Wales 1889-1914' (London MPhil., 1969); B. Weekes, 'The A.S.E. 1880-1914' (Warwick PhD, 1970); F.J. Lindop, 'A History of Seamen's Trade Unionism to 1929' (London MPhil., 1972); K. Laybourn, 'The Attitude of Yorkshire Trade Unions to the Economic and Social Problems of the Great Depression, 1873-1896' (Lancaster PhD, 1973); P.J. Leng, 'The Dock, Wharf, Riverside and General Labourers' Union in South Wales and Bristol, 1889-1922' (Kent MA, 1973).

(3) **Parliamentary Commissions and Reports:** *Report on the Strikes and Lockouts of 1889* 1890 LXVIII, *of 1890* 1890-1 LXXVIII, *of 1891* 1893-4 LXXIII pt 1, *of 1892* 1894 LXXXI pt 1, *of 1893* 1894 LXXXI pt 1; *Report on the Relation of Wages in Certain Industries to the Cost of Production* 1890-1 LXXVIII; R.C. on Labour 1892 XXXIV and XXXVI; Board of Trade, *Report on Agencies and Methods for dealing with Unemployment* 1893 C. 7182; R.C. on the Port of London 1902 XLIII and XLIV.

(4) **Contemporary Works:** B. Tillett, 'The Dockers' Story', *Engl. Ill. Mag. 7* (1888-9) 97-101 and for further writings by Tillett *see* his biography above; Anon., 'The Seamen's Strike', *Sat. Rev.*, 15 June 1889, 731; H. George, 'The Warning of the English Strikes', *N. Amer. Rev. 149*, no. 395 (Oct 1889) 385-98; H. Manning and J. Burns, 'The Great Strike', *New Rev. 1* (Oct

1889) 410-22; F. Harrison, 'The New Trades Unionism', *19th C. 26* (Nov 1889) 721-32; *Great Dock Labourer's Strike 1889: manifesto and statement of accounts* (1889) 16 pp.; A.H. Smee, *The Great Strike and its Lesson: labour, capital and investment* (Carshalton, 1889) 16 pp.; H.L. Smith and V. Nash, *The Story of the Dockers' Strike* with an Introduction by S. Buxton [1889]; G. Shipton, 'Trade Unionism, the Old and the New', *Murray's Mag. 7* (Jan-June 1890) 721-33; T.R. Threlfall, 'The Labour Revolution: II. The New Departure in Trades Unionism', *19th C. 28* (Oct 1890) 517-25; Anon., 'The Strike of the Docks', *Sat. Rev.*, 8 Nov 1890, 521-2; H.H. Champion, *The Great Dock Strike in London, August 1889* (1890) 30 pp.; D.M. Charleston, *New Unionism* (1890) 7 pp.; G. Howell, *The Conflicts of Capital and Labour Historically and Economically considered, being a History and Review of the Trade Unions of Great Britain* (1878, rev. ed. 1890); N.F. Robarts, *Strikes and Lock-Outs* [1890] 20 pp.; U.A. Forbes, 'The New Trades-Union Movement', *Engl. Ill. Mag. 8* (1890-1) 8-17; *Dockers' Record* (monthly report of the Dock, Wharf, Riverside and General Labourers' Union) (1890-2); G.N. Barnes, *Trade Unionism: the case plainly stated* (1891) 8 pp.; T.S. Cree, *A Criticism of the Theory of Trades' Unions* (Glasgow, 1891) 39 pp.; G. Howell, *Trade Unionism, New and Old* (1891, rev. eds 1894, 1900); idem, 'The Provident Side of Trades Unionism', *New Rev. 5* (Dec 1891) 546-8; T. Neill, *Strikes and Lockouts, a Suggestion for their Prevention* (Greenock, 1891); T.J. O'Keeffe, *Rise and Progress of the National Amalgamated Labourers Union of Great Britain and Ireland* (Cardiff, 1891) 16 pp.; J. Burnett, 'Strikes and Lock-outs in 1890', *JRSS 55* (Mar 1892) 127-32; T. Mann, 'English Royal Labor Commission: report on the hours of labor', *Social Economist 2* (Mar 1892) 296-304; J.G. Adderley, 'Some Results of the Great Dock Strike', *Econ. Rev. 2* (Apr 1892) 202-13; C. Black, 'The Coercion of Trade Unions', *Cont. Rev. 62* (Oct 1892) 547-54; H.W. Massingham, 'The Trend of Trade Unionism', *Fortn. Rev. 58* (Oct 1892) 450-7; H.L. Smith, 'Chapters in the History of London Waterside Labour', *Econ. J. 2* (Dec 1892) 593-607; C. Booth, *Dock and Wharf Labour, 1891-2* [1892]; idem, 'London Riverside Labour' [inaugural address], *JRSS 55* (Dec 1892) 522-7; J.S. Ramsome, 'Master and Man versus New Unionism' two articles from the *Globe* repr. in R.C. on Labour 1892 XXXVI pt II App. xcii; C. Dilke and T. Mann, 'The Labour Problem: i. Pressing Reforms; ii. The New Unionism', *New Rev. 8* (Mar 1893) 257-80; C. Edwards, 'Labour Federations' pts I and II, *Econ. J. 3* (1893) 205-17 and 408-24; idem, 'The Hull Shipping Dispute', ibid., 345-51; H. Hayman, 'The Triumph of Free Labour at Hull', *Liberty Rev.* (July 1893) 1-9; E.G. Stubbs, 'The Great Strike in the Cotton Trade', *Econ. Rev. 3* (July 1893) 413-16; J.W. Cunliffe, 'Modern Industrial Warfare', *West. Rev. 140* (Aug 1893) 109-14; C.H.D'E. Leppington, 'The Teachings of the Labour Commission', *Cont. Rev. 64* (Sep 1893) 388-404; T. Mann, *An Appeal to the Yorkshire Textile Workers* (1893) 32 pp.; H.R. Smart, *Trade Unionism and Politics* (Manchester, 1893) 16 pp.; L. Hall, *The Old and New Unionism* (Manchester, 1894) 15 pp.; S. and B. Webb, *The History of Trade Unionism* (1894, rev. ed. 1920); J.M. Ludlow, 'The National Free Labour Association', *Econ. Rev. 5* (Jan 1895) 110-18; T. Mackay, 'The Methods of the New Trade Unionism', *Q. Rev. 180* (Jan 1895) 138-59; M. Stobart, 'Wanted, a Newer Trade Unionism', *West. Rev. 143* (Jan 1895) 23-30; P. de Rousiers, *The Labour Question in Britain* (1896); B. Taylor, 'A Study in Trade Unionism', *19th C. 43* (Apr 1898) 679-92; J.T. Baylee, 'New Unionism', *West. Rev. 150* (Oct 1898) 396-403; G.N. Barnes, 'Uses and Abuses of Organisation among Employers and Employed. The Old Trade Unionism vs Wisely-organised Labour', *Engineering Mag. 20* (Jan 1901) 560-7; G. Howell, *Labour Legislation, Labour Movements and Labour Leaders* (1902; 2nd ed. 2 vols, 1905).

(5) **Other Works:** C. Booth, *Life and Labour of the People in London* (1902 ed.); P. Longmuir, 'The Possibilities of a New Trade Unionism', *Engineering Mag. 23* (Apr 1902) 90-6; W.E. Bohn, 'The Breakdown of the Old Unionism', *Int. Soc. Rev. 11* (Jan 1911) 430-4; F. Popplewell, 'The Gas Industry' in *Seasonal Trades* ed. S. Webb and A. Freeman (1912) 148-209; W. Collison, *The Apostle of Free Labour* (1913); G.N. Barnes, 'Thirty Years of the Trade Union Movement', *Co-op. Annual* (1914) 189-210; G. Barker, 'Should the Workers be

organised by Industries', *Int. Soc. Rev. 16* (Sep 1915) 147-8; G.R. Carter, 'The Triple Alliance of Labour', *Econ. J. 26* (Sep 1916) 380-95; F. Bramley, 'Craft versus Industrial Organisation', *Soc. Rev. 15* (Apr 1918) 164-8; Sir J. Broodbank, *History of the Port of London* (1921); T. Mann, *Memoirs* (1923); W. Thorne, *My Life's Battles* [1925]; J.H. Wilson, *My Stormy Voyage through Life* (1925); F.C. Coley, 'Trade Unionism, Old and New', *Engl. Rev. 44* (Mar 1927) 312-21; H. Gosling, *Up and Down Stream* (1927); H. Tracey, 'Trade-Unionism, New and Old', *Labour Mag. 8* (Sep 1929) 194-7; J. Sexton, *Sir James Sexton, Agitator* (1936); T. Mann, 'The Dock Strike of 1889 and after', *Lab. Mon. 20* (Sep 1938) 548-51; G.D.H. Cole, *British Working Class Politics 1832-1914* (1941); E.J. Hobsbawm, *Labour's Turning Point, 1880-1900* (1948); idem, 'General Labour Unions in Britain 1889-1914', *Econ. Hist. Rev.* 2nd ser. *1* (1949) 123-42; NUGMW, *Sixty Years of the National Union of General and Municipal Workers* (1949); L.H. Powell, *The Shipping Federation: a history of the first sixty years 1890-1950* (1950); K.D. Buckley, *Trade Unionism in Aberdeen, 1878-1900* (Aberdeen, 1955); H. Pelling, 'The Knights of Labor in Britain, 1880-1901', *Econ. Hist. Rev. 9* (1956) 313-31; D. Torr, *Tom Mann and his Times* (1956); B.C. Roberts, *The Trades Union Congress 1868-1921* (1958); J. Saville, 'Trade Unions and Free Labour: the background to the Taff Vale decision', in *Essays in Labour History* ed. A. Briggs and J. Saville (1960) 317-50; E.H. Phelps Brown, *The Growth of British Industrial Relations* (1959); A.E.P. Duffy, 'New Unionism in Britain, 1889-1890: a reappraisal', *Econ. Hist. Rev.* 2nd ser. *14*, no. 2 (Dec 1961) 306-19; A. Stafford, *A Match to fire the Thames* (1961); J. Brophy, 'Bibliography of British Labor and Radical Journals 1880-1914', *Labor History* (NY) *3*, no. 1 (Winter 1962) 103-26; L.J. Williams, 'The New Unionism in South Wales, 1889-92', *Welsh History Rev. 1*, no. 4 (1963) 413-29; H.A. Clegg et al., *A History of British Trade Unions since 1889*, vol. *1: 1889-1910* (Oxford, 1964); E.J. Hobsbawm, *Labouring Men* (1964); P. Thompson, *Socialists, Liberals and Labour: the struggle for London, 1885-1914* (1967); J. Lovell, *Stevedores and Dockers: a study of trade unionism in the Port of London, 1870-1914* (1969); R. Hyman, *The Workers' Union* (Oxford, 1971); R. Bean, 'A Note on the Knights of Labour in Liverpool, 1889-90', *Labor History 13*, no. 1 (1972) 68-78; idem, 'Working Conditions, Labour Agitation and the Origins of Unionism on the Liverpool Tramways', *Transport History 5* (1972) 173-93; R. Brown, *Waterfront Organisation in Hull 1870-1900* (Univ. of Hull, 1972); R. Bean, 'Aspects of "New" Unionism in Liverpool, 1889-91' in *Building the Union: studies on the growth of the workers' movement, Merseyside 1756-1967* ed. H.R. Hikins (Liverpool, 1973) 99-118; idem, 'The Liverpool Dock Strike of 1890', *Int. Rev. Social Hist. 18* (1973) 51-68; E.L. Taplin, *Liverpool Dockers and Seamen 1870-1890* (Univ. of Hull, 1974); J. Lovell, *British Trade Unions, 1875-1933* (1977).

WALSH, Stephen (1859-1929)
MINERS' LEADER AND LABOUR MP

Stephen Walsh was born at Kirkdale, Liverpool, on 26 August 1859, the son of John and Mary Walsh, who were of Irish descent. His father died a few months before he was born and his mother before he could remember her. His first recollection was of being found by a policeman on the steps of St Nicholas Church, Liverpool. At the age of four he was living with an uncle in Kirkdale, and spent most of his boyhood in an industrial school at Kirkdale, where on his own evidence he was happy and well cared for, and where he received a good elementary education. While at school he expressed a desire to become a teacher but was told he was 'too small'. He was brought up in the Roman Catholic faith, but became a member of the Church of England when he was about twenty-one years of age. (It should be noted that there are several versions of the story of his origins.)

When he left the industrial school at the age of thirteen he went to live with his brother in Ashton-in-Makerfield, near Wigan, where he was employed at Pewfall Pit as a pony boy. His working day normally extended to ten hours, for which he received ten pence. 'Reckoning Day', when wages were paid, was every fortnight.

Walsh found that his elementary education gave him an advantage over many of his fellow colliers, a large number of whom were illiterate; and as he wrote later, 'No doubt I caught something of the art of public speaking in delivering little expositions or lectures to my mates on things I had read about.' From his early years he was an avid reader, and in 1906 he set down for W.T. Stead the books that had influenced him:

> But from very early years Shakespeare has been a prime and constant favourite. Falstaff, Brutus, Mark Antony, Cassius, quaint old Dogberry, and the tender, half petulant, yet innocent old Verges – all these have been almost living realities with me. The first book I ever bought was a shilling volume of *Pilgrim's Progress*, over thirty-two years ago, although I was then a Roman Catholic. Perhaps the book that has most influenced me on the social, economic and inquisitorial side has been Buckle's *History of Civilisation*, while in the event of feeling a little run down I almost invariably turn to my well-thumbed *Ingoldsby Legends*. But Dumas, Mark Twain, Carlyle, Cervantes, John Stuart Mill, Victor Hugo (particularly *Les Misérables* and the *Hunchback of Notre Dame*), all these and many more have left upon me an abiding and, I hope without egotism, a salutary influence.
>
> But I had almost forgotten the greatest of all – Dickens. His is, indeed, an inexhaustible banquet, and I prize him for practical everyday life above all the rest.

Walsh began to take an active part in trade union affairs early in his adult life, probably in 1881. Although small in stature, he had great natural energy and determination. He was at one time a member of the 'England's Glory Lodge' of the LCMF, and later became checkweighman at the Garswood Hall Colliery. He was elected district officer and secretary of the Ashton and Haydock Miners' Union from 1890 – although still working in the mines – and in 1901 he was appointed agent for the Wigan area within the Lancashire and Cheshire Miners' Federation. On this last appointment, he left Ashton and went to live in Wigan. The Miners' Federation in Lancashire and Cheshire was particularly attracted to the idea of a Labour Party, separate and distinct from the other two parties. There were a number of reasons for this attitude, among them the political divisions among its own members which had prevented the Federation from co-operating fully with either Tories or Liberals. There was also the fact that the Lancashire coalfield, with Wigan at its centre, provided working conditions worse than in most other fields in Britain; and demands for parliamentary legislation evoked immediate responses among the rank and file. Until 1906 Lancashire and Cheshire had been the least successful of all the big miners' unions in securing parliamentary representation, but it was the first to affiliate to the Labour Representation Committee in 1903, and it voted decisively in 1908 to join the Labour Party. In the 1906 general election there were two candidates sponsored by the LCMF, Walsh at Ince and Thomas Glover in St Helens. Both had a straight fight with Tory opponents. Walsh faced the Conservative – Colonel H.H. Blundell, who had been the MP for many years and who owned a large colliery in the constituency where the miners were actually on strike during the election period; the Labour majority was over four and a half thousand. From this time, until his death, Walsh sat continuously in the House of Commons as member for Ince.

Long before he went to Westminster, Walsh had served his apprenticeship in public work. In the early 1890s he began to take a prominent part in the management of the Park Lane Co-operative Society, Ashton-in-Makerfield, and served as auditor; and in 1894 he was elected as one of the first Labour members of the Ashton-in-Makerfield District Council. He resigned from the Council when he removed to Wigan. From 1894 to 1900 he was president of the Wigan Trades and Labour Council. It was, however, only after his election to Parliament that he became known nationally, although he first represented the LCMF on the MFGB executive in 1904.

He was on the NEC of the Labour Party in 1912. He took an even greater part in the affairs of the Parliamentary Labour Party, being its vice-chairman at one time and always one of their main speakers on mining questions. He was particularly involved in the debates which led to the Mines Act of 1911, and he was also especially concerned with compensation matters. With other Labour MPs, Walsh presented a Bill in July 1913 to nationalise the mines. As a moderate he found himself increasingly at odds with the industrial unionist and syndicalist trends in the years immediately before the outbreak of war in 1914, and in 1912, when the Minimum Wage Bill was in the Committee stage, Walsh declared that citizenship was higher than trade unionism, and that if the national interests were in danger, he would stand by the State. Afterwards, defending himself before miners' meetings in Lancashire, he said:

> There had been extremists, mainly from South Wales, who advised the conference to defy the Government and to bring out the transport workers and so strangle the life of the nation. That would have meant starvation, and women heartbroken, and desperate men with policeman's batons and soldiers' bayonets in their bodies. It would have meant civil war.

When the war came, Walsh took a strongly patriotic line. He campaigned vigorously for recruitment to the armed forces, and helped to raise Pioneer Battalions in Lancashire. In 1915 Walsh was a member of the Departmental Committee set up by the Home Office to report on the loss of manpower in the mines due to the considerable enlistment of miners. He voted for conscription in 1916, and supported the aims and objectives of the British Workers' National League. After the Lloyd George Coalition Government was formed Walsh was invited to serve, first as parliamentary secretary to Neville Chamberlain at the Ministry of National Service – known among some trade unionists as the Ministry of National Slavery [Pankhurst (1932) 424] – and then at the Local Government Board, where his successive chiefs were Lord Downham, Sir Auckland Geddes, and Dr Addison. Walsh fought the general election of December 1918 as a supporter of the Coalition until the terms of a just peace had been secured, and on a definite programme of resistence to the idea of a class war. John Hodge, George Roberts and George Barnes took similar positions. Walsh was opposed by the Socialist Labour Party candidate, William Paul, whom he defeated by 12,651 votes; but the Labour Party, aided by mounting opposition within the LCMF and his own constituency, compelled him to withdraw his support from the Government in 1919. He continued, however, in company with other right-wing members of the MFGB and the Labour Party, among them Brace, Hartshorn and Hodges, to maintain secret contacts with Lloyd George and other Coalition leaders [Cowling (1971) 39-40].

Walsh became vice-president of the MFGB in 1922, but he resigned when Ramsay MacDonald formed the first Labour Government. Walsh was offered the War Office and there was much gossip at the time, reported by Sir Philip Gibbs among others, that Walsh was 'entirely unable to conceal his reverence for generals' [Gibbs(1923-4)621]. Walsh was certainly warmly commended by members of the Conservative Opposition. As a former serving officer said in the Commons: '. . . we in the Army realise that in the person of the present Minister for War we have a friend on whom we can rely and who will not let us down' [Hansard, 13 Mar 1924]. The only criticisms of Walsh came from his own back-benches. After the defeat of the Labour Government, Walsh continued to speak in Parliament on mining matters, but on the whole took a less prominent part in national affairs. In 1927, when he was appointed a member of the Indian Statutory Commission, he had to resign on medical grounds. He was president of the LCMF from 1927 to 1929, and he continued to take an active interest in the co-operative movement, as a member of the Park Lane Co-operative Society and also of the Wigan Co-operative Society. He was a JP for Wigan Borough and Lancashire County, a Deputy Lieutenant and a PC.

Walsh married Anne Adamson, a local Ashton girl, on 16 August 1885. At the time of their marriage she was working on a colliery pitbank. Their married life was happy and there were four sons and six daughters. Their eldest son, Arthur, who was a graduate of Manchester University and of the Sorbonne, was Modern Languages Master at Nelson Grammar School in 1914. He enlisted in the Army, was awarded the Military Cross, but was killed on active service in 1918. Two other sons entered the legal profession: Leslie, who became a barrister in 1927 and

Stipendiary Magistrate for Salford in 1951, and Leonard, who was a solicitor. The fourth son, Wilfred, was a colliery manager. Of the six daughters, four entered the teaching profession and one of these became a JP for Lancashire. Walsh died on 16 March 1929 and left an estate valued at £7927 (net). He was survived by his wife, three sons and five daughters. After a service on 20 March conducted by Canon Raven for the Bishop of Liverpool in Holy Trinity Church, Ashton-in-Makerfield, Walsh was buried in the Church cemetery. The funeral service was the occasion for many tributes, including speeches from J. McGurk of the LCMF, and W.P. Richardson on behalf of the MFGB.

Sources: (1) MSS: Labour Party archives: LRC. (2) Other: *Liverpool Post*, 3 Jan 1906; 'How I got on', *Pearson's Weekly*, 29 Mar 1906; *Liverpool Post*, 26 Jan 1910; *Wigan Observer*, 2 Mar 1913; *Hansard*, 8 Mar 1921; *DNB* (1922-30); S.V. Bracher, *The Herald Book of Labour Members* (1923); Sir P. Gibbs, 'Labor's Blow to Caste in Britain', *World's Work 47* (Nov 1923-Apr 1924) 619-25; *Hansard*, 13 Mar 1924; *Wigan Examiner*, 18 June 1924; *Labour Who's Who* (1927); *Dod* (1929); E.S. Pankhurst, *The Home Front* (1932); R. Page Arnot, vol. *1 The Miners* (1949); idem, vol. *2 The Miners: years of struggle* (1953); C.L. Mowat, *Britain between the Wars* (1955); R.W. Lyman, *The First Labour Government 1924* [1957]; R. Gregory, *The Miners and British Politics 1906-1914* (Oxford, 1968); M. Cowling, *The Impact of Labour 1920-1924* (Cambridge, 1971); biographical information: T.A.K. Elliott, CMG, Helsinki; personal information: L. Walsh, Manchester, son and W. Walsh, Midsomer Norton, son. OBIT. *Times* and *Western Mail*, 18 Mar 1929; *Wigan Examiner* and *Wigan Observer*, 19 Mar 1929; *Liverpool Weekly Post*, 23 Mar 1929 [by J. Sexton]; *Labour Party Report* (1929).

JOHN SAVILLE

See also: †William FOSTER; †Thomas GLOVER; †Charles Butt STANTON.

WARD, John (1866-1934)
TRADE UNIONIST AND SOCIALIST, LATER LIB-LAB MP

John Ward was born at Oatlands Park, Weybridge, Surrey, on 21 November 1866, the son of Robert Ward, a journeyman plasterer and his wife Caroline, née Edmonds. His father died when he was three years old, and his mother then went to live in her native place of Appleshaw, near Andover, Hampshire, and it was here that John was brought up. He had very little formal schooling, and began work on a farm at the age of seven. After three years he went to work greasing axles. 'It was pretty hard work, and well do I remember the bitter winter of 1878. To this day I carry the marks of open chilblains and other wounds caused by coupling wagons when it was so cold that my hands stuck to the couplings, and could only be released at the expense of my skin' [*Pearsons' Weekly*, 15 Mar 1906]. Ward later worked on the building of the Andover to Marlborough railway, and then on the construction of the Manchester Ship Canal, for which he was paid at the rate of $4\frac{1}{2}d$ an hour. During his early teens he joined evening classes in the village of Weyhill conducted by a Mrs Stock and her daughter Ellen. At the end of a year he was able to read a chapter of the Bible, and from then on he became a voracious reader. Reading, he wrote later 'changed the whole course of my life'. In 1885 he enlisted for railway construction work with the British Army in the Sudan, for which he was awarded the Queen's Silver Medal and the Khedive's Bronze Star, medal and clasp. His experiences in the Sudan made him '*anti war* and anti many other things' [*Rev. of Revs* (1906) 571], and a reading of Hyndman's translation of Kropotkin's *Appeal to the Young* helped to move his ideas towards acceptance of a radical reconstruction of society. Personal contact with Tom Mann and John Burns completed the process, and he joined the Battersea branch of the Social Democratic Federation. Ward quickly became active in the Socialist movement, and in the autumn of 1886 he was chosen by the SDF to test the legality of the ban on unemployed demonstrations imposed by the

Commissioner of London police. He was arrested at an unemployed demonstration in Trafalgar Square on 9 November 1886, the day of the Lord Mayor's Show. There was an enormous mass of foot and mounted police mobilised for the meeting, and Ward was charged with unlawful assembly and assaulting the police. He was remanded for a week, and then appeared wearing his two Sudan medals. W.M. Thompson, defending him, made much of his youthful war services. Ward was fined 10s. [Also arrested on the day of the demonstration was George Bateman, a compositor and ex-soldier and author of a pamphlet addressed to soldiers: *Socialism and Soldiering; with some Comments on the Army Enlistment Fraud*, with an Introduction by H.H. Champion (1886) [Torr (1956) Ch. 13]].

Ward became chairman of the Battersea branch of the Gas Workers' Union in 1889, with De Mattos, a Fabian, as secretary. In the same year he founded the Navvies, Bricklayers' Labourers and General Labourers' Union, and after a series of strikes in west London, he and Jack Williams of the Gasworkers established the National Federation of Labour Union, which by the end of 1889 had thirteen branches, mainly in south-west London. The history of the National Federation is obscure, and it disappeared in the nineties; but the Navvies' Union continued although it was never very effective. In 1906 the *Labour Leader* described Ward's union as 'simply a benevolent friendly society' in which the 'working expenses' absorbed sixty per cent of the contributions from a membership of 1988.

By the end of the eighties Ward had become involved in the political side of the movement. In the November 1888 London School Board election he stood as a candidate of the Central Democratic Committee, along with Annie Besant, Harry Quelch and Mrs Amie Hicks. Annie Besant alone was elected, although John Ward polled over 8000 votes. In March 1892 he stood, but was defeated, in the LCC elections. His failure led him to follow John Burns into the Progressive camp, with unfortunate consequences for the Wandsworth branch of the SDF. He was adopted as parliamentary candidate for Wandsworth in 1894, but he did not contest the seat. Like Burns, Ward began to move steadily towards a more Liberal stance in politics, and by the end of the nineties he had more or less renounced his social-democratic past. He took a similar line to that of Burns in opposition to the Boer War, arguing, at the 1900 TUC, 'that practically £100,000,000 of the taxpayers' money had been spent in trying to secure the goldfields of South Africa for cosmopolitan Jews, most of whom had no patriotism and no country.' In the following year Congress refused to suspend standing orders to allow debate on a resolution by Ward in favour of the cessation of hostilities.

The most important political development for Ward at the turn of the century was the foundation of the National Democratic League. W.M. Thompson, the editor of *Reynolds's News*, decided in the summer of 1900 to establish a broad alliance of the Left around his journal. Arrangements were delayed by the general election, and the founding Convention did not meet until October. It then agreed on a programme of seven points, all concerned with constitutional changes, Tom Mann was elected full-time organiser, and John Ward became a member of the executive and vice-chairman. The Labour Representation Committee were considerably disquieted at the appearance of the League, but it was to make little progress except in London and South Wales, where C.B. Stanton acted as its adviser. Tom Mann emigrated to New Zealand in 1901, and the anti-union decisions of the judiciary served to divert the attention of many industrial leaders from the new political initiative. Ward became chairman of the NDL in 1902, and in February 1903, at the Newcastle annual conference of the LRC, he moved as chairman of the NDL an amendment to the constitution which would have allowed the League to affiliate to the LRC. His request was defeated by 118 votes to 48, and this led to Pete Curran's important resolution that executive members of the LRC, and officials of affiliated organisations, should not identify with, or promote the interests of 'any section of the Liberal or Conservative parties'. The resolution, amended but still insisting upon independence, was easily passed, and it became known as the 'Newcastle Resolution' – an important policy statement in the history of the Labour Representation Committee.

Ward had already staked his own parliamentary claim. As early as April 1902 he began negotiations at Stoke-on-Trent, and with Richard Bell's assistance, he finally concluded a satisfactory arrangement with the local Liberals, despite the fact that the Navvies' Union was affiliated to the LRC. In 1903, along with Richard Bell and W.C. Steadman, Ward refused to sign the LRC constitution, and was removed from the LRC lists. In the general election of 1906 Ward therefore stood, successfully, as a Labour candidate without the LRC support, and retained the seat in 1910. He once stated in the Commons that at the time of his first election to the House he was earning thirty-five shillings a week [*Hansard*, 22 Apr 1920]. At the 'Coupon' election of 1918 he was returned unopposed as a Coalition Liberal and in 1922 was re-elected as a National Liberal with a majority of 6163 over the Labour candidate. He held the seat in 1923 with a smaller majority (617 votes) and at the 1924 election fought and won as a Constitutionalist with both Conservative and Liberal support. In 1929, however, he was defeated by the Labour candidate, Lady Cynthia Mosley, the first wife of Oswald Mosley.

There is a brief account of Ward in the Commons before the First World War in Griffith-Boscawen's memoirs. 'In those days', the latter wrote, 'he was not a popular person with the Conservatives. We had not then had the chance of appreciating the splendid qualities which he displayed in the War, as Colonel of a Battalion of the Middlesex Regiment, the old and original Die-Hards. He used to sit in the House, below the gangway on the Government side, wearing a huge sombrero hat – looking like a cross between a navvy and an Italian brigand; the very type of Liberal-Labour member most abhorrent to us' [*Memories* (1925) 150].

Ward still continued active in trade union affairs before 1914. He was elected to the management committee of the General Federation of Trade Unions in 1901, and he represented the Federation at a Joint Board of the TUC, the LRC and the Federation, established as a permanent co-ordinating committee of the three organisations. The first meeting was on 29 November 1905. Ward served on the management committee of the GFTU until 1929, and for the last sixteen years he was treasurer. The Federation offered him a very suitable niche within the trade union movement, and he was a close friend of W.A. Appleton, its general secretary. Ward contributed a brief preface to Appleton's book *What we want and where we are*, published in 1921, and Appleton's general approach – anti-Socialist, favouring a minimum of state interference in private enterprise and supporting 'responsible' trade unionism – was wholly acceptable to Ward himself. In November 1907 Ward gave evidence before the R.C. on the Poor Laws. He presented a report on unemployment prepared by the joint board of the Parliamentary Committee of the TUC, the General Federation of Trade Unions and the Labour Party.

At the outbreak of the First World War Ward became very active in army recruitment, especially in the county round his own constituency. The first company he raised consisted mostly of labourers, and it became known as the 'Navvies' Battalion'. Altogether Ward helped to recruit five labour battalions, and he was given the rank first of captain and later of lieutenant-colonel. He saw service on a number of fronts, and then, in the summer of 1918, he went to Siberia as part of the interventionist force against the Bolsheviks. His battalion was attached to the forces of Kolchak. Between Ward and Kolchak there developed 'peculiarly strong ties of mutual respect and affection' [Pares (1931) 525-6], and there is an account of the Middlesex regiment that Ward commanded in Siberia in P. Fleming's book, *The Fate of Admiral Kolchak* (1963). Ward wrote his own story in *With the Diehards in Siberia*, published in 1920. He was created a Cossack Hetman, of which he was especially proud, and he received a number of other foreign decorations. In 1918 he was awarded the CMG by the British Government and the CB in the following year. He was abroad at the time of the 'Coupon' election but returned to Britain in 1919, with an articulate hatred of Communism that continued until his death.

After his defeat in the 1929 general election he retired to Appleshaw, where he took a keen interest in village affairs. He was already a JP of the County of London (from 1908), and took his seat on the Andover bench. He also became president of the Andover branch of the British Legion.

His wife Lilian, whom he had married in 1892, had died in 1926 and his youngest son, a doctor, two years later. Ward himself died on 21 December 1934, leaving two sons, one of whom was a solicitor, the other a businessman in America, and a married daughter. He left an estate valued at £5234.

Writings: 'The Rise of a Ploughboy', *Pearson's Weekly*, 15 Mar 1906; Evidence before R.C. on the Poor Laws 1910 VIII Qs. 83501-768; *Socialism, The Religion of Humanity* (n.d.) 15 pp.; *Notes from a Navvy's Diary* (n.d.) 30 pp.; *The Soldier and the Citizen* (1914) 50 pp.; *With the Diehards in Siberia* (1920); Preface to W.A. Appleton, *What we want and where we are* (1921).

Sources: (1) MSS: Labour Party archives: LRC. (2) Other: *Annual Reports* of the GFTU from 1899 to date: GFTU, London; *Reformers' Year Book* (1902); *Labour Leader*, 21 Sep 1906; *Rev. of Revs 6* (1906) 571; *Dod* (1909) and (1929); Pall Mall Gazette 'extra', *The New House of Commons 1911* (Jan 1911); *Hansard*, 22 Apr 1920; *Who's Who in the New Parliament*, ed. T.W. Walding (1922); *Staffordshire Weekly Sentinel*, 7 Nov 1922; Sir A. Griffith-Boscawen, *Memories* (1925); W. Thorne, *My Life's Battles* [1925]; *WWW* (1929-40); *DNB* (1931-40); B. Pares, *My Russian Memories* (1931); H.W. Lee and E. Archbold, *Social-Democracy in Britain* (1935); W.P. and Z.K. Coates, *A History of Anglo-Soviet Relations* (1944); H. Pelling, *The Origins of the Labour Party 1880-1900* (1954, 2nd ed. 1965); D. Torr, *Tom Mann and his Times* (1956); F. Bealey and H. Pelling, *Labour and Politics 1900-1906* (1958); P.P. Poirier, *The Advent of the Labour Party* (1958); B.C. Roberts, *The Trades Union Congress 1868-1921* (1958); P. Fleming, *The Fate of Admiral Kolchak* (1963); H.A. Clegg et al., *A History of British Trade Unions since 1889* vol. *1: 1889-1910* (Oxford, 1964); P. Thompson, *Socialists, Liberals and Labour: the struggle for London 1885-1914* (1967); *The Labour Party Foundation Conference and Annual Conference Reports 1900-1905* (Hammersmith Reprints of Scarce Documents no. 3, 1967); biographical information: T.A.K. Elliott, CMG, Helsinki. OBIT. *Evening Sentinel* [Stoke], 19 Dec 1934; *Times*, 20 Dec 1934; *Andover Advertiser*, 21 Dec 1934; *Times*, 22 Dec 1934.

JOHN SAVILLE

See also: †Richard BELL; *William Charles STEADMAN.

WARNE, George Henry (1881-1928)
MINERS' LEADER AND LABOUR MP

George Warne was born on 15 December 1881 at Burton Cottages, Blue Top, Cramlington, Northumberland, a row of two-roomed houses. His father William Warne and his mother Elizabeth Toms were both natives of Cornwall. George was the third in a family of thirteen children. The only school he attended was East Cramlington Elementary School, at which his parents contrived to keep him until he was twelve, although before that time they had two other children at school, and the fee was 1s 2d a fortnight for each child. The rest of his education he owed to himself. His daughter remembers that 'he quoted freely from Burns and the Scriptures' (he belonged to no denomination, however), and that 'for a working-class household we had a fairly large library' – she mentions the poems of Shelley, Keats, Burns, Carlyle's *Sartor Resartus* and Dennis Hird's *Evolution of Man*. When George reluctantly left school he started work as a trapper boy at Shankhouse Colliery, Cramlington. Four years later his parents moved to Ashington, and George worked at Woodhorn Colliery, where he passed through the various grades to reach the top position of coal-hewer. He achieved this even although, in his own words, 'I had never wanted to be placed in the mines, and I dare say many a convict has enjoyed his work as much as I did' (*T.P.'s & Cassell's Weekly*, 27 Feb 1926). He was a coal-hewer when he was elected to Westminster in 1922; unlike all the rest of the forty mining MPs in that Parliament he had had no intervening period of work as checkweighman or agent.

At eighteen years of age Warne became interested in trade unionism. His abilities were quickly perceived by his fellow-workers in the Woodhorn branch of the NMA; he became branch average-taker, then secretary and delegate to the county executive meetings, then president and compensation secretary. In 1909 he was elected to the executive committee of the NMA and was again a member when he won his parliamentary seat in 1922. He stood as a candidate for the general secretaryship of the MFGB in 1918.

From 1904 Warne belonged to the ILP, for to his mind trade unionism and politics were inseparable. He was secretary of the Ashington ILP from 1906. Along with a few other progressives he formed the Wansbeck Divisional Labour Party, and was its secretary until 1918, when the town of Ashington was transferred to the Morpeth constituency and Warne became chairman of the Morpeth Divisional Labour Party. In 1919 he stood for the NAC of the ILP.

In 1907, when he was only twenty-five, he was elected to the Ashington Urban District Council, on which he served for fifteen years. He was its chairman in 1919 and 1920, and for three years chairman of its housing committee. This latter position took much time, patience, and organising ability, because of the acute housing shortage which followed the First World War. For five years (1919-24) he served on the Northumberland County Council, and for some of this time was a member of its education committee. The curtailing of his own schooling made him zealous for the education of the next generations. One of his dearest wishes was that all children should be enabled to go to school until they were sixteen years old – a wish realised forty years after his death.

Warne took a deep interest in the Northumberland and Durham Miners' Permanent Relief Fund and was a member of its committee. He helped to start the building in Ashington of a two-ward hospital which the heavy incidence of pit injuries made essential, and which was maintained by contributions from the miners' wages; later he was president of the hospital committee. In 1926 he was president of the Northumberland and Durham Miners' Approved Society.

In 1904 George Warne married Dorothy Isabel Fenwick, daughter of George Fenwick of Ashington; they had nine children, six daughters and three sons. Their early family life was spent in a colliery house, in the middle of a row of nineteen houses with very small gardens attached, called Maple Street. There were many such rows in Ashington, built front to front, forming a large congested complex of white brick houses crowded together – a design characteristic of this mining town. There were no trees, and few flowers. George Warne conceived the idea of a park to give some amenity to these drab surroundings. On the edge of the area were two small fields which had formerly been used as a refuse tip. Warne persuaded the Council to have these fields levelled and turned into a park, where trees and flowers grew, and tennis and bowls were played. Some people at the time referred to this park as 'Warne's Folly'; but it has been enjoyed by countless families, and still exists as – to quote Warne's own words – 'an oasis in the desert'.

During those years in Maple Street, as compensation secretary for the Woodhorn Miners' Lodge George Warne often had to meet the manager of Woodhorn Colliery, to argue cases for compensation after accidents to his fellow-workers. Heated disagreements sometimes arose, and on one occasion about 1919, unable to cope with Warne's arguments or weaken his persistence, the manager lost his temper and dismissed him. This meant that Warne lost tenure of his house as well as his job at the pit. Public protests caused the dismissal to be rescinded, and the manager apologised; but the realisation that his family could so easily be deprived of a home made Warne determined to have a house of his own and he found one in Woodhorn Road, Ashington.

When the First World War broke out, George Warne was exempt, as a miner, from military service. If he had not been exempt, he would have been a conscientious objector, for he was a pacifist, and strongly opposed the war, both speaking against it and attending pacifist meetings.

Warne was Labour agent for Wansbeck in the election of 1918 and a member of the NEC of the Labour Party. In 1922, at the age of forty, Warne was chosen as Labour candidate for the Wansbeck Division to fight in the general election of 13 November. Wansbeck was a miners' seat, and Warne was the third miners' representative to contest it. The first was Charles Fenwick

(Liberal; also born in Cramlington, in Paradise Row, not far from Burton Cottages); he held the Division from its formation in 1885 until his death in 1918. Ebby Edwards, who followed him as a miners' candidate, was defeated both in the by-election and general election of 1918 and withdrew his candidature after having accepted a post with the Northumberland Miners' Mutual Confident Association. In the 1922 election Warne defeated three candidates (a Unionist, a National Liberal, and an Independent Liberal) by the solid majority of 4883. This was a Labour gain. At the general election of 6 December 1923, in a straight fight, his majority over the Conservative, Captain H. Philipson, was 4452; and even the notorious Zinoviev 'Red Letter' scare of the election of 29 October 1924 did not oust him from his seat, which he held with a majority of 2284 over the Conservative candidate, Mrs Hugh Middleton. (It is indicative of Warne's quality that during his last illness Mrs Middleton urged him to come and stay for convalescence at her home, Belsay Castle.)

At Westminster Warne was soon well known as an able, reliable, principled and generous man. In 1924 he was made a Junior Lord of the Treasury, and remained a Party Whip. His speeches in Parliament were generally on mining affairs, although the first which impressed his fellow Members (28 June 1923) concerned the health and welfare services, especially those for mothers and children. On 31 March 1925, the day after the disastrous flooding of the Montague Main Pit, in which thirty-eight men were killed, Warne impressed the House even more. He controlled his strong feeling about this and other pit accidents, and made a temperate and reasoned speech on the causes and prevention of such disasters. Many pit accidents occurred, he said, because plans of workings were not kept. The Montague Pit area was honeycombed with old mines; he had discovered the record of one close to the Pit itself. The 1911 Act had never been properly applied, and he called on the Minister to see that it was enforced and that a new survey was speedily undertaken.

On 10 December 1925, five months before the General Strike of May 1926, Warne spoke in the debate on the mining industry which had been opened by the Chancellor of the Exchequer, Winston Churchill. The debate centred on the situation that would arise when the government subsidy should be ended in April 1926. Warne's speech combined moderation of tone with commitment to the miners' cause. In an article written at this time under the heading 'Ministers of To-morrow', Commander Kenworthy, Liberal MP for Central Hull, referred especially to George Warne, and said that after this speech he 'was cheered in all parts of the House for his constructive statesmanship' (*Evening Standard*, 22 Dec 1925).

In the debate of 6 May 1926 Warne again impressed the House, as a correspondent reported: he spoke 'with a forceful moderation', and 'performed the feat, which is so difficult for a private member, of keeping a large audience at the end of an absorbing interchange between the party leaders' (*Newcastle J.*, 7 May 1926).

During the first half of 1926 Warne had been travelling strenuously all over the country to speak on the problems of the mining industry. He worked almost without rest, disregarded his health, and finally broke down in June, when he became seriously ill with chest trouble. A holiday in the north of England brought no improvement, and in October, on medical advice, he went to a clinic in Switzerland, where he stayed for seven months. In April 1927, although not really well, he was able to come home, but not to return to his parliamentary work. In early 1928 he and his family moved from Ashington, a smoky colliery town, to Gosforth, where it was hoped the cleaner air would benefit his chest. By December 1928 he felt so much better that he went to London, visited the House of Commons and attended a meeting of the PLP ('no man was ever more warmly received', as J.R. Clynes wrote to Mrs Warne on 28 December). That winter was severe, however, and London full of fog. When Warne went home to Gosforth for the Christmas holiday, he had an attack of chest trouble on 21 December. He seemed to recover, but on the night of 23 December he had a sudden seizure and died in the early morning of the 24th.

Warne left an estate of £802. He was survived by his wife (who died in 1938) and his children. All the children, as he would have hoped, were enabled by their education to take up professions, such as teaching, secretarial work, nursing, police service.

George Warne was a man of high principles and strong, though disciplined feelings, with an acute intelligence and a pretty wit. It is clear that he was warmly liked and much respected by his fellow-workers in the many fields in which he was active. For instance, at the PLP meeting of 17 July 1928 'it was unanimously decided', Warne was told, 'to re-elect you right away as one of the Junior Whips' – this although for two years he had been ill and off work, and still was. Again, his constituents in Wansbeck seem to have very willingly accepted virtual disenfranchisement during these two years; and the Northumberland miners contributed generously to the expenses of his stay in Switzerland. The trust and affection he inspired is plain in many letters written to him during his illness and after his death, to his family about him. 'I feel the House to be the poorer when you are not there,' the Speaker, J.H. Whitley, wrote to him on 1 September 1926. A letter from Sir Charles Trevelyan written to Miss Warne on the day after his death, includes the simple statement, 'There was no one I was more fond of in the House.' On the same day Philip Snowden also wrote, to Mrs Warne, 'I cannot express to you adequately how greatly he was loved and respected. His loss at such an early age is irreparable.'

During the First World War, when George Warne was one evening addressing an open-air meeting at Blyth and no doubt putting the pacifist as well as the Socialist case, an old lady brandished her umbrella at him and told him excitedly what she would do with him if she could. Warne conquered her with the cheerful reply, 'It's all right, mother, the only difference between you and me is that I love you better than you love me.' The same point was made by Joshua Ritson, the Labour MP for Durham Division, who wrote to Mrs Warne about her husband, 'He was loved because he himself loved.'

Writings: 'Can we stop Mine Disasters?: what might be done if we had the will and the courage', *Reynolds's Illustrated News*, 5 Apr 1925; 'In the Days of my Youth', *T.P.'s and Cassell's Weekly*, 27 Feb 1926.

Sources: *WWW* (1916-28); S.V. Bracher, *The Herald Book of Labour Members* (1923); *Dod* (1923) and (1927); *Hansard*, vol. *165*, 28 June 1923; vol. *182*, 31 Mar 1925; vol. *187*, 28 July 1925; vol. *189*, 10 Dec 1925; *Labour Who's Who* (1927); J.J. Lawson, *The Man in the Cap: the life of Herbert Smith* (1941); biographical information: T.A.K. Elliott, CMG, Helsinki; NUM, Newcastle upon Tyne; personal information: Mrs E. Stimpson, Morpeth, daughter, to whom the editors are indebted for an earlier draft. OBIT. *Times*, 27 Dec 1928; *Morpeth Herald* and *Newcastle J.*, 28 Dec 1928; NMA, *Monthly Circular* (Jan 1929); *Labour Party Report* (1929).

MARGARET 'ESPINASSE

See also: †Thomas ASHTON, for Mining Trade Unionism, 1900-14; Alexander BLYTH; †Arthur James COOK, for Mining Trade Unionism, 1915-26.

WHITEHOUSE, Samuel Henry (1849-1919)
MINERS' LEADER

Samuel Whitehouse was born on 14 February 1849 in Swan Village, Staffordshire, the eldest of the nine children of a collier. He entered the pit before he was nine, as a door-boy; at ten he took part in a strike and by the time he was twelve he had had two pit accidents, and had kept watch alone for a whole night over a miner who was dying, crushed by a fall of coal [*Beacon* (July and Sep 1909)].

At sixteen he was 'a full blown collier'. He joined a trade union as soon as he could, and by 1867 was secretary of his lodge and represented it at district meetings. In the following year he was dismissed from his job for speaking on behalf of a Liberal candidate for Parliament, and was unable to get work for many months.

He had become keenly interested in the progressive movements of the time, and this had made him determine to learn to read, a task which he accomplished by means of Sunday school and night school. At some point he was elected checkweighman at one of the pits, a post he held for a number of years. He had also held office with the Amalgamated Association of Miners, which was founded in 1869, and was agent to the West Bromwich Miners' Federation.

Whitehouse was one of the founders of the Midland Miners' Federation, in the 1880s. When the Federation was definitely established in 1886 he became secretary; the president was Enoch Edwards, secretary of the North Staffordshire Miners' Association. Whitehouse continued to act as secretary for the next two years, until in 1888 the miners of Somerset invited him to become their agent, and he left the Black Country.

His task of organising the union in Somerset was at first very difficult. The colliery owners threw every obstacle in his way. In 1888 judgement was given against him in a suit brought by a proprietor, and when he refused to pay the fine and costs, the bailiffs were put in. However, he persevered in the work of organising, and succeeded before very long in establishing an efficient and stable union.

Whitehouse continued as agent for Somerset until he retired in 1917. He was a delegate to the Newport Conference of 1889 which brought into being the MFGB, and he represented Somerset on the national executive of the Federation on six occasions between 1889 and 1912. He took an active part in the great lock-out of 1893, which was ended by the direct intervention of the Liberal Government; and he represented the Midland Federation at the Rosebery Conference which followed and which resulted in the setting up of the National Conciliation Board in 1894.

Both when he was in Staffordshire and later in Somerset, Whitehouse took an active part in local government. He was for many years a very useful member of the West Bromwich School Board, and he served on the Radstock (Somerset) Urban Council from 1893 to 1898, as chairman in 1896. He was a member of the Clutton Board of Guardians for many years; a supporter of the co-operative movement, and was on the committee of a small society before he was twenty. He was a lifelong Liberal. As a representative of the Somerset Miners' Association, Whitehouse travelled widely, investigating mining conditions in Canada and the U.S.A. as well as in a number of European countries.

Whitehouse developed a talent for competent journalism and for editorial work. He was a member of the staff of the mining paper *Labour Tribune* in the years before he went to Somerset, and was sub-editor in 1887. In the *Beacon* for 1909 he gave an interesting account of his early life, and of industrial and political conditions in general in the 1850s and 1860s.

Ill health caused Whitehouse to retire from work in 1917. He died on 20 December 1919 at his home in Clutton, Somerset. After a service at Radstock Parish Church he was buried in St Nicholas's churchyard. He was survived by at least two sons and a daughter and left effects valued at £379.

Writings: Letters and articles in *Labour Tribune* (1886-9); 'Some Incidents in the Life of an Agitator', *Beacon* (May, July and Nov 1909); 'Universal Peace', ibid. (Apr 1911) 61.

Sources: W. Hallam, *Miners' Leaders* (1894); R. Page Arnot, *The Miners* vols *1* and *2* (1949) and (1953); biographical information: NUM (South Wales). OBIT. *Somerset and Wilts J.*, 24 Dec 1919 and 9 Jan 1920; *Times*, 24 Dec 1919; *Somerset Guardian*, 2 Jan 1920.

MARGARET 'ESPINASSE

See also: †Thomas ASHTON, for Mining Trade Unionism, 1900-14; †Enoch EDWARDS; †Benjamin PICKARD, for Mining Trade Unionism, 1880-99; †Fred SWIFT.

WILLIAMS, David James (1897-1972)
MINERS' LEADER AND LABOUR MP

David Williams was born at Gwaun-cae-gurwen, Glamorgan, on 3 February 1897, the son of Morgan Williams, a miner, and his wife Margaretta (née Jones). In the local elementary school he reached Standard VI at the age of thirteen, and was therefore qualified to be issued with a Labour Certificate, and leave school a year before the normal age. He began working underground, and took an early interest in trade union affairs. D.J. supplemented his education by evening classes. The authors and books that most influenced him were Marx's *Capital*, Dietzgen's *Positive Outcome of Philosophy*, and Rosa Luxemburg's *Accumulation of Capital*. Williams was especially impressed by the last named and her general advocacy of a revolutionary social democracy. In 1917 he joined the Socialist Labour Party, and before he was twenty-one he became chairman of his local miners' lodge. He remained active in the SLP for several years, and was a member of its South Wales district committee.

In 1919 Williams won a South Wales Miners' Federation scholarship to the Central Labour College in London, and he remained there for two years. Among his fellow students from South Wales were Nye Bevan, Ness Edwards, Bryn Roberts and J.L. Williams. On his return to South Wales he was unemployed for a year. In 1923 he passed a Club and Institute Union examination which gave him a one-year scholarship to Ruskin College. While he was at Oxford he joined the local branch of the ILP and became its propaganda secretary, addressing a great many open-air meetings in the town and the surrounding districts. He found time, however, to engage in research, and the resulting book was published in 1924 under the title *Capitalist Combination in the Coal Industry*. The book was issued by the Labour Publishing Company, and had a foreword by Tom Richards, who was at the time secretary of the South Wales Miners' Federation and vice-president of the MFGB.

After his Ruskin years, Williams went to Scotland as a tutor for the National Council of Labour Colleges, and held classes in Fifeshire, Clackmannanshire, Stirling, Perth, Dundee and Aberdeen. He continued in this post for six years. During the General Strike of 1926, Williams was secretary of the Fife, Kinross and Clackmannan Workers' Council of Action, and editor of the Council's daily strike bulletin. In the course of the strike he was charged with 'incitement to riot'; but the verdict was 'Not Proven'. His ideas at this time may be gauged from an article he wrote in 1927 for *Plebs*, 'The Passing of Parliamentary Democracy'. He was doubtful whether it would be possible, because of the power of the media, for the Labour Party to win a parliamentary majority, and even more doubtful whether, in the event of its doing so, it would be permitted to legislate for Socialist policies. The capitalist class he wrote, 'will abandon democracy, as they have abandoned it before, when their needs as a class demand such a step' [(Oct 1927) 327].

In 1931 Williams returned to South Wales, and was elected miners' checkweigher and lodge secretary at the Gwaun-cae-gurwen Collieries. He served on several committees of the SWMF, and in 1937-8 was chairman of the Anthracite Miners' Combine Committee, covering thirty-four collieries. In the same year, 1931, that he returned to his native county, he was elected to the Pontardawe Rural District Council. He was chairman of the council in 1938-9, and remained a member until his election to the House of Commons in 1945. He was also a member of the Board of Guardians as long as they lasted, and served as a JP in 1938-9 in his capacity as chairman of the Pontardawe RDC.

Williams suffered from a protracted illness during the early years of the war – from 1940 until 1942 – and his trade union and public activities were severely curtailed; but he recovered his health, was elected to the executive council of the SWMF in 1943, and chosen as parliamentary candidate for the Neath division of Glamorgan early in 1945. He became an MP in 1945 through a by-election very soon after VE Day, with the general election following very quickly. The by-election of May 1945 was noteworthy for the candidature of the first Trotskyist to stand in a parliamentary election in Britain. This was Jock Haston, of the Revolutionary Communist Party, who polled 1781 votes against over 31,000 for Williams. Williams retained Neath at all subsequent elections until ill-health forced him to retire in 1964. As might be expected, his main concerns in the House of Commons were mining, and Welsh industry and agriculture (including afforestation). He was chairman of the Welsh parliamentary group from 1950 to 1951, and secretary of the group from 1946 to 1962. Williams was notably critical of the way in which the nationalisation of coal had been organised; in particular, of the lack of participation in management affairs by working miners. During 1946-7 he was strongly opposed to the National Service Bill, which introduced peace-time conscription. In foreign affairs, he was opposed to the rearmament of Germany in the mid-1950s; and was always against the use of the atom and hydrogen bombs. He had much sympathy with the broad principles of CND, but never became a member, mainly because he disagreed with the methods used to attract publicity.

Williams was a highly intelligent man, and unusually well read – especially, but not at all exclusively, in the fields of economics and politics. He possessed a good memory and an excellent private library. All these things made him a 'dungeon of learning' for fellow MPs in search of information. They also made him a good public speaker; but it was his innate feeling for language, his flair for expression, that made him a distinguished one. He prepared his speeches with studious concentration; they remained in his memory, and so he had no need to use notes, and scarcely ever did. His ability to speak without them was admiringly noted by a number of his friends. His speeches were not rhetorical in the popular sense – emotive or flamboyant. On the contrary, the quality of his speaking resided in his ability to analyse a theme, to select the relevant facts and order them to a logical conclusion, to convince by good reasoning; equally important, to choose precisely the right word, and to be completely in command of his tone. All this can be seen in, for instance, the speech he made in a House of Commons debate on foreign affairs, in July 1949. The first paragraph set the tone:

A number of speakers in this debate have stressed the need for defence, but so far no one has said what is to be defended. One Member has said that democracy should be defended, another brought in feudalism and oil in the Middle East; and the hon. Member for Lancaster said that we must defend China and the Far East and nationalism. If all these things are to be defended, then we are faced with a formidable task. I would remind the Committee that only on Monday we debated what was called a serious economic crisis, and that that crisis has not yet been solved. Moreover, no one has said how all these things are to be defended and, most astonishing of all, no one has said against whom they are to be defended.

He continued with an admirable analysis of the economic and political implications of the Atlantic Pact, and included a wish that its authors were clearer whether they were afraid of 'territorial aggression or ideological aggression? . . . Stalin as a marshal or as a Marxist?' America, he continued, is afraid – 'psychologically and pathologically afraid' of Communism. Because of this fear, Europe is to be obliged to rearm. 'Armaments', he ended, 'are no answer to the modern challenge of Communism. Indeed, the armaments programme of the democratic nations is Stalin's secret weapon, and the most effective weapon in the armoury of Communism.'

In another debate of the same year, on the National Coal Board, answering attacks on the Coal Board as a monopoly, Williams gave an eloquent account of the private monopoly previously controlling the anthracite coalfield in South Wales: he called its establishment 'a squalid affair' managed not by coalowners but by 'financiers, speculators, sharepushers and "spivs" from the City of London'; whose operation of squeezing out the independent owners 'was governed by the economics and ethics of the jungle. If hon. Members opposite care to pay a visit to the anthracite coalfield we will show them the ruins and the relics of free enterprise.'

During the 1950s Williams's speeches and questions in the House of Commons gradually became fewer. His health was failing and he resigned in 1964, before the general election of that year. He had married Janet Scott Alexander of Alloa at Dunfermline in 1939. His wife served as a JP for Glamorgan from 1951-70 and is now (1975) on the supplemental list. There were no children of the marriage. Williams's mother was a deeply religious woman although, so far as is known, Williams did not hold any religious beliefs in his adult life but he was always tolerant towards the beliefs of others. He died on holiday at Llandudno on 12 September 1972, and was cremated at Conway. He left investments of £2600 in addition to his house, which was owned jointly with his wife.

Writings: 'What next in the Mining Industry?', *Lab. Mon. 5*, no. 4 (Oct 1923) 224-8; *Capitalist Combination in the Coal Industry* (1924); 'Two Stages of Capitalism', *Plebs 17*, no. 2 (Feb 1925) 72-5; 'Problems of Dictatorship', ibid., *19*, no. 3 (Mar 1927) 103-6; 'Capital's Next Step in Coal and Iron', ibid., *19*, no. 6 (June 1927) 192-6; 'The Passing of Parliamentary Democracy', ibid., *19*, no. 10 (Oct 1927) 322-7; 'Rationalising the Robot', ibid., *20*, no. 7 (July-Aug 1928) 152-3; 'Future of Coal', *Spec. 176*, 8 Feb 1946.

Sources: *Labour Who's Who* (1927); *South Wales Voice*, 19 May 1945; C. Bunker, *Who's Who in Parliament* (1946); *Dod* (1946); *Western Mail*, 17 Feb 1950; *WW* (1959) and (1966); *Election Address*, 8 Oct 1959; *Kelly* (1960); W.W. Craik, *The Central Labour College* (1964); biographical information: G.I. Lewis, Univ. College of Swansea; personal information: D.J. Williams, letter of 26 Sep 1966; Mrs J.S. Williams, Neath, widow; D.J. Evans, Bridgend; H.J. Finch, Pontllanfraith, Mon.; W.R. Hopes, Neath; L.C. Williams, Neath. OBIT. *Western Mail*, 15 Sep 1972; *Neath Guardian*, 29 Sep 1972.

MARGARET 'ESPINASSE
JOHN SAVILLE

See also: †William ABRAHAM for Welsh Mining Trade Unionism; †Arthur James COOK, for Mining Trade Unionism, 1915-26.

WILSON, Joseph Havelock (1858-1929)
TRADE UNIONIST AND LIB-LAB MP

Havelock Wilson was born on 16 August 1858 at Sunderland, the third son of John Blenkin Wilson, a foreman draper, and Hannah Wilson (née Robson). His father died when he was three years old and his mother was left with seven children. She provided for her family by opening a greengrocer's shop, and then later became proprietor of a small boarding house. Havelock Wilson was christened in the Church of England, but it was the chapel which had most influence upon him in his early years. His maternal grandfather, John Joseph Robson, a master joiner and patternmaker, took him to the local Methodist chapel during his boyhood days in Sunderland. At the age of six Havelock began selling newspapers out of school hours, and at nine, after a few years at the Boys' British School, Sunderland, he went to work as an errand boy [*Pearson's Weekly*, 29 Mar 1906]. He was apprenticed at thirteen to a local lithographic printer, but within a few months he ran away to sea. After several short voyages, his family accepted his determination to become a seaman, and he was apprenticed to Mr Sanderson, a Sunderland shipowner. During the next eleven years, Wilson shipped out in many different types of vessel and in capacities ranging from boy steward, cook, able seaman to boatswain/second mate. Mostly he seems to have sailed as AB/Cook, but he always considered himself to be an AB, and after 'extra training' it was at this rating that he served five years in the Royal Naval Reserve.

On 30 March 1879, Wilson married Jane Anne Watham at Monkwearmouth Parish Church. At the time of his marriage he was in the coasting trade, but in 1882, mainly in deference to the wishes of his wife (whose father had been drowned at sea), he came ashore permanently. With some savings, and possibly with help also from both his mother and his mother-in-law, he opened a small 'cook-shop' in Church Street, Monkwearmouth. Two years later he moved to larger premises in High Street East, Sunderland, and the business became known as 'Wilson's Temperance Hotel and Dining Rooms'. In his early days as union organiser his business interests afforded him the important security of independence.

Wilson had gained his first trade union experience while he was working in the Australian coasting trade. In May of 1879, just after his marriage, the North of England Sailors' and Seagoing Firemen's Friendly Society was established. Wilson became a member; the first mention of his name is in December 1883. By June 1885 the Society was meeting in his hotel, and within a few months he became president of the Society. He gave evidence in 1886 for the Society before the R.C. on Loss of Life at Sea, and before two government committees, the S.C. on the Employers' Liability Act and the Departmental Committee on the Life Saving Appliances Bill. He was also the Society's delegate to the Sunderland Trades Council, and he was present, according to his autobiography, at the small conference of the British seamen's unions held in Leith in August 1885. Wilson was eager to widen the influence of the Society, and for a short time branches were opened in North and South Shields and Middlesbrough; but many of the leading personalities of the union, including the new secretary, Rutherford, were unwilling to accept the idea of expansion; in particular, they feared the loss of their special relationship with the Lambton family, the leading shipowners of Sunderland. Unable to persuade his colleagues, Wilson withdrew, and established his own union in August 1887. This was the National Amalgamated Sailors' and Firemen's Union of Great Britain and Ireland. Much was made in later writing of the help in drafting the rule-book which Wilson received from local miners' leaders, but there is little direct evidence of this assistance, except that he undoubtedly took over some regulations from the rule-book of the Durham Miners. Help did come from a local solicitor, B.W. Brown, and from William Foreman of the ASRS. Wilson became general secretary, and the union with a membership of 500 affiliated to the TUC in 1888, with Wilson attending as its delegate. This first appearance at the TUC was important in producing offers of help from a number of political and trade union figures, among them Chisholm Robertson, of the Stirlingshire miners, and John (Jack) Gardner of the Cardiff Trades Council. His objectives at the beginning of his career as a national trade union leader were those which, broadly speaking, remained throughout his life. They included improvements in the manning scale, the establishment of professional certificates, changes in maritime law, and a uniform wage list.

Wilson had established his union at an opportune time. Foreign trade expanded rapidly during the closing years of the decade and during 1889 there were strikes in most of the large and small ports for an advance of wages. By the time the 1889 TUC was held in Dundee in September, the NASFU was affiliated with 65,000 members and thirteen delegates attended the Congress. Wilson himself was elected to the parliamentary committee, and remained a member until 1898. For a critical comment on Wilson's election in 1889 by John Burnett, see B. Webb, *Our Partnership* (1948) p.23; and his poor attendance in later years was specifically deplored by the parliamentary committee in a resolution passed on 8 June 1898 [Clegg et al., (1964) 261n].

The rise and decline of union organisation on the waterfronts of Britain has been documented in many places [Saville (1960); H.A. Clegg et al., (1964); Lovell (1969); Brown (1972); Taplin (1974)]. That Wilson had imagination and energy as a union organiser, many of his contemporaries recognised, although these qualities were offset by his incompetence in financial matters and his autocratic personality. It was not, however, personal defects that were mostly responsible for the disintegration of his union in the early 1890s. The counter-offensive against the unions of both dockers and seamen was organised by the Shipping Federation, established in August 1890; and the Federation's onslaught on the organised workers, perhaps induced, and certainly supported, by shrinking trade and growing unemployment, proved remarkably successful. The Federation's pioneering development of the techniques of blacklegging was crucial in the victory of the employers over the NASFU and the Dockers' Union. Over the years the Federation also sponsored rival unions, and financed legal actions by opponents of Wilson in order to force him into bankruptcy. During a seamen's strike in Cardiff in 1891 Wilson was convicted of 'unlawful assembly and riot' and was imprisoned for six weeks. With unsuccessful strikes in Bristol in late 1892, and the major defeat of the waterside trade unions in Hull in the spring of 1893, the end of the Seamen's Union soon came. Wilson had resigned the general secretaryship to become president in the autumn of 1893, and in the following summer of 1894 the union went into voluntary liquidation. A new National Sailors' and Firemen's Union of Great Britain and Ireland was formed, with Wilson again as its president. One feature of the constitution of the new body was the complete centralisation of the union's funds; and strict centralisation of finance and power was henceforth to be a guiding principle of Wilson's leadership and a continual source of friction and tension throughout the subsequent history of the union. For many years, however, the reorganised union remained extremely weak, and it was not until the period of unrest preceding the outbreak of the First World War that membership again became significant.

Before his first union had collapsed, however, Wilson had become an MP. He had had political ambitions from his early days as a national union figure, as is shown by what he wrote in 1889 in *Seafaring*, the union journal. In September 1889 he helped to form a branch of the Labour Electoral Association in Sunderland, even though he and his family had already moved to London along with the Union headquarters in the previous July. He nearly stood as candidate for Dundee and the East Toxteth division of Liverpool: his first actual campaign was in a by-election at East Bristol in May 1890. Bristol Trades Council disapproved of his last-minute candidature, but nevertheless endorsed him. Wilson stood as a representative of Labour, with a radical programme, and he polled 602 votes against the Conservative's 1900 and the Liberal's 4775. He then became prospective Lib-Lab candidate for Deptford, but withdrew to fight Middlesbrough in the general election of 1892. There, having failed to gain the Liberal nomination, he stood on an independent Labour platform. A majority of 629 over the Liberal made him the first Labour candidate to win a three-cornered fight. He retained the seat in 1895, losing it to the Unionist in 1900, and regaining it in 1906.

Yet Wilson was a Liberal throughout his life. Immediately after his election victory in 1892 won as an independent Labour candidate he made a speech closely identifying himself with the Liberal Party; this alienated many of his most enthusiastic supporters in Middlesbrough, but made his peace with the Liberal Party, who thereafter allowed him a straight fight with the Conservatives. Wilson often stood on Liberal Party platforms in opposition to ILP and, later, LRC candidates, and in the early years of the new century he was 'organising opposition to the LRC throughout the North-East' [Bealey and Pelling (1958) 152] – although he was a delegate to the LRC as late as 1904. In the 1906 general election, in which he stood as a Lib-Lab candidate, the Middlesbrough LRC, without the support of the national executive, ran George Lansbury against him. MacDonald and Hardie tried very hard to give Lansbury official backing, but they failed because of rather complicated local difficulties. Lansbury, whose candidature was largely financed by Joseph Fels, came a poor third on voting day [Purdue (1973)].

Inside the House of Commons Wilson was mostly concerned with extending the work for the improvement of seafaring conditions already begun by Samuel Plimsoll. He took an active part in the debates on the Merchant Shipping Consolidating Act of 1894 and the amending Act of 1906. He was a member of, or gave evidence to, many Commissions and Select Committees dealing with the various aspects of the seaman's life and working conditions. He always regarded politics as an adjunct to industrial action and for this, as well as for many other reasons, he never became a parliamentarian of any stature. One notable feature of Wilson's public life was what he himself described in his autobiography as 'almost a mania for law' [(1925) 236]. He was involved in legal cases almost continuously. A few examples were the case against *Fairplay* in 1891; against William Collison, leader of the National Free Labour Association in 1896; against the Shipping Federation and others in 1913. The Shipping Federation was especially active in encouraging Wilson's litigious propensities, and on more than one occasion he had to be declared bankrupt as a result of damages and costs which he was unable to meet.

The most important union development of the depressed years between the middle 1890s and 1910 was the establishment of the International Transport Workers' Federation (ITF) in 1896.

Wilson helped in its foundation; he saw the ITF as a means of cutting off the supply of foreign strike-breakers during disputes in Britain, and its longer-term objectives as the organisation of European seamen and dockers to raise wage rates and improve working conditions. His evidence to the 1903 Committee on Mercantile Marine (para. 5410) set out clearly his policies for the ITF. There were many problems and difficulties. In 1904 the headquarters of the ITF removed to Germany, with Hermann Jochade as general secretary. The importation of British strike-breakers into Germany and Sweden to smash strikes of dockers and seamen put the ITF under strain and there were also rather bitter personal conflicts, although a formal split was avoided; and there was little support for Wilson when he began developing his ideas for international strike action in the later part of 1910 and early 1911. Nor did he get support from the newly established National Transport Workers' Federation in Britain. This was formed by sixteen unions concerned with the seagoing, waterside and road (but not railway) transport trades, who came together in October 1910 and in November elected a committee of five to draft a constitution. A week before the seamen's strike of 1911 was to begin, this new Federation decided not to take part. They may have endorsed the contemporary opinion which regarded the strike, in the words of Robert Williams, as 'a gambler's last chance' [Mogridge (1961) 381]; the Shipping Federation took the same view.

The background to the calling of the strike is still unclear. Wilson later tried to present its development as a well thought-out plan; but this is unlikely. Wilson called the strike on 14 June 1911, and that same day the demands of a group of striking seamen and firemen at Southampton, who had come out five days earlier, were agreed by the shipping firm which was the other party in the dispute. This pattern was to be repeated round the country. Company after company bought peace with both wage increases and other concessions. There was an upsurge of solidarity strikes by other waterfront and transport workers, and these included major confrontations between strikers and their employers in London and Liverpool, where Ben Tillett and Tom Mann were the outstanding leaders.

Wilson's Union came out of the strikes with a greatly increased membership, with the beginnings of official recognition by some shipping companies, and with the majority of firms within the Shipping Federation no longer accepting the Federation's 'ticket' as compulsory for those seeking employment. The bitter conflicts of the past were, however, far from being ended. The other major concession was the move towards local standardisation of wage rates. Altogether, the events of the summer of 1911 were a considerable achievement for Havelock Wilson – and this in spite of worsening health. It was in these years that both 'Captain' Edward Tupper and 'Father' Hopkins began working as close colleagues with Wilson. Edward Tupper was not a captain, but a bankrupt company promoter and ex-private detective who became the union's national organiser. Father Hopkins, an American-born Anglican priest, was founder of the Society of Saint Paul, concerned with seamen's welfare work while he was a chaplain in Calcutta and became the union's research officer some time before 1910. He actively supported Wilson in the disputes with dissident branches in 1911-12, acting for Wilson (along with Tupper) on investigation committees. He was obviously very much impressed with Wilson's character; like Tupper, he saw his own role in the union very much in terms of personal loyalty to Wilson and his policies.

Relations with the Shipping Federation continued difficult – as they did until the war years – and Wilson had further problems with the emergence of two new unions. The first, the Cooks' and Stewards' Union, was established by Joe Cotter in March 1909, and the second was the British Seafarers' Union (BSU) composed of the Southampton branch of Wilson's Union, which broke away after the strike of 1911, and the Glasgow branch, which also broke away, in 1912. The BSU was politically and industrially more militant than the NSFU.

The years of the First World War were to witness important changes in the position of Wilson's Union in the British shipping industry. The executive of the Sailors' and Firemen's Union met soon after the outbreak of war and decided to co-operate fully in the war effort. Wilson himself had always considered himself a 'true Britisher'. He had served in the Royal

Naval Reserve, was always vigorous in his support of the Royal Family, – and had already demonstrated his political patriotism by his positive support of the Boer War: in the election of 1900, although he lost his parliamentary seat, his statement of aims had been a stoutly imperialist one. He became known during the First World War for the vigour of his anti-German sentiments; but in the early years he took quite a moderate nationalistic line. At the beginning of the war, the NSFU established, at considerable financial cost, an open internment camp for its own German and Austrian members. Wilson was still urging caution in anti-Germanism at the 1916 annual conference of the NSFU. There were a number of incidents and features of the conflict – submarine warfare in particular – that helped to push Wilson into anti-German attitudes that can only be described as pathological; but not, probably, before the closing months of 1916. His anti-Germanism was also bound up with his virulent opposition to the Labour Party, and above all to those within the labour movement who took an anti-war stand. The most spectacular examples of Wilson's phobias were the refusals to transport certain Labour and Socialist personalities on missions overseas. In May 1917 union members in Aberdeen refused to allow Ramsay MacDonald and Fred Jowett on board a ship which was taking a Labour delegation to Russia. This decision, prompted by Havelock Wilson and carried out by his close colleague, 'Captain' Tupper, enjoyed considerable rank-and-file support. There were other examples. Wilson's anti-Labour attitudes also encouraged him to seek allies among trade unionists and Socialists who supported the war; and he became vice-president of the British Workers' League [Douglas (1972); Stubbs (1972)].

Wilson's ultra-patriotic views and deeds, combined with membership of such organisations as the National Alliance of Employers and Employed (1917), served to alter the attitudes of leading members of the Shipping Federation towards him and his union. The pressure of war conditions inevitably worked in the same direction. There was a growing shortage of seamen for British shipping, and from March 1916, with amendments to the La Follette Act, it was no longer possible to imprison deserting foreign seamen in American ports. When the United States entered the war in April 1917, with wages in American ships some eighty per cent. higher than in British ships, the numbers of deserters increased quite rapidly. By July 1917, with the rapid growth of unrest, the Ministry of Shipping was forced to intervene. By November a National Maritime Board had been established, and the shipping owners had at last been forced to concede many of the demands for which Wilson had been fighting for so many years. The purposes of the new body are set out in Hopkins (1920) 155-8 and Mogridge (1961) 389-90. The National Maritime Board was continued after the war (without government representation), with the Sailors' and Firemen's Union as the main union representing the workers' side, a provision which was to cause considerable bitterness and conflict in the post-war period. For his service to shipping, recruitment and national savings Wilson was awarded the CBE in 1918, and he was made a Companion of Honour in 1922.

The effect of the four years of the war on Wilson had been to move him to even more conservative political and industrial positions. He completely dominated his union; and as a result of his attitudes and policies, the Seamen as an organised body became increasingly isolated from the rest of the labour movement.

Wilson himself continued to contest parliamentary seats. He had not stood in the election of 1910, but in 1913 he campaigned on an independent Labour, free-trade platform and received 7088 votes in Wandsworth, South London, where he was defeated by Samuel Samuel, a banker and shipowner, with 13,425 votes. Later, in 1914, he was adopted by Great Yarmouth, but never contested the constituency. At a by-election in October 1918 he was returned unopposed at South Shields, and at the general election of the same year, he stood as a Coalition Liberal, defeating his Labour opponent G.J. Rowe by 19,514 votes to 6425. Between then and the general election of 1922, his Union had balloted affirmatively for affiliation to the Labour Party; but Wilson continued to present himself to the electorate of South Shields as a National Liberal, and was opposed in 1922 by Will Lawther, the official Labour Party candidate. Wilson came third in this election, and his parliamentary career ended. The Union was refused affiliation to the Labour Party in 1923, accepted in 1924 and then disaffiliated in 1927.

The complicated post-war history of unionism in the shipping industry continues to be dominated by Wilson until his death in 1929. In the reorganisation of the National Maritime Board in January 1920, the British Seafarers' Union had no seat, but the National Union of Ships' Stewards, Cooks, Butchers and Bakers represented the catering departments. Recognition of the BSU at a local level in two areas was forced upon the National Maritime Board by the strength of the union at Glasgow and Southampton; but this recognition was terminated in 1921. The ending of the short-lived post-war boom in the spring of 1920 saw freight rates plummetting downwards. Unemployment increased rapidly and wages declined sharply. A strike by Joe Cotter's Cooks' and Stewards' Union failed disastrously in the summer of 1921; for to the efforts of the shipowners in organising blackleg labour were added those of the Sailors' and Firemen's Union. A few months earlier Wilson had promoted strike-breaking action at the time of the miners' strike in April 1921. His union seceded from the National Transport Workers' Federation, to forestall its expulsion, and after the failure of the Cooks' and Stewards' strike the leaders of the NTWF decided to encourage an amalgamation between the Cooks' and Stewards' and the British Seafarers' Union. Robert Williams, secretary of the NTWF, acted as chairman of the various conferences which considered the amalgamation, and on 1 January 1922 the Amalgamated Marine Workers' Union (AMWU) was officially established.

Havelock Wilson was now confronted with a potentially serious rival to his union, and he was also faced with considerable discontent and unrest within his own union. Local rank-and-file committees established themselves and organised a number of unofficial disputes, the most important taking place during August and September 1925 in Liverpool, London, South Africa and Australia. Wilson waged an unceasing struggle against both the new union and the rank-and-file rebels. The union's constitution was amended repeatedly to make opposition to the leadership more difficult, and to strengthen those groups likely to support Wilson. The post-war years saw an interaction between the increasingly conservative political line of the Sailors' and Firemen's Union, its growing subordination to the employers, and the continuous weakening of its democratic practices. Wilson was always ready to use his own union members in strike-breaking; he made stringent use of the rule-book to expel recalcitrant members and officials; he was always willing to have recourse to the courts; and above all, he used the document known as PC5. This, in effect, was the old Shipping Federation ticket now endorsed by the Union. The PC5 was introduced in April 1922. Any sailor or fireman seeking employment had to obtain from the Sailors' and Firemen's Union a card – the PC5 – duly stamped, and then have it stamped by the owner's organisation. Only paid-up members of the Union were given cards. To the new Amalgamated Marine Workers' Union the scheme was, of course, a serious blow, although the PC5 did not come to be used immediately in every port. Merseyside, for example, was an area where the PC5 was not universally used, and the AMWU, although seriously weakened by the attempt at a closed shop by Wilson's Union, managed to keep for a few more years several thousand members, particularly in liners sailing from Southampton and Liverpool. But its days were numbered. In its short history – from January 1922 until early 1927 – it was involved in three major strikes; and all three were defeated by the combined strike-breaking efforts of the Shipping Federation and Wilson's Union, with 'Captain' Edward Tupper acting in his well-known role of hatchet-man for Wilson himself.

In the spring of 1924 the TUC managed to bring the two unions together in order to explore the possibilities of ending the bitter inter-union fight. Discussions dragged on for over a year, but it became abundantly clear that Wilson was only prepared to negotiate seriously on terms that meant the continued domination of his own union. One of his conditions for an agreement was the retirement from seamen's affairs of the three leading personalities of the AMWU: Emanuel Shinwell of Glasgow, Thomas Lewis of Southampton, and James McKinlay, head of the Union's insurance department. By April 1925 the deadlock was complete, and negotiations were abandoned. One interesting development concerned Joe Cotter, whose enthusiasm for the AMWU had long disappeared, and whose obstructionist policy inside it was finally met by his expulsion in June 1925. Within a few months he had become an official of Wilson's Union. The AMWU came to an end early in 1927. Its demise was hastened by an ingenious legal action – prompted by Wilson – as a result of which the AMWU was denied the right to take over the funds of the old Cooks' and Stewards' Union; and the financial problems thus created proved insuperable.

Throughout the decade after the war ended Wilson ranged himself against the main movement of British labour. He refused in the immediate post-war to rejoin the ITF because of its German connections; and at the Sankey Commission in 1919 he gave evidence which broadly supported the mineowners' case. In the General Strike Wilson aligned his Union with the Conservative Government. He characterised the strike as part of a vast Communist plot; he refused to obey the instructions the General Council that all transport workers should withdraw their labour, and he took to court a number of his own officials who did support the strike. In one particular instance his actions led to a legal decision which at the time provided important support for Sir John Simon's statement that the General Strike was illegal. Wilson had encouraged an application to the High Court to restrain officers in one of the London branches of his Union from calling members out on strike. On 11 May (five days after Sir John Simon's speech in the House of Commons) Mr Justice Astbury in the Chancery Division of the High Court granted the injunction being applied for, and added certain *obiter dicta* which characterised the general strike as 'illegal and contrary to law', and suggested that there was no protection under the 1906 Trade Disputes Act, since 'no trade dispute' could exist between the TUC and 'the Government and the nation' [Crook (1931) 472-3]. In late 1926 Wilson organised a number of meetings for the Industrial Peace Union of the British Empire; and when breakaway unions from the MFGB were established in Nottinghamshire and elsewhere, Havelock Wilson supplied cars, officials and financial assistance. This vigorous support for the Spencer Unions was opposed by a number of Wilson's own officials, including J. Davies, the general secretary who had held office for only eight months; they were all expelled. Wilson had also expelled after the General Strike most of the Mersey District officials of the union, all of whom had been loyal to him throughout the unofficial Vigilance Committees. In turn, Wilson's Union was expelled from the TUC in 1928, an event which provided the opportunity for the powerful Transport and General Workers' Union to begin recruiting seamen. Ernest Bevin had long been pressed to organise a maritime section within the TGWU, but he had refused on the ground that poaching on a union affiliated to the TUC was inadmissible. When it came to Bevin's notice that Wilson's delegation to the 1929 ILO Conference was going to vote against the eight-hour day for seamen, the TGWU began to organise its own seamen's section. This was in the later months of 1928.

Bevin, however, did not pursue an aggressive policy of recruitment. He was aware that some of the other officials of the Seamen's Union were out of sympathy with Wilson's views and actions, and that from October 1928 the latter was a very sick man. Havelock Wilson died, in his union office, on 16 April 1929, survived by his wife Jane Anne, two sons, who were both union officials, and a daughter, Mrs Macalmson. He left £428.

In his younger days Wilson was known for his physical stamina but during the 1890s he began to suffer from ill-health. He was seriously ill in the autumn of 1890 and again in 1895, when he broke a blood vessel in his neck. After about 1910, when rheumatoid arthritis began seriously to impair his physical movements, he never returned to full health, despite frequent rest cures. He gradually became obsessed with quack remedies, especially for his arthritis. In his later years he began also to suffer heart trouble.

Wilson's career was a fairly unusual one in the history of the British labour movement. It has not been uncommon for youthful militants to be translated into political and industrial moderates; but Wilson's despotic and successful control over what gradually became a company union was a rare phenomenon. Naturally members of the Shipping Federation in later years saw him very differently from his trade union contemporaries. One of them wrote in his memoirs:

Havelock Wilson was almost a dictator in the affairs of the seamen's side. This was not because of any direct inclination upon his part to adopt such a role. It was that he stood head and shoulders, through experience, ability, and consequently influence, above his contemporaries within the Union, which he had been instrumental in forming. Indeed he was one of the few really constructive thinkers in the trade union movement [Sanderson (1967) 133].

This was not at all how Wilson was looked at by his fellow trade-unionists. Robert Williams, secretary of the NTWF, replied in 1923 to a vicious attack on himself and some of his colleagues which had been published in the *Seaman*. Williams accused Wilson of 'conspiring with the shipowners to smash the resistance of his own members to wage reductions and worsened conditions' and the whole of the four-page pamphlet is a documented indictment of Wilson's collaboration with the shipping employers. On Wilson's death the *Miner* wrote:

We do not propose to overstep the bounds of good taste in our comments upon Havelock Wilson, whose death is announced as we go to press. In his early years he performed magnificent work in organising the much ill-used seamen of this country. The war had a most disturbing effect upon his outlook, and in post-war years he has been, in plain language, a faithful ally of the employing class. His Union organisation has been the faithful servant of the shipowners and he himself used the whole of his own and his Union's influence to disrupt and demoralise other sections of the workers.

We miners were honoured by the major share of his attentions. It cannot be said that his efforts met with a considerable degree of success; but they must necessarily have the effect of causing him to be remembered less as the organiser of the seamen 30 years ago than as the step-father of Spencerism in the coal industry. Havelock Wilson will go down to history as one of the tragedies of the twentieth-century working-class movement in Britain. We would very much rather it had been otherwise [20 Apr 1929].

It is certainly true that the war had important effects upon Havelock Wilson, and in particular upon what developed as a growing obsession with international Communism. He was, however, already moving to a committed anti-Socialist position before 1914. Much of the writing on Wilson tends to emphasise the changes in his attitudes over time, but it is possible to argue that his basic philosophy did not, in fact, alter in fundamental ways, but that he reacted, rather, with different emphases to different circumstances. His periods of militancy can be seen as the product of both the aggression of his members and the intransigence of the employers, which left him with little room to manoeuvre; and there is no doubt that the collapse of 1891-3 had a profoundly conservative influence upon his later policies. We still lack a full biography.

Writings: Evidence before S.C. on Employers' Liability Act (1880) Amendment Bill 1886 VIII Qs 5834-923; R.C. on Loss of Life at Sea 1887 XLIII Qs 18745-972; R.C. on Labour 1892 XXXV Group B Qs 9191-10375 and 10649-54; Departmental Cttee on Continuous Discharge Certificates for Seamen 1900 LXXVII Qs 1419-544; Board of Trade Cttee on Mercantile Marine 1903 LXII Qs 5175-6626 [Wilson was also a member of this cttee]; Departmental Cttee on Supply and Training of Boy Seamen for the Mercantile Marine 1907 LXXV Qs 10987-1586 [Wilson was also a member of this cttee]; Wilson was a frequent contributor to *Seafaring*, 1888-92 *Seaman's Chronicle*, 1896-7 and the *Seamen*, 1912-28. Other of his publications include: *Objections to joining the Union answered* [189-?] 8 pp.; 'How I got on', *Pearson's Weekly*, 29 Mar 1906; *The Dublin Dispute: a statement of the seamen's case* [1913] 27 pp.; 'An Appreciation: Father Hopkins [founder of the Order of St Paul] the sky pilot', *Messenger* [1922?] 133-5; *My Stormy Voyage through Life* (1925); *The Red Hand. Exploiting the Trade Union Movement; the Communist Offensive against the British Empire* (1926) 39 pp.; *The Real Truth about the Soviet Government of Russia* (1927); 'Peace and Goodwill', *Engl. Rev. 44* (Jan 1927) 20-4; *Havelock Wilson's Appeal on Behalf of the Industrial Peace Union of the British Empire* n.d. 6 pp.

Sources: (1) MSS: Webb Coll., BLPES; K.A. Golding, 'Transport Workers International' [1965]: ITF, HQ. London; Minute book of NASFU, 1887-90: NUS, HQ. London. (2) Thesis: F.T. Lindop, 'A History of Seamen's Trade Unionism to 1929' (London MPhil., 1972). (3) Newspapers, journals etc.: *Sunderland Daily Echo* (1879-91); *Workmen's Times* (1890-4); *Clarion*, 23 July 1892; *Free Labour Gazette* (1894-5); *North Eastern Daily Gazette* (1905-6); *Shipping Gazette* (1911-14); *Fairplay* (1913). (4) Other: *TUC Reports* (1887-1929); NASFU of GB & I: *Rules* (Cardiff, 1889), *Reports* of AGM (1890-2) and (1912-25); *Dod* (1894); [W. Collison], J. *"Havelock" Wilson, M.P. Daylight on his Career. Exposure and Challenge Astounding Revelations* (1894) P; 'From a Ship's Forecastle to the House of Commons: life and labours of J. Havelock Wilson, M.P.', *Special Double Supplement to Seafaring* [May 1900] 22 pp.; T.G. Duffy, *The Merchant Shipping Bill: a Liberal fraud* (ILP, [1907]) 20 pp.; A.W. Humphrey, *A History of Labour Representation* (1912); NTWF, *Report of Third Annual General Council Meeting* (1913); *Labour Party Reports* (1915-29); M. Eden, *Saviours of the Empire: J. Havelock Wilson, C.B.E., and "Captain" Tupper* (Glasgow, 1918) 16 pp.; C.P. Hopkins, *"National Service" of British Merchant Seamen 1914-19* (1920); *DNB* (1922-30); Robert Williams replies to Joseph Havelock Wilson, C.B.E., 30 June 1923, 4 pp. [in Webb Coll., BLPES, section B vol. CV, item 31]; *Report of speeches* [by J.H. Wilson, J. Cotter and A.H. Roston] *... at a meeting ... of the crew of the Mauretania ... at New York on ... 20th September 1925* (1925) 16 pp.; NUS, *Reports of AGM* (1926-30); G. Hardy, *The Struggle of British Seamen* (Minority Movement, [192-?]) 47 pp.; C.E. Fayle, *The War and the Shipping Industry* (1927); *WWW* (1929-40); W.H. Crook, *The General Strike* (Chapel Hill, 1931); J. Sexton, *Sir James Sexton Agitator. The Life of the Dockers' M.P.: an autobiography* (1936); E. Tupper, *Seamen's Torch: the life story of Captain Edward Tupper* (1938); B. Webb, *Our Partnership* (1948); L.H. Powell, *The Shipping Federation* (1950); K.G.J.C. Knowles, *Strikes – a Study in Industrial Conflict* (Oxford, 1952); F. Bealey and H. Pelling, *Labour and Politics 1900-1906* (1958); P.P. Poirier, *The Advent of the Labour Party* (1958); B.C. Roberts, *The Trades Union Congress 1868-1921* (1958); J. Saville, 'Trade Unions and Free Labour: the background to the Taff Vale decision' in *Essays in Labour History* ed. A. Briggs and J. Saville (1960) 317-50; S.W. Lerner, *Breakaway Unions and the Small Trade Union* (1961); B. Mogridge, 'Militancy and Inter-Union Rivalries in British Shipping, 1911-1929', *Int. Rev. Social Hist. 6*, pt 3 (1961) 375-412; H.A. Clegg et al., *A History of British Trade Unions since 1889* vol. *1: 1889-1910* (Oxford, 1964); Y. Gyllin, *Förbund på sju hav. Handelser och gestalter i sjofolkets historia* [Seven Seas' Union. Events and Figures in Seamen's History] (Malmö, 1964) 35-42 and 71-2; H. Pelling, *Social Geography of British Elections 1885-1910* (1967); Lord Sanderson of Ayot, *Ships and Sealing Wax* (1967); J. Lovell, *Stevedores and Dockers: a study of trade unionism in the Port of London, 1870-1914* (1969); K.A. Golding, 'In the Forefront of Trade Union History 1896-1971', *ITF J. 31*, no. 2 (Summer 1971) 29-52; W.C. Balfour, 'Captain Tupper and the 1911 Seamen's Strike in Cardiff', *Morgannwg 14* (1971) 62-80; R. Brown, *Waterfront Organisation in Hull 1870-1900* (Univ. of Hull, 1972); R. Douglas, 'The National Democratic Party and the British Workers' League', *Hist. J. 15*, no. 3 (1972) 533-52; J.O. Stubbs, 'Lord Milner and Patriotic Labour, 1914-1918', *Engl. Hist. Rev.* (Oct 1972) 717-54; A.W. Purdue, 'George Lansbury and the Middlesbrough Election of 1906', *Int. Rev. Social Hist. 18* (1973) 333-52; E.L. Taplin, *Liverpool Dockers and Seamen 1870-1890* (Univ. of Hull, 1974); biographical information: Dr.H.H. Borland, Hull Univ.; T.A.K. Elliott, CMG, Helsinki; F.T. Lindop, London. OBIT. *Shields Gazette* and *Times*, 17 Apr 1929; *Brixton Free Press* and *South London Press*, 19 Apr 1929; *Miner*, 20 Apr 1929.

J. McConville
John Saville

See also: †Allen Clement EDWARDS; Harry GOSLING; †George LANSBURY, for British Labour Party, 1900-13; *Tom MANN; Benjamin (Ben) TILLETT, and for New Unionism, 1889-93.

Consolidated List of Names

Volumes I, II, III and IV

ABBOTTS, William (1873–1930) I
ABLETT, Noah (1883–1935) III
ABRAHAM, William (Mabon) (1842–1922) I
ACLAND, Alice Sophia (1849–1935) I
ACLAND, Sir Arthur Herbert Dyke (1847–1926) I
ADAIR, John (1872–1950) II
ADAMS, David (1871–1943) IV
ADAMS, John Jackson, 1st Baron Adams of Ennerdale (1890–1960) I
ADAMS, William Thomas (1884–1949) I
ADAMSON, Janet (Jennie) Laurel (1882–1962) IV
ALDEN, Sir Percy (1865–1944) III
ALEXANDER, Albert Victor (Earl Alexander of Hillsborough) (1885–1965) I
ALLAN, William (1813–74) I
ALLEN, Reginald Clifford (Lord Allen of Hurtwood) (1889–1939) II
ALLEN, Robert (1827–77) I
ALLEN, Sir Thomas William (1864–1943) I
ALLINSON, John (1812/13–72) II
AMMON, Charles (Charlie) George (Lord Ammon of Camberwell) (1873–1960) I
ANDERSON, Frank (1889–1959) I
ANDERSON, William Crawford (1877–1919) II
APPLEGARTH, Robert (1834–1924) II
ARCH, Joseph (1826–1919) I
ARNOLD, Alice (1881–1955) IV
ARNOLD, Thomas George (1866–1944) I
ASHTON, Thomas (1844–1927) I
ASHTON, William (1806–77) III
ASHWORTH, Samuel (1825–71) I
ASKEW, Francis (1855–1940) III
ASPINWALL, Thomas (1846–1901) I
AUCOTT, William (1830–1915) II

BAILEY, Sir John (Jack) (1898–1969) II

BAILEY, William (1851–96) II
BALLARD, William (1858–1928) I
BAMFORD, Samuel (1846–98) I
BARBER, Jonathan (1800–59) IV
BARKER, George (1858–1936) I
BARNES, George Nicoll (1859–1940) IV
BARNETT, William (1840–1909) I
BARRETT, Rowland (1877–1950) IV
BARTLEY, James (1850–1926) III
BARTON, Eleanor (1872–1960) I
BATES, William (1833–1908) I
BATEY, John (1852–1925) I
BATEY, Joseph (1867–1949) II
BATTLEY, John Rose (1880–1952) IV
BAYLEY, Thomas (1813–74) I
BEATON, Neil Scobie (1880–1960) I
BELL, George (1874–1930) II
BELL, Richard (1859–1930) II
BENTHAM, Ethel (1861–1931) IV
BESANT, Annie (1847–1933) IV
BING, Frederick George (1870–1948) III
BIRD, Thomas Richard (1877–1965) I
BLAIR, William Richard (1874–1932) I
BLAND, Thomas (1825–1908) I
BLANDFORD, Thomas (1861–99) I
BLATCHFORD, Montagu John (1848–1910) IV
BLATCHFORD, Robert Peel Glanville (1851–1943) IV
BLYTH, Alexander (1835–85) IV
BOND, Frederick (1865–1951) I
BONDFIELD, Margaret Grace (1873–1953) II
BONNER, Arnold (1904–66) I
BOSWELL, James Edward Buchanan (1960–71) III
BOYES, Watson (1868–1929) III
BOYLE, Hugh (1850–1907) I
BOYNTON, Arthur John (1863–1922) I
BRACE, William (1865–1947) I

BRADBURN, George (1795–1862) II
BRAILSFORD, Henry Noel (1873–1958) II
BRANSON, Clive Ali Chimmo (1907–44) II
BRAY, John Francis (1809–97) III
BROADHEAD, Samuel (1818–97) IV
BROADHURST, Henry (1840–1911) II
BROOKE, Willie (1895/6?–1939) IV
BROWN, George (1906–37) III
BROWN, Herbert Runham (1879–1949) II
BROWN, James (1862–1939) I
BROWN, William Henry (1867/8–1950) I
BRUFF, Frank Herbert (1869–1931) II
BUGG, Frederick John (1830–1900) I
BURNETT, John (1842–1914) II
BURNS, Isaac (1869–1946) IV
BURT, Thomas (1837–1922) I
BUTCHER, James Benjamin (1843–1933) III
BUTCHER, John (1833–1921) I
BUTCHER, John (1847–1936) I
BUTLER, Herbert William (1897–1971) IV
BYRON, Anne Isabella, Lady Noel (1792–1860) II

CAIRNS, John (1859–1923) II
CAMPBELL, Alexander (1796–1870) I
CAMPBELL, George Lamb (1849–1906) IV
CANN, Thomas Henry (1858–1924) I
CANTWELL, Thomas Edward (1864–1906) III
CAPE, Thomas (1868–1947) III
CAPPER, James (1829–95) II
CARPENTER, Edward (1844–1929) II
CARTER, Joseph (1818–61) II
CARTER, William (1862–1932) I
CASASOLA, Rowland (Roland) William (1893–1971) IV
CATCHPOLE, John (1843–1919) I
CHARLTON, William Browell (1855/7?–1932) IV
CHARTER, Walter Thomas (1871–1932) I
CHATER, Daniel (Dan) (1870–1959) IV
CHEETHÁM, Thomas (1828–1901) I
CIAPPESSONI, Francis Antonio (1859–1912) I
CLARK, Fred (1878–1947) I
CLARK, Gavin Brown (1846–1930) IV
CLARK, James (1853–1924) IV
CLARKE, Andrew Bathgate (1868–1940) I
CLARKE, William (1852–1901) II
CLAY, Joseph (1826–1901) I
CLUSE, William Sampson (1875–1955) III

COCHRANE, William (1872–1924) I
COLMAN, Grace Mary (1892–1971) III
COMBE, Abram (1785?–1827) II
COOK, Arthur James (1883–1931) III
COOK, Cecily Mary (1887/90?–1962) II
COOMBES, Bert Lewis (Louis) (1893–1974) IV
COOPER, George (1824–95) II
COOPER, Robert (1819–68) II
COOPER, William (1822–68) I
COPPOCK, Sir Richard (1885–1971) III
CORMACK, William Sloan (1898–1973) III
COULTHARD, Samuel (1853–1931) II
COURT, Sir Josiah (1841–1938) I
COWEN, Joseph (1829–1900) I
COWEY, Edward (Ned) (1839–1903) I
CRABTREE, James (1831–1917) I
CRAIG, Edward Thomas (1804–94) I
CRAWFORD, William (1833–90) I
CROOKS, William (1852–1921) II
CURRAN, Peter (Pete) Francis (1860–1910) IV

DAGGAR, George (1879–1950) III
DALLAS, George (1878–1961) IV
DALLAWAY, William (1857–1939) I
DALY, James (?–1849) I
DARCH, Charles Thomas (1876–1934) I
DAVIES, Margaret Llewelyn (1861–1944) I
DAVISON, John (1846–1930) I
DEAKIN, Arthur (1890–1955) II
DEAKIN, Charles (1864–1941) III
DEAKIN, Jane (1869–1942) III
DEAKIN, Joseph Thomas (1858–1937) III
DEAN, Benjamin (1839–1910) I
DEAN, Frederick James (1868–1941) II
DEANS, James (1843/4?–1935) I
DEANS, Robert (1904–59) I
DENT, John James (1856–1936) I
DILKE, Emily (Emilia) Francis Strong, Lady (1840–1904) III
DIXON, John (1828–76) I
DIXON, John (1850–1914) IV
DOCKER, Abraham (1788/91?–1857) II
DRAKE, Henry John (1878–1934) I
DREW, William Henry (Harry) (1854–1933) IV
DUDLEY, Sir William Edward (1868–1938) I
DUNCAN, Andrew (1898–1965) II
DUNCAN, Charles (1865–1933) II
DUNN, Edward (1880–1945) III

DUNNING, Thomas Joseph (1799–1873) II
DYE, Sidney (1900–58) I
DYSON, James (1822/3–1902) I

EADES, Arthur (1863–1933) II
EDWARDS, Alfred (1888–1958) IV
EDWARDS, Allen Clement (1869–1938) III
EDWARDS, Enoch (1852–1912) I
EDWARDS, John Charles (1833–81) I
EDWARDS, Wyndham Ivor (1878–1938) I
ENFIELD, Alice Honora (1882–1935) I
EVANS, Isaac (1847?–97) I
EVANS, Jonah (1826–1907) I
EWART, Richard (1904–53) IV

FALLOWS, John Arthur (1864–1935) II
FENWICK, Charles (1850–1918) I
FINCH, John (1784–1857) I
FINLEY, Lawrence (Larry) (1909–74) IV
FINNEY, Samuel (1857–1935) I
FISHWICK, Jonathan (1832–1908) I
FLANAGAN, James Aloysius (1876–1935) III
FLANAGAN, James Desmond (1912–69) IV
FLEMING, Robert (1869–1939) I
FLYNN, Charles Richard (1883–1957) III
FORMAN, John (1822/3–1900) I
FOSTER, William (1887–1947) I
FOULGER, Sydney (1863–1919) I
FOWE, Thomas (1832/3?–94) I
FOX, James Challinor (1837–77) I
FOX, Thomas (Tom) (1860–1934) II
FRITH, John (1837–1904) I

GALBRAITH, Samuel (1853–1936) I
GALLAGHER, Patrick (Paddy the Cope) (1871–1966) I
GANLEY, Caroline Selina (1879–1966) I
GEE, Allen (1852–1939) III
GIBBS, Charles (1843–1909) II
GIBSON, Arthur Lummis (1899–1959) III
GILL, Alfred Henry (1856–1914) II
GILLILAND, James (1866–1952) IV
GILLIS, William (1859–1929) III
GLOVER, Thomas (1852–1913) I
GOLIGHTLY, Alfred William (1857–1948) I
GOODY, Joseph (1816/17–91) I
GOSLING, Harry (1861–1930) IV
GRAHAM, Duncan MacGregor (1867–1942) I

GRAY, Jesse Clement (1854–1912) I
GREENALL, Thomas (1857–1937) I
GREENING, Edward Owen (1836–1923) I
GREENWOOD, Abraham (1824–1911) I
GREENWOOD, Joseph (1833–1924) I
GRIFFITHS, George Arthur (1878–1945) III
GROVES, William Henry (1876–1933) II
GRUNDY, Thomas Walter (1864–1942) III
GUEST, John (1867–1931) III

HACKETT, Thomas (1869–1950) II
HADFIELD, Charles (1821–84) II
HALL, Frank (1861–1927) I
HALL, Fred (1855–1933) II
HALL, Fred (1878–1938) I
HALL, George Henry (1st Viscount Hall of Cynon Valley) (1881–1965) II
HALL, Joseph Arthur (Joe) (1887–1964) II
HALL, Thomas George (1858–1938) II
HALLAM, William (1856–1902) I
HALLAS, Eldred (1870–1926) II
HALLIDAY, Thomas (Tom) (1835–1919) III
HALSTEAD, Robert (1858–1930) II
HANCOCK, John George (1857–1940) II
HANDS, Thomas (1858–1938) II
HARDERN, Francis (Frank) (1846–1913) I
HARES, Edward Charles (1897–1966) I
HARRIS, Samuel (1855–1915) III
HARRISON, Frederic (1831–1923) II
HARRISON, James (1899–1959) II
HARTLEY, Edward Robertshaw (1855–1918) III
HARTSHORN, Vernon (1872–1931) I
HARVEY, William Edwin (1852–1914) I
HASLAM, James (1842–1913) I
HASLAM, James (1869–1937) I
HAWKINS, George (1844–1908) I
HAYHURST, George (1862–1936) I
HAYWARD, Sir Fred (1876–1944) I
HEADLAM, Stewart Duckworth (1847–1924) II
HENDERSON, Arthur (1863–1935) I
HEPBURN, Thomas (1796–1864) III
HERRIOTTS, John (1874–1935) III
HETHERINGTON, Henry (1792–1849) I
HIBBERT, Charles (1828–1902) I
HICKEN, Henry (1882–1964) I
HICKS, Amelia (Amie) Jane (1839/40?–1917) IV

HILL, John (1862–1945) III
HILTON, James (1814–90) I
HINDEN, Rita (1909–71) II
HINES, George Lelly (1839–1914) I
HIRST, George Henry (1868–1933) III
HOBSON, John Atkinson (1858–1940) I
HODGE, John (1855–1937) III
HOLBERRY, Samuel (1814–42) IV
HOLE, James (1820–95) II
HOLLIDAY, Jessie (1884–1915) III
HOLYOAKE, Austin (1826–74) I
HOLYOAKE, George Jacob (1817–1906) I
HOOSON, Edward (1825–69) I
HOPKIN, Daniel (1886–1951) IV
HOSKIN, John (1862–1935) IV
HOUGH, Edward (1879–1952) III
HOUSE, William (1854–1917) II
HOWARTH, Charles (1814–68) I
HOWELL, George (1833–1910) II
HUCKER, Henry (1871–1954) II
HUDSON, Walter (1852–1935) II
HUGHES, Edward (1854–1917) II
HUGHES, Hugh (1878–1932) I
HUTCHINGS, Harry (1864–1930) II

IRONSIDE, Isaac (1808–70) II

JACKSON, Henry (1840–1920) I
JACKSON, Thomas Alfred (1879–1955) IV
JARVIS, Henry (1839–1907) I
JENKINS, Hubert (1866–1943) I
JENKINS, John Hogan (1852–1936) IV
JOHN, William (1878–1955) I
JOHNS, John Ernest (1855/6–1928) II
JOHNSON, Henry (1869–1939) II
JOHNSON, John (1850–1910) I
JOHNSON, William (1849–1919) II
JONES, Benjamin (1847–1942) I
JONES, Patrick Lloyd (1811–86) I
JUGGINS, Richard (1843–95) I
JUPP, Arthur Edward (1906–73) IV

KANE, John (1819–76) III
KELLEY, George Davy (1848–1911) II
KENYON, Barnet (1850–1930) I
KILLON, Thomas (1853–1931) I
KING, William (1786–1865) I

LACEY, James Philip Durnford (1881–1974) III
LANG, James (1870–1966) I
LANSBURY, George (1859–1940) II

LAST, Robert (1829– ?) III
LAWRENCE, Arabella Susan (1871–1947) III
LAWSON, John James (Lord Lawson of Beamish) (1881–1965) II
LEE, Frank (1867–1941) I
LEE, Peter (1864–1935) II
LEES, James (1806–91) I
LEICESTER, Joseph Lynn (1825–1903) III
LEWIS, Richard James (1900–66) I
LEWIS, Thomas (Tommy) (1873–1962) I
LEWIS, Walter Samuel (1894–1962) III
LIDDLE, Thomas (1863–1954) I
LINDGREN, George Samuel (Lord Lindgren of Welwyn Garden City) (1900–71) II
LOCKWOOD, Arthur (1883–1966) II
LONGDEN, Fred (1886–1952) II
LOVETT, Levi (1854–1929) II
LOWERY, Matthew Hedley (1858–1918) I
LOWERY, Robert (1809–63) IV
LUDLOW, John Malcolm Forbes (1821–1911) II
LUNN, William (Willie) (1872–1942) II

MACARTHUR, Mary (1880–1921) II
MACDONALD, Alexander (1821–81) I
MacDONALD, James Ramsay (1866–1937) I
MACDONALD, Roderick (1840–94) IV
McGHEE, Henry George (1898–1959) I
McSHANE, Annie (1888–1962) IV
MADDISON, Fred (1856–1937) IV
MANN, Amos (1855–1939) I
MARCROFT, William (1822–94) I
MARLOW, Arnold (1891–1939) I
MARTIN, James (1850–1933) I
MAXWELL, Sir William (1841–1929) I
MAY, Henry John (1867–1939) I
MELLOR, William (1888–1942) IV
MERCER, Thomas William (1884–1947) I
MESSER, Sir Frederick (Fred) (1886–1971) II
MIDDLETON, Dora Miriam (1897–1972) IV
MIDDLETON, George Edward (1866–1931) II
MILLERCHIP, William (1863–1939) I
MILLINGTON, Joseph (1866–1952) II
MILLINGTON, William Greenwood (1850–1906) III
MITCHELL, John Thomas Whitehead (1828–95) I

MITCHISON, Gilbert Richard (Baron Mitchison of Carradale) (1890–1970) II
MOLESWORTH, William Nassau (1816–90) I
MOORHOUSE, Thomas Edwin (1854–1922) I
MORGAN, David (Dai o'r Nant) (1840–1900) I
MORGAN, David Watts (1867–1933) I
MORGAN, John Minter (1782–1854) I
MORLEY, Iris Vivienne (1910–53) IV
MUDIE, George (1788?–?) I
MURNIN, Hugh (1865–1932) II
MURRAY, Robert (1869–1950) I
MYCOCK, William Salter (1872–1950) III

NEALE, Edward Vansittart (1810–92) I
NEWCOMB, William Alfred (1849–1901) III
NEWTON, William (1822–76) II
NOEL, Conrad le Despenser Roden (1869–1942) II
NORMANSELL, John (1830–75) I
NUTTALL, William (1835–1905) I

OAKEY, Thomas (1887–1953) IV
O'GRADY, Sir James (1866–1934) II
OLIVER, John (1861–1942) I
ONIONS, Alfred (1858–1921) I

PALIN, John Henry (1870–1934) IV
PARE, William (1805–73) I
PARKER, James (1863–1948) II
PARKINSON, John Allen (1870–1941) II
PARKINSON, Tom Bamford (1865–1939) I
PARROTT, William (1843–1905) II
PASSFIELD, 1st Baron Passfield of Passfield Corner. See WEBB, Sidney James II
PATTERSON, William Hammond (1847–96) I
PATTISON, Lewis (1873–1956) I
PEASE, Edward Reynolds (1857–1955) II
PEASE, Mary Gammell (Marjory) (1861–1950) II
PENNY, John (1870–1938) I
PERKINS, George Reynolds (1885–1961) I
PETCH, Arthur William (1886–1935) IV
PICKARD, Benjamin (1842–1904) I
PICKARD, William (1821–87) I
PICTON-TURBERVILL, Edith (1872–1960) IV
PIGGOTT, Thomas (1836–87) II

PITMAN, Henry (1826–1909) I
POINTER, Joseph (1875–1914) II
POLLARD, William (1832/3?–1909) I
POLLITT, James (1857–1935) III
POOLE, Stephen George (1862–1924) IV
POSTGATE, Daisy (1892–1971) II
POSTGATE, Raymond William (1896–1971) II
POTTS, John Samuel (1861–1938) II
PRATT, Hodgson (1824–1907) I
PRICE, Gabriel (1879–1934) III
PRINGLE, William Joseph Sommerville (1916–62) II
PRYDE, David Johnstone (1890–1959) II
PURCELL, Albert Arthur (1872–1935) I

RAE, William Robert (1858–1936) II
RAMSEY, Thomas (Tommy) (1810/11–73) I
READE, Henry Musgrave (1860–?) III
REDFERN, Percy (1875–1958) I
REED, Richard Bagnall (1831–1908) IV
REEVES, Samuel (1862–1930) I
REEVES, William Pember (1857–1932) II
REYNOLDS, George William MacArthur (1814–79) III
RICHARDS, Thomas (1859–1931) I
RICHARDS, Thomas Frederick (Freddy) (1863–1942) III
RICHARDSON, Robert (1862–1943) II
RICHARDSON, Thomas (Tom) (1868–1928) IV
RICHARDSON, William Pallister (1873–1930) III
RITSON, Joshua (Josh) (1874–1955) II
ROBERTS, George Henry (1868–1928) IV
ROBINSON, Charles Leonard (1845–1911) III
ROBINSON, Richard (1879–1937) I
ROBSON, James (1860–1934) II
ROBSON, John (1862–1929) II
ROEBUCK, Samuel (1871–1924) IV
ROGERS, Frederick (1846–1915) I
ROGERSON, William Matts (1873–1940) III
ROWLINSON, George Henry (1852–1937) I
ROWSON, Guy (1883–1937) II
RUST, Henry (1831–1902) II
RUTHERFORD, John Hunter (1826–90) I

SAMUELSON, James (1829–1918) II

SCHOFIELD, Thomas (1825–79) II
SCURR, John (1876–1932) IV
SEDDON, James Andrew (1868–1939) II
SEWELL, William (1852–1948) I
SHACKLETON, Sir David James (1863–1938) II
SHAFTOE, Samuel (1841–1911) III
SHALLARD, George (1877–1958) I
SHANN, George (1876–1919) II
SHARP, Andrew (1841–1919) I
SHAW, Fred (1881–1951) IV
SHEPPARD, Frank (1861–1956) III
SHIELD, George William (1876–1935) III
SHILLITO, John (1832–1915) I
SHURMER, Percy Lionel Edward (1888–1959) II
SIMPSON, Henry (1866–1937) III
SIMPSON, James (1826–95) I
SIMPSON, William Shaw (1829–83) II
SITCH, Charles Henry (1887–1960) II
SITCH, Thomas (1852–1923) I
SKEVINGTON, John (1801–50) I
SLOAN, Alexander (Sandy) (1879–1945) II
SMILLIE, Robert (1857–1940) III
SMITH, Albert (1867–1942) III
SMITH, Alfred (1877–1969) III
SMITH, Herbert (1862–1938) II
SMITHIES, James (1819–69) I
SPARKES, Malcolm (1881–1933) II
SPENCER, George Alfred (1873–1957) I
SPENCER, John Samuel (1868–1943) I
STANLEY, Albert (1862–1915) I
STANTON, Charles Butt (1873–1946) I
STEAD, Francis Herbert (1857–1928) IV
STEVENS, John Valentine (1852–1925) II
STEWART, Aaron (1845–1910) I
STRAKER, William (1855–1941) II
STOTT, Benjamin (1813–50) IV
SULLIVAN, Joseph (1866–1935) II
SUMMERBELL, Thomas (1861–1910) IV
SUTHERS, Robert Bentley (1870–1950) IV
SUTTON, John Edward (Jack) (1862–1945) III
SWAN, John Edmund (1877–1956) III
SWANWICK, Helena Maria Lucy (1864–1939) IV
SWEET, James (1804/5?–79) IV
SWIFT, Fred (1874–1959) II
SWINGLER, Stephen Thomas (1915–69) III
SYLVESTER, George Oscar (1898–1961) III

TAYLOR, John Wilkinson (1855–1934) I
TAYLOR, Robert Arthur (1886–1934) IV
TEER, John (1809?–1883?) IV
THICKETT, Joseph (1865–1938) II
THORNE, William James (1857–1946) I
THORPE, George (1854–1945) I
TILLETT, Benjamin (Ben) (1860–1943) IV
TOOTILL, Robert (1850–1934) II
TOPHAM, Edward (1894–1966) I
TORKINGTON, James (1811–67) II
TOYN, Joseph (1838–1924) II
TRAVIS, Henry (1807–84) I
TROTTER, Thomas Ernest Newlands (1871–1932) III
TROW, Edward (1833–99) III
TWEDDELL, Thomas (1839–1916) I
TWIGG, Herbert James Thomas (1900–57) I
TWIST, Henry (Harry) (1870–1934) II

VARLEY, Frank Bradley (1885–1929) II
VEITCH, Marian (1913–73) III
VINCENT, Henry (1813–78) I
VIVIAN, Henry Harvey (1868–1930) I

WADSWORTH, John (1850–1921) I
WALKER, Benjamin (1803/4?–83) I
WALLHEAD, Richard [Christopher] Collingham (1869–1934) III
WALSH, Stephen (1859–1929) IV
WALSHAM, Cornelius (1880–1958) I
WARD, John (1866–1934) IV
WARDLE, George James (1865–1947) II
WARNE, George Henry (1881–1928) IV
WATKINS, William Henry (1862–1924) I
WATSON, William (1849–1901) III
WATTS, John (1818–87) I
WEBB, Beatrice (1858–1943) II
WEBB, Catherine (1859–1947) II
WEBB, Sidney James (1st Baron Passfield of Passfield Corner) (1859–1947) II
WEBB, Simeon (1864–1929) I
WEBB, Thomas Edward (1829–96) I
WEIR, John (1851–1908) I
WEIR, William (1868–1926) II
WELSH, James C. (1880–1954) II
WESTWOOD, Joseph (1884–1948) II
WHITE, Arthur Daniel (1881–1961) III
WHITEFIELD, William (1850–1926) II
WHITEHEAD, Alfred (1862–1945) I

WHITEHOUSE, Samuel Henry (1849–1919) IV
WHITELEY, William (1881–1955) III
WIGNALL, James (1856–1925) III
WILKIE, Alexander (1850–1928) III
WILLIAMS, Aneurin (1859–1924) I
WILLIAMS, David James (1897–1972) IV
WILLIAMS, Sir Edward John (Ted) (1890–1963) III
WILLIAMS, John (1861–1922) I
WILLIAMS, Ronald Watkins (1907–58) II
WILLIAMS, Thomas (Tom) (Lord Williams of Barnburgh) (1888–1967) II

WILLIAMS, Thomas Edward (Baron Williams of Ynyshir) (1892–1966) III
WILLIS, Frederick Ebenezer (1869–1953) II
WILSON, John (1837–1915) I
WILSON, John (1856–1918) II
WILSON, Joseph Havelock (1858–1929) IV
WILSON, William Tyson (1855–1921) III
WINSTONE, James (1863–1921) I
WINWOOD, Benjamin (1844–1913) II
WOODS, Samuel (1846–1915) I
WORLEY, Joseph James (1876–1944) I
WRIGHT, Oliver Walter (1886–1938) I
WYLD, Albert (1888–1965) II

General Index

Compiled by Barbara Nield with assistance
from V. J. Morris, G. D. Weston and Joyce Bellamy.
Numbers in bold type refer to biographical entries

Abbeyfield Society, 49
Adams, David, **1–2**
Adams, William Edwin, 145
Adamson, Janet (Jennie) Laurel, **2–4**
Adamson, William Murdoch, 2, 3, 4
Addams, Jane, 162
Addison, Dr Christopher (*later* 1st Viscount Addison of Stallingborough), 189
Admiralty, 49; Royal Dockyard Discharges, 109
Agricultural Wages Board, 70
Agricultural Wholesale Society, 57
Airedale College, Bradford, 161
'Ajax' (pseud.): *see* Besant, Annie
Aldridge, (Harold Edward) James, 131
Allan, William, 10
Allen, James, 94
Allen, Reginald Clifford (*later* 1st Baron Allen of Hurtwood), 123, 155
Allenby, Edmund (Henry Hyndman) (*later* 1st Viscount Allenby of Megiddo and of Felixstowe), 96
Allied Engineering Trades Federation, 158
Allotments movement, 57
Amalgamated Association of Tramway and Vehicle Workers, 135
Amalgamated Engineering Union, 54, 80, 81, 158, 159
Amalgamated Marine Workers' Union, 205, 206
Amalgamated Society of Dyers, 45, 70
Amalgamated Society of Engineers, 1, 8, 9, 10, 11, 124, 157
Amalgamated Society of Railway Servants, 68, 120, 135, 201
Amalgamated Society of Watermen and Lightermen, 84, 85, 86, 183
Amalgamated Stevedores' Union, 178
Amalgamated Union of Co-operative Employees, 136, 137; Manchester Federation of, 136
Amalgamated Union of Foundry Workers, 53, 54
American Convention of Labor (1894), 90
American Federation of Labor, 149
American Revolution, 113

Anderson, James, 85–6
Anderson, John, 8
Andover, 190, 192
Annand, James, 145
Anthracite Miners' Combine Committee, 198
Anti-Corn Law League, 6
Anti-Semitism, 102
Appleton, William Archibald, 149, 192
Argosy, 63
Argus (South Shields), 165
Army Education Corps, 111
Arnold, Alice, **4–6**
Ashington, 193–4
Ashton, Margaret, 169
Ashton-in-Makerfield, 187–8
Asquith, Herbert Henry (*later* 1st Earl of Oxford and Asquith), 181
Associated Shipwrights' Society, 109, 110
Association of Municipal Corporations, 49
Association of Operative Bleachers, Dyers and Finishers (Bolton Amalgamation), 45
Association of Registered Medical Women, 20
Association of Supervisory Staffs, Executives and Technicians, 49
Ataturk, Mustafa Kemal, 139
Atholl, Katharine Marjory, Duchess of, 73
Atlantic Pact, 199
Attlee, Clement Richard (*later* 1st Earl Attlee), 47, 184
Attwood, Charles Matthias, 112
Australia, 179, 180, 181
Authors, influence of
  Addison, Joseph, 177; Austen, Jane, 104; Barrie, James, 50; Beattie, James, 177; Blair, Robert, 177; Blatchford, Robert, 69, 100, 165; Booth, William, 165; Buckle, Henry Thomas, 157, 188; Bunyan, John, 34, 148, 188; Burns, Robert, 13, 112, 148, 193; Carlyle, Thomas, 35, 153, 177, 188, 193; Cervantes Saavedra, Miguel de, 188; Cobbett, William, 34, 35; Comte, Auguste, 21, 157; Darwin, Charles, 21, 100, 148, 157, 177; Dickens, Charles, 34, 148, 165, 188; Dietzgen, Joseph, 198; Drummond, Henry, 148; Dumas, Alexandre, 129, 188; Eddy, Mary Baker, 77; Emerson, Ralph Waldo,

Authors, influence of—*contd.*
35; Engels, Friedrich, 100, 103; Frazer, Sir James George, 100; George, Henry, 8, 22, 165; Gibbon, Edward, 104, 157; Haeckel, Ernst Heinrich, 39; Hardy, Thomas, 13, 69; Hazlitt, William, 177; Hird, Dennis, 193; Hugo, Victor, 188; Huxley, Thomas Henry, 177; Hyndman, Henry Mayers, 35; Johnson, Samuel, 177; Keats, John, 193; Khayyam, Omar, 35; Kidd, Benjamin, 148; Kingsley, Rev. Charles, 153; Knowlton, Charles, 22, 23; Kropotkin, Prince Peter Alexeivitch, 190; Lamb, Charles, 177; Lenin, Vladimir Il'ich, 103, 129; Lewes, George Henry, 100; Lowell, Russell, 148; Luxemburg, Rosa, 198; Macaulay, Thomas Babington, Lord, 153, 157; Malthus, Thomas Robert, 23; Marx, Karl, 8, 80, 100, 103. 129, 198; Massey, Gerald, 148; Mazzini, Joseph, 122; Mill, John Stuart, 21; Milton, John, 153; Morris, William, 8, 35, 69, 148; Newman, Henry, 177; Pope, Alexander, 177; Richmond, Rev. Wilfred, 161; Ruskin, John, 153, 177; Shakespeare, William, 188; Shaw, George Bernard, 50; Shelley, Percy Bysshe, 148, 164, 193; Smiles, Samuel, 35, 165; Spencer, Herbert, 157, 177; Spinoza, Benedict de, 21; Strachey, John, 129; Tolstoy, Leo, 161; Twain, Mark, 188; Whitman, Walt, 148; Winstanley, Gerrard, 130; Wordsworth, William, 177. *See also Bible*
'Autolycus' (pseud.): *see* Petch, Arthur William
Auxiliary Territorial Service, 175
Aveling, Edward Bibbins, 22, 23, 24
Aveling, Eleanor: *see* Marx, Eleanor

Bakers' Society, 109
Ballancé, James, 134
Ballot Society, 145
Barber, Jonathan, **6–7**
Barnes, George Nicoll, **7–15**, 66, 68, 189
Barnsley, 46, 66–7, 68. *See also* Parliamentary Constituencies
Barnsley Chronicle, 46
Barrett, Rowland, **15–16**, 141
Bartley, James, 35, 76
Bateman, George, 191
Battley, John Rose, **16–18**
Bax, Ernest Belfort, 24
Beacon, 197
Beard, John, 71
Beaumont, Hubert, 45
Beckett, John, 47
Beddows, Rev. F. Seaward, 16
Bedfordshire Mercury, 15
Belfast, 2

Bell, Richard, 120, 148, 149, 192
Bell's Life, 35
Benedict, Sir Julius, 52
Beniowski, Major Bartłomiej, 114
Bentham, Dr Ethel, **18–20**
Bentham, Jeremy, 19
Besant, Annie, **21–31**, 154, 191
Besant, Digby, 21
Besant, Rev. Frank, 21, 23
Besant, Mabel, 21, 23
Besant, Walter, 21
Besterman, Theodore, 28
Betts, Barbara: *see* Castle, Barbara
Betts, Frank, 124
Bevan, Aneurin, 73, 125, 126, 198
Beveridge Report on Social Insurance and Allied Services (1943), 3
Bevin, Ernest, 4, 40, 71, 87, 88, 89, 124, 125, 182, 183, 184, 206
Bible, influence of, 34, 77, 99, 193
Bi-metallism, 76
Bingley, Henry William, 50
Birks, James, 95
Birth control, 22, 23, 150–1
Black, Clementina, 90
'Black Friday' (15 Apr 1921), 88
Bland, Hubert, 24
Blatchford, Dorothea Glanville, 34, 40
Blatchford, Louisa, 31–2, 34
Blatchford, Montagu John, **31–3**, 34, 36, 37, 167
Blatchford, Robert Corri, 38, 40
Blatchford, Robert Peel Glanville, 31, 32, **34–42**, 166–7. *See also* Authors
Blatchford, William, 31–2
Blatchford, Winifrid Norris, 38, 39, 40, 167
Blavatsky, Helena Petrovna, 27
Blindness, Departmental Cttee on Causes and Prevention of, 150
Blundell, Henry Blundell-Hollinshead, 188
Blyth, Alexander, **42–3**
Board of Trade, 79, 86, 149; Departmental Cttee on Merchant Shipping (Life Saving Appliances) Act of 1888, 201; Labour Correspondents, 121
Boards of Arbitration and Conciliation, 70. *See also* Mining
Boards of Guardians
Bradford, 76, 135; Cardiff, 110; Chester-le-Street, 146; Cleveland, 79; Clutton, 197; Hackney, 48; Hemsworth, 47; Lincoln, 2; Pontardawe, 198; Poplar, 154; Stepney, 154
Boer War, attitudes to, 17, 38–9, 60, 66, 69, 121, 191, 204
Boilermakers' Society: *see* Friendly Society of Boilermakers
Bolshevism: *see* Russia

Bonar, Dr James, 83
Bondfield, Margaret Grace, 28, 92, 110, 138
Bookbinders' Society: *see* Consolidated Union of Bookbinders
Booker, Thomas, 94
Booker, William, 94
Boon, David John, 110
Booth, Charles, 9
Boscawen, Griffith: *see* Griffith-Boscawen, Sir Arthur
'Bounder, The' (pseud.): *see* Fay, Edward Francis
Bow and Bromley Institute, 177
Bowerman, Charles William, 12, 180
Brace, William, 189
Braddell, Maurice, 128
Braddell, Sir Thomas de Multon Lee, 128
Bradford, 39, 45, 76, 135, 180; Social Reform Union, 76; Unemployed Emergency Cttee, 76
Bradford Labour Union, 35, 76
Bradford Pioneer, 124
Bradlaugh, Charles, 21, 22, 23, 24, 25–6, 27, 99, 177
Brailsford, Henry Noel, 125
Bristol, 182; Socialist Society, 182
Bristol, West of England and South Wales Trade Operatives, 65
British Ally, 63
British Association, 52
British Federation of Co-operative Youth, 111
British Legion, 47, 49, 192
British Medical Association, 20
British Red Cross Society, 118
British Seafarers' Union, 203, 205
British Socialist Party, 15, 39, 91, 157, 158, 181. *See also* Social Democratic Federation
British-Soviet Friendship Society, 132
British Union of Fascists, 47
British Workers' League, 141, 189, 204
British Workers' National League: *see* British Workers' League
Broadhead, Samuel, **44**
Brooke, Willie, **45**
Brooks, Canon Joshua William, 7
Brown, B. W., 201
Brown, George Alfred: *see* George-Brown, Baron
Brown, Ivor John Carnegie, 123
Browning Hall Mission (*later* Settlement), 9, 161–2
Brownlie, James Thomas, 149
Buchman, Frank Nathan Daniel, 183
Bulgaria, 59
Burne-Jones, Sir Edward Coley, 169
Burnett, John, 201
Burns, Isaac, **46**–7, 67

Burns, John Elliot, 8, 35, 85, 89, 90, 178, 179, 184, 190, 191
Burrows, Herbert, 22, 26, 89
Burt, Thomas, 43
Butler, Harold Beresford (*later* Sir), 12
Butler, Herbert William, **47–50**
Buxton, Charles Roden, 170
Byron, Kathleen, 133

Cadbury, Elizabeth, 140
Callaghan, (Leonard) James, 49
Cambridge University, Girton College, 169; St Catherine's College, 96
Campaign for Nuclear Disarmament, 199
Campbell, George Lamb, **50–2**
Campbell, J. R. (Johnny), 107
Campbell, Sir John, 94
Canada, 10, 76, 80, 82, 116, 147, 175, 197
Cardiff, 109–10
Cardiff Shipwrights' Society, 109
Carmarthen, 96
Carson, Edward Henry (*later* Baron Carson of Duncairn [Life Peer]), 179
Carstairs, Peter, 144
Casasola, Rowland (Roland) William, **52–5**
Casey, Fred, 105
Castle, Barbara (Anne), 124, 125
Castleford, 133–4
Catholic Herald, 79
Cattle Committee, 72. *See also* Livestock Commission
Central Democratic Committee (London School Board election, 1888), 191
Central Labour College, 45, 123, 159, 198
Chainmakers' Union: *see* Operative Chain Makers' Union (Newcastle upon Tyne)
Challenge to Britain, 54
Chamberlain, (Arthur) Neville, 57, 189
Chamberlain, Joseph, 39
Chamberlain, Sir (Joseph) Austen, 10
Champion, Henry Hyde, 89, 178, 191
Charlton, William Browell, **55–6**
Charter, 112, 142, 143, 164
Chartism, 37, 89, 93–5, 142, 143, 164, 176
  Conventions: (1839), 113; (1842), 114
  in Carlisle, 112, 113; Cornwall, 113; Lancashire, 113; London, 112; Manchester, 164; Newcastle, 112–16; North Midlands, 113; Nottingham, 6, 171, 172; Scotland, 112, 113, 114; Sheffield, 93–5; South Yorks., 93–5, 113
  Land Company, 172
  Newport Rising, 93, 113
  Plug Plot (1842), 164, 171, 176
Chater, Daniel (Dan), **56–8**
Chicago, 162

China, 73
Christian Socialism, 16, 26, 97, 109, 161; Christian Socialist League, 69
Chronicle and Echo [Northampton], 72
Churches and religious groups
   Baptist, 17, 93, 97; Christian Evidence Society, 22; Christian Scientist, 77; Church of England, 7, 20, 113, 120, 135, 138, 187; Congregational, 33, 75, 161, 162, 177–8; Episcopalian, 7; Free Church, 117; Methodist, 45, 80, 83, 113, 159, 200: Primitive Methodist, 112, 147, 152, Wesleyan Methodist, 56, 162, 109; Roman Catholic, 9, 47, 65, 78, 79, 118, 134, 155, 176, 187; Society of Friends (Quakers), 20, 115; Theosophical Society, 27, 28; Unitarian, 122, 123. *See also* Christian Socialism; Labour Church; Spiritualism; Theosophy
Churchill, Sir Winston Leonard Spencer, 57, 195
Citrine, Walter (*later* 1st Baron Citrine of Wembley), 158
Civil Wars, English, 129, 130, 132
Clapham, 17, 18
Clarion, 31, 32, 36, 37, 38, 39, 40, 69, 167
Clarion Movement, 32, 37, 38, 39, 40; Cinderella Clubs, 37; Cycling Clubs, 37, 157, 159; Fellowship, 37, 39; Field Clubs, 37; Holiday Camps, 37; *Scout*, 37, 157; Vans, 37, 57; Vocal Unions, 32, 33, 37
Clark, Gavin Brown, **59–61**
Clark, Sir George Norman, 123
Clark, James, **62**
Clarke, Frank Edward, 3
Claxton, James (Jim), 80
Clayton, John, 94, 95
Clifton, Sir Robert, 172
Clynes, John Robert, 150, 182, 195
Coalition Governments: (1915–16), 149; (1916–18), 11, 12, 149, 189; (1940–5), 77
'Cogers', 81
Cold War, 58, 131, 199
Cole, George Douglas Howard, 123, 124, 125
Cole, Margaret Isabel (*later* Dame), 36, 37
Coleridge, John Duke, 75
Collieries: Aldwarke Main (Yorks.), 98; Baddesley (Warwick), 74; Burnhope (Durham), 62; Chapel Pit (Yorks.), 44; Darfield Main (Yorks.), 152; Darton Main (Yorks.), 152; Denaby Main (Yorks.), 74; Do Well (Derbys.), 98; Dudley (Northumberland), 42; Edmondsley (Durham), 55; Felton (Durham), 62; Fryston (Yorks.), 133, 134; Garswood Hall (Lancs.), 188; Glass Houghton (Yorks.), 133, 134; Gwaun-cae-Gurwen (S. Wales), 198; Haigh Moor (Yorks.), 133; Hamsteels (Durham), 55; Hartley (Northumberland), 42; Haydock (Lancs.), 51; Hetton (Durham), 55; Lintz Green (Durham), 83; Littleburn (Durham), 55; Mitchell's Main (Yorks.), 152; Montague Main (Northumberland), 195; Ouston 'E' (Durham), 83; Pewfall (Lancs.), 187; Rawmarsh (Yorks.), 44; Robin Hood (Yorks.), 44; Roundwood (Yorks.), 98; Seaham (Durham), 55; Shankhouse (Northumberland), 193; South Kirby (Yorks.), 46; Usworth (Durham), 55; Washington (Durham), 146; Westwood (Durham), 62; Whitburn (Durham), 78; Woodhorn (Northumberland), 193–4
Collins, John, 114
Collison, Rev. W., 7
Collison, William, 202
Coloured Women, Committee for Protection of, 20
Comintern: *see* International, Third
Commission for World Labour, 12
Common Cause, 169
Commonweal, 90
Communism, 101, 106, 192, 199, 207
Communist, 103
Communist Party of Great Britain, 46, 48, 50, 53, 54, 55, 79, 80, 81, 103, 104, 105, 106, 107, 124, 125, 126, 132, 158; Unity Convention, London (1920), 158, Leeds (1921), 103
Communist Party of the Soviet Union, 103
Communist Party (U.S.A.), 129
Communist Review, 104
Complete Suffrage Union, 114
Comrades of the Great War (*later* British Legion), 47
Condor, Rev. G. W., 7
Confederation of Shipbuilding and Engineering Unions, 54
Connolly, Cyril (Vernon), 63
Connolly, James, 102
Conscientious Objection: *see* First World War; Second World War; and *see also* No More War Movement; Peace Pledge Union *and* War Resisters' International
Conscription, 40, 70, 122, 124, 189, 199
Conservative Party, 40, 78, 150, 174, 191, 192
Consolidated Union of Bookbinders, 9, 164
Contagious Diseases Acts: *see* Parliamentary Acts
Conway, Ellen Dana, 21
Conway, Moncure Daniel, 21
Cook, Alfred George, 27
Cook, Arthur James, 46, 48, 49
Cook, Sam, 171
Cook, William, 143

Cooks' and Stewards' Union, 203
Coombes, Bert Lewis (Louis), **62–5**
Cooper, Robert, 7
Co-operative College, Manchester, 82, 111
Co-operative Comrades' Circles, 111. *See also* British Federation of Co-operative Youth
Co-operative Congress: *Post-Rochdale* 1960, Blackpool, 111
Co-operative Dry Goods Trade Association, 111
Co-operative Insurance Society, 127
Co-operative Political Council, 48
Co-operative Printing Society, 13
Co-operative Productive Federation, 111
Co-operative Societies: *Post-Rochdale* Brandon, 56; Chelsea and Fulham, 8; Coventry and District, 5, 141; Eccles Provident Industrial, 136, 137; Huddersfield, 159; Lincoln, 2; London, 57, 111, 147; Norwich, 148; Park Lane (Ashton-in-Makerfield), 188, 189; Royal Arsenal, 3, 8; Walsall, 127; Wigan, 189
Co-operative Union, 81, 82, 111
Co-operative Women's Guild: *see* Women's Co-operative Guild
Co-operators and local government, 57, 118, 119, 127, 136; and religion, 118
Corri, Clarence, 36
Cotter, Joe, 203, 205, 206
Coulton, George Gordon, 122
Council of Action for Peace and Reconstruction, 45
Courtneidge, Dame Cicely, 36
Courtneidge, Robert, 36
Cousins, Frank, 54
Coventry, 4, 5, 15, 140, 141
Coventry Sentinel, 15, 141
Cowen, Joseph, 142, 143, 144, 145, 146, 165
Cowey, Edward (Ned), 66
Crawfurd, Helen, 48
Cremer, Sir William Randal, 122
Cresswell, Gertrude, 127
Cripps, Sir (Richard) Stafford, 72, 125
Crooks, William, 10, 85, 148, 153
Cullington, Albert, 47, 48, 50
Cunninghame Graham, Robert Bontine, 8, 60
Curran v. Treleaven, 66
Curran, Peter (Pete) Francis, 46, **65–9**, 121, 191
Czechoslovakia, 72

Daily Citizen, 149
Daily Express, 131
Daily Herald, 20, 57, 123, 124, 125, 126, 154, 167, 175, 181, 183
Daily Herald League, 154
Daily Mail, 40

Daily Mirror, 64
Daily News, 169
Daily Post [Sunderland], 165
Daily Worker, 104, 106, 107, 128, 131, 132
Dallas, George, **69–74**
Dalton, Edward Hugh John Neale (*later* Baron Dalton of Forest and Frith [Life Peer]), 28, 72
'Dangle' (pseud.): *see* Thompson, Alexander Mattock
Daniel, Professor Glyn, 97
Davies, Rev. Charles Maurice, 22
Davies, William John, 206
Davis, Stanley Clinton, 49
Davis, William John, 149
Davitt, Michael, 65
Dawson, Julia, 37
Day, Anne, 106
Deakin, Arthur, 54, 184
De Mattos, W. S., 191
Democratic Federation, 59, 89
Demonstrations
    'Bloody Sunday' (Nov. 1887), 8, 26; Bulgarian Atrocities (Oct. 1876), 59; May Day (1926), 80; Unemployment (1885–6), 190–1, (1905), 162, (1908), 39
De Morgan, William, 169
Denaby and Cadeby Main Case, 98
Denmark, 139
Derby, Lord (16th Earl), 60
Derry, John, 121
Despard, Charlotte, 103
Deutsch, André, 132
Devonport, Lord (1st Viscount of Wittington), 85, 86, 181
Dickens, Charles, 99, 105, 163. *See also* Authors
'Disque' (pseud.): *see* Holyoake, George Jacob
Disraeli, Benjamin (*later* 1st Earl of Beaconsfield), 23, 59
Distributive Industry Training Board, 111
Divorce reform, 23, 169
Dixon, John, **74–5**, 99
Dobbie, William, 53
Dock Labour, Shaw Court of Enquiry into, 88, 182
Dock, Wharf, Riverside and General Labourers' Union (*later* . . . and General Workers' Union), 85, 109, 153, 179, 180, 181, 182, 183, 201
Dollan, Patrick Joseph (*later* Sir), 125
Doubleday, Thomas, 112, 142
Downham, Lord (1st Baron Downham of Fulham), 189
Drew, William Henry (Harry), **75–7**
Dublin, 19
Duffy, James, 94

Duncan, Abram, 112, 113
Duncombe, Thomas Slingsby, 163
Dunnico, Rev. Herbert (*later* Sir), 147, 170
Durham Aged Mineworkers' Homes Association, 56
Durham Coal Owners' Association, 56
Durham University, 117
Dyson, Levi, 134

East London Ropemakers' Union, 90
Eastern Question, 59, 145
Eccles, 136, 137
Eddy, Mary Baker, 77
Edinburgh, 114
Edinburgh University, 59, 117
Education, 20, 38, 89, 90, 109, 110–11, 112, 119, 123, 135, 140, 152, 155, 158, 159, 164, 174, 177, 187, 193, 197; Half-time, 140; Ragged Schools, 17. *See also* University Extension Movement; Workers' Educational Association
Edwards, Alfred, **77–8**
Edwards, Ebenezer (Ebby), 195
Edwards, Enoch, 197
Edwards, Ness, 198
Edwards, Walter James, 49
Egypt, 97, 145
Eight Hour Day Movement, 8, 66, 67, 119, 120, 206. *See also* London Joint Union Committee
Elias, J. S., 124
Employers' Federation of Engineering Associations, 8
Employers' Liability: *see* Parliamentary Acts *and* Select Committees
Engels, Friedrich, 80, 105
European Coal and Steel Community, 167
European Economic Community, 167
Ewart, Richard, **78–80**
Ewer, Monica, 124
Export Credits Scheme, 174

Fabian Research Committee, 123. *See also* Labour Research Department
Fabian Society, 1, 19, 24, 25, 26, 27, 28, 33, 35, 36, 59, 66, 97, 123, 154, 167, 191; and Boer War, 66
Fairplay, 202
Farrow, Sam, 80
Fascism, 47, 49
Fawcett, Millicent (*later* Dame), 138, 169
Fay, Edward Francis, 32, 35, 36, 167
Fellowship of Reconciliation, 17, 166
Fels, Joseph, 202
Female Charter Association, 95

Fenwick, Charles, 10, 194
Ferguson, John, 60
Finley, Lawrence (Larry), **80–1**
First World War, 28, 47, 53, 57, 60, 96, 134, 138, 166, 169, 196, 207; attitudes to, 10, 11, 17, 40, 46, 87, 88, 102, 123–4, 135, 141, 147, 149, 153, 157, 162, 167, 181, 189, 192, 194, 203, 204; Commission of Enquiry into Industrial Unrest, 11; conscientious objection, 11, 16, 17, 102, 147, 154, 157, 166, 194; conscription, 40, 70, 124, 189, Derby Scheme, 63; Jewish Regiment, 96; Parliamentary Munitions Cttee, 199; Pensions, 10, 11; Port and Transport Executive Cttee, 87; War Savings Cttee, 11; Wounded Allies Relief Cttee, 60. *See also* War Emergency Workers' National Committee
Flanagan, James Aloysius, 81
Flanagan, James Desmond, **81–2**
Fletcher, Christine, 32
Fliegende Blätter, 168
Foot, Michael, 125
Ford, Isabella, 138
Foreign Affairs, 170
Foreman, William, 120, 201
Formosa (Taiwan), 73
Fortnightly, 63
Forward, 60, 70
France, 113, 170; Paris Commune, 101; Revolution of 1848, 6
Free Library Movement, 52
Free Trade, 39, 109, 204
Freehold Land Movement, 115
Freemasonry, 49, 52, 146, 183
Freethought Publishing Company, 22, 23
French, Sir John (*later* 1st Earl of Ypres), 182
Friendly Societies, 148; Foresters, 75, 165; Good Templars, 59, 178; Oddfellows, National Independent, 164
Friendly Society of Boilermakers, 164
Friendly Society of Ironfounders, 53
Friends of Free China Association, 73
Frith, John, 44, 75, 98
Frost, John, 93
Fun, 32
Fyfe, Henry Hamilton, 124

Gaelic Society (London), 117
Galbraith, Samuel, 83
Gandhi, Mahatma, 28
Gardner, Jim, 55
Gardner, John (Jack), 201
Garibaldi, Giuseppe, 145
Geddes, Sir Auckland Campbell (*later* 1st Baron Geddes), 189

Gee, Allen, 76
General Federation of Trade Unions, 66, 68, 182, 192
General Labourers' National Council, 87
Geographical Magazine, 63
George, Henry, 35, 59, 65. *See also* Authors
George-Brown, Baron [Life Peer], 72
Germany, 1, 9, 40, 72, 79, 162, 167, 170, 181, 203, 204, 206; rearmament of, 54, 199
Gibbs, Sir Philip, 189
Gill, George, 172
Gilliland, James, **82–3**
Gladstone Clubs, 148
Gladstone, Herbert John (1st Viscount Gladstone), 148
Gladstone, William Ewart, 28, 59, 60, 99, 145, 179
Glasgow, 65, 69
Glasgow University, 59, 117, 161
Goff, Sir Park, 174
Gonne-Macbride, Maud, 103
Gosling, Harry, **83–9**, 183
Gould, Barbara Ayrton, 72
Graham, William, 139
Grand National Consolidated Trades Union, 112, 115
Grant, William, 163
Grayson, Victor, 39
Green, J.F., 66
Griffith, (Frank) Kingsley, 123
Griffith-Boscawen, Sir Arthur, 12–13, 192
Groom, Tom, 37
Guild Socialism, 123, 124, 155; National Guilds League, 124
Gunning, James, 11

Hackney, 47, 48, 49, 50
Hague Conference (1899), 162
Hales, John, 59
Halford, Edwin, 135
Halifax, 31, 32, 33, 34; Art Society, 32
Hall, Joseph Arthur (Joe), 83, 134
Hall, (William) Leonard, 35
Hallsworth, Joseph (*later* Sir), 137
Halstead, J.F. Blandwood, 163
Hamilton, Mary Agnes, 169
Hannington, Wal, 48
Hardie, James Keir, 9, 37, 38, 39, 59, 60, 66, 68, 147, 202
Harford, Edward, 68, 120
Harney, George Julian, 95, 113, 142, 143
Harrison, George, 6
Hartley, Edward Robertshaw, 15
Hartshorn, Vernon, 189
Haslam, James, 154
Hastings, Sir Patrick, 151

Haston, Jock, 198–9
Hayhurst, Joseph, 135
Headlam, Rev. Stewart Duckworth, 26–7
Headlam, T.E., 144
Hemsworth, 46, 47
Henderson, Arthur, 10, 11, 12, 48, 138, 139, 149, 182
Henderson, (James) Frederick, 149
Herriotts, John, 83
Hewart, Gordon (*later* 1st Viscount Hewart of Bury), 15
Hewitt, Alfred, 136
Hicks, Alfred, 89
Hicks, Amelia (Amie) Jane, **89–92**, 191
Hicks, Frances Amelia (Amy), 90
Hicks, Margaretta, 89, 91
Hicks, Ron, 80
Hicks, William James, 89
Highland Land League: *see* Scotland
Hill, Dr (John Edward) Christopher, 132
Hindmarch, Thomas, 55
Hinduism, 27
Hobson, Samuel George, 123
Hodge, John, 11, 149, 189
Hodges, Frank, 152
Hodgson, Richard, 144
Hohler, Gerald Fitzroy, 110
Holberry, Samuel, **93–6**
Holmes, David, 90
Holmes, Walter, 104
Holyoake, George Jacob, 6, 7, 143, 145
Home Office, 86
Home Work, Conference on (1897), 91
Hong Kong, 139
Hopkin, Daniel, **96–8**
Hopkins, Rev. Charles P., 203
Hopper, Joseph, 56
Horner, Arthur, 83, 134
Hoskin, John, **98–9**
Housing, working-class, 1, 5, 15, 19, 20, 35, 49, 118–19, 127, 135, 141, 162, 165, 174, 180, 194; tied cottage system, 15, 72. *See also* National Housing and Town-Planning Council
Housing Reform Council, 165
Huddersfield, 157–9
Huddersfield Worker, 157
Hull, 116, 119–20; Radical Club, 119
Hull House Settlement, Chicago, 162
Hulton, Edward (*later* Sir), 32, 35, 36, 166, 167
L'Humanité, 54
Hungary, Soviet intervention in, 54
Hunger Marches, 129
Hutt, Tom, 141
Hyndman, Henry Mayers, 24, 25, 35, 65, 66, 89, 121, 180, 190. *See also* Authors

Ideas, 167
Ilford, 57
Illingworth, H. Holden, 76
Illustrated Sporting and Dramatic News, 32, 33
Imperial War Graves Commission, 88
Independent and Nonconformist, 161
Independent Labour Party, 1, 8, 9, 19, 38, 39, 46, 50, 53, 67, 68, 70, 76, 77, 91, 118, 124, 125, 146, 154, 157, 158, 165, 169, 180, 182, 202:
  Branches: Ashington, 194; Barrow, 66; Battersea, 17; Bradford, 45, 135; Bristol, 101; Chester-le-Street, 68; Coventry, 15, 141; Crewe, 15; Dewsbury, 39; Halifax, 33; Hull, 121; Ilford, 57; Lincoln, 173; London, 17; Manchester, 35, 36; Motherwell, 70; Norwich, 148, 149; Oxford, 198; Rochdale, 8; Wolverhampton, 15
  Conferences: 1893, Bradford, 37, 66, 180; 1896, Nottingham, 38
  and First World War, 147
  and Leeds Convention, 182
  Manchester Fourth Clause, 36–7, 39
  National Administrative Council of, 1, 19, 38, 66, 155, 180, 194
  Relations with Labour Party, 154, 155
India, 27, 28, 59, 137, 138, 139, 154, 155. *See also* Indian Home Rule League
Indian Affairs, Standing Joint Committee on, 155
Indian Home Rule League, 28, 154
Indian National Congress, 28
Indian Statutory Commission, 189
Industrial Co-partnership Association : *see* Labour Association for the Promotion of Co-partnership
Industrial Council (1911), 86
Industrial Peace Union of the British Empire, 206
Industrial Syndicalist, 181
Industrial unionism, 181. *See also* Spencerism
Industrial Women's Organisations, Standing Joint Committee of, 3, 19
Inns of Court OTC, 173
Institute of Secretaries' Association, 137
International, First, 59
International, Second, 72; Conferences: Paris (1889), 27; Paris (1900), 66; Copenhagen (1910), 1; Berne (1919), 12; Vienna (1931), 72
International, Third, 49, 104, 105
International Alliance of Women's Suffrage Societies, 139
International Arbitration League, 122
International Brigade, 80. *See also* Spanish Civil War

International Co-operative Alliance, 82
International Labour Office, 12
International Labour Organisation, 12, 13; Conferences, 12, 206; Conventions of, 12
International Literature, 105
International Socialist and Trade Union Congress (1896), 91
International Transport Workers' Federation, 183, 202–3, 206
Ireland, 23, 35, 59, 65, 93, 103, 105–6, 145, 170; Home Rule for, 9, 67, 99, 102, 113, 120, 146
Irish Citizen Army, 103
Irish Land League, 59, 65. *See also* Irish National League *and* United Irish League
Irish National League, 65
Irish Nationalist Party, 9, 68
Ironfounders: *see* Friendly Society of Ironfounders
Irving, David Daniel (Dan), 121

Jackson, Thomas Alfred, **99–108**
Jacob, Alaric, 129, 130, 131
James, Clara, 90, 91, 92
Jameson Raid, 60
Jenkins, John Hogan, **109–10**
Jessel, Sir George, 23
Jewson, Dorothea (Dorothy), 150
Jochade, Hermann, 203
Johnston, Thomas, 60, 70
Joint Industrial Councils: *see* Whitley Committee
Jones, Ernest, 176
Jones, William Ernest, 134
Jowett, Frederick William, 135, 204
'Judex' (pseud. of G. D. H. Cole and W. Mellor), 123
Jupp, Arthur Edward, **110–11**
Justice, 89, 90
Justices of the Peace, 1, 17, 19, 48, 52, 56, 68, 71, 73, 79, 83, 97, 109, 110, 122, 141, 151, 153, 166, 189, 190, 192, 198, 200. *See also* Miners

Kelly, Thomas, 178
Kenya, 139, 155
Kenyon, Barnet, 154
Kerensky, Alexander Feodorovich, 11
Kiernan, Professor Victor Gordon, 132
King of the Road, 38
King, Sir H. Seymour, 121
King, P. J., 38
King, Dr William, 159
Kingsley Hall, 154
Kinnaird, Emily, 138, 139

Kirkwood, David (*later* 1st Baron Kirkwood of Bearsden), 125
Knight, Sam, 80
Kolchak, Admiral Alexander Vasilievich, 192

Labour and Socialist International: *see* International, Second
Labour and Socialist Women's International Committee, 3
Labour Association for the Promotion of Co-operative Production, 121
Labour Charter (or Chapter), 12
Labour Church, 33
Labour Co-partnership Association: *see* Labour Association for the Promotion of Co-operative Production
Labour Electoral Association, 120, 180, 202
Labour Governments: (1924), 88, 151, 170, 189; (1929–31), 124, 155–6; (1945–51), 3, 53, 55
Labour Information Bureau, 165
Labour Leader, 15, 37, 40, 68, 155, 191
Labour Magazine, 167
Labour, Ministry of, 10, 11, 12, 149, 150
Labour Party, 2, 9, 10, 11, 12, 13, 15, 16, 17, 18, 19, 28, 39, 40, 47, 53, 54, 57, 68, 71, 73, 77, 78, 83, 109, 111, 125, 138, 139, 146, 147, 150, 154, 158, 166, 167, 170, 174, 175, 180, 181, 182, 188, 192, 194, 198, 204, 205; Advisory Cttee on Agriculture and Rural Problems, 171; Advisory Cttee on International Questions, 170; Advisory Cttee on Public Health, 19; Commission of Enquiry into the Distressed Areas, 72; and Communist Party, 48, 53, 54, 125, 158; and First World War, 10, 11, 204; and ILP, 154, 155; Labour Representation Committee, 1, 9, 19, 39, 66, 77, 135, 141, 148, 149, 150, 157, 188, 191, 192, 202; League of Youth, 80; National Executive Committee, 3, 11, 19, 48, 49, 54, 71, 72, 118, 125, 127, 135, 150, 188, 194; Parliamentary Labour Party, 1, 10, 11, 66, 71, 77, 155, 181, 188, 195, 196; and Socialist League, 125; Women's Section, 19
Annual Conferences: 1913, London, 149; 1917, Manchester, 11, 154; 1926, Margate, 71; 1932, Leicester, 125; 1936, Edinburgh, 3; 1937, Bournemouth, 72; 1939, Southport, 72; 1949, Blackpool, 53; 1953, Margate, 54; 1954, Scarborough, 54; 1958, Scarborough, 54
Branches: Bethnal Green, 58; Bradford, 41; Clapham, 17; Cleveland, 79; Coventry, 4, 5; Eccles, 136;

Hackney, 47; Huddersfield, 158; Ilford, 57; Lincoln, 173, 174; Morpeth, 194; Newcastle upon Tyne, 1; Salford, 80; South Hammersmith, 57; Walsall, 118, 119, 127; Wansbeck, 194. *See also* Independent Labour Party, Labour Governments *and* London Labour Party
Labour Publishing Company, 198
Labour, R. C. on: *see* Royal Commissions
Labour Representation Committee: *see* Labour Party
Labour Research Department, 105, 155
Labour Tribune, 197
Labour Women's National Conference, 3
Labourers' Union, 109
Ladies' Medical College, 90
La Follette Seamen's Act (U.S.A.) (1915), 204
Land, Departmental Cttee on the Employment of Sailors and Soldiers on the, 149
Land Nationalisation Society, 165
Land Reform, 23, 59, 60, 65, 67, 71, 73, 115, 117, 119, 158, 165, 172
Lang, Rev. Gordon, 53
Langley, J. Batty, 121
Langley, J. Baxter, 144, 145
Lansbury, George, 28, 77, 124, 138, 153, 154, 162, 181, 202
Laski, Harold Joseph, 125
Latham, William (Bill), 138
Law, Andrew Bonar, 9, 10
Law and Liberty League, 26
Lawn, William E., 159
Lawrence, Arabella Susan, 19
Lawther, Will (*later* Sir), 204
Leach, William, 135
League of Nations, 1–2, 12, 170, 174
League of the Blind, 165
League to Abolish War, 12, 162
Lee, Peter, 55, 83
Leeds, 101–2; Convention (3 June 1917), 182; National Conference of Reformers (Nov. 1861), 145; Parliamentary Reform Association, 114
Left Book Club, 63, 126
Lehane, Con, 102
Lehmann, John Frederick, 63
Leicester, 161
Leicester Co-operative Printing Society, 148
Leicester Pioneer, 15
Lenin, Vladimir Il'ich Ulyanov, 80. *See also* Authors
Levellers, 130, 132
Lewin, Sir Gregory, 94
Lewis, Thomas, 205
Lib-Lab MPs, 10, 121, 192, 202

Lib-Labourism, 39, 66, 68, 120, 146
Liberal Party, 15, 39, 42, 46, 56, 59, 60, 66, 75, 109, 117, 119–20, 121, 145, 148, 165, 191, 192, 196, 197, 202, 204; National Federation of Liberal Associations, 59
Library Association, Annual Meeting (1882), 52; Southport Conference (1899), 52
Liddall, Walter Sydney, 174
Light, George, 183
Lincoln, 2, 173, 174
Lindsay, Alexander Dunlop (1st Baron Lindsay of Birker), 73
Lindsay, Jack, 63
Link, 26
Linton, William James, 143
Liverpool Financial Reform Association, 145
Livestock Commission, 72
Llantwit, 96
Lloyd George, David (later 1st Earl Lloyd George of Dwyfor), 10, 11, 45, 149, 189
Local Government Board, 189
Local Government Representation, 15, 49, 73; in: Ashington, 194; Ashton-in-Makerfield, 188; Barry, 110; Bradford, 45, 135; Cardiff, 109; Coventry, 4, 5, 141; Durham (County), 55, 56, 83, 146; Eccles, 136; Halifax, 33; Hemsworth, 46; Huddersfield, 158; Hull, 120; Ilford, 57; Lincoln, 173, 174; Mexborough, 75; Middlesbrough, 77; Newcastle upon Tyne, 1, 19; Northumberland (County), 194; Nottingham, 172; Pontadawe, 198; Poplar, 154; Radstock, 197; Rawmarsh, 98; South Shields, 78–9; Sunderland, 165, 166; Walsall, 118, 119, 127; Washington, 146; Wombwell, 153. See also London County Council
Local Option, 67, 120, 121. See also Temperance
Lockwood, John Cutts, 3
London, Metropolitan Boroughs Standing Joint Cttee, 154; Metropolitan Radical Federation, 153
London County Council, 3, 17, 18, 19, 26, 39, 48, 50, 58, 85, 87, 88, 91, 154, 155, 175, 180, 191
London Highland Law Reform Association, 60, 117. See also Highland Land League
London Joint Union Committee, 8
London Labour Party, 3, 48, 49, 88, 110, 154
London Labour Women's Advisory Committee, 3
London Reform Union, 91
London School Board, 26–7, 89, 191
London School of Economics, 69
London School of Medicine for Women, 19
London Society of Compositors, 17, 122, 148

London Tailoresses' Union, 90
London University, 24
Longman, Mary, 19
Lord's Day Observance Society, 109
Loughlin, Anne (later Dame), 184
Lovett, William, 114, 115, 172
Lowerison, Harry, 37, 38
Lowery, Robert, **112–17**
Lunn, William, 67
Lutyens, Lady Emily, 28
Luxemburg, Rosa, 198
Lynch, Arthur Alfred, 48

Macarthur, Mary Reid, 70
McCarthy, Tom, 178
Macdonald, Alexander, 42
MacDonald, James Ramsay, 10, 66, 71, 92, 125, 138, 139, 148, 149, 154, 155, 156, 169, 174, 189, 202, 204
MacDonald, Margaret Ethel, 19, 92
Macdonald, Roderick, **117–18**
MacDougall, Archibald (Archie), 54
McGurk, John, 190
McKenna, Reginald, 10
McKinley, James, 205
Maclean, John, 13, 102
Macmillan, (Maurice) Harold, 14
M'Owen, J., 95
McShane, Annie, **118–19**
McShane, John James, 118
Maddison, Fred, **119–22**
Magistrates' Association of Great Britain, 97
Maisky, Ivan, 175
Malaya, 139
Malthusian League, 23
Manchester, 2, 35, 39, 164, 169, 175–6; Cheetham's Hospital, 164; Federal Labour Parliament, 38
Manchester Grammar School, 166
Manchester Guardian, 37, 169
Manchester Ship Canal, 190
Manchester, Phyllis Winifred, 131
Mann, Tom, 8, 68, 85, 123, 178, 181, 190, 191, 203
Manning, Cardinal Henry Edward, 178, 179
Mansion House Unemployment Committee, 178, 179. See also Strikes and Lockouts—Docks, London (1889)
Mappin, Sir Frederick Thorpe, 121
Marjoribanks, D.C., 144
Markievitcz, Countess Constance Georgina, 103
Marquand, Hilary Adair, 78
Marriott, Sir John Arthur Ransome, 1
Marryat, Frederick, 21
Marx, Eleanor, 24, 101, 178

Marx, Karl, 25, 37, 80, 102, 105, 107, 130. *See also* Authors
Marx House, Manchester, 80
Marxism, 24, 25, 49, 81, 101, 102, 103, 105, 107, 129, 132, 180
Marxism Today, 81
Mary Macarthur Holiday Homes for Working Women, 175
Masterman, Charles Frederick Gurney, 154
Mather, James, 112, 113
Matthews, John, 65
Maxton, James, 70, 102, 125
Means Test, 57
Mechanics' Institutes, 42, 172, 176; Winlaton, 142
Mellor, William, **123–7**
Merchant Shipping: *see* Board of Trade
Merrie England, 32, 37, 39, 100. *See also* Authors—Blatchford, Robert
Michel, Louise, 101
Middlesbrough, 77–8
Middleton, Dora Miriam, **127–8**
Middleton, Mary, 19
Middleton, Mary K. (Mrs Hugh Middleton), 195
Midland Counties Illuminator, 172
Midland Counties Tribune, 15
Mills, Leslie, 175
Miner, 167, 207
Miners
   and accident insurance and compensation, 42, 43, 50, 51, 52, 194
   election to school boards, 75, 146, 197
   and First World War, 46, 63, 134, 153, 189, 194, 196
   and freemasonry, 52
   and the Independent Labour Party, 46, 146, 194, 198
   as Justices of the Peace, 56, 83, 153, 189, 198, 200
   and Labour Party, 83, 147, 194, 198
   and Liberal Party, 42, 46, 66, 196, 197
   and local government, 46, 55, 56, 75, 83, 98, 146, 153, 188, 194, 197, 198
   and pacifism, 46, 194, 196
   and provident associations, 42, 43, 50–1, 56, 98, 146, 152, 194, 195: attitude of coal owners towards, 42, 43, 51
   and religion
      Church of England, 187
      Congregational, 75
      Methodist, 56, 62, 83, 147, 152
      Roman Catholic, 47, 134, 187
   and Socialism, 46
   and Temperance, 42. *See also* Collieries
Miners' Unions
   Local and Regional

Ashton and Haydock Miners' Union, 188; Durham County Colliery Enginemen and Boilerminders' Association, 55; Durham County Federation Board, 55, 56, 62; Durham Deputies' Mutual Aid Association, 62; Durham Miners' Association, 62, 78, 83, 146, 201; Lancashire and Cheshire Miners' Federation, 188, 189, 190; Midland Miners' Federation, 197; North Staffordshire Miners' Association, 197; Northumberland Miners' Association, 194; Northumberland Miners' Mutual Confident Association: *see* Northumberland Miners' Association; Nottinghamshire Miners' Association, 171; Somerset Miners' Association, 197; South Wales Miners' Federation, 198; South Yorkshire Miners' Association, 44, 74–5, 98; West Bromwich Miners' Federation, 197; West Yorkshire Miners' Association, 44, 75; Yorkshire Mine Workers' Association: *see* Yorkshire Miners' Association; Yorkshire Miners' Association, 44, 46, 67, 75, 98, 99, 133, 134, 152
   National
Amalgamated Association of Miners, 197
Miners' Association of Great Britain and Ireland 44
Miners' Federation of Great Britain, 46, 48, 83, 99, 133, 147, 152, 188, 189, 190, 194, 197, 198, 206; Newport conference (1889), 197
National Federation of Colliery Enginemen and Boiler Firemen, 55
National Union of Mineworkers, 83, 134
Mining
   Boards of Conciliation, 46, 98, 134, 146, 152, 197; colliery disasters: Hartley (1862), 42; Haydock (1878), 51; Montague Main (1925), 195; Whitehaven (1928), 48; Wigan district (1868–71), 50; Royalties, 120, 137
Mining Association of Great Britain, 83
Mitchell, G. W., 3
Mitchison, Gilbert Richard (*later* Baron Mitchison of Carradale [Life Peer]), 125
Mollet, Guy, 54
Mond, Sir Alfred Moritz (*later* 1st Viscount Melchett), 183
'Mont (Mong) Blong' (pseud.): *see* Blatchford, Montagu John
Moral Re-Armament, 183
Morel, Edmund Dene, 169, 170
Morley, Iris Vivienne (Mrs Alaric Jacob), **128–33**
Morley, Samuel, 172

Morning, 179

Morris, George, 4

Morris, William, 24, 26, 35, 36, 38, 89, 125, 169. *See also* Authors

Morrison, Herbert Stanley (*later* Baron Morrison of Lambeth [Life Peer]), 48, 49, 84, 88

Mosely Industrial Commission, 9

Mosley, Lady Cynthia, 192

Mosley, Sir Oswald, 47, 58, 77

Muit-tsai, Government Commission into (1936), 139

Mundella, Anthony John, 121

Municipal Socialism, 67, 158–9, 165, 167

Munro, Dr Hector, 135

Murphy, John Thomas, 48

Nation, 169

National Agricultural Labourers' Union, 70

National Alliance of Employers and Employed, 149, 204

National Amalgamated Furnishing Trades Association, 15

National Amalgamated Sailors' and Firemen's Union of Great Britain and Northern Ireland, 201, 202

National Amalgamated Union of Labour, 165. *See also* Tyneside and National Labour Union

National Amalgamated Union of Shop Assistants, Warehousemen and Clerks, 69, 109, 173, 174

National and International General Federation of Trade and Labour Unions, 38. *See also* Manchester, Federal Labour Parliament

National Assistance Board, 3

National Coal Board, 199

National Committee of Organised Labour, 9, 162. *See also* Old Age Pensions

National Council of Agriculture for England, 72

National Council of Labour Colleges, 53, 102, 106, 137, 158, 159, 160, 198

National Council of Women Citizens, 139

National Democratic League, 191

National Federation of Discharged Soldiers and Sailors (*later* British Legion), 47

National Federation of Labour Union, 191

National Federation of Women Workers, 70, 71

National Free Labour Association, 202

National Government (1931), 3, 139, 174

National Guilds League: *see* Guild Socialism

National Housing and Town Planning Council, 1

National Maritime Board, 204, 205

National Organisation of Girls' Clubs, 91

National Reformer, 21, 23, 24, 25, 27

National Sailors' and Firemen's Union of Great Britain and Ireland, 109, 179, 202, 203–4, 205, 206

National Secular Society, 21, 23, 27, 101

National Service, Ministry of, 189

National Society of Operative Printers and Assistants (NATSOPA), 167

National Transport Workers' Federation, 85, 86, 87, 88, 181, 182, 183, 203, 205, 207

National Unemployed Workers' Movement, 80

National Union of Agricultural Workers, 15, 16

National Union of Allotment Holders, 57

National Union of Bookbinders, 47

National Union of Boot and Shoe Operatives, 178

National Union of Distributive and Allied Workers, 137

National Union of Dyers, Bleachers and Textile Workers, 45

National Union of Ex-Servicemen (NUX), 47

National Union of Foundry Workers, 53. *See also* Amalgamated Union of Foundry Workers

National Union of Gasworkers and General Labourers, 65, 191

National Union of General and Municipal Workers, 57, 78, 79

National Union of Journalists, 15, 82

National Union of Railwaymen, 110, 125

National Union of Ships' Stewards, Cooks, Butchers and Bakers, 205, 206

National Union of Shop Assistants, Warehousemen and Clerks, 47

National Union of Textile Workers, 45

National Union of Women Workers, 91

National Union of Women's Suffrage Societies, 19, 169

Nationalisation, 54, 58, 67, 68, 77, 120, 174; Bank of England, 125; Banks, Joint Stock, 125; Engineering, 53, 54; Iron and Steel, 77; Land, 59, 60, 65, 67, 71, 73, 119, 165; Mines, 63, 67, 146, 147, 189, 199; Railways, 67, 68

Navvies, Bricklayers' Labourers and General Labourers' Union, 191. 192

Neath Guardian, 63

Nehru, Jawaharlal, 28

New Age, 123, 124

New Clarion, 40

New Dawn, 137

'New Deal' (U.S.A.), 129

New India, 28

'New Party': *see* Reid, Andrew

New Statesman, 54

'New Unionism' (1889), 8, 26, 35, 66, 84, 178–83
New Writing, 63
Newcastle Daily Chronicle, 143, 144, 145, 146
Newcastle Foreign Affairs Committee, 142
Newcastle upon Tyne, 1, 19, 112, 114, 116, 142, 144
Next Five Years Group, 14, 139
1917 Club, 2, 20, 170
No-Conscription Fellowship, 17, 166
No More War Movement, 17
Normansell, John, 44
Norris, Joe, 35
North East Coast Institution of Shipbuilders, 1
North of England Sailors' and Seagoing Firemen's Friendly Society, 201
North of England Shipowners' Association, 1
North Shields, 112
North Shields Political Union, 112
Northamptonshire Rural Community Council, 73
Northern Daily Express, 144, 161
Northern Echo, 161
Northern Liberator, 112
Northern Political Union, 112
Northern Reform League, 145
Northern Reform Record, 144
Northern Reform Union, 142, 143, 144, 145
Northern Star, 6, 95, 114
Northern Tribune, 142
Norwich, 148, 151
Nottingham, 6, 7, 171, 172, 173; Secular Society, 7
'Nunquam Dormio' and 'Nunquam' (pseuds): see Blatchford, Robert Peel Glanville

Oakey, Thomas, **133–4**
O'Brien, James Bronterre, 115
Observer, 130, 131, 169
O'Connor, Feargus Edward, 6, 112, 114, 172; Lunacy Commission Enquiry, 172
O'Connor, Thomas Power, 10, 151
Odhams Press, 40, 124, 183. *See also Daily Herald*
O'Donovan, Dr William James, 156
O'Grady, Sir James, 149
Old Age Pensions, 9, 127, 162
Olivier, Sydney Haldane (*later* 1st Baron Olivier of Ramsden), 24
O'Neill, Ellen (Mrs L. Finley), 80
Openshaw, James, 80
Operative Chain Makers' Union (Newcastle upon Tyne), 142
Operative Dyers' Society, 176
Orage, Alfred Richard, 123

Orange Order, 93
Orbell, Harry, 178
Orwell, George (pseud. of Eric Blair), 105
Our Corner, 24, 25, 27
Owen, Robert, 69, 115, 116
Owens College, Manchester, 161, 169
Oxford University, 123; Exeter College, 123

Pacifism, 17, 18, 38, 46, 141, 154, 162, 166, 170, 194, 196. *See also* First World War, conscientious objection
Packman, Lydia (Mrs T. A. Jackson), 105
Paget, Charles, 172
Palestine, 96, 97
Palin, John Henry, **134–6**
Pall Mall Gazette, 25, 27
Palmer, Sir Charles Mark, 68
Palmer, Godfrey Mark, 68
Palmer, Robert Alexander (*later* 1st Baron Rusholme), 36
Palmer, William, 32, 36, 167
Palmerston, Lord, 14
Pankhurst, Emmeline, 138, 169
Pankhurst, Estelle Sylvia, 154, 169
Paris Commune: *see* France
Paris Peace Conference, 12
Parker, Ralph, 131
Parkin, Ben, 54
Parliament, Members of, intellectual influences upon, 13, 69, 77, 138, 148, 153, 165, 177, 188, 190, 193, 198
Parliamentary Acts
    1834, Poor Law Amendment, 115
    1854, Corrupt Practices Prevention, 144
    1866–9, Contagious Diseases, 90
    1875, Conspiracy and Protection of Property, 66
    1880, Employers' Liability, 43, 51, 90
    1885, Redistribution of Seats, 144
    1886, Crofters' Holdings (Scotland), 60
    1894, Merchant Shipping, 202
    1897, Workmen's Compensation, 51
    1902, Education, 76, 102
    1906, Merchant Shipping, 202
    1906, Trade Disputes, 206
    1909, Trade Boards, 150
    1911, Coal Mines, 189, 195
    1914, Defence of the Realm, 102
    1916, Military Service, 11, 124
    1917, Corn Production, 70
    1924, London Traffic, 88
    1926, Trade Facilities, 174
    1930, Land Drainage, 71
    1931, Coal Mines, 83
    1939, Personal Injuries (Emergency Provisions), 3, 57–8

Parliamentary Acts—*contd.*
  1946, National Health Service, 58
  1947–8, Local Government, 73
Parliamentary Bills
  1859, Representation of the People, 143
  1860, Representation of the People, 145
  1866–7, Representation of the People [Reform Bill], 145
  1886, Crofters (Scotland) (No. 2), 117
  1894, Employers' Liability, 91
  1908, Pensions (Old Age), 9–10, 162
  1911, Labour Disputes, 10
  1911, National Insurance, 10
  1912, Coal Mines (Minimum Wage), 189
  1913, Nationalisation of Coal Mines and Minerals, 189
  1923, Housing (No. 2), 1
  1924, Port of London Authority, 155
  1924–5, Commonwealth of India, 28
  1925, Government of India (Civil Service), 155
  1928, Rating and Valuation, 155
  1928, Shops (Hours of Closing), 174
  1930, Education (School Attendance), 155–6
  1930, Mental Treatment, 20
  1930, Nationality of Women, 20
  1930–1, Sentence of Death (Expectant Mothers), 139
  1944–5, Family Allowances, 3
  1946–7, National Service, 18, 49, 199
Parliamentary Committees: Anglo-Russian, 155; Ecclesiastical, 139
Parliamentary Constituencies: Aberdeen, 114; Barnard Castle, 83; Barnsley, 46, 66, 68; Barrow-in-Furness, 1, 66; Batley and Morley, 45; Belper, 72; Berwick-upon-Tweed, 144; Bethnal Green: North-East, 57, South-West, 154; Bexley, 3; Blackburn, West, 53; Blackfriars and Hutchesontown (*later* Gorbals), 9; Bradford: Central, 135, East, 35, 36, North, 135, West, 135, 180; Brightside (Sheffield), 120, 121; Bristol, East, 202; Buckingham, 154; Burnley, 121, 122; Bury, 53; Caithness, 60; Cannock Chase, 2; Carmarthen, 97; Chatham and Gillingham, 109, 110; Chesterfield, 154; Clapham, 18; Colne Valley, 39; Consett, 1; Coventry, 141; Darlington, 122; Dartford, 3; Dewsbury, 39; Doncaster, 153; Dunbartonshire, 45; Durham, 196; Eccles, 180; Edinburgh, 114; Enfield, 126; Exeter, 75; Gateshead, 47; Gorbals, 13; Great Yarmouth, 204; Greenock, 157–8; Hackney: Central, 48, 49, North, 48, South, 48, 49; Hammersmith, South, 57; Hull: Central, 120, 121, East 120; Ilford, 57; Ince, 188; Ipswich,

154; Islington: East, 20, North, 138; Jarrow, 68, 122; Lambeth: Kennington, 88, North, 88; Leicester, 15; Lincoln, 173, 174; Maldon, 71; Manchester, Moss Side, 53; Middlesbrough, 77, 202, East, 77; Morpeth, 194; Neath, 198, 199; Newcastle upon Tyne, 144, 145, East, 78, West, 1, 135; Northampton, 23; Norwich, 148, 149, 150; Nottingham, 172; Paisley, 74; Pontefract, 46; Port Talbot, 138; Rochdale, 8; Ross and Cromarty, 117; Roxburgh and Selkirk, 71; St Helens, 188; Salford, North, 182; Sedgefield, 83; Shipley, 135; South Shields, 204; Stalybridge and Hyde, 53; Stepney, Mile End, 154; Stockport, 53, 126; Stoke-on-Trent, 192; Stroud, 138; Sunderland, 79, 165, South, 79; Swansea, 180; Uxbridge, 88; Walsall, 118; Wandsworth, 204; Wansbeck, 194; Wellingborough, 71, 72; Whitechapel, 88; Whitehaven, 146, 147; Workington, 79; The Wrekin, 138; York, 1
Parliamentary General Elections
  1841, 114
  1857, 144
  1859, 144
  1880, 23, 59
  1885, 117
  1886, 117, 145
  1892, 117, 120, 180, 202
  1895, 8, 39, 66, 121, 180, 202
  1900, 60, 121, 202, 204
  1906, 9, 68, 77, 109, 121, 135, 149, 165, 180, 188, 192, 202
  Jan. 1910, 68, 110, 122, 149, 165, 180, 192
  Dec. 1910, 88, 122, 146, 149, 192
  1918 'Coupon', 1, 13, 46, 71, 88, 135, 147, 150, 157, 174, 182, 189, 192, 195, 204
  1922, 1, 13, 48, 71, 83, 88, 135, 138, 150, 154, 174, 182, 192, 194, 195, 204
  1923, 57, 71, 138, 150, 192, 195
  1924, 1, 40, 57, 71, 138, 154, 173, 174, 182, 192, 195
  1929, 20, 45, 57, 71, 97, 118, 135, 138, 154, 174, 182, 192
  1931, 1, 45, 57, 71, 97, 118, 126, 135, 139, 156, 174, 182
  1935, 1, 3, 45, 53, 57, 72, 77, 97, 126
  1945, 3, 18, 48, 49, 72, 77, 79, 198
  1950, 53, 78, 79
  1951, 53, 78, 79
  1955, 49
  1964, 49
  1970, 49
Parliamentary Labour Party: *see* Labour Party
Parliamentary Reform, 67, 71, 99, 114, 117, 119, 121, 142, 143, 144, 145

Parnell, Charles Stewart, 65, 99
Parrott, William, 66
Paterson, Emma, 90
Paul, William, 189
Pavitt, Laurence Anstice, 49
Peace Negotiations Committee, 170
Peace Pledge Union, 166
Peart, (Thomas) Frederick (*later* Baron Peart [Life Peer]), 79
Pease, Edward Reynolds, 35
Peat, Sir William Barclay, 71
Peel, Sir Robert, 34
PEN Club, 20
Pensions, Ministry of, 3, 11, 13
People's League, 115
Perceval, Spencer, 117
Petch, Arthur William, **136-7**
Peterloo, 113
Peters, Samuel, 178
Pethick-Lawrence, Emmeline, 28
Phelen, E. J., 12
Philipson, Hilton, 195
Phillips, Dr·Marion, 19, 28
Phillips, Morgan Walter, 54
Pickard, Ben, 66
Pickard, William, 50, 51
Picton-Turbervill, Edith, **137-40**
Picture Post, 63
Plan for Engineering, 54
Plebs, 137, 198
Plebs League, 57, 159
Plimsoll, Samuel, 202
Plug Plot (1842): *see* Chartism
Poland, 73
Pole, David Graham, 154
Pollitt, Harry, 103, 107
Poole, Stephen George, 4, 15, **140-1**
Poor Law, 123, 146, 155. *See also* Boards of Guardians and Royal Commissions
Poplar, 153, 154, 155
Poplar Labour League, 153
Popular Front (U.K.), 72, 125
Port of London Authority, 85, 155
Priestley, John Boynton, 63
Pritt, Denis Nowell, 125
Progressive Party, London, 39, 85, 91, 191
Proops, Marjorie, 64
Provident, 43
Punch, 32, 33

Queen, The v. Charles Bradlaugh and Annie Besant, 22
Quelch, Harry, 24, 39, 191

Railway Review, 120, 121

Ramage, Cecil Beresford, 1
Raynor, Oscar, 17
Reade, Henry Musgrave, 35
Reader's Digest, 63
Reasoner, 7
Reckitt, Maurice Benington, 123
Reed, Sir Joseph, 146
Reed, Richard Bagnall, **142-6**
Reform League, 172
Reid, Andrew, 38; and the 'New Party', 38
Republican Brotherhood, 142
Republicanism, 6, 22, 23, 120
Reuters News Agency, 129
Review of Reviews, 162
Revolutionary Communist Party, 198
Reynolds, A. H., 15, 16
Reynolds's News, 191
Richards, Thomas (Tom), 198
Richardson, Kenneth, 5
Richardson, Thomas (Tom), **146-7**
Richardson, Thomas Alfred, 79
Richardson, William Pallister, 83, 147, 190
Ridley, George, 144
'Right to Work' Council, 68, 154
Ritson, Joshua (Josh), 196
Roach, John, 164
Roberts, Benjamin Charles, 87
Roberts, Bryn, 198
Roberts, George Henry, 11, **148-52**, 189
Roberts, William Prowting, 21
Robertson, John Mackinnon, 22
Robertson, Robert Chisholm, 201
Robson, James, 83
Roebuck, Samuel, **152-3**
Rogers, Frederick, 9, 162
Rogerson, John Bolton, 163, 164
Roosevelt, Eleanor, 129
Rosebery Conference (1893), 197
Rossa, O'Donovan, 106
Rotary Club, 17, 77
Rowe, G. J., 204
Royal Academy of Dramatic Art, 129, 133
Royal Commissions
    1841, Children's Employment, 6
    1845, Framework Knitters, 6
    1871-4, Friendly and Benefit Building Societies, 43
    1884, Crofters and Cotters (Highlands), 60
    1887, Loss of Life at Sea, 201
    1891-4, Labour, 51, 76, 90
    1905-9, Poor Laws, 192
    1906, Coast Erosion and the Reclamation of Tidal Lands in the United Kingdom, 165
    1910, Divorce, 169
    1919, Agricultural Industry, 70-1
    1919, Coal Industry (Sankey Commission), 206

Royal Institute for International Affairs, 170
Royal Literary Fund, 64
Royden, (Agnes) Maude, 138, 140
Rushton, Martha Agnes, 170
Ruskin College, 16, 123, 174, 198
Ruskin, John: *see* Authors
Russell, Bertrand Arthur William (*later* 3rd Earl Russell), 73
Russia, 11, 53, 58, 73, 103, 118, 130, 131, 132, 139, 145, 204; Anglo-Russian commercial relations, 174; 'Hands off Russia' movement, 158; and Hungary (1956), 54; Intervention in, 128, 170, 182, 192; 1917 Revolution, 49; February/March, 2, 102, 170, 182; October/November, 124, 132; TUC delegation to (1924), 183
Rutherford, Alfred, 201

Sabbatarian Movement, 115. *See also* Temperance
St John's Ambulance Brigade, 64
Salaman, Dr Myer, 96
Salaman, Dr Redcliffe Nathan, 96
Salford, 80
Sanitary Associations, 35
Scardifield, F., 16
School Boards, 75, 76, 121, 146, 148, 161, 197. *See also* London School Board *and* Miners
School feeding, 27, 67, 89, 135
Scotland, Highland crofters, 59, 60, 65, 117; Highland Land League, 60, 117; Home Rule for, 60, 61
Scott, Charles Prestwich, 169
Scott, Leslie (Frederick) (*later* Sir), 149
Scott, Thomas, 21
Scottish Labour Party, 60
Scottish Land League, 65
Scurr, John, **153–6**
Scurr, Julia, 156
Seafaring, 202
Seaham Weekly News, 165
Seaman, 207
Second World War (1939–45), 3, 19, 49, 57, 72–3, 81, 97, 106, 111, 130, 139; Personal Injuries (Civilians) Scheme, 3, 57–8, 77
Secularism, 6, 7, 21, 22, 23, 27, 33, 39, 101, 123, 177
Select Committees
  1886, Employers' Liability Act (1880), 201
  1903, Certain Questions affecting the Mercantile Marine, 203
  1918, Emergency Legislation, 150
  1920, Indemnity Bill, 150
  1929, Capital Punishment, 20
  1929, Electoral Reform, 71
  1930, Shop Assistants, 20, 174
  1932, Agricultural Tied Cottages, 72
  1936, Farm Workers in Scotland, 72
  1943, Equal Compensation, 3
  1946, Expenses of Members of Local Authorities, 73
Sexton, James, 182
Shackleton, Sir David James, 12
Shaw Court of Enquiry into Transport Workers: *see* Dock Labour
Shaw, Fred, **156–60**
Shaw, George Bernard, 22, 24, 25, 26, 123, 167, 169. *See also* Authors
Shaw, Rev. George William Hudson, 138
Shawcross, Sir Hartley William (*later* Baron Shawcross of Friston [Life Peer]), 79
Sheffield, 93–5
Sheffield and Rotherham Independent, 121
Sheffield Mercury, 95
Sheffield University, 64
Shepheard, George, 65
Shinwell, Emanuel (*later* Baron Shinwell of Easington, Durham [Life Peer]), 205
Shipping Federation, 201, 202, 203, 204, 205, 206
Shirland Colliery Co. Ltd., 44
Shop Assistants' Union: *see* National Amalgamated Union of Shop Assistants, Warehousemen and Clerks
Shop Stewards' Movement, 124
Shops (Early Closing) Acts of 1920 and 1921, Departmental Cttee on, 174
Sickert, Walter Richard, 169
Silverman, Sydney, 54
Simon, Sir John Allsebrook (*later* 1st Viscount Simon of Stackpole Elidor), 206
Sinclair, Clarence G., 60
Sinclair, Upton, 141
Skinner, J., 121
Smillie, Robert, 67
Smith, Herbert, 48, 133, 152
Smith, Walter Robert, 150
Smith, Ward, 3
Snell, Henry (Harry) (*later* 1st Baron Snell of Plumstead), 28
Snowden, Philip (*later* 1st Viscount Snowden of Ickornshaw), 139, 180, 196
Social Democratic Federation, 15, 24, 25, 27, 35, 36, 37, 38, 65, 89, 100, 121, 141, 153, 178, 180, 181, 190, 191. *See also* British Socialist Party
Social Democratic Party, 181
'Social Gospel' movement, U.S.A., 162
Socialist Labour Party, 102, 157, 189, 198
Socialist League, 8, 89, 90, 125
Socialist National Defence Committee, 181
Socialist Review, 155

Socialist Sunday Schools, 80, 159
Society for Cultural Relations with the U.S.S.R., 132
Society for Socialist Inquiry and Propaganda, 124, 125
Society for the Suppression of Vice, 22
Society of Authors, 64
Society of Saint Paul, 203
South Africa, 58, 60, 61, 155; Co-operative movement in, 58
South African Agricultural Union, 58
South African Republic, 60
Southwell, Charles, 7
Sowter, James, 6
Spain, 79
Spanish Civil War, attitudes to, 5, 53, 80, 129
Spencer Union: see Spencerism
Spencerism, 83, 206, 207
Spiritualism, 5, 27, 40
Sporting Chronicle [Manchester], 35
Stacy, Enid, 68
Stamp, Reginald, 53
Stanton, Charles Butt, 191
Stead, Francis Herbert, 9, 12, **161–3**
Stead, Professor John Edward, 161
Stead, William Thomas, 22, 26, 27, 40, 122, 161, 162, 188
Steadman, William Charles, 192
Stephens, Rev. Joseph Rayner, 112
Stevedores' Union, 85
Stockholm (Peace) Conference (1917), 11, 149, 157
Stokes, Richard Rapier, 73
Stopes v. *Sutherland and Another*, 151
Stopes, Dr Marie Carmichael, 151
Storey, Samuel, 165
Stott, Benjamin, **163–4**, 177
Strauss, George Russell, 125
Strikes and Lockouts
    Builders, London (1914), 28
    Cooks' and Stewards' Union (1921), 205
    Docks
        London (1889), 8, 84, 90, 178–9
        Bristol (1892), 202
        Hull (1893), 121, 202
        London (1911), 153, 181
        London (1912), 85, 86, 87, 181
    Dye workers, Dunbartonshire (1911), 70
    Dyers, Manchester (1853), 176
    Engineers
        (1897), 8–9
        Clyde (1903), 9
        (1921–2), 158
    File Trade, Black Country (1915), 2
    General Strike (1926), 2, 46, 80, 103–4, 124, 159, 174, 183, 195, 198, 206; Women's National Strike Committee, 2

Lightermen
    (1900), 85
    (1909), 85
Manningham Mills, Bradford (1890–1), 76
Match Girls, London (1888), 26
Miners
    Durham (1844), 44
    Northumberland (1844), 44
    Wigan (1881), 51
    Silksworth Colliery (1890), 62
    National Lockout (1893), 197
    Minimum Wage (1912), 152
    (1921), 99, 205
Plymouth Coal Harbour (1890), 65, 66
Railways
    (1919), 88
Seamen
    Cardiff (1891), 201
    (1911), 203
Thread workers, Nielston (1910), 70, 71
Transport
    (1911–12), 86–7
Workers' Union
    Braintree (1913), 70
Strutt, Edward (Gerald), 149
Stuart, James, 165
Sturge, Joseph, 114
Suffrage Alliance Congress, 169
Summerbell, Thomas, **165–6**
Summerbell, Thomas (Jr), 166
Summerbell, Walter, 166
Sunday Chronicle, 32, 35, 36, 40, 166, 167
Sunday News, 40
Sunday Times, 131
Sunday Worker, 103, 104, 105
Sunderland, 165–6, 200, 201
Suthers, Robert Bentley, 36, 39, **166–8**
Swallow, David, 44
Swan, John Edmund, 83
Swanwick, Frederick, 169, 170
Swanwick Helena Maria Lucy, **168–71**
Sweated Industries, 26, 56, 90, 138, 154; House of Lords S.C. on the Sweating System (1888–90), 178
Sweden, 203
Sweet, James, 6, **171–3**
Sydenham, Lord (1st Baron Sydenham of Combe), 11
Syndicalism, 123, 181, 189

Taff Vale Case, 9, 68, 98, 180
Tariff Reform, 39, 68, 167, 174
Tate, Mavis Constance, 77
Taylor, Dr John, 113
Taylor, John Wilkinson, 147
Taylor, Peter Alfred, 144

Taylor, Robert Arthur, **173–5**
Tea Coopers' Association: *see* Tea Operatives and General Labourers' Association
Tea Operatives and General Labourers' Association, 178, 179
Teer, John, **175–7**
Temperance, 1, 17, 22, 42, 59, 113, 114, 115, 116, 120–1, 172, 178
Temperance Societies
  Central Temperance Association, 115; London Temperance League, 115; National Temperance League, 115, *Weekly Record of the Temperance Movement*, 115; Scottish Temperance Association, 115
Temple, William, 71
Teynham, Lord (16th Baron), 145
Theosophy, 27, 28, 154. *See also* Churches and Religious Groups
Thomas, James Henry, 12, 182, 183
Thompson, Alexander Mattock, 32, 35, 36, 38, 40, 167
Thompson, Laurence Victor, 32, 34
Thompson, Mrs Lilian Gilchrist, 92
Thompson, Thomas Perronet, 143
Thompson, William Marcus, 191
Thorne, William James (Will), 68, 182
Tiffin, Arthur Ernest (Jock), 54
Tillett, Benjamin (Ben), 28, 85, 86, 149, **177–87**, 203
Tillett, Louis John, 148, 149
Timber Control Board, 73
Times, 6, 28, 112, 131
Toby [Leeds], 35
Tolstoy, Count Lev Nikolaevich: *see* Authors
Tomkinson, Clifford Leslie, 127
Tomkinson, Grace, 127
Torr, Dona, 105
Town and County Councillor, 124
Trade Union Monetary Reform Association, 76
Trade Union Worker, 70
Trades and Labour Councils: *see* Trades Councils
Trades Councils: Barnsley, 66, 67; Bradford, 76, 135, 180; Bristol, 202; Cardiff, 109, 201; Dewsbury, 39; Eccles and District, 81, 136; Hackney, 48; Halifax, 33; Huddersfield, 158; Hull, 119, 120; Irlam and Cadishead, 136; Lincoln, 173; London, 90, 91; Norwich, 148, 150, 151; Plymouth, 66; Poplar, 153; Sunderland, 165, 201; Swinton and Pendlebury, 136; Wigan, 188; Yorkshire Federation of, 159
Trades Union Congress, 9, 38, 53, 59, 66, 71, 85, 87–8, 104, 121, 124, 127, 149, 158, 180, 182, 183, 191, 201, 205, 206
  and Communism, 48, 53

Delegation to U.S.S.R. (1924), 183
General Council, 88, 183, 206
Joint Board with TUC and GFTU, 192
Parliamentary Committee, 9, 66, 85, 87, 148, 180, 192, 201
annual conferences: 1886, Hull, 119
  1888, Bradford, 201
  1889, Dundee, 201
  1893, Belfast, 180
  1895, Cardiff, 109
  1900, Huddersfield, 191
  1901, Swansea, 180, 191
  1911, Newcastle upon Tyne, 10
  1916, Birmingham, 87
  1929, Belfast, 183
Transport, Ministry of, 88
Transport and General Workers' Union, 4, 54, 71, 88, 135, 179, 182–3, 206
Transvaal: *see* South African Republic
Treleaven, George F., 65
Trevelyan, Sir Charles Philips, 156, 196
Tribune, 126
Triple Alliance, 88, 182
Trotskyism: *see* Revolutionary Communist Party
Turkey, 139. *See also* Eastern Question
Tupper, 'Captain' Edward, 203, 204, 205
Turner, Ben (*later* Sir), 28, 45, 76, 157, 183
Turnway Societies, 84
Twentieth Century Club (U.S.A.), 90
Tyler, S., 59
Tyne Improvement Commission, 1
Tyneside and National Labour Union (*later* National Amalgamated Union of Labour), 165
Typographical Association, 119, 148, 149, 150, 151, 165

Unemployment, 49, 76, 80, 161, 162, 165, 190–1, 192, 205; Insurance, 174. *See also* Demonstrations *and* Means Test
Union of Democratic Control, 169, 170
United Irish League, 65, 155
United Nations, 82
United States of America, 9, 46, 77, 113, 129, 197, 204; Marshall Aid, 79. *See also* La Follette Act
Unity Manifesto (1937), 125
University Extension Movement, 169
University Socialist Federation, 123
'Unstamped' Press, 112
Urquhart, David, 114, 115
U.S.S.R.: *see* Russia

Vacant Lands Cultivation Society, 57

Vansittart, Lord (of Denham), 72
Varley, Julia, 135
Versailles Peace Treaty, 170
Vincent, Henry, 59
Vivien, Henry Harvey, 121
Voysey, Rev. Charles, 21

Waddington, A.W., 16
Waddington, Joseph, 35
Wadsworth, John, 152
Waggon and Carriage Workers' Union, 109
Wales, 97, 101; Home Rule for, 109
Wallhead, Richard [Christopher] Collingham, 155
Walsall, 118-19, 127
Walsh, James, 67
Walsh, Stephen, **187-90**
Walton, Sir Joseph, 66
War Emergency Workers' National Committee, 11, 182
War Resisters' International, 166
Ward, John, **190-3**
Warehouse Workers' Union, 137
Warne, George Henry, **193-6**
Watermen's Company, 84
Watson, William, 42, 43
Watts, Charles, 22
Webb, Beatrice, 91, 123
Webb, Catherine, 91
Webb, Sidney (*later* 1st Baron Passfield), 24, 25, 123
Webber, Laura (Mrs R. A. Taylor), 174, 175
Weekly Dispatch, 40
Wells, Herbert George, 123
Wells, William, 94
Welsh, James, 74
Welsh Parliamentary Party, 199
Welwyn Garden City, 71
Werth, Alexander, 131
West Bromwich, 197
West Indies, 165, 175
West Riding Power Loom Weavers' Association, 75
'Whiffley Puncto' (pseud.): *see* Palmer, William
Whiston, John, 119
White, C. H. (pseud. of Marcelle Boutier), 80
'Whiteboys', 93
Whitehouse, Samuel Henry, **196-7**
Whitley Committee, 150
Whitley, John Henry, 196
Widdrington, Rev. Percy Elborough Tinling, 16, 141
Wigan, 50, 52, 188
Wigan Observer, 50
Wilde, Arthur, 81
Wilde, Oscar, 169

Wilkes, John, 105
Wilkinson, Ellen, 77
Wilkinson, W. Tom, 36
Willey, Frederick Thomas, 79
Williams, David James, **198-200**
Williams, Ethel, 19
Williams, Jack, 80
Williams, John (Jack) E., 191
Williams, John Lloyd, 198
Williams, Robert, 86, 87, 181, 205, 207
Willis, Charles Armine, 139
Wilson, Henry Joseph, 121
Wilson, Joseph Havelock, 68, 77, 149, 179, 182, **200-8**
Windham, William (*later* Sir), 10, 11
Winfrey, Sir Richard, 15
Winlaton and Blaydon Health Association, 142
Wise, Edward Frank, 125
Women, International Conference of, (London, 1899), 91
Women, rights of, 5, 20, 22, 23, 90, 91, 138; war injuries, compensation for: *see* Second World War, Personal Injuries (Civilians) Scheme
Women Folk, 38, 39
Women's Co-operative Guild, 91, 110, 118, 127, 169
Women's Council, 91
Women's Industrial Council, 19, 90, 91, 92; Clubs' Industrial Association of, 91
Women's Industrial News, 91
Women's International League, 170
Women's Labour League, 19, 71
Women's Peace Conference (Zurich, 1919), 170
Women's Suffrage Movement, 2, 19, 28, 138, 146, 154, 169, 170, 174
Women's Trade Union Association, 90
Women's Trade Union Council (Manchester), 169
Women's Trade Union League, 90
Womersley, Sir Walter, 3
Woods, Sir Wilfred, 139
Workers' Art Club, 80
Workers' Daily, 104
Workers' Educational Association, 71
Workers' Film Society, 80
Workers' Municipal Federation, 135
Workers' Union, 2, 4, 70, 71, 181
Working Men's Association, 6, 93, 171
Working Men's Club and Institute Union, 174, 198
Working Women's Organisations, Standing Joint Committee of, 3. *See also* Industrial Women's Organisations
Workman's Times, 36
Workmen's Compensation, TUC and LP Joint Cttee on, 3

Yorkshire Factory Times, 75–6, 157
Yorkshire Post, 131
Yorkshireman, 35
Young Communist League, 80. *See also* Communist Party of Great Britain
Young Women's Christian Association, 138

Younger, Sir George (*later* 1st Viscount Younger of Leckie), 11

Zinoviev Letter, 135, 138, 195